FAMILIES AND THEIR RELATIVES

Kinship in a Middle-Class Sector of London

An Anthropological Study by

RAYMOND FIRTH
JANE HUBERT
ANTHONY FORGE

with the team of the 'London Kinship Project'

LONDON
ROUTLEDGE & KEGAN PAUL
NEW YORK: HUMANITIES PRESS

First published in 1969
by Routledge and Kegan Paul Ltd
Broadway House, 68–74 Carter Lane
London, E.C.4
Printed in Great Britain
by C. Tinling & Co. Ltd
Liverpool, London and Prescot

SBN 7100 6431 4

To

THE SUBJECTS OF OUR STUDY

who endured our enquiries with fortitude
and good humour and who
by our promise must remain anonymous

Contents

Introduction

The project which is the subject of this book is a continuation of studies of kinship in urban conditions begun as early as 1947.[1] But in its present form this project was conceived in discussions between David Schneider and Raymond Firth at Palo Alto in 1959. Both of us had been interested for some time in studying the structure and meaning of kinship in modern Western society.[2] Schneider and I then considered the possibility of undertaking an exploratory study of a novel, comparative kind. Most studies in the Western kinship field so far had been done either in rural communities or, in Britain at least, among urban working-class people. We proposed, one working in Chicago and the other in London, to examine kinship ties outside the elementary, nuclear family in urban conditions in a middle-class sector of the society. We hoped, by maintaining close contact between the British and the American teams in the course of the investigation, to contribute not only towards a further understanding of the theory of social relations in modern industrial society, but also to examine some problems of methodology of field study. In particular, the experiment of trans-Atlantic co-operation in an anthropological investigation seemed to us to be both new and worth trying. Our proposal in this form seemed imaginative enough to attract the interest of the National Science Foundation of the United States, to whose generous support the British side of the investigation in particular must be regarded as being most indebted.

This book, on our findings in the London area, gives the main part of the results of our investigation. The results of the parallel Chicago study are appearing separately,[3] while the intention is to relate the findings of the two studies comparatively in a further publication. Reports on aspects of the London study at various stages have been given: by Anthony Forge to a conference on family and kin ties in Britain and their social implications, under the auspices of the British Sociological Association and the Association

[1] Raymond Firth, ed. *Two Studies of Kinship in London*, London School of Economics Monographs on Social Anthropology No. 15, 1956.

[2] v. e.g. D. M. Schneider and G. Homans, 'Kinship Terminology and the American Kinship System', *American Anthropologist*, 57, 1955, pp. 1194–208.

[3] David M. Schneider's *American Kinship: A Cultural Account*, Prentice-Hall, Englewood Cliffs, 1968, is the first fruit of this study.

of Social Anthropologists, in 1961; by Raymond Firth, Jane Hubert, Dorothy Crozier and Sutti Ortiz to a Working Party on kinship studies and to other discussion groups at various dates. Articles giving a few preliminary results of our London study have already been published.[4] While this book has been delayed, then, many of its methodological and theoretical findings have been circulated among interested people.

We have not been able to make any reference to the interesting work by Colin R. Bell, *Middle-Class Families*, which was published while this book was in press.

London R.F.
July 1968

[4] Raymond Firth, 'Family and Kinship in Industrial Society', *Sociological Review Monograph*, No. 8, 1964, pp. 65–87; Dorothy Crozier, 'Kinship and Occupational Succession', *The Sociological Review*, vol. 13, 1965, pp. 15–43; Jane Hubert, 'Kinship and Geographical Mobility in a Sample from a London Middle-class Area', *International Journal of Comparative Sociology*, vol. 6, 1965, pp. 61–84; see also Raymond Firth, 'Family and Kin Ties in Britain and their Social Implications: Introduction', *British Journal of Sociology*, vol. 12, 1961, pp. 305–9. A detailed description of the methodology of the enquiry has been issued in duplicated form as an Occasional Paper of the Department of Anthropology, London School of Economics and Political Science, under the title of *Methods of Study of Middle-Class Kinship in London: A Working Paper on the History of an Anthropological Project*, 1968.

Acknowledgements

Many acknowledgements are necessary in a work of this kind.

To the National Science Foundation of the United States our gratitude is very great; the imaginative interest of the Foundation and its advisers in the comparative findings and methodology of our investigation gave us not simply the finance for the study, but also an increased respect for the significance of international co-operation in the social sciences.

We are also extremely grateful to the London School of Economics and Political Science, who made it possible for Jane Hubert to extend the analysis of data from the project for some months after the Foundation's grant had ended.

Valuable advice on the planning of the project in its initial stage was received by Raymond Firth from colleagues at the Center for Advanced Studies in the Behavioral Sciences at Palo Alto, especially from Fred Eggan, Lloyd Fallers, Meyer Fortes, Clifford Geertz, G. P. Murdock, Kaspar Naegele and Melford H. Spiro. The scheme was put forward with the special advice and active assistance of David M. Schneider. Further advice on the later planning and conduct of the study was received from Lorraine Barić (Lorraine Lancaster), Maurice Freedman, Hildred Geertz, Hilde Himmelweit, J. B. Loudon, C. A. Moser, Colin Rosser, Alice Rossi, Margaret Stirling, Paul Stirling. A preliminary investigation by Helen J. Stocks in the Highgate area was very helpful to the field planning.

For consultation at various stages, basic contribution in the onerous work of field interviewing, and help in the analysis of results we are much indebted to the members of 'the Kinship Team'. Those who participated full-time in the fieldwork of the project were: Connie Dawson (1960–61); Helga Jacobson (1960–63); Julyan Fancott (1961–62); Diana Russell (1961–62); Gill James (1961–64); Alison Murray (1962–64); Sutti Ortiz (1963–64). Those who participated for shorter periods were: Brenda Beck, Martha Bladen, Audrey Hayley, Jennifer Mouat, Anne Sharman, Teresa Spens, Ann Whitehead.

We are also indebted to Roger Warren Evans for sociological analysis of some of the data. To the historian of the team, Dorothy Crozier (1960–64), we owe much for her patient assembly and presentation of background materials, and for safeguarding our historical interpretation. We are indebted to the Highgate Literary and Scientific Institution for help in this investigation. For preliminary drafts of special sections of our work we are very grateful to Dorothy Crozier, Helga Jacobson, Gill James, Alison Murray, Sutti Ortiz and Diana Russell.

We are also very grateful to Mrs D. H. Alfandary for her continued interest in the project and her patient typing of case histories, tabular and other materials during the progress of the work.

As 'Principal Investigator' in the project, I must also pay a tribute to my co-authors, Anthony Forge and Jane Hubert (Jane Forge), who acted successively as team leaders of the project, and who have contributed in a very large measure to its achievement. As co-planners of the project, both on the theoretical and the practical side, and as field workers and organizers of the day-to-day activities of the team, they have made an essential contribution, which is appropriately represented by their co-authorship.

Finally, we have to acknowledge the contributions of our informants. Though they must remain anonymous,[1] according to the terms of our study, their willingness to submit to extensive interviewing, and their own stimulating, sometimes challenging, suggestions and questions, have helped us a great deal and we are very grateful to them all.

R.F.

[1] The case histories cited most frequently in this book, forty in all, are listed under their code names at the end, with references to where they appear. In some cases descriptive details have been slightly modified: O – female; △ – male; M – mother; F – father; Z – sister; B – brother; D – daughter; S – son; W – wife; H – husband; = or — – married; ≠ – divorced; Ø – dead or otherwise inactive; — siblings, i.e. brothers and/or sisters. (For examples see Figure 5 and p. 192.)

Tables

Tables

Figures

PART I

1

Kinship and Class in Metropolitan Society

How important is kinship in modern British society? The question itself is quite a recent one in sociological enquiry, and it is due largely to anthropologists that it has become meaningful. That the answer to it is still not very clear suggests that, however important it be, its effects are hard to isolate and identify.

NATURE OF KINSHIP

What is meant by *kinship*? To a social anthropologist or sociologist kinship is broadly concerned with what English people usually call their 'relatives'. More precisely, kinship is a set of ties socially recognized to exist between persons because of their genealogical connection, that is, in terms of the relationships thought to be created between them by marriage and/or procreation of children. There has been much argument on the question of how far kinship ties are based upon a concept of biological relationships or at least have biological relations as their ultimate referent. But it is generally acknowledged that kin relations are not reckoned in simple biological terms. Marriage implies sex union of husband and wife, but sex union alone does not create kinship. In the classification of kin social categories and functions are of great significance and the biological referent is often indirect.

The social component itself is not simple, and may vary according to the type of society. In every society the principle of legitimacy of children is important – whether or not their putative biological father should ideally be legally married to their mother, every child should have as social father a man who is or has been so married. In many societies this principle of legitimacy is carried so far that legally the male person who is socially recognized as having prime rights over a child, and corresponding obligations towards it, is that man who is (or has been) the mother's husband, irrespective of who is thought to be the progenitor of the child. But the content of the notion of 'social' is not exhausted by the legal provisions. In many societies, too, in a case of illegitimacy, where the child's mother is unmarried, whether the law is invoked or not, and whether physiological paternity is fully admitted or not, a man may agree that he is the 'father' of the child and assume the social role without being the woman's husband. But the main field of interest of kinship is broader than this. Biologically, no modern Western industrial society is a breeding isolate, and over relatively few generations elaborate genetic relationships will have been formed by intermarriage between a large number of the members. Yet the kinship networks, in terms of traceable genealogical connections, will be much more attentuated. Social processes of selection will have taken place whereby some people who are biologically related have been retained in recognition whereas others, perhaps the majority, have been lost to memory. It is a fair assumption that these processes of selection are not random, but have relation to the social interests and needs of the people concerned.

In his comparative study of human societies a social anthropologist has learned to look to kinship as a major element in the operations of a society. Among the ties of kinship those of the elementary family (the simple or nuclear family as it is termed by many writers) are primary.[1] But in most of the societies historically studied by anthropologists the extra-familial kin – to use a rather cumbrous but useful expression – are at least of comparable social significance. So much is this the case that the structure of the society may seem to depend upon groups such as lineages recruited on an extra-familial kin basis, and the elementary family may even be denied recognition as a structural unit. Ties to maternal uncle or to father's sister may assume a rigour much more evident than with ties to parents, and be reinforced by sanctions of strong social or even supernatural kind.

A special point concerns relatives by marriage, known as affines, for example the kin of spouse, or of siblings' spouses. Some difference of terminology exists here among anthropologists themselves, as to whether affines are to be included with consanguines as kin; or whether only consanguines should be termed kin, and affines put under a separate head.[2] The latter narrow usage is popularly expressed in English by the distinction sometimes drawn between

[1] For some qualifications to this, see Raymond Firth, 'Family and Kinship in Industrial Society', *The Sociological Review Monograph No. 8*, 1964, pp. 65–87.

[2] The former usage has historical precedent, as in L. H. Morgan's pathbreaking work, *Systems of Consanguinity and Affinity of the Human Family*, Washington City, 1871.

'relations' and 'connections' (see later). But the broad usage of calling them all kin is convenient. In many societies, consanguines merge with affines through marriage with kin. But whether they do or do not, it is common for affines, especially close 'relatives-in-law', to be treated with particular formality, with respect and even with avoidance of all bodily contact, near presence, use of personal name, rough language, immodest jokes, etc. This is apart from or in addition to the elaborate exchange of goods and services that take place between the groups of kin so connected by a marriage.

The comparative studies of social anthropologists have revealed the structural and organizational significance of kinship in a great range of societies. Kinship is a core of social relations, a basis of education, a medium of transmission of economic rights, a framework for social obligations and often for political alignment, even (as in ancestor worship) a focus for moral ideas and ritual procedures.

THE PROBLEM OF KIN TIES IN ENGLISH SOCIETY

What now is the position in modern English society? It is clear at once that the student of social affairs does not find himself confronted by kinship at every turn, as the overt framework for economic and political action. It is obvious, for instance, that kin groups outside the family do not constitute firmly structured units of the social system.[3] There are some indications of kinship operations and attitudes outside the elementary family. These vary from the crude stereotyped 'mother-in-law joke' behaviour, to suspicions that in the upper echelons of business and political circles ties of 'family' and marriage account for jobs that the claims of efficiency alone could not justify.

Occasional references in literature, including the Press, indicate that in some ways kinship has meaning at widely separate levels of British society. In working-class circles, for example, in Covent Garden market the sons of porters had until 1957 a monopoly of porters' jobs, and still are said to have preference; 'family groups of a dozen are common' and one 'family' with its collaterals is said to

[3] This has been often pointed out. See e.g. Raymond Firth, *Two Studies of Kinship in London*, London 1956, p. 14; O. R. McGregor, 'Some Research Possibilities and Historical Materials for Family and Kinship Study in Britain', *British Journal of Sociology*, vol. XII, 1961, p. 310; Talcott Parsons, 'The Normal American Family', in *The Family's Search for Survival*, ed. Seymour Farber *et al*, New York, 1965, p. 35. See also R. O'R. Piddington, 'A Study of French-Canadian Kinship', *International Journal of Comparative Sociology*, vol. II, 1961, pp. 15–16.

have ninety members in the market. Father to son succession in dock labour still seems often to operate. In the business field small family-owned concerns are common in lighterage companies – 'it is a great kith and kin way of life'. Kinship ties in circus ownership seem important. At the other end of the social scale, some exclusive regiments of the Guards, it seems, not only recruit all their officers from the public schools but also earmark sons of officers in the hope that they will join the regiment too. One regiment has been reported even to have a 'baby book' containing the names, scholastic records and sporting interests of its officers' sons – the officers of the future – who are later approached by the regiment to see if they are interested in following in their father's footsteps.[4] Yet what is of interest in these examples is only partly the element of extra-familial kinship. It is also the recognition given by a sector of society to the tie of kinship as a recruitment and co-operation principle. This kin tie is recognized as valid by other people not necessarily related genealogically to those immediately concerned, and it is made a basis for social action. *All* Covent Garden porters, *all* officers of the regiment, recognize the prior claim of sons of *some* of their number to participate in the privileges of employment in the group. Even if not all porters or officers share in these views, the principle of kinship recruitment in the form of father-son succession is sufficiently well-established to have become part of the custom of the group.

But what also these examples suggest is that they are relatively rare in modern society. Yet we have no idea how atypical such a principle of recruitment may be. The instances given are like rocks appearing above the surface of a sociological sea; they give little indication of what in fact may be the reality of the structures that lie below. Moreover, the examples given are mainly upper-class and working-class; what is the position in the middle classes?

In modern Western industrial society, with its great complexity, its divorce of major formal education and of occupation from the home, and its focus upon national, impersonal goals and responsibilities, it would be unrealistic to expect any very thorough-going

[4] *Sunday Times*, 21 April 1963; for Covent Garden see 19 April 1964. For the significance of recruitment of dock labour in London by reference to kinship, especially the father to son tie, see *The Times*, 28 December 1964, under heading: 'Following Father's Steps into a Dock Job. Harder for Outsiders than Entry to Eton'. For barge and lighterage companies see the *Sunday Times*, 3 March 1968. For 'a strong family affair' in the circus world, see the *Observer*, 14 December 1965. For some information regarding the 'dynasties of headmasters' of public schools, see the *Observer*, 8 April 1962. For the 'Smith Family Club', the patrilineal descendants of Thomas Smith, the seventeenth-century banker, see the *Observer*, 24 October 1965. See also T. Lupton and Sheila Wilson, 'Kin Connections and the Bank Rate Tribunal', *Manchester School*, 1959–61.

operation of kinship principles in productive organization or in other large-scale institutional fields. The role of kinship, assuming that it has one, is to be sought in the less formal social arrangements – co-operation in daily affairs, public festivals, anniversaries and crises in personal life. It is likely to be found in the interplay of personalities which is part of the whole process of individuals maintaining themselves in and contributing to the society of which they are members. But to what extent are such kin ties of significance?

That kin ties are expected to have force even in a modern industrial society is indicated obliquely by a remark attributed to N. Kruschev in speaking about the partition of Germany as an established fact. 'People today are distinguished not so much by kinship as by ideological standpoints', he said.[5] This warning, taken in context of the scenes of kin reunion that occurred when the Berlin wall was breached for a time, is a clear reminder of the strong affective character of kin ties, especially after a period of separation. Any modern Western society, indeed any society at all, would presumably show the same characteristics.

But, it may be objected, such reunion scenes concern the elementary family members alone, and it is only natural that their kinship should be of prime moment to them. We have a vast anthropological and sociological literature already which demonstrates the importance of such family relationships over the range of human societies. In Britain there has been much systematic investigation of family relationships, in historical and in contemporary terms, and from it a great deal of cardinal importance for an understanding of modern social problems has been learnt. But on the whole this family literature has been focussed on the internal functioning of the elementary family – on marital adjustment, on parent-child relations, on sibling attitudes – or on the relationships of the elementary family with external agencies and institutions such as school, church or housing authorities.

Two large areas of social interest have gone uninvestigated until quite recently. One is the relations between what have been termed family of orientation and family of procreation, family of birth and family of marriage, or natal family and conjugal (or marital) family. In one's *natal family* into which one has been born, one is a junior member, a child and a sibling. In one's *conjugal family*, created by one's marriage, one is a senior (indeed founding) member, a spouse and a parent. But when one has married one is now involved also with a further group, the spouse's natal family, which may be termed the *family of affinity* (*affinal family*). Now the great mass of literature on the topic of 'family' ordinarily deals only with the natal family

[5] As reported in *The Times*, January 1963.

of a young person or the conjugal family of an adult. Relations with the natal family of an adult and with the affinal family are commonly omitted from consideration altogether. In concrete terms, for example, despite all the popular views on the subject, what exactly are the relations in general English society between sons-in-law and mothers-in-law? What role does a woman have as mother, wife's mother and grandmother to the various members of an elementary family in a home in which she does not live, but in which she usually has a very lively emotional interest?[6]

The other great area of social interest is the relationships with kin outside these family circles. What are the social relationships with aunts and uncles, cousins of various kinds, and their children, who are known genealogically, recognized socially and kept in some sort of contact, if only at periodic intervals? Here too the 'family' literature is usually unrevealing.

What degree of influence, if any, such kin exert on the elementary family members, what they represent as factors of sociability, resources in time of trouble, sentimental links with elders who have died, is generally speaking unknown. Questions of this order are sometimes dismissed because it is thought that behaviour as regards kin outside the family is either 'natural' or 'random'. Either it is assumed to need no explanation beyond a rather obvious assumption of emotional linkage, or it is thought to be so dictated by idiosyncratic impulse and interest as not to be capable of meaningful generalization.

It is against this background that the present study has been conceived and carried out. A certain number of studies have already explored parts of this field. Some, such as those of Rees, Curle, Williams, Loudon, Fox, Vallee, Littlejohn, have demonstrated the importance of extra-familial kinship in rural areas of Britain, where relationships of this order can be relatively easily traced and seen to have material effect. Other studies, such as those of Young, Willmott, Marris and their colleagues of the Institute of Community Studies, Townsend, Bott, Stacey, Rosser and Harris, have shown that kinship in urban conditions can have considerable significance.

KINSHIP IN METROPOLITAN CONDITIONS

One would expect that kinship relations would tend to vary in scope

[6] Members of the Royal Family seem to share conventional kin patterns here as elsewhere. When Princess Margaret was about to have her second child, her first was sent to stay with his grandmother, the Queen Mother, to make room for midwives, medical equipment, etc. (Reported in the *Evening Standard*, 28 April 1964.) The role of wife's mother at confinements is discussed in the context of the present study, Chapter 11.

and intensity according to whether the people concerned live in a rural or an urban physical and social environment. But the distinction may not be clear-cut. Kinship in a country town which is a centre of a large farming district may in fact assume much the quality of that interlocking network of ties characteristic of the surrounding rural area.[7] The most striking contrast to rural social conditions is probably to be found in metropolitan conditions. People living in a large city often do not know their neighbours on either side, and therefore are ignorant of who are their neighbours' kin. Occupational diversification may mean that their own kin may live far away. Even if they do have kin in the metropolis, distance alone may make communication difficult. What may be called 'pockets of sociability' may develop in a metropolitan area – a 'local interest group' of a cultural or political kind, a 'street', a 'village', may provide a medium in which residents do know something of the lives of their fellow-residents, and share even in relationships with these residents' kin. But this is probably fairly rare, at any rate in a metropolis such as London, and such 'social pockets' are not usually composed of kin.

The nature of metropolitan living can raise very serious problems for the conduct and personality of the people living therein. The impersonality and 'anonymity' of a large city may be overemphasized and their alleged deleterious effects misconceived. But it seems clear that a person in a large city may have very few social contacts indeed, apart from at his work and in his family circle. If he is living 'away from home' (as the phrase goes) the influence of his natal family may be largely removed from him. Can he do without kin in his personal life? Where then does he get support if he runs into difficulties? How are his judgments formed and checked; how is his conduct regulated? Sanctions against gross breaches of conduct exist, in the form of police and other official guardians of society. But in the subtler fields of everyday behaviour, what kinds of sanctions operate in controlling him and guarding him against failures of obligation? Workmates, professional colleagues, fellow-students, friends, church or other associational members all have their role in this, and probably supply many outlets for personal interest and guidance in judgment and in response to obligations. But these sources of social control arise for the most part when a person is already mature. Therefore, they supply a framework within which his conduct expresses itself, rather than build the basic set of norms by which his life is controlled. They may limit deviation and provide immediate rules for behaviour.

[7] See J. B. Loudon, 'Kinship and Crisis in South Wales', *British Journal of Sociology*, vol. XII, 1961, p. 334.

But for the provision of basic standards, school, family and early peer-group have a primary responsibility. But how far does the family as an elementary or nuclear unit in society exist in isolation from members of other families with which it is genealogically connected? In adult life kin outside the family may help to provide the social sanctions brought to bear on a person. How far do such extra-familial kin take part in family affairs? What is their role in the array of people with whom an individual has social relationships in the course of his ordinary life and in crisis? How far do extra-familial kin have a part to play in forming or maintaining an individual's standards of aesthetic and moral evaluation? To what extent are they involved in the individual's definition of his own personality?

In this form the problem is a difficult one to tackle since it demands a close scrutiny of intra-familial behaviour and studies on a developmental scale. But it is perhaps approachable more easily from another angle, that of the type and quality of social contacts. In modern metropolitan life a person may be expected to have several types of social contact. With his friends, he has a sentimental bond though they may live at a distance from him. With his occupational colleagues, he has a bond of co-operation in production though possibly no close tie of residence or sentiment. To a more limited degree he may co-operate with his neighbours, because of shared local facilities and problems, though no other ties of work or sentiment with them may exist. Other social contacts may occur on the basis of shared aesthetic or recreational interests. Yet there are some people with whom a person maintains social contact despite the fact that they do not live near him, nor are they linked with him by common issues of work, art or recreation; nor are they necessarily classified as friends and may even be said to be disliked. What is their place in an individual's social scheme of things? Who are they? For the most part these are his kin.

A metropolitan situation such as that of London presents kinship operationally in a very different light from that in rural or indeed many urban studies. When people live in separate independent units, not related by kinship to their neighbours or others living close by; when their actions are free from daily oversight on the part of their kin; when their behaviour at work, at home or in recreation need not depend at all on kin; then this is the nearest thing to 'pure' kinship we are likely to get. For these people undertake social relations with their kin because they *are* kin, either from voluntary choice or because of their sense of obligation, and not because they are dealing with workmates or neighbours who happen also to be kin. In this sense the theoretical significance of such studies of metropolitan kinship can be great, in isolating more rigorously than is often possible in rural or small town studies the principle of kinship itself.[8]

One of the most significant features of kinship is that it consists of social relationships the ultimate basis for which is independent of the choice of the central individual concerned. When it comes to the selection of a wife a person in modern Western society is responsible for his own decision – in some other modern societies he is still not responsible for the choice of his spouse. But a person cannot decide, in basic genealogical terms, who shall be his consanguineous kin. He must also accept, in genealogical terms, his spouse's consanguines as his affines. From the genealogical point of view then a framework of kinship is largely constructed for a person without his volition. This implies that a capacity for actions and decisions which may radically affect a person's life is placed in the hands of people of pre-selected status, irrespective of their fitness for such a role. Where the person can exercise choice is in the degree to which he will accord social recognition to the genealogical facts. His life is not unique in this respect; if he enters a business firm he has to accept the hierarchy of his colleagues – and it may be the hierarchy of their wives also – as a given factor in his situation. But what is unique about the genealogical frame of kinship is that it starts at birth and endures through all of life, and that the ties and obligations associated with it are therefore given a 'built-in' quality which is unlike other forms of social linkage.

SOCIAL RECOGNITION OF KIN

The separation between genealogical framework and social recognition of kin creates some interesting and important problems in modern Western society. In most societies of the type studied traditionally by social anthropologists there is a high degree of coincidence between recognition of genealogical framework and recognition of social obligation. Kin are treated in personal terms, but tend to be regarded as falling into categories, each of which has its own set of terms, code of duties and requirement of privileges. Moreover, each member of the society tends to follow the same patterns – to adopt the same type of address, usage of respect, avoidance, familiarity, exchange of service to the same type of kin. Such is not normally the case in a modern Western society, above all in a metropolitan environment (cf. Firth, 1956, pp. 13–14, for further observation on this point).

[8] Cf. also D. M. Schneider, 'The Nature of Kinship', *Man*, No. 217, 1964; *American Kinship: A Cultural Account*, Englewood Cliffs, N.J., 1968.

Basically, the patterns of kin observance are not clear-cut. There are general patterns of respect, for instance, for an uncle, but no *specific* ways laid down in which one should behave to a mother's brother as distinct from a father's brother. Then, the sanctions making for conformity are equally vague and highly personalized, residing more in the opinions and actions of other immediate kin than in the opinions and actions of society at large. Moreover, even if sanctions of a fairly developed and formal kind did exist, to promote fulfilment of kin obligations, their enforcement would be practically impossible in a metropolitan environment. Hence in such conditions there is a high degree of individual variation in the recognition and implementation of kin ties. One might think that a person in a metropolitan household who lives alone can select kin ties he will maintain, and ignore the rest. His neighbours and friends are unlikely even to know, let alone take responsibility for, his relationships with any of his kin. Even if he is a resident member of a family, their collective sanctions may be hard to apply, and there will almost certainly be a large area of his life in which his individual decisions about his behaviour to his kin must be allowed to take their course.

Yet the theoretical choice is hardly ever seen by the person concerned as a real choice. It is a matter of experience that even those who live alone are apt to maintain some linkage with some kin, and that those who live in a family are likely to be linked with some kin outside the family. The very possibility of choice in itself may give rise to questions and difficulties. The genealogical aspect of kinship is a 'given factor' in a person's existence, even though he may not realize it consciously as such. What he may have to interpret is the validity of such links for social purposes. How important and how right is it that he should 'see something' (as the odd expression goes) of an old aunt who is living alone? Does the discovery that a cousin has come to live in the neighbourhood mean that he is obliged to make social contact in the face of a sinking feeling that they have few interests in common? What is the obligation upon a woman to entertain a husband's sister whom at heart she really dislikes? How far are one's own relationships and obligations in the kinship sphere to be regulated by the interests of one's spouse and of one's children, or of one's ageing parents? What regard should one have to the feelings of elderly kin who think they have a right to interfere in advice on one's child's education? If one is proposing a course of action of which one knows one's wife's mother will disapprove, how far is one entitled – or even wise – to disregard her view?

In many households such questions appear to be very relevant and to involve individuals in very serious concern. Taken item by item they may seem trivial, but in the aggregate they help to make up the stuff of family existence. Moreover, however 'natural' and obvious the questions may appear, the answers to them do not come 'naturally'; they involve a complex set of reasonings, emotional attitudes, divided loyalties, self-interested and 'disinterested' considerations which make up the totality of social behaviour on any such issue. Take the commonest stereotype of all in the English kinship field – that of mother-love and corresponding affection for the mother. A married daughter naturally, it is thought, has close ties with her mother. But if it be thought 'natural' for a married daughter to keep close contact with her mother and give great weight to her opinions, is it 'unnatural' if the daughter keeps away from her mother and regards her as an interference in the family affairs?

A few opinions from our study are relevant here. The stereotype view of a mother in our society is epitomized by the description of one of our informants, who regarded her mother as a 'wonderful person' and remembered with loyalty and gratitude the way she had worked to bring up her family. But there were other views. One woman said her mother was terrible to her children and did nothing but read detective novels all day and completely neglect them; she told them quite often how glad she would be when they were grown up, had left home, and she could do what she liked. Another woman said she felt desperately sorry for her mother. She didn't really love her mother 'except in a filial sort of way – she *is* my mother – but I can't love her as a person'. Her mother's sister, a widow, was the person whom she described as 'the angel of the family'. There are many cases in our records where a substitute for maternal love has been provided by a relative outside the nuclear family.

Sociologically, an obvious question is then; what is the *prevalence* of these various types of behaviour? How idiosyncratic or 'random' are these cases and the issues they represent? How far are kinship ties inside and outside the family a significant part of the fabric of social existence of individuals and households in British society? Putting it another way, how far is kinship a significant element in decision-making – as regards what job to take, where to live and to what school to send the children; in economic affairs – inheritance of property, aid in buying a house or a car, or with a child's education; in providing some comparative standards of evaluation of social achievement? How far on the other hand do kinship ties seem to involve people in situations of strain, tension and social friction; or to help provide them with elements of security, moral support and social expression? What are the social mechanisms by which such processes occur and are handled by the individuals most concerned?

It is this sociological viewpoint which we are taking in this study.

Our aim is descriptive and analytical. Our object is *not* to try and 'make a case' for kinship, to try and demonstrate that kinship is *everywhere* important in social life; in modern complex industrial societies this clearly would not be true. But we are concerned to see if kinship is important in the sectors of social life we have chosen to investigate, and if it is, *for what kinds of people, in what kinds of conditions*, and with what kin.

KINSHIP AND CLASS

Patterns of kinship in Britain may be assumed to have been responsive to many variables, including residential distribution of the population, housing types, household composition, occupation, religious affiliation and moral ideas of the nature of obligation. But three variables of major importance may be briefly mentioned: large urban agglomerations; economic changes; and class differences. We have already considered some of the isolative effects of metropolitan living on the character of extra-familial kin relations, and would add only that with urban living the patterns of kin services must inevitably change. As regards economic change over time, it seems fairly evident that, taking a long-period view, in the eighteenth and nineteenth centuries in Britain, kinship ties were of greater significance than they are nowadays.[9] But with regard to class influences the situation is not so clear.[10] It might be held that in modern times extra-familial kinship is most marked at either end of the social scale, corresponding to social needs of very different kinds. Kin ties of the aristocracy and the landed gentry and of upper-class politicians and business men would seem to be still important in the transmission

[9] T. S. Ashton, *An Economic History of England: The 18th Century*, London, 1955, p. 18 (on 'the strength of the ties of kinship'); G. E. Mingay, *English Landed Society in the Eighteenth Century*, London, 1963, p. 17. 'Individually gentlemen, collectively the landed aristocrats formed a series of families, so linked by intermarriage that they have been likened to tribes. The family interest and the family reputation were normally superior to the claims of any individual within it . . .' This is borne out by data for professional and commercial families in the nineteenth century (see Dorothy Crozier, 1965). The interest of British historians in problems of family and kinship in the earlier centuries seems to have been decidedly less than that of French historians. See review article on work by Duby, Aries, Mandrou and others, by Joan Thirsk, 'The Family. Past & Present'. *A Journal of Historical Studies*. No. 27, 1964, pp. 116–22.

[10] Joan Thirsk has pointed out that it is almost certainly true that the history of the rich family was not also that of the poor – since differences in the size of household, in the education available to children, in the amount of leisure of the parents, were class distinctions. But there were many local differences. (1964, p. 121.)

of economic and political assets.[11] Among the working classes, on the other hand, where such assets are rare, the extent and strength of kinship sentiment have also been demonstrated by Young, Willmott, Townsend, Marris, Firth, Kerr and others. There has been an implication here, though not very precisely stated, that the strength of working-class kin ties is to be correlated with their relatively weak and unprotected social and economic position. The matri-centred kin structure and close-knit nucleus of female kin – which have been often stated to be characteristic of British working-class circles – fit this notion of compensation for relative lack of resources, and for the strains of living in modern urban conditions, by giving a day to day system of mutual aid and support.

Views on the kinship situation among the middle classes seem to be more diversified.[12] Elizabeth Bott, from a detailed study of only three families but a more general study of a score more, found a great deal of variation in the relationship of these families with their kin. There is a hint in her book that the more established middle-class families had less elaborate kin ties than the others, but on the whole she is of the opinion that the degree of variation could not be correlated at all closely with class status.[13] Other writers, however, see class differentials more obviously. Geoffrey Gorer has some evidence that middle-class people, especially in the south of England are most often separated from their kin and dependent on friends and neighbours for help and companionship. Ronald Fletcher, in broad agreement, holds that interest in perpetuating kinship ties, and kind and degree of mutual aid between kin, may differ between social classes. Young middle-class parents, he states, may desire and obtain help from elderly relatives, as in sending their children to a public school, but beyond such help and some indirect financial influence there may be little sentimental attachment and little desire for closer interdependence. The situation is likcly to be different, he implies, with young working-class parents, whose sentimental feelings are likely to be strong as their financial expectations are weak. The study by Willmott and Young shows that, as compared with working-class people, middle-class people in Woodford live

[11] See T. Lupton and Sheila Wilson, op. cit.; S. Aaronovitch, *The Ruling Class: A Study of British Finance Capital*, London, 1961.

[12] Robin Fox has stated generally 'In some working-class enclaves . . . kinship networks seem to be important. It is in the less conservative and more mobile middle-classes that kinship now seems to be of little relevance beyond the level of parent-child relationships, and even these have a looseness about them that would shock many of our primitive contemporaries. . . . (*Kinship and Marriage*, Pelican Books, 1967, pp. 14–16.)

[13] Elizabeth Bott, *Family and Social Network*, London, 1957, pp. 114–58, esp. p. 122.

further away from their parents but use car and letters more to communicate with relatives.[14]

Crudely generalized, such views seem not too implausible. They place the kinship attitudes of the middle classes somewhere between the interest – both co-operative and competitive – in perpetuation of economic and political assets shown by the upper classes and the warm protectiveness of the propertyless working classes. It would probably be unreasonable to ask even the authors of such views to accept the class-linked contrast between kin materialism and kin sentiment in this bald form of statement. But it is clear that there is a problem here, of trying to establish just what the middle-class kinship structure is.

But something must first be said on the concept of middle class itself.

THE CONCEPT OF 'MIDDLE-CLASS'

The literature on the definition of social class, and on class structure, is vast, and we think it unnecessary to enter on any very elaborate argument of a general kind here. Our concern is to identify our selected cases in such terms as to allow them to be reasonably admitted to the 'middle-class' category on most of the ordinary criteria used.

One of the difficulties in discussions about social class – or simply 'class' as it is often called – is that two major principles of categorization are employed, and that while they do overlap they are not coincident. One principle, associated especially with the analyses of Karl Marx though by no means restricted to Marxist usage, bases class categorization upon the different major roles taken by people in the productive processes of society. Hence the recognition in modern Western conditions of a ruling class of capitalists and landowners; a bourgeois middle class of professionals, tradespeople, small merchants; and a proletarian labouring class of manual workers. On this view, the notion of class is closely connected with that of political power. What creates a class is recognition of identity of interests between those who are engaged in the same type of economic role, and outcome of this recognition is political action. It is assumed that similar positions in the production scheme, that

[14] Geoffrey Gorer, *Exploring English Character*, London, 1955, p. 46; Ronald Fletcher, *Britain in the Sixties: The Family and Marriage*, Penguin Books, 1962, pp. 169–70; Peter Willmott and Michael Young, *Family and Class in a London Suburb*, London, 1960.

is, similar economic conditions of existence, tend to develop similar modes of life, interests and culture.[15]

Here comes in the second major principle. While stratification according to production role may be termed class, and stratification according to role in consumption be termed status, the term class is often applied to the latter kind of group differentiation also. Such categorizations of class emphasize primarily similarity of way of life, common cultural patterns (including perhaps speech patterns in a highly differentiated society). They do not deny a broad association between way of life and role in production – if only because income, a considerable determinant of way of life, is so obviously usually associated with economic role. But they attach less significance than does Marx to those 'economic conditions that lie at a deeper level'[16] in the determination of class position, hence they separate occupational status from social status in other fields.

When classes are defined in terms of similarity of style of life, two methods of classification have been used, one of relatively objective kind, the other more subjective. The more objective indices, often used in combination, include occupation, source of income, house type, dwelling area, type of education. The more subjective indices tend to rely on how people evaluate themselves or others they know in class terms – by references to membership of clubs and other associations, to whom their friends are, from whom they are descended, with whom they marry.

Related to the conception of class as style of life is a rather special sense of the term, indicated by A. R. Wagner, writing as Richmond Herald: 'A social class for him (a genealogist) means an endogamous class, one, that is, whose members normally marry within it.'[17] Wagner links this intermarrying pattern with a sense of belonging together, reflected in, fostered and even formed by community of speech, manners, outlook and education. While generally valid, this index of class is however no more definite in practice than any other. The rule against marrying out of the class[18] has been consistently

[15] Karl Marx, *18th Brumaire of Louis Bonaparte*, quoted with other passages, by T. B. Bottomore and M. Rubel, 1963, pp. 196, etc. It may be held, however, that Marx's categorization referred specifically to the early or mid-nineteenth century.

[16] Karl Marx, *Capital*, I, Everyman ed., London, 1930, p. 117.

[17] A. R. Wagner, *English Genealogy*, Oxford, 1960, p. 86.

[18] Lawrence Stone, Marriage among the English Nobility in the 16th and 17th centuries. *Comparative Studies in Society and History*, vol. III, 1961, pp. 182–206, holds that while the trend should not be exaggerated, wealth was the most important single consideration in very many seventeenth-century marriages. 'Whereas social and political factors had influenced many earlier marriages, the growing fluidity of society inevitably led to a growing emphasis upon more strictly financial considerations.'

ignored in English history, and this breach is abundantly illustrated at the present day, from Royalty downward. Although superficially attractive to an anthropologist therefore, the genealogist's definition is not adopted here.

In Britain, the lead given by the Registrar-General, T. H. C. Stevenson, in the Census of England and Wales 1911, has been commonly followed. An attempt to give more precision to fertility statistics led to the construction of a scheme of 'social classes' by reference to a grading of occupations of male householders. While a series of occupational categories rather than of social classes in a full sense of the word, this scheme has proved a very useful means of sorting the population into major sets for many analytical purposes. We, however, have adopted a well-known modification of it as a basis for our identification of middle-class families in this study (see Chapter 2).[19]

There are certain features of social classes which are very important for the interpretation of any social material which uses them as a referent. One is that class arrangement is not haphazard but regular; the classes are conceived to be related in ranked order. In general categories, though not in individual cases, this ranking is linked with the occupational structure. As Lipset and Bendix remark (1960, p. 1), 'In every complex society there is a division of labour and a hierarchy of prestige', and these are associated. Positions of leadership and major responsibility in the industrial, commercial and administrative spheres tend to be assigned the highest status, unskilled manual workers under direction the lowest, with a great range of statuses in between, varying according to economic function, skill and training of those involved. A problem here is how this multitude of statuses and prestige attributions, of differing quality, sometimes of small variation, sometimes overlapping and blending into one another, become crystallized and generalized into major social divisions of a class order. Simple difference of status does not necessarily imply hierarchy, nor need a hierarchical scale necessarily connote stratification. Yet it is a matter of empirical experience that in common

[19] For general discussion of these issues, including combination of occupational and other criteria in the study of social classes, see especially John Hall and D. Caradog Jones, 'Social Grading of Occupations', *British Journal of Sociology*, I, 1950, pp. 31–55; D. V. Glass, *Social Mobility in Britain*, London, 1954; S. M. Lipset and R. Bendix, *Social Mobility in Industrial Society*, Berkeley, 1960; W. Lloyd Warner and P. S. Lunt, *The Status System of a Modern Community*, Yankee City Series, vol. II, New Haven, 1942. The use of indices of social participation and social reputation in combination with more 'objective' indices for computing the status characteristics of Americans has been promoted forcefully by W. Lloyd Warner and associates in their 'do it yourself' manual, *Social Class in America*, Chicago, 1949.

estimation in a country of complex industrial development such as Britain there are broad class distinctions.

Class distinctions are relative, a function of relationship to other classes in the economy and society as a whole. (The concept of 'station' in life in vogue in for example the nineteenth century, if stripped of its rather fatalistic and moralistic overtones, seems to have had reference to this functional interdependence of classes.) A further point is that neither class structure nor class position of individuals and groups is firmly fixed. Unlike mobility in a caste system (which theoretically is impossible and in practice even yet is rare) social mobility between classes is not only theoretically possible but in fact has been achieved and continues to a considerable degree in every complex industrial society. Finally, although it is often convenient to use a term such as working-class or middle-class in singular form, it may be contended that the classes are not unitary in their composition, but represent rather belts or bands of people who all share some of the characteristics of their major social category, but are by no means uniform in all their characters.[20]

In popular estimation, then, the notion of class is a complex one. It involves concepts of difference in productive role, in economic reward, in position in a hierarchy of control and authority, in position on a status ladder, in general cultural assets, interests and 'background'. Moreover, it implies some degree of social distance between members of the different classes, though not denying the possibility of communication and even mobility between them.

Turning now specifically to the middle-class, our conception in terms of both historical evidence and of contemporary classification is that in England we are not dealing with a unitary social element in a clearly stratified series. The term 'middle-class' implies a ranking intermediate between people in manual, skilled operative and simple clerical categories – most of whom at least are conventionally termed 'working class' – and people in a category which nowadays is a compound of aristocracy and plutocracy, and constitutes what is often referred to as an 'upper class'. But the relativity of the definition of the middle class is plain; the term itself suggests that the categorization of its members exists only by reference to two other classes. Certainly their production role is less clearly defined by autonomous criteria than is the case with capitalist/landowners or with the working class. The middle class, it may be argued, tends to be a kind of omnibus category; its components are by no means all on the same scale. So far from forming a neat sector of a class structure, unambiguously recognizable by their function in pro-

[20] See for example Roy Lewis and Angus Maude, *The English Middle Classes*, Pelican Books, 1953, esp. p. 18.

duction, these people constitute a highly diversified collection of contributors to the economic process: the great mass of civil servants with administrative roles; the 'free' professionals; merchants and traders of medium range; managers and agents of various kinds; scientific and other technical personnel with some degree of responsibility; people living on moderate fixed incomes. They must be looked at as occupying not the same rung on a ladder but a set of different positions on a distribution chart, with different evaluations for different criteria. As mass-consumption products and standards have spread, as higher education has become more generally available, the recognition of special strata of people by dress, recreational habits and even accent becomes increasingly difficult. Yet still, different combinations of occupation, income source, wealth, education, speech style, consumption standards give different configurations on the social map. Moreover, mobility in and out of their ranks is considerable. Hence, what is termed the 'middle class' has been more appropriately termed in recent discussion the 'middle classes', and regarded in British society as a broad band of composite structure.[21]

Historically, was there anything analogous to the middle class or classes in the eighteenth or nineteenth centuries? The question is relevant since one of the objects of the present study is to consider in terms of our data how far there have been changes in the structure of kinship over time, and for this purpose it is necessary to compare families of roughly similar social standing.

Close analysis of the materials for English social history in the eighteenth and nineteenth centuries has revealed the inadequacy of the old terms of aristocracy, landed gentry, middle class and working class to describe the configurations of a rapidly changing society. From about 1800 onwards the divisions between the 'middle class' or 'classes' and the 'working class' or 'classes' were in process of formation, but in their classic form did not fully emerge until the 1880s, although there were premonitions of what was to come in the 1840s. The use of the contemporary term 'interest', with its vertical not horizontal connotation, has been widely adopted. Interests were not necessarily conflicting, but they were different. The two main interests in the eighteenth, and indeed for much of the nineteenth

[21] Cf. Josephine Klein, *Samples from English Cultures*, vol. I, London, 1965, pp. 303–10, for demonstration of this. To give a working basis for investigation, a formal criterion of classification has sometimes been adopted – e.g. a middle-class family is one in which a white-collar job with an income of £800 p.a. or more is held by at least one member of the family. (Mark Abrams, the *Observer*, 23 October 1960; quoted by Peter Willmott, *Evolution of a Community*, London, 1963, p. 97.

centuries were the landed interest and the commercial interest. Both, should the need arise, could be broken down into a series of specific interests such as the 'City interest', the 'East Indian interest', the 'cotton interest' and later on the 'railway interest'. The 'City interest' was referred to as much in the 1860s as it was in the 1760s.[22] The Reform Act of 1867 marked the end of the 'classic' period of parliamentary government by 'interest'; then, consequent upon the extension of the suffrage, the modern national party system with its more complex association with class interests gradually emerged.

English society in the period under consideration was hierarchical in form. It was composed of a large series of social gradations, but the criteria whereby a family was included in or excluded from any particular gradation differed according to locality – with the exception of those families who occupied the apex of the national pyramid. Complexity and mobility of middle class in southern England about the end of the eighteenth century would seem to have been illustrated by Jane Austen. The criteria for social aspiration of men wishing to enter the gentry in a small country town society may be summarized as including a 'good'education, a small independence, abandonment of the 'more homely pursuits', entry into the militia as an officer, marriage to a woman of 'good family'. Most or all of these, with the possession of 'manners', marked the 'respectable family, which for the last two or three generations had been rising into gentility and property' (*Emma*, 1932, p. 10).

The novelist's view, of course, with its ironic touch, and interest in personality rather than in category, may have lacked judicial emphasis. But in any case Namier and Brooke have drawn attention to the remarkable fluidity of English society in the last half of the eighteenth century. 'A family could rise or fall in social standing in a single generation',[23] Thompson, using a 10 per cent sample, has shown that about a quarter of the families entered in the 1846 edition of *Burke's Landed Gentry* had disappeared by the time of the 1871 edition, and that about a quarter of the entries of 1871 related to families which had acquired their country seats since 1790.[24] Namier and Brooke perhaps go too far when they assert that 'a man's social standing in the last resort depended on his own estimate'. But they do draw attention to an important difference between the English society with which they are concerned and English society of the last half of the nineteenth century. The speech, manners and

[22] Asa Briggs, *The Age of Improvement*, London, 1959, p. 405.

[23] Sir Lewis Namier and John Brooke, *The House of Commons*, vol. I, London, 1964, p. 99.

[24] F. M. L. Thompson, *English Landed Society in the Nineteenth Century*, London, 1963, p. 125.

customs of the gentleman had not yet been standardized by the universities and the public school system. There was no hierarchical educational system. Education 'was a commodity to be bought and sold like other commodities, and of which there were both cheap and expensive varieties', and education was not considered to be an essential requisite in the life of every child. Boys from every social grade mixed in what schools there were. The traditional professions of the law, the church, the army and the navy were the only ones the eighteenth century recognized. Namier and Brooke exclude medicine. Although physicians were graduates, their social standing was ambiguous, and while the sons of gentry and aristocrats could become barristers or clergymen or accept commissions in the army and navy or even enter trade, they did not yet practice medicine.[25] Medicine, however, could be a means of social mobility upwards. One of the characteristic movements of the nineteenth century has been the growth of 'professionalism'[26] and the consequent closure of the professions as well as their proliferation. But until the second half of the century, and indeed for many professions until the twentieth century, the situation was still fluid. It was not until 1870 that entry into the administrative ranks of the Home Civil Service was restricted to those who had received a 'liberal education'. Gladstone's avowed object was 'to strengthen and multiply the ties between the higher classes and the possession of administrative power' and by the 'separation of *work* . . . into mechanical and intellectual . . . open to the highly educated class a career and give them a command over all the higher parts of the civil service, which up to this time they have never enjoyed.'[27] Gladstone's upper classes included not only 'the aristocracy' but all 'those who may be called gentlemen by birth and training'. The underlying assumption in mid-nineteenth-century England was, as Briggs has pointed out, that it was possible to reconcile economic change and individual mobility with traditional social balance and stability – a view epitomized by a pronouncement by Palmerston, 'We have shown the example of a nation, in which every class of society accepts with cheerfulness the lot which Providence has assigned to it; while at the same time every individual of each class is constantly striving to raise himself in the social scale.'[28] Yet increasing professionalism and the capture by the

[25] Namier and Brooke, op. cit., pp. 15, 110, 126.

[26] Institutions of civil engineers, mechanical engineers, and architects were founded at various dates between 1818 and 1847, and the Medical Act regularizing some aspects of the medical profession was passed in 1858.

[27] Quoted in E. Hughes, *Civil Service Reform*, 1853–5, in *History*, vol. xxvii, 1942.

[28] A. Briggs, op. cit., p. 404.

well-to-do of the public schools and the universities were to make individual social mobility from the lower rungs of the ladder difficult, if not impossible, in the latter half of the century.

Both Mingay[29] and Thompson have criticized the traditional classification of the landed interest into aristocracy, landed gentry and freeholders, and have shown that the peerage and great landed magnates were not synonymous. Many of the greater landlords were commoners and some had far greater incomes than the poorer peers. Functionally, there was a clear-cut distinction between landlords and owner occupiers, but when incomes are taken into account the accepted social categories again break down, many farmers being far wealthier than the poorer landed gentry. The great magnates were related by marriage and kinship through younger sons with the lesser gentry who in their turn were likewise related to the freeholders. All three were also related to the merchants, manufacturers, traditional professions, country town traders, and even to husbandmen and labourers. In 1726 Defoe had pointed out that

> Trade is so far here from being inconsistent with a gentleman, that in short trade in England makes gentlemen, and has peopled this nation with gentlemen; for . . . the tradesmen's children, or at least their grand-children, come to be as good gentlemen, statesmen, Parliament-men, privy-counsellors, judges, bishops, and noblemen, as those of the highest birth and the most antient families.[30]

Kitson Clark in his Ford Lectures has poured scorn on the use of the concept 'middle class' in discussing Victorian England, and has asked the very relevant question 'Who precisely were the middle class?'[31] The absurdity of grouping into one social category the great merchants of Liverpool and London with the small town trader is patent. If the term is to be used at all, it needs to be defined very precisely in relation to the particular context in which it is used. E. P. Thompson has drawn attention to the changing patterns in relationships between individuals in this period, and is convinced 'that we cannot understand class unless we see it as a social and cultural formation, arising from processes which can only be studied as they work themselves out over a considerable historical period.[32] He would see identity of interests as one of the essential

[29] G. E. Mingay, op. cit.

[30] Quoted by Sir Lewis Namier in *England in the Age of the American Revolution*, 2nd ed., London, 1963, p. 9.

[31] G. K. Clark, *The Making of Victorian England*, London, 1962, p. 5.

[32] E. P. Thompson, *The Making of the English Working Classes*, London, 1963, p. 11.

criteria of class. It is this lack of identity of interests which has led to misgivings of the use of class concepts in the analysis of much of the history of this period. The occupational classification of the 1851 census was functional and conceived in terms of particular 'interests', and this is not without significance. Individuals and families, whatever their position in the various social hierarchies were linked through kinship and marriage with other individuals and families representing different interests and occupations, and occupying very probably different positions in the social hierarchies. Within the same family of procreation there would be members engaged in commerce and the professions, while the eldest son might be heir to a landed estate and yet draw a large part of his income in the eighteenth century from East India merchantmen or in the nineteenth from railway shares.

It is possible at certain given times by using census data to distinguish families of roughly similar social standing in a specific area and to compare them with those of today. But unlike today, if any family were removed from that particular area to another area, the gradation of its social standing would be different – with the exception of families at the apex of the social pyramid. In Chapter 3 the 'middle-class' people of one such specific area are examined from this historical point of view.

In the latter half of the twentieth century we are dealing with the conception of a 'middle class' which in metropolitan conditions is of very diverse social origins, occupational composition, income range and cultural interests. There may be some hierarchy of an objective kind vis-à-vis a 'working class' on the one hand and an 'upper class' on the other – in terms of gross income levels, or type of status-ranked symbols of a social and recreational kind. But there is considerable overlapping – as in the incomes of popular entertainers and of top-level business men. The class structure may be looked upon in some ways – especially by members of the different classes themselves – as a set of horizontally-ranked strata. But figuratively regarded, as with the historical situation, it is more significantly seen as a set of vertically-cut social sectors. The differentiation is in terms not of grading as high or low, but of interest-groups of various nature and position. This is not to deny the importance attached by middle-class people to differences in income level and correspondingly to differences in housing and general style of life. But what also seems characteristic, especially in metropolitan conditions, is the high degree of geographical and social mobility, and correspondingly, the relative lack of clear-cut exclusive group formation.

All these elements in the situation would seem to be relevant to the character of kinship outside the elementary family. The people who were the subjects of our investigation were clearly middle class by any ordinarily accepted criteria. Most of them so regarded themselves, though the criteria they used in definition of their position were not always the same. One point of view which may epitomize the attitude of many professional people was that of a woman who described her family as 'utterly middle class' for the last 150 years, and who characterized the middle classes as 'not having to work for anyone, not being anyone's servants, and having the means to be independent' – though not necessarily having their own businesses. In this study of the kinship of middle-class people in London, we are not assuming that to be middle class necessarily involves having a different kind of kinship system from people of other classes. This has indeed been suggested by some general preliminary statements. But our approach to the question is both more sceptical and more pragmatic. We were concerned to find out what sort of kin ties they had, and what use they made of them, without postulating in advance any particular sort of class-kin typology.

POSSIBLE CORRELATES OF MIDDLE-CLASS KINSHIP PATTERNS

There are certain elements in the social life of the middle classes which may be relevant to the patterning of their kin relations. These include:

(i) relatively high economic level as compared with manual workers. This can allow middle-class people to provide for themselves some paid services of an alternative kind to those, such as domestic aid, given by kin among the working classes, and so can remove an economic dimension of service from kin relations. But higher income also can allow of more commodious housing, with possible provision of accommodation for kin in need; or it may allow of financial support of kin living elsewhere. So, in a situation of kin dependence, alternative solutions and differing patterns of reciprocity may be open.

(ii) much greater economic security, as salary earners, than is apt to obtain among manual workers and their families. This can mean more economic independence from kin in times of crisis. On the other hand, among middle-class families property relations may be more extensive, and inheritance may be much more significant than among working-class families. In the direct line of property transmission this could mean a greater importance of father-son tie among the middle classes as contrasted with the strength of the mother-daughter tie noted in working-class families.

More widely, it would mean a maintenance of social relations with kin from whom there were property expectations.

(iii) greater geographical mobility associated with the professions and the middle classes generally could mean more scattering of families and loss of contact with kin. But there could have been, until the diffusion of the automobile through the working classes, a much greater access of middle-class people to travel facilities, and hence much greater possibility of keeping up contacts with scattered kin.

(iv) greater cultural diversity, bringing with it the possibility of contacts with friends in a wide range of interests, and so militating against the needs for social relations with kin.

(v) an ideology of child independence – exemplified by attitudes to boarding schools – which might lead to a different expression of ties with home and kin than in families from which a child is rarely separated.

(vi) a probable tendency towards greater independence for young women in middle-class households – at least until recently, when young working-class women have also gained greater freedom. This could lead to their earlier emancipation from home, before marriage, with consequent reaction upon mother-daughter and other family ties, and possible lessening of ties with kin outside the family circle.

The possible effects of these various elements in middle-class social relations do not all point in the same direction. They do not indicate *a priori* any particular type of middle-class extra-familial kin structure. But consideration of them does suggest that middle-class people are likely to differ significantly in their kin arrangements from working-class people, with perhaps diminished kin ties in some directions and increased ties in others. It is possible too that in their relative lack of landed property and major industrial assets, and still relative lack of control of political power, the middle classes may differ recognizably in their kinship patterns from 'upper-class' people. But at this stage of sociological and anthropological enquiry in Britain we do not know whether significant differences in kin patterns exist on such basis and if they exist what they are, and how pervasive they are. A major aim of this study is to help in the elucidation of these problems.

One further question may be raised here, and answered briefly – what is the use of such enquiries? Three reasons seem to us to be valid.

1. In a very limited way, this book describes a sector of North London, especially Highgate, society at a recent period. But its

value is as an analytical symptom rather than as an historical record. The results of the study are a contribution to the ethnography of Britain – to understanding in a more scientific, systematic way, the customs and institutions of ordinary people in a sector of metropolitan society. There have been still many gaps in this ethnography – we know much about families, something about friendship and neighbourhood relations, a very great deal about economic, legal and political institutions; there is also much material of uneven quality about religion. Studies of kinship such as these help to fill a gap in our knowledge which is wider than we often realize. This book then should contribute to a further understanding of middle-class values and behaviour patterns.

2. The study is a contribution to the comparative theory of social systems. British kinship patterns in a metropolitan area suggest comparisons with other types of kinship patterns in other conditions. British kinship is a type of bilateral kinship, which covers a great range of phenomena which have been the subject of much theoretical analysis. The conceptual problems of structure and process involved in this are of great complexity, and British data and generalizations give help in clarification. A particular effort in this direction is the collaborative study undertaken with our colleagues in Chicago, with exchange of information and creative discussion of theories and methods.

3. The study has practical implications. These are of several kinds. First of all, it may serve to widen the horizon of those in British society who have a curiosity about their own social origins, and become concerned to trace back their forbears. Many people wish to know more about their ancestors. This study will not give them any direct information. But it may provide for the more systematically-minded a basis for interest in the social implications of kin relations and not merely in the formalism of genealogies or 'pedigrees'.[33] More important, it should help to provide some theoretical underpinning for the many practical studies made of family problems by psychologists, social workers and sociologists. Too often in the past many of these studies have ignored extra-familial kinship ties such as relations with aunts, uncles, parents-in-law, which have been important conditioning factors in intra-family behaviour.[34] But perhaps most of all it may be of value in

[33] See Arthur J. Willis, *Introducing Genealogy*, London, 1961; L. G. Pine, *Trace Your Ancestors*, London, 1953 (paper, 1966); and the scholarly study by Wagner, op. cit.

[34] An admirable demonstration of the involvement of client families with their kin in an American Jewish setting has been provided for family caseworkers by Hope Jensen Leichter and William E. Mitchell, *Kinship and Casework*, Russell Sage Foundation, New York, 1967.

helping to provoke a wider interest in personal kinship – an aspect of social behaviour of all of us which is still too little understood. In any walk of life people seem apt to think that the way they get on with their relatives depends primarily on individual character and temperament, or is a matter of luck. Part of the purpose of this study is to reveal the kinds of interconnection that exist between factors of personality, including individual selection and forces of self-expression, and factors of social patterning, including norms of convention and moral evaluation.

2

Methodology of this Study[1]

The history of this kinship project can be divided broadly into four phases: formulation; development of the framework; field collection; and analysis and writing-up. There was considerable overlapping between these phases.

FORMULATION OF THE PROJECT

As mentioned in the Preface, the project was originally conceived in Anglo-American discussion about the character of bilateral (cognatic) kinship systems, especially those in Western society. At the outset it was specifically entitled 'A Study of British Middle-Class Families, with the ultimate aim of comparison with American Kinship Structures'. The research took as a major hypothesis that in industrial society families were not isolated from their kin, and kinship had positive functions. We postulated that extra-familial kinship ties are of great importance, especially in conditioning the interplay of intra-familial roles and in affording to individuals sources of social support outside the family. Since most of the research on kinship in Britain has been done on working-class families we decided to concentrate on the middle class.

The aim of the research was not to try and throw immediate light on family and personality problems, though it was contended that ultimately many phases of social work would have to take account of these significant structural features.[2]

The primary methods used were to be the intensive first-hand methods of enquiry of the social anthropologist. These would be

[1] A detailed account of the methods used in this study has been issued as *Methods of Study of Middle-Class Kinship in London: A Working Paper on the History of an Anthropological Project*, 1960–65, by Jane Hubert, Anthony Forge and Raymond Firth. Occasional Paper of the Department of Anthropology, London School of Economics and Political Science, 1968.

[2] In American conditions this has been borne out by Hope Leichter and W. Mitchell. op. cit.

modified where necessary by the nature of the situation, e.g. full-scale observational techniques would not, it was thought, be usually possible, but direct observation would be sought wherever feasible to confirm the results of interviews. Great use would be made of the genealogical techniques of enquiry. But it was intended also to examine documentary materials on the communities from which the samples would be drawn, to help in selecting the samples and to give historical and sociological background. It was reckoned that the intensive methods of enquiry would allow only a relatively small number of families to be studied, the preliminary estimate being about 100 families (with associated kin) in the British sample.

In organizational terms the project was seen as involving direct co-operative planning of research by British and American scholars – something which, as far as we knew, had not been attempted before in the social sciences. It was proposed that ultimately there would be two sets of enquiries, each to be undertaken by a small team, one in United States and one in Britain. The investigations would be autonomous as regards control but associated as regards aim, planning and the comparison of methods and results. It was hoped that part of the ultimate value of the enquiry would lie in the comparability of the results and in the methodological gains from this Anglo-American co-operation. Links between teams would be facilitated by ties of personal knowledge and confidence between the major investigators. It was thought that at some stage personal consultation between team members in a trans-atlantic conference might be valuable.

It was recognized that for adequate comparison it was essential that the number of possible variables in the samples chosen should be reduced as far as possible, and that certain factors be held as constant. Hence, considerable thought was given to the possible matching of samples in Britain and the United States – in terms of area, age factor, occupation, marital state, spatial mobility, etc.

It was recognized too that one of the more difficult aspects of the investigation would be to find comparable indices in the United States and Britain for the measurement of the intensity and significance of kin relations. The main problem would lie in systematization of data on quality and structure of kin roles and the social implications of extra-familial kin ties. But it was thought that possibly some ancillary problems might be studied – e.g. differences in the kin relations of the single child from those in a family with several children; and differences in the kinship universe of 'traditional' middle-class families from that of 'rising' middle-class families. (In the upshot it was not possible to undertake these special enquiries.)

The period proposed for the project was three years, divided approximately as follows: preliminary enquiries, 3 months; field research, 21 months; analysis, drafting and final checking, 12 months.

The project went forward in this form, with only minor modifications from the original draft. Originally intended to begin early in 1960, it did not get under way until almost the end of that year, and concluded formally in mid-1965. It thus took four and a half years, not the three years originally planned. Moreover, when the project officially came to an end the collection and analysis of materials had been completed but the drafting of the results in publishable form had been only about half finished. Other claims on the time of the principal investigator and his colleagues then prevented the job being completed at once. It became clear that in this as in other comparable projects final synthesis of the results in publishable form demanded an effort of personal focus which had to be continued far beyond the work of analysis and preliminary drafting of conclusions by the working team.

Co-operation with the American study was most fruitful. The original aim of direct close comparison proved not to be very applicable – there were too many variables which could not be eliminated. On the other hand, many parallels stimulated theoretical discussion and frequent exchanges of interview guides, progress reports, memoranda and comment on special topics were most enlightening. Three special transatlantic visits helped to crystallize procedures for interviewing, analysis and reporting of results, to develop agreed strategies for further work, and to provide a forum for discussion of a range of theoretical problems of kinship.

DEVELOPMENT OF THE FRAMEWORK

The work of the project began formally at a meeting of the principal investigator and three members of what came to be known as the Kinship Team on 30th September 1960.

We had already decided on the first field of study, a housing estate in North London, which for purposes of the investigation we named Greenbanks. The chief advantage of this area was that it contained a high proportion of professional people, who clearly fell well within the 'middle-band' social class range which was our object of study. Moreover, the area was reasonably accessible for our field workers, and offered facilities of introduction to some informants. Later for comparison we decided to undertake the study of a second London area. After consideration of various alternatives, including a country town and a London square, we fixed upon a middle-class sector of the population of Highgate, which lay in the same geographical area as Greenbanks, the northern heights of London. By contrast with the Estate, an area of fairly recent settlement, Highgate had a long history, and we thought it possible that we might find families of a different type there. (A brief description of the area is given in Chapter 3.) For this reason we had already started historical research in Highgate while Greenbanks was still being investigated.

We now consider from an analytical viewpoint the development of the techniques we used in the enquiry.

Intensive Interviews

On the field work side the first basic question which faced us was how best to get the information required. The use of structured questionnaires for collecting data was rejected. The main reason was that we wanted intensive qualitative material, not relatively superficial answers to simple questions. Although empirical information was required at all levels, our interest was not only in this, but in the way questions were answered, the discussion that a question or answer might provoke and the ideology and values and norms that became apparent. Informants were encouraged to talk freely and, within obvious limits, talk about what they wanted. It was essential not to prevent anyone from raising and discussing matters which he or she felt were relevant, since what they considered relevant to kinship added to our overall picture and, to some extent, provided the material of kinship ideology. For example, a simple question regarding frequency of contact with a specific relative will often provoke more than a quantitative answer of frequency. Certainly with further questions it may lead an informant to a statement of ideology and evaluation of a kin relationship. Without a set of formal questions to be ploughed through at a sitting, interviewers were free to follow up any answer, where they saw interesting leads, without feeling tied to a rigid programme. This tendency toward discussion rather than question-and-answer interviewing also in most cases enabled rapport to be established between interviewer and informant – which was of great importance in a relationship which had to be maintained through five to ten or so interviews, and dealt with very personal matters.

Although interviews in themselves were unstructured, this did not mean that the information collected was arbitrary – most of the material was essential to each case, and had to be obtained at some point. Certain basic material, in fact, had to be collected in the first interview (or at least before any other data was collected, since with a difficult informant the first interview might be spent merely discussing the project). The basic tool, the framework around which all the material was gathered and placed together, was the *genealogy*.

Genealogies

As soon as possible and, if it could be managed, before kin were discussed at all, genealogies were obtained systematically. These started from the informants and their children (if any) working out to siblings (and their spouses and descendants), parents, parents' siblings (and their spouses and descendants, etc.) and so on, until all relatives were accounted for, dead or alive, whether link to informant ('Ego') or name was known or not.

It should be noted that the genealogy as obtained and used by social anthropologists is different in several respects from the document sought by professional genealogists. When tracing a pedigree the anthropologist is hardly interested at all in family origins as such. 'To trace descendants from persons whose lives are known to history' is a reasonable aim of genealogical research.[3] It is true that a genealogist may be interested as much in the contemporary 'lateral ties' as in the ancestral 'vertical ties'. But an anthropologist is concerned not with the *fact* of linkage, but with the *recognition* of linkage and the use made of this recognition. He may even be concerned less with historical accuracy than with imaginary links, provided that these are recognized as a basis for social 'kinship' ties between the parties.

There is a further point, in regard to the use of the term 'Ego' as the personal focus of a genealogy. A social anthropologist's use of 'Ego' is different from that of the psychologist or psycho-analyst. We are not concerned with problems of the consciousness of the 'Ego', its relation to the self, etc. For the social anthropologist 'Ego' is the central point of a genealogical construction, the point of reference in regard to which the map of social relationships expressed by the genealogy can be identified. Usually, 'Ego' is also the major informant from whom the information on the genealogy was derived. But even if information was derived from several people equally, the anthropologist will still label one of them as 'Ego' for genealogical purposes in discussing the kin relations involved.

Various empirical data were collected by all interviewers from all informants in the first interviews. For each relative the following information was asked for, and a note was made where this was not known: all names, age (or date of death), sibling order (where age

[3] A. R. Wagner, *English Genealogy*, 1960, p. 370.

not known), occupation and residence. These were all recorded on the genealogy, which was then used as reference point throughout the interview sequence. Other information collected systematically for all relatives appearing on the genealogy was education, frequency of contact (seeing, writing, telephone, etc.) and whether or not services of any kind were exchanged. After this information had been gathered, interviewers were free to follow the *aide-mémoire* (see later) as they liked.

At various phases in the field work we compiled specific check lists for different sorts of data. But generally they proved to give more trouble than they were worth. The basic material was checked in other systematic ways; and material such as attitudes or kinship ideology was not 'checkable' in any simple list form. However, at the beginning of the study it had been realized that some general summary record of the more empirical data was useful as a guide, apart from yielding the information in a relatively manageable form. Consequently, apart from the case history for each family, forms were filled in for husband and wife on various topics: contact with kin (and type of contact); occupation of all kin; services exchanged with kin (including hypothetical situations as discussed later). In early stages forms were filled in separately for relationships with siblings and parents, but these were later incorporated into one or other of the more comprehensive forms.

After preliminary analysis of the non-random sample, and a great deal of unnecessary counting and recounting from the genealogies, a condensed form was devised which was referred to as the '*primary data form*'. All information on the genealogy was recorded here: relationship to Ego; name; age; residence; occupation; education; 'boundary category' (see Chapter 7); and frequency of contact.

Aide-Mémoire

The *aide-mémoire*, which developed from three to twenty-three pages during the pilot stages of the study, was divided in its later form into twenty main sections, each with further sub-divisions. Each section consisted of a reminder to interviewers of the most important aspects of the material to be obtained in the section, and a series of questions relating to these. These questions were not intended to be asked parrot-wise of the informant; rather they were questions to the *interviewer*, to which she must supply the answer. Interviewers were obviously not expected to remember the whole thing at any one time. They were expected, however, to know it quite thoroughly, and to be able to remember the most important questions in it at any time, should they or the subject come round to any of the topics in an interview. The usual practice was to brush up the sections that were going to be tackled at the next interview. The main point is that at no time did interviewers arrive at an interview with the *aide-mémoire* in hand either for reference or to tick off questions as they were answered.

Obviously, the use of a large, rather amorphous, schema such as this had some great disadvantages. There was even the question how far the term '*aide-mémoire*' was strictly applicable. It became obvious that all the questions in it could not be answered by all informants. Interviewers complained because, given an unco-operative or an untalkative informant, or someone too busy to give enough time to the project, they could not, using the *aide-mémoire* as it stood, know which questions were more important than any others. In the absence of some indication of 'priority', at first different interviewers were choosing different points in each section which they felt should be covered in any event. In other instances, because of the nature of a particular case, one section would be covered in great detail, leaving too little time to cover another section adequately. Because of this, before interviewing in the second sample area began, the *aide-mémoire* was marked up, indicating with an asterisk the most important questions that had to be answered in each section.

The use of closed-question interviewing techniques, or even open-ended types of questionnaire, was precluded by the nature of the material and the depth of investigation we wanted to make. By choosing to use the anthropological technique of intensive, unstructured interviews, however, we increased the possibility of non-comparability between cases, because of the variability of informants and interview situations, and the variations of personality, interest and approach between different interviewers. (But see pp. 52–3.) Another serious problem was the analysis of the material gained from this sort of interviewing. Yet the *aide-mémoire* method did allow great freedom to interview, let fresh topics be opened up as the informant responded, and yielded a rich supply of data. Without having their minds made up in advance, interviewers could record anything relevant to the general problem.

Participant Observation

One of the main anthropological techniques, apart from intensive interviewing of informants, is participant observation. In the classical anthropological 'field', anthropologists live among the people they are studying, watch or take part in social functions, keep an eye on all that goes on and try to be as much a part of the community as they can. Obviously in this way they are able to see what happens rather than just be told what happens, though how far they actually become *participants* varies a great deal according to context and personal qualities. In a kin-oriented society kin relationships will be manifested freely and publicly in statements and non-verbal behavioural patterns, and the articulation of behaviour can be easily observed. In a modern urban community the situation is quite different. There are not, in any comparable sense, geographically corporate groups of kin, and kinship behaviour is not observable in the same way. Dwellings are more individualized, most kin behaviour occurs in private, is relatively infrequent and is interspersed with a whole range of other sorts of behaviour in all sorts of contexts: work, recreation, religious activities.

In early stages of the study, before interviewing began, and again later as well, a great deal of discussion took place on the advantages and disadvantages of one or more members of the team living in the area of study. It was finally decided that the advantages would be few, and the drawbacks probably considerable. We did acquire a room on the Estate as a resting-place for members of the team in between interviews, but did not use this as an effective living-room.

All possible opportunities were taken to participate, especially on the Estate, in local and family affairs. Local newspapers were taken weekly. Local events were noted and attended by one or more team members and some local clubs were joined. These activities added to the general picture we had of the area, but further confirmed us in the view that in a metropolitan district such as this, with few identifiable social units, participant observation of kin relations at the community level is quite limited. The only club that yielded useful information and sidelights on any of our informants on the Estate was a local Parents' Club, but again its value was limited since members of the club were mainly mothers living off the Estate. A more cohesive group of people than a set of local residents would perhaps have been a group of young mothers attending this Parents' Club. Although they lived fairly scattered through the general area, they had more in common and probably more contact (apart from casual meetings) than had the residents of the Estate.

Apart from local events and associations, interviewers sometimes attended family affairs in the houses of their informants. Where this did occur, much valuable material was gathered. In many cases, too, interviewers ate meals in the house, met the odd relative at various times, chatted to the children and so on, which meant that information gathered in actual interviews was often elaborated on, argued about, checked and validated in other contexts.

Interview Notes and Case Histories

Interviewers did not go into the field with interview 'schedules' which had to be filled in. Instead, in anthropological fashion, they went armed with small notebooks, in which they endeavoured to write down as much as possible of what was said by the informants, including answers to questions and remarks by themselves. Naturally no one could record everything verbatim, but a great deal was in fact recorded as it was said. In the later writing up of the cases, only those words which were recorded verbatim were used as actual quotations. Often, of course, information could not be recorded straight away. The informant would say, 'Don't put this down, but. . . .' Sometimes information would be given during meals, or walking round the garden, or while washing-up. In a few cases informants only started producing interesting material as soon as the interviewer's notebook was closed.

When interviewers returned from a field interview notes were written up from the notebooks into readable form. When a sequence of interviews was completed with a household the interview notes were used as the basis of a case history. Each case history contained all the material on one family, organized according to the headings of the *aide-mémoire*, and was then used as the basic document for all further discussion or analysis of the case.

It was considered important that there should be some record of interviews, apart from the final case history, that could be checked through by the team leader, or consulted by any member of the team. It was important, too, that these interview records should preserve the original form of the interview, and not be rearranged as they were written. (In a few cases interviewers were found to be rearranging and in some cases interpreting notes from the field notebooks in the process of typing up, in order to make the task of case history writing that much easier. At all times this was discouraged, since the way the interview developed was obviously very important, and if the sequence was changed, remarks often came to mean something quite different and thus were misleading.)

So, all field notebooks, written-up interview notes and original genealogies were preserved, but once a case was finally written up they were only consulted when there was an apparent gap or contradiction in the case history.

This three-stage process of recording in the field, then writing up of interview notes and then writing up of case histories was a slow business. It was essential however – since there were a number of interviewers and change-over of team members at various points between and during interviewing and analysis phases – to have interviews written up in the form that they actually occurred. It was also necessary, given the variations in the order and complexity of interview material, to have the data for each family finally organized in a similar way. Without this organization into case histories, the material would have been unmanageable when it came to analysis of all the cases. (This point is obvious when it is realized that the longest case histories amounted to over one hundred foolscap pages.) Genealogies, too, were drawn up in a similar fashion for each informant, and dyeline copies made of each for analysis and for file.

Although case histories were largely factual reports, interviewers were encouraged at this stage to give in special sections their own interpretations and ideas about their cases. Space too was given to their own impressions of the informants, and a general assessment of the material. Later, when a case history was completed, it was discussed at meetings with the rest of the team; comments upon it of a more theoretical order were entered in the meeting record.

The final case histories were written in coded form. All surnames were changed according to a simple code, and some first names where they were particularly unusual, and therefore possibly recognizable by other people. The original reason for coding was that early in the project it was thought that various colleagues who were 'consultants' to the project might be given access to the material, and since we had given our word to our informants that they would remain anonymous to all but ourselves, coding was necessary. Genealogies were not coded (except one or two sent to America for comparison) since sight of these was intended to remain exclusively within the team. However, at a later stage it was agreed that, in any case, all original material about informants should not be seen by anyone outside the team, since it might still be possible to identify informants if they happened to be known to the 'consultants'. Although this decision was taken, coding of case histories continued. It still served a purpose since team members, in discussing cases among one another privately and in team meetings, used the code names regularly and thus got accustomed to referring to their informants by pseudonyms. All these precautions minimized the risk of taking away the anonymity of our informants. It also had the effect of allowing us to treat the material more dispassionately, much as a medical man views a patient in hospital as a case.

The fact that almost all members of the team were social anthropologists, and that all were graduates, is important. At no stage were assistants employed solely to act as interviewers. Throughout the study, right from the beginning, all members of the team were participants in the planning and development of the research. It was seen to be essential for a study of this depth and complexity that field workers were not merely interviewers but had a full grasp of the theory and concepts involved. This was one reason why they did not need to be provided with a stereotyped questionnaire.

Great importance was attached from the beginning to team discussions, which were held at first almost daily, and later as formal meetings once a week, with many interim informal discussions between all members of the team. The formal meetings, which were presided over by the director of the project, were recorded in detailed meeting reports. These reports, which grew to over four hundred pages by the end of the study, constitute a history of the project from the first week. Altogether 146 'formal' meetings were held, from the opening of the project in the autumn of 1960 until the summer of 1964, when the majority of the team dispersed.

At these meetings all members of the team were free to discuss and argue anything relevant to the project. Decisions about procedures to be adopted and such matters as the type of samples to be taken, where they should be taken from, modifications or additions to the *aide-mémoire*, etc. were made by the team as a whole, not necessarily by any individual.

The reports of these meetings not only give an account of the procedures adopted, but show what alternatives were considered, how decisions were arrived at, and the stages in the development of our thinking and the theoretical position in critical areas of the study. At various stages in the project papers were written for anthropology seminars, kinship 'working parties' and other groups on such problems as kinship terminology, sibling solidarity, parent-in-law/child-in-law relationships, methodology of the study. Detailed answers were also written to memoranda sent over by our colleagues engaged on the Chicago project, concerned with changes in kin networks over time, family typology, kin 'boundaries' and 'kin-keepers'.

FIELD PROCEDURES

Choice of Sample Areas

The traditional anthropological techniques with which we intended to operate as far as possible were developed primarily for the study of small-scale primitive communities, and obviously had to be modified in a modern, urban context. In a primitive society there are usually residential groups of some kind, with recognizable boundaries, which correspond to some more or less precise social units, and form communities. Rural areas of Britain also show such communities. In London, or its suburbs, there are not such geographically determined localized social units. There are, however, certain areas which have fairly well-defined geographical boundaries (e.g. the foot of a hill, a wood), and although these areas are by no means precise social units it would be reasonable to expect that there would be more interaction between residents in them than in a similar but undefined London area. By the very nature of such an area a certain degree of identification with it is unavoidable for the residents, since the physical boundaries exist, and they live within them rather than outside them. This, then, is what we have called a 'quasi-community'.

It may be asked why it was necessary to approximate to a community at all. Firstly, we recognized that our intensive methods of enquiry were such that relatively few households could be studied out of any population. If these households were completely isolated from one another all the information that could be obtained would be from each one individually and there would be no possibility of obtaining additional material which might be relevant. In a 'quasi-community' we could expect some interaction between residents (however small this in fact might be), whether friendly, hostile or neutral. The intention was not to 'check-up' on information given to us, but to fill out the picture given to us by individuals, especially with respect to the extent of exchange of services between households – something which was obviously important in an assessment of the need for, and use of, relatives. In addition, any participation of interviewers in social activities with their informants was more likely to involve other informants and their families. Moreover, the relations between neighbours and other members of the community might act as a foil to the relations between these people and their kin. Study of community relations could not only give a background to the kinship relations of the informants but also could enable us to observe some of the alternatives presented to them in the areas of sociability or exchange of services.

The relevant factor, which relates to both these points, is that in a modern urban society people do not live in general with their kin in any identifiable unit larger than the household, nor do their lives consist only, or even chiefly, of a series of kin encounters. If we had taken families from a wider, undefined area our total knowledge of them would have been obtained from information given by them in interviews and, to a lesser degree, from observation during interviews and time spent in the household. By choosing an area where there was likely to be a significant amount of interchange of services, and general acquaintanceship, we increased our sources of knowledge about our informants by being able to observe, if only in a limited fashion and largely through the chatter of other people, the sphere of day-to-day life. As anthropologists we were also initially interested in studying the nature of the relations between neighbours and the degree of their commitment to the notion of community.

The first sample we studied, in Greenbanks, was of households acquired in snowball fashion on a non-random basis. This gave us time to develop our methods of investigation and decide on the most efficient means of getting information. It also enabled us to sort out themes which seemed deserving of special attention from others which were only of peripheral interest, and showed us which areas were going to be especially difficult to tackle. From the beginning, however, the intention had been to follow the pilot sample with a randon sample of residents on the Estate. Although primarily an anthropological study, the use of certain techniques usually considered to be 'sociological' was obviously necessary. After investigation of our initial 30 cases, and three months after the start of the project, a random sample of 60 households was drawn from the population of Greenbanks. This sample constituted roughly 25 per cent of the Estate.

The need for a random sample was primarily because the inhabitants of the area were heterogeneous in terms of occupation, income, age, family stage and marital status, religion and origin (both class and ethnic). Ideally it would have been preferable to study the whole population. But within the limits of time and number of workers 250 households could not be studied intensively, and the aim was to investigate relatively few families as intensively as possible rather than many families superficially. It was realized at the beginning, and substantiated by subsequent comparisons, that the non-random pilot sample was biased in various ways. For example, the two professional contacts we had in Greenbanks introduced us to a largely professional set of people; there tended also to be age clustering, and even religious clustering. There was also the danger that people would recommend those of their friends and acquaintances whom they knew to have 'interesting' families, or who were known to 'love talking about their family', or whom they thought of as 'typical' families.

Since our aim was to assess the importance of different factors in the field of kinship, as many elements of bias as possible had to be eliminated. By our previous 'snowball' method of getting informants we were liable to miss whole groups of people whose lives did not overlap with the people we first met, and since we were also trying to study the degree of community participation this was an additional drawback. By taking a 25 per cent sample we could at least claim to have a set of people who were representative of the Greenbanks population.

The population to be studied was defined as all dwellings on the Greenbanks Estate shown to be occupied by Electors according to the Electoral Roll of 2 February 1960, as amended on 28 November 1960, the qualifying date for inclusion being 10 October 1960. The unit of population was the house except where it was clearly separated into more than one residence and was indicated as such on the Electoral Roll. Where a house drawn in the sample was found to contain more than one household the household that had been longest in residence was selected.

It was decided that we would keep the number actually studied at 60 households. This meant that as soon as a family was disqualified for any reason, or gave a final refusal, another family had to replace them. Thus, after the first sample of 60 had been drawn, another set of households was drawn randomly from the same population, and listed in order of drawing. The first supplement of 20 households was drawn in July 1961, and since these did not prove to be enough, another 15 were drawn in May 1962. When a household was dropped out of the first 60, either by disqualification or because of a refusal, the first one on the supplementary list was put in to replace it. This process was continued until 60 households were successfully contacted and the sample therefore complete. To obtain this sample 92 households were contacted in all, of which 12 were disqualified and 20 refused to co-operate.

The average number of interviews held with each family was four, and was the same for each category of households, i.e. married couples, widows and widowers, and single women. The number of hours spent with each household varied greatly, the average being eight hours; and although the range was from two hours to seventeen, in 43 out of the 60 cases (72 per cent) seven or more hours were spent with the family.

The Highgate Sample

The study of the random sample taken from the total population of the Greenbanks Estate had shown us that for many purposes the heterogeneity of the household in terms of age, marital status and family stage had made analysis difficult. In some respects the isolation of factors relevant to kinship behaviour and ideology was almost impossible. The category of households least like all the others were those consisting of single, mainly elderly, women; since there were only seven of them little could be said about the 'kinship of single women', but on the other hand they obviously differed in attitude and behaviour from the married couples with children. Similarly, the three widowers and three widows could be expected to differ – at least in terms of certain needs which kin might fulfil. The remaining 47 households, all consisting of married couples, also varied. Some were elderly and childless, others had grown-up children and several grandchildren, while yet others were young with dependent children. Our analysis shows to what extent these factors seem from our material to be relevant in the field of kinship. Results of such analysis, however, can only suggest certain possibilities, given the limited and uneven nature of the sample.

Hence, for the second sample, it was decided that we would concentrate on married couples from a few stages in the family cycle, e.g. pre-children couples (of which we had no example on Greenbanks); families with schoolchildren (at least one dependent child); and others with only adult children. Finally it was decided that we would concentrate on one type of family, that with at least one dependent child. In this way we would limit the factors involved in family stage, and have a set of families that were comparatively homogeneous. Various possible ways of stratifying the sample occupationally were considered, but rejected. It became clear to us that we did not in fact want to stratify the sample but rather take a cross-section of the middle-class population in the area as it came.

One of the main reasons for the decision to study families with dependent children rather than any other type of family was that the material from Greenbanks had been particularly fruitful in this field. Not only were younger couples involved in child-rearing generally the least difficult to establish rapport with, but the whole field of confinements, birth and bringing up of children had proved one in which the role of kin was most easily identifiable. It should also be added that the team of interviewers, all young women (apart from one male interviewer in the pilot stages of the project), tended to take great interest in this sort of material, which both they and their informants were generally able to discuss freely and at length. It should be noted that while husbands (and other men in the Greenbanks sample) were used wherever possible as informants, by far the greater proportion of data was obtained from women informants by women interviewers.

In order to discover which households in the delimited area were of the required family stage it was necessary, if we wanted a fully random sample, to take some sort of preliminary census of the whole area. This was also necessary in order to identify the right occupational groups. The population of Highgate is socially and economically heterogeneous, and a random sample from the total population of Highgate (which here in the following text refers to the geographical area delimited later) would include a lot of households which would be totally unsuitable, e.g. those in which the head of the household was involved in manual or semi-skilled work.

The alternative to this, which was adopted, was a quick survey of the area in the form of doorstep interviews in which only a few vital questions were asked and recorded on cards. We had at an earlier stage identified 'married couples' on the Electoral Roll. If the card survey was regarded solely as a screening of the area, to *identify* the relevant population in terms of occupation and family stage, and not as a means of acquiring background information about all households in the area, then it was possible to limit the number of households which had to be visited to these 'married couples'.

Using the most recent Electoral Rolls and Amendments, all households with two people of opposite sex with the same name were numbered and listed. As a plausible preliminary, it was assumed that these people were likely to be married couples. It would not matter if some turned out to be, e.g., widowed mother and son. The total of 'married pairs' identified in the area was 199. A card was drawn up and stencilled, and the name and address of each 'married pair' was typed on to a copy of it. The card was designed to record the following information: (1) name (if not the same as on the Electoral Roll, i.e. on the card); (2) marital status; (3) number and age range of children; (4) occupation of husband; (5) names of any other married couples in the house. In addition, for comparative purposes, two questions were included on length of residence in Highgate: of the married couples themselves; and of any other relative.

In order to have a base of operations, a room was taken in Highgate, in which interviewers could rest and make notes for the duration of the card survey. Each member of the team was given a section of the area to cover, and had to go back to houses again and again where the occupants were out, until they got the relevant information.

Because of very bad weather conditions at the time of the pilot survey (which had already been postponed for some weeks in the hope that the snow would clear) it was necessary in some cases to forego the collection of all the material asked for on the cards. But successful results were obtained from a very high proportion of households.

The population of actual married couples in our area from which we could draw a sample was found to be 176. (199 – 1 vacant – 6 moved – 2 moving – 1 non-resident – 7 refused – 6 disqualified [non-marital].) There were then two variables which concerned us: family stage and occupation of husband. For four families, exact family stage could not be discovered, but these were Irish labouring families and were thus occupationally unsuitable anyway. Of the rest (172), 46 had no children, 62 had children over 18[4] only, and 64 had at least one child eighteen or under. This last category being the one we were interested in, they were then sorted out according to occupational category. The 64 husbands were arranged on the Hall-Jones scale[5] of occupation according to the information we had at that stage. In some cases it was difficult to attribute a man to one class, and in that case he was allotted to alternative classes.

Since we were interested only in those people who could be considered 'middle-class', some line had to be drawn to exclude those people who were not suitable for our study. For our purposes the best place to draw this line was between the third and fourth Hall-Jones categories. Class 4, though undoubtedly containing some occupations which may be considered middle-class did, however, contain a wide range of occupations which fell well outside the general level we were concerned with, i.e. professional people and others at a similar socio-economic level. By limiting the sample population to the top three categories we were not drawing a line between the 'middle' and the 'working' classes. It was simply that for our purposes, since a line had to be drawn somewhere to mark off a manageable set of middle-class people, this was the most appropriate place to draw it.

Having thus limited the sample population to the top three categories of the Hall-Jones scale, we were left with 49 households containing families at the appropriate family stage, i.e. with at least one dependent child. In order not to limit ourselves to any specific number in a sample, we drew the whole 49 in random order. Later the decision was made to study 30 of these, in due sequence.

As in the approach to Greenbanks, an initial letter from the project director with a covering note and card from the interviewer was sent to informants in Highgate. This explained the nature of the study, the importance of co-operation in a random sample, etc., but also mentioned the historical aspect of the study, which was thought might interest some people who might not be too keen on an investigation of their present-day kinship situation. It was also stressed that we were interested in anyone drawn in the sample, irrespective of the origin, type or size of the family concerned. This was in order to counteract the response, or non-response, from people who thought they were 'unsuitable' for the study.

[4] Since we had no way at this stage of determining whether a child was dependent or not some method had to be adopted in order to categorize family types. The age of 18 was taken as the upper age limit of dependent children.

[5] John Hall and D. Caradog Jones, op. cit., p. 33.

Interviewing Phase

In Highgate nearly every family received interviewers in a very friendly way. As on the Estate, there were a few cases of extreme involvement with the study and/or the interviewer (see section on Interviewer and Informant). Out of the 30 families interviewed in Highgate, in only one case did a spouse in a married couple refuse personal discussion. In this case (a husband allegedly too busy to be interviewed) the material was checked with him by post. The genealogy was given by his wife, who was also only minimally co-operative, and attempts to see her husband were abortive in spite of telephone conversations with him by the interviewer and the team leader. The genealogy was eventually sent to him to be checked; he returned it unaltered, though it is likely that he could at least have added a few more details to his wife's version. In a couple of other cases husbands proved almost impossible to get hold of, and were often stubbornly protected by their wives. In all other cases some contact was made with both spouses.

The average number of interviews with each household was five, one more than on the Estate. In Highgate no household had less than four interviews, and in one case a family was seen eleven times and in another ten times. The number of hours spent with each household also varied, the average being eleven hours, ranging from three hours in the least satisfactory case to 36 hours in a particularly interesting and fruitful case. In all cases except the minimal one just mentioned, seven or more hours was spent with each family, i.e. with 96 per cent of cases as opposed to 72 per cent of Greenbanks cases.

The difference between Greenbanks and Highgate in the amount of time devoted to each family was largely a matter of policy. Apart from the fact that certain information was required from the Highgate families that we had not asked for in Greenbanks (e.g. detailed genealogical information on consanguines of affines of kin), more pressure was put on interviewers to cover all major aspects of the *aide-mémoire* thoroughly. Analysis of the Estate sample had revealed certain inadequacies in the systematic coverage of data, which meant that some features in the analysis had to be abandoned or the missing bits of material rather belatedly extracted by telephoning the informants. (In areas where the analysis was considered to be particularly important, the latter was done.) However, this was obviously an unsatisfactory and tiresome way to proceed; thus, material from Highgate informants was more carefully checked at each stage to make sure that all information was systematically obtained.

INTERVIEWER AND INFORMANT

A major characteristic of this kinship project was that field interviewers conducted most of their work inside the houses of their subjects in situation which in many respects resembled the social relationships of visits of other kinds. They concentrated at an early stage on recording a genealogy of the family by methods already described and they endeavoured to obtain the answers to a set of questions indicated in the *aide-mémoire*. But the relatively unstructured interview situation allowed of issues of great diversity being raised between interviewer and informant. It also allowed the interview process to slide over almost imperceptibly into conversation and other social interaction of other kinds. In particular, as the material in this book demonstrates, it promoted in a number of cases very frank interchange on the subject of investigation and on the methods used to conduct it.

The individual character and temperament of interviewer and informant were variables which affected the situation to a considerable degree. But it is worth recording that in most cases relations between them were not only polite but also amiable, and that in various instances practical demonstrations of this were given by informants to the interviewers. All this gave a quality of 'free flow' to much of the information obtained so that it could often catch up one detail in terms of another, relating quite often to intimate affairs, and helping to build up a pattern of relationships and attitudes of informants concerning their kin.

The interviews varied very much in degree of formality. In some cases interviewers were treated as visitors on a scientific mission. For instance, members of one family were all extremely friendly and helpful. At interviews they insisted:

> on sitting formally around the dining-table on which the genealogies had to be spread out, and each interview commenced with a few comments about relative extent of knowledge of Ego's long family history. After this they would wait for me to ask questions. It was almost impossible for me to get them to 'chat'. The sitting around the table induced an atmosphere of waiting always for me to take the lead, and this of course I would have preferred to avoid. I did try and change the pattern, even suggesting that they would be more comfortable if we were sitting somewhere else. But they said no, I would need the genealogies and somewhere to rest my notebook, so it proved impossible to alter the situation. I also found it extremely difficult to take notes as wherever I put my book they could see what I was writing, and it was therefore diffi-

> cult to get down many of their comments, and anyway I found it inhibiting to have my notebook in the limelight. I found it made no difference whether I had my notebook out or not, that is, I tried interviewing without it once but conversation was no easier and also they seemed anxious that I got everything perfectly clear, so I brought my notebook out again, and again we went through the routine of waiting while I found questions to ask. Most interviews (elsewhere) were far less formal.

On many occasions interviewers abandoned genealogy and notebook and joined members of the family in social activities. In one case the husband was seldom in until late in the evening and it was only possible to see him once. He seemed tired and insisted that his wife knew almost as much as he did about all his relations and added only a few names to his genealogy. But his wife, well-dressed and friendly, far advanced in pregnancy, was glad to sit down and just talk. She was always willing to give information and really think about what her relationships were with her kin, although she was never completely clear what the purpose of the enquiry was and considered it all to be 'in the social sciences line'.

> She has proved to be an informant with whom it has been possible to establish very friendly relations, with prolonged talks over tea and washing up, shopping expeditions, feeding the baby, potting the older child, cooking supper and so on.

On several occasions our interviewers found themselves taking unexpected exercise. One, invited to lunch to get a list of people to whom Christmas cards had been sent, and meeting the son of the family, was taken for a walk by him and other young guests. Another, interviewing a small, lively man, springing with energy, was taken for a long tramp across Hampstead Heath on a bitter winter's morning. On many occasions interviewers were given meals – an informant once offered to cook breakfast for her interviewer! Sometimes they were driven home if they had been interviewing late at night. It seems clear that by many of our informants these young women were treated with special courtesy, as visitors who either had an interesting subject to discuss or who had to carry out a working role whether they wished to or not; they were therefore treated as guests and helped to accomplish their end.

Some of our informants seemed to find this role especially stimulating, and obviously found great interest in discussing their kinship affairs and attitudes. Others found it of marginal interest and were in turns neutral to, bored or even embarrassed by certain aspects of the enquiry.

What was particularly striking to the investigators was the apparent freedom with which most people seemed to talk on quite intimate matters. Sometimes this was with the expressed view that a scientific enquiry demanded frankness in reply; sometimes they appeared to have a kind of urgency to relieve their feelings on matters about which they very rarely spoke. (It was in such contexts particularly that our promise of anonymity was most necessary.) In one case the informant:

> was very kind and sympathetic throughout the time I was interviewing her and talked very easily. She seemed pleased to have someone to talk to sometimes about things that worried her. She discussed her children's education at some length because she needed to sort things out in her own mind, and when we got on to talking about specific kin relationships she said she was glad to talk to me about the relationship with her husband's mother, brother and brother's wife and with her own father and stepmother. She was sure it did her good to get it off her chest. It worried her that she didn't get on with these people, although she didn't blame herself for the fact that she didn't.

Another angle to this aspect of the situation was the way in which participation by an informant in the study appeared to have almost a cathartic effect. In one case it seemed that three of our informants (husband, wife and neighbour) who were close acquaintances had gathered that each family was the subject of enquiry. When it was completed one of them, very pleased to have copies of the genealogy, launched into an account of how they, as neighbours, had come to a mutual agreement of how they felt about the study. They sat discussing it in a pub, egging each other on to more and more revealing statements! This informant said she felt quite relieved when the study was over. She had got to a point when she felt she could not go on; she was so nostalgic and too emotional, and now she could be herself again. 'I don't regret doing it (the study) now I have got it in proper perspective.' The interviewer commented:

> So three of our informants, though apparently very willing to co-operate with the study and apparently enjoying the interviews while they lasted, once the latter were over got into a huddle and decided they had all emerged shaken as it were from a rather dramatic, traumatic experience!

But acceptance of interviewer did not necessarily mean being in complete accord with the purpose of the enquiry. One woman obviously wanted someone to talk to – and telephoned the interviewer repeatedly with no other purpose. A few people who were very interested indeed in the idea of research into kinship of families, treated the enquiry as a kind of genealogist's field day. They were interested in tracing their own kin connections historically – or putatively – and saw the genealogies our interviewers prepared for them as evidence of these relationships. Others saw the sociological import of the enquiry, but disagreed with it on grounds either of its smallness of scale or its apparent lack of practicality. One woman who was very interested in the study wanted to know how many families we were interviewing and how long the study would last. She had seen a programme on 'The Family' on television and wanted to know if we had had anything to do with it; she criticized this programme for stating the obvious. She thought that it said nothing about families that could not have been said by any intelligent person who sat down and thought about the matter. She said that one didn't need to go and live in 'Bethnal Green or wherever it was' to come to the conclusions that the programme presented. Other people were intrigued, especially by being drawn in a 'Random Sample'. Some realized fully the aims of the investigation and co-operated wholeheartedly in helping us to achieve them.

By implication such comments as these put us on our mettle. For the individual interviewer and for the team as a whole a reaction of scepticism about the enquiry especially, if based upon serious consideration, could be as helpful in stimulating us to elaborate the material required as an attitude of unquestioned support.

The most difficult set of problems was presented by informants who felt that for one reason or another the enquiry was an invasion of their privacy. Apart from the very few cases where this attitude resulted in firm refusal, there were several cases in which it was clear that the informant was co-operating out of good manners or from a sincere desire to assist the enquiry, but that the pursuit of the enquiry was a troublesome, even embarrassing or painful, matter. There were those who were disconcerted when they found that the interviewing was going on for so long, and who felt, as one woman said each time an appointment was made to see her, 'I'm sure I've told you *everything* already. There can't be anything left'.

When informants appear to feel very keenly the admission of an interviewer into their home and discussion of intimate affairs of family and kin relationship, the problem of invasion of privacy presents some delicate moral aspects. To the project director and interviewers the legitimacy of scientific curiosity is assumed, but the question is at what cost should it be satisfied. The costs are paid primarily by the informants and only they can say what real embarrassment is caused by allowing themselves to be subjected to such intensive and personal scientific enquiry. There seems no satisfactory answer to this problem except use of tact and judgment by the interviewer in terms of a kind of balance of sacrifice.

In such circumstances, the problem which faces the anthropologist is apt to be much more acute than that which faces either the ordinary questionnaire interviewer or the social worker. From the nature of the questionnaire situation the replies required are usually brief, and painful topics can frequently be blocked off by the person questioned. In an anthropological enquiry such as ours the development of the social situation in the direction of exchange of courtesies tends to inhibit any blunt refusals of information. This problem is, of course, very familiar to a social worker. But the rationale of the situation is rather different for the anthropologist. The social worker can point to some direct practical objective to which the information desired is expected to contribute, whereas the anthropological field worker can be regarded as pushing the enquiry simply from curiosity, however scientifically motivated. The fact that in several cases where the personal circumstances of the informants were of great delicacy our interviewers still managed to obtain what appeared to be basic information on kin relationships and attitudes indicates not only the ability of the field workers but also the logical implications of such a social situation once begun.

In summary, then, one of the cardinal features of the relation between interviewer and informant in such situation is that it allows combination of a systematic process of enquiry and record with a dynamic approach which takes account of the developing character of the communication between them.[6]

ANALYSIS AND EVALUATION

The methods used in the analysis of data and writing-up of results are described in the body of this book. Here it is sufficient to consider questions of comparability and reliability of the material.

Comparability of Material

The techniques used in this study were basically anthropological, i.e. the use of genealogical methods, participant observation (where possible) and intensive unstructured interviews. The latter technique – i.e. of unstructured interviewing – could be considered to be a possible adverse influence on the comparability of the material.

[6] An illuminating study in this field has emerged from the comparative project of our American colleagues: Linda M. Wolf, *Anthropological Interviewing in Chicago: Analysis of a Kinship Research Experience*, University of Chicago, Department of Anthropology, 1964.

Broadly, the material can be divided into four categories:

(a) genealogical data;
(b) other quantitative material (e.g. contact frequencies, geographical scatter);
(c) personal-historical and straight descriptive data;
(d) qualitative data such as discussion of relationship and kinship ideology.

Genealogical data were gathered systematically and exhaustively in the earliest interviews. The genealogy was then used as a framework for later interview discussions, and mistakes could be found or additions could be dealt with on many occasions. Every genealogy was obtained in a similar fashion, i.e. by working outwards from the informant until information ran out. There was little room here for variations in approach and personality of the interviewer to affect the nature of the data obtained. This genealogical enquiry took place on the first occasion that the informant saw the interviewer, or at least before the informant got to know her, thus strong personality or attitudinal influences did not yet have a chance to enter the situation. Most important, however, is the fact that this material was gathered systematically, and recorded in such a form that it could be easily checked and quantified; hence gaps in information were identifiable as informants' lack of knowledge rather than as interviewers' omissions.

A possible disadvantage of the open interview was that a discussion on one occasion might affect the nature of a later discussion on a different subject. But in fact most subjects were gone over in a variety of different ways, on different occasions and in varying contexts. It would have been extremely limiting to have kept to any particular order within the interviews or interview sequences. With material of this complexity, interviews were a prolonged discussion, steered by the interviewer only in a general way to follow themes she wanted to have covered. Only in the least satisfactory cases were interviews reduced to a series of questions and answers.

Differences between interviewers were carefully considered. There are various areas in which individual differences between them might have been significant, i.e. in personality, perceptiveness, interests, approach and individual kinship situation. An interviewer's personality might affect the degree of rapport that was established with different sorts of people, and some interviewers found it more difficult to establish rapport at all than others. Personality could also be reflected in the attitudes of the interviewer, which were bound to emerge in the course of discussion, even if only to a very small extent. This could possibly influence statements and even attitudes of the informants. Although all interviewers were graduates in anthropology (or a related subject) there were variations in perceptiveness and overall intellectual ability. This could affect the extent to which they took informants' statements at face value, especially in the sphere of kinship ideology. Instead of developing sophisticated discussion, interviewers sometimes tended to accept bald statements about, e.g., presence or absence of a sense of obligation to kin. In some cases, too, the informants were exceptionally sophisticated people; a few were expert in anthropology or related disciplines, with a level of argument occasionally above that of the interviewer.

Differences in the interests of the interviewers might also be important since they could be expected to affect the amount of time and attention spent on various topics in the *aide-mémoire*. Differences in approach were also relevant; this is in fact one of the most widely discussed aspects of non-structured interview techniques. Obviously in some spheres the way questions were asked would affect the answer – perhaps one of the more radical difficulties. Lastly, the personal kinship situation of interviewers might be thought to influence the assessment of the informants' kinship situation and ideology.

All these factors were considered, both before interviewing began and after the completion of the case histories. At the onset of the project (and at the appointment of each new team member) interviewers were instructed in the theory and practice of the project.

Frequent comparative discussion of cases kept the problem to the fore. In general terms, we did find some differences between the degree of detail in each interviewer's case histories, but no evidence of bias in approach, or in the basic quality of the resulting material. In a study of this kind the advantage gained from formalizing many of the questions would have been seriously outweighed by the disadvantages. The fact that all shared the same theoretical approach, and were aware of the problems involved, were the chief safeguards against the effects of individual differences.

Reliability of Material

Since this study was intended to rely on ego-oriented material, there was no consistent attempt to give more than the individual's own picture of his or her kin universe and relationships within it. This does not mean that information (or attitudes) from other kin or from written sources was not made use of when available, but this was considered as additional comparative information, not as 'verification' or disproof of the picture presented by the informant.

Obviously, however, we were interested to see to some extent how far the picture given to us was in fact a reflection of reality. With a large proportion of the material there was no reason to believe that we were deliberately misled or misinformed of the facts, though in many cases the information was incomplete, and in some cases questionable in detail – points of caution often suggested by informants themselves.

Popular among anthropologists is a belief that people are inclined to 'invent' genealogies, or at least to distort them for social reasons. This is probably true in some circumstances. However, since we showed ourselves to be more interested in the contemporary situation than in the ancestral origins of our informants there was very little incentive on this latter score to alter the facts. The genealogical information given to us was often far from a complete picture of what the facts must have been on the ground, even in terms of the contemporary situation. But we have no evidence that anyone deliberately misinformed us, and much evidence that many informants went to considerable trouble to recollect or obtain what they regarded as the correct version of their ancestral and lateral kin relationships.

There are ways in which it can be seen that the material given to us about genealogies was substantially correct, in the view of the informant. There were constant internal checks on the data. A genealogy was not given to us on one occasion and then put away – it was produced at almost every interview, and information regarding people on it and relationships between them discussed on many occasions and in various contexts. It would have been very difficult for an informant, even if he wanted to, to have continued to discuss a mythical character, or even a false set of characteristics, in a series of interviews. A genealogy might be full of small mistakes, exaggerations, understatements, even fictions, but it was a picture of the informants' views about their kin. In so far as we were interested primarily in this individual picture we did not need independent 'historical' corroboration of their stories. This did not mean that we were interested only in attitudes and not in facts, but that we accepted that the selection and mode of presentation of facts to some extent expressed individual attitudes.[7] The fact too that copies of genealogies were generally accepted with pleasure at the end of a sequence of interviews implied that they did represent a reality, a kind of compressed experience to the informants. It should be remembered that in most cases this 'reality' was corroborated by comparison of data provided by both husband and wife.

[7] For purposes of analysis it was the informants' own knowledge of kin that was counted, i.e. excluding information added from any secondary sources whatsoever.

Another relevant factor was that in some cases relationships cited by an informant were known independently to a member of the team, and thus known to be correct. In no case was there a discrepancy found between a section of the genealogy as given by an informant and that as known to a team member – although there were sometimes variations in the interpretation of the affective nature of a relationship.

Another reason for accepting the genealogical data was that a certain proportion of it was backed by documents produced by informants. These included copies of 'family trees' and copies of birth, marriage and death certificates. 'Family trees' were, of course, not necessarily historical. (In so far as a genealogy given by an informant without reference to documents did in fact correspond to an 'official' family tree, then the personal genealogy was in a similar position *vis-a-vis* the actual situation as the document already drawn up.) With regard to the 'historical' data, i.e. about past generations, empirical checks were provided for a few genealogies by other documentary scrutiny during the investigation of 'old Highgate families' stretching back into the early or mid-nineteenth century.

As far as the qualitative material was concerned, the question of reliability did not arise in the same way. When an informant talked about his relationship with a kinsman it was his picture that was of interest, and it was accepted that the kinsman concerned might give a quite different account of the relationship. That in many cases these things were discussed with both husband and wife (where possible both together and separately) meant that there was a chance to see how far a picture given by one of them was a reflection of a situation described by the other and so presumably actual. Sometimes discussions with husbands and wives separately yielded quite contradictory accounts of a relationship. This was so most usually with a relation with a parent or a parent-in-law, a situation in which the relationship was sometimes idealized, or hostility was postulated for which there was no concrete evidence. Such contradictions, of course, did not invalidate any of the material, but rather increased the body of data for interpretation.

In some areas of the material, 'reliability' was of no relevance at all. This was so, e.g. in the sphere of kinship ideology. The problem here was an academic one, i.e. how far someone could be said to possess an ideology if his behaviour did not conform to it. Informants were asked many questions about their sense of moral obligation towards their kin, and the obligations involved in kinship in British society in general. Many positive statements were elicited, although according to other evidence when relevant situations arose in the past these 'obligations' were not always met. This did not mean that the informants' statements about their sense of responsibility were thereby invalidated. The mere necessity felt to state these obligations was itself significant. The fact, e.g. that nearly everyone felt that they had some obligation towards 'aged relatives', but that the majority in fact left it to someone else to *do* anything, was one of the most interesting aspects of these kin relationships. The discrepancy in no way meant that the ideology did not exist.

In this discussion of the reliability of the material the significance should be noted of obtaining the main part of the data from informants in interviews, rather than by participant observation, or indeed any systematic observation of behaviour patterns. It could be said that since all our data were merely reported to us by informants, then all we have is in the realm of 'ideology', i.e. that it is not valid empirical material but merely expression of attitudes. In the interview records and the case histories, however, we distinguished ideology and statements about behaviour in hypothetical situations from reported 'actual' behaviour, i.e. what informants said they or others *did*. We also noted any observed behaviour seen or heard by the interviewer. These remain valid distinctions, in spite of the fact that in nearly every case our statements about the behaviour of our informants and their kin were in fact statements about what they said they did. We rarely could check the accounts given to us, but there was no reason to believe that they were not factual. Just because the data we had on kin behaviour were as reported to us, rather than from our direct observation, did not mean that we were not entitled to talk about this behaviour as if it were empirical fact.

This issue was brought to our attention mainly by other anthropologists to whom the conventional field situation was familiar. For instance, it was suggested that the very nature of the questions we asked our informants might influence their replies, e.g. that there might be a danger of imparting guilt feelings when we asked people questions about kin contact. But in fact this type of problem enters into any intensive anthropological investigation. It should be remembered that although 'living among' a small rural community obviously allows for a great deal more direct observation than does field work in an industrialized metropolitan area, in fact a large amount of data in any field situation is obtained only through the statements of individual informants. Certainly it is true that it is customary in a 'primitive' field situation to try to compare the story given with the reality on the ground. But every field worker knows that in his notes are many statements about what people do which are in fact based primarily on what people have told him they do. Such is often the case with data on seasonal festivals or personal life crises, which may not have occurred during the field worker's period of residence. This is one sphere, perhaps, where studying one's own culture is an advantage. Although in many cases we cannot observe the actual behaviour of our informants with their kin, we can nevertheless assess their reports of their behaviour in terms of our own experience and knowledge of their cultural background. In a completely strange society this is not possible.

3

Social Character of the Areas and Samples Studied

One of our first problems in this study of English middle-class kinship was to decide on the scale and place of the investigation. Should we try to examine a national sample or a metropolitan sample, or be content with a much smaller local sample? Bearing in mind the multitude of variables involved, we decided that we would at least try and reduce the effects of variation in one set – those of local environment. To get neighbourhood relations, transport facilities and immediate amenities open to each of our subjects as similar as possible we selected our cases from only two areas, each of fairly small size, which would give the likelihood of some common social experiences to those living in each area. After careful consideration, we took both areas close together in the mid-outer residential ring of the metropolis, in North London. This meant that we could dispense with having to bring in as background a fresh set of socio-geographic and historical features, which might have affected the kinship patterns of contact differently if our areas or cases had been chosen at random from the country at large.

CHARACTER OF THE AREAS

The first area chosen was a housing estate, of fairly recent construction, which we decided to treat as anonymous; it is referred to in this book as Greenbanks. The second area was a population centre of long standing, a staging-post on one of the ancient routes out of London to the North. Since its history seemed to afford the opportunity of comparison with present-day conditions we decided that there was distinct point in being able to refer to it by name; it is in fact the area known as Highgate Village.

The Greenbanks Estate is within easy reach of both the centre of London and the country; it is also enclosed, with no through traffic, and is thus attractive to parents with young children. Highgate is in some respects in contrast to this (see p. 61).

In neither area has population turnover been rapid (see Table 1). One section of the Estate was built about forty years ago, another about thirty years ago. At the time of the survey about one quarter of the total survey population of households had lived there for more than twenty years, and over half for more than ten years. In general, the individuals in the Highgate sample were of slightly longer residence than were those of Greenbanks. But Greenbanks is a much smaller geographical area than Highgate, and in fact many of the Estate residents had moved in from the area immediately surrounding it. Thus, though they were 'new' residents of the Estate, they were often 'old' residents of the area.

TABLE 1

Length of residence of individuals in North London samples[1]

	1–5 years	*6–10*	*11–15*	*16–20*	*21–25*	*26–30*	*Over 30 years*	*Total persons*
Highgate	14	16	10	7	2	6	5	*60*
Greenbanks:								
Segment A*	20	17	10	7	0	2	0	*56*
Segment B	1	14	8	6	3	7	12	*51*
Total	*35*	*47*	*28*	*20*	*5*	*15*	*17*	*167*

* For 'segments' see p.78.

The Greenbanks houses, of which about one-third were semi-detached, were in the majority of 'good middle-class' appearance, though in fact their size, their siting, their quality and hence their property values varied considerably. (The range in 1961 was from about £4,400 – quite common – to upwards of £20,000 – very rare.) The Estate was a private one, with residents' responsibility for keeping up streets and verges; these and other matters were arranged by a residents' committee, which had some difficulty in obtaining the necessary financial resources. There was some pressure indeed for the local Council to assume the care of the Estate. Residents tended to be divided on the issue of whether it was socially appropriate to maintain the Estate as an area of privilege, or throw it open to general access.

Despite its geographical unity, Greenbanks could be described as a quasi-community rather than as a tightly-knit social unit. Though

[1] Data for this and other tables were obtained for Greenbanks mainly in 1961 and for Highgate mainly in 1963. For convenience the date of 1961 cited in the text covers both.

churches, cinemas, pubs and shopping centres of various kinds were close at hand, there were none on the Estate itself. Facilities such as a restaurant and a community centre formerly existed there, but had lapsed, to the regret of some older residents. A fairly active Dramatic Society recruited its members from outside the Estate as well as from within, and seemed to owe much of its vigour to this.

The people of Greenbanks, while all to be described as 'middle class', varied considerably in their origins, their incomes and their interests. Some came from middle-class families with public school and University connections; others came from working-class families with a greater educational range. Some, such as a number of elderly single women, were living on small incomes in retirement, having bought their houses for around £1,000 some thirty years ago; others – including young fathers of families – were earning substantial incomes from professional or business activities.

In Chapter 2 the community status of the area of our study was discussed in its possible relation to kinship and to the general type of interaction between neighbours, friends and associates which could serve as a contrast to kin behaviour. An established community could display interaction in daily life, mobilization of members in a crisis, conceptualization of themselves as a whole, which could imply patterns of behaviour and sanctions for behaviour which could affect attitudes to kin.

Some of the residents referred to the notion of community only when asked about it; others volunteered opinion in such terms. Some of the older residents said that before the War the Estate was a community, but they had seen a change in this respect over the years. In general, at the time of our study, the people of Greenbanks did not seem to see the Estate as a 'community'. But their criteria often differed, and opinions varied greatly.

As far as a sense of community was concerned, this also varied: one woman said 'I don't think there's much community life here', and held that there had been more in the days when there was a community centre; another resident said that the idea that it was anything like a village was 'a lot of rubbish'. On the other hand, it was often felt that although not a community the Estate was a rather more 'friendly' place than other areas of London. One said 'For London it's quite friendly. It's helped by being an entity. Here there's a lot of neighbourhood; it's easier with small children . . .'

Children did seem often to serve as a link. They seemed to have considerable interaction with their neighbours, some being often 'in and out' of one another's homes. People who knew one another often co-operated in taking children to and from school. Other services were also exchanged, and even those who found the place least friendly seemed to know one or two people on the Estate on whom they could call in a crisis.

Socially, there did not appear to be a great deal of mixing in any formal way. Coffee or tea parties for fellow residents, especially among the women, seemed the pattern; dinner parties were not common in the area of our survey. From our information the most intensive contact seemed to be between people living in the same street, often between neighbours, and, according to the cross-section talked to in the survey, few broader circles existed. But one woman characterized the Estate as 'posh' and 'snobby'; though she had young children, in her experience people kept so much to themselves that she found it difficult to get to know anyone. Some others thought that, compared with the district bordering one end of it, the Estate – far from being posh and snobby – was considerably lower in the social scale.

Highgate is in some respects in strong contrast to Greenbanks. It is a long-established settlement whose growth has been determined by a complex geographical and economic history, and not by any specific act of fairly recent planning. Its population is not a fairly uniform social stratum of a 'middle-class' kind, but a mixture containing people of almost every socio-economic grade. It is not enclosed in any way, but is split administratively into two parishes, which meet at its centre, and is right on one motor route leading across London and another leading north and south. Its residents have relatively easy access to various shopping areas, such as those of Kentish Town or the Nag's Head in Holloway Road, but more important to most of them are the shops right in their midst. These include not only grocers, newsagents, ironmongers, pubs and wine-shops but also high-class bakers, florists, a picture-framer and an antique bookseller's. There are churches but no local cinemas.

Highgate has a wider variety of dwellings than Greenbanks in terms of size, period, appearance and general desirability. At one extreme are the very large seventeenth-century houses of the Grove – perhaps some of the most coveted houses in London – and at the other extreme are small workmen's cottages and, in the main street, many flats over little shops. In a few streets middle-class and working-class families are very much mingled together, whereas others are identifiably 'middle class'.

One cannot say that the population of the centre of Highgate, the 'Village', forms *more* of a community than does that of Greenbanks, but it is anyway a *different sort* of community. Certainly a higher proportion of inhabitants of Highgate felt that it had to some extent a village-like character. Theoretically, one might have imagined that the people of Greenbanks, all of the same general class and relatively isolated on their Estate, would have constituted a social unit of a fairly highly integrated kind, whereas the opposite would have been the case with Highgate, with its social heterogeneity. But the diversity of Highgate seemed to allow it to have assumed a more integrated character, with the variety of occupations, class relationships and institutional allegiances providing a kind of functional complementarity.

But while the general attitude was that Highgate was more of a community than most areas of London, that there was a sort of 'village' atmosphere, there were exceptions. The young married couples in Highgate varied in the extent to which they thought of themselves as being part of a community, or thought that a community existed at all. One woman said that it was not a community: 'It is very close and reserved', and another that 'It's not much of a community but it can be in times of trouble'. To a great extent the degree to which individuals considered it to be like a village, or a friendly place, depended on the degree of participation they were prepared to give. The ones who felt there was no community spirit were largely people who did not 'entertain' in the way they thought was expected of them, and the most extreme case was of a woman who never invited anyone to her house, and never did local shopping. In some streets women complained that they were quite isolated, and never saw their neighbours; in others, the inhabitants 'practically lived in each other's houses' and had a more or less permanent system of inter-exchange of children.

The fact that Highgate Village has a core of old-established and, in some cases, family-based shops is obviously one reason why many inhabitants felt that it had some village quality. But this may well be coming slowly to an end. One man felt that the gradual modernization of the shopping centre was breaking up the 'village character' or 'personal service and chatter'. Nowadays, shopping in the Village still consists of 'more than a mere exchange of goods' across the counter. Not only have many shopkeepers and housewives other local interests in common as well, but also shoppers in the High Street still very frequently meet their friends there, and sometimes kin as well.

As foci of interest, in very different ways, there are several important institutions, each with its material base. There are the School; the Church; the Literary and Scientific Institution; and recently, the Highgate Society.

Highgate School is an ancient foundation, established by Sir Roger Cholmeley in 1565. After a period of degeneration in the eighteenth century it was revived in the nineteenth century, especially through the efforts of the famous Headmaster Dr Dyne, 1838–74 (whose granddaughters still lived near Highgate Village at the period of our survey). Part boarding and part day school, it has long since ceased to serve Highgate alone, but it still draws a significant part of its now large intake from there and the areas immediately around. With local Governors, its public events such as fêtes and choir performances, as well as its locally resident staff, the School still plays a definite part in Highgate life. When recently Highgate appeared to be threatened by the establishment of a one-way lorry route to the North, it was Highgate School, under the energetic leadership of its Headmaster, which provided much of the organization which successfully opposed the proposal, mobilized the activities of many local citizens as well as of parents of boys at the School, and drew together people of all types of occupation and social class in the common cause. The role of the Headmaster and of the School in this was perhaps no more than would have been provided by efficient leadership in any local area so threatened. But it was in fact the School that, at an early stage, took over the initiative from other hands.

The Church in Highgate was essentially a development of the nineteenth century as far as a separate social entity is concerned. In earlier times the people of the hamlet of Highgate could either go two miles to worship at St Mary's, Hornsey, or they used the School Chapel, to which an ancestry of great antiquity has been attributed. The efforts to 'restore the School' led to the building of St Michael's, Highgate, consecrated in 1832, and its establishment in a separate ecclesiastical district, with a vicar and a vestry. This church was used by the School until the gift to it of the Crawley Chapel, consecrated in 1867. Meanwhile, the School Chapel was disused and there was some conflict between the Governors of the School and the churchwardens of St Michael's in the early mid-nineteenth century, particularly over the School's rights to free pews. These pews were a source of some embarrassment to the church authorities since St Michael's was not endowed, and therefore needed all the revenue it could secure. But the church was an important social as well as religious centre, marking off a population of the Established order from Nonconformist members of the community, for whom provision had been available as far back as the seventeenth century.

The Highgate Literary and Scientific Institution (called colloquially the 'Instie' by old residents) was founded in 1839 and still is an active centre of cultural life, with its library and reading-room, its annual programme of lectures and discussions, its shows of Highgate prints and pictures, its 'bring and buy' fêtes. Its membership is largely middle class, but it draws in a selection of other residents. It tends to represent the 'old Highgate', the 'solid' middle class, the

Establishment, but it is one important nodal point for community interest. In the past, although its membership was drawn considerably from Church of England supporters, it served as a common meeting place where sectarian rivalries could be forgotten and community collaboration achieved.

In some contrast to the Literary and Scientific Institution, with its sober intellectualist flavour and traditional outlook, has come the Highgate Society. Founded in 1966, after the lorry-route threat had galvanized the more socially conscious residents, this organization has a broadly based approach to the problems and advantages of living in Highgate. Its membership is probably wider in class terms than that of the Institution, and its major executive members probably younger, though there is no necessary clash between them. The Society has developed a very energetic programme of lively interest in current Highgate affairs. Holding that Highgate is an area of considerable architectural and historic value, and also a community with many social links between residential areas, shops, public buildings and buildings and open spaces, the Society has investigated the road and traffic problems of the area and made specific proposals to protect the local amenities. It has also sought to create and develop interest in community affairs by a series of exhibitions, club meetings, dancing classes, 'cook-ins' and bridge 'teach-ins', and by the publication of periodical diary cards of events and a quarterly magazine. Whether or not Highgate is a community, the Society has consciously tried to make it such.

It is evident that not all middle-class people in Highgate participate in these social activities. Many have done so, among them some of our informants. But, as is characteristic of metropolitan living, many people depend partly or even primarily on social facilities outside the Highgate area.

HISTORICAL BACKGROUND

The contrast between Greenbanks and Highgate presents an interesting question – how far can this be seen to have any significance for the kinship relations of the people studied in the two area? The contrast might be thought to be especially relevant in one respect – that of historical background. Greenbanks as a populated area has a very recent history, comprising still only that of a single generation for the older inhabitants. One would not expect then any very elaborate kin arrangements to exist, in the form of 'old families', local patterns of inheritance, or kin networks through marriage. In Highgate, on the other hand, all these phenomena might be looked for. Since some historical records for Highgate go back for more than 500 years, and are rich for at least the last 200 years, we might expect to be able to examine the changes in such kinship patterns and relations over a considerable span of time.

It must be said at once that any expectations for a substantial kinship history of Highgate, with a large number of 'old families', marriage alliances and kin 'networks' persisting for centuries right down to the present day, must be disappointed. This lack of historical depth in the present-day population is in accord with historians' views about the mobility of London's inhabitants, in the past as well as in modern times. In the middle-class field at least very few of the present-day families living in Highgate have any long ancestry there (vide data on residence and birthplace, Tables 1 and 2 and Chapter 9), and what information we have about families in other social classes is of the same kind. Not only did not one of the families in our Highgate sample bear the same name as any family in the 1851 Highgate Census – i.e. no descendants of those families in the male line were to be found living in the area – but also in only two of the sample of 30 families was there a person (in each case a wife) whose ancestors were living in Highgate at that date. Outside our sample were 4 cases known to us (all female) of modern representatives of families in the 1851 Highgate Census, and in about 3 other cases the modern representatives had either recently died or moved away. Even these survivals for over more than a century of the families of 1851 may be thought to be surprising. It is relevant that the Highgate population of today, though not biologically a modern extension of the population of a century ago, is a social replacement of it, the area having been one of continuous middle-class occupation for well over a century. Yet in recruitment the middle-class community of Highgate is of relatively new formation, with fairly high geographical mobility of its residents. Out of a sample of approximately 200 married couples in Highgate in 1963 – the 'middle-class' section of the Electoral Roll sample (see Chapter 2) – few if any appeared to have had relatives there in 1851.

In examining the kinship of the North London families we studied, we were interested in problems of historical depth – the extent to which past conditions of the areas might have affected the present condition of the people concerned. It is clear that the present population had almost no ancestry in the area a century ago, so that any direct inheritance of kinship patterns, property rights, residences, is ruled out. But what were the general social conditions of the people of Highgate, say, a century ago, providing the matrix within which the modern population has developed? Though the people of the mid-nineteenth century were of different stock, what type of kinship relations did they tend to have, living in the same area and sharing some of the same facilities? How far can any comparisons be made between the kinship structure and institutions of the people who lived there formerly and kinship now?

Not all the aims of this historical research could be achieved. But investigation of a range of sources, including the enumerators' schedules of the 1851 Census, manorial records, family histories, rate books, directories and maps, has tended to show at least the main lines of development.[2]

A brief outline of certain aspects of the social history of Highgate in the nineteenth century will show how it developed its middle-class character.

Highgate has never possessed a separate administration, lying as it does athwart the boundaries of two parishes and three manors. But socially it has long had a separate identity. From medieval times the village was a natural staging-post for wayfarers climbing the steep hill on the road to the North from the capital. (It was long notorious for the number of inns which grew up on the brow of the hill to cater for the thirst and needs of travellers.) From the seventeenth century onwards its salubrious northern heights were a favourite resort of wealthy merchants and members of the aristocracy whose business kept them in the proximity of London and yet who desired to escape from the pestilence and noisome smells of the City. As the metropolis expanded these moved still further out. Their place was taken from about 1820 onwards by smaller merchants, retailers, attorneys, solicitors, barristers, publishers and other professional men, whose standard of living was rising and who, like their predecessors, were desirous to escape from the congestion and unhealthy living conditions of London, and to find good schools for their children. This was London which still suffered from filthy streets, from outbreaks of cholera and typhoid and from riots.

The modern social character of Highgate is closely related to the type of housing which emerged as a result of such settlement. Even to

[2] For many details (not all completely accurate) on Highgate, including eighteenth- and nineteenth-century houses – see John H. Lloyd, *The History, Topography and Antiquities of Highgate*, Highgate, 1888. Among various sources see Thomas Cromwell, *Walks Through Islington*, London, 1835; Percy W. Lovell and William McB. Marcham, *London County Council*, *Survey of London, vol. XVII, The Village of Highgate* (The Parish of St. Pancras, Part I), London, 1936. *St. Michael's Highgate, Parish Magazine*, 1863 *et seq.*, covered all the local events in the latter half of the nineteenth century. It was not confined to parish activities, and contained articles on the history of Highgate School, etc. For information on some prominent Highgate families, see Dorothy Crozier, 'Kinship and Occupational Succession', *The Sociological Review*, vol. 13, No. 1 n.s. March, 1965, pp. 15–43.

the present day Highgate has had for the most part a variety of family houses, set in spacious gardens, rather than the closely packed terrace houses developed by building speculation in many areas to the south. How was it that Highgate for so long escaped the attention of the speculative builder? The answer lies in part in topography and communications, and in part in the nature of the land tenure.

In 1851 Highgate lay across the boundaries of metropolitan London and extra-metropolitan Middlesex. Its physiognomy was part-urban, part-rural, with farms and orchards, stately homes, and the congested High Street. The great building development took place in Highgate only towards the end of the nineteenth century and during the twentieth century; it was a slow process, accelerated only by conditions prevailing after the two World Wars. The cable tramway up Highgate Hill was not built until 1884. There had been a local horse-driven omnibus service since 1851 or earlier, but this could not cater for a large-scale 'commuter' traffic. Most of the workmen and petty traders and craftsmen who lived in Highgate were employed locally; the professional and business men had their own means of transport. Stables with their fields for horses and cottages for coachmen were not only a mark of status but as essential to the mode of life of the well-to-do gentry of Highgate at that time as is the motorcar to their successors.[3] Small rows of terrace houses had already made their appearance, but the rents were too high to be within the reach of any but the well-off. The usual congested 'rabbit warrens' housed the working classes, but these were scattered amongst better-class dwellings and were the result of the nature of the land tenure in Highgate and the investments of local traders, not of speculative builders.

It was not until the end of the nineteenth century that there was substantial demand for relatively uniform upper middle-class dwelling in this area. This alone could provide sufficient return in the form of ground rents to justify the capital expenditure involved on the part of the Ecclesiastical Commissioners – who administered the old church manorial lands – and the various private builders. In 1851 much of the land and many of the houses in Highgate had been in the hands of absentee owners, many of whom were the descendants of eighteenth-century merchants who had gone on to acquire country residences. But the nature of the copyhold tenure, with its fines on the granting of leases and on transfer, payable to the Lord of the Manor, together with the latter's residual rights on the failure of heirs, made it unsuitable for speculative building. Moreover, many of the holdings were small. If copyhold land was developed, this was

[3] The motor car is more economical of space and manpower than a carriage and pair.

done by the copyholder as a private investment, on a very small scale, determined by the size and shape of the holding. Also (what is very striking) there was a lack of ready capital available to the copyholder in the nineteenth century; mortgages had to be fully secured and interest rates were high. Before copyhold could be successfully developed individual lots had to be bought and amalgamated as they came on the market and then enfranchised, i.e. the residual rights of the Lord had to be bought out together with the manorial incidents. This was a process which, under the aegis of the Ecclesiastical Commissioners, was liable to be fairly expensive. There were instances of this being done by enterprising individuals: the famous Grove in the eighteenth century and Holly Terrace in the early nineteenth century, built as a post-Napoleonic War speculation, were examples of development by individual copyholders for investment purposes, but this was rare. Hence the topography of Highgate and its social character even today is in part determined by the location of the titles of the ancient manors recorded in Domesday; many of its inhabitants, among their documents proving title, still retain copies of the court rolls.

Relevant to this social situation also were the aspirations of the City merchants. There was a general tendency for merchant and trader to invest capital acquired from commerce in land. This was in keeping with the generally accepted notion that ownership of land (realty) conferred a social prestige that ownership of other property (personalty) by itself did not. Moreover, until the Second Reform Act (1867) the possession of realty was the basis of all major political rights. Hence, it would seem that the acquisition of a copyhold estate in Highgate by the rising merchant, trader or solicitor in the City was a step in the process by which he or his children would emerge as landed proprietors. This is borne out by the court records, which indicate that the children of the successful original immigrants from the City rarely stayed in Highgate but moved further out into the counties, where they acquired landed estates. This did not always happen, but Highgate would appear to have been a halfway house where trader or merchant from the City could become separated physically if not occupationally from his counting-house, and by residence become a gentleman, perhaps even an esquire.[4] In many cases they or their children retained the original copyhold in Highgate.

Significant in the Highgate society of the period is the status of these immigrant traders from the City, especially in regard to that of

[4] E.g. in 1851 No. 6, 'The Grove', was occupied by the widow of Thomas Jones of Highgate Esquire, who in a surrender of 1805 was described as Thomas Jones of Highgate Merchant.

the local traders. It would seem that a City merchant with a Highgate estate was classed locally as a member of the gentry, looked up to and served by the local traders, who formed a class apart. In constituting the vestry for the new church in 1832 the Reverend Samuel Mence wrote to the Church Commissioners, '. . . The fact is, that certain tradesmen of this place having subscribed more than some, who live here as gentlemen, their occupations being in London, I do not like to pass over the former, though certain that the latter will feel offended.'[5] The status of gentleman, and more so the ascription of esquire, presumably depended to some extent on the socio-geographic context. A merchant, solicitor or stockbroker who had achieved this status[6] in Highgate would not necessarily have been so recognized in the Counties, though their children might be so in time, especially if they had received the appropriate education.

The role of public schools in the educational system is significant here. Public school education, offering an important means of entry to the growing Civil Service in the nineteenth century, was also a great attraction to men who wished to mark the emergence of their family from trade into the ranks of the gentry by securing the social position of their sons. This was very relevant in the case of Highgate, which had in Sir Roger Cholmeley's School an ancient but impoverished institution that could be put to new use. There was accordingly pressure to raise its status and secure its recognition as a public school (which was effected by a legal decision in 1830), and also to restrict entry to the sons of the 'gentry' by excluding the sons of the local traders. At the same time, as a result of analogous process, the school lost pupils to more famous or more fashionable schools as the parents increased in wealth.[7]

[5] C.C. 18119, Pt. 3.

[6] The status of esquire could be given to a City merchant in Highgate, but not to a local trader. If he retired from business and continued to reside in Highgate he might be given the ascription of gentleman, which has a legal connotation of a man of no occupation.

[7] In the early part of the nineteenth century the school drew largely on Highgate and the neighbourhood for its scholars. Between 1833 and 1851 out of about 425 admissions, 155 or rather more than one-third were drawn from Highgate itself and nearly another third from Hornsey, Muswell Hill, etc. Later the proportions had changed greatly. Between 1851 and 1937 out of about 6,300 admissions, only a few more than 1,200, or less than 20 per cent, were from Highgate and the neighbourhood, the majority being from elsewhere in London, outside London and even from various other parts of England and abroad. (E. W. Reeves, ed., *Highgate School: A Roll of the School*, 2nd edn, London, 1913; J. Y. Boreham, ed., *Highgate School Register 1838–1938*, 4th edn, London, 1938. T. W. Bamford, Public Schools and Social Class, 1801–1850 (*British Journal of Sociology*, Vol. 12, 1961, pp. 224–235) points out that in leading public schools of this period an early spread of entry across the social classes, especially in schools of local catchment,

COMPARATIVE SOCIAL STRUCTURE, 1851 AND 1961

This general indication of earlier social conditions in Highgate (especially in the nineteenth century) has shown how, through the recognition of Highgate as a stage in the conversion of City merchants into gentry, and through the existence of its public school, its character of a desirable middle-class residential area came to be promoted. We now pass to a closer consideration of the character of the nineteenth-century, middle-class population, relating it later to the present-day situation. For this purpose the data of the 1851 Census have been used. As a point of methodology it should be noted that the results have been obtained through our historian's analysis of the original enumerators' schedules.

For comparative purposes the heads of households in these schedules have been classified into three social categories. These, categories represent broadly the gentry; the local traders and minor professionals; and the manual workers. The categories do not appear as such in the original data of the 1851 Census, but have been constructed by our historian's independent assessment.[8] The primary purpose of the categories was to elucidate relative social status, and they were designed particularly to isolate the set of people corresponding most nearly to the modern middle-class. The criteria used for this were primarily occupation, number of resident servants, ownership of the residential property, and gross annual rental. Judged by the criteria of the mid-nineteenth century (which differed materially in some respects, e.g. servants kept, from modern criteria) the social categories I and II of Highgate of 1851 did correspond broadly to the class 1 to 3 of the Hall-Jones scale which we had adopted for the modern material.

Table 2 summarizes the initial results of this analysis. The heads of households (some being women) in Highgate on the night of the 1851 Census have been listed by occupation and arranged in categories according to the criteria mentioned. The proportion of households in

[8] Dorothy Crozier, 1965, pp. 16–20. As far as we know, this was the first time that an analysis in such terms, with kinship implications, has been made from census enumerators' schedules. Compare independent comment by O. R. McGregor (1961, p. 313) on the use of enumerators' manuscript books (schedules) by agricultural historians, and the possible use of other tabulations of the data for kinship study.

gave way to a trend towards more exclusive entry – of sons of landed gentry and people of independent means who accepted the gentry way of life and standards. Cf. F. Musgrove, Middle-Class Families and Schools, 1780–1880 (*Sociological Review*, n.s. vol. 7, 1959, pp. 169–78).

TABLE 2

1851 Census of Highgate: occupations of household heads

Social category	*Occupation*	*Number*	*Total*
I	Merchants	16	
	Manufacturers and Retailers	19	
	Banking, Insurance and Stock Exchange	11	
	Civil Servants and Clerks	17	
	Professions	52	
	Rentiers	30	145 (17%)
II	Semi-Professions	35	
	Merchants' Agents and Dealers	17	
	Manufacturing Craftsmen	13	
	Farmers, Graziers and Nurserymen	10	
	Minor Civil Servants, Clerks and Officials	18	
	Local Traders	125	
	Minor Rentiers	45	263 (32%)
III	Shop Assistants and Petty Traders	44	
	Petty Officials	22	
	Skilled Artisans	59	
	Labourers	65	
	Farm Labourers	35	
	Servants	172	
	No occupation	24	421 (51%)
I, II and III	Total		829

each social category thus constructed would seem to indicate that we can reasonably classify Highgate as a 'middle-class oriented' suburb of London in 1851. Not only did most of the households in the social categories II and III render some form of service to those in social category I, but many in social category II were themselves employers of service in various forms. The number of farmers, graziers and farm labourers suggest that the metropolis at that date was only gradually advancing and engulfing the local farm land. Given the limited means of public transport available and the cost, only those who were comparatively wealthy and could afford their own carriages would live away from their places of business in the City and the West End. For the same reason, most working-class people lived near their place of employment, and the majority of the domestic requirements of the more wealthy would therefore have been supplied locally. The stage of organization of the retail trades is reflected in the number and specialization of the local traders.

The heads of households in social category III were primarily of 'working-class' status; and it will be noted that over 40 per cent of them were classified as servants; nearly all were engaged in some form of domestic service, presumably in Highgate. In addition, there were 149 dependent members of households (not counted in the Table) in social categories II and III who were similarly employed. Probably many of these servants were employed in Highgate; they comprised 76 gardeners, 16 coachmen, 6 grooms, 51 dressmakers, needlewomen and sempstresses. Here is a very strong contrast with the Highgate of today.

What now was the kin character of the households whose heads followed the occupations listed? In broad kin terms the household composition has been expressed in Table 3.

So, in 1851, nearly half (43 per cent) of all households in Highgate, and more than one-third of these in the upper social bracket, consisted of elementary families. The fact that only one-fifth of upper-class households were extended family or composite kin units is one further piece of evidence to show how false would be a Victorian stereotype of a large household of variously assorted kin as the commonest type.

It is interesting to compare the distribution of household types of social categories I and II of the Highgate population in 1851 with that of the middle-class Greenbanks sample[9] of North London in 1961: see Table 4.

In both cases the most common household unit was the elementary family, but the proportion of extended family and composite kin units was rather higher for 1851. Markedly there were many more denuded families in 1851, presumably reflecting the higher mortality in middle-age a century ago.

In our study we examined the households in the 'upper bracket' social categories I and II only, from the point of view of age in familial residence.[10] By this is meant the composition of households in

[9] The Highgate sample was restricted to married couples with at least one dependent child, and is thus not representative of the present-day Highgate middle-class population as a whole. But within this restricted category of households it shows a similar lack of extra-familial kin living with the elementary family.

[10] The concept of familial residence is used here rather than marital status and family stage since the information applies only to the composition of the household on the actual night of the Census. It would, therefore, not be valid to infer that the married couples with no children resident on the night of the Census were childless; the same remark also applies to the husbands, wives, widows and widowers grouped under single persons. In the households with children, a number of children could have been absent at school or University (this remark applies particularly to sons in social category I); in social category II a number of children in their teens and over 21 were probably away working. There is some evidence that in both social categories this was the case. For the same reason it is impossible to determine the number of grandparents or of those with all their children independent or married.

TABLE 3

1851 Census of Highgate: household types

Social category	*Married couple only*	*Elementary* family*	*Denuded family*	*Extended family*	*Composite kin unit*	*Siblings only*	*Single person*	*Total households*
I	15	58	17	8	27	8	12	145
II	30	101	33	16	32	4	47	263
III	59	193	66	29	27	5	42	421
Total	104	352	116	53	86	17	101	829

* By elementary family is meant parents and their dependent child/children. By denuded family is meant an elementary family from which one parent has been lost (by death, divorce, desertion, etc.). By extended family is meant a kinship unit where relations of the family type operate lineally over more than two generations, e.g. with grandparent(s), parents and their children. This is distinguished from composite kin unit, consisting of any other set of kin, say, siblings and their children, or aunt and niece, living in this case in one household.

TABLE 4

1851 and 1961: 'upper-bracket' social categories

Social category	*Married couple only*	*Elementary family*	*Denuded family*	*Extended family*	*Composite kin unit*	*Siblings only*	*Single person*	*Total households*
1851 Highgate I and II	45	159	50	24	59	12	59	408
%	11	39	13	6	14	3	14	100%
1961 Greenbanks	13	29	2	3	4	1	8*	60
%	22	49	3	5	7	1	13	100%

* This figure includes three persons living with non-kin.

terms of the age of children of the head of the household and their relationship of economic dependence upon him or independence (as indicated by the 1851 Census data). The limitations of the 1851 Census data made it impossible to construct a life cycle table comparable to that available for the contemporary data. Yet although precise comparison was not possible, the information available for 1851 in the original data showed certain differences in the patterns of familial residence from those of today. These differences may denote a change in the pattern of the life cycle between 1851 and a century or so later. Tabular data on familial residence in 1851 are not presented here. But two particularly interesting facts emerged from the analysis. The first, perhaps obvious, was the very large age range of children in some of the families. Unlike the wives in the present-day sample, the 1851 wives started having children at an early age; without the advantages of modern methods of birth control, they went on to produce a large number of offspring. The second point was the number of families in which there were still resident adult children – just over 40 per cent of all households in which there were resident children contained one or more child over the age of 21. There is fairly strong contrast in these respects with our 1961 sample.

We now compare the immediate origins of our Highgate populations in 1851 and in 1961. It would be easy to assume that the population in 1851 was of long standing in the area. But an elaborate and painstakingly slow tracing-out of birthplaces produced a different result.

Mention was made earlier of the fact that the modern middle-class population of Highgate is of relatively recent advent there. But much the same was true also of the 1851 population. Table 5 illustrates this, and includes for comparison our data relating to Greenbanks and to Highgate Village as modern North London populations.

So, in the 1851 sample, less than 10 per cent of the husbands and of the wives were really local, i.e. Highgate born, and less than 50 per cent of either were born in London. A century later, no husbands in the Highgate sample and very few wives had been born in Highgate, and less than 30 per cent had been London-born. But whereas in the 1851 sample, outside the London area by far the greatest contingent came from the Midlands and South-East England, by 1961 recruitment had taken place from much further afield. It may be noted that a greater proportion of the modern sample was born abroad.

In order to try and determine more closely what sort of people we were studying, we collected information where possible in 1961 on the birthplaces of the *parents* of our informants as well. Many details were not known, but for more than 80 per cent of the 334 parents of our subjects we were able to obtain data on their country of birth.

TABLE 5

1851 and 1961: birthplaces compared

	1851				*1961*					
	Highgate				*Highgate*		*Greenbanks*		*H & G*	
	Husb.	*Wives*	*Total*	%	*H*	*W*	*H*	*W**	*Total*	%
Highgate	26	20	46	9	—	3	—	—	3	2
London (Other)	96	100	196	37	10	9	26	26	71	43
S.E. England	24	26	50	10	5	4	4	6	19	11
S.W. England	12	15	27	5	1	1	1	1	4	2
Midlands	66	56	122	23	1	2	3	6	12	7
E. Anglia	17	22	39	7	—	—	—	—	—	—
Wales	—	1	1	—	—	—	1	1	2	1
Lancs/Yorks	7	6	13	3	5	3	2	5	15	9
N. England	4	6	10	2	—	—	2	3	5	3
Scotland	4	4	8	1	3	3	1	1	8	5
Ireland	2	1	3	—	1	—	2	—	3	2
Abroad	8	9	17	3	4	5	8	8	25	15
Total	266	266	532	100%	30	30	50	57	167	100%

* The figures under this head include the 7 single women of our sample, 4 being London-born, 1 in South-East England and 2 abroad. (Highgate as a birthplace was not relevant for the 1961 Greenbanks sample, but just less than 50 per cent were London-born.)

Where this was Britain some indication of the town or county of birth was usually also obtained. For our total sample, only 28 per cent of the parents had been born in London, but 80 per cent were from the British Isles (64 per cent in England and more than half of the remainder from Scotland). Of the 20 per cent of parents born abroad, a few had been born in India, presumably for the most part of British stock; the majority, however, had been born in Russia, Poland or Germany, and came to England as refugees before or after the birth of their children. This foreign component of our middle-class population was somewhat larger proportionately in Greenbanks than in Highgate, but was significant in both samples.

PROFILE OF NORTH LONDON SAMPLES, 1961 FAMILY STAGE

In the previous section we have considered the household types, occupations and birthplaces of Highgate residents of 1851, according to the available information, in order to give some historical frame to the present-day social picture of Highgate and the other North London area of Greenbanks. Now we focus on the modern material.

TABLE 6

Greenbanks and Highgate, 1961: household composition

	Married couple only	*Elementary family*	*Denuded family*	*Extended family*	*Composite kin unit*	*Siblings only*	*Individuals not with any kin*		*Total*
							With non-kin	*Alone*	
Highgate	—	28	—	1	1	—	—	—	30
Greenbanks									
Segment A	—	26	—	1	1	—	—	—	28
Segment B	13	3	2	2	3	1	3	5	32
Total	13	57	2	4	5	1	3	5	90

We first set out the household composition of our North London material, to show the social situation of informants in each sample, relative to their kinship position. It will be remembered that in Greenbanks we took 60 households as they came 'across the board' in a random sample of what was a fairly homogeneous 'middle-class' neighbourhood. In Highgate we chose households which were not only 'middle-class' but were families with at least one dependent child – though the actual cases were randomly selected from a universe of this type. Hence the Highgate sample consisted almost solely of elementary families. The Greenbanks sub-sample segment (A) comprised those Greenbanks families which corresponded to the Highgate sample.

Of the Greenbanks household units 28 (Segment A) were at the same family stage as the 30 Highgate families. The remaining Greenbanks households (Segment B) were not at that stage; they were a miscellaneous set of mainly older people, either married with adult children, childless couples or elderly unmarried women. Only two of these households contained young families, both cases of young widows with children. There were no young married couples at the pre-children stage, and this was obviously because few young married couples would want a house of the type on the Estate before they had children, even if they could afford such a house.

OCCUPATION

We now examine the constitution of our two modern North London samples in terms of occupation.

Both samples were drawn from the middle-class occupational range. As discussed fully in Chapter 2, the Highgate sample was drawn from a population restricted to the top three categories of the Hall-Jones scale of occupation. This was necessary, not because it was considered that this was where the 'border' between the middle and working classes fell, but because some objective line had to be drawn in order to avoid, in our sample, families who would completely fall outside a study of middle-class kinship. (In a general sample this would certainly have happened since Highgate is socially and occupationally heterogeneous.) The Greenbanks sample, on the other hand, was drawn from the total population of the Estate, since the latter was far more homogeneous in terms of housing, occupation and general living standards. But although all residents of the Estate could be said to be middle class by most criteria, two male informants did technically fall below the Hall-Jones categories 1–3. (One of

TABLE 7

Greenbanks and Highgate, 1961: family stage of households

Family stage	*Households*			
	Highgate	*Greenbanks*		*Total*
		A (*Sub sample*)	*B* (*Misc.*)	
1 Married: no children				
A Pre-children	—	—	—	—
B Childless	—	—	10*	10
2 Child-rearing:				
A At least one child under 5 years	13	10	—	23
B All 18 years or less but none under 5	8	14	2†	24
3 Transitional: One child 18 or less; others over 18	9	4	—	13
4 Post-childbearing:				
A All over 18, no grand-children	—	—	8	8
B All over 18, at least one grandchild	—	—	5‡	5
5 Single Women	—	—	7	7
Total Households	30	28	32	90

* includes one widow and one widower
† two widows
‡ includes one widow and one widower.

these was a highly skilled craftsman, the other the owner of a small business; only the latter appears in Segment A.)

The types of occupations of the husbands in both Highgate and Greenbanks are shown in Table 8. The differences between the samples were small. About half the men in both were in professional occupations or the Civil Service. Of the rest, the Greenbanks men were mainly in some sort of business, varying greatly in size, whereas in Highgate a smaller proportion were in business and a significant number were concerned with the arts or some branch of entertainment.

As might have been expected, most of the women in the samples had also worked outside the home, at least until they married. In Highgate only three married directly after leaving college, though two others had worked only in war time. In Greenbanks, too, only three wives had never worked – all of them older women (none included in

TABLE 8

Greenbanks and Highgate, 1961: occupations of husbands

Types of occupation	*Highgate*	*Greenbanks* A (*Sub sample*)	*Greenbanks* B (*Misc.*)	*Total*
Religion	—	1	—	1
Law	2	—	2	4
Medicine	5	3	2	10
University teaching/research	1	4	1	6
Schoolteaching	1	—	2	3
Engineering	—	2	2	4
Other professions	4	3	1	8
Civil Service	2	2	2	6
Business	8	11	8	27
Arts and Entertainment	6	1	1	8
Skilled trades, Crafts, etc.	—	1	1	2
Institutional Management	1	—	—	1
Total	30	28	22	80

the matching Segment A); apart from these all the women had worked at some time. So 79 out of the total 87 in the two samples had had some regular employment outside the home for some period.

More relevant here is the extent to which wives in Highgate and the Greenbanks Segment A were going out to work at the time of the study. That is, as mothers of still dependent children and, also important, as the wives of predominantly financially secure business and professional men, how far did they want to be completely domestic? In fact, none of the wives with a child under school age was going out to work, though two did part-time work at home. Of the rest of the mothers whose children were all at school, slightly more of the Greenbanks wives were working (56 per cent as opposed to 35 per cent). But all these latter working mothers were part-time except for two in Greenbanks and one in Highgate – these three all had only children over twelve years old.

The types of occupations followed by these wives varied widely – they included medicine, University work, school-teaching, nursing, professional acting and secretarial work.

EDUCATION

Greenbanks and Highgate showed more differentiation in education. Over three-quarters of the husbands in the Highgate sample were educated at public schools, or schools represented at the Headmasters' Conference or other private schools. Less than one-quarter went to elementary schools or secondary schools not included in the Headmasters' Conference. A high proportion of all these husbands (exactly two-thirds) attended a University or received some form of higher education. All were educated in this country, even those who were born abroad.

In Greenbanks well under half of the husbands were educated at public schools or other fee-paying schools in England. Within Segment A 40 per cent went to such schools, 40 per cent to State schools and the other 20 per cent were educated abroad. Of Segment B an even higher proportion were State-educated. Of Segment A 57 per cent and of Segment B 54 per cent received higher education.

The women in the two samples showed a similar difference. In Highgate over 70 per cent had been at private (or girls' public) schools, and in Greenbanks less than half. Over 70 per cent of Highgate wives had some form of further training or higher education compared with less than 60 per cent of Greenbanks women.

RELIGION AND ETHNIC ORIGIN

The two samples showed considerable diversity in religion and also, to some degree, in ethnic origin. Table 9 shows the religion of all informants. In order to bring out in particular the situation of the married people, the figures are given first of all in terms of number of households, as well as of individuals. Where the religion of the spouses was the same, the household is so listed; where it was different, the household is listed as 'Mixed'. In many cases attribution to a particular religion was based only on nominal criteria, e.g. baptism, and did not imply anything about on-going religious activities. The only informants labelled as atheists were those who not only stated themselves to be non-believers, but whose parents also called themselves atheists.

Only a minority of informants, of any religion, took part in any regular religious activities, i.e. attended church, chapel or synagogue every week. Many, however, kept up a minimal amount of activity – about half of the informants from both samples attended a place of worship at least once a year.

It can be seen from Table 9 that the Highgate sample was more homogeneous in religion than was the similar set of individuals in Segment A of Greenbanks. Among the former, e.g. almost two-thirds of the marriages were between Anglicans and there were only three people of Jewish origin. In Segment A less than a third of marriages

TABLE 9

Greenbanks and Highgate, 1961: religion of informants by household

Sample and type of household	Same religion						Mixed religion				
	CE.	Other Prot.	RC.	Jew.	Ath.	Other	CE. & other Prot.	RC. & Prot.	Jew. & Prot.	Ath. & Prot.	Total
Highgate											
Married couples	19	—	3	1	1	1	2	—	1	2	30
Greenbanks											
Segment A:											
Married couples	9	2	—	5	—	—	3	1	6	2	28
Segment B:											
Married couples	13	1	1	2	—	1	—	1	—	—	19
Single and widowed	9	2	1	—	—	1	—	—	—	—	13
Total households	50	5	5	8	1	3	5	2	7	4	90
Total individuals	91	8	9	16	2	5	10	4	14	8	167

were Anglican and there were eleven households in which one or both partners were Jewish. Segment B, consisting mainly of older people, was less diverse.

As regards ethnic origin, the diversity among the married couples in Segment A was not confined to a range of differing English backgrounds. Eleven of the 56 individuals were born (and another brought up) abroad. Only one of these was born of British parents. Thus, although by 1961 all were British subjects, 20 per cent of them were of immediate foreign origin, and thus often had relatives living outside this country. Some of these were Jewish families, but not all.

This mixture of backgrounds did not necessarily mean that the Segment A of Greenbanks was any less 'representative' for our purpose than the Highgate sample (of which nine informants were born abroad but only one of non-British parents). It serves to illustrate how British middle-class people, particularly of the metropolitan middle class, do not only come from families established in this country for generations. While people tend to accept recent European immigrant origin as normal for the United States of America, it is not so often recognized that to a lesser degree the same is true of much of the population of Britain.

SUMMARY

The 167 individuals whose kinship forms the subject of this book have been shown to vary widely in terms of age, family stage, occupation, education, religion and ethnic origin. Other differences obviously exist too, in regional and class origins as well as in cultural interests and ideology. The range of differences (apart from that of age and family stage in the total Greenbanks sample) is not restricted to one sample only. The Highgate sample and Segment A of Greenbanks largely consist of similar sorts of people. In each sample are minorities that differ, but the differences are mainly in the size not the nature of the minorities. The differences between the two samples are relevant only in so far as they may affect or be affected by the nature of the communities or quasi-communities from which they are drawn. Beyond this we are not concerned with comparing and contrasting the samples *qua* samples, since to do so would be to mask the really significant variations that exist within the total number of individuals and specific families.

In the subsequent analysis of kinship knowledge and behaviour the samples are mostly tabulated together as a sector of middle-class London material. In a few cases, where their origin from different areas seems relevant, they are given separately to show the degree of their correspondence or difference. Any disparity which may occur between them is to be attributed not to the nature of either sample as a whole, but to specific factors of relevance.

PART II

4

Kinship Ideology

Is there an ideology of kinship among the English middle class? In its general meaning ideology is a set of ideas concerning phenomena of social life. Such ideas are expected to be formulated in words, and expressed in relatively consistent verbal and non-verbal behaviour. In this sense, we are looking to see how far ideas about kinship are expressed in speech and action as a coherent whole, and are so interrelated that one kind of idea depends in some logical way upon the others. This is so in most societies of a pre-industrial kind, where kinship is commonly one of the major organizing principles of the social order.[1] The ideas of North London middle-class people about their kin, we can predict, will be found almost certainly not to be of such clear-cut, systematic kind. But granted this, what are the ideas which people do have about the nature of kinship, the patterns of behaviour characterizing it, and the responsibilities attaching to it? How far are they expressed as articulate generalizations? How far do people integrate these ideas and conceive of a kinship system? How far do they think there are any rules of kinship as such? How far do they link ideas with action, and what kinds of sanctions do they think operate to produce the right kind of action?

Whatever be the ideas of kinship held by North London middle-class people and however systematic be these ideas, these may still not constitute an ideology in a more specific sense. Ideologies appear, it has been argued, whenever apparently factual systematic assertions about society embody, usually by implication, evaluations about the structure of society, primarily in reference to the distribution of power. Much study of ideologies has focussed upon an attempt to reveal the relation between such assertions about the nature of society

[1] In a society such as that of the Trobriands, for instance, a classic matrilineal form, the ideas of descent in the female line, responsibility for economic support of a married woman and her children by her brothers, authority of the woman's brother over her children, and even denial of physiological paternity in favour of a theory of impregnation by matrilineal spirits, are all linked together in a series of principles which are treated as interrelated and as empirically demonstrable as such, by the people.

and the presence of interest-groups; it has been concerned with the ways in which social 'facts' present themselves to people according to the differences in their social setting.[2]

We have referred in Chapter 1 to the composite character of the 'middle-class' sector of British society. From the outset it has seemed improbable that we should find a middle-class kinship ideology which was a direct and obvious rationalization of class interests, a reflection of power distribution in the way in which kinship ideas may have been among the landed gentry in the politics of eighteenth-century England. But stripped of any immediate political connotations, and of any necessary reference to a common basis of class-consciousness and solidary economic status, this notion of ideology can nevertheless offer suggestive problems for our consideration of middle-class kinship. If assertions are made about kinship, how far do these imply meanings which are something more than face-value interpretations? Without looking for crude *determinants* of kin ideology, how far can we find that expressions about the nature of kinship and its obligations are *congruent* with elements in the social and economic situation of the people we have studied?

Take concrete examples. Some of the middle class are propertied, i.e. possessors of personal estate. To what degree does this seem to affect their generalizations about kinship and specific kin roles? Is kinship different among those of the middle class whose position depends on income and not on inherited property? Do people with high earned incomes and no particular economic pressure have the same kind of kinship ideology? Are we to expect different kinship ideology in cases of rising social mobility? These are not simple questions. Theoretically, widespread distribution of property in significant amounts throughout the members of the kinship unit might have either positive or negative results for kin ties. Positively, such ties might be kept up and regarded as appropriate because of prospects of gain or inheritance between kin or because of the obligations felt to support poorer kin from one's own resources. Negatively, knowledge of the relative poverty of kin might inhibit a wish to keep up kin ties which might threaten the conservation of one's own property. Again, the values attributed to property might be such that recognition that one's kin possess more substantial property than one does oneself might result in an embarrassed assertion of one's own independence and a reluctance to maintain kin ties.

There is a further point. Comment upon social phenomena by

[2] See e.g. Karl Mannheim, *Ideology and Utopia*, esp. pp. 238 *et seq*., 1936; N. Birnbaum, 'The Sociological Study of Ideology (1940–60),' *Current Sociology*, IX, pp. 91–117, 1960.

members of a society usually combines assertions of fact with some assumptions about values. In getting general formulations of middle-class views about kinship then, we ask if what are presented as factual statements about kin ties and kin behaviour bear a moral loading. This may be especially likely where ideas of family solidarity are backed by religion. Empirically, as far as we know, no data have hitherto been available from the contemporary situation to enable any informed opinion to be given as to whether any or all of these factors operate, and if so to what extent.

Our study of kinship will be concerned with doing as well as saying – or at least with what people say they do in connection with their relatives. But at this stage we consider primarily people's expressions of opinion about their kin in general.

CONCEPT OF 'FAMILY'

The terms kin and kinship were used very little by our informants, who spoke primarily about 'family' and 'relatives'. (The terms 'relations' and 'connections' were also used, though less often.) As a specific part of our study, we made detailed enquiry as to what our informants meant by these terms, and what they covered.

In general English usage these two terms are not at all precise. Even the dictionary offers a range of meanings which are not all consistent. *Family* historically can mean the body of persons living in one house and including servants as well as parents and children, or the group consisting of parents and their children whether living together or not, or in a wider sense all those who are 'nearly connected by blood or affinity'. It can also mean those descended or claiming descent from a common ancestor. A *relative*, according to the dictionary, in this context is one connected with others by blood or affinity, a kinsman. It is equivalent to *relation*, a connection between persons arising out of the natural ties of blood or marriage or a person so related. Historically then a very broad interpretation of these terms is possible, and the usage of our informants was in accord with such scope.

By our informants the term 'family' was by far the most generally employed for kin. It was used as the sole term by about twice as many informants as used the term 'relatives', or 'family' and 'relatives' interchangeably. (In only one case did the informant talk of her 'relations' consistently.) Wherever the term 'relatives' was used consistently to the exclusion of the term 'family', this seemed to be fairly clearly correlated with the existence of some social distance between the informant and his/her kin. The informant's general behaviour indicated some degree of isolation – restricted contact, lack of emotional security among kin, feeling that kin in practice had not lived up to the ideals expected of them, separation of duty and affection towards kin.

The term 'family' was regarded generally as the most intimate. With every married couple it included in the first place self, spouse and children – the conjugal family or 'family of procreation'. It then normally but not always included also the parents and siblings of the speaker – his or her natal family or 'family of orientation'. This was epitomized by one informant as, when he thought of his family, '. . . primarily of my family, then of my mother and father, then of my brother.'

But there was great variation in the use of the term 'family'. This was not surprising, if the lack of homogeneity of even a small middle-class sector such as that which we are studying be taken into account. But it must be noted, because the differences in content of the concept of family reveal much about the range of ideas concerning kinship in general. At least a third of our informants used 'family' in a general rather vague sense, and made no attempt even when encouraged to give more precision to the term. Ranged around this usage, however, were others of more definite application. One difference in usage, between 'my family' and 'our family', appeared to be largely a matter of verbal convention by different informants rather than an indication of deeper significance in conceptualization.

But as part of our enquiry we want to look at the conception of 'family' in the light of the structure of relations of the people concerned. The expression 'our family' did sometimes seem to correspond to the existence of a sibling group with which the informant felt in some rapport. But the main difference in usage lay in inclusion or exclusion of four categories of kin – ascendants, descendants, collaterals and affines. In general, live ascendants, i.e. usually only parents, were counted as 'family'. Where they occurred, descendants also – children (always) and grandchildren (usually) – were included in the informant's 'family'. But as regards collaterals and still more affines, there were two contrasting usages. The one gave a wide connotation to 'family'. Thus, in one household 'family', to the wife, comprised her mother and father, her mother's sister and her husband; by the husband, it was defined to include his wife's mother, his wife's mother's sister and this woman's husband. Here both husband and wife included affines in their 'family'. Another informant used 'family' to describe both her own and her husband's kin. 'Family' when defined meant her mother, her brother and his 'family', her husband's brother and sister and their children. As 'relatives' outside the family this woman indicated her two cousins and her uncle, but her brother's wife, formerly not included in the 'family', was so reckoned once she had children.

In such categorizations both collaterals and affines within close range were included as 'family'. In contrast to this were categorizations which excluded such kin. Exclusion of all affines except the spouse from the 'family' concept was not as common as might be imagined; at times some uncertainty was shown as to where they should be placed. One woman, when asked to define her family, said 'I think of my sisters and parents.' On being asked if she would include her sisters' husbands, she added 'They are sort of – I suppose they are really.' On the whole, however, the only affines included in an informant's 'family' were the spouse's siblings and occasionally spouse's parents. What is striking, however, is to find how often even relatively close consanguine kin are excluded from the 'family'. One husband, who showed a sense of filial duty to his parents, acknowledged only minimal other kin contacts. For him 'family', in addition to spouse and children, comprised only his parents and siblings; he positively excluded his aunts, uncles and cousins from this sphere.

But what comes out from our material most strongly are two points of general interest. The first is that 'family' is essentially a relative term, not a constant. One variable seems to be the general configuration of the kin group as a whole. Where there are many siblings 'family' tends to be restricted to them. The term is also defined empirically by the context, its content often varying with the same informant. It may be relative to the residential situation. On the whole a spouse's parents tend not to be included in the individual's 'family', but such a parent is almost certain to be included if he or she is living in the same household with the person concerned. This is not a simple confusion between 'family' and 'household' – a kinship unit and a residential unit, as anthropologists would see it – but a recognition that for the informant 'family' is an operational social concept (*vide* Chapter 9). When spouses discuss 'the family' the parents of both may well be included. Again, the term 'family' may be differently used by the same informant, depending on the situation being described. One informant talked of 'family' as 'the people that are close to you – brothers and sisters' (she was a single woman) and this connotation was the one she most consistently used. But to her 'family' also connoted moral responsibility, and such responsibility could on occasion extend to aunts, uncles, cousins, nephews and nieces, who in such context were also taken to be part of the 'family'. On the other hand, for this woman affines were definitely not included in the definition of 'family'. 'She is not a relation, only by marriage', and such persons were referred to as 'the secondary lot'.

The second point is that 'family' is not simply a term of demarcation of certain categories of kin. It tends to be *a term of affective significance*, and the inclusion or exclusion of kin in 'family' is a mode of classifying people not so much by degrees of consanguinity and affinity as by the affective quality of their relation to Ego. In other words, 'family' is really a way of expressing a sense of identity with specified persons who are members of one's kin universe. The kinship relation of the persons specified may vary greatly from one Ego to another and even on different occasions for the same Ego. This sense of identity may have complex components, negative as well as positive, but for a person to be recognized as part of the 'family' means that the relation to him or her is not neutral.

An implication of some importance from all this is the superficiality, in discussions of the significance of 'the family' in social life (as affecting the development of the individual personality and his socialization), of treating this as a simple, clearly defined uniform unit of parents and children. Not only for the anthropologist, but also for the social worker or social administrator, 'family' should be taken as what the people concerned take it to be, in the operation of their social affairs and the formation of their character.

This view should not of course be pushed too far. To begin with, it must be made clear that the notion of 'family' as an area of kin identification does not mean simply an area of positive love and mutual help among the persons concerned. The 'family' may be an area of conflict as well as of support. It may also be identified by some of its members as a stronghold of tradition and conservatism hampering individual development. The remark of one of our informants about her husband's mother was revealing. 'His family, and his mother, was very Victorian. She believed in the family and was very narrow-minded. His father was much better. . . .' Aspects of such family relations will be discussed in later chapters. Of more direct concern at this point is that many – though by no means all – informants made a differentiation between a concept such as an 'immediate family circle' or 'more immediate family' and some larger collection of kin, termed the 'bigger family,' 'larger family' or 'relatives' more generally. But such 'immediate family' was not necessarily the elementary or nuclear family of the anthropologist or 'the family' of the sociologist's case-book. Take this example, more clearly formulated than most, but no more limited in its scope. The wife in this case referred to her 'more immediate family', which included not only her husband and daughters, but also her husband's siblings and parents and her own parents; with all these there was 'a special closeness'. The 'larger family' on the other hand was for this woman the network of ties which a young adult inherits from 'his family'; he has an initial, unalterable tie with all blood relations, she thought, and this tie exists whether they have been met or not, though it weakens in proportion to genealogical distance. The wife in another case had a strong feeling of responsibility towards what she described as her 'immediate family' – 'I would help all the immediate family, certainly'. By this category, she explained, she meant her father, father's brother, father's sister, father's brother's daughter and this woman's husband, and her mother's sister. Apart from the last, whom Ego visited as a child, she had her mother's kin 'not the same sense of responsibility as I have towards my father's family'. In another case still, that of a male informant, even where there was a heavy stress on the elementary family and feeling that this was the most important social unit, he included in his 'immediate family circle' not only his wife and his children but also his wife's mother and his wife's mother's sister. On the other hand, he did exclude his own brother from this circle. He would have liked the brother to be closer, it was evident, but there were difficulties in the relationship. (The constitution of the 'immediate family circle' will be examined more systematically in Chapter 9.)

CONCEPT OF RELATIVES

With the term 'relatives' there tends to be a similar lack of definition, but the whole concept is a much more amorphous one. There is apt to be a very great variety in the recognition and implementation of the more complex kin relations. Yet while the notion of 'relatives' bears a much more neutral affective quality than does that of 'family', it is not devoid of sentiment. On the whole, it seems, whereas 'family' connotes closeness, even identity with Ego, and emotional warmth, 'relative' connotes some social distance, and moral duty rather than stronger affectivity. 'I suppose you'd help any of your relations if you heard they were in trouble' epitomizes an attitude of some generality in the definition of the term. Or, if an unknown relative turned up on the doorstep and needed help, 'I'd have sufficient family feeling for that – yes, I'm sure I'd do what I could.' The quality attaching to the notion of 'relative' is expressed in another way, by the contrast sometimes drawn between 'relative' (or 'relation') and 'connection'. This is illustrated by the pithy generalization (by an informant from outside the area of study): 'One may *love* one's connections, but one has a *duty* to one's relations.' 'Relative' usually means in this context a consanguineal kinsman, and 'connection' an affinal one, or more colloquially a difference between 'blood' and 'marriage' relationship is recognized. Sometimes the distinction is between 'close' and 'distant' kin. But essentially the contrast is between the optional element in dealing with kin by marriage or distant kin, and the obligatory element in dealing with kin by blood or close kin.

The notion of a relative 'by blood' often had a very special quality, though it was hard to get people to define this. One informant who used 'family' in a very broad sense to cover all those related to her by any kinship bond laid a very definite stress on consanguines. 'Blood relations are rather different. Blood relations are "my relations"; the others come into the family, but are more or less outsiders.' A peculiar, almost mystical, quality is sometimes attributed to consanguinity. Expressions such as the well-known saying 'Blood is thicker than water' were quoted to us by various informants. One said reflectively, 'It's odd; blood *is* thicker than water. There *is* a difference. One's feeling is of a warmth for no real reason . . . it doesn't do to think of it too closely or it would wear off.' Another, asked if he felt more under obligation to relatives than to non-kin, said yes, he did, and if he could help them he would; giving in explanation his own deprecatory version of the cliché: 'blood-is-thicker-than-water sort of thing'. It is a plausible speculation that some recognition of this special quality lies at the root of a paradoxical linguistic usage – the use of the very general terms 'relative' and 'relation' without further description to denote kin, particularly consanguineous kin. A friend, a business colleague, a fellow committee-member is *in* a relation (of a social or economic kind) to Ego, but he is not '*a* relation'. When the substantive is personalized it denotes a kinsman,[3] and nothing else. It is as if the conception of a 'relation' in its living form can be only that of someone linked by kinship, and who potentially links one to other kin. 'Relation' (or 'relative') is the term for someone in the most important category of social linkage.

But specifically, who are one's 'relations' or 'relatives'? Not all persons who are related genealogically are necessarily classed as 'related' in the technical kinship sense, i.e. as 'relations' or 'relatives'. Moreover, in our London study the classification differed with different people. A few tended to include only their own consanguines as relatives. Most included also their immediate (or direct) affines, i.e. persons married to their consanguines (e.g. 'A nephew by marriage – he married my niece'). Most also included as their own relatives the immediate consanguines of their own spouse – husband's (or wife's) parents and siblings. But most people excluded remote (indirect) affines, e.g. the kin of direct affines, though some people

[3] A similar usage seems to exist in some other European language, e.g., in German – '*Eine Verwandte*', a kinswoman.

were willing to include these too. These differences may now be exemplified.

There is no case in our material where known consanguines were not allowed as relatives, in theory at least, though in practice some were ignored. 'My mother always said "beyond first cousins don't count" . . . but Uncle Ansel thinks that from the tenth generation the people come into the net like the Indians do . . .' The link was often fairly distant. For example, in one case a set of people known as 'the Irish relatives' were the husband's mother's mother's mother's sister's sons and their children – showing incidentally that such ties were traced through females as well as through males. In the same case, the husband said he felt 'a sort of cousinly bond' with his mother's father's father's brother's son's son's son, whom he saw occasionally. 'Relative' has then a basic definition of consanguine. But hardly any informant restricted the term to this. One man did indeed include in his 'family' his three sisters and their children, but would not admit even the fathers of these children as relatives. 'I would always refer to them as my sisters' husbands.' Another informant commented when asked to define what she understood by relative: 'Goodness, that's difficult; definitions are . . . a blood relative, I suppose.' But she went on to say that she included her husband's brother and this man's son, as well as her husband's mother and his mother's sister's daughter and family, as kin.

> Yes, I think of them as relatives . . . if ever they wanted anything we would be pleased to help them . . . but I don't think of the others as relatives . . . they are older and it is not likely for us to ask them for any help as friends . . . and not the distant ones . . . my husband has hundreds of them . . . whenever his mother comes into the house she has a photo of various people [kin].

Diverse points of view in regard to the recognition of affines as relatives were expressed. Everyone accepted that basically relatives are people related to one by blood. When these people marry it is difficult to leave their spouses out of the 'relative' category, especially when they have children, and most people included them. Many people said emphatically they considered all the people on their own genealogy as their relatives, i.e. including all spouses of their consanguines. But there was a view expressed in one case that a spouse of a consanguine was a relative only if the couple had children. Again, there was some obscurity about the position of such a spouse when the consanguine partner (Ego's own relative) was dead or the parties were divorced (cf. p. 375). In regard to the dead there seemed to be a tendency to slough off affines when the relative connecting them died, or at least this opened up the possibility of more choice.

For a family party where consanguines were invited and their spouses as a matter of course, a mother's brother's widow was not invited – 'Well, she's sort of an in-law, isn't she' – nor was a father's sister's daughter's widower asked for the same reason.

But the dividing line in the definition tended to be drawn in regard to the inclusion or exclusion, not of the spouses of consanguines, but of the kin of such direct affines. With regard to consanguines of spouses generally, attitudes were highly selective. The tendency was for only those with whom Ego had some personal relation to be regarded as kin. One woman said 'Relatives of in-laws? No; they are not family . . . we don't make contact.' Another woman defined a relative as someone related by blood and marriage, the latter including any person who has 'married in', and any member of this spouse's family whom Ego and her husband knew well. Again, one woman classed her mother's sister's son's wife as a 'relation', and helped her because she felt the wife had been misunderstood by the family in general. On the other hand, of a father's sister's husband's second wife a woman remarked, 'She is a connection, I should say.' (cf. p. 93). Another woman who had a strongly negative attitude towards her family – she had no siblings and felt that her responsibility finished with her parents – not unnaturally refused to consider her mother's brother's son's wife's parents as relatives, but also contended that they should be left off the genealogy we were compiling! (Her husband did not agree, and thought they should be put on.) A fairly clear definition according to the same informant was that 'relatives' include all one's relations by blood and those who marry such kin. A mother or sibling of such an affine is not a relative since he or she is not the one who has done 'the actual marrying into the family'. This field definition has the merit of simplicity, but its use was implicit rather than explicit among most of our informants. (What this may imply is that contrary to the theory of the situation in many primitive societies, siblings may not consider themselves to have an identical set of relatives. When one of our informants was asked if she considered her brother's wife's brothers and sisters as her relatives she replied, 'No, they're not my relatives, but they are my brother's relatives'.)

What did emerge, rather unexpectedly, was a much less clear but understandable operational definition. In general, 'relatives' were admitted to include all consanguines and in nearly every case direct affines. People in the debatable category of kin of affines who were said to be relatives, were not necessarily any more closely related to Ego than others who were excluded. The term was a way of putting a ring round a certain category – there are others too – of socially acceptable persons. Such kin of affines were regarded as relatives when circumstances gave their relationship special significance. In one case both husband and wife considered spouses of their consanguines as relatives, and included consanguines of these affines as well; this inclusion seemed to depend on a strong affective bond with them. In another case the informant said of her mother's father's sister's daughter's son's wife's kin, 'They only came into my life ten years ago, and they're a very big clan on their own and rather nice, but I would hardly call them relatives. I would have called them relatives if I'd known them longer.' Reinforcing this attitude from the other side was the woman who said that she didn't see her sister's husband as a relative. She was emotionally very close to her sister, but her relationship with the sister's husband was rather strained, in her view because he was jealous of the sisters' close tie. In the same vein, though less definitely, was the woman who said she thought of her parents-in-law, her mother's brother's wife and her siblings' spouses, as relatives . . . 'somehow one thinks of them as the family . . . one still thinks of them as a unit where one grows up.' But she didn't feel related, in her view, to the relatives of these in-laws . . . 'no, perhaps because I've never seen them . . . I don't feel personally involved with them.' Even spouses might disagree as to a categorization. In a discussion with our field-worker one husband asked his wife 'But are your in-laws relatives?' She answered about her brother's widow 'No! She's not a relative, she's a friend.' But her husband held a different view. He said of his wife's brother 'He was so close to her that, yes, he was a relative . . . his widow – we've just accepted her as a friend, as a relative; someone who's welcome in the house. I feel rather responsible, very responsible for her in fact.'

Significant in this discussion is that while one can give a definition in structural terms of the concept of 'relatives', as of 'family', based on the empirical delimitations, this may not correspond at all closely to people's own definitions. It is essential for a full understanding of what these terms mean to consider people's own operational categories. Relevant here are elements of personal knowledge, duration of contact, performance of services and affective attitudes, which all go to make up not merely the content of the idea of kinship but also the demarcation of its boundaries, within as well as outside the consanguineal circle. Neither 'family' nor 'relatives' represent clear-cut kin units to our informants. Their definitions expressed in behaviour can vary, even in small middle-class samples such as we have been considering, both between individual informants and according to individual circumstances.

Later we examine the ambiguity in the classification of kin, as to who fall within and without these categories, and in what conditions. We propose to show how such ambiguity, offering a flexibility in social relationships, is a mechanism which has both utility and disadvantage in modern urban life.

INTEREST IN KINSHIP STUDY

In considering the ideas of family and 'relatives' we have noted the affective character underlying some aspects of the usage of these terms. But the operational definitions we obtained were extracted piecemeal from our informants. With lack of precision and even of articulation in the notions of what kinship meant to them went also lack of interest in the general implications of our kinship study.

In both Greenbanks and Highgate most people regarded our activity as external to their own intellectual concerns. Though willing to help the members of our research team and often generous with their time, they tended to treat the subject of our enquiries as not of prime interest to themselves. Their answers were intended to help the team members to do their job rather than to be contributions to a subject which they felt to be relevant to an understanding of their own lives. An aspect of this attitude was epitomized by one woman who remarked several times that, as far as family relationships were concerned, 'it all seemed so natural' to her that she couldn't imagine what we were trying to find out; it must be so 'boring' to the interviewer to sit and listen to people talking about their families! (But in contrast to this was the attitude of a woman who said she thought investigation of our own society probably quite a lot more interesting than the ordinary job of anthropologists of studying 'those boring old primitives'.) Even to some who were social scientists, the idea of kinship as a general social phenomenon, to be studied in their own sector of society, tended to be an alien notion.

Some people did however show interest. One set of people were simply intrigued to find themselves in a random sample, as an object of study. Another set, several other social scientists, tended to have a professional concern for the enquiry. Though in some cases they had reservations about the aims or methods of the study, as being unorthodox from the viewpoint of their own training, they nevertheless appreciated the general intent of the investigation, and were prepared to judge it by its results as contributing to further understanding of contemporary social relations in Britain. Another set of people were those who thought in terms of contrast of family life a generation or so ago and today, who felt that family affairs were better, kin ties stronger, moral bonds more accepted in the past, and that our study would help to point up how much degeneration had taken place. One woman, for instance, said that it would have been interesting if such a study had been done about thirty years ago and the present one were a follow-up. In her opinion family life had changed much in this period. In those days there was always a 'Grannie' or a sister nearby who could look after the children; now, she said, this is no longer so, as people live further away from their kin because of movement entailed by their jobs.

Parallel to lack of interest in the objects of our study was a lack of capacity to formulate generalizations about kinship as a general theme. There was little concern for the abstract theory of family and kin relations in modern society, and most generalizations that were produced were a reflex of either the informant's personal knowledge of other people's circumstances or his experiences with his own family and kin.[4] Roughly only one-half of our informants showed some capacity for or interest in generalizing about family and kinship topics, and about half of these in turn based their statements primarily on their own experiences. One woman, with a developed sense of responsibility towards her own kin, was very willing to give views about relationships in general, but illustrated her propositions by references to cases she had encountered as a hospital almoner. 'Kinship' as such did mean something to this woman. She pointed out that she preferred to seek help for her patients among their relatives because usually they knew the background of the patient, and why the patient was in his precise situation. Help, she thought, was a matter of good relationship between the kin, regardless of whether they were close or distant in genealogical terms.

From all this one significant inference emerged – that for our samples at least, people's generalizations about the state of family life, responsibilities for relatives, solidarity of kin, and the like, tended to be to a very considerable extent a reflection of their own personal involvement in kinship arrangements, and not a dispassionate set of observations on the state of society external to themselves. There was no uniform concept of an ideology of kinship, what it meant and what it stood for; at the most there was a set of particular ideologies but even here not clearly formulated.

Not unexpectedly we found rather more interest by informants in our investigation of their own kin than in the general nature of our study. Broadly speaking, this interest was of a threefold kind. One aspect of it was the attraction to some informants of exploring in a systematic way by genealogical techniques the range of kin of whom they had knowledge but previously no co-ordinated scheme in mind. Some of these, while indifferent to the study of their kinship in its

[4] A similar finding in regard to generalizations about standards of conjugal behaviour was obtained by Elizabeth Bott, Urban Families: The Norms of Conjugal Roles', *Human Relations*. IX, p. 334, 1956.

operational sense, were passionately interested in genealogies. A number of our informants had some previous documents of their own (see pp. 119–26), but the majority had not, and to most our offer of a copy of the final genealogy we prepared was welcome. One informant said,

> It's rather fun, isn't it? Amusing? All those boys (named) after my grandfather, and the girls after my grandmother . . . You suddenly see how large the family is. And when you showed them to me, all drawn up (in the genealogy) it was enormous. I'd never really thought of them as so many like that . . . It's so big and funny. But it's interesting, and you see things . . . I'll pin it round the wall, and pass it on to one of the younger generation so that they can add to it.

Another woman, though formerly uninterested in her family history, had had her curiosity stimulated by her husband's mother, who was fascinated by such matters, and by her participation in our study, and now felt she would like to know something about her ancestors.

Another aspect of the interest taken by informants was clearly a wish to impart information about their own family and kin. In a sense they were describing an extension of their personal ego, and the process gave them pleasure. As an example of this category was the woman who, kindly and thoughtful, and with a developed social conscience, enjoyed talking about her relatives and thinking of answers to questions. She swiftly became enthusiastic about the study, and at the end thanked the interviewer profusely – as did others – and said how much she had enjoyed the interviews.

To some people another feature of the interest in exploring their kin relations was the kind of cathartic effect it had. Once the initial reserve had been overcome, they were able to talk freely, and with some relief, about their relatives, which was also in fact a way of talking about their personal situation. Occasionally it might be a marital irregularity in the family or some other lapse from conventional morality, a note of which they thought was demanded by the record. But for the most part it was difficulties with relatives, sometimes economic, sometimes worries about health, often concerning the assumption of responsibility.

A marked feature of the interest in kinship, whether as a general subject or as an investigation of one's own family and wider relationships, was not only the wide range of attitudes displayed, but also its distribution. Nearly twice as many women as men showed definite interest, both in their own kin materials and in the study as a whole. This may have been partly due to the fact that women were interviewed at greater length and had opportunity to become more involved. But on the whole it seemed that women were more interested in the social relations of kinship and men in the genealogical aspects. A few men showed extreme interest in the investigation of their own kin. One was almost obsessively so, lacking concern for personal detail but being 'fanatical about dates, documents, etc.' Very interested in his own genealogy, he tried continually to improve it, and would return to it from all topics in the interview; he appeared convinced that we were interested in 'tracing' kin rather than in contemporary kinship.

Another aspect of the distribution of interest was occasional difference between husband and wife. As regards interest in the study as such, conjugal opinions tended to coincide; in only about one-tenth of the married pairs in our Greenbanks sample, for instance, was the interest or lack of interest by one partner not paralleled by similar attitudes by the other. But when it came to specific interest in the study of their own kin varieties of view were more marked. In one case both husband and wife were very interested in and proud of his family crest and his formal genealogy. But the husband, whose knowledge of his ancestors had been stimulated by portraits owned by his parents and their siblings, gave his opinion that he thought it more worthwhile to probe the sorts of responsibilities people feel towards living kin rather than to collect information about the dead. In another case the wife was interested in locating what place her ancestors came from, but not in her genealogy as such or in the general study of kinship. Her husband, on the other hand, while curious about his family roots, was very interested also in study of the function of the family in present-day society.

There was divergence of view also between spouses in regard to interest in their own and in each other's kin. This threw up more than anything else the main characteristics of 'interest' in kinship. It will have been recognized that the use of the term 'interest' has covered a set of very complex factors, and that the indications of proportion or magnitude of interest shown are only very rough approximations. What has been termed lack of interest, for instance, included a positive attitude of withdrawal, associated with the idea that the details of the informant's family and kin were essentially private concerns, not to be discussed with a professional investigator. But this attitude did not seem to bulk large in the interviews. One of the few cases was that of a husband who, according to his wife, had said that family information was none of our business and that in no circumstances was she to participate or divulge any information to us. He was said by his wife to be completely uninterested in his kin, and not to feel that he should have anything to do with them. She, on the other hand, had a very close relationship with her sisters, and believed that kin have definite obligations to one another – e.g. a father should put his son into a business if it be financially possible.

But reluctance to give what was regarded as private information must be distinguished from a refusal to co-operate. Where one spouse seemed reluctant to discuss family and kin affairs as such, she was reported as 'friendly, but having no wish to discuss her family with anyone'; as having corrected the purely formal genealogical information, but not going further. This was a lack of interest in, or involvement in, our study, not a lack of involvement in kin. Conversely, an involvement in our study did not necessarily mean an interest in the informant's own kin, though it usually did. The husband in the case just cited was both interested in our study and willing to supply information, and interested in his own kin, in regard to whom he clearly had a strong sense of moral responsibility. But there were the cases of people who were very anxious to help, who had an obvious sympathetic identification with the study or with the interviewer, or both, but whose interest in kinship, either generally or as affecting themselves, was relatively slight.

More generally, absence of interest in kin had a diversity of aspects or manifestations. In one case a wife was curious about our study because of her own past academic experience. But by her own account she disliked most of her kin and lacked interest in them, and her husband too apparently disliked all his kin except his mother. In other cases the interest was a matter of level; close contemporary kin were highly regarded, but there was no wish to seek out distant links depending on records of the past or to preserve the memories of the past. A wife in one of these who was interested in our investigation, thought the study of families a fit subject for a scientific research grant and seemed surprised that others should think otherwise. She liked to describe the ideal type of family in terms of her mother's family, and insisted that those people were interested in keeping up with family news and remembering names and pedigrees. Yet she herself was not interested in the investigation of her past kin and had thrown out an album of kin photographs, keeping only those in which she herself figured. Another wife, not interested in the study of her family, had never bothered to read a book that had been written about it, and had taken down photographs of kin which used to be in her main room because they cluttered the room up. She said that her mother had been very interested in the family, as her brother and sister still were, so her own lack of interest did not reflect the attitude of the rest of the family. A third case was that of a wife who varied in the interest she showed in the enquiry on different occasions, but whose attitude was summed up by the statement, 'It is all in this family tree and I haven't bothered to remember'.

An important consideration is suggested by these examples,

namely that lack of interest in kin may be not simply a disinterest or lapse of attention but a reaction in the presence of alternatives. For some people a knowledge of or interest in all kin outside their immediate family circle is felt to be a matter that can be left to others. Some other member of the family, it is thought, will take care of this, will serve as source of information and channel of communication, or 'has put it all down' in a book or on a genealogical chart (see later Kin-keepers, Pivotal Kin). More generally, we are dealing here with sets of interrelated patterns, not with individual isolated relationships.

This general point will come out in our analysis. But it may be illustrated by one of the cases just quoted. Here the wife said her husband disliked most of his kin. She herself seldom referred to her own or her husband's kin as 'family'; her use of the term 'relative' instead probably indicated her own lack of interest in and contact with kin generally. She defined a relative as 'anyone who is related by blood (to me) in the family', and looked on her husband's kin as his, not hers. 'I do tend to look on my husband's relatives as his. They're his, not mine; something I took on with him.' Husband and wife did not seem to look for emotional security among their kin, but in each other. They appeared to rely on themselves in most situations, and turn for assistance only to the wife's mother, for help in illness. The impression given was that the married couple had each other and were quite self-sufficient.

But it is relevant to point out that the wife had no siblings and the husband's only brother was dead. They themselves were childless. Both had had considerable contact with their kin as children, but had since sloughed off the greater number of relatives either because they were not interested in or wanted to have nothing to do with their kin. They did have a bond with their parents, a sense of moral responsibility tempered with affection. With the wife's mother's brother too there was a common bond of sympathy, so that he was classed as a friend as well as a relative. They may well have felt that others were a burden rather than a benefit. In addition to financial help given to the husband's mother, husband and wife obviously felt they had a financial responsibility for the husband's dead brother's widow and two children. Neither acknowledged any affective bond with these kin, but they thought they should help, especially with the children's education, since they had the money to do so and no children of their own. Here, then, attitudes to extra-familial kin would seem to have been complicated and affected by the almost complete lack of siblings, the strength of the conjugal tie and the strength of the filial tie. Thus, only by looking at the pattern as a whole can one understand the significance to the wife of the moral and economic responsibility assumed together with her husband for the husband's sibling's widow and children.

VIEWS OF MORAL OBLIGATION TO RELATIVES

Running through all discussions about the meaning of kinship in modern conditions is the notion of some moral quality, and some degree of moral imperative, attaching to the relationship. The moral quality envisaged in a kinship relation might from an abstract viewpoint be wide-ranging – to cover, for example, the obligation to accord a kinsman social recognition and make social contact with him; to give respect to his opinions and to seek his advice on issues with which he is known to be concerned; to acknowledge his right to intervene in family disagreements and to rebuke for unconventional behaviour.

In this Chapter we consider the 'moral charge' borne by kinship ties in its more general aspects and forms of expression. In Chapter 11 we examine the matter in more detail, with attention to particular circumstances and types of kin.

With our North London informants the moral obligations of kinship were focussed largely on the question of their own responsibility to help kin. (This was not due to the form of the enquiry, which also raised the question of responsibility of kin to help the informant.) The emphasis on acknowledging obligation can perhaps be looked upon as a reflex of life in relatively comfortable middle-class circumstances in which the people who were our informants were not in much need of help from others.

But recognition of moral obligation was complex. There was first the standard view, which in a sense may be taken as an ideal norm, that kinship, especially consanguinity, in itself imposes an obligation to help if required. One markedly strong statement which may be taken to represent this viewpoint was that families 'ought to stick together', that the informant's own sibling group was 'good' in that 'we are very clannish; we all rush to one another's rescue'. This woman held that the education of her siblings' children was partly her concern though she had children of her own – 'after all, education's a family thing'. She also displayed a strong feeling of responsibility towards her parents' aged siblings, being prepared to furnish a nurse (her own children's ex-nanny) to go and look after her father's sick sister if need be, though this woman was in no financial difficulty.

But this general norm was often interpreted as variable in its incidence according to genealogical distance – the further away in genealogical terms kin were, the less was the obligation to help them. The idea was further qualified by one of three considerations: of need on the part of the relative concerned; of interest on the part of the person concerned; and of his ability to assist. Moreover, words did not always correspond to deeds. A person might acknowledge the obligation but not be moved to act upon it; or might deny the obligation verbally and yet assist if needed. Even if the obligation of kinship was recognized and help given, at the same time the obligation might be resented, felt as onerous. It might even be described as 'unfair' – that is, moral norms were felt to be in conflict. This tended to be especially so when contrasted with performance by other kin.

The obligation to help a relative obviously is a function of age as well as economic and social circumstances. Since the great majority of our informants were able-bodied, young to middle-aged people, married with children, their responsibilities tended to be incurred towards those either much younger than themselves or much older. In fact, nearly all the kin thought to need help were of the older generation.

This sense of responsibility for elderly relatives is a marked feature of the middle-class kinship picture, though clearly not restricted to the middle class. It has various constituents, ranging from actual monetary help or advice on financial problems, to performance of small manual services, visiting, entertainment and provision of a place to live. A positive statement along these lines was that of a woman who said she felt strongly that the young should be taught to like and respect elderly relatives. 'They appreciate visits from the young . . . Something the young people should be educated to remember. I've always thought this was rather nice in the Chinese. They honour their relatives . . . and if it's purely a duty, neither would get any pleasure out of it.' This woman felt that the only relatives she herself ought to see were her mother and her husband's mother. Both were elderly people, who had each lost her husband, was no longer surrounded by her family and was therefore rather lonely. In this sort of situation, our informant said, she felt that children should make an effort to see something of their parents, and let the latter meet their grandchildren.

Undoubtedly to many people one of the most important obligations is that of visiting, of 'seeing something' of the relative. Most people have a kind of 'model' of social existence. There is a tacit assumption that it is necessary to maintain some social relationships in order to keep going as a fully functioning personality. There is also a common admission of an onus on close kin to supply such relationships if no other sources are available. The notion here is that a person exists through his own activities primarily while he remains able-bodied, but that he continues to be socially effective as he grows older increasingly through the efforts that others make on his behalf. The kind of image which he represents to them depends on their initiative. Hence, 'elderly relatives like to be remembered', and in this way they continue as social entities.

An articulate view of the general norms of obligation to kin was given by Mrs Maskell as follows:

> I was brought up very strongly by my mother that everyone should be independent and able to look after themselves. But I've changed my views on the subject . . . Just looking at people, and how nasty it was to look at people who had no one in particular to look after them in any way.

(She said that she had been shocked by the number of people who seemed to be uncared for by relatives and foisted on to impersonal state institutions which can hardly give a person the sort of relationship and security and companionship and feeling of belonging, present in greater or less degree if such a person is in constant contact with relatives.)

> Relatives shouldn't do anything unless they want to . . . but if a situation arises then they should cope with it to some degree. . . . Unless they like them (their kin) I feel they have only duties towards them, in times of trouble I think. And then I think they have very strong duties towards them because it is very unpleasant, and very difficult, in times of difficulty, to get outsiders to cope at all. . . .

Institutions such as hospitals and old people's homes are 'unpleasant' – because knowing little about the background of an inmate their functionaries cannot cope as successfully as relatives. This informant seemed to feel keenly her sense of responsibility towards kin, especially elderly relatives. 'There are five old ladies I feel responsible for . . . some of them I like.' They included her mother (about whom she was ambivalent – 'I do quite like her, I suppose; but there are too many family troubles for me to feel entirely easy about her'); her father's sister (whom she preferred to her mother); her mother-in-law; and a sister of her mother's sister's second husband.

This is a fairly straightforward sample of recognition and assumption of responsibility for kin and performance of duties. But in other cases the obligation was if not rejected overtly, at least qualified strongly, though in fact it was tacitly accepted.

Two examples will illustrate common variations in such behaviour. In one the husband, Mr Woollcombe, came from a 'farming family', a term in which he seemed to embrace nearly all his paternal kin, with many of whom he had had contact as a child and from some of whom he had had assistance. He recognized a moral obligation towards his kin, though he qualified this in terms of distance of relationship, and relative need. 'Not if it hurts your own family, but I believe very much in the principle of helping the family all round.' Referring to some of his third cousins and beyond, he said, 'I wouldn't feel the need to help in any way, irrespective of demands'. Yet to a kinsman whom he had not formerly met he was prepared to give help over a property deal and not charge him if the deal fell through – as he would to an unrelated client. This man was his MFBDDH. Again, he gave hospitality to two cousins from Australia, distantly related to him by links unknown, who turned up 'out of the blue', having been given his address by a kinswoman out there. He welcomed them as relatives though he didn't know how he and they were related. Here his strong feeling for kinship ties and his interest in finding out more about his kin overcame his more cautious general formulation of the moral obligation.

A detailed example with genealogy (Figure 1) will illustrate the complexity of the situation.

The case of the Dingle family shows even more marked contrasts of

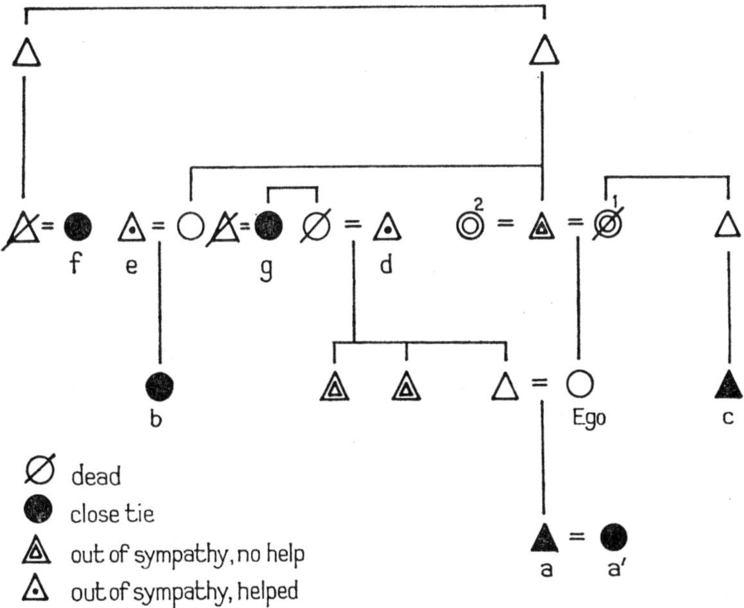

FIGURE 1. Moral Obligation in Kinship

attitude. Mrs Dingle recognized kinship in terms of a moral obligation, but qualified this by putting friends in the same category. 'If *anyone* turned up (needing help) I'd do the same for anybody, not just a relation. A friend or their friend.' Friends afforded her sociability, emotional security and a safety-valve with whom she could 'let off steam'. 'You wouldn't discuss your family troubles with your relatives as you would with friends, because you're never quite sure which side they're sitting on.' With some of her most intimate kin this woman had for long had little social contact. With her own mother she had been out of sympathy because of her mother's opposition to her marriage. With her father she was also out of sympathy because he remarried secretly after her mother's death and told her only after he had introduced her to his second wife. She had no siblings. With her mother's brother's son ((c) in Genealogy) she had had close ties as a child, but geographical distance and his social affluence had reduced their contacts to an occasional visit to him at his place of work and an annual letter. The most important relationship to her, side by side with that to her husband, was that with their son (a) and his wife, with both of whom contact was warm and frequent. With her father's sister's daughter (b), who counted as a friend, Mrs Dingle also had a close relationship. Her husband's father ((d) in Genealogy) was living with her and her husband, but showed little gratitude and complained about the food. Both she and her husband showed a sense of responsibility towards him; they had had him living with them for seventeen years, entirely at their own charge, though neither of them really liked him. Of her two husband's brothers one was rarely seen though he had the old father over to his house weekly and the other was not seen at all – primarily because he had rejected all responsibility for the old man and thrust it on her and her husband. The general ambiguity of Mrs Dingle's situation was expressed in this form: 'Relatives are a perishing nuisance. The more I have to do with relatives the better I like my dog. I don't have anything to do with them. They're no use to me except Alice (her father's sister's daughter). We're a most disunited family.' In fact, she *did* maintain at least minimal contact with some of them and also with some of Mr Dingle's kin, the operative element in her sense of duty being her involvement with her husband and with her father's sister's daughter. For instance, she kept up some contact with her father's sister's husband (e), the father of her cousin and friend, including visiting him when he was in hospital with a broken leg. She rather disliked this man but saw him because she was close to the daughter. ('She's all I've got in the family line and I'm all she's got.') So when asked to go she felt it her duty, as she expressed it. She also kept up some contact with her father's father's brother's son's wife (f), and with some of her husband's kin because he wished her to, though from lack of time and of inclination he himself did not always visit them. She gave assistance too to one of her husband's mother's sisters (g), whom she liked and whose husband's grave she tended as an act of liking. (See also Chapter 11, p. 389.)

In this case the feeling that conformity to a kin obligation is a burden, not matched by pleasure in social contact with the relative concerned, emerges very clearly. This would seem to be quite an important feature of the ideology of kin responsibility. There is a reciprocal relation between the *quality of social relationship* between the parties and the *degree of moral responsibility* felt.

A classic question in moral philosophy, whether a person can be properly regarded as having a sense of moral responsibility if he states his obligations but does not fulfil what he says he ought to do, is not one with which our informants were concerned. Rather, a problem that worried some of them was, assuming that they had a sense of responsibility towards certain relatives, how much or what quality of performance was proper to the situation?

There was sometimes a difference between what an individual said he (or 'people') should do – or would do – in certain circumstances, and his description of his behaviour when these circumstances had actually arisen. This was not unexpected. Many informants, when considering questions of moral responsibility to kinsmen, were making this explicit to themselves for the first time. Questions about duty to parents (and other very close kin) could usually be answered spontaneously. About relatives on the periphery of the kin universe (either genealogically or affectively speaking) there was often hesitation. But sometimes there were sweeping statements to the effect that they would 'help any relative who was in trouble'. The fact that an individual said this but had not done anything when an occasion arose did not mean that the statement was not valid. The statement might have the implicit qualification (often in fact made explicit) that closer relatives of the person in trouble should be the first to offer help; that our informant himself would help if there was really no one else to do it – which after all is an acceptance of a limited obligation. Apart from this, statement and practice might differ because when we extracted formulations about obligations with some difficulty, the informants might have been echoing a moral code with which they were brought up. Moral values are, to a great extent, acquired from the natal family during childhood. These may not be consciously replaced by others and thus verbal loyalty to them may continue – they may even still be thought to be the 'right thing' – although behaviour may deviate from them.

There is too a difference between saying 'I would help any relative who is in trouble' and 'It is my duty to help any relative who is in trouble'. The first statement, often the form of answer given in this context, may merely imply a *willingness* to help; the second recognizes the existence of a moral obligation to help.

Analysing the material further leads to the perception of at least three significant types of response in a situation of kin obligation. The first is related to the theme of reciprocity (Chapter 11, p. 396). What is conceived to have been the prior conduct of the kinsman is used as a test or justification of a person's own fulfilment or non-fulfilment of kin obligation. This test was sometimes used even for parents. One woman said she believed that people had a duty to look after their mothers and that this was the strongest kinship obligation that existed. She herself never felt that she had any obligation towards her father, who was a 'strange man' and 'never there'. She believed that fathers who had fulfilled their obligations to their children ought to be looked after when they got old, but not otherwise. Towards siblings, she thought, people didn't have such a great obligation as towards their parents because 'they are more on a level with you'. (This instance illustrates the point made in Chapter 12, that contrary to a common moral stereotype, no automatic affection or obligation is conceded to parents.)

Another type of response is the development of a sense of guilt in respect of inadequate fulfilment of obligation (or of what is regarded as inadequate). This may in turn lead to or be associated with a heightening of the intensity with which the relationship is regarded. A kind of self-consciousness about it develops and may well make for some embarrassment in social contacts.

Mrs March, wife of a professional man, said that she felt when people were well-off financially they should give help to less-well-off relatives if the latter should need it, and in fact she and her husband did indeed appear to give such help. Moreover, she said that she felt very strongly concerning the problem of loneliness among the aged – she had organized a party for her husband's elderly relatives including her own mother-in-law and some other elderly people she knew locally. But her relation to her mother-in-law obviously worried her. She didn't much like her mother-in-law, finding her dull and trying (a view confirmed by the field worker, who met her), with no common interests. 'I don't disagree with her . . . but I've absolutely nothing in common with her.' She said that her husband too found his mother slow and conventional and generally rather uninteresting. Yet despite all this he saw his mother every week as he knew how much it meant to her; and his wife also saw her frequently. But clearly the wife felt that she could do more, and that she had to justify why she was not doing it.

> I'm very conscious about this family business . . . I think the saddest business today is the matter of no time . . . but anyway I don't want to rush off and see people (relatives) because I ought to . . . I suppose that's very bad? But my husband says that if you can't do something willingly you might just as well not do it at all . . . my husband says that if there is no common ground and you don't enjoy it (visiting relatives) then the relatives won't enjoy the visit, so it would be better not to go in the first place . . . I like my husband's aunt much more than my mother-in-law . . . I've been talking to friends about this business of relatives, and they said exactly what my husband said . . . I feel from one's conscience point of view I ought to help my mother-in-law . . . I don't go round there to talk with her. That I suppose I ought to do, but I have very little in common with her and there's two generations difference (in age) . . . But I do feel that if my mother-in-law needed anything I would do it . . . What people do for relatives is very dependent on their circumstances anyway . . . I think in definite emergencies, and the essential problem is loneliness, and one should really like to spend time with people . . . but it's no use, with my mother-in-law, if I ask her round, because she doesn't want to.

And on the general issue, 'I suppose you *might* feel that because they're relatives you should keep on seeing them, but I find it very tedious to have to see people when there's nothing in common with them.'

Here was a case of initial responsibility assumed, but felt to be imperfectly met in practice, with the result that a rationalization had been set up. The proposition that lack of interest reacts upon recipient of good offices as well as on giver was a shrewd piece of sophistication, with various possible levels of interpretation. But it will be noted that sanction given for both the obligation and for the rationalization was the attitude of the husband. This was an illustration of the importance of third-party relations in kin ties – a point taken up again later. A significant aspect of many kin ties is that they depend ostensibly at least upon a third party – a wife feels she owes obligations to her husband's kin because of him; a man keeps up ties with his mother's sister's children because of his mother; a woman may even see her own mother, with whom she has been out of sympathy, partly for the sake of her own children, so that they have a granny, and because she recognizes the grandmother's rights to see her grandchildren. This *contingent* aspect of many kin ties implies also that if the third party is no longer there, the kin tie may lapse – a point which is relevant for an understanding of some aspects of social process.

A further type of response to kin obligation, also linked with third-party behaviour but in a different way, is to use a comparative standard in looking at kin responsibility and duty. The obligation may be admitted but not performed because other kin – perhaps better placed – have been willing to carry it out instead; or it is performed grudgingly with a critical eye kept on what other kin have or have not done. Mrs Nudley said she obviously felt a great sense of responsibility towards her mother and would always help her if there was need (cf. Chapter 11, p. 388). She said that she also felt responsible for her brother, his wife and his children – 'I feel quite strongly about this' – and for her husband's brother, because apart from her and her husband there was no one else who cared. But, she said, 'We're always being landed with the aged'. She and her mother had taken on responsibility for her mother's father's sister, now almost blind, who had refused to move into an old people's home, and she and her husband kept an eye on her husband's godmother, whose son had been killed in the war and whose daughter was a Mother Superior in a convent far away. Both these old ladies were visited and had to stay. In addition, she and her husband had earlier contributed towards the keep of the husband's mother's sister in a home, and visited her regularly. What irked Mrs Nudley particularly about this last relationship was that the husband's sister took so little share in it. When the mother's sister retired from work she lived for a while with the husband's sister, who eventually found it too much for her. A family conference was held, consisting of our informant and her husband, the husband's sister and husband, the husband's two brothers and the wife of one of them. They all agreed to contribute towards the old lady's keep. (Our informant and her husband, from rather slender means, contributed ten shillings per week.) 'It seems strange, considering how wealthy my sister-in-law and her husband are, that we had to contribute when we had so little. They could easily have afforded to keep her themselves.' The husband's sister rarely visited the old lady in the home, and when she died it was our informant whom the authorities notified, not the husband's sister, 'even though, as the wife of the youngest son, it wasn't really my responsibility'. She thought it was her sister-in-law's responsibility, and blamed this woman for not assuming it – though in general relations with her were good. Yet she seemed to think that such responsibilities should fall more strongly upon female than upon male kin, and so did not blame her husband's brothers for ignoring their aunt.

Here a sense of grievance, possibly well-based, was directed not against the elderly relative who was the cause of the difficulty but against the (husband's) sibling whose response was judged by comparison to be meagre. (But the husband's sister might perhaps have argued that in having had her aunt to live with her earlier she had discharged her obligation, and that it was now the turn of her brothers.) So, responsibility for kin in certain circumstances is felt to be a moral obligation, but this obligation is not construed as absolute. The response to it is conceived as properly to be a function of the total kin situation, relative to the position and resources of other kin in the field. Another informant, Mrs Gamba, explained such priorities of obligation to help kin in a clear, schematic manner. She did not think of aunts and uncles as individuals in a particular relation with her, but as parts of 'lots'. Her mother's brother's 'lot' would not need any help as there was enough money for any one of them to help the other. Her mother's sister's 'lot' would also not need any help, though when the children were younger they received financial help from their mother's brother. The same was true for father's brothers' 'lots'. Financial help to any member of a 'lot' should be first met by any other member of the 'lot', otherwise by the next sibling; cousin help would come at the third stage.

We can now draw a general conclusion about kinship ideology which is relevant to all the further treatment in this study. *The ideology of kinship in its moral aspect is not a series of one-to-one relationships, each with its separate moral content, but a constellation in which the moral responsibility of each party is regarded as relative to that of others in the field.* In such conditions performance of obligation by any party takes on its character by comparison with that of any other party thought also to lie under obligation. Here another important point may be made – that it is *not the amount of performance which tends to be regarded as relevant, but its relative value when set against what others do.* Hence, it is a matter of common observation that *great significance is attached in kin relations to what may appear to outsiders to be quite trivial differences in conception of obligation and in level of performance.*

If now we put together three elements of the kin situation: that kin relations represent something 'given' in advance in social life; that they are thought to have a peculiar, inescapable moral quality of obligation attached to them; and that fulfilment of such obligation at even a trivial level is often felt to be onerous, then we can understand how it is that consideration of such kin matters tends often to acquire such emotional importance and occupy such a specific position in the lives of people.

KIN AND FRIENDS

An aid to the estimation of the quality and strength of ties of relationship is to compare them with those of friendship. (This was seen by one of our informants, who observed at an early stage in her interviews that the trouble about our enquiry – as she then saw it – was that it was all about relatives and nothing about friends.) This was realized in planning the investigation, and from the start an attempt was made to find out how our informants would define friends, whether they would put them in a different category from relatives, how they would compare attitudes towards kin and friends, degree of reliance upon them and obligation towards them. An interesting range of views emerged, revealing some polarization in terms of those who gave priority of attention and social regard to kin and those who gave such priority to friends. But there was much intermediate ground covered also, including a tendency by some informants to merge the 'kin' and 'friends' categories.

A main theme which came out in our informants' views in various ways was the contrast between voluntariness in the choice of friends and involuntariness in the assignment of kin. 'You can't choose 'em, you've got 'em' was the succinct expression which epitomized a great deal of discussion of the kin theme. The result of this pre-allocation of kin to a person was, it was implied, a certain inescapable element in social relations with kin – an obligation to help if the relative was in need. But what our informants did not stress, and which comes out very clearly from the material, is *that empirically the principle of choice operated with kin* as well as with friends. This worked in two ways. Some informants selected from the total kin universe – the complete genealogical range known to them – only certain categories of people whom they were prepared to call relatives. Thus, one man neither wanted nor expected any services or social relationship with those kin outside his narrow range set of relatives – 'all that is finished'. Those kin who were inside this narrow range he saw out of affection and duty. When his father was sick, as frequently happened, he telephoned his mother every night otherwise she would get upset. He would even assist these kin financially, but he did not share either his entertainment or the intimacy of his home with them. Though he went to call on his parents, his sister and his half-sister occasionally, they were never invited to his house. 'This is my castle and I do not want relatives in it.' With friends, on the other hand, this man and his wife had an active social life, with frequent exchange of dinner invitations. He did not rely on his friends for advice and help, but he did rely on them, and on them alone, for sociability.

The selection of relatives by this man was primarily by category. What most of our informants did was to leave the category of relative quite wide, but to choose within it on a personal basis those to whom they would apply the appropriate behaviour. But here came a consequence of the arbitrary or 'given' nature of the kin tie. Friends were by definition liked; their company was sought. But relatives, even those who might be selected as objects of obligation, might be viewed in an ambivalent way, or even be disliked, and their company not sought. Yet in such cases there was an inescapable minimum of social contact held necessary to fulfil the obligation. It was the relative prevalence of this 'against the grain' behaviour that was so characteristic of relations with kin, as compared with friends.

Another main theme which was stressed by many of our informants was that the ease of relationship with friends was precisely the opposite of the tensions of that with kin. 'Somebody with whom one can talk and on whom one can rely for help, from whom one hopes to obtain some degree of sympathy . . . I'd turn to my friends . . . I don't really know – but even one's own relatives are rather distant' said one woman. Friends are 'people you can relax with'; 'mean much more' in every way than do relatives; people 'with whom I could talk about absolutely everything . . . they would know all my comings, goings and latest doings . . . they'd have the same interests.' A vivid definition was, 'A friend is someone I could invite into my kitchen and still go on working in front of'. Another definition (by Mrs Savage) expressed what many will feel to be the essence of friendship, if rather touching in its optimistic aspiration: 'Someone with whom you have quite a lot in common, with whom you can just be yourself and with whom you don't have to be careful. You don't have to be emptying your soul every minute with a friend, but you can if you want to.'

The general point of all this is that in many cases relatives are not people with whom one can feel comfortable, 'be oneself'. One has to be 'careful' with them. This is intelligible when one takes into consideration their permanent character; since the relationship is an enduring one, if it is to remain viable it must be conducted with discretion. From this point of view too it is easy to see why so many of our informants declared that they kept their friends and their relatives separate. Obviously it is difficult to feel free with some people and not with others in the same company. Yet the two categories were not regarded by all as completely incompatible. Certain specified kin were commonly admitted to a considerable degree of intimacy (see Chapter 9), and some of these, usually siblings or other consanguines of the same generation, were then often classified as friends. Not surprisingly, such classification might differ as between husband and wife in a family – where a wife considered her brother to be a friend, though her husband really did not, since he had to be 'careful' with him on some subjects. Three further points can be briefly made, two in particular of semantic interest.

The first point is that the category of friends, like that of relatives, is a graded one: it is with the notion of 'close friends' or 'real friends' that the definitions given above are mainly concerned. Various informants separated out the category of 'acquaintances' from 'friends', but even those who did not seemed to recognize some gradation. As a second point, what was of peculiar interest was the semantic difference which some informants drew between the substantive 'friend' and the adjective 'friendly'. In several cases a relative such as a brother or brother's wife was described as being 'friendly' with the informant, but 'not a friend'. While semantic divergence has not proceeded as far as it has with 'relative' as person and as adjective, 'being a friend to' and 'being friendly with' cover rather different areas of meaning. The third point, also one of linguistic usage, throws up again the ambiguity underlying the concept of close kinship. In several cases a close friend was described by some of our informants as 'almost one of the family', 'part of the family'; 'almost as close as a sister'; 'like a sister'; or called by a kinship term such as 'Auntie'. Or an informant said that 'a close friend becomes a relative', meaning that 'one takes responsibilities for them as for relatives'. On the face of it, this would seem to deny the proposition that it is friends with whom one can be comfortable and kin with whom one must be careful. But clearly, in thus equating friends with kin, just as in equating kin with friends, what is envisaged are the most positive if not idealized qualities of both. (It is important to note that the friends were not equated with kin just because actual kin were lacking; most of the people concerned had brothers or sisters of their own.)

In general, the relative significance of kin and of friends to our informants seemed to lie in the fact that they fulfilled separate functions; they did not appear on the same scale of values. A few informants said that their friends were more important to them than their kin; some, that their kin were more important, or that their kin took the place of friends. But for the most part the two categories were kept distinct, each with its own special quality; one was not a substitute for the other.

The criteria cited by our informants for the selection of people as friends, in addition to compatibility, included belonging broadly to the same age range, having the same kinds of interests, and being uninvolved in other ways with the family affairs of the person concerned. The implication of this last criterion was that the friend could be relatively objective in listening to and commenting on one's troubles, and could not spread gossip around about one among one's kin. This aspect of the social role of friend invites comparison with conditions in societies where friendship is institutionalized, and has as one function the provision of an alternative mode of social relationship and support to that provided by kin ties. In such societies bonds and obligations of kinship and descent are often highly formalized. What ties of bond-friendship do is to help to give an individual some wider field of choice, some greater flexibility in social arrangements, and even at times some avenue of escape from the demands of kin.[5] The kinship and friendship system of London middle-class people is not of this formalized character. But it is interesting to note that even here relations with friends do to some extent fill a similar antithetical and complementary role to those with kin.

The function of structural non-involvement is relevant to such situations. In some pre-industrial societies the role of mediator has been institutionalized. In some of these societies, the mediator is a person who is a kinsman related to both sides to the dispute, and who is therefore in theory at least equally committed to the interests of both and can therefore be trusted to work for a fair solution. In other societies the mediator must be a person who is *not* related to either side, and therefore being uncommitted may be regarded as unbiased.

The question then arises, in the case of those of our London subjects who have assimilated some of their kin to the friendship pattern, whether such kin are expected to perform a mediator's role? It does not seem so, for two reasons. The first is that most of the kin who are admitted to the category of friends are in a very close genealogical position – siblings, siblings' spouses, spouse's siblings – and therefore often stand in the same or very similar relation as Ego to any potential disputant in the kin field. The second reason is that the evidence does not show any different pattern of kin disputes, whether kin or non kin enter as friends. But what does seem to be indicated in some cases is that where kin have been selected or included as specially intimate friends, the history of the family has shown some particularly striking events which have affected the participants deeply.

IDEAS OF FAMILY STATUS

What kind of a family and kin universe did our informants think they and their spouses belonged to? Considering the diversity of their origins, from the outset one would hardly expect any great degree of uniformity in the family and kin backgrounds of this middle-class population. But did these people themselves tend to try and impose

[5] See Raymond Firth, 'Bond-friendship in Tikopia,' *Custom is King: Essays Presented to R. R. Marett*, London, 1936, reprinted in *Tikopia Ritual and Belief*, 1967, pp. 108–115.

the illusion of uniformity upon their background, to identify what might be called middle-class characteristics in the kin units from which they sprang and of which they were members? If not, how did they characterize these units – by reference to ancestry, to property, to careers, to moral qualities of an external kind such as service to the State or internal such as a reputation for integrity, for industry or for helping others? Or were our informants uninterested in the conception of their family and kin as having any identifiable quality and simply adopting a pragmatic attitude of concern for their immediate personal affairs?

Elements of all these attitudes were revealed by our enquiry. In the next Chapter we see just what distribution of views existed, and what shape they took.

5

Factors in Kin Knowledge

In the last Chapter we examined the ideas people in our sample had about family and kinship generally – the kind of ties they thought these institutions implied and the meaning they attached to these ties. We now consider the knowledge these people had of their own kin, and the extent to which they implemented this knowledge in terms of social contact.

Before considering quantitative data we set out briefly the most important social factors which give a basis for this knowledge. We are not here concerned with such psychological characters as differences in individual memory or interest, but with social elements which serve as predisposing factors for presence or absence of knowledge about kin. These elements are of diverse kinds. Some, such as possession of family documentation or family portraits, are the material expression of a particular kind of family life – sometimes an active part of it, sometimes a mere legacy or residue from an earlier period. Other elements, like relationship to family firms or estates, or membership of a family of a particular socio-cultural type, are of an institutional character. Others, the existence of so-called 'kin-keepers' or 'pivotal kin', are of a personal kind; still others, such as residential clustering, are really series of events. Few except family firms or estates and particular socio-cultural types of family can be regarded as specifically middle-class in type.

Among the major factors affecting kin knowledge those relating especially to kin of earlier generations have obvious importance.

DOCUMENTARY INFORMATION

In our enquiry we were particularly interested in the amount of documentary information available to our informants. Part of this interest lay in the idea that possibly the kinship patterns of urban middle-class people might be thought to have been basically influenced by some system of literate record-keeping – more so perhaps than among working-class people, who might be thought to have a more purely verbal mode of transmission of kin information. Rather to our surprise, we found that there was relatively little formal documentation of kin in the possession of our informants. Few people had family records, though some knew of such documents in libraries or in the possession of relatives. In all, only about 12 per cent of our informants actually had genealogical or other critical documents about their kin in their possession, and another 8 per cent knew where such were to be found.[1] In other words, we think of our society as a literate one, but in the kinship field, even among the middle-classes, knowledge is transmitted very largely by oral means and not through written materials.

The basic position about kin documentation is shown in the following Table.

TABLE 10

Formal documentation about kin
(Greenbanks and Highgate samples)

Informants possessing own genealogical material	14
Informants possessing other documentary material only	7
Informants possessing some sort of documentary material	21
Informants knowing location of genealogical material	14
All informants with some documentary background to their kinship knowledge	35
Total informants	(167)

For documentation in the possession of our informants we specifically enquired about genealogies formally drawn (by professionals or by amateurs), about books on family history and books written by ancestors or other kin and about wills. We also asked about other family papers such as letters, birth, marriage and death certificates and entries in family bibles, but made no systematic observations on them. There is much popular talk about the significance of the 'Family Bible' in English middle-class society. Yet it is interesting to note that as far as we observed family bibles were rare for kinship documentation. (We recorded only 6 informants who definitely had them, and for 3 of these entries in the bible were the only documentary source they had for their kin of past generations.)

On the whole, the proportion of people who were furnished with

[1] The unsupported assertion by Michael Young and Hildred Geertz: 'In England it is comparatively rare for anybody outside the aristocracy to know anything about their pedigrees'. 'Old Age in London and San Francisco' (*British Journal of Sociology*, XII, 1961, p. 133) thus receives partial confirmation from our middle-class sample.

documents or who knew where documents about their kin were to be found seemed to be higher for the Highgate sector than for the Greenbanks sector, and certainly more informants in Highgate could trace back for four generations or more. In general, documents referred to paternal ancestors rather than to ancestors on the mother's side. Moreover, genealogical and other documentary material about kin tended to be rather more in the hands of men than of women.

The possession of such material, however, did not make much difference to the kinship position of the owner. Comparison of these people with others revealed no marked differences in numbers of effective kin or in type of family ideology, though these cases did show knowledge of rather more generational depth.

The most significant part of the documentation was the genealogies, since they provided the majority of the names which made up the framework of knowledge of kin of the more remote past. The owners of these documents were very generous in allowing our investigators to see them, and where we wished in allowing us to make photographic copies. These genealogies varied considerably in their scope, their style and their professionalism, and from an anthropological point of view offered some very interesting material. A few had been drawn up by accredited genealogists, from extracts from records at the College of Heralds, London, endorsed by a King of Arms, and were embellished by coats of arms in colour. Others, the majority, were much simpler, and seemed to have been compiled from parish records and private papers, as well as from county histories and other printed sources. Technically, the material was presented in a variety of forms, mostly of the common divergent style, descending from ancestors to the present day, but occasionally in rising linked 'box' style with original ancestors at the bottom and most recent descendants at the top. One of the most interesting was the genealogy of a Polish Jewish woman who was related to prominent Viennese families; her FMF's parents, who lived in the early nineteenth century, were each traced back to rabbis of the sixteenth and seventeenth century. This genealogy was drawn up as a 'tree' (*Stammbaum*), in which marriage was represented as a vertical line, joining the names of the spouses, and the children branched off as lines from it. When they married, a new 'tree' of similar form was given to them and their children. While this system of record had the advantage of easy indefinite extension, it was difficult to link people on it genealogically, even when a system of annotation was used.[2]

[2] An analogous treatment (seen not in our samples but elsewhere) of an English middle-class genealogy is to construct it around the primary ancestors, with concentric circles of kin representing the different generations, the most recent on the periphery.

These genealogies – at least those in which the ancestors were born in Britain – seemed, in accord with the generality of such documents, to have been mainly nineteenth- and early twentieth-century productions. Most of them went back no further than the seventeenth century, though one of the most highly authenticated mentioned an ancestor who died in 1350, and another mentioned a Freeman of a Suffolk town who died in 1294. Another more daring still, referred to a 'poet prince' ancestor living in A.D. 1038! That there was guesswork involved in some early attributions is suggested by one entry: 'If he died at the age of 72 he would have been born in 1450. From the date of his birth the pedigree is traced. Seventy-two years would be a long life for those days, but it brings the beginning of the pedigree to a convenient half-century date, 1450'!

Some of these documents contain material of considerable significance for an historical study of kinship. Such is the following:

> The family of A. of M. had possessed M. for a long time. They and the B's of N. had long been connected by marriage, and finally Jane B. the last of that family married Henry A. of M; and their only daughter Susannah Maria (who married the Rev. A.T., who took her name) died childless. [The Rev. A.T., who had a son and a daughter by a previous marriage, was left an estate by a kinsman whose surname he further assumed; he left this estate to his son on his death.] Susannah Maria, his widow, was *of course* [our italics] mistress of M. in her own right, and she left M. to her husband's daughter, Mrs C. and her husband, who are the ancestors of the present family of C. of M.

Such lateral transmission of landed estates to affines, through women heirs, must have been a significant feature in the acquisition of property in the early nineteenth century, long before modern legal provisions facilitated the control of property rights by married women. But there is probably much scope still for investigation of the extent of this practice. Others of these genealogical compilations contained notes of a more personal, sometimes more painful character, such as: 'James. Went to South America. Became rich. Married Spanish lady of fortune. Ceased to communicate with relatives.'

But our major concern has been with the contemporary significance of this genealogical material. Three points seemed fairly clear about this. The first was that most of the genealogical material had not been spontaneously accumulated by our informants themselves; it had been handed on by kin. Only a very few of our informants had specifically taken the trouble to seek out and collate documentary evidence of their past and of their collateral kinsfolk. The second point was that genealogical interest on the part of our informants in general was very restricted. It was not merely that their possession of this type of documentation was very limited, it was also that, with the exception of the few amateur genealogists, their wish to acquire or enlarge it seemed very small indeed. With these few, however, the interest was keen. For example, a man had taken the initiative in having a family genealogy drawn up by the College of Heralds, because an aunt of his had collected a lot of material and he thought it should be properly recorded; he intended to forward to the College of Heralds further information on births, deaths, etc. of his kin, and hoped to delegate this duty later to a younger interested member of the family, ideally to his son.

The third point of sociological interest indicated by some of our observations was that opinion about the validity or the value of the formal genealogy was not always shared by members of the same household, including spouses. The husband of the woman with the elaborate genealogy traced back to sixteenth- and seventeenth-century rabbis was critical of it. He was inclined to argue that the record could not be wholly accurate because of the relatively late development of Jewish surnames and birth registration, and frequent change of name to avoid military service – even after compulsory registration was introduced (he said) in A.D. 1780. According to another possessor of a genealogy, this was 'like a red rag to a bull' to his wife – though this was a charge which she denied hotly, saying that she had always taken a great interest in it. But what these examples suggest, even if they do not illustrate, is that in some cases a genealogy is regarded as a kind of status symbol, and if not shared by husband and wife, may become a bone of contention.

Compare this situation with that in a primitive society without written records, where a genealogy is usually a public instrument or status symbol, not merely a private one. It is used to secure for an individual or a descent group some particular social privilege, or to validate their title to land, or to allow them to claim prestige in some special social context. The important point about such a genealogy is usually that the possession of it and the use of it are publicly known; it is only by using the material in relation to or in opposition to the genealogical claims of others that its significance becomes apparent. Even where the exact names in a genealogy are kept secret for ritual reasons, there is public recognition that the owner of the genealogy does indeed have a set of names of proper antiquity as a basis for his claims and operations. Some such public recognition applies also to the use of genealogies by English aristocracy and 'old families' of the gentry; the names of their ancestors are not known to the general public, but it is generally believed that they can trace their ancestry far back into the history of our country, and because of this they have a certain social status and prestige. But it is otherwise with the written genealogical material of our North London middle-class families. For the most part, members of the wider society, even their neighbours, are completely ignorant that they possess such material, and no social status or prestige accrues to them on this account, at least outside their own kin circle. The satisfactions which their owners receive are essentially personal in character; they are a source of private esteem, not of public status. The putative genealogies of primitive social groups are not at all immune from challenge and scepticism, but this tends to be by other social groups.[3] In the sector of North London society we have been studying any challenge tends to come from within the domestic circle or immediate kin group; the society outside ignores the whole situation. This conversion of genealogies from public into private objects of interest would seem to be one of the many kinship concomitants of the geographical and occupational fragmentation consequent on the development of our industrial type of society.

What further can be said of the genealogies we have been examining, as evidence of interest in the past and a sense of history on the part of our informants? Social anthropologists are well used to the idea that in primitive societies genealogies are not simply historical but have social functions which often mean that their historical validity assumes a secondary place. Hence, as much anthropological analysis has pointed out, in non-literate societies genealogies are *transmuted* when being *transmitted.* What about genealogies in the field we studied? The genealogist critic, Round, has written of the 'fabric of fiction' woven round the 'actual evidence' of a pedigree, and how the desire for ancestry in English society led to the construction of a set of 'monstrous fictions' in genealogical form. Our scrutiny of data from the North London enquiry has not led us to think that in this middle-class field there has been any widespread invention of aristocratic ancestors or faking of ancestral links in order to give greater depth to a pedigree. Most of the documents refer to 'solid bourgeoisie' and are of a quite sober type with a great air of plausibility. But on the other hand, we cannot agree with Goody and Watt, who argue that in a pre-literate society 'the individual has little perception of the past except in terms of the present; whereas the annals of a literate society *cannot but enforce* (our italics) a more objective distinction between what was and what is'.[4] Empirically,

[3] See e.g. Firth, *History and Traditions of Tikopia*, Wellington, N.Z., 1961, pp. 78–80, 175–6.

[4] Jack Goody and Ian Watt, 'The Consequences of Literacy,' *Comparative Studies in Society and History*, vol. V, 1963, pp. 310–11.

we have found that in the kinship field this 'more objective' distinction is very dubious. An important distinction should be drawn here between *public annals* and *private annals.* The 'private annals' of our society refer to a past of shallow depth and are very unevenly distributed. Many people in the middle-class field have no such private annals of a personal kind, nor any immediate access to public annals which have concerned their own ancestry. (Generally speaking, they have no idea where to go to consult such public annals.) This lack of personal documentation of the past means that for them the literacy of the society has brought no very clear sense of objectivity in differentiating past from present. Again, even where they have such documentation, in kinship terms at least, our observations have shown that with rare exceptions the documents are not treated in critical terms, with historical canons of objectivity in mind. The literate urban middle-class and the pre-literate peasantry are far closer together in their attitudes to past and present than has been alleged.

Moreover, the existence of genealogical and other documentary material in the hands of a person does not necessarily mean that the information contained therein has been integrated into his or her body of knowledge of kin. A distinction is drawn later (Chapter 6, p. 155) between a 'personal universe' of kin and a 'literary universe of kin'. It may be that the latter, in the form of documentation, has been fully incorporated into memory, and mobilized historically as occasion offers, to describe the precise genealogical relation of A to B and to give details of where A lived and what he did. Or again, there may be no attempt to carry any of the information in memory, but the documents may be specifically kept as a reference source, and looked up whenever any questions of relationships arises. But on the other hand the genealogical data may be merely vaguely apprehended with no particular interest in checking what is thought to be so against the actual documents – here past fact and present interest tend to merge. A plausible hypothesis is that where there has been full incorporation of the data supplied by the documents into the current knowledge of kin, or conversely where discrepancy between memory and documents is ignored, emotional factors are involved which either give stimulus to memory or block it. Where on the other hand the documents are used as a reference or check source primarily, one can postulate that this rests upon some economic or allied interest, such as a possible inheritance or the appearance of a kinsman as a resident in one's neighbourhood.

Realising that availability of family history does not always mean that the owner has memorized it in terms of family trees, we analysed the 21 cases where some sort of basic documentary information about ancestors was in the possession of an informant, to try and see how far such material may have formed the basis of kin knowledge. In fact, one can never isolate very rigorously the influence of this factor from that of others – such as oral tradition acquired from grandparents, or association of ancestors with a family business. But we did find that while in 12 of the 21 cases knowledge of ancestors coincided with the genealogical data available from documents, in the other 9 cases knowledge of our informants, unaided by their documents, stopped at the great-grandparental generation and not even all grandparents could be named. Moreover, however much the informants had learned from the documents available to them, they had garnered this knowledge selectively, restricting themselves in almost every case to one or two lines of ancestors, and seldom bothering to learn the names, e.g. of ancestors' siblings. What we concluded from this then was that acquisition and retention of kin knowledge is not a fairly freely floating process, but is highly selective and linked with a set of specific interests of the person concerned. In a primitive society, with no written records, this conclusion might be thought reasonable, but it is noteworthy in a literate society that documentation is used so directly in an instrumental manner.

PORTRAITS AND HEIRLOOMS

Allied in a sense to documents as sources of information about past kin are portraits of them. Our informants possessed portraits of various kinds: paintings in oil and water-colour, daguerrotypes, silhouettes and ordinary photographs. This portrait material was held by both men and women, though the photographs tended to be for the most part in the control of women. Our evidence about this type of material is not complete. Our investigators enquired about kin photographs in almost every case in Highgate, but not so in Greenbanks. They did not make specific enquiry about family portraits in oils or analogous media, but in a number of cases they were shown such by informants, or saw them hanging on the walls. Our observations under this head are therefore to be taken as generally indicative rather than as a full record of conditions.

Original portraits of kin in the form of paintings, including miniatures, seemed to be relatively few. They were noted for only 10 of our cases, nearly all in Highgate. These portraits depicted a variety of kin, some in the direct line, others collateral; some identified, others not. In several households there were paintings of FFF, FFZ and father's sister, kin of the husband in each case. One informant had his mother's father's maternal grand-uncle's likeness in his sitting-room, as well as several other paintings of eighteenth- and nineteenth-century gentlemen, very tentatively identified only by their family surnames. In another case, of portraits given by the husband's mother, while they were known to be of ancestors several generations back, their exact identity was not known.

In several other cases portraits of forbears and other kin of past generations were known to exist, though not in the possession of our informants. They were 'in the family', as the expression goes; some, though by no means all, might be inherited in due course by our informants.

> In the Smith family (Ego's mother's mother's) there are quite a lot of family portraits. Aunt Jane (mother's sister) has one of her mother. And my mother has one of a Smith ancestor, and one of a great-aunt of hers – I don't know who – and a relief of *her* mother – a plaque thing. . . . The paintings are not very good ones – they're of interest to the family, but not much – they are probably put away in cupboards. . . . There wouldn't be any of the Jones's (father's family); they were not rich. They were East End people – and not arty either.

Some interesting sociological points are indicated by such statements: that paintings (as distinct from photographs) are a prerogative of the rich or at least very well-to-do; that they are kept for their sentimental rather than for their aesthetic value; and that the sentiment is of a dormant rather than active kind in that the paintings may be stored and not displayed. This seems too to indicate a prior component in our middle-class sample, of junior members of gentry families, for whom family portraits were not linked with land and other property interests and so had no built-in reason for preservation of identity. (The major portraits in the direct line were held elsewhere by senior representatives of the family.)

In a sense, having a portrait of a kinsman may be regarded as a kind of extension of the personality of the owner. One woman brought up a painting of her HFFZ from her house in the country to show to our investigator, and displayed it with the remark 'Don't you think Alice (her daughter) is *exactly* like her?' Here the perception of ancestral physical likeness gave an added dimension to the daughter's personality – and that of the mother – by giving her continuity with the past. But such incorporation of these portraits into the intellectual and emotional fabric of the kin universe of our informants who possessed them was very uneven.

Possession of photographs of kin was considered by our observers in household terms; to separate out exactly to whom the various kin photographs might be said to belong was difficult, and in itself was a point of sociological interest. Our material was incomplete. Out of a total of 90 households, we have no data for 26 (nearly all Greenbanks cases). No photographs at all were seen in the house in 3 other cases, and two more households possessed no kin photographs. In one of these the wife used to have a family album, but threw it away – she 'didn't know why'; not, it seemed, from any emotional crisis. In the other, a single woman living by herself had an enlarged photograph of her goddaughter on her mantelpiece, but none of true kin. That this was not due to lack of sentiment alone was shown by the fact that she had preserved a small china doll given her by her mother when she was a child.

Of the 59 remaining cases of households with kin photographs, in 3 the kinds of kin depicted were unspecified. To get some idea of the range, kin given photographic cover in the other 56 cases were divided broadly into four main categories: immediate household members – informants and their children; informants' natal family – parents, siblings – and siblings' children; grandparents, parents' siblings and their children; great-grandparents, grandparents' siblings and their descendants, including second cousins and more distant kin. It appeared that hardly any informants had photographs of more distant kin, but that in these categories the material was fairly evenly distributed in household terms. About one-third of the households had photographs of a personal nature only, limited to household members and their parents, siblings and siblings' children. Households with photographs of grandparents, uncles, aunts and first cousins comprised just over a third of the total. But households with great-grandparents and/or second cousins also in their photographic collection amounted to just over a quarter of the total.

What did these photographs mean to those who had kept them? Were they a mnemonic, a focus of sentiment, a means of implementing kin ties, a demonstration of solidarity, an object of curiosity? What is notable is that they seemed to serve several purposes; there was great variety of attitude in the people who had them and commented upon them.

In a few cases production of family photographs for our investigator served to jog the informant's memory; one man, Mr Arthur, was prompted thus to remember a second cousin once removed and her daughter, a third cousin (MMMZDDD), whom he had forgotten to mention earlier. In other cases photographs acted as a kind of identificatory memorial. One informant said that he had never met his grandfathers, and knew them only from their photographs. Many photographs of dead people in past generations served to show their kin what they had been like in life. But the process of identification was not always an easy one, and this illustrated how the personality of someone of an earlier generation could be obliterated from the kinship field by a simple lapse of memory. One woman produced a photograph of her mother's family, showing her maternal grandmother and grandfather (the latter 'bearded, Victorian and prosperous-looking') and all their children, four boys and four girls. The informant was unclear about which name went with which child, and gave different versions of sibling order on different occasions. Yet even when kin photographs are unidentified they do not necessarily cease to be of significance. They may be cherished as evidence of a family past in which individuals cannot be specified, but which is given a solid body by these concrete representations. So in one case of a man who was almost obsessed by family documentation; he had a large stack of old photographs inherited from his parents. Most of the faces he no longer recognized, and often there were no names written on the backs. But he seemed to take great delight in going through them slowly, each in turn, and musing who each might have been. It was with great difficulty indeed that the interviewer managed to divert his attention to a discussion of more contemporary aspects of family life.

Some informants showed a negative or fairly lukewarm attitude towards kin photographs. Several, but not all of these, were single women. One, who had an album, no longer put photographs in it. 'People don't take them (family photographs) now. The family do send them occasionally, of the children and things. But I don't think I want them to bother.' An old woman, her case illustrated the point that the old do not necessarily want to be 'kept in touch' in all the ways that their kin think advisable; the expenditure of energy needed to 'keep up' may be more than they feel that they can bear with equanimity. They also tend to be more highly selective. Another equally elderly single woman said of kin photographs 'I won't have them stuck about'. She used to have albums a long time ago but got rid of them; all that she retained were a few photographs of an aunt with whom she had spent most of her childhood. Whereas with single people the selectiveness in kin photographs may tend to be retrospective, with married people it may rather focus on spouse and children. An elderly married woman said that she used to keep photographs of kin on display, but they cluttered the room up so she took them down. But she then took the investigator upstairs and with great pride showed her photographs of her husband and her daughter. Another married woman said they had no photographs at all. After a little thought, however, she said they had a few of her husband and herself, her son, and her dogs (of whom she was very fond). 'They're only of interest to yourself some little while, and then, well, they lose their joys, I think.'

Another attitude was to regard keeping and transmission of kin photographs as a function of having young children. Several informants said: 'The children are all grown up and therefore people don't send photographs any more'; or 'I think it's a thing one does when they're little.' Here the developmental aspect is significant – the photographs sent to kin can express parental pride in the child's development, and also allow the kin to keep pace with changes which otherwise could render the child unrecognizable after a few years. An outstanding example of this was where the Nevilles sent the husband's mother a batch of photographs every three months, mainly of their young son, so that she could see his progress – she had never seen him personally. Out of a batch of twenty coloured photographs taken by the husband on a Christmas Day, the son alone, plus Christmas toys, was the subject of thirteen. One showed the boy holding a present his grandmother had given him, and was designed to show her how much he had liked it. The only reason this family took so many photographs of themselves and their son was to send to the husband's mother and to exchange with the husband's brother and wife (who sent in return photographs of themselves and their own small son).[5]

Another aspect of the more positive interest in kin photographs is their reminiscent value – they recall relationships and episodes connected with the personality in times long past. Mrs Woollcombe said 'My mother has a lot and so has my grandfather and these will come to me – all of the immediate family. . . . Now the photos are mainly of the children. They reflect the different phases of my life: as a child, of me and my mother, as a schoolchild, my schoolfriends. Now it's back to the children.' Mr Woollcombe, equally interested in his own family photographs, produced a batch, including a group of kin at his parents' wedding – thirty close kin and three friends. A photograph of himself and his younger brother called forth the remark 'This was when I was at the resentful stage'. Such photographs tend to serve as pegs upon which to hang stories about family and kin. Mrs Gibbon had a photograph of her mother at the age of seventeen, which was said to have won a beauty competition. 'She could have had a film career', but when she went for an interview she took fright at the last minute and ran away. This behaviour was explained by 'Well, she had no parents, and had to look after herself'!

The function of kin photographs as helping to provide family depth and continuity, and as aids to personal reminiscence is given additional complexity by the peculiar aesthetic quality of such memorials. There is often an interest of a quasi-scientific kind in the

[5] Photographs were sometimes exchanged between branches of a family long separated but who discovered each other anew through some accident.

costumes, hairstyles and postures of the past as displayed in these reproductions. Mrs Maskell, though not particularly interested in having photographs of the range of kin of past generations, did say it was interesting to see what aunts and uncles looked like when they were young, all dressed up in the clothes of that age. Mrs Gamba, who had inherited a lot of family photographs, particularly from her mother who had practised photography, commented 'It is curious to look at old photographs, different fashions, different poses and techniques'. Her interest in them was an attachment to her maternal property, as a sort of curiosity about the changes they depicted, rather than as portraits of individual kin.

But much of this interest in fashions of a bygone era was less sociological, and more personal. It was not fashions in general but what 'Aunt Mary' was wearing that was striking; it was the personal incongruities and changes in people whom one knew to be connected with oneself that seemed to be of most significance. It was a record of change in a sphere of personal interest. One woman said 'It's quite pleasant to have odd snapshots of people. They're always good for a laugh ten years later. Odd snapshots and photos do remind you of people and of things – how they've altered.' Said Miss Lamb, 'Photos of the family are kept because it's quite amusing to see what they looked like then, now.' And again 'We had far more old photos which my father got rid of, I don't know why. I like to look at them now and again. It's always jolly to look at them – amusing. If they were taken quite a few years ago one looks so funny, and one's family and the fashions.'

The element of humour evoked by these photographs is sociologically relevant. It would be going too far to say that the photographs are kept for their incongruity, but by contrast the oddities of the past give reassurance to the present. These photographs illustrate and give a basis for some of that rather wry interest in the definition of one's own personality,[6] and of personalities related to one's own, which finds material in a record of persistence and change in looks, clothing and behaviour.

Our field workers did not make complete, systematic observations on heirlooms. But in the Highgate sample the existence of inherited property, including some heirlooms, was recorded in at least half the cases. For the most part this consisted of furniture or jewellery, often objects in ordinary use in the household. The range of kin from whom the articles were inherited was not very wide: a piano from a father's brother, antique chairs from a mother's mother, a silver

[6] Anecdotes about past kin serve in some cases an analogous function as 'verbal portraits'. Some of our informants seemed to have a great deal of their kin knowledge in this anecdotal form.

sugar sifter from a father's sister. Both husbands and wives inherited such property. Of special remark was that in a number of cases heirlooms in the possession of the wife had been inherited from a kinswoman of the husband. The principle here seemed to be that the property was sex linked, i.e. feminine rings and other jewellery, but that it was regarded as appropriate that it should be transmitted to the wife of a male member of the family. The most notable case of this was where a wife got jewellery from her HFMBD, i.e. her husband's first cousin once removed, specifically because this woman thought it should go to her cousin's wife. Here is a principle of patrilineal inheritance, the actual property being held by daughters or spouses of the men concerned. Such heirlooms seemed to serve as concrete reminders of dead kin, though their presence in the home seemed to be not so much a direct factor in retaining knowledge of kin as in a reinforcement of ties of sentiment for kin. (see also section on Kinship and Money in Chapter 11.)

FAMILY FIRMS AND ESTATES

Economic interest and genealogical knowledge would seem to demand a high degree of correlation in a family firm, or family estate. In all, 20 informants mentioned that there had been family firms or landed estates with which they or their forbears had been associated. (This excludes family firms started by informants or their parents.) In most cases this implied some inheritance of family property but by no means always did the informant benefit from these business concerns.

Knowledge of the kin history of these concerns varied considerably. Two informants could name all ancestors connected with family firms started six generations ago. Firms started by great-grandparents numbered five, though in only three of these cases were the names of the founders known to their descendants. Another eight firms were started by grandparents, and the particular founder could always be named in every case, even when the informant had not actually met him.

One informant, whose family had been mainly skilled craftsmen for many generations, said that there was a family history that could be dug out of local records. He said he knew many generations of his father's family, and did give a list of names from his father to an ancestor five generations above, though he placed this man rather improbably in the early seventeenth century. According to his account, his FMF was a craftsman in a similar trade and this man and his FFF met at the Paris Exhibition of 1840.

There were altogether seven family estates mentioned by our informants, but two of them were also connected with family businesses. Rarely could informants trace their ancestors back to the original owner of the estate. One informant could trace back to the original farming owner in the seventeenth century, another to an original family owner four generations back. But in the other three cases knowledge reached back only two generations, though one of these informants who professed great interest in the subject had material both published and unpublished which could have extended the record.

In general, it would appear that in about half the cases of a family firm or family estate its existence may have helped to extend kin knowledge by stimulating the interest of descendants to learn the names of forbears associated with the concern and fixing the names in memory.

Where our informant retained a financial interest, direct or indirect, in the affairs of the firm or estate, this tended to strengthen kin knowledge or maintain it, by necessitating a channel for contact. Many of the members of Mrs Underwood's father's family had a financial interest in or were employed in the family foundry in the Midlands. When the father was alive he had organized an annual dinner and dance for the firm, and this became an occasion of family reunion. Our informant continued to attend, even after the father's death, since the arrangement was carried on by the father's sister, a director of the firm. This annual celebration provided an occasion for our informant to meet her paternal kin – an opportunity which she would perhaps not have provided otherwise since she did not seem to have much in common interest with them. 'I was conscious on Saturday (when she attended the reunion) how little I have to say to my male cousins. I found that I was asking them the same things as I asked them the year before.' Nevertheless, at the reunion she did gather news about other kin who did not attend. Moreover, on the last occasion we recorded she arranged for her son to visit the family firm for a fortnight and learn something of its work and traditions, and of the local business world.

Even withdrawal from a family firm may provide a focus of kin interest, if it creates financial problems such as that of 'buying-out' the retiring partner, or emotional problems such as that of accusations of breach of family loyalty. In such case the strong negative attitudes aroused may well tend to help in the maintenance of knowledge about kin and transmission of it to children.

The existence of a family firm may help to perpetuate kin knowledge in another way – by facilitating the entry of certain affines who otherwise might remain in the periphery of interest and knowledge.

The process may be illustrated from an example of a firm started by one informant's own father. Our informant was the only son, but he had a sister and a half-sister, both of whom were given shares in the firm by their father. On this basis both their husbands became members of the board of directors of the firm, though they did not otherwise work in the firm since they both had separate businesses of their own. Our informant, who was very restrained in contacts with his kin and who otherwise would have seen little of these men, did have some contact with them at board meetings and informally in social chat afterwards; otherwise his relations with them were minimal. In this firm, with father as chairman of the board, his son as managing director, and father's brother, mother's brother, sister's husband, half-sister's son and half-sister's husband as directors, the appearance of a tightly-knit kinship unit is presented. But here was a case where the kin tie was the basis of the financial association, but the financial association had not promoted closer social contacts outside the business realm. Kin knowledge was facilitated by the business association, but this did not imply more personal relationships. Indeed, there had been some difficulties and disagreements among the partners, though they had been ironed out. Our informant, who obviously felt no particular validity in a kin tie as such, said that in principle he preferred not to have kin as business associates.

The point here is that the existence of a family business, whether or not our informant was a member of it, can serve as a stimulant and focus for kin knowledge, but does not necessarily promote closer kin contact.

NOTABLE ANCESTOR OR FAMILY NAME

We were dealing with a cross-section of an urban middle-class population, and therefore did not expect to find many families with a notable record of public service or any particular title to fame in the annals of the country. Such a record might have been expected to provide an additional stimulus to kin knowledge. We did find a few families well-known for their professional services, as in banking or the theatre. But it was mostly individuals rather than families who were significant. In all, fifteen informants were able to trace their genealogical connection to an ancestor noted for a special accomplishment or action, some of distinct historical note. The most spectacular of these was Guy Fawkes, who according to one of our informants was the direct ancestor of an old-established family of gentry from whom her MMMF came!

An illustration of the kind of family and kin lore in the possession of some of our informants is the story of this great-grandmother's father. The Fawkes (we were told) were an old Yorkshire family but some members migrated to Warwickshire and had a large family. The eldest son of this branch left home and got a job in another part of the country as a builder's labourer. The foreman noticed that the lad's hands were not those of a manual worker, and enquired about him; it then transpired that the lad had nowhere to spend the night. The foreman took him home. In due course the young man married the foreman's daughter, and when his family learned of his *mésalliance* they 'cut him off' in classic style. As time went on the couple had seven or eight children. The eldest daughter, ancestress of our informant, when in her teens was sometimes taken up to London by her father's kin, wined and dined, and bought many clothes 'to give her a taste of what life should have been'. When she returned home to her six or seven siblings her new wardrobe was shared among them.

This kind of charter of gentry origins is relatively rare among our informants. But what is especially interesting is that for a modern middle-class person the line of ancestry, starting in the gentry, dips into the working-class field and then slowly emerges again.

On the whole details about noted ancestors were relatively obscure. In one case an ancestral surname (of FFM) was remembered because her grandfather (FFMFF) was reported to have been extraordinarily tall (7 ft.), to have come from Cornwall to Western Ireland and to have fought with great valour for the French when they invaded Ireland in 1798. But for the most part not much more than the role of the noted ancestor as actor or writer was remembered, or the fact that he had inherited a title or been knighted.

PLACE OF ORIGIN

In some cases there was a coincidence between the name of a village or other place in the British countryside and the surname of an informant or of one of his or her ancestors. This coincidence aroused the curiosity of some of our informants, who sought for documentary materials which would make more precise the nature of the tie (if any) between the ancestor and the place. The result had been not necessarily a proof of any specific local origins but at least an enlargement of knowledge of ancestors and past kin. In fact, however, there were very few cases in which data about place of origin was relevant for increase or confirmation of kin knowledge.

More usually, knowledge of kin and of their geographical location was held side by side.

PERIOD OF GRANDPARENTS' DEATH

The factors discussed so far which may affect kin knowledge have been of a fairly concrete kind, external to the informant's own position. Now we come to a structural feature of demographic type, involving a relationship between informant and kin of past generations. From our enquiries, it seems evident that knowledge of a person about his kin of grandparental generation – meaning primarily the ability of the informant to name grandparents and their siblings – in effect related to the age of the informant at the death of grandparents. In some cases a grandparent's house was a meeting place for kinsmen, including the informant, and such family gatherings were a source of memory information. Even if the house was not a meeting place, while grandparents were alive names and information about their siblings tended to be a fairly common topic of conversation. In some cases correspondence served as a key. Mrs Ackroyd had to read to her grandmother the letters which this old lady received since she could not read well any more; so our informant acquired a very full genealogical knowledge, equal to that of her own mother.

When informants had met their grandparents they were usually able to name them for us, and add something about their siblings; in Highgate this happened in 70 per cent of the cases. If the grandparents had died before our informants were born it was unlikely that there would have been much contact with great-uncles and great-aunts. So in only two-thirds of the cases where grandparents had been personally unknown to our informants were they able to name them, and in less than half of these cases did they know anything about the grandparents' siblings. Where in such case they were able to name a grandparent's sibling, this was apt to be because of some alternative source – in 14 cases out of 24 there was documentary evidence of the name, or some item of property had been inherited from the kinsman in question.

VERBAL TRANSMISSION

It is clear from the foregoing data that a person's knowledge of his or her grandparental generation, especially of grandparents' siblings, is very incomplete in the urban circles we have been examining.

Moreover, it seems clear also that many opportunities for accumulating information about the kin of past generations have not been taken. In a great number of cases it was not possible for us to determine why kin knowledge was so limited. But one aspect of the situation which did seem relevant was the obvious lack of any explicit tradition of transmission of kin knowledge. Not only are there no rules for securing that children are made aware of their parents' kin, there is also no sense of obligation to hand on such information. No view exists that a knowledge of the family and kin past in any way constitutes an element in the make-up of the social personality of an individual. 'Not to know his ancestors' and his ancestors' kin is a stigma in some societies; not so in urban middle-class London.

So, ignorance of grandparents' siblings means that parents do not deliberately pass on information about their own uncles and aunts to their own children. Only if a person has known these great-uncles and great-aunts personally, or has known his grandparents who have talked about their siblings, has he been furnished with data about them. The transmission of kin information tends to be a function of immediate family relationships. People talk about their own siblings – beyond that there has to be some special reason for them to communicate information. Only about a dozen informants in both our samples mentioned their parents as a specific source of kin information; in most instances it was the mother who supplied the knowledge. Occasionally a parent was reticent about kin information – 'My mother is very secretive about the family; we cannot make her talk'.

This did not mean that there was little concern for the elementary family relationships as such, just that on the whole parents did not attempt to instruct their children about the background of their family or about their ancestors.

SOCIAL INTERACTION

Our informants learned about their kin, including those of earlier generations, not by any simple verbal transmission of information about them, but by a process of social interaction. The majority of the kinsmen they could name were contemporaries with them or with their parents. Informants' parents were usually in contact with their own siblings, so informants learned through participating in such contact, of the existence, names and characteristics of aunts, uncles and first cousins. The social interaction included exchange of letters and Christmas cards, visiting and family gatherings. It varied in quality – friendly, indifferent, critical, unfriendly, or of that curious mixed affective character which seems especially liable to occur in kin contexts. Interaction was often indirect, not face-to-face with the kin concerned but through parents or other kin. For example, a person heard about a mother's first cousin not through personal sight or correspondence but because of an argument between his mother and the cousin, which the mother discussed openly with him.

The importance of social interaction rather than simple verbal transmission as a medium of kin knowledge explains how kin get dropped off the mental genealogical map. The fact that kin knowledge has been acquired through such interaction, directly or indirectly through one's parents, explains why it decreases as genealogical distance increases. But the parents have not remained in touch with all their uncles, aunts, cousins, equally (for data see Chapter 6), so informants themselves knew only some, not all, of their great-aunts and great uncles, as well as their second cousins and senior first cousins once-removed.

The Highgate sample was analysed to determine how knowledge of the more distant kin, those of the second or third collateral line, had been acquired. Of the 41 cases of informants having knowledge of kinsmen at this degree of collaterality, up to third cousins, only 13 informants had known about these kin just because they had been *told* of their existence and their names. The remaining 26 (excluding 2 informants not intensively interviewed) mentioned that they had *met* all these people when they were young. Only 2 informants remembered having met kinsmen about whom they could give no details. In one case a man mentioned that his mother had 25 maternal first cousins and was sure that he must have met them all, some probably several times, but after making an effort he was able to cite only two of them. Another man could not tell us anything about his father's father's family though his paternal grandfather had lived with him and his parents when he was a child, and had been very interested in 'family trees', about which he talked a great deal.

In general, extensive knowledge of kin can be explained by active participation in the social life of the elementary family and wider kin set, usually when the individual was a child, though sometimes as an adult. On the other hand, if parents were withdrawn and had little contact with their kin an individual had scant opportunity to meet them. In some cases of little kin knowledge it seemed that parents of the person, while themselves maintaining some contact – as in a family gathering to which they did not take their children – did not always bring their kin into the family or household environment; they did not often write to or talk about kin they met outside the household. In such cases a household did not always act as a unit in kinship interaction.

'KIN-KEEPERS'

In some of our cases knowledge of kin and social interaction with kin were mediated primarily not through parents but through a particular relative, usually a woman, who made it her special interest to keep posted with kin information and to impart it to other kin. In an earlier study (Firth, 1956, p. 39) such specially informed kinsfolk were termed *pivotal kin*, 'relatives who act as linking points in the kinship structure by their interest in, and knowledge of, genealogical ramifications'. But adopting a term introduced by Alice Rossi, one of our Chicago colleagues, we now term such relatives *kin-keepers* or kin repositories, since they act as retaining mechanisms for kin knowledge. We distinguish them where possible from kin-mobilizers, who serve in particular to get kin together for family gatherings and for aid to any member in difficulty. (See also p. 211.)[7]

Such a kin-keeper may seldom be seen by some other kin of the wider kin group, although he or she knows of them. Moreover, the kin-keeper tends to have information about a large number of kin which is not necessarily shared by other kin. Conversely, other people in the kin universe tend to look upon this particular person as a repository of extensive kin knowledge. Such knowledge, sometimes based on keeping genealogies or other records about kin, is apt to be regarded as something unusual, idiosyncratic. A kin-keeper is not necessarily prime mover in getting kin assembled together or in putting them in touch, but may be applied to when kin information is wanted. The disparity between the kin knowledge of any ordinary informant and the kin-keeper may be very striking. In one case (in the early non-random section of our study) our informant had a fairly small total knowledge of kin – 38 persons in all. His sister, a kin-keeper, had a total kin knowledge of 234 persons. When our informant was first interviewed, he could remember few of his kin so immediately wrote to his sister for information, and she supplied him with a genealogy, a large proportion of the names on which our informant had not known even existed. This relative disparity in kin knowledge existed at every generation level.

How far can the role of kin-keeper be regarded as a structural role in the kinship system, or how far is it primarily a function of the operations of people with a rather strong organizing type of personality, or a strongly developed sense of curiosity about other people? At first sight structural elements do seem to be present.

[7] Cf. also R. Piddington, 'The Kinship Network among French Canadians,' *International Journal of Comparative Sociology*, VI, p. 150, 1965.

Parents (about a dozen) could be characterized as kin-keepers. Members of the elementary family and kin of wider range orientated their knowledge of one another's activities around a central parental figure, in most cases the informant's mother. Occasionally the father fulfilled this role. Exceptionally, the father of Mrs Mitchie wrote a letter each week to his daughter giving her all the local news. Duplicates of this letter were sent to his five other children and also to his FZD. Our informant and her siblings replied 'theoretically once a week' and in practice rather less often, though our informant usually telephoned. Mrs March regarded her husband's mother as a kin-keeper. She said of our study 'My mother-in-law would love this; you ought to interview her. . . . She knows a lot of relatives. . . . There isn't a day goes by without her writing a letter to some relative or getting one . . . I always go to her for an address if I want one.' The mother-in-law herself said that she felt an interest in relatives was 'rather nice really and it gives me something to do. I have always been interested in my relatives.' Yet despite this interest she declined a copy of the genealogical information we had accumulated and collated. 'I don't think I want one, thank you – I would rather go on writing to them. I don't need a genealogy really because I know about them.'

It may be argued that the role of kin-keeper comes naturally to a parent, especially to a mother. If this is so, it is surprising that so few parents, including mothers, could be found who filled this role. Our information on kin-keepers is not complete, so it may not be significant to find that in only about a quarter of the Greenbanks cases was a kin-keeper specifically recorded. But for the Highgate cases, where a more definite enquiry was made on this point, only about half gave any clear indication of such a role. Moreover, the range of kin types concerned went very definitely outside the parental field. It included informants' sisters, mothers' sisters, fathers' sisters and mothers' mothers, and even a MBS and a mother's brother's third wife filled such a role. In the majority of cases the kin-keepers were aunts of the informants and were often unmarried. The MBS was a bachelor and seemed to find considerable satisfaction in tracing out all his kin ties. In a few cases a relative from abroad came over to Britain and acted as a kin-keeper by 'looking-up' as many relatives as he could in this country and making overt to them the nature of the kin ties between all. All this does indicate a structural component involved – of a person on the fringe of the kin system rather than central to it, and using knowledge of the system as a means of maintaining integration with it.

The role of kin-keeper was not always conceptualized by members of the kin universe, but in some cases was clearly realized. Descriptions of kin-keepers were given in such terms as 'a colossal one for relatives', 'a great collector of people', 'very family conscious', 'keeping up with a large number of relatives', 'knows a lot about the family', 'avid for family news', 'quite a family man', 'makes an effort to keep up'. Occasionally the role was objectified in a piece of family colloquial language. In one case our informant did not consult anyone for genealogical information, but made it clear that one of her sisters was most interested in kin. This woman had a copy of a book which had been written about some of the very distant relatives (though our informant had not bothered to read it). Our informant was one of seven siblings and the house where two of the sisters lived was called 'Central Office' because when their mother lived there she used to circulate all the news. (In her mother's lifetime the house was also called 'Elastic Villa' because so many relatives 'descended' on her to stay.) Her eldest sister seemed to have taken this role over from their mother. When our informant discussed kin such as her MBD or her MZS, she referred to her sister as the person with whom they had more contact than with herself; about her nieces' relations with this sister she said, 'They feel that she is the sort of head of the family'.

Some of these kin-keepers tried to cultivate the interest of some of their kin, especially in the younger generation, in 'family' matters, but from the evidence of our case histories this was usually without success.

One infers from such material that 'kin-keeper' is not simply a structurally defined role. Among the members of an elementary family contact and knowledge are usually multi-stranded, and there is no particular need for one single person to hold all these strands together. Outside the elementary family in the wider kin universe there is a job which can be done in serving as a central information point and repository of knowledge about kin. Structurally this job would seen to be most efficiently done by women of a senior generation, especially those who have not the obligations of a growing family on their shoulders. But it is clear that not every kin universe has such a kin-keeper, even when people of the appropriate structural position are available. Factors of personality as well as opportunity obviously enter into the situation.

The role of kin-keeper can be closely associated with that of *kin mobilizer*, but they need not be combined in the same person. There were instances, however, in which a kin-keeper, usually a mother of one of our informants, was described not merely as knowing all about the family but also 'holding the family together'. (For example see Chapter 7, p. 211.) In some cases 'kin mobilizer' is a succession role. Family ideology may require that as many members of the kin group as possible meet at intervals, and as one organizer of such gatherings dies another may serve as a replacement. There is a suggestion in our material that roles of 'kin-keeper' and 'kin-mobilizer' tend to be more necessary and significant in large kin units of semi-corporate type.

GEOGRAPHICAL CONCENTRATION

One factor helping to structure an informant's kin universe was the geographical distribution of his kin. In the next Chapter we discuss the relation between this distribution and the degree of contact – the constitution of the *effective* set of kin. But here we are concerned only with the way in which the places where kin lived in relation to one another and to North London, where our informants lived, affected the amount of knowledge of kin.

It is clear that mere distance of kin from our informants did not in itself diminish the knowledge about them. But when the distance had involved overseas migration, then this tended to interpose a barrier. In particular, as had happened with several of our informants, geographical separation had left them with a knowledge of the older generation of kin, their contemporaries, but lack of personal acquaintance with younger kin meant that their knowledge at this level was very slender. Some kinship links had been dropped through severance of communication in the past, and hence knowledge of the younger generations was lacking altogether. But in at least one case this had been revived by an accident of meeting with a visitor from abroad, which led to exchange of correspondence and photographs and an addition of a whole new set of kin to our informant's knowledge.

Conversely, what seemed to be especially important for maintaining kin knowledge was a solid concentration of kin in one area, as an interacting group. Where such an identifiable kin group remained, even though our informants had deserted it residentially, it was of great significance in serving as a focus for kin interest and in allowing knowledge to be kept up, not only of close kin but also of more distant kin in touch with these. Such a 'nodule' of localized kin made the retention of kin knowledge easier. When a visit was paid to one kinsman, there was every stimulus to visit others too, or for these to come and see the visitor. So the most recent news of births, marriages and other events was easily acquired and absorbed into the body of kin information. (In the next Chapter some examples of these 'kin nodules' are illustrated.) This process is not painless. Mrs Mitchie said 'It's rather a chore, having to go round and visit everybody. Sometimes I think it would be nice to go home and only see one's parents.' But the multiplication of kin by natural growth may well defeat the social process. She pointed out that she was not likely to have a kin knowledge comparable to her mother's when she would be the same age, because even if she returned to live in the kin centre she would not keep up with her relatives as much as her mother did. Although she kept in touch with all her siblings, she didn't maintain contact with all their children (see p. 391).

On the whole, however, though geographical contiguity facilitated kin knowledge, and especially kin contact, these did not depend upon unified location of kin. An illustration of this is given by Mrs Outram whose father's father was one of seventeen siblings. Their father was in the cotton business in Liverpool, inherited from his father and father's father, and passed it on to one of his sons. But none of the siblings seemed to have any particular attachment to Liverpool and became very scattered, at least four of the sons going abroad. Yet our informant's knowledge of them did not seem to have suffered particularly because of this – she had information about ten of them and their children.

SOCIO-CULTURAL TYPE

One of the most significant factors affecting the knowledge of kin in English middle-class circles is probably the socio-cultural type to which a family belongs. The English middle-class has to be regarded as a composite social category, and certain elements in it have a much more marked interest than others in the hereditary transmission of what may be termed cultural assets. In our society as at present constituted, some middle-class families are either more interested than others or more in a position to be concerned with such cultural assets. These include social status and public reputation of their members, titles of rank, landed and other property, membership of fairly exclusive associations such as certain religious or professional bodies or leading public schools. In some sectors of the middle-class, families as such are not particularly involved with these kinds of assets; individuals in them may be, but lacking any particular hereditary transmission of them, or sharing of them on a family basis, no tradition of common family interest in them has developed. But in other sectors such an asset-oriented interest has developed, and is one of the ways in which a family expressed a collective personality. In such conditions there is a predisposition for members of the family to have knowledge of a more substantial kin universe than in others.

Three socio-cultural types which have emerged most clearly from our material are: (a) those families which have multiple connections with the gentry and share in some of the assets of the landed gentry without possessing their major endowment – the 'para-gentry', as they might be called; (b) families with an immediate rural background and a tradition of independent farming; and (c) families of exclusive, primarily religious, association.

Aspects of these different types will be discussed further in considering the quality of kin relationships. Here we are concerned only with the way in which the focus of attention upon cultural assets such as status tends to affect the knowledge of kin, for example as regards the size, depth and range of the kin universe.

(*a*) *Families with multiple connections with gentry*

Under this head come half-a-dozen families (less than 10 per cent of the total) in which our informants, husband or wife or both, trace descent from a family of landed gentry or, in a few cases, from nobility. Empirically, this means that ties with gentry in such cases are multi-stranded, a situation to be distinguished from that in which some member of our informant's kin has married someone from a gentry family. Almost all these multi-stranded gentry-connected families were in our Highgate sample. In these cases we were dealing not with members of the landed gentry as such but with offshoots, members at one or two removes, e.g. whose mother's father or father's mother was a son or daughter in a landed gentry family. The people we were concerned with had gentry among their kin, and shared some of the common status assets, e.g. by inheriting a family portrait, by visits to the ancestral home, or by using the family name as a personal name. They might also have received some monetary inheritance. But they did not themselves own the major assets – the title, the landed estates, the associated family firm, which are the normal concomitant of gentry status.

Yet their direct interest in the transmission of the minor assets, and their indirect interest in the character of the major assets, including the intangible asset of the prestige of the family name, helped to maintain a recognition of a wide range of kin. It would seem to be no accident that these cases of 'para-gentry' families tend to provide those cases of largest sets of *recognized* kin. (They do not necessarily have the largest number of *effective* kin, since this involves some form of contact, and personal selectivity enters in here to a marked degree.) An illustration of this kind is given in Figure 2, the Outram case, in which both husband and wife traced descent from landed gentry, the husband's mother's mother being

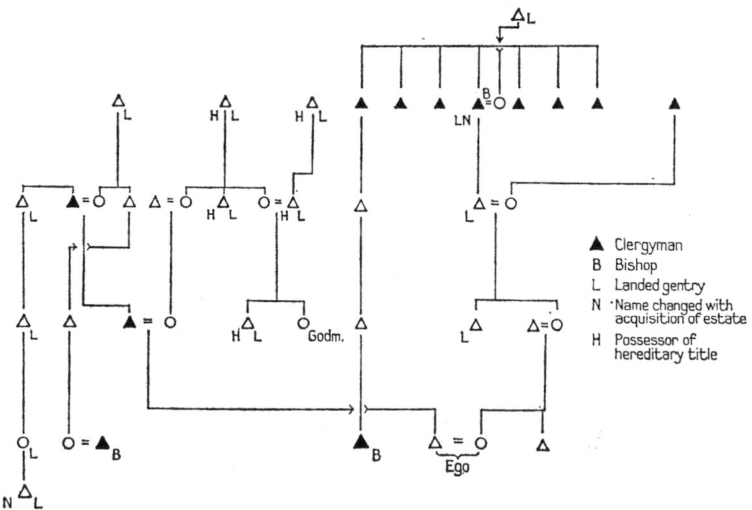

FIGURE 2. Linkage of Church and Landed Gentry in Upper Middle-Class Kin Set

the daughter of a peer. Both Mr and Mrs Outram were among the half-dozen instances of the largest sets of recognized kin in our whole collection of cases.

Circumstances of this kind imply that the family concerned is likely to be able to trace back for a number of generations on one side or both in its genealogy, to base the recognition of kin on some substantial documentation. This was so in the present case. Yet it must be noted that despite the association of kin documentation with this socio-cultural type of family, and the considerably greater genealogical depth than the average, the range of kin recognition was not significantly greater. It could be said of a Scottish Highlands or a Polynesian chieftain that he is 'a man of many cousins', meaning that he could trace his consanguineal kinship out very widely to many degrees of relationship. This was not so with our North London middle-class families sprung from the gentry; like the husband and wife in this case illustrated, none of them had a knowledge of more than third cousins.

The character of the kin universe of these families did not depend upon the occupation of their members. But it tended to be associated with a fairly limited range of occupations, mainly of the higher professional type, and of the financial rather than commercial order. In some cases, as that illustrated in Figure 2, the Church, the traditional resort of younger sons of landed gentry, tended to be of some importance – though a consistent row of seven sons all in Holy Orders, as shown there, must be rare indeed! In another striking example of this occupational clustering was a number of kin in merchant banking: the wife's brother was in one firm, her husband in another, her sister's husband in a third; both the husbands of her MFZDD and of her MMZSD came from well-known merchant banking families, and the son of the latter recently went into merchant banking. One can understand then if 'all the merchant bankers in the City are related to one another. . . . It's all a network, and the merchant bankers all know one another socially as well as through business.'

The significance of these occupational clusters from a kinship point of view lies in the fact that in these fields a man's job and his reputation are very closely associated; not only that, but his own success is very closely bound up with the reputation of his associates. To select associates from a fairly closely-knit group, where there is a pervasive knowledge of personal character and common sanctions of some restraint, is reasonable, and these conditions are provided to a considerable degree by using existing kin ties and creating new ones.

The upper middle-class type of family is well-known for its interest in education – at least as concerns its own sons and to a lesser extent its daughters. This preoccupation has been by no means only with an eye to job and income. As much as anything it has been focussed on securing that by going to the 'right kind' of school the sons and daughters are helped to emerge as young adults with the 'right kind' of social personality. This does not mean, of course that it is desired that they should all fit the same mould – though even eccentricity should have its more appropriate spheres – but that the individual should be endowed with enough knowledge, self-respect and cultural mores to take his place in the more responsible administrative, even 'governing' categories of society. In this process the public school, as the chosen instrument of this kind of education, has been of prime importance, the reputation of particular schools – their 'name' – being a peculiar compound of historical flavour, scholastic standards, public role of past pupils, individual usages, special facilities and families of recruitment.

The kin element in recruitment is well-known in some of the major public schools; it is to be expected then that we should have found it among the upper middle-class families in our sample. One of the most obvious cases is that of the Herberts, where over only two generations as many as 42 consanguines and affines in a particular kin network (ranging from members of the nuclear family outwards through nephews as far as third cousins) went to Eton. This kin universe was one of the largest in our study. Here the common schooling of so many young men almost certainly helped to reinforce the retention of knowledge about kin, if not the kin bond itself. But the families of our survey as a whole presented a wide range of variation in the patterns of education of their kin. The Table of educational distribution of close kin given in the next Chapter indicates the relatively sparse occurrence of male principals and their close kin in the 'top bracket' public schools, and therefore the fairly limited force of an upper middle-class education as a factor in kin knowledge.

(*b*) *Farming Families*

Common occupation provides a bond of interest, and when kin follow the same employment this seems to serve as a factor of integration among them. One of the outstanding examples in our

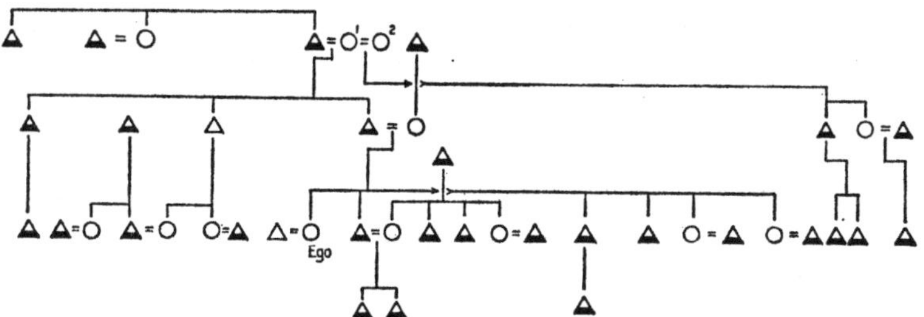

FIGURE 3. Farmers in a Kin Set
(Farmers indicated by half-filled symbol)

survey was that of Mrs Mitchie, a woman from a farming family who married a man with a craftsman's family background. His universe of kin amounted to 21 kin in all, hers to 114, and the reason she gave for the size of hers was that she herself had grown up surrounded by kin. Figure 3 shows the genealogical distribution of her farming kin. There were in all 28 farmers on her genealogy; apart from her dead mother's father, all were of her father's kin, consanguines and affines. The complete kin universe cannot be shown, but it is noteworthy how many farmers' sisters married farmers, with the result that the farming kin included such relatives as brother's wife's sister's husband. (Figure 8B in Chapter

7 indicates the geographical concentration of these kin, and their significance in terms of kin grouping is examined in Chapter 9.)

In another example Mr Woollcombe's family had been farmers. His wife had a kin universe of 22 individuals, his numbered 240, one of the largest in the sample. His father had been educated at a small private school which catered mainly for sons of farmers, but went into engineering. This man's eldest brother took over the family farm from our informant's father's father, who had been a miller and farmer of a family property in the Eastern Counties. Other farmers included FFB, FMF, FB, FBS, FBWB, FBWZD. His father's brother's daughter had married a man who came from a big family of old-established farmers, and who had five brothers all with farms in Lincolnshire and a sister married to an agricultural surveyor. Here again, the common agricultural interest and the fairly close rural concentration were factors stimulating a sympathetic concern for kin.

There were very few families with extensive farming connections in our sample, and from the metropolitan nature of our sample the rural focus could be only of a somewhat retrospective, sometimes nostalgic, kind. People who belonged to such sets of kin seemed to approve of them. One woman, for instance, who said she came from a 'farming family', stressed how such families were always giving help to one another in a friendly way, compared with the lack of helpfulness and friendliness she had found when she first came to London. She said that she had missed the sort of assistance and company provided by a family of siblings and other relatives, and that Londoners were suspicious by contrast.

(*c*) *Families of Exclusive Association*

One would expect membership of an exclusive association to promote extensive kin knowledge and a compact kin universe, especially if reliance upon in-group rather than out-group members was expressed in intermarriage of the former. We have already noted one aspect of this in the public school alignment of kin in upper middle-class families, where common schooling and affinal connection are well linked. But it is in some religious fields that kin knowledge and exclusiveness might seem to be most closely associated. This could be assumed to be so where the religious ideology lays great stress on family solidarity, such as Roman Catholicism does, or on uniqueness of physical as well as religious transmission of membership, as does Judaism. (Cf. Chapter 9 on Mixed Marriages.)

We had in our sample no members of the more exclusive Protestant Nonconformist sects such as the Brethren. A member of the Eastern

Orthodox Church, Mrs Savage, while giving the impression that such people in London formed a close-knit community because they were members of a minority group, did not stress their exclusive nature. (She had a kin universe of no more than average size; that of her husband, a convert to the Orthodox Church, was much larger.)

The relation of kin knowledge to religious association might seem to be more relevant with Roman Catholicism. Yet rather contrary to our expectations, this did not seem to be the case. With the six Catholic families in our sample, the size of the kin universe of husbands and wives was not noticeably greater than those of non-Catholics; they showed much the same distribution over the entire range. The largest of all in the Catholic group,[8] with a kin universe of 179 relatives and an effective kin set of 26 with whom she was in contact, was that of Mrs Lander who was a convert. (It should be noted that two of her sisters had independently become converted and married Catholics.) While the issues of a Catholic education for their children and Catholic spouses for their close kin seemed important, most Catholics did not appear to link their kinship as such with Catholicism. Mrs Gilroy, who had a relatively small kin universe, regarded her FFBD, a non-Catholic, as her closest friend among her kin. Another who took it for granted that her kin would be 'very very strict Catholics', said that Catholics were more broadminded than Protestants; they accept Jews, Protestants and probably 'Blacks' without making them feel uncomfortable! However, she did admit that it was 'funny' to have a great-uncle in a Protestant seminary. With another Catholic, an emigré from Central Europe, it was his nationalism rather than his religion which, he said, 'linked him in spirit' with his kin a thousand miles away.

The relation between character of kin universe and socio-cultural type of family might be expected to be very close with Jewish families. Inside as well as outside Jewry the stereotype of Jewish family and kinship is of a large close-knit group, with widely ramified knowledge, elaborate communications and ample support among its members. Yet we have some reason to question the validity of this stereotype, at least as far as Jews who are members of a mixed London middle-class area are concerned. No adequate study has yet been made of the kinship of Jews in Britain[9] and this cannot be attempted here. But our very limited material at least suggests some possibilities.

There were 23 Jews in our whole sample, but from the point of

[8] In the earlier non-random sample, the largest kin universe of a Catholic husband was 163 and of his wife 101.

[9] Cf. M. Freedman, *The Structure of Jewish Minorities*, London, 1957, p. 24.

view of study of Jewish *families* one woman, a convert from Christianity, should be omitted. In terms of marital units, there were seven Jewish marriages; another seven in which a Jewish partner had 'married out' of the faith (five out of these seven were men); and also one case in which a Jewish man married the convert just mentioned, making in effect eight 'out' marriages.

There were certainly large kin aggregates of the stereotype kind among the 22 Jewish-born in our sample. In Greenbanks, out of twelve people recognizing 100 or more live kin, eight were Jews; two of these, women, each had nearly 200 apiece in her kin universe, by far the largest of all. In Highgate, of the three Jews in our sample one, again a woman, had the largest number of live kin in her universe, 295, and on her genealogy appeared nearly all the best-known names of English Sephardi Jewry. In Greenbanks, of the ten people only who maintained contact with 40 or more kin, six of these were Jews. In all except two of eight mixed marriages the kin universe and set of live kin of the Jewish spouse were larger than those of the non-Jewish spouse. One exception was a case where, owing to the war, the Jewish member had had to leave his home in Poland in boyhood, and his mother, siblings and many other relatives had been killed. In the other case the man's mother's parents came over from Russia, and nothing was known of the kin left behind.

Yet the picture of the large, closely-knit group of Jewish kin is not consistent throughout. Of the 22 Jews in the sample, nine had a kin universe of less than 100 each (though two of these were only just less); and ten maintained contact with less than 20 of their kin. One man, very low on the list of kin size, had only ten people in his own kin universe and kept contact with only seven of these; the reason was perhaps in part that his parents came over to England when they were eighteen. This man was said by his wife not to be able to do much about meeting family, not to feel the need or urge to exchange family visits – she quoted him as saying he didn't belong to a particular family but to a group with similar interests. On the other hand, he had his compensation in his wife's kin, who were very many and with the nearest of whom he was on very good terms. It is pertinent also to note that neither this man nor his wife belonged to a synagogue. In two other cases, each with about 40 total kin and only three kin in contact each, similar reasons of emigration had applied, and in addition the mother of one had died when he was a child.

Although it is possible to say, therefore, that some of our Jewish informants had a wide kin knowledge, it is clearly not true of all of our Jewish informants. Moreover, it is equally not true that with all informants the largest aggregates of kin were those of Jews. In the Greenbanks sample while it is true that a high proportion of Jews was found to have a high recognition of kin, out of eleven persons with a kin universe of over 150, five were non-Jews, and in the Highgate sample the largest kin universe of all (live and dead kin known) was that of a non-Jewish woman. In other words, the reputed size of Jewish sets of kin is a matter of averages, not applicable in all cases. It is superficial then to attempt to characterize 'Jewish families' as a type without trying to discover what it is that makes such families vary so considerably in the size of their kin sets. Apart from a factor of 'Jewish ideology' (see Chapter 9) issues of Eastern European or Mediterranean origin, of immigrant status, of minority group consciousness, may well be partly responsible for the particular pattern which the kin universe assumes in any case. To sort out the issues on any scale would demand a more extensive investigation than has been possible here. But the whole subject of kinship among Jews in London and in Britain generally seems to us to be well worth further research.

RELATIVE IMPORTANCE OF FACTORS BEARING ON KIN KNOWLEDGE

The importance of these various factors discussed as affecting knowledge of kin is clearly very different. For knowledge of kin of previous generations the most important factor would seem to be documentary records, though as we have shown the possession of documents does not necessarily imply an equivalent knowledge of what they contain. Portraits, especially photographs, seem to be ancillary sources of information only; often not provided with names, their identification depends upon memory, and verbal transmission of the information often fails. The economic element involved in participation in a family firm or family estate is a more significant factor in preserving kin knowledge. This often operates even when the economic interest has ceased for a generation or so, and the status element would seem to be relevant here. A definite geographical focus in the past – 'the place the family came from' – also serves as a useful peg upon which to hang knowledge of kin.

For recognition of contemporary kin a different set of factors tends to be relevant, more closely related to nuclear family constitution and procedures. Parental influence in verbal transmission of information about kin, and in social interaction with kin; the existence of a 'kin-keeper' who assumes the role of furnishing information; the presence or absence of 'strategic kin' such as a parent or grandparent, whose early death deprives a person of important sources of knowledge about kin – these appear to be the most important factors. Very important also appears to be the particular socio-cultural type to which a family belongs – whether or not its combination of ideology and interest tends to be kin-positive, kin-neutral or kin-negative.

6

Structure of the Kin Universe

Modern British society has a domestic structure based on the elementary, primary or conjugal family. 'Family' and household are normally expected to coincide, and many statements on social phenomena use the two terms almost interchangeably. Yet the household as a social entity often does not coincide completely with the primary family. Sons or daughters at work or in a University or other college may live elsewhere than 'at home'. Marriage of a son or daughter splits the conjugal family in residential terms, and ties between different households are created. The process of residential diversification and social linkage need not stop there since members of a conjugal family may have knowledge of and keep contact with other kin outside their family unit altogether. In this Chapter we describe and analyse the structure of these social relationships.

The kinds of ideas which people have about these relationships have been discussed in Chapter 4 on kinship ideology, and factors relevant to the knowledge they have of their kin have been examined in Chapter 5. Here we are concerned with the actual patterns of knowledge and of contact – the ways in which people behave in this sector of their social life. 'Structure' in this sense is the set of patterns elucidated from observation of behaviour. In a Western industrial society there is very little formal structure in kin relations outside the conjugal family; there are very few overt rules which express the principles of conduct and provide moral sanctions for guidance. Yet, as we show, behaviour towards kin is not simply random, unstructured; regularities are involved, though not followed by everyone to the same degree. Hence, the 'structure' that we expose here is a matter of relative frequencies, based for the most part on quantitative estimates. We are concerned with questions such as these: How many and what sorts of kin are known and kept in touch with? What kind of relation do the numbers involved bear to other facets of the social life? How far does the documentary evidence about them serve as a basis for kin ties? What is the quality of these recognitions of kin and contacts with kin?

Before tackling these questions we discuss briefly some of the basic terms we use to distinguish important categories of kin relationships.

Budgets of terms professionally used by anthropologists in discussing the problems of kinship exist, but for the most part they have been constructed with reference to the data from non-industrial societies. In various contexts in this book we discuss the relevance of some of them for our study. But to some extent we have reconstructed them in our own terms, partly to take account of categories of kin distinguished by our subjects themselves, and partly for more general theoretical reasons.

UNIVERSE OF KIN

We start from the concept of a *kin universe*. Every person may be said to have a social universe, consisting of the persons with whom he is in more than physical contact (as in a train or bus) – by holding speech with them, engaging in co-operative acts with them or entering into conflict with them. Many social contacts are brief and peripheral – as with the newspaper seller from whom one buys an evening paper and exchanges a conventional word of greeting – the persons concerned are only on the periphery of one's social universe. But other contacts are protracted and intimate, as with members of one's conjugal family. The notion of social universe is a very general one. But kin are among those who may form a significant part of this universe, and the notion of a *kin universe* is more precise. The limits of a kin universe at a given moment are *genealogically* defined. By common convention then, though not factually so, the links are *biologically* given. It is true, as N. W. Thomas[1] pointed out sixty years ago, that whereas consanguinity is deemed to be physiological, kinship is sociological, and their range is not coincident. But whereas not all people related physiologically may be admitted as kin (the lines of recognition varying according to the society), only by some kind of 'fiction' such as adoption or ignoring the results of extra-marital unions can persons not related physiologically be included in the kin universe.[2] The 'biological' basis of kinship means that in general kin ties are unalterable. (There is one major exception in adult years, that choice in marriage gives a spouse a set of affines. But even here the choice of spouse involves a set of affines who are, in turn, given not chosen.) It is important, however, to realize that in any kinship system a process of social closure

[1] *Kinship Organisations and Group Marriage in Australia*, Cambridge, 1904, p. 4. On this point also see Chapter I, p. 4.

[2] Even the legal incorporation of a person into a family by adoption does not fully integrate him or her into a genealogical relationship.

can be applied, such that not all the genealogical endowment is utilized.

The terms we use for kin are of two kinds. The first comprises those of general ascription in vogue among the people themselves, to indicate the kind of social box into which they put the persons with whom they are concerned. These are terms of the order of 'relative', 'relation', 'family', and (more rarely) 'kin', the significance of which has been analysed in Chapter 4. In our samples there was some range of variation in the way in which different individuals defined the kin who entered into their social field. Some included and others excluded not only the spouses of any of their own consanguine kin but also any consanguines of these spouses whom they knew. For purposes of genealogical comparison and analysis in quantitative terms we have excluded from our major tabular counts the consanguines and affines of immediate affines (relatively few in all), though we have included them (where they have been recognized) in separate calculations. (Discussion of the criteria used is given in Chapter 2.) The second kind of term is that used by ourselves as social scientists to order our description of the social relationships of the persons we are discussing. Here, while we have been guided by the behavioural distinctions made by our informants, we do not follow their own terminology. A 'model' of kin categories that can be given some precision and related in a logical sequence is as follows:

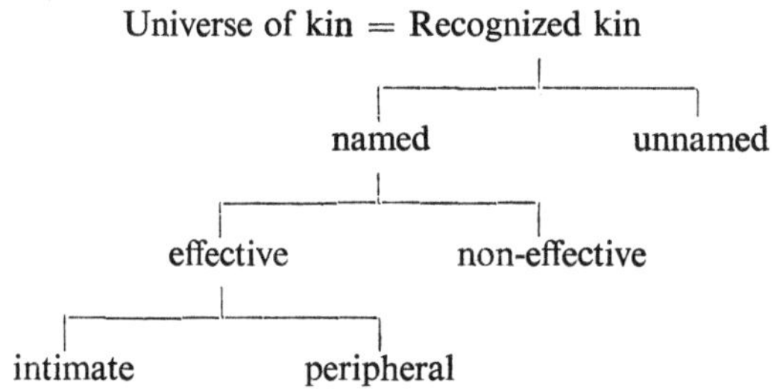

Some explanation of these terms has been given in earlier studies.[3] Briefly, by 'universe of kin' we mean all persons known to our informant (Ego) as related to him by genealogical ties, whether of consanguinity or of affinity, i.e. all persons 'recognized' by him as kin.[4] 'Recognized' kin comprise two sectors. One sector, usually by

[3] See Raymond Firth (ed.) *Two Studies of Kinship in London*, 1956, p. 45; 'Bilateral Descent Groups: An Operational Viewpoint', *Studies in Kinship and Marriage*, ed. I. Schapera, R.A.I. Occasional Paper No. 16, 1963.

[4] As noted earlier, it may be necessary to distinguish a 'personal universe' of kin embraced by an individual as part of his ordinary knowledge from a 'literary universe' of kin known to him only from consultation of documents (see p. 125).

far the largest, comprises persons whose names are known (called in the earlier study 'nominated' kin). Another sector is of persons known to be genealogically related, but, such as small children of distant cousins or siblings of grandparents, whose names are not known.' (Also in the category of 'recognized kin' but not able to be located precisely on the genealogical map, are some persons classed in kin terms as 'cousin', without the informant being able to specify the precise genealogical position.) These unnamed kin are defined only by relationship, so that their personality is in a sense incomplete as far as the informant is concerned. Named kin in turn are divided into effective and non-effective kin. 'Effective kin' in our terms are those with whom social contact is maintained, as by correspondence, occasional visits, services, or attendance at family gatherings. By non-effective kin is meant those kin who are recognized to be related, but with whom no contact of any kind is maintained – though contact may be initiated or revived. In the category of effective kin one may distinguish 'intimate kin' and 'peripheral kin'. Unlike effective and non-effective kin, which can be clearly demarcated, exclusive categories, the line between intimate and peripheral kin is much less easy to draw. The indices are much less objective, consisting much more in what people say about how they regard such kin than in the more empirical behavioural measures. But the difference is by no means entirely that of the social analyst; in most cases our informants themselves tended to draw such distinctions, and to specify those kin who fell in each category. By intimate kin then we mean those with whom contact tended to be purposeful, close and frequent, and the set of persons involved tended to be described by our informants in such terms as 'immediate family circle' (cf. Chapter 4). By peripheral kin we mean those with whom contact tended to be casual or accidental, distant and sporadic.

What is the validity of such a framework or 'model' of analysis? How far is such a procedure of successive fractionating of the field useful? The answer is that it is valid to the extent to which it has helped us to classify and explain the behaviour of the people whose kinship we are investigating. The relationships with which we are concerned here are primarily known genealogical relationships ('primarily' because they may include a few of the 'cousin' variety where the genealogical tie is unknown – but even here there is a *putative* genealogical link). The criteria isolated for the ordering of these social relationships are: *recognition* of persons as related to one by (putative) genealogical ties; *contact* with such persons as a kind of social behaviour; and *quality* and *frequency* of such contact, as demonstrated especially by transactions between kin, in particular the provision of services. These criteria of knowledge, contact and transaction or service seem meaningful in understanding how and why people act as they do towards other people whom they categorize as their 'relatives'. Our problem in this Chapter is to examine the range of our informants' knowledge of their kin by particular reference to the genealogical material we have accumulated.

Logically, it might be argued that the universe of kin, which we have equated with all those kin recognized to exist as such by an informant, should include a hypothetical category of 'unrecognized' kin, i.e. those who are not known to exist by our informant, though they are known to other persons as being related genealogically. Such a hitherto 'unrecognized' kinsman may occasionally appear and claim kinship, which is acknowledged, or his existence may be made known by, say, a parent or grandparent. But this hypothetical category was useless for our purposes since we could engage in very little independent genealogical enquiry, and were hence unable to control, to define or indeed even to indicate the actual existence of 'unrecognized' kin in any instance. Moreover, the existence of such kin is an historical, not a sociological, datum. So for all the purposes of this study a person's 'universe of kin' is equivalent to the kin he or she knows to exist, and the question of 'latent' kin who can be activated by someone else is no more than indicated, where relevant. An analogous problem is raised by the question of whether 'named' kin include those whose surname only is known.

Another question concerns the position of dead kin. To ask if they are included in a person's universe of kin or not sounds a very academic, if not absurd, question. But it is relevant because we continually encounter references to dead kin in the discussions of our informants, and they are cited for themselves and as links in large numbers on genealogies; therefore, we have to try and estimate their real significance in a conceptual sense. This question must be answered by reference to different levels of inclusiveness. At the level of effective kin, that is, those with whom some contact is maintained, obviously the point does not arise.[5] But at the level of knowledge and affective reaction as contrasted with that of actual contact, dead kin must be included in some sections of the study. (See later in this Chapter for the social significance of dead kin, and the relatively constant proportion of dead to living kin in each person's kin universe.)

Again, there is the question of comparability of material in the kin universe of the range of informants in our samples. Having

[5] Anthropologists are familiar with societies in which alleged communication with dead kin occurs; socially speaking, such kin should be included in the 'universe', though in fact the observer can argue that the people are really communicating with themselves, exteriorizing their problems.

considered just what persons can be comprised in an individual's kin universe, the question arises of how the universe of kin of different individuals can be compared. Criteria of an objective kind are provided in the *size* of the kin universe – the number of kin contained therein; its *depth* – the number of generations involved; its *range* – the number of degrees of cousinship or other distance from Ego at which kin are recognized; and its *symmetry* – the extent to which there is balance between paternal and maternal kin, and kin of earlier and later generations. We suggest that these criteria can be used – as they have been less systematically by many other anthropologists – for the comparison of kinship systems of various other kinds as well.

We now examine our material from the point of view of each of these criteria.

SIZE OF KIN UNIVERSE: NUMBERS OF KIN KNOWN

First, we consider empirically the size of a 'kin universe' in our field of study. The question of how many kin the persons in our North London areas knew, both on the average and in extent of individual variation, is in itself not especially significant. But the figures have comparative interest for other sections of British society. Relative kin numbers may be indicative of relative social assets. In societies where kin ideology and obligations are strongly demarcated, actual numbers of kin may be less important than the range of types of kin available. But where kin ideology and obligations are weak, the extent of the kin field available may be important irrespective of type, in indicating the range of possibilities which may be open for mobilizing assistance. But the cultural position of kin may be important here. So we consider what kinds of kin in genealogical, education and occupational terms these were. (Factors which may have affected the variations in amount and kind of kin knowledge have been discussed in Chapter 4.)

The amount of kin knowledge was more considerable than might be commonly thought, for a society with a high degree of individuality of the primary family in occupational and social matters. Excluding children and grandchildren, as direct descendants, and the consanguines of affines, who presented a special problem of interpretation, the total number of kin, dead and alive, recognized by all our informants in both Greenbanks and Highgate at the time of study was 13,937. The total number of live kin alone recognized was 9,142. For our set of 166 informants[6] the overall average was

[6] Total informants were 167, but a husband and wife, first cousins, have been counted only once since their kin were identical overall.

84 kin per person. Of this total rather more than a third, 5,572, were kin of our 60 Highgate informants, while the other 8,365 were the kin of our 106 Greenbanks informants. The difference in averages of 93 for Highgate as against 79 for Greenbanks, can hardly be regarded as very considerable.[7]

The range of kin known varied from 7 to 243 in the Greenbanks field and from 8 to 388 in the Highgate field. But the distribution was not at all even thoughout the total range. Taking kin knowledge per informant in groups of 20 and then of 100, the range, for Greenbanks and for Highgate in actual numbers of cases, and for the combined material in percentages, was as follows:

TABLE 11

Number of kin known, living and dead

No. of kin Known	*Greenbanks informants*	*Highgate informants*	*Total %*
0– 19	9	3	7
20– 39	16	10	16
40– 59	22	8	18
60– 79	16	8	14
80– 99	12	9	13
100–119	9	10	11
120–139	6	3	5
140–159	6	2	5
160–179	5	3	5
180–199	1	0	1
200–299	4	2	4
300–399	—	2	1
	106	60	100%

These figures show a heavy concentration (60 per cent) of cases with kin in the range between 20 and 100, and about another 25 per cent between 100 and 200, with very few cases recognizing fewer than 20 or more than 200 kin. Greenbanks concentrates half its cases in the kin-range between 20 and 80, while the Highgate cases show a greater upward spread, but the patterns of kin knowledge in both are much the same, falling off heavily after a range of about 120 kin per informant.

[7] The presence of eight old people in their seventies or more in the Greenbanks sample was not responsible for the difference, since half these people had numbers of kin above the average. But the five members of the sample not personally interviewed gave figures below the average.

What kind of kin are so recognized? The first distinction that can be considered is how precisely are these kin identified? Are they thought of simply as being 'related' in a general sort of way, with kinship terms – such as cousin – applied to them to categorize them for social purposes of status recognition and of exchange of gifts and services, as happens in many primitive societies? Or are they conceived as being definitely pin-pointed in genealogical terms, located specifically on a mental chart with links traceable throughout? Considering the comparative lack of highly structured kin relationships in our society, the former might be expected. But in fact it is the latter which obtains. Acknowledgement of an individual as a kinsman rests on awareness that both parties are bound by a specifiable genealogical tie. Conversely, without a demonstrable genealogical link a person is apt to be classed as 'not related'. In a few cases of rare surnames the sharing of a common patronym may give a presumption that there is a genealogical link between the parties; but ordinarily, with the complexity of modern society, this is not regarded as having any validity. Unlike the situation in Chinese society, not only the Smiths and Browns but also people bearing much less common surnames are not usually regarded as kin-linked.[8] When a person refers to another as a 'relative' it is normally because he knows precisely how he is genealogically connected or because he accepts the relative's or a third person's assertion of a genealogical connection as valid. Only in relatively few cases (22 out of 166 informants) did our subjects name as kinsmen – e.g. 'mother's cousin' – any persons whose genealogical connection was unknown. On the average, only a couple of individuals with 'links unknown' were so characterized as kin. (In two unusual cases, with 45 and 49 unknown links respectively, each of the informants could list a very much larger number of kin whose genealogical ties were known to them.)

The small proportion of persons recognized as kin with genealogical links unknown is an indicator of the general attitude to kinship in our field of study. Kinship is not recognized as a pervasive, compelling principle of social organization and obligation, as it is in many societies of a less complex order. The mere categorization of someone as kin is not enough; there must be a precise identification of him in the social universe, by an unambiguous tie such as a genealogy provides. It is plausible to link this attitude with the lack of opportunity for enforceable reciprocity in the society. Vague kin

[8] The brother of one of our principals, of landed gentry family, once gave a party for all the people of the same surname he could find in the (London) telephone book. According to our informant he did it 'for a lark' and 'all kinds of strange people turned up – one being the owner of a cat circus.'

ties are not recognized, it may be argued, because, if obligation is admitted and service performed, there is no likelihood in our complex society with diversified personal relations that the service will ever be repaid by the recipient. Nor will some other person generally identified as a kinsman act in his stead to repay the obligation.

In so far as our impressions go, it seemed that the kin characterized as being of 'links unknown' were inferentially for the most part of not very distant relationship – cousins of parents, or children of such.

Within the total kin universe of any informant his or her knowledge of kin varied considerably. But one obvious differential was knowledge of name. Considering only the total number of live kin recognized, 9,142 in all, 6,416, or rather more than two-thirds, were known by name. In contrast to this, 2,726, or nearly one-third, were known by their genealogical position to be kin, but their personal names were not known to our informants. (More than half of these kin whose names were not known were either abroad or their place of residence was not known.) Typical of such cases was the informant who knew that his father had a brother but did not know his personal name nor where he was living at the time of our enquiry. Except in the rarest cases, informants knew the personal names of their parents and their own siblings. (Where the parent or sibling died when the informant was a very young child this item of knowledge was sometimes lacking.)

Another obvious differential could be by sex of kin. But here no significant difference was perceptible between numbers of male and of female kin, either in the total or in either sample. Out of the total of approximately 13,900 kin recognized, approximately 6,700 were males and 6,600 females, with about 600 sex not known. Treating Greenbanks and Highgate separately, almost exactly the same proportions were obtained, and if consanguines and affines were separated only a very slight difference was perceptible. In other words, as a general principle, sex of kin was not a significant factor in their recognition.

What *was* significant was the sex of the principal. On the whole, throughout this total of about 13,900 kin recognized, the men of our combined sample knew on the average 76 kin apiece, whereas the women knew 90 kin apiece. The difference for Greenbanks was only just over 10 per cent (73 as against 84), while for Highgate (where our enquiries were pushed rather harder) it was more than 20 per cent (80 as against 103). To this extent, then, the popular notion that women in our society are the repositories of kin knowledge is borne out – though not to any very marked degree.

RECOGNITION OF DEAD KIN

A major distinction to be drawn is between living and dead kin. The numbers involved were as follows:

TABLE 12
Living and dead kin

	Living kin	*Dead kin*	*Total*
Greenbanks	5,441 (65%)	2,924	8,365
Highgate	3,701 (66%)	1,871	5,572
Total	9,142 (65%)	4,795	13,937

It is striking, and probably not coincidental, that the proportions of live and dead kin recognized should be almost identical in our two samples. The reasons why kin are recognized are complex, and are not to be put in terms either of simple memory or of sentiment. While in our study we did secure some independent genealogical material from documents, we did not include such data in our primary kin counts, but restricted ourselves to what informants knew. Yet it is obvious that no person recollects his complete genealogical universe, at least for more than a very few generations; wittingly or unwittingly he makes some selection from a range of possible kin. In such selection the dead would seem to be at a disadvantage, since strong ties of sentiment for their memory are likely to operate only for a very few of them, usually those who have been closest to Ego. The living are always capable of bringing themselves to attention, especially in a literate society, by correspondence! That the proportion of dead kin recognized is only about half that of the living indicates this to be so. Yet the fact that in our two separate samples the average proportion of dead kin recognized was much the same suggests that there are regularities in the process by which recognition is accorded them. The factors involved may be partly structural, partly idiosyncratic.

The proportion of dead kin in the kin universe of our subjects did show a fair range of variation. It would be a plausible hypothesis that in those cases where there was a high proportion of dead kin, the person concerned was old, with most of his own generation already dead before him.

From this point of view it is of interest to look especially at those cases in which the number of dead kin recognized exceeded the number of live kin. Age of the informant alone was not the determining factor in all cases where the proportion of dead kin recognized was high. But it had relevance. Of the 27 cases where dead kin recognized exceeded live kin, 21 of the informants were 50 years old or over, nine of these being 60 or over. Of the rest, four were in their forties and two in their thirties.

Among the reasons for such recognition of an unusually high proportion of dead kin might be that this was particularly a characteristic of women's attitude to kin – to remember the dead in a sentimental way. It is significant then to note that this suggestion was not borne out by the data. Cases where recognition of dead kin exceeded that of live kin were divided almost equally between men and women. More relevant seemed to be aspects of the personal history of the informants, especially their residential history. A woman who was brought up by her mother's mother knew a great deal about that woman's mother's siblings, all of whom were dead long before. A man whose mother died early was brought up largely with friends; most of his kin were in the United States and his knowledge tended therefore to be of the dead in this country rather than of those who were living abroad. Other informants, some Jewish, had migrated to this country while young and lost touch with their kin in their home country. They knew much about relatives of the older generation there, many of whom were now dead, but little about relatives of the younger generation, nearly all living but whom they had never seen. In a few cases an informant's mother or other elder relative, wishing that he should not lose all knowledge of the kin abroad, had furnished him or her with a genealogy or other material referring primarily to the past.

But the general distribution of live and dead kin in terms of the age distribution of our subjects did not show any very consistent trend. On the contrary, apart from the elderly people mentioned, what did appear was a fairly even concentration in the recognition of dead kin. Indeed, the data suggested the existence of some tendency to a fairly regular limitation or cut-off of the dead from the genealogical chart. This appeared in a difference between the proportion of affines of dead kin and of live kin. With the live kin there was one affine recognized for every two consanguines; with dead kin the proportion dropped to one affine for every three consanguines. If the kin count had been restricted to adults only, this difference would have been even more marked.

The numbers of dead kin recognized by our informants were not spread out randomly, but nearly all fell within the 50 belt. This indicates a kind of unconscious closure applied to the genealogical reckoning, an erosion of memory, which, it is noteworthy, occurs on the part of both young and old. Some anthropologists have referred to the 'structural amnesia' that seems to have taken place in respect of genealogies which provide the charter for the relationships of unilineal descent groups in many societies. What was evident from our analysis here was that an analogous process takes place in systems of bilateral kin reckoning. The genealogical cut-off, which could be postponed almost indefinitely, and which might be expected to vary unpredictably according to individual memory, tends to take place fairly soon, and to yield in the sphere of dead kin approximately similar numbers irrespective of the circumstances of the persons concerned. This regularity is to be looked upon, we would argue, as a function of the operation of kin relations in a complex social field with many competing relationships. Dead kin have their uses, but to only a limited degree.

Some of these points will now be taken up in more detail, in reference to knowledge of earlier generations of kin, and to factors involved in kin knowledge generally.

DEPTH OF KIN UNIVERSE: KNOWLEDGE OF PAST GENERATIONS OF KIN

We consider now the range of recognition of kin in the generations above the parents of our informants. Here the element of personal knowledge rapidly diminishes and soon reaches a point at which any personal contact between informant and kinsman specified was impossible.

One of the characteristic features of the kinship of our North London middle-class subjects was the general lack of interest they displayed in their forbears. Some certainly enjoyed talking on the subject, but the type of information which seemed significant to them varied a great deal from case to case. One informant thought her family background would be of interest because it was representative of a certain period and type of community in London – coming from a Jewish family of good social standing, she had contracted a mixed marriage. Her interest was to place 'her family' (in this case the descendants of her great-grandparents) in its socio-historical context. It was not to trace as far back as possible, nor to attempt to clarify some of the intricacies of her very complex genealogy. Her knowledge was extensive and she could tell a great deal about almost every one of the 366 individuals on her genealogy, yet she could name only one great-grandparent and no further back. Had she wanted to learn the names of members of earlier generations she would have been able to do so because there was documentary material available elsewhere. Another informant, who had an outstanding knowledge of previous generations of his kin, could trace six generations back, but had a total kin count of only 137 kinsmen. He had a formal genealogy passed down from his paternal grandfather who had employed a professional genealogist to draw it up, and also a number of books written about his family. He was proud of his ancestors and interested in learning about them, yet all this information did not lead him to clarify the exact genealogical connection of some of his third cousins. Many other informants expressed no interest whatever in past generations.

We were particularly concerned to determine whether knowledge about family and kin background was being passed on to members of younger generations, and if so, what sorts of information about past generations were of the expected order: details about kinship volunteered by parents and other elder kin or given in response to a child's enquiry; details arising in the course of some incident in the family history, such as the discovery of an old photograph; details gained from documentary sources such as wills, family letters, funeral cards and formal genealogies. It was quite clear that in general no very widespread effort was made by people to *learn* about their past kin, nor was there any corresponding enthusiasm by their elders to *teach* them about the history of their family. The informants with most knowledge of their kin of three or more generations back were those who had an ancestor who had compiled a genealogy or who possessed printed biographical information about a famous ancestor, or who had documents referring to family property. But almost without exception such information was restricted to the particular famous ancestor concerned or to the particular line of inheritance involved. Oral information was rare for generations earlier than those of grandparents; even where there was documentary information about siblings of grandparents and their predecessors, this was usually not incorporated into informants' stock of personal knowledge of past kin.

Knowledge of grandparents, though not complete, was fairly full. Our informants were able to say something about 71 per cent of their grandparents: 62 per cent of them were named and either the place of residence or the occupation of the other 9 per cent was given. Gaps in information could be accounted for by the fact that some grandparents had died long before informants were born. Paternal grandparents were just as likely to be known as maternal grandparents, if informants had ever met them.

But knowledge of grandparents did not mean that informants could necessarily name or even be sure of the existence of grandparents' siblings. While 141 informants could tell something about at least one of their grandparents, only 107 could add something about grandparents' siblings. The existence of some great-uncles or great-aunts could be inferred from second cousins, but in all 107 cases the informant did have some independent precise information about them, including their name in most cases. Lacking independent genealogical information, we could not ascertain what kind of gap lay between our informants' knowledge of their grandparents' siblings and the reality. But many informants themselves were doubtful if their knowledge was complete. While in only 9 per cent of the cases did informants manifest any uncertainty about the completeness of their knowledge of their parents' siblings, in 35 per cent of cases they said that they thought their information about grandparents' siblings were incomplete. Informants had knowledge of a few more maternal than paternal great-uncles (267 as against 234). Moreover, though not many more than half of these could be named, the proportion was rather greater on the maternal side (68 per cent as against 56 per cent). The somewhat greater knowledge of close collateral kin on the mother's side was consistent from the grandparental generation down to the youngest generation of kin. It could not be explained by chance circumstances of death and of geographical distribution, which were factors responsible for differential knowledge of the informants' own grandparents. The same pattern of bias towards the maternal side held also in regard to the kin with whom our informants were in contact (see later, pp. 200).

Knowledge of generations further back than grandparents tended to fall away rapidly; few of our informants were historically-minded

TABLE 13

Knowledge of great-grandparents

No. of great-grandparents known	*No. of informants with knowledge of name*	*No. of great-grandparents named*
One *only*	25	25
Two	21	42
Three	10	30
Four	5	20
Five	4	20
Six	1	6
Seven	2	14
Eight	2	16
Total	70	173

as far as their own families were concerned. Less than half of our informants (78) could tell anything of their great-grandparents, and only about two-fifths (70) could name one or more of them. Of the eight great-grandparents whom every person (except the product of a first cousin marriage) has had, most of our informants could name only one or two. Table 13 illustrates the position.

Our informants altogether must have had nearly 1,328 great-grandparents (assuming few intra-kin marriages, as we know to be the case). But of these only 13 per cent could be named, which is in marked contrast with the 62 per cent of grandparents named. In cases in which all or most great-grandparents were known by name, this knowledge did not seem to rest on any special social circumstances – though one was Gentleman-in-Waiting to Queen Victoria – but rather on efforts made by a grandparent or other senior relative to impress it on the younger relative. Knowledge of siblings of great-grandparents was equally small. By comparison with the 65 per cent of our informants who knew of at least one great-aunt or great-uncle, only about 15 per cent knew of a great-great-aunt/uncle.

Knowledge of ascending generations of kin is conveniently summarized in two more Tables. The first (Table 14) indicates *how many generations* back an informant could trace his genealogy by naming an ancestor or a collateral kinsman, and by giving other pertinent information such as occupation or residence about him. The second Table indicates the distribution of knowledge as among the various *lines of ancestors*.

In view of differences found between the Greenbanks and Highgate samples in occupational distribution and educational history, it is worth noting that while more informants in Highgate could trace

TABLE 14

Generation depth

	No. of informants with:	
Generations back	*Knowledge of name*	*Any other knowledge*
One *only*	30	19
Two	78	70
Three	37	51
Four	14	20
Five	6	5
Six	1	1
Total	166	166

four or more generations back, the difference was small – overall both samples had almost equally shallow-depth kin sets. Again, there was nothing to indicate that either men or women were better genealogists in depth. Husbands and wives appeared to trace equally far back – or rather to be equally unable to do so. Furthermore, such knowledge of kin of the distant past as did exist was almost entirely of persons in the direct ancestral line; for the most part nothing was known about their siblings, and we have only two cases where a sibling of an ancestor of four generations back was mentioned.

TABLE 15

Ancestors whose names were known[9]

Ancestor	*Total No. of ancestors known in category*	
FFF	34	
FFM	18	
FMF	16	
FMM	6	
MFF	29	
MFM	19	
MMF	30	
MMM	21	173
FFFF	8	
FFFM	3	
FFMF	2	
FFMM	3	
MFFF	5	
MFFM	1	
MMFF	1	
MMFM	2	
MMMF	3	
MMMM	2	
MFMM	1	31
FFFFF	5	
FFMFF	2	
FFMMF	1	
MMFFF	1	9
FFFFFF	1	1
		Total 214

[9] Note (i) Ancestors of category for which no case gave information have been omitted from the Table.

(ii) By 'name known' is meant either personal name, or surname if not simply inferred from other information, e.g., a maiden name of a married woman is counted as fresh information, but a repeated patronym is not.

In the total of 214 names in this ancestral kin count, males outnumber females by two to one, i.e. 138 as against 76. This is in strong contrast to the general position of maternal *vis-à-vis* paternal kin, as discussed in the next section. But it should be noted here that apart from any substantial reasons such as patrilineal transmission of property to account for any preference for males in ancestral kin knowledge, there is a possible factor which may help to give the bias seen in the Table. In remembering remote kin, when a name of a married person is called to mind, it may be that of a husband rather than that of a wife; the surname is his, and to recall her maiden name is probably harder without special reason. The predominance of males over females in the list may be due in part to this. But while in the direct male line the names recorded are personal names – the patronym not being repeated – the names of women recorded are often their maiden surnames.

What is the significance of the shallow depth of kinship traced and numbers of kin involved? The general pattern was for a person to know relatively little of his or her forbears. In the second ascending generation it was usual for an individual to know the names of one or two of his grandparents and a few great-uncles and great-aunts. Knowledge of three generations upwards was limited usually to being aware of the name of one or two of the eight possible direct ancestors. Very few individuals could trace further back, and even when they could their knowledge was apt to be incomplete and erratic. (In an outstanding case of extensive knowledge of ancestors, our informant could name only seven out of the eight possible great-grandparents, seven out of the sixteen possible direct ancestors in the next generation, three out of the 32 in the fifth generation, and only one out of 64 in the sixth generation.) There is thus a rapid falling-off in kin knowledge with generation. Considering also the lineal focus of the knowledge that is retained, it is clear that this involves a very restricted set of collateral kin, and consequently a relatively small kin universe for social action.

RANGE OF KIN UNIVERSE

The problem of how far laterally and in depth does the recognition of relatives go in a particular social system is obviously important, if this recognition implies any concrete action, as by gifts, services or exchange of sociability. The posing of this problem in theoretical terms in respect of a middle-class sector of English society is not new; it was formulated two hundred years ago by William Blackstone, and it is interesting to consider briefly why and how he did it, to compare the results with our own material.

Blackstone's 'Essay on Collateral Consanguinity, its Limits, Extent and Duration' (1750) (in *Law Tracts*, vol. I, Oxford, 1762) originated in a claim made on All Souls' College early in the eighteenth century by a 'descendant' of the fifteenth-century founder, who had given a degree of preference and also certain peculiar privileges to his kinsmen in the election of Fellows. To the observance of every part of these statutes the Warden and Fellows were bound by a solemn oath at their admission. The College had suffered in the past in that such appeals, based on infinity of descent, had succeeded. It was therefore a matter of serious concern to them to establish what persons were or were not 'comprehended under so general name as that of kindred'. Blackstone, a Fellow of the College, therefore set himself to show that such tenuous collateral claims were invalid, that the relation of kindred was 'bounded at some certain period and degree' (p. 13). How far did that relation extend, which entitled the persons related to the privileges of kinsmen? – he asked.

He pointed out that the strict significance of *consanguinitas* by the Roman civil law (with the authority too of Calvin) was only that relation which subsists between brethren born of the same father;[10] more distant kinsmen are comprised under the terms *agnatio* and *cognatio* (p. 13). But this sense must be enlarged as it had been by the canon and our municipal laws, to signify all collateral relations. Yet the popular view will never teach us to look on collateral kindred as subsisting for ever.

> On the contrary, the affection, the remembrance, the very name of cousins ceases after a few descents. When we speak of *our relations*, we only mean such as are within a few degrees of us; nor do we pretend to argue that because all our kinsmen are descended from one common ancestor, therefore all who are descended from one common ancestor are to be reputed our kinsmen! (p. 17).

Blackstone argued that the Founder of all Souls' made his statute undoubtedly because of his affection and regard for his '*real* kindred', that such affection implied that distant kin must be excluded or by their very number they would reduce the benefits enjoyed by the close kin to nothing, and that such distant claimants should be regarded as 'pseudo-kinsmen' (pp. 19, 23). He held that it was really lineal consanguinity, not collateral consanguinity, that was meant in this case, giving elaborate reasons, and citing the

[10] In this sense consanguine is opposed to uterine, born of the same mother.

various legal boundaries including those of marriage prohibition which had been imposed on collateral kinship in the past.

Despite some special pleading, the essay demonstrates very clearly and convincingly a principle of kinship closure – the difference between the recognition of kinship in a formal genealogical relationship and in an operationally valid social and economic tie.

How then with our modern North London informants? Do they recognize the range of their kinship in theory almost indefinitely and have to restrict it in practice, as Blackstone's exposition might indicate? In fact they are much more summary. Certainly their range of *operational* recognition of their kin is very limited, in accord with Blackstone's view. But not only this – their knowledge of their kin was almost equally restricted, unlike Blackstone's case. It would have been interesting to have known what would have happened if a similarly advantageous claim had been made on our subjects by distant kin beyond the conventional limitation; but no such case was evident. (That reported on p. 107 has some analogy.)

We now specify the constitution of the kin universe of our informants in terms of the closeness or remoteness of kin they recognized. Before giving the empirical evidence it will be useful to summarize in a diagram the formal English terminology of reference in this field[11] (Figure 4).

When relationship was traced through affines by our informants, some quite elaborate kin links were given recognition (see later, pp. 270–4). But in terms simply of consanguineous relationships the kin universe was of very limited genealogical range. All informants had in their kin universe parents and siblings. In 5 per cent of cases the informant could list only these kin (together with siblings' children), though in a few of these cases they had a good idea that they had other kin not so closely related. About 40 per cent of informants could list no further than first cousins, whereas another 50 per cent knew at least one second cousin. But third cousins were much less frequently known – only 10 per cent of informants knew of any. *Not a single person could list a fourth cousin*, i.e. of the order of FFFFBSSSS. No one then could trace beyond the seventh degree of collateral kinship.

Again, though half of the informants did know some of their second cousins and their descendants or ascendants, this knowledge was not as complete as for the first degree of lateral remove. Demographically, in normal cases an individual is likely to have *more* second cousins than first cousins, yet the total number known of second cousins, and other kin of more than first degree

[11] See also Chapter 10 on Kin Terminology.

remove, was much *smaller* than the total number of first cousins together with their children, and aunts and uncles.

Moreover, the quality of knowledge tended to taper off with genealogical distance. Of the 84 informants who could list some second cousins, 62 stated that they knew there might be more, either because they were sure their grandparents had more siblings than they could reckon, or from some other hint. On the other hand, of the 149 informants who could list first cousins, only 45 said that they thought their knowledge of them was incomplete. Furthermore,

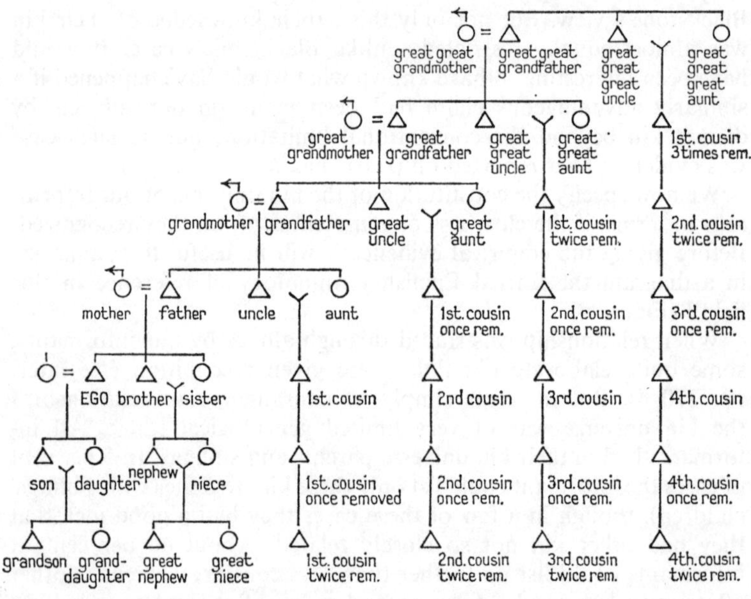

FIGURE 4. Table of Consanguinity

the knowledge about second cousins was more superficial than that regarding first cousins. Often informants did not know if their second cousins had descendants, or what occupation they followed, whereas such information was usually known about first cousins. Only 61 per cent of second cousins could be named, whereas 74 per cent of all cousins known could be named.

Some examination of the factors relevant to such differences in knowledge was given in Chapter 5. But it can be stressed that what one sees here is the operation of a process of closure whereby a selection is made out of a theoretically indefinite genealogical universe, according to interest and opportunity, with an element of personal idiosyncracy.

The element of personal idiosyncracy may be expected to be most marked in regard to affines (i.e. those related by marriage) and particularly with the consanguines of affines, who are linked by still more tenuous bonds. There are many possible degrees of affinal relationship here, but broadly affines separate into two main types: spouse of consanguine of Ego, and consanguine of spouse of Ego – exemplified by my brother's wife, and my wife's brother. But additional complications are introduced by the idea of consanguine, not of Ego's own spouse, but of his consanguine's spouse, hence, brother's wife's brother. Increasing distance and the introduction of further affines may result in a quite complex relationship.

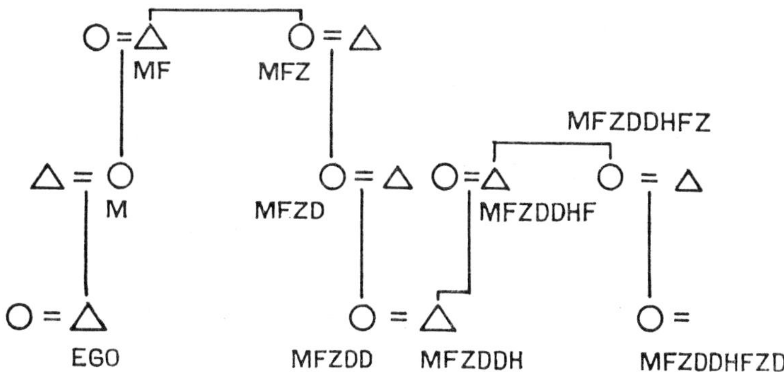

FIGURE 5. Recognition of a Distant Affine.

What is particularly interesting is the remoteness of some such people specifically recognized as kin. For the Highgate sample of 60 persons, all married, for whom we took the material most systematically, there were approximately 200 kin recognized, who were consanguines of affines or affines of consanguines. (This number did include a few of marginal category, such as divorced former spouse of present spouse of consanguine.) An example of the recognition of a distant relative of the spouse of a close consanguine in our Highgate material was that of BWMZHZ; and of a fairly close relative of the spouse of a distant consanguine was FMZDS-WFB. The most distant affinal tie of a person in a social relationship with an informant in our Highgate sample was that of MFZDDHF-ZD (see Figure 5). This woman, with whom our informant, Mr Tintern, had some community of professional interest, had her mother and father living in Highgate. The mother, who also had common interests with our informant, was seen about three times a week and the daughter about once a year, apart from some professional telephoning. Possibly because some of the parties concerned were well known in the scientific field, the kinship tie was well recognized.

So, the frame of genealogical recognition of affines and consanguines of affines is not simply a lateral spread but may cover two or more generations. But for many people such an affinal tie is not classed as a kin tie (*vide* Chapter 4); the person concerned is not regarded as a 'relative', but as no more than a 'connection'.

In the constitution of the kin universe its size, depth and range are all to some degree related. Factors affecting recognition of persons as kin and knowledge about them as they tend to determine the dimensions of the kin universe, are considered later. Now a brief mention may be made of the symmetry of the kin universe.

SYMMETRY OF THE KIN UNIVERSE

In the general pattern of kin knowledge there seemed to be no significant difference between male and female kin (see above p. 161). In recognition of paternal and maternal kin, it might have been expected that the English use of patronyms as surnames would give a bias – that people would tend to bear in mind those kin who shared the same surname as themselves, and to drop out of recognition those (e.g. mother's kin) who bore a different surname. But this was not so. Our evidence showed that at the first degree of collateral removal people were just as likely to have learned about the existence of mother's siblings as of father's siblings and knowledge of their children was shared fairly equally, regardless of the social background and sex of the individual concerned. Not only that – for the second degree of collateral removed, about 13 per cent *more* kinsmen were known on the maternal than on the paternal side. As regards contact with kin, however, the patterns were rather different.

This was the situation at the level of overall recognition of kin; in any particular case, of course, there was by no means always an even distribution of kin on both mother's and father's sides. (See also Chapter 9.)

GROSS DIFFERENCES IN RANGE OF PERSONAL KIN KNOWLEDGE

Are there any special features about individuals who have very extensive genealogical knowledge of their kin or who are very sparsely equipped with knowledge even about those kin who are their contemporaries?

Take the latter first. If we use an arbitrary figure of 25 total kin as representing a fairly low level of kin knowledge then in the combined sample there were eighteen instances of people with less than 25 kin, twelve from Greenbanks and six from Highgate. In four of these (from Greenbanks) the person concerned was unco-operative and was not interviewed, the information being obtained from the spouse in each case, and therefore quite likely not representing the full facts of the situation.

No very clear-cut correlates of a low level of kin knowledge were obtained. It was not just a matter of the sex of the person concerned – with men having less memory of and interest in their kin than women. Of the eighteen cases two-thirds were men, but the six women were distributed among them. More relevant were the following four sets of conditions:

i *A demographic gap* – a lack particularly of parents' siblings and consequently a lack of first cousins. This seemed to be relevant for five informants two of whom had apparently no father's siblings, and two others only one first cousin each. One case, that of a woman, was unusual in that she herself, her father, her father's father and her father's mother were all single children, without siblings. (She herself had only one son.) Hence her father had no aunts or uncles at all, and because her own mother was one of a sibling set of only three she herself had only one aunt and one uncle. (The aunt was also her first cousin once removed, owing to an intra-kin marriage.) But it is important to stress that demography alone did not account for the differences we found.

ii *Early deprivation of parent.* The effects of this were particularly obvious in two cases, both men. In one both his parents had died when he was about eleven years old, and he and his sister had been brought up quite separately; he knew very little of his kin, and after his marriage his wife's relatives had clearly provided the context of kin relations for him. In the other case the boy's father deserted his mother when he was about four years old and she herself died when he was about seven. Both he and his sister were adopted separately, and he knew far more of his adoptive kin than he did of his own.

iii *Geographical separation.* This seemed to have had some effect in a few cases partly because of emigration of close kin from Britain, but more so when parents came from abroad when young and severed ties with their homeland. But other factors were clearly relevant here, such as a low level of literacy hampering communication with the separated kin or, as possibly happened in cases from Eastern Europe, sudden death of kin in a pogrom in the homeland.

iv *Family strain.* In a few cases divorce and its attendant strains seem to have led to severance of relations with kin on one side of the family at an early age of the child, and to consequent lack of kin knowledge. But it seemed to us that rather than a simple failure of communication leading to a gap in knowledge, such cases showed some indication of block. In two cases at least there was clear evidence to the interviewer of disturbance resulting from strain which showed itself in confusion and painful uncertainty.

Any of these factors, however, cannot be regarded as being by itself a sufficient explanation of a low level of kin knowledge. For example, a demographic gap produced by lack of parents' siblings produces a lack of first cousins. But if, as sometimes happens, the parents compensate for their lack of siblings by taking their own first cousins into a quasi-sibling role, then the child could be furnished with an effective set of second cousins, which could give him a sizeable kin universe. But in fact very few people in our sample had second cousins but no first cousins; it was as if the implications of a kin gap were accepted, once the gap occurred beyond the confines of the natal family. The same was true of other forms of deprivation. Out of the eighteen cases of low level of kin knowledge, five of the subjects were single children, without siblings. But this in itself was not sufficient reason for a low level of kin knowledge, since there were in all eighteen individuals without siblings in our total sample, and the average of their kin knowledge was about 75 kin apiece. (Several had well over 100 people in their universe of kin.)

To sum up, a very small knowledge of one's kin is not an accident or a failure of memory; it depends on social factors. But these factors do not usually operate singly; they act in combination to turn low potential into actual poverty of kin knowledge and kin relations.

To consider those people in our sample who had very extensive knowledge of kin we took as an arbitrary figure a knowledge of 150 kin, six times as many as the upper limit of kin of those with sparse knowledge. In this category there were nineteen cases, twelve in Greenbanks and seven in Highgate. Of the total about a dozen have already been cited by the discussion of socio-cultural family types and other factors in Chapter 5. Two had strongly localized sets of farming kin. One, Mr Woollcombe, had kin with fourteen farms among them in the vicinity of an eastern counties cathedral town; the other, a woman, was a member of an Irish Catholic set of farmers and hotel-keepers, all of the same patronymic, 'a real clan', with whom she identified strongly. A man and a woman (Mrs Outram) had upper middle-class kin networks with aristocratic connections (see Fig. 2). Half a dozen others, men and women, belonged to Jewish families of the pervasive, highly integrated type. The rest were less easily identifiable in specific terms, but tended to be characterized by several features in combination. One factor was usually a large parental sibling group – cases of (two) fathers with 9 siblings apiece, a FF with 14 siblings and another with 16 siblings are recorded. Another factor was reasonable material comfort which obviated an early break-up of the elementary family. Still other factors were a business firm serving as an economic rallying point; and a positive kin ideology expressed in a sentiment for the 'ancestral home' or for family reunions at weddings and funerals. Additional factors were proximity of parents or other 'kin-keepers' to supply a stream of information about kin not seen; and similarity of tastes and interests in husband and wife, which tended to promote the exchange and retention of kin data.

DISTRIBUTION OF MALE KIN BY EDUCATION

We pass now to a consideration of some of the distributional aspects of the structure of the kin universe. The subjects of our study have themselves been classified by occupation and education; this in combination with their surroundings and way of life indicated them as middle-class. But what about their kin? How far did these form part of a relatively homogeneous sector of the society, or, in so far as there was variation among them, what was its range? To put it in crude analogy, were we dealing with people whose kin too were of the same kind as themselves, or with a series of middle-class islands in a sea of working-class or upper-class relatives? The most significant indices we can take to answer this question are education and occupation of the kin.

Our material on the education of kin was collected as systematically as possible, but naturally tended to become more imperfect as the genealogical distance of our informants from their kin increased. Moreover, material was harder to get systematically for female than for male kin. We have therefore restricted our major analysis here to consideration of the education of the fathers, brothers, sons, wives' fathers and wives' brothers of our male principals, in conjunction with their own education; our information on these kin is complete for purposes of our classification. We were interested in the type of training these people had received in the light of the occupational level they had ultimately achieved. We were also interested in the social quality of their education, with particular reference to the proportion who had or had not been to a public school. (The problems of definition of a public school are well known, and we therefore used as an arbitrary criterion that of membership of the Headmasters' Conference, an organization which came into being in 1869 – before any of the individuals in our sample went to school.)

The results of our analysis are given in Table 16. It has already been shown (Chapter 3, p. 8) that rather less than half of our principal male subjects were educated at a public school. We can now see that about the same proportion of their brothers and wives' brothers, and a rather higher proportion of their sons, were educated in this way also. But of their fathers and wives' fathers, less than a quarter had a public school education. In other words, if education be related to job and social position, we are dealing on the whole with an upwardly mobile sector of the population. (This refers only to these two generations – our data are too fragmentary for the grandparental generation.)

But we wished also to get some measure of differentiation between those who had been to one of the 'great' public schools and the rest. We therefore selected on an exclusive basis those six public schools which are generally recognized as leading the list, and which a century ago apparently regarded themselves as constituting the 'Public Schools Club'[12] and put them in a separate category. From this it appears that less than a twelfth of our principals and their close male kin went to any of the 'great' public schools; as a whole their education was 'middle-class' in the public school field.

But the difference between the Greenbanks and the Highgate samples is interesting here. In all cases there was considerably less public school education among the fathers of the male principals and of their wives than among the succeeding generations. But if the, samples be separated (not shown on the Table) and compared, Highgate shows a markedly higher proportion of public school men, including a higher proportion who went to the 'great' public schools.

[12] i.e. Charterhouse, Eton, Harrow, Rugby, Westminster and Winchester. (See Board of Education, *The Public School*, HMSO (The Fleming Report) 1944, pp. 25, 123.) The Public Schools Act of 1868 dealt with Shrewsbury as well as those schools cited above, while the Clarendon Commission of 1861 had concerned itself with nine schools, including Merchant Taylors' and St Pauls' as well as the others mentioned. For our purposes it matters little which basis is chosen. If Shrewsbury be added to the top category of our Table, only one individual is added and the percentages remain unaltered. If Merchant Taylors' and St Pauls' be included also, five more individuals are transferred up, but the percentage in the top bracket is thus increased only from 7 per cent to 8 per cent.

TABLE 16

Education of male kin

Type of education	*H*	*HF*	*WF*	*HB*	*WB*	*S*	*Total*	
1 Eton, Winchester, Rugby, Westminster, Charterhouse, Harrow	6	6	2	4	6	8	32	7%
Other Headmasters' Conference Schools	30	11	16	37	24	20	138	29%
2 Secondary Education (excluding Secondary Modern)	23	11	14	15	21	13	97	20%
3 Elementary Education (before 1944); Secondary Modern (after 1944)	6	17	18	9	3	4	57	12%
4 Other:								
a Other Private Education	4	5	7	2	9	4	31	7%
b 'Progressive' Schools	3	—	—	1	2	5	11	2%
5 Educated Abroad	9	12	11	12	9	0	53	11%
6 Education not known	2	21	15	8	6	0	52	11%
Totals	83*	83	83	88†	80‡	54	471	

H = Husband *W* = Wife *F* = Father *B* = Brother *S* = Son (over 13 years old).

* This total includes 3 deceased husbands

† This total includes 4 deceased brothers

‡ This total includes 6 deceased brothers

Male kin of single women have been excluded.

In Greenbanks, only 2 per cent of the male principals and their close male kin went to the top public schools (only 4 per cent even if the nine schools of the Clarendon Commission be taken) and only 25 per cent to any other public schools of the Headmasters' Conference category. But in Highgate 15 per cent went to the top public schools and another 37 per cent to other public schools, meaning that just over half of a total of 185 men had had a public school education compared with not much over one-quarter in Greenbanks.[13] However, if the Highgate sample be compared not

[13] If the Clarendon Commission criterion be taken, the Highgate figures remain unaltered.

If other kin than those cited in the Table were taken into account the figures might be altered somewhat probably still more in favour of Highgate. Thus in one set of kin of a Highgate family already cited (p. 147) forty-two men went to Eton. Girls from some families also went to St Paul's. But our information about the education of kin in general is too incomplete for a general survey.

with the Greenbanks whole sample, but with the sub-sample of those families in it which had a child of school age – i.e. a rather younger set of household heads – the education of the male principals at least was much more in conformity; exactly half the men in this Greenbanks sub-sample were educated in public schools, and their kin too showed more public school education than the generality.

It is commonly held – probably with reason – that the public school tradition tends to perpetuate itself from father to son. But this was not necessarily the case as far as any particular school was concerned. In one marked instance, a man and his brother attended a particular public school, but whereas his brother did well there he himself disliked it so much that he refused to send his own son there, although it was relatively near. The boy's mother said

> It is a school where cricket is thought of very highly, and if you are not good at it, then you don't enter into anything. My husband prefers rugger. Harrow plays rugger, and we put him down for Rugby too, but the latter is a long way off, and an expensive and awkward place to stay; we have always been rather a united family, and we were introduced to one of the housemasters at Harrow, and he got him a place when he met us, and the boy and we were very pleased, and it's so near and very convenient . . . and one school is probably as good as another . . . and it is a good thing for him to go to a boarding school.

In some ways these remarks epitomize many parental attitudes to the subject.

DISTRIBUTION OF MALE KIN BY OCCUPATION

In occupational terms our subjects were mainly professional men and businessmen, i.e. by conventional definition, middle-class. In the analysis of social relations it is interesting to know what these people thought about the distribution of occupations of their kin. We accordingly consider: were our subjects part of a universe of genealogically related people of fairly similar occupational grade to themselves, with sets of kin following the same types of calling – or did they have relatives distributed throughout the whole socio-economic field? In terms of generations, did fathers and sons particularly tend to follow the same occupational lines? In marital terms, had our male subjects tended to marry women whose own fathers and brothers were occupationally linked with them – as an architect might marry an architect's sister, or a barrister a solicitor's daughter?

We can answer these questions, if only in part. We made no independent empirical enquiry of our own about the occupations of people's relatives. Apart from a few fortuitous pieces of information which gave us checks (see Chapter 2), the results we obtained are based on what informants stated about their kin. They therefore represent the reality as seen through the special lens of our informants' knowledge and prejudices. But even so, the distribution of kin occupations as these were represented by our informants was interesting. In Table 17 below we give the general result of our enquiry in this field, taking all kin whose occupation was known, but separately listing the Greenbanks and Highgate data, and the kin of our men and of our women informants.

Our information about occupations, covering as can be seen more than 3,000 male kin of our 166 principals, is certainly not complete (total male kin, including children, numbered approximately 6,700). But it does deal with a high proportion of the male adult kin. The data of course varied greatly in precision. Many occupational labels were fairly straightforward – e.g. doctor,

TABLE 17

Occupations of male kin

Occupational group	*Men's kin*		*Women's kin*		*Kin of special case**	*Totals*		
	G	*H*	*G*	*H*		*G*	*H*	*All*
Religion	45	23	24	32	1	70	55	125
Law	22	36	27	39	—	49	75	124
Medicine	32	25	51	36	1	84	61	145
University	18	21	7	21	—	25	42	67
Engineering	28	29	37	30	1	66	59	125
Schoolteaching	16	16	30	31	1	47	47	94
Arts and entertainment	23	20	38	35	—	61	55	116
Other professions	58	65	80	42	2	140	107	247
H.M. Forces	27	72	56	49	1	84	121	205
Civil Service	45	36	74	48	7	126	84	210
Business	354	252	423	231	12	789	483	1,272
Farming	85	45	78	69	1	164	114	278
Skilled trades and crafts	33	17	14	3	—	47	20	67
Other	8	10	18	1	—	26	11	37
Totals	794	667	957	667	27	1,778	1,334	3,112

G = Greenbanks *H* = Highgate

* A case of husband wife in first-cousin marriage, hence their kin must be considered together (additional to Greenbanks).

solicitor, quantity surveyor, hospital anaesthetist, chartered accountant, heating engineer, leather gilder, quarryman, pianoforte maker. Some were more difficult to place, and occasionally unclassifiable – 'something in oil'; 'something on the railways', as the odd expressions go. In other cases a little ingenuity had to be used in interpreting the grading. A man who was 'something in the City', and went up to London every day 'wearing a bowler hat' was plausibly inferred to be of at least middle occupational grade in business, while one who 'made glasses' and had 'two children and a Rolls-Royce' could be reasonably classed as an optician of managerial status. Ancillary information often helped to confirm the classification. For example, in a set of three siblings in the Willmott family, one brother made a decision to study medicine, probably with encouragement from his father's sister and her husband, both practising doctors. This seemed to act as incentive to the other siblings, and first the other brother and then the sister followed in his footsteps; the details given of their training and posts all fitted the picture. Sometimes the description was of more social than economic detail, but this also helped to give content to the occupational classification – as with a cousin of Mrs Arthur who wrote books ('rotten novels') and married a woman who was a principal boy in pantomime; 'none of his relatives thought very much of that, though she was quite nice.'

What the Table does bring out, even if only approximately, is how wide was conceived to be the spread of kin over the various occupational groups. The more senior professions of the Church, law, medicine and engineering, and the professions directly a part of the State apparatus, such as the Civil Service, schoolteaching and the Armed Forces, each comprised about one-sixth of the total occupations of kin, while the arts and entertainment, and other professions, together with farming, accounted for about one-fifth of the total. But all these together were only half as much again as the number of kin engaged in business, which was by far the largest occupational category of all. Of special interest was the number of farming kin. None of the principals himself could be a farmer (fairly obviously in the heart of London), but many of them had farming kin at one or two removes.

In all these respects there was not much difference between our two samples. Among the kin of the Highgate sample there were more lawyers and University teachers, and members of the Armed Forces – including many Army officers – but for the most part the proportions of Greenbanks and of Highgate kin in the various major occupational types were of the same order; both samples had a professional and business occupational setting as far as most of their kin were concerned.

But what now of individual cases? Did doctors tend to have medical kin and lawyers to have legal kin; did architects marry surveyors' daughters and barristers marry solicitors' daughters? We found no evidence of this on any scale. There were particular cases of kin aggregates in one profession, as in the example quoted above, of a man, his brother, sister, father's sister and father's sister's husband all in the medical profession. There was also a spectacular case of six doctors among the husband's kin and seven doctors and ten dentists among the wife's kin. But these seemed relatively rare. Two architects had no other architects among their kin, though they did have fourteen engineers among their own and their wives' kin. Two lawyers, who had eight other lawyers among their own and their wives' kin, also had eleven doctors; and five doctors, who had twelve other doctors among their own and their wives' kin, also had eleven lawyers. Six men in arts or entertainment had only seven of their own or their wives' kin in the same general field, whereas they had fourteen engineering kin, ten lawyers and 42 farmers. What appears is that these professional men did have quite a lot of relatives, their wives' as well as their own, in professional fields *in general*, but not necessarily particularly in their own professional field. Moreover, what comes out in very striking fashion is the intermingling between business and the professions in the kin universe of our informants. The two architects cited above had only eighteen businessmen among their and their wives' kin – equally divided; but the two lawyers had 52 businessmen as kin, the five medical men had 67, and the six arts and entertainment professionals had 72 businessmen as kin, their own and their wives'. It was clear, however, that businessmen as such did tend to have a higher proportion of kin in the same general field. Eight businessmen in Highgate, while having a fair scatter of kin in the medical, legal, engineering and other professional fields, had over 170 kin of their own and their wives' in business likewise, or 50 per cent more than the businessmen kin of a similar number of lawyers, medical men and University teachers.

But now what about the general classification of kin not by occupational group but by the social rank of the occupations? If one took the information at face value one might be struck at once by the overwhelmingly middle-class character of the male kin of our informants, judging by these occupational alignments. As listed, there are only about 2 per cent of the total kin engaged in specifically working-class occupations – the skilled trades and crafts. But in many cases, notably in the groups of H.M. Forces, the Civil Service, business and farming, the descriptions of kin occupations were not at all precise as to the exact type of job performed. While the evidence as to occupational *grouping* of kin is therefore probably a reasonably good guide to the actual situation, that in regard to *grading* of the occupations is much weaker. It may well be that some of this vagueness on the part of our informants concealed a status awareness which has led them, perhaps unconsciously, to suppress those details of kin occupations which detracted from their own image of themselves as essentially middle-class people. Yet there seemed to be few cases in which any reluctance to state what was known about the working-class occupations of kin was evident, and some in which a kind of curious amusement was shown at having a relative who was in a relatively low status job. What did seem to happen was that the statements about such kin took a deprecatory form. A mother's sister wasn't mentioned in one informant's house when she was young because this woman had run away to marry the son of the local garage proprietor; our informant said that her mother was ashamed of this sister (this must have been about forty years ago), though other sisters kept in touch with her. Though not clearly demonstrable it seems plausible that such wide differences of occupational ranking have supplied one of the factors inhibiting contact between kin, but not knowledge of them, or the imparting of information about them.

Granted the qualifications mentioned, the relatively middle-class nature of the kin universe of our informants can be reasonably inferred from the data given. If we take as middle-class all the kin in the various professions, and reckon at similar level only, say, 50 per cent (probably a low figure, judging from the details we have), of those in the Forces, Civil Service, business, the arts and entertainment, and farming, we get as a total more than 2,000 kin. That is, more than two-thirds of the total kin universe of our informants is of middle-class ranking in occupational terms. Our middle-class principals are then seen to be not an island in a sea of largely working-class linkage, but an integral part of a large middle-class occupational configuration, in family and kin terms.

The kin of relatively low occupational grading comprised a number of collaterals who had found their own job level in manual or routine employments, and a number of spouses of female kin who had married away from the occupational stratum of their fathers and brothers. But other kin of relatively low occupational grade were in past generations and were the fathers or grandfathers of our principals. This raises the question of occupational mobility in successive generations. An indication of occupational mobility can be obtained by taking sets of closely associated kin of three successive generations, comprising a man, his father, father's father, wife's father and WFF. This is as far back as our information goes in most cases. The total number of individuals so concerned in our Greenbanks sample was 265,[14] and for our Highgate sample, 150; we have occupational information for 211 and 137 of these respectively, or 348 in all. When the occupations of all these kin were arranged in terms of the Hall-Jones Scale (see Chapter 2) the results were as follows:

TABLE 18

Occupational spread of kin

Occupational category	*Ego*	*F*	*FF*	*WF*	*WFF*	*Total*
I Lawyer, Surgeon, etc.	42	31	14	35	18	140
II Farmer, Schoolteacher, etc.	17	11	8	15	13	64
III Small business, Musician, etc.	21	18	10	19	12	80
IV Clerk, Greengrocer, etc.	1	7	3	7	5	23
Va Commercial traveller, etc.	1	4	2	2	2	11
Vb Butcher, Tailor, Coachman, etc.	1	9	11	2	6	29
VI Warehouseman, etc.	—	—	—	1	—	1
Total occupations	83	80	48	81	56	348
Total occupations not known	—	3	35	2	27	67
Total individuals						415

What emerged from the Table initially is the general middle-class character of the fathers and grandfathers of our informants and their spouses. Even if we reckon the 'not known' occupations of these forbears as in the lower ranking, about 70 per cent of our total sample were in the upper three occupational categories, and 50 per cent in categories I and II; while among the fathers and grandfathers alone, about 45 per cent were in the top two categories. On the whole, the slightly greater proportion of wife's fathers and grandfathers than of husband's fathers and grandfathers among the upper occupational categories suggests that men married into families of at least as high social status as their own.

An example which shows a strong middle-class occupational succession and kinship distribution is the family of Mr Tintern, who was in one of the most respected professions. The family had been associated with the ownership of landed property, and some members had been farmers in addition to their other occupations. Mr Tintern's mother's family were concentrated in a country town in the Eastern

[14] That is, for the 53 married men, including three deceased husbands (whose fathers' occupations were not known).

Counties. His mother's father was a banker, and three of his mother's brothers and four others of his mother's kin were in banking. One mother's mother's brother had been in the regular Army, and had been followed by his son and son's son; another was a family solicitor as was his son also. Mr Tintern's father's father had a family furniture business, which he left for the Church; two of the grandfather's brothers were also in the family business; our informant's own father was also a clergyman. His mother's father's brother was a judge; this man's son also became one and his son in turn was a barrister. On Mrs Tintern's side, her father's father had been the owner of a shipping firm, her father and mother's father had been in the Indian Navy and four of her father's sister's sons were in the merchant navy. This case, by no means the only one of its kind in our sample, illustrates a typical middle-class field of occupations in successive generations: banking, a family business, the law, the Army, the Church, the Navy. Family solicitor and merchant navy are perhaps at the far end of the traditional field, but this might be taken as the epitome of the solid middle-class family.

On the other hand, there has clearly been some upward occupational mobility in most of our samples. Leaving out the 'occupation not known' cases, the proportion of husbands' and wives' fathers and grandfathers who were in occupations of the lower middle-class and skilled tradesman category was nearly 25 per cent (61 out of 265) as against 4 per cent only among our male principals themselves. Illustrative of this situation were senior University staff and leading medical men whose fathers had been tailors or railway clerks and whose grandfathers were paper-makers or quarrymen. In this respect there was a marked difference between Greenbanks and Highgate (not shown in the Table). Taking direct forbears of the men in our sample, there was a much higher proportion of the fathers and grandfathers of the Highgate men in occupational categories I and II. Whereas the Highgate figures for fathers and grandfathers for occupational categories I, II, and III and below are: 55 per cent, 23 per cent and 22 per cent respectively, the corresponding figures for Greenbanks are: 21 per cent, 9 per cent and 70 per cent. This different balance is very striking. Occupational mobility in the Greenbanks cases over two generations had obviously been much greater than in the Highgate cases.

Upward mobility as far as two generations are concerned is shown most clearly when fathers and sons are plotted against one another occupationally. The following Table 19 covers both Greenbanks (50 cases – excluding 3 deceased husbands) and Highgate (30 cases).

In general terms, this Table shows that out of the 80 cases of father–son occupational comparison, there were 38 cases in which son

TABLE 19

Fathers' and sons' occupational grade

Husband's occupational grade	*Husband's father's occupational grade*							*Total*
	I	*II*	*III*	*IV*	*V*	*VI*	*VII*	
I	24	5	4	3	6	—	—	42
II	4	3	4	3	2	—	—	16
III	4	3	9	1	3	—	—	20
IV	—	—	—	—	—	—	—	0
V	—	—	—	—	2	—	—	2
VI	—	—	—	—	—	—	—	0
VII	—	—	—	—	—	—	—	0
Total	32	11	17	7	13	0	0	80

remained on the same broad occupational level as his father, 11 cases in which he dropped to an occupational category below that of his father, and 31 cases in which he rose to an occupational level above that of his father. This is clear evidence that on the whole the trend has been towards maintenance of, or improvement upon, the father's position. (Though not shown in the Table, this happened especially with the Greenbanks men.)

DISTRIBUTION OF KIN BY RESIDENCE

Some data on geographical distribution of kin have been given in Chapter 3 in regard to birthplaces of parents of our informants, and in Chapter 7 the significance of residence for kin contact will be considered. Here we are concerned primarily with the location of the large number of live kin recognized by our informants.

London is a magnet, and so we expected to find that our informants came for the most part from far afield (*vide* Chapter 3). But where were their kin? Certain obvious possibilities arise here:

(a) The kin whom informants recognize are those who have also migrated *en bloc* to London.

(b) The informant remains in touch with kin who have stayed in the home area after his migration.

(c) The kin have dispersed, and are now to be found scattered in various parts of the country or indeed further away.

(d) In accordance with a pattern known from other areas, e.g. Ireland, the Hebrides, there has been migration of kin chain-wise – one man gets a job and is followed by his relatives seriatim as opportunity and capital allow.

TABLE 20

Residence of kin

Category	*Within 3 miles*	*Within Greater London*	*Home Counties*	*British Isles*		*Abroad*	*Residence not known*	*Total*
				70–200 miles	*Over 200 miles*			
Kin in contact	88	849	911	627	293	543	89	3,400
Kin known by name but not in contact	17	364	351	487	145	787	865	3,016
Kin not known by name, not in contact	1	277	275	309	201	685	978	2,726
All living kin	106	1,490	1,537	1,423	639	2,015	1,932	9,142

From our evidence the overall pattern of kin residence showed no marked tendency in any single one of these directions. But in general it was a phenomenon of dispersion rather than concentration. If we take a set of concentric circles, so to speak, from our area of investigation, the total live kin of all our informants in both Greenbanks and Highgate were situated at the time of study as shown in Table 20 on p. 188.

Residence of kin

Degrees of contact with kin will be discussed in the next Chapter. But it is interesting to note that the proportion of kin with whom our informants were in contact was considerably less than the proportion with whom, whether known by name or not, they were not in contact. About one-sixth of the whole universe of kin of our informants was to be found in Greater London. (It is significant that contact was maintained with only three-fifths of these, while another two-fifths were known to live in London but no contact with them was maintained.) Of rather less than one-fifth not even the names were known. Rather more than half of kin lived within the British Isles. About a quarter of these were known by name, without contact being kept, and another quarter were not even known by name. It seems clear too that if one looks at the great area fanning out from London, those kin who were known but not kept within social range by contact tended to increase in numbers as one goes outwards, up to about two hundred miles. Those kin with whom contact was maintained, however, were to be found concentrated for the major part within the Home Counties. Beyond about two hundred miles within the British Isles the number of kin known fell off whether kept in contact or not. It is interesting also to see that of the 2,000 odd kin abroad, although about three-quarters were still known to live in specific places, contact was kept with only about one quarter, and rather more than a quarter were not even known by name. Yet out of the total universe of live kin of about 9,000, there were less than 2,000 whose place of residence was unknown. So although no active social relation was maintained with nearly 6,000 kin, information about where two-thirds of these lived was available.

A striking feature of the distribution of kin by residence is the variety of highly localized patterns which emerge when individual cases are considered. It is seen particularly when such distributions are plotted on a map. Examples of these are given in Figure 8 in Chapter 7. It is to be remembered that we are describing the kin universe of London residents. We might expect to find then that most middle-class families of this type had the majority of their kin concentrated in the Greater London area. But this was not so; nor on the contrary were their kin widely distributed throughout the British Isles. Families of one type (e.g. the Ackroyds), did have a heavy concentration in London and the Home Counties, with only rather sparsely scattered kin elsewhere. But another type had very few kin in or immediately around London but a heavy concentration throughout a region elsewhere, often the industrial Midlands (as with the Underwoods) or, as with Mrs Mitchie's family, a rural area such as the north of Scotland. Another type seemed to have two major concentrations, one in the London area and another elsewhere in the country, not infrequently in the Midlands. A variant of this type (Nedd) had a concentration of kin in the London area, another major concentration in Southern Scotland, with many kin in rural areas, and several other secondary concentrations – one in the far north of Scotland, one in the North of England and one in an industrial area near Portsmouth. In most cases a major concentration of kin occurred in the area in which an informant had been born, or in which a parent had been born.

MARITAL CONDITION IN THE KIN UNIVERSE

A social class is sometimes regarded as an intermarrying group (cf. p. 17). It is relevant to ask then how far the genealogical material we have accumulated indicates intermarriage among kin.

The canon law of the Church of England, with which the Statute law of the land is in close parallel, sets out a Table of Kindred and Affinity 'wherein whosoever are related are forbidden by the Church of England to marry together'. The 25 categories prohibited for marriage to a man or a woman in the modern canon may seem a formidable restriction. But in fact they cover only a sector of persons who are 'related', and their restrictive scope is sanctioned sociologically by generation difference as well as by moral, religious and legal scruples. For man or woman the forbidden kin comprise twelve categories in kin grades two generations above and below, and another ten categories one generation above and below. Only three categories – own sister and two kinds of half-sister – are forbidden to a man in his own generation. To a man, the categories barred reduce in effect to daughters of grandparents, parents and siblings; direct female ascendants and descendants of self and wife;[15]

[15] Many people seem unaware of these legal barriers. In a case reported in the press a husband fell in love with, committed adultery with and wished to marry his mother-in-law. Relations between his wife and her mother had been very strained, as between wife and husband, and after the husband left his wife he

wives of one's own male ascendants or descendants not otherwise included – e.g. father's wife other than one's own mother; daughter's son's wife. The categories forbidden in marriage to a woman correspond.

Before the modern revision, the prohibitions of the canon dealing with the Table of Kindred and Affinity were commented upon by Malinowski.[16] He stressed, in line with his general view, the incompatibility between sexual approaches and typical family sentiments; and by an extension of this argument he justified the prohibitions of the canon. But he did recognize the case for less stringency in rules relating to certain affines, especially because the greater freedom of women in modern social conditions had broadened the range of social intercourse and lessened the significance of household and kin relationships in erotic temptation. He also argued for the minimum of restrictions in order that the law might be obeyed, and deprecated any divergence between the law of the State and that of the Church.

Especially now that the canon has been modified, effective restrictions on marriage choice are few. Permitted in marriage are not only the whole range of cousins, including first cousins, but also aunts and deceased wife's sister and deceased brother's wife, from whom the ban formerly obtaining has been removed. The possibilities for marriage with kin in the modern English system are therefore considerable.

But it is clear that in our middle-class sample these possibilities have been largely ignored. Only in rare cases have the people concerned, and those related to them as shown on the genealogies, married with their kin. Among our immediate informants only one kin marriage is recorded – that between first cousins, the children of two brothers (Tomlinson). In the total genealogical record of kin, approximately 4,700 marriages are listed. Of these, as few as 43 appear as marriages between people known to be consanguine kin. Even for a population which contracted a high proportion of its marriages in an urban environment this figure of less than 1 per cent may seem low, especially since it includes a wide range of people

[16] B. Malinowski, 'A Sociological Analysis of the Rationale of the Prohibited Degrees in Marriage', App 3 to *Kindred and Affinity as Impediments to Marriage*, being the Report of a Commission Appointed by His Grace the Archbishop of Canterbury, London, 1940 (pp. 101–6). (We owe this reference to our colleague Isaac Schapera.) See also *The Canon Law of the Church of England* – being the Report of the Archbishops' Commission on Canon Law – London, 1947 (which presents the modified Table, p. 127).

---

turned to her mother for comfort. According to the Divorce Court judge, only on the eve of the husband's divorce did the couple discover they were within the prohibited degrees of marriage (*Evening Standard*, 28 February 1968).

related through affinal ties. Commonest was marriage with first cousins, nearly half of the total kin unions, with marriage with FBD as most popular. The remaining marriages were spread over a great variety of kin, including such seemingly remote relatives as ZHZH-MBD or MZHZDD. In about a score of marriages to affines, a person's sibling married a sibling of his spouse – the 'brother–sister exchange' of anthropologists, though mostly lacking the simultaneity of this custom as generally found.

In addition to this also were a few marriages between more distant affines. One of these (from the Herbert case) is illustrated in the diagram.

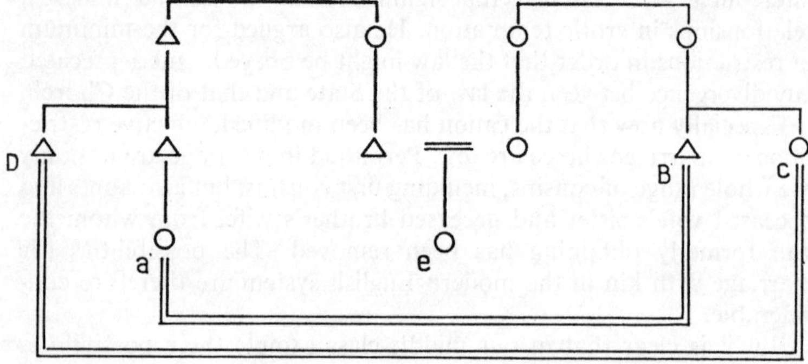

FIGURE 6. Intra-kin Marriage.

From the point of view of the narrator (e), her FMBSD (a) married her MMZS (B); and her MMZD (c) married her FMBS (D). In relation to one another (a), who apparently married (B) first, was united with her FFZSWMZS; while (c) then married her BWFB. In other terms, (B) and (c), who were both first cousins of (e)'s mother, married a niece and an uncle. If the disparity in kinship grade between (a) and (B) be disregarded, this example is in effect a brother–sister exchange.

One possible significance of intra-kin marriages is the strengthening of solidarity between the kin groups concerned, and helping them to maintain a more unitary character. But it is not at all clear that this is in fact what happens. It might seem indeed that such marriages are a result and not a cause of the solidary nature of the sets of people concerned. Common economic and social interests and background would seem to provide the basis for marriage, with ties of kinship closely intermingled with those of friendship. For instance, as an extension of the case just cited, (e)'s sister's husband had a brother who married a woman whose family were well known to (e)'s parents; this woman's brother married a friend of (e)'s.

A special case was presented by Jewish marriages. None of our Jewish principals had married a known relative, but at least two instances of this had occurred among the kin of one of the families studied. The father of one of our principals, after the death of his wife, had married his deceased wife's brother's daughter. Our informant, referring to this, was of the opinion that while one shouldn't marry an aunt or uncle it was not forbidden by religious rule; yet it was preferable to marry outside one's own kin group. Our interviewer, however, thought that uncle/niece marriage was a 'preferred' form, and on checking this was found to be correct.[17] Discussion of other forms of 'preferred' marriage produced the following examples. Our informant, who was brought up in Central Europe, had a younger brother who died, leaving a widow. According to custom, it was stated, our principal, then unmarried, should have married the widow, but she went through a formal ceremony of rejection, thus relieving him of the obligation. Another brother of his was left a widower. But his dead wife had an unmarried sister, and 'according to custom', though she was a cripple, the widower married her. (She too died later and the brother remarried again.) But the rarity of such special forms of intra-kin marriage in our material indicates that whatever the rules may be among special groups, action in such terms is unlikely to have any wide currency in modern British conditions.

What is perhaps more significant than intermarriage about the marital condition of the kin of all our subjects is that according to the record 177, or nearly 4 per cent of all the 4,700 marriages ended in divorce. In three-fifths of these cases of divorce one of the spouses at least remarried.[18] The incidence of divorce was on the whole spread fairly evenly through the sample, almost exactly one-half of

[17] *Schulchan Aruch* [Code of Jewish Law], Chapter CXLV, section 9 – 'It is mandatory upon one to marry either the daughter of his sister or the daughter of his brother; but regarding another relative, whether she be related to himself or to his deceased or divorced wife, or if she be related to the woman to whom he gave *halizah*, he should not marry any of these without consulting the wise.'

[18] This figure may be compared generally if not too closely with the estimate given by O. R. McGregor (op. cit. p. 38) for 1954, of 6·7 per cent of marriages contracted 5–15 years earlier terminating in divorce. That the figure from our material is lower may be due to lack of knowledge of our informants about their kin, or reluctance in some cases to speak of the divorce. There is a possibility, however, that it is due in part to the quality of the sample as a fairly stable sector of middle-class families. McGregor (p. 39) cites figures to show that roughly two-thirds of divorced persons remarry. Our data, probably for the first two reasons given above, suggest a rather lower figure of remarriage for all divorced persons in our sample.

the principals in our sample knowing of one or more divorces in their kin universe. For the most part each genealogy had only one or two divorces, but a few had more, one family having as many as nine divorces. The effects of divorce upon relations between the kin of the divorced pair, and of remarriage upon the creation of new kin ties, will be considered later (p. 440).

It has been pointed out in anthropological literature that one possible effect of frequent marriages between persons who are already kin is to lessen the resort to divorce in cases of marital strain, since the kin of the spouses, being kin in other ways as well, try and keep them together in the interests of the wider unity of the group. Nothing of this kind can occur with our London subjects and their kin. But it does mean that when ties have been severed by divorce, social relationships between the kin of the divorced pair can continue only by reference to the children of the marriage, or from some ties of sociability that have already been forged.

Over the whole field, then, the kin of our subjects showed no particular signs of any tendency to intermarriage among themselves. On the other hand, though the evidence is not complete, there did seem to have been a very high proportion of intra-class marriages.

If our subjects had married people who were already kin to them, they would have shared the same kin universe, as did one pair of our informants. This was not so in general. But the question remains, how far did a married pair, and still more the members of a natal family, share the same kin universe because of their intimate relations with one another. The answer seems to be, to a considerable extent. Children in an elementary family obviously have as their kin, as far as knowledge goes, all the kin of their parents. But even a childless husband or wife shares to some extent the kin knowledge of the other spouse. Sometimes a spouse, especially a woman, is better informed about the kin of the other than the latter is. The married couple, and still more the family, is a unit of kin knowledge to a significant degree. But usually the sharing of kin knowledge is not complete, and we have found it more accurate as well as more convenient to discuss the universe of kin of our informants separately as far as recognition goes. When it is a matter of contact with kin, however, the family as a unit becomes more important.

7

Contact with Kin: The Effective Kin Set

In Chapter 6 we examined the structure of the kin universe as a whole, kin of past generations as well as contemporary kin, kin simply known about as well as kin in active social relation. We now consider in structural terms those kin of most interest to our enquiry, those with whom our informants were in *active social relation*. These are the sets of people whom we have termed 'effective kin', meaning by this that they are more than a name and a description, that the recognition of the relationship has some effect, however minimal, on the social life of the informant. As the simplest criterion of 'effect' we have taken *contact* of any kind with the kinsman, whether by telephone, correspondence, visiting, exchange of services or common attendance at family gatherings. In all such cases some form of *social action* is involved. In later Chapters we examine the quality of such contact and its significance for the social life of our informants; here we are interested primarily in mapping the field, in stating in more precise terms the kinds of kin who are effective.[1]

The kind of questions to which an answer is sought are these:

i How large is a person's set of effective kin, both on the average and with what range of variation? Is there any relation between this and his whole universe of kin so that the more/less kin he knows of, the greater/smaller is likely to be the number with whom he keeps contact? Are there significant differences in size or character of the effective kin sets of men and women, husbands and wives? And how far do husbands and wives have complementary kin sets?

ii Is there any particular boundary to an informant's effective kin set, or does the choice of kin with whom contact is maintained seem to have been quite random out of the whole kin universe? If there does seem to be a boundary, where on the average does it run, and

[1] As before, kinsmen whose genealogical connection with Ego is unknown and all consanguines of affines are discussed separately from this analysis; they are only a small proportion of effective kin.

what degree of variation is to be found within it, both in size and in type of kin relation?

iii Within any boundary, do contact preferences seem to be for kin of older or younger generation, male or female kin, paternal or maternal kin?

iv Finally, what relation does geographical distance bear to maintenance of kin ties?

SIZE OF EFFECTIVE KIN SET

The number of one's effective kin, i.e. those with whom there is some contact, will normally be less than the total number known. But how much less? Keeping contact with kin, as with anybody else, demands expenditure of time and energy – perhaps money too. Is there a tendency then for the *number* of effective kin any person has to be fairly constant irrespective of the total number of kin he knows? Or does the *proportion* of effective kin tend to remain constant, so that a person with very few kin known keeps in contact with even fewer, whereas a person who knows many keeps in contact with many? In other words, is there a functional relation between his area of knowledge and his area of social action, as far as kinship is concerned? Or again, if a person knows very few kin, does this in itself tend to make him prize them the more and so tend to make contact with all of them.

The answer is that the principle of economy of resources does operate. On the whole, the number of effective kin which any person has is fairly limited. Taking both our samples together, the total number of effective kin recorded for our 166 informants was about 3,400, giving an arithmetic mean of about 20 kin per person, or about one-quarter of a person's total kin, or one-third of the average number of live kin. The distribution differed markedly between the two samples, the Highgate people having in general more effective kin than the Greenbanks people, with modes of 21 and 13 respectively. The figures are given in Table 21.

Effective kin numbers varied considerably from one person to another, roughly in proportion to the total number of kin recognized. On the whole, men seemed to make rather more of their recognized kin than did women.

The pattern of kin relations between husband and wife is of interest. Effective kin sets tended to vary according to the attitudes of married pairs. Some married couples in our samples largely ignored kinship, and the effective kin sets of both husband and wife were very small. Others put great store on kin ties, so the effective kin

TABLE 21

Range of effective kin

No. of effective kin	*Greenbanks*	*Highgate*
Under 10	36	8
10– 19	35	17
20– 29	15	19
30– 39	10	7
40– 49	5	5
50– 59	2	2
60– 69	3	0
70–120	0	2
Totals	106	60

sets of both partners were large. But it seemed that the majority of married people could operate only a fairly limited range of kin contacts effectively, so if one spouse was closely linked to a number of kin – say, through a large sibling group – the effective kin of the other tended to be a small set; conversely, if for reasons of distance or demographic lack of kin one spouse's effective kin set was quite small, that of the other tended to expand to fill the gap. So it looked as if the constancy of the effective kin set was a *marital* not an *individual* phenomenon. Either husband or wife might operate the major element of effective kin for the pair, but there was a complementary relationship in their kin contacts. This strengthens the idea that while the *genealogical* ties of kinship are derived from each spouse separately in a married pair, the *effective* social ties of kinship tend to be shared. Kinship as a basis for social action tends to involve married couples and families, not individuals alone.

BOUNDARY OF EFFECTIVE KIN SET

While there was no rigid line demarcating the kin with whom our informants were in contact, it is noteworthy that for a high proportion of them (62 per cent) their effective kin set *did not go beyond their first cousins*. The distribution of informants in terms of the lateral extension of their effective kin is shown in Table 22.

This seems to correspond approximately to the relative magnitudes of these categories in the kin universe, i.e. as a whole people tended to make and keep contact with kin in proportion to the number of such kin whom they recognized to be available.

But the variations are interesting. Of the few informants having

TABLE 22

Boundary of effective kin

Restriction of effective kin set to:	*Number of cases*
Siblings and their descendants	22
First cousin collateral line	82
Second cousin collateral line	57
Third cousin collateral line	5
Total	166

knowledge of third cousins, half had contact, i.e. some social relationship, with at least one of them. But no woman in either of our samples had any contact with a third cousin[2]. Of the men who did, one was a solicitor who handled the legal affairs of some of these kin and so saw them on business anyway; another, a business man, made contact with some third cousins on holiday abroad, stayed with them and went round to visit others. Members of families with fairly long ancestry had definite genealogical interests to aid and stimulate their social contacts with kin. Yet despite such genealogical knowledge usually only one or two of the many cousins of this range were actually kept in contact. Out of a total of 78 third cousins recognized, social contact existed only with 18, less than 25 per cent. The process of kin linkage in social as distinct from genealogical relationship is a highly selective one, and seems to rest upon an attitude of personal liking akin to friendship rather than on the kinship tie as such.

The meagre utilization of genealogical possibilities for social relationships is made clear by the diagram below (Figure 7). For the whole of our samples, out of the eight possible types of great-grandparents whose siblings could have supplied descendants for kin contact only three types had been used – presumably by our informants' predecessors – and in only 5 cases out of the whole 166 informants. To judge from our samples, the metropolitan middle classes are not strongly kinship oriented at the periphery of their kinship universe, whatever they may be at the centre.

Whereas the number of our informants with third cousins known and alive was very few, those with second cousins were nearly half of our samples. Of these cases with known live kinsmen in the second

[2] But one woman had contact with an affine – a FFFWZSD – of equivalent distance.

collateral line, 64 per cent of informants had contact with at least one of them. Those with first cousins known and alive were about three-quarters of our total informants, and of them 78 per cent had contact with at least one of these cousins.[3] It is evident that the closer the cousinship, the higher the proportion of people who avail themselves of cousins for social contact – and as will be shown later, the higher the proportion of cousins used.

But the principle that contact increases proportionate to the nearness of kinship is not without qualification. Most siblings were seen or written to, but not all step-siblings and half-siblings, and with step-parents, and even parents, in cases where there was much

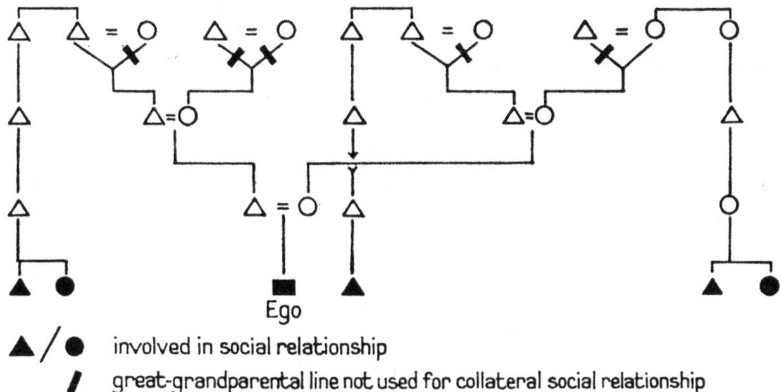

FIGURE 7. Types of Third Cousin used for Social Relationship

tension, contact was not always maintained (cf. p. 401). In 7 cases out of 60 in Highgate and 15 out of 107 in Greenbanks informants had no contact with at least one living member of their natal family. Some of the reasons for such neglect of the social bond are discussed elsewhere (pp. 175, 401–4, 431–2). But it is a spectacular demonstration of the range of variation and degree of selectivity which operate in the effective kin field. While the pattern of the effective kin set does conform to some degree to a genealogical framework, this framework itself is not sufficient to describe the situation.

[3] These categories are not exclusive; most of the informants who included second cousins in their effective kin had some first cousins in this set as well. In other words, those who had second cousins in their effective kin did not utilize them simply because they lacked, or were in bad relations with, first cousins.

PREFERENCES IN EFFECTIVE KIN SETS

What major distributions show up when the total numbers involved in the effective kin sets of all our informants are analysed along structural lines?

There is a significant point concerning kin of different generations. It might be supposed that the effective kin set of any individual would be composed primarily of people of his own generation, with whom he could feel most at home in social contact. This was in fact not so with our informants. For instance, about five out of every six people in our samples with uncles or aunts alive had contact with at least one of these. Indeed, contact was maintained with a slightly higher percentage of kin of the parental generation than of first cousins. This may mean either that there was much less opportunity, or less interest or feeling of obligation, to remain in touch with first cousins, people of one's own generation, than with aunts and uncles, people of a generation above. Here the inference would be either that the aunts and uncles were influential in the earlier life of the person concerned and the tie persisted, or that a parent's siblings were kept in contact as a kind of extension of parental obligation. Both these factors may operate together. Not only did individual informants differ in such attitudes; they also tended to be selective as between such aunts and uncles.

In general, what appeared in significant though not very marked terms was a *maternal* bias at various genealogical levels. On the whole, there was slightly more tendency to incline towards social contact with mother's brother's and mother's sister's children, and mother's father's and mother's mother's siblings' descendants than to the corresponding kin on the father's side. The following Table illustrates this.

TABLE 23

Maternal and paternal cousin distribution in total effective kin

Kin type	*Total no. recognized*	*Effective kin*	
Mother's siblings and descendants	2,622	902	34%
Father's siblings and descendants	2,517	751	30%
Mother's Parents' siblings and descendants	1,084	237	22%
Father's Parents' siblings and descendants	1,008	204	20%

At this level of analysis the percentage differences are small, though statistically significant.[4] If these gross categories are broken down the difference becomes clearer. If, for instance, the maternal cousins of the second collateral line, i.e. mother's parents' siblings' descendants, be separated into mother's mother's siblings' descendants, and mother's father's siblings' descendants, not only are there considerably fewer of the latter known (less than 450 as against 650) but the proportion of these with whom social contact exists is also much smaller (16 per cent as against 26 per cent).

This picture of a maternal focus is altered somewhat, however, if we look at the relations of our informants with their parents' siblings, their own uncles and aunts. More aunts than uncles are kept in contact. It is the sex of the parent's sibling, not the sex of the parent, that seems a significant factor here. The following Table shows a focus in social relations overall not on the mother's siblings to the detriment of the father's, but on *sisters as against brothers* of either parent.

TABLE 24

Contact with parents' siblings

Kin	*Total no. known*	*No. in contact*	*Proportion in contact*
Father's brother	74	42	57%
Mother's brother	109	60	55%
Father's sister	101	64	63%
Mother's sister	139	92	66%
Totals	423	258	61%

Will the picture now be modified still further if we break up this Table to separate the contacts of men with their uncles and aunts from those of women with theirs? In general, women have more kin, including effective kin, than men do. For example, taking 105 of the informants of our Greenbanks sample (excluding the first cousin marriage case), the women of the sample had a rather higher number of effective kin apiece (36) than did the men (28). Not only this, they had effective social relationships with a slightly larger proportion (38 per cent) of their recognized kin than did the men (35 per cent).

[4] Tests of significance indicate a probability of only 4 in 1,000 that the percentage difference between maternal and paternal first cousins could occur by chance. Similar tests have been applied to the other differences discussed.

The Table below indicates the degree to which men and women in both random samples had contact with the different kinds of uncles and aunts. (The case of first-cousin marriage has been excluded since the spouses shared the same kin; this has slightly reduced the totals from those in Table 24.)

TABLE 25

Contact of men and women with their parents' siblings

	Men			*Women*		
	Recognized	*No. in contact*	*Per cent*	*Recognized*	*No. in contact*	*Per cent*
Father's brother	21	11	52%	52	30	58%
Mother's brother	49	28	57%	59	32	54%
Father's sister	35	21	60%	65	42	65%
Mother's sister	63	37	59%	76	55	72%
Totals	168	97	58%	252	159	63%

It is clear from the data that the women of the samples had more uncles and aunts in their kinship sphere than did the men. (The inference here is that this was in part a recognition factor, not a simple genealogical factor.) But what also emerges from the Table is that in three out of the four categories, a greater proportion of contact was maintained with parents' siblings by women than by men, and a greater contact by both men and women with aunts than with uncles. Yet for the most part the proportional differences are not very great, and statistically speaking the probability of their not being due to chance is relatively low.

In one direction, however, a significant relationship appears. The women of the sample were more active in the kin field than were the men: they recognized more kin and they had contact with a higher proportion of their kin than the men did. What emerges markedly from the Table is the high degree of contact of women with their mothers' sisters. The total number of such kin recognized by women was the largest in the four categories and so also was the proportion of contact.

This female linkage is in accord with the relative frequency of contact between sisters as compared with that between sisters and brothers or brothers with one another. (See Chapter 12 for data.) Indeed, if children assume the kin patterns of their parents the greater maintenance of contact between sisters may well set the frame for persisting kin relations between women in the broader field.

KIN CONTACT AND GEOGRAPHICAL DISTANCE

In a large-scale complex society such as that of Britain one expects to find kin separated by considerable geographical distances, even when they are genealogically closely connected. The job requirements of industrial life alone tend to produce this. One obvious question is then, how far separation by geographical distance means separation by social distance – how far people tend to drop social relations with kin who live far away? An obvious limiting condition is that if kinsmen are separated by great distance – as for example between London and Edinburgh – very frequent personal contact is ruled out because of the cost in time and money. But if kin are living in the same area of London, say within three miles, meeting and other social relationships are relatively easy. How far did this geographical factor really seem to affect the maintenance of kin relations?

A great deal of data was collected in our study on frequency, quality and type of contact between informants and their kin. From data concerned in particular with exchange of visits, a rough frequency of contact was established for each informant with every one of his or her relatives.[5] The rough measures of contact – daily, weekly, monthly, quarterly, yearly or less than yearly (but within the last five years) though crude, did give some indication of the weighting of social relationships, and the results were supported by a great deal of qualitative data. Against this measure of frequency of contact a scale of distances from the sample area was devised. Table 26 indicates the relation between distance and frequency of contact with all live kin of our 166 informants in Greenbanks and Highgate.

In the first place it is clear that nearly five-sixths of the kin with whom any contact at all was kept were living in the United Kingdom, but that less than one-third of these lived within the greater London area. Significant contact was maintained then with a large number of kin living at some distance from the individual concerned. But frequency of contact did on the whole tend to vary with the distance of the kin from the informant. With those kin who lived outside the Home Counties relations were overwhelmingly yearly or less frequently. Yet even with those living within the Home Counties and within Greater London itself, a smaller proportion of kin were seen quarterly or more frequently than were seen yearly or less frequently.

[5] This topic has been treated more extensively by Jane Hubert in 'Kinship and Geographical Mobility in a Sample from a London Middle-Class Area' (prepared for a Symposium on Kinship and Social Mobility edited by R. O'R. Piddington), *International Journal of Comparative Sociology*, vol. vi, 1965, pp. 61–80.

TABLE 26

Distance and frequency of contact with kin

Category	*Distance from Informant* *A*	*B*	*C*	*D*	*E*	*Total in U.K.*	*Abroad*	*Not known*	*Total*
i. Personal visit:									
W	42	62	12	—	—	116	—	—	116
M	13	128	91	15	1	248	—	—	248
Q	8	128	155	76	9	376	2	3	381
Y	13	209	292	236	113	863	53	10	926
L	9	277	279	232	147	944	330	58	1,332
Total	85	804	829	559	270	2,547	385	71	3,003
ii Distant contact only: Xmas Cards etc. Letters Telephone	3	45	82	68	23	221	158	18	397
K1	88	849	911	627	293	2,768	543	89	3,400
K2	17	364	351	487	145	1,364	787	865	3,016
K3	1	277	275	309	201	1,063	685	978	2,726
Total	106	1,490	1,537	1,423	639	5,195	2,015	1,932	9,142

A = residence within 3 miles; *B* = within Greater London; *C* = within 70 miles of London (approx. within Home Counties); *D* = within 70–200 miles; *E* = British Isles over 200 miles from London.
W = weekly; M = monthly; Q = quarterly; Y = yearly; L = longer than a year.
K1 = in contact; K2 = name known but not in contact; K3 = name unknown.

So common residence within Greater London was hardly more significant for keeping frequent contact with kin than was residence within a range of seventy miles. Only in the case of kin who lived within about three miles of the informant were relations much more frequent. And here it is significant that such kin in fact tended to include a high proportion of parents and siblings.

In general, contact tended to be maintained with members of the natal family regardless of where they lived (cf. Chapter 12, pp. 406–407). It was with kin outside this range that geographical distance seemed to play a much more important part.

But what our detailed data have shown especially is the selective quality of contact between kin. In urban conditions geographical proximity in itself does not imply that contact between kin should be frequent or intense. The metropolitan character of London may have something to do with this, but probably the same is true for any large city. Out of the total of 1,600 London kin of our informants, only 65 per cent were in contact with them. If parents and siblings and their descendants be excluded, only about half the kin in London were 'seen' at all, and only about 1 per cent of these were seen as often as once a month. Genealogical distance was not the determining factor. What operated was a series of personal preferences in which elements of obligation and responsibility seemed to play a very considerable part. Our informants then were highly selective in their choice of social contacts from among their kin, however close they might live. They did not feel that living in the same city meant that contact must be maintained, nor if it was maintained that it must be very often. Metropolitan proximity, unlike rural proximity, rarely means that the persons concerned are engaged in any common set of interlocking social and economic relationships and are therefore involved in frequent contact and interchange of services. Social relations between them must be a matter of individual initiative, and in this personal choice is at least as significant as kinship ideology.

What is very evident here is the high degree of personal variation in these kinship patterns.

The significance of personal factors is brought out very clearly if we examine the patterns of contact with kin in comparison with the residential distribution of these kin. For illustration we have taken four contrasting cases from our sample, showing differences in these distributional patterns. In each case we have plotted on a map of Britain the kin recognized by our informants, differentiating between those with whom contact was maintained and those with whom there was no contact (Figure 8 – see also Chapter 6, p. 190). In each case the kin of the husbands have been separated from those of wives.

Two things are striking about these distributional maps. One is that in general the kin of our informants were not scattered randomly through the British Isles, but were to be found in tight concentrations in relatively few areas in each case. In some cases (e.g. Nedd) there was a fair degree of scatter of kin, but even here the number of localities in which kin were to be found was only about a dozen at the most. The second point is that while as an overall pattern for the totality of our cases there was a decrease of contact as geographical distance from London increased, this occurred only as an average phenomenon. In the individual cases contact was commonly maintained with some of the more distant kin, while others – much closer to the informant's residence – were out of contact. We have not shown on the distributional maps the degree or quality of contact,

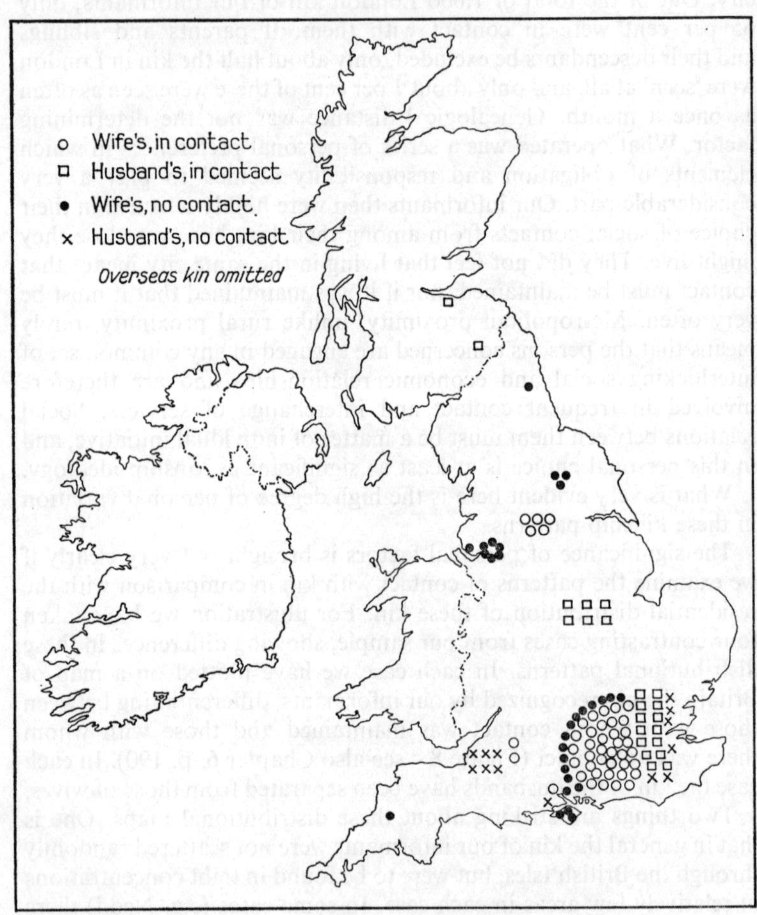

FIGURE 8A. Ackroyd

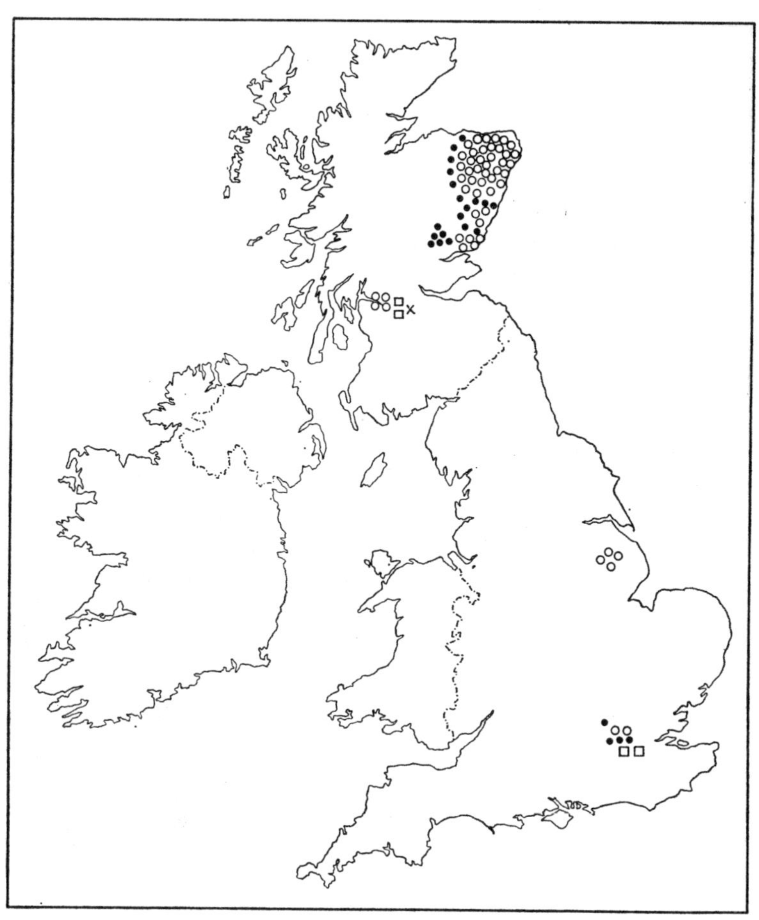

FIGURE 8B. Mitchie

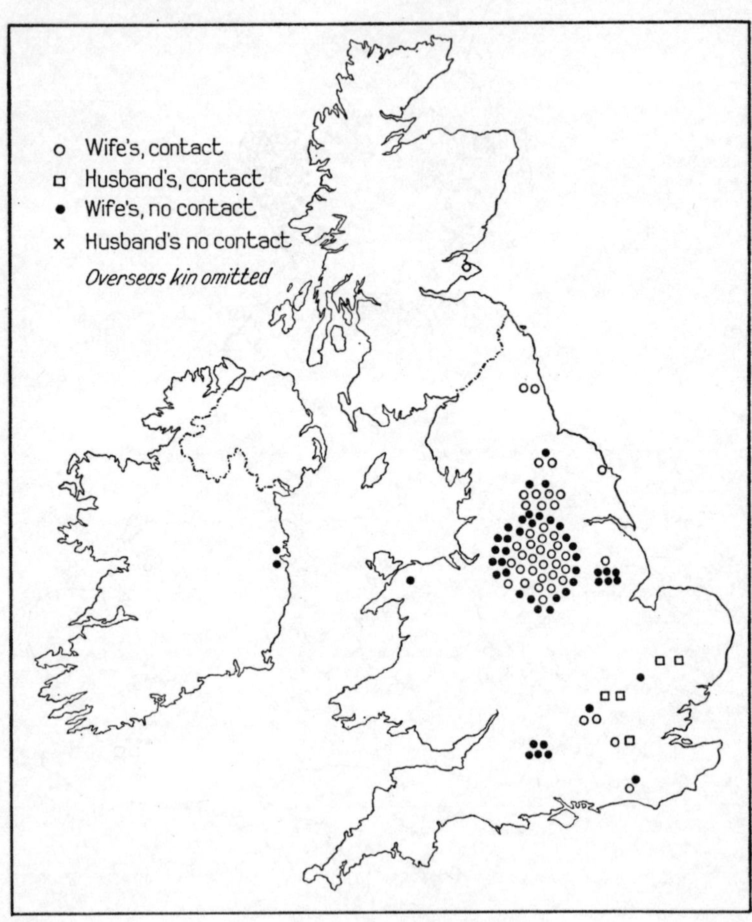

FIGURE 8C. Underwood

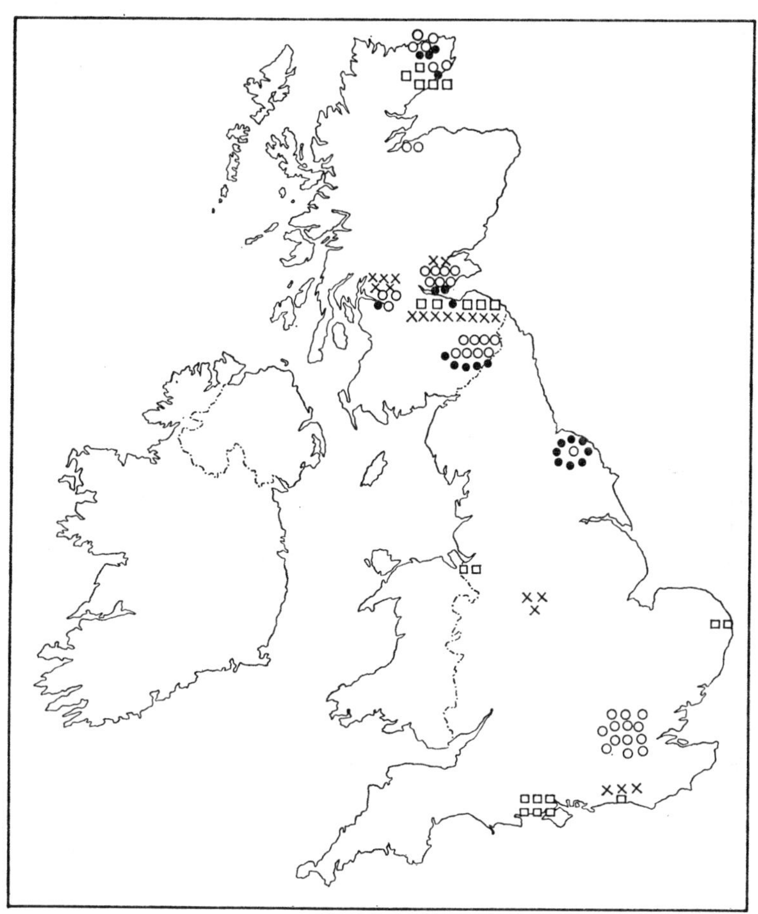

FIGURE 8D. Nedd

but if it had been possible to portray this, it would have emerged that intensive contact was often maintained with some relatively distant kin, while other relatively close kin were ignored. Genealogical propinquity was of some significance, but childhood association and personal temperament often had significance. Economic factors too could be very important.

EXAMPLES OF DISTRIBUTION OF EFFECTIVE KIN

Kin contact resting primarily on an economic base was demonstrated by the Underwood case (Figure 8C). Mrs Underwood had come from a family of manufacturers in the Midlands, and the family firm held an annual dinner dance. Our informant travelled north for this occasion regularly, and this gave her opportunity to maintain contact with father's siblings and their children. But for this dinner dance our informant would have seen her relatives only at weddings and funerals. Her contact with her own brother, who also lived in the Midlands, was included in an economic category. She said she had always felt ill at ease with him ever since childhood. However, they were joint trustees of money left by their father for their children's education, and her brother had assumed the responsibility of administration of these funds. ('He must spend hours on our children's financial affairs – he is very conscientious.') Letters were frequently exchanged between them, about once a fortnight, though they were largely of a business nature, typed by a secretary, with a footnote added by her brother to the effect, 'Please sign these. . . . Are the children well?' Three times a year documents had to be signed jointly by our informant and her brother in order to finance the children's schooling, and this in itself involved knowledge of kin matters. 'One must know what people are doing, their addresses and any changes in their children's schooling.' Yet the economic relationship was overlaid by social elements. On Christmas morning our informant and her brother telephoned each other, and Christmas cards and presents were exchanged between the two families. All our informant's children had been to stay at her brother's country house. Our informant's son stayed with her brother when he visited the family firm; conversely, the brother's daughter stayed with our informant when she came to London to take a University entrance examination. (In this case the aunt was also the girl's godmother.)

Kin contact was reinforced by Mrs Underwood's father's sister, a spinster aunt who had stopped at home to look after her parents (from whom she had inherited 'plenty of money') and who was devoted to her brothers, her nephews and nieces. Being well off, she gave her nephews and nieces expensive toys, took them to London for holidays and had large Sunday tea parties which many kinsfolk, often as many as twenty, attended. 'She kept us all together' – a succinct description of a 'kin mobilizer' (cf. Chapter 5, p. 139). Yet our informant had no contact with two of her father's brothers (who appeared to have been eliminated from the family firm). One was the black sheep of the family, 'with all sins possible attributed to him'. Nor had she contact with a mother's brother – 'a real bad hat, he was so awful and he drank all the time'. However, she visited a mother's sister in the Midlands about three times a year, feeling a sense of responsibility towards her and being legally the executor of her will. With this mother's sister Christmas and birthday presents were exchanged, and our informant wrote to her about every six weeks.

With our informant's husband's relatives there was no such economic focus. Yet with her husband's unmarried sister and brother Mrs Underwood's contact was close. The sister, 'an extraordinarily bad correspondent', was telephoned to come and look after an Underwood child if our informant wanted to go away for the weekend. She regularly came to stay at Christmas, and Christmas and birthday presents and cards were exchanged. Mr Underwood's brother was named by our informant as one of her favourite relatives. When he came to London he telephoned and usually stayed the night. More indeed was seen of him than of his sister. 'It is exceedingly personal; he is sociable and she is not.' Mr Underwood, too, had a mother's sister who, according to him 'kept us all together'. She maintained contact with kin in South Africa, but since her death this contact had been lost.

Another pattern of kin contacts which had some resemblance to this was that of Mrs Mitchie, nearly all of whose kin lived in the north-east of Scotland (Figure 8B). In this case too there was a strong economic base to the residential clustering of these kin, but it was not as a single family firm but as an aggregate of farmers that these kin (Mrs Mitchie's father and a number of her siblings) had strong common economic interests. She visited this area regularly twice a year, staying on her father's farm, and while there she always visited a number of kin who lived near by. She took her children, leaving her husband at work. She felt that her husband 'missed something' by having few relatives and so, in addition to giving her children contact with some kin, she intended to tell them about others whom they didn't see. 'I think it is a good thing for them to know where they have come from.' A secondary kin cluster had developed in Lincolnshire, where siblings also had farms. Mrs Mitchie and her children went to stay on the farm of one of her sisters there about three times a year, and she and her sister saw each other six to eight times a year and wrote or telephoned monthly. The selective principle, however, was shown in distinctions drawn between different cousins and even siblings. Our informant said she felt much closer to her sisters than to her brothers, whom she thought conventional. She regularly visited and was very fond of one of her FBD in Scotland, but had no contact with another, nor with a son of her mother's sister who lived quite close to London.

The close contact of Mrs Mitchie with many of her kin stood in strong contrast to the relations of Mr Mitchie to his kin. These people were categorized as 'unfamily sort of people', viewing their relatives 'very objectively – there is no warmth'. Her husband, however, got on very well with his parents and Mrs Mitchie herself seemed to be very much at ease with them. These parents were seen once a fortnight, either visiting the Mitchies or visited in their own home. When the Mitchies were first married the husband's mother used to call very frequently, 'but never uninvited. She never dropped in'. On the other hand, when later she had a heart attack Mrs Mitchie and her children flew back from Washington to look after her. 'It was awful for her to come straight from a convalescent home to the house with no one but her husband and a home-help to look after her. She has no relatives apart from us, and very few friends.' In contrast to this relationship, Mr Mitchie had had very little to do with her parents. 'He has hardly seen them, and they are so much older anyway.'

This case illustrates a fairly frequent phenomenon – one spouse maintains active, strong connection with his or her own relatives and perhaps also embraces some of the partner's kin within this effective set, whereas the other spouse operates a minimal set of contacts with kin.

A more dispersed distributional pattern of contact with kin is shown by the Nedd case (Figure 8D). This had no significant economic base, but depended upon the strength of kin sentiment combined with an interest in the social aspects of travel. Once a year husband and wife travelled north. Until recently these trips, which concluded in northern Scotland, were intended as visits to one of Mrs Nedd's sisters of whom the couple were extremely fond and with whom they stayed. A very generous, maternal kind of person, she obviously enjoyed having her brothers and sisters around, and visiting her was made the occasion for maintaining various other kin contacts. Kinship alone, however, was not the motivating force along the way. The Nedds stopped usually first in the Midlands where they had a number of close friends with whom they stayed for a few days. They often by-passed Glasgow and Edinburgh, though they both had kinsmen living there or nearby. Visits were made to various parts of northern Scotland in order to see both husband's and wife's kin. On other vacations an annual visit was made to Norfolk to see Mr Nedd's father, who lived there with his second wife. This woman was not regarded as a close relation and indeed was not liked, but contact was maintained not only by visits but also by Christmas and birthday cards and presents. The visit to Norfolk was also made a means of maintaining contact with Mr Nedd's father's sister. Her second husband was connected with marine affairs, and spent some part of the year on the coast, his wife usually accompanying him. The Nedds then tried to arrange their visits so that at times they coincided with the stay of the father's sister with Mr Nedd's father. The visit to Norfolk was also an occasion for maintaining contact with a sister's son and his wife, who lived near the father. With them too Christmas and birthday cards and presents were exchanged. Mr Nedd had a strong sense of kinship obligation. He had a sister with whom he was not very close and whom his wife disliked exceedingly. Contact between them was not frequent, but once a year the sister and her family were visited on Mr Nedd's initiative, and Christmas and birthday cards and presents were sent to them – though reciprocated by only a single Christmas card. Mr Nedd attached great importance to contact with his genealogically close kin, although the quality of that contact was not very positive. Conversely, he appeared rather shocked by his wife's reluctance to initiate contact with one of her own sisters who was an eager correspondent, 'too frequently for my taste, oh dear'. But it did seem that Mrs Nedd, with a large and fairly accessible sibling group, maintained fairly frequent contacts with most of them in the London area as well as with her kin in Scotland. Between husband and wife in this case there were eleven siblings, so that some degree of selectivity might be expected. To some extent a significant factor here was the character of the relationship with the sibling's spouse.

It is clear from these examples that there is no exact correlation between closeness of contact with kin and either closeness of genealogical connection or closeness of geographical location. But where contact *is* maintained these factors have relevance for frequency and for quality of relationship. On the whole, it is from among those kin who are genealogically near that the effective kin set is selected. Within this set greater frequency of contact is maintained with those who live in the most accessible position.

All this may sound very plausible, indeed predictable. But what is not predictable is that for any individual case there are kin, equally close genealogically and equally close residentially, who are *not* part of the effective kin set, with whom contact is minimal in frequency and effect, or who even may not be in contact at all. Every individual and every married couple have some kin in effective social relationship, others not. The patterns of this relationship are personally determined, in an elaborate configuration of estimations and transactions.

8

Kin Gatherings

Kinship, even in our relatively atomistic North London society means more than dyadic relations. Collective social action by kin, or participation by kin in gatherings of a wider composition, definitely occurs. Apart from ordinary social calls or the occasional cocktail party, occasions on which kin assemble comprise mainly celebration of personal events in the individual life cycle and seasonal festivals. We know that weddings, funerals, Passover or Christmas dinner are occasions when kin inside and outside the immediate household are likely to come together. But not much systematic information has been available about such gatherings – how frequent and big they are; what types of kin usually come; how significant they are to the people concerned.[1]

The data we obtained on family and kin gatherings varied greatly in depth and precision.[2] But enough was collected to show the importance of such gatherings in general and to throw light on the difficult problem of identification of kin groups (see Chapter 9).

It was clear that practice varied greatly in different families. Some husbands and wives rarely attended any general gatherings of their kin. Geographical separation might be thought to be responsible for this. Mr Newfield, Jewish of Continental origin, and his wife, mid-European Calvinist, had no Christmas gathering of kin apart from their own children. The parents of each spouse lived abroad, and visits to them though frequent were not made to coincide with any festive season. 'We go and see the relatives. We always come in between the festivals, so there are not the reunions.'

[1] In the United States some interesting data on 'family reunions', annual assemblies of cognatic kin regarded as descended from the same ancestor, have been gathered and analysed by Millicent Ayoub. Adapting a term from Firth (1958, 1963, p. 26) she has classified these as 'occasional kin groups'. (Millicent R. Ayoub, 'The Family Reunion', *Ethnology*, vol. V, 1966, pp. 415–33).

[2] All but one of the gatherings mentioned in this Chapter are described from hearsay. From the timing of the events concerned, and the fact that many of them took place outside the North London area, it was not usually possible for our investigators to apply any first-hand checks. But some cross-reference was made and one family party (Offord) was attended by our investigator, upon invitation.

With this relatively low level of kin activity may be contrasted that in another family of mixed origins – the husband nominal Church of England and the wife nominal Roman Catholic of Continental extraction. The couple saw the wife's brother and family once a month, exchanging visits, usually on a Sunday and spending the day together; and the wife spent the day with her mother, a widow, about twice a week. She always had her mother and sometimes her brother and family for Christmas, and two of her MZS, students from abroad, for Boxing Day. She, her husband and children went to visit her mother on her birthday and also tended to visit the mother when her brother went. She said that she liked to keep in touch with her family, and that she tended to invite kin to visit her rather than the other way round. Sunday, she said, was the day for visiting kin, and she tended to have small informal family gatherings on that day. Though her own and her husband's available kin were not many, when all their children had grown up and married it would be a considerably larger set, she argued, and such a custom of family gatherings might play an important part in wider kin contacts. This woman also participated in family gatherings organized by her mother in Southern Europe (the mother had a house there as well as in London) to allow her Continental relatives to meet her. All this activity was not restricted to her own kin, but was made to embrace her husband's kin too. Her husband's brothers and sister came to stay frequently, she and her husband went often to stay with his parents in the country, and she organized birthday parties for them, attended by the husband's siblings and families. Here an outgoing attitude on the part of the wife seemed to lead to kin gatherings on both sides.

In another case frequent kin gatherings seemed to be linked with strong in-group attitudes. The Tomlinson husband and wife were first cousins; her brother had married his sister, thus making for a very tightly knit immediate kinship system. (The husband's mother, who spent Christmas with them, was mother to one pair of siblings, and both aunt and mother-in-law to the other pair.) The couple had strong northern connections, and at Christmas time parties were given in London by them, and in Cumberland by some other members of the family living there. Telephone calls were exchanged between the London and the Cumberland parties, and 'we speak to five or six people at the same time'. Anyone who couldn't get to either party generally telephoned during the course of it. Any member of the family who happened to be in London at the time would spend Christmas with the Tomlinsons. So, 'at crises, weddings and things, we all rally round': these were all occasions for family gatherings. (See also Chapter 11, p. 371.)

A general point arises from all this – that some families seemed to use almost any pretext of personal crisis or achievement for a gathering of kin, while others seemed to do their best to avoid such gatherings.

But an important point about such family gatherings is their selective character. It is often not enough to be closely related to someone and live near; there must be some common interest or bond of sympathy or element of commiseration to provide a basis for activating and maintaining the kin tie. This is a highly significant feature of the kinship system of the sector of London society we have been studying. The following is an example. Mrs Maskell's first cousin (MZD), with her husband, had annually a cocktail party to which they invited quite a number of their kin and friends. The Maskells had been always invited and gone. Nearly always present had been: a sister of the hostess, with husband and two children; the hostess's mother (aunt to our informant) with her second husband; this second husband's sister, and his son by a former marriage, with the son's wife, and a number of this wife's kin. The intent of the party was not to have a family gathering, but a gathering of people whom the cousin liked, which happened to include some kin. Mrs Maskell had always been asked, she thought, because she gave some artistic instruction to three of the cousin's children, and because she got on well with the cousin's husband – 'I have slightly literary interests with him'. But her sister had not been asked, nor her brother and his wife, though just as closely related; the sister 'because she's been so rude' and the brother and wife 'because their ages are so different'. Now it is true that this was not supposed to be a family party. But the point is that it *was* a party for friends, and the implication was that the sister and brother were not the cousin's friends – which could be just as wounding as being left out of a 'family' party. Yet in the system we are studying – and which has obvious analogies elsewhere in Britain – the exercise of overt personal choice between kin even if it involves discrimination, is admitted as a right and not usually challenged. This is not so in many kinship systems in other parts of the world.

Another feature of many of these family gatherings is their contingent, haphazard nature. In many societies, especially those of a rural pre-industrial character, the regular seasonal events and the irregular but fairly predictable personal events are used as groundwork, so to speak, for kin gatherings. This was so with some of our informants; others relied on sporadic, almost accidental, circumstances to provide them with a basis for meeting kin, or a specific kin gathering.

There have been indications of change in custom in family gatherings from the last generation, particularly where there has been migration from a rural or small town environment to the city. An illustration was a description of Christmas in Derbyshire when Mrs Pillerth was a child. The Christmas season was always spent with her father's parents. These were 'colossal' affairs, with meals in three different houses – 'at Grannie's, Aunt Liz's and Aunt Isobel's (two father's sisters). You know what it's like in the Midlands and the North – these fantastic family gatherings.' Our informant apparently didn't really *enjoy* these gatherings as a child, but she valued their memory immensely and had tried to recreate something like them. She tried to arrange a Christmas meeting with her kin – a father's sister, husband, children and children's children – who still lived in the north, and who, she held, still had a 'northern-type' family gathering each Christmas. She felt that this type of family gathering was 'terribly important' for children, because it gives them a great sense of security. She and her sister both tried to collect as many people as possible for their own Christmas gatherings because they thought 'it's so good for the children'. Even if this was an idealization of a childhood situation, it was not merely a sigh for times past but an idealization with social force, and therefore significant. Moreover, nearness of residence, lack of easy transport, and other factors affecting mobility may well have meant that the picture given of those days was substantially accurate. Nevertheless, in some cases there is a question of why such gatherings were not continued. Moving away to work, dispersion during the War, the death of pivotal kin, seem to have been among the factors responsible.

A somewhat similar situation was described by some of our Jewish informants. Mrs Garson in particular insisted that whereas formerly there were large gatherings of a ceremonial nature among her kin, especially her father's mother's kin, these were now quite a thing of the past; ceremonies such as *barmitzvah* (cf. p. 227) were now attended only by close kinsmen such as siblings and first cousins. Our informant put these large-scale kin gatherings of the past generations down to two main causes. One was that a set of these kin 'were all very clannish'. They all lived in the same area, within walking distance of the synagogue; (they were all quite orthodox, were regular synagogue attenders, and so could not live far away). The nucleation of elderly kin, especially father's mother's brothers, in this area for religious purposes made possible frequent informal visits among these families. The second reason was that her kinsmen were all 'comfortably off; lived in those large Victorian houses with plenty of rooms and plenty of servants', and their womenfolk did little but entertain, visit and do charity work. This social environment, the product of money and leisure, accounted for their ample kin gatherings. The only regular reunion that Mrs Garson herself used to attend was a very large Passover feast at her FMB house, attended by most of her father's mother's family. But as she grew older, her father became less orthodox and ceased to attend many of the functions given by the more orthodox members of the family. One family gathering was special. Her mother, helped by a sister, arranged a 'get-together' with all the siblings and descendants of the mother's own mother because of the interest shown by Mrs Garson and many of her cousins in the family history and in former members of the family. Her mother asked the two oldest members of her own mother's family to come and give a talk to the younger generation. (Mrs Garson did not know these people or their exact genealogical relation, nor could she remember their names.) As circumstances changed with other members also – including the need for the women to look after the children or to go out to work – these family reunions became smaller, less important and less frequent. With this drifting away from orthodox precepts and from association with orthodox Jews came more radical changes too, such as marriage with non-Jews.

KIN GATHERINGS ON RITUAL OCCASIONS

Many events in personal life may be marked by some kind of ceremony and some assemblage of friends, colleagues and possibly kin. Conventionally, in modern English middle-class society such major occasions include birthdays, weddings, engagements to marry, arrivals from or departures for countries abroad, and achievements such as passing an examination or receiving an honour. A special category of personal occasions is provided by funerals, which sociologically can be classed under the same head. Weddings and funerals have normally a ritual component and a religious sanction, as also by definition have such symbolic personal occasions as acceptance into a Church, or confirmation of such status on reaching maturity. We now explore the significance of such celebrations for kin relations, especially with reference to the problems of kin grouping. We take account of the presence of non-kin such as friends in order to keep perspective, but it is primarily with kin relationships in social action that we are concerned.

First consider christening and other personal religious rites.

CHRISTENING

'Christening' is a rite of baptism which from its name applies only to Christians, nominal or practising. Of 120 children for whom information was available in our sample, approximately 90 had been christened (including three who had been baptized with sponsors but not godparents). Of the remainder, about half were of Jewish parents, and their celebrations will be discussed later, while the rest were of professed atheist or agnostic parents, or parents of different faiths who did not decide to bring up their children in one religion or the other.

These figures of christening and non-christening throw some light on kinship influences in decision-taking. Having a child christened is an optional act, but the option is not exercised on one's own behalf. It is one of the decisions for which parents take responsibility, with the child as a passive, unknowing participant, yet it is the child whose status is changed. Parents often seem to feel a need to justify to themselves and to others the assumption of such responsibility, with its possible lifelong implications. Almost certainly the majority of people in our North London area who had their children christened did so out of their own belief in the religious values involved. They felt that they were right to act thus on the child's behalf, to make this initial committal for him or her to a Christian name and a Christian relationship to a religious body.

But the sanctions involved were not simply religious. No legal sanction attaches to christening, but there are fairly explicit moral sanctions, exemplified in part in the duties laid down for godparents. There are also sanctions of a more secular social kind. There are still sectors of English society where it is the 'done thing' to have a child received into the Church by the administration of baptism. For a parent to neglect to have this performed is regarded as a dereliction of duty, leaving the child without a formally bestowed name, without an assigned place in the social universe and without the putative support of godparents in the social and economic as well as the moral sense. (This is why some non-religious parents still enlist friends as 'godparents' of secular order for their children – or 'anti-God parents', as they have been sometimes described!) In such circles convention is flouted if a child be not christened.

How does this bear upon the kinship situation? First, the basic kinship tie of parent and child is reaffirmed by the fact that a duty is laid upon Christian parents to take the responsibility of initiating the christening of their own child. It is they who nominate the godparents who assume a spiritual and moral obligation as the child's quasi-kin. This special responsibility attaching to parents is sometimes expressed by a parent as that while not particularly concerned about religion himself he wanted his son to have something to belong to if he felt he needed it when he got older. But the kinship element in decision-taking reaches further. According to the rules of the Church the child's parents have the say in whether the child shall be christened or not – in consultation with the priest or other religious dignitary. But according to the practice of society in the sector we are discussing, other kin may exercise a strong, even deciding voice. This may well be the first formal occasion on which the views of parents of the married couple as grandparents are brought to the fore; it may also see conflict of views between the two sets of grandparents. In one case two sons were christened, to please the husband's parents, it was said; in the Gamba household, two sons and a daughter were christened 'not to shock the family'. In both cases the parents belonged nominally to the Church of England, but were not churchgoers. The notion of a family pattern can work the other way. The Maskell husband and wife, who were declared atheists, had not christened their son – 'We don't go in for that sort of thing, the family doesn't'. In a case where the husband was Church of England and the wife Jewish, the husband's mother wanted their son christened and the wife's mother wanted him circumcised. (By Jewish law, since his mother was Jewish, the boy was also.) The husband said 'no' to the christening, and eventually the infant underwent neither operation.

Sometimes 'godparents' are appointed though the child is not christened. An interesting case of this was of a woman who came from a Methodist background and whose children had not been christened, but for whom 'godparents' agreed to act in a social capacity. The main motive here was to have trusted people who would look after the children should the parents die. 'I thought with horror what might happen if the children got into my mother's hands.' After hearing a radio programme about the difficulties of orphans, the parents appointed a legal guardian for their son. But it became clear that the 'godparents' of the two girls would step in and take charge of the children in emergency, and the wife later thought it a bit silly to have gone the length of making a legal arrangement for the boy.

How far did a christening serve as a focus for kin assembly, and illustrate solidarity among kin? One index of kin solidarity is the prevalence of kin as godparents. In a score of cases in our samples a sibling, sibling's son, or other relative (e.g. mother's sister's son's wife) filled this role. There was great variation in the conscientiousness with which godparents carried out the obligations, both ritual and social, which they had assumed, but this practice of enlisting kin shows a wish on the part of parents and others to bring the child into closer contact with relatives of an earlier generation on either its father's or its mother's side.

Data about attendance at christenings are of special interest.

Of the 90 christenings recorded we have details about kin attendance for 67 cases. In 10 of these cases no kin of the child at all were present except its parents (whose presence is assumed in all cases in the following discussion). In a couple of cases although pressure of parents or other relatives was responsible for the christening, this rite in itself was deemed enough and no kin, not even those who influenced the decision, were invited to attend. In another case two sons were christened, but (according to Scots custom, it was maintained) it was a small ceremony, and no one was invited to witness it. Christenings in Nonconformist circles, especially in those such as Congregationalists, who do not have godparents, tend to be small.

Considering that the principal party is normally an infant,[3] unable to take a very active role in the proceedings, one might expect that the people, either kin or friends, attending a christening ceremony would do so primarily because of the child's parents. Now there were 57 cases of christenings where some kin attended, and in 51 of them one or more parents or siblings of husband or wife were present. Out of a total of about 270 kin attending all the christenings, about 150 were parents and siblings of the parents of the christened child. Roughly, out of an average kin attendance of 5 people, 3 were parents and siblings, in the proportion of two to one respectively. Wife's parents were nearly twice as frequent as husband's parents, but husband's siblings and wife's siblings were of similar frequency. Fathers and brothers, though less numerous than mothers and sisters, were still in the proportion of two to three in the total parent–sibling category; christening is by no means only an affair of women.

What is interesting is that in only a quarter of these cases were parents, or siblings, of husband or wife the only kin attending; in three-quarters of the cases other kin, either consanguine or affine, were present too. So the natal families of the parents of the christened child were strong in their support, but they were not alone. Uncles and aunts of the parents of the christened child were strongly represented – about one-third of the total kin outside the parent–sibling category. What is remarkable is that out of these 40 or so uncles and aunts, 90 per cent were kin of the wife, i.e. the child's mother. They were fairly evenly distributed between her mother's and her father's kin, and though aunts were distinctly in the majority, there was a respectable showing of her uncles, especially father's brothers. The implication here is that at a christening there is a strong interest for kin, men as well as women, in the association of

[3] We have at least one case where christening was performed for a child aged 4 years – a son and daughter were christened together because before this the people whom their mother wanted to be godparents were abroad, and she and her husband couldn't get them all together for the ceremony.

the child with the woman from their group who has borne it.

Other kin present at these christenings were widely distributed. Among consanguines, there were a couple of grandparents and a couple of great-aunts; about a dozen nephews and nieces; half as many first cousins and a couple of first cousins once removed. But there was only one second cousin – there was no great lateral use of kinship. Among affines, by far the most numerous were siblings' spouses (about a score); there were also half-a-dozen spouses of uncles and aunts and a few spouses of first cousins. There were also a couple of spouses of first cousins once removed – FMZSW and FFBDH. Most of these spouses, like the few children of parents' former marriages, attended as supporting members of marital pairs or conjugal family units. The most notable case of this was the presence at the same christening (Danby) of the husband's mother's third husband and his father's second wife, both accompanying their spouses! But this was exceptional. Sometimes a distant affine appeared in his or her own right, usually as a godparent. Such were a FMZSW and a MZHZS (Fortescue), the latter serving as godfather to the infant because his father had been godfather to the infant's father.

In what kinds of combinations were these kin present at the christenings? In very few cases were kin alone present. Nearly always friends seem to have been there as well. Comparatively few in the smaller gatherings, they constituted from about a half to three-quarters of most of the larger gatherings. An 'ideal type' of kin combination at a christening of a March child some years before our study was: Mrs March's father, her mother, Mr March's father and mother, Mrs March's brother (godfather), Mr March's brother and his brother's wife (godmother), Mrs March's mother's sister; there were no non-kin friends. But another example, a combination of kin and non-kin, consisted of: Mrs Underwood's father, her mother, brother, brother's wife, father's brother and his wife, father's brother's son and his wife, father's sister, mother's sister, two mother's brothers and a daughter of one of them; Mr Underwood's brother and sister; also the curate and his wife, the doctor and his wife, and five godparents – none of them kin. The christening in this case was performed by Mr Underwood's father.

In two cases a double christening took place, the children of two sisters being christened at the same time. At one of these the sister's husband was godfather to our informant's child – whose father, incidentally, was a non-practising Jew. This was a small affair, but after the other a christening party was held, with 23 kin present – nearly all relatives of the wife. All this is evidence of family and kin solidarity.

A further index to kin interest and linkage is the christening robe. Sometimes this is made by the wife's mother or other kinswoman; sometimes it is inherited. In a few cases the infant was specially clothed in a garment worn formerly by one of his kinsmen. One boy was christened in the same robe as his father wore. Mrs Gilroy's christening robe had 'come down' in her mother's family and was stated to be 130 years old. Her mother received the dress and her mother's brother the lower section of the robe; as the daughter, our informant received the dress in turn; she has had all her children christened in it and, she said, if it survives it will 'go' to her eldest daughter.

Yet if christenings often demonstrate family and kin solidarity, they can also be used for show of kin resentment, and so illustrate family and kin tensions. Of a christening where two sisters of our informant had been invited and came, she remarked that another sister 'would have had an invite unless we were on fighting terms'. In another case, of the Pillerths, a mother's brother and his wife did not attend 'because they do not approve of me; I'm rather a black sheep as far as they are concerned'. (This woman was not one to flout kin relations; she took her baby some distance to see her HMZ, HMMBD and HMMBS after the christening, to show them, because they were too old to attend.) Mrs Potts related how she wanted her father to baptize the child, and thought that her husband and his family expected that as a clergyman he would do so. So she, her husband and child went down to her parents' home in the country, to stay for a week. There was a good deal of tension over the arrangements for the ceremony. Her mother, apparently a generous but rather bossy, unsympathetic woman, took over the whole affair, decided who would be invited, and even baked the cake without consulting her daughter! This was the last straw; her daughter was very hurt as she had been planning the cake and had even bought the ornament to go on top. Her nanny and she were to bake it and she had been very excited at the prospect; she certainly did not want to use her brother's christening cake ornaments, as her mother intended. The matter was finally settled and she was allowed to make her own cake. But then trouble arose over the invitations. Her mother, who had already asked all her own local friends, had not considered asking any of her daughter's husband's kin except his mother. Actually, the daughter had wanted only a small christening ceremony, with just the god-parents, her husband and her natal family. But since her mother had already issued these invitations, about which her husband was terribly annoyed, it was decided to invite her husband's sister who lived nearby, together with her husband and daughter. Another sister had also to be invited, because she lived close to the husband's mother and would have felt slighted otherwise when she heard of the affair. But this sister did not bother to come (her relations with her own mother were rather strained). This illustrates how the decisions to hold such events and the decision about their organization may show up the complications in kin relations and their strengths and weaknesses.

JEWISH RITUAL PATTERNS FOR CHILDHOOD

Christening ceremonies of the great majority of our informants have demonstrated regularities in their kinship behaviour. What, sociologically studied, are broadly the corresponding Jewish patterns? It would be presumptuous to think that from our few cases we can throw much light on the question of whether these illustrate religious institutions or merely social conventions. But our material does show a range of variation in the intensity, scope and kin components of the occasion comparable with those found in the non-Jewish sector. Moreover, while this range is to be largely equated with the varying degree of traditionalism found among our Jewish informants, it is not completely so.

The approximate Jewish equivalent of christening is circumcision (combined with naming), as the equivalent of confirmation is *barmitzvah.* In orthodox Jewry both of these are ceremonies performed only for males. The female analogue of circumcision, practised in some Muslim communities (clitoridectomy), does not occur. Modern ideas of the equality of the sexes have led to the introduction of a form of confirmation for girls.[4]

Like a christening, a Jewish circumcision may have three components, a physical act, a religious rite and a social celebration. But unlike a christening, where the physical act of baptism either by aspersion or by immersion can hardly be regarded as being very meaningful in itself, or effecting any significant alteration in the child's make-up, the physical act of circumcision permanently alters the child's genitalia. Moreover, the act may be performed for medical reasons, and is sometimes so performed on a child of Christian parents by their wish.[5] It would be quite meaningless for nominally Christian agnostics to have their child baptized but not christened – simply sprinkled with water, without the religious utterances. It

[4] This is generally held in the synagogue on a Sunday afternoon, for three or four girls at the same time. In British Jewry the practice goes back some distance in time.

[5] The Nudley parents, Church of England, who had invited a family of Jewish friends to their daughter's christening, had their son circumcised privately by a Jewish practitioner.

would be using the symbol without the symbolism. But it is not quite meaningless for nominally agnostic Jews to have their child circumcised without a religious rite; the surgery can be given another meaning. One suspects that both non-practising Christians and Jews have the equivalent performance carried out for much the same complex of social reasons – pressure of kin opinion, safeguarding a possible future religious orientation of the child's views, etc. But Jews can put forward a more rational-seeming excuse and keep themselves more free from a false-seeming religious profession.

Circumcision of male children in our samples appears to have been practised by all parents who considered themselves Jews, of whatever degree of religious practice or non-religious agnosticism. In one case of a non-practising Jew married to a Christian woman, their two sons were circumcised without any ceremony. The husband explained that apart from any question of Jewry the practice was in conformity with the ideas of the wife's family – though if he had been in close relation with his mother, from whom he had been estranged, a ceremony might have been performed as well. Three sons of the Liberal Jewish Arden parents were also circumcised without ceremony and, it was explained, for health reasons rather than for religious reasons. (But there may also have been an element of 'insurance-policy' here, in the event of the boys later themselves wishing to take up the religious side of Jewry.) The husband's father, who was present in the home during the circumcision, though not in every case at the actual performance, was 'not too happy' at the omission of ceremony, nor was the circumciser.

Whether or not a religious ceremony accompanied the circumcision, a social celebration was common and in this kin played a prominent part. In view of the popular ideas about the stereotype of a large, active Jewish kin group, it is interesting to examine the composition of the kin in attendance. The Regan parents were Liberal Jews, though they described themselves as 'very unreligious' and visited the synagogue only about once a year. A rabbi performed the circumcision ceremony for their son, their doctor's father held the child at his own request, and the others present turned away while it was done. Present at the ceremony also were: Mr Regan's father and mother; Mrs Regan's father and mother; her brothers; the family doctor and some friends. (The presence of women indicated a modern departure from tradition.)

In contrast was a ceremony in a more orthodox household. At the actual circumcision of the elder son only the husband, his father and his wife's father were present besides the circumciser, and at the circumcision of the younger son only the husband, his brother, his father, his wife's MZH and a FFBDH of his own; no women attended. But at the ensuing social celebration for the younger son these men (except the brother) attended with their wives, as well as MZS and MZD and ten Jewish neighbours. The wife's mother's sister and her daughter came over particularly to help to prepare food for the gathering. For the elder boy the traditional ceremony of ('Redemption of the firstborn' *Pidyon haben*) took place. (By religious rule the firstborn son of a family 'belongs' to the synagogue, and to make the child their own the parents have to make a token offering to the appropriate person – a member of the priestly Cohen name-group.) Kin present for this ceremony were: Husband's father; wife's father and mother; wife's sisters; wife's mother's sister, her husband and children; wife's FFBDD and her husband (visiting from the United States); husband's FFBDS and family; and husband's mother's sibling's daughters, son and family. All except the rabbi and his wife, and two members of the Cohen group, were kin.

All this material is insufficient for more than a suggestion. But it seems probable that while Jewish residents of this North London district had no wider recognition of kin than did other non-Jewish residents, and about as much variation in behaviour, they could if they wished activate their kin relations rather more effectively and consistently for such operational purposes as ceremonies connected with their children. On the other hand, the mobilization of their kinship ties was probably more liable to be interrupted by doctrinal or ritual differences than was the case with others than Jews.

Data about *barmitzvah* indicate the involvement of kin behaviour with religious affiliation. *Barmitzvah*, which may apparently even be spoken of as 'confirmation' in Liberal Jewish circles, is a ceremony in which an adolescent boy demonstrates publicly his acquisition of religious learning, and thereby achieves the status of full membership of the religious congregation. It is a 'transition rite' of great importance in all practising Jewish circles. So it is attended with pride by the boy's parents, and celebrated afterwards by them, their kin and friends, often at considerable financial cost. In an Orthodox synagogue the ceremony takes place when the boy is aged 13; in a Liberal synagogue it tends to take place later, at the age of 15 or 16 'when they feel the boy is intellectually ready'. A Jew of Liberal persuasion, even a non-practising Jew, may attend *barmitzvah* of one kinsman in an Orthodox synagogue and of another in a Liberal synagogue – as did Mr and Mrs Ghent. But an orthodox Jew may well refuse to attend the ceremony of a kinsman in a Liberal synagogue. Mrs Arden said that she and her husband intended to have their sons 'confirmed' in a Liberal synagogue, and that her father-in-law would come, but 'none of the others, because they are too orthodox'. (See also Chapter 11, p. 368.)

Barmitzvah as a time of rejoicing may sometimes come into conflict with other more gloomy events. One such 'coming-of-age' ceremony (presumably *barmitzvah*) of a MBDS of one of our informants was to be held about Christmas time, and all the celebrations were arranged. The day before, however, another mother's brother's daughter died, after having been ill for some time. The conflict was what to do in the circumstances – whether to go on with the celebrations or to hold the funeral. It was decided in the end by some sort of family discussion not to tell the dead woman's mother of the death until after the coming-of-age ceremony for her grandson. The boy's mother telephoned our informant to ask whether his own mother ought to be told of her niece's death or not, and he decided to do so, thinking that she would prefer it. Neither he nor his brother attended the coming-of-age ceremony, though they both went to the funeral; this did annoy his mother, who had wished constantly that he would involve himself more with the family affairs. As our informant pointed out, this was an interesting sociological example of resolution of conflicting kin obligations.

KIN OBLIGATION IN WEDDING ATTENDANCE

Though we did not make a detailed study of marriage in all its kinship bearings, we have data for 75 weddings. These include 45 weddings of the principals in our study – the remainder comprise weddings of sons and daughters of the principals, their siblings and a variety of other kin. In the following account, information is drawn from any of the whole series, but where figures are quoted they refer only to the 45 cases of our principals, for closer comparability.

First look at the approximate figures of attendance. In rough magnitude, for these 45 weddings the total number of guests seems to have been of the order of 2,150, while a careful count of the total number of kin said to have been present gave about 460. This gives an average guest attendance of about 50 people, of whom about 10 on average, or 20 per cent, were kin.

Very few weddings (only between about 10 per cent and 15 per cent) occurred without any kin support. Where such support was lacking, it was not a matter of simple neglect but of special circumstances often almost completely beyond personal control: e.g. a wartime wedding; a wedding in a foreign country away from kin. In a few cases absence of kin was a response to ideological or moral pressures: a husband who regarded marriage as simply a means of getting a legal certificate – and whose relations with his mother were at the time not good anyway; a woman who was marrying a divorcee of whom she was sure her kin would not approve; a woman, herself divorced and resolved not to remarry, who had been enticed into the Registry Office by a subterfuge and once there had yielded to persuasion. These were weddings with very few people present, sometimes only official witnesses.

Overall, the number of wedding guests, whether at the actual marriage ceremony or at a reception afterwards, varied greatly from a handful to several hundreds. Both the number and the proportion of kin among the guests also varied considerably. At very few weddings, not more than half-a-dozen, were kin alone present.

Weddings have a popular image – of large numbers of relatives and friends assembled to celebrate the change of state of the groom and bride, with speeches and drinking of toasts and merriment. It is significant that a wedding which is 'small', i.e. attended by few people, is also known as a 'quiet wedding'[6] – as if the amount of noise were a direct function of the number of people assembled. In fact, most middle-class weddings of the kind recorded in our study seem to have been very decorous affairs. The stereotype of a wedding includes the notion of a plentiful assembly of kin. Weddings are 'times when people come together', meaning that they draw kin in particular. The stereotype may take on an exaggerated form. One informant said that at the wedding of his first cousin there were 650 guests, of which a considerable section were family – about 75 per cent – though he couldn't remember who were there. Considering that the largest number of kin actually recorded as being at a wedding covered by our study was 28 (though in a couple of other cases as many as 50 kin may have been present) the estimate of 450 kin or more sounds like a wild guess.

In general, kin represented for the most part the customary, even the obligatory, guests at a wedding. As a rule the smaller the wedding the higher the proportion of kin; the larger the wedding the lower the proportion (though not the number) of kin. If from the figures given earlier the totals for the only two large weddings – of about 400 and 500 guests respectively – be subtracted, then the total guest members fall to about 1,250, of whom about 430 were kin – which means 35 per cent as against 20 per cent overall.

But a small or medium-sized wedding (both very vague terms, their conception varying with the standing and resources of the informants) did not necessarily imply a higher proportion of kin. The very size of the 'kin group' might lead to a guillotine being applied to kin participation. One woman's fiancé had 'millions of relatives', so only about half-a-dozen kin on her side were invited so as to avoid having

[6] This is probably associated with a trend towards civil rather than religious marriages, i.e. towards decreased ceremonial.

to invite all the groom's kin. Another bride, Mrs Woollcombe, had only her 'immediate family' present. The groom's parents were dead, and his brother was on the other side of the world, and none of his relatives were there at all. 'We didn't invite any of them because if we'd invited any one, we'd have to have invited them all – about twenty to thirty.'

The conventional middle-class wedding shows a very definite attitude of *obligation* to kin. Failure of any party to fulfil what is regarded as their obligation may result in considerable emotional upset and disturbance of social relations. There are three separate elements here: the obligation to invite to the wedding; the obligation to reply and attend if possible; the obligation to give a wedding present, even if not attending. Each element has its own canons of 'correct' behaviour, but is open to interpretation according to individual taste and interests. The same obligations apply also to friends, but to less degree.

What is particularly interesting about some of these situations is that while the obligation to invite kin is recognized, *this is regarded as avoidable so long as there is no discrimination* between kin of bride and of groom. It is tacitly agreed by both sides that economic and social circumstances may make it difficult or impossible to fulfil the obligation, and that this is acceptable so long as there is not differential treatment.[7] (This situation is likely to be incomprehensible in most primitive societies where the claims of kinship tend to be regarded as paramount.)

Typical of the sense of obligation to invite kin was the reiterated expression of 'having' to ask someone, or if *a* was asked then *b* would 'have' to be asked too. The emotional component in the view that close kin should be invited to a wedding may be quite strong. Mrs Gibbon went to her sister's daughter's wedding and said: 'We'd have been very upset if we weren't invited.' Likewise the obligation to answer the invitation and to attend the wedding if there is no reasonable excuse is regarded as fairly strong. But in both these situations the sanctions for fulfilment are not always purely internal; the sense of kin obligation is expressed also through the pressures put upon people by relatives, usually senior relatives, to conform to invitation procedures. In a few cases this was overtly expressed by our informants.

Mrs Potts described her wedding as mostly an affair *for her mother*, who invited all her friends to the wedding while the bride invited only a few of hers – she would have much preferred a very small wedding since it was a time of strain and family argument. Conversely, attend-

[7] Rosser and Harris (1965, p. 261) emphasize the importance of the notion of 'balance' in marriage at Swansea.

ance at a wedding may be largely in response to a sense of obligation, not to the kinsman or kinswoman who is marrying, but to the respondent's own parents. One pair of informants reckoned that on the average they attended a wedding or funeral every nine months or year, conforming to 'emotional blackmail' by their own parents, who wished them to retain contact with their kin. Having been to weddings of six first cousins and a second cousin, they did not want to see any more of their cousins! They met the vast majority of their families only at weddings and funerals, and wished to avoid the links so recreated. They described the 'aftermath' of one wedding as a 'terrifying flood of telephone calls' by relatives who simply could not believe that they wished to live in comparative isolation from their kin!

But in the modern highly differentiated type of society from which our examples come, response to such obligations is not at all uniform, and the obligation itself may be denied. In a few cases specified relatives in close relationship were not invited because of tensions. A bride did not invite one of her mother's brothers and his wife, whom she disliked, whereas other parent's siblings were invited, including another mother's brother, her godfather, who paid for the wedding celebrations for 100 guests. In another case a man who had many cousins invited no members of his 'family' to the wedding except his mother – he just did not want them there.

Embarrassment at contracting a second marriage after divorce may have accounted for some shrinking of expression of obligation to invite kin to the wedding. But in accord with general sociological interpretations, there is also the feeling that a second marriage demands less formalization than the first, which has been the critical entry into the married state. As one man put it: second marriages tend to be small; ceremony is then so unimportant.

Attendance at a wedding may be in direct response to the obligation felt to conform to the invitation, and to support bride or groom; or it may be motivated by wish to conform to the views of a spouse or parent whose interest in the wedding is much greater. Representation of a collective interest, or interest of another close kinsman may be an important feature. A brother's wife will attend a wedding of his sister if he cannot, or one son or daughter in a family will attend to show that the family supports the occasion. So, a daughter went to a FZS wedding in place of her parents, who were unable to go; this was at her father's suggestion, although there had not been much contact with the father's sister's family. Other kin may also take on the representative role. A married couple among our principals were invited to the marriage of the husband's MBS. The husband, a doctor, was on duty that weekend and his wife said she had no one with whom to leave the three children. So the husband's mother and sister went 'to represent the family'. Where another bride had many kin ties in Wales, her mother's BWZ and her husband came to the wedding 'to represent that branch of the family'. The recognition of such 'representative status' is a way of meeting the obligation to attend a wedding to which several people have been invited. But the converse does not hold. It seems to be regarded as inappropriate to issue invitations representatively; hence the occasional decision noted earlier, to invite no kin since one 'would have to invite them all'.

The way in which reasons were given for non-attendance at a kin wedding to which an invitation had been received acknowledged the weight of kin obligation. Great distance, advanced age, illness (including pregnancy) were all accepted as genuine reasons. A plea of work was also usually received as valid, though grudgingly. Some non-attendance was due to kin tensions between bride or groom and kin – even their parents – or between other kin who could not bear to meet one another, even on neutral ground. Sensitivity provoked by a refusal to attend was illustrated where a MMB and his daughter did not come to a wedding; this was put down to their being 'a bit grander than the rest' of the kin who did come – it was said that they 'dropped in' at family gatherings only at Christmas. If differentiation in inviting kin could give offence, so could abstention from going to a wedding when other kin went. Social feelings in such situations are like a very sensitive barometer. An important point here is that whereas there are no clearly objective criteria for judging the grading of friends in such circumstances, kin can be graded by genealogical relationship and judged accordingly.

The invitation to perform a service at a wedding can also have emotional significance. Acting as usher to the guests, on behalf of bride and groom; supporting the bride by 'giving her away' or the groom by acting as 'best man'; attending as bridesmaid or matron-of-honour or page boy; conducting the marriage ceremony; signing the marriage register – all these may be roles which kin may be asked to perform, and which they themselves may be *expecting* to be asked to perform. Failure to ask to officiate may be interpreted as a slight, just as may failure to respond. Other more substantial services which may be a subject of expectation may be helping to organize or to pay for the wedding reception, or lending a house or car for the honeymoon.

Examples of all of these services occur in our records. Mrs Mitchie's wedding was held in her parents' farmhouse; her married sister was matron-of-honour; all her brothers and sisters attended, and though her parents wanted to keep the wedding as small as possible, there was so many local kin that there were about 50 people there in the end. Her brother's son played the bagpipes after the wedding; the reception was held at her parents' house; her mother, 'a great organizer', arranged the lunch with her sisters helping. Finally, since she had forgotten to engage a photographer, one of her sisters made the arrangement with a local man, the result being 'a ghastly wedding photograph' which made her look, she said, like a hospital almoner and her husband a country yokel! In this mobilization of kin it is normally the bride's kin who bear the greatest burden of responsibility since convention holds that it should be from her side that the social accompaniments to the wedding should come. But sometimes the situation is reversed. The Nebworth wedding took place where the husband's family lived, because his mother wanted it there, and the bride's parents were indifferent. Mr Nebworth's mother was planning to move house soon, and she thought that if the wedding was held where she still lived, and she gave a party beforehand, it would be like a farewell. The wedding was in church, also at the wish of Mr Nebworth's mother, though not for any particularly religious reason. The bride had wanted a Registry Office marriage, but the groom said they couldn't because of his mother, and the bride complied because she said, 'You always give people the benefit of the doubt at the beginning'. The role played by the bride's father was unorthodox. He and her mother had been divorced, and neither of them showed any particular feeling of responsibility for the bride's marriage, and she was glad about this. However, her father's second wife had just left him when she herself was getting married, so the father was very much in evidence at the time. He gave her away at the church, and the bride said that it didn't seem to worry him that everything was the wrong way round – that Mr Nebworth's mother paid for everything. He was her only relative present at the wedding; her sister was working and did not come. Mr Nebworth's brother was best man, and a few others of his kin attended, but more friends than kin were there.

TYPES OF KIN AT WEDDINGS

Examination of types and proportions of kin involved in weddings shows that the distribution of kin in the attendance lists was not haphazard; some very definite patterns emerge.

What might also stand as the stereotype or model of such patterns is indicated by the attendance at a 'small' wedding held at a Registry Office because the wife's mother was too ill to stand the strain of a large social gathering. Those present were only the natal families of bride and groom, with appropriate spouses:

Wife's mother and father
Wife's brother and his wife
Wife's sister and her husband
Wife's brother's wife (the other brother was away).

Husband's mother and father
Husband's brother and his wife
Husband's sister and her husband.

Many more kin would have attended had the bride's mother not been ill.

But how far does this stereotype represent a general balance? Two plausible hypotheses must be qualified at once. One might imagine that in weddings overall husband's kin and wife's kin would be fairly evenly represented. One might also imagine that in both cases those attending would be mainly women, considering that most weddings occur during the day and that they are often regarded as 'women's business' anyway. Each of these views has some substance, but neither is fully borne out. Out of an approximate total of 460 kin attending the 45 weddings of our principals, husband's male and female kin were (in round figures) 90 and 100 respectively and wife's male and female kin 110 and 160. So, wife's kin were to husband's kin roughly as 3:2; but women were to men in a less relation, of nearer 5:4. It is evident that a groom is supported by his male kin nearly as strongly as by his female kin, and not much less strongly than a bride by her male kin. What does emerge most markedly is the way in which a bride's female kin rally round her – even taking into account some relative shortage of husband's male kin available to him.

When the kin attending weddings are analysed into types, the preference patterning appears more marked. Broadly, for the total kin count of about 460 people attending 45 weddings, the kin can be divided into five major categories of roughly equivalent size, as in the following table (the figures have been rounded slightly and four 'others' of uncertain status omitted).

These numbers do indicate certain major configurations in kin attendance. But when (by a piece of rather laborious calculation) the attendance figures have been set against those of the available kin in each category, they become much more significant. To put the result in very general terms – the principals of the 45 weddings had among them upwards of 5,000 live kin at the period of study; even if the total number had been rather less when the various marriages actually took place, only about 10 per cent of their kin, on the average, attended the weddings. The figures for parents, siblings and parents' siblings, being of prime interest, have been calculated more precisely.

TABLE 27

Types of kin at weddings

Parents of bride and groom	95		21%
Siblings	90		19%
Parents' siblings	80		17%
Other consanguines:		265	
First cousins	40		
Nephews/nieces	15		
Second cousins, etc.	40	95	21%
Affines:			
Sisters' husbands and			
Brothers' wives	40		
Other affines	60	100	22%
	Total	460	100%

For these first three categories in the Table we have calculated the number of kin in each who were alive at the time of each particular marriage, and who therefore were definitely available (in theory) to attend the wedding. Some of course might have been dangerously ill, others in distant parts of the world. But the fact that the wedding could be held without them is to some extent a measure of the relative weight of the kin factor on such an occasion, since it is conceivable that the wedding could have been postponed until they recovered from illness or held in a more accessible place if they were far away.[8]

TABLE 28

Kin attending and available: weddings

	Parents			*Siblings*			*Parents' siblings*			*Totals*
	Wife	*Husb.*	*Total*	*Wife*	*Husb.*	*Total*	*Wife*	*Husb.*	*Total*	
'Available'	70	65	135	95	100	195	230	170	400	730
Attended wedding	50	45	95	50	40	90	50	30	80	265
Attendance %	72	72	72	49	40	44	21	18	20	36

[8] Note that a christening was postponed in one instance for four years (p. 222 above) until the desired godparents could be present. The wedding of a Tomlinson son was postponed until an uncle of the bride, an Army chaplain, could be home on leave to marry them.

Comparison of the 'available' kin in these three close categories with the numbers who actually attended the weddings is shown in Table 28.

Of major significance is the regular drop in the attendance ratio as one compares the different types of kin – from average attendance of nearly three-quarters of the available kin for parents to about two-fifths for siblings and then to one-fifth for parents' siblings.[9] (From available cousins and other types of kin, only about 5 per cent attended.)

Figures for wife's kin were broadly the same as for husband's kin as far as parents are concerned. For siblings, if the detailed figures (not cited here) be examined, there was a marked discrepancy in the attendance of husband's brothers as compared with other kinds of siblings; sisters were fairly strongly represented on both sides. Among the older generation, mothers' sisters were most strongly in attendance and fathers' sisters much less so. That personage so prominent in anthropological accounts of kinship, the wife's maternal uncle, was very low on the attendance list – husband's maternal uncles did much better. On the whole, the view that wife's kin are more in evidence than husband's kin is only partly borne out by these figures. As a hypothesis it may be suggested that it is the social and economic role of wife's kin on the occasion that is much more prominent, and this may give rise to the popular impression of great superiority in numbers.

What is clear from these figures is the very large measure of support that a person got on marriage from his or her natal family. Gaps in attendance of parents of the marrying pair, where they were still alive, were due to causes largely beyond their control – illness or great distance. In only 10 per cent of such cases did absence of parents from the wedding seem to be deliberate, due to bad relations with the son or daughter who was marrying. (A strong contributory factor here was alien religion, especially conversion of son or daughter to the spouse's faith.) But in some instances, when there had been severe tension between child and parent before the marriage the parent came to the wedding – as did a husband's mother who had tried to break up the marriage and then attended the wedding under sedation.

With siblings the effort to attend a wedding was obviously not so great, and work was often given as an excuse for not being present. Where a specific reason for non-attendance could be obtained, it was

[9] The explanation for the very much lower number of 'available' parents' siblings of husbands than of wives may lie in part to the fact that, according to statements made to us, a number of the husbands came from Germany, Russia or Poland, and their parents' siblings were exterminated during the War, or died in some earlier pogrom, or had been only imperfectly remembered.

of the order of: bride's sister having a baby; bride's brother away at boarding school; groom's sister living in South Africa; groom's brother away at the War; and, in one instance groom's sister very ill – she died the night of the wedding.

Members of the natal family, then, formed the core of the wedding guests, about 40 per cent in all, and turned up in some force, equivalent to about 55 per cent of their theoretically available numbers. In this they were supported by parents' siblings, whose proportion of attendance was relatively much smaller, but whose numbers were considerable. Typologically, all four types of these siblings appeared in the attendance lists, the category of mother's sister being most frequently found.

The number of other consanguines, while considerable, was spread over a wide range of relationships, particularly of the 'cousin' variety. All eight types of first cousin appeared, none in great numbers, though the category of mother's sister's daughter was rather more frequent than the rest, corresponding to the greater frequency of mother's sisters. For first cousins once removed (parents' first cousins), less than half the available categories were represented at these weddings. The few such kin who did appear showed no marked concentration. Of the thirty-two kinds of second cousin, only seven were represented at these weddings. Two only of these, MMBSS and MFZDS, were on the mother's side, the others being on the father's side. But in these various categories never more than two instances were recorded. Out of the whole range of 45 weddings no consanguineal kinsman more distant than second cousin attended. All this reinforces the view that a wedding, as regards kin participation, is mainly an affair of the natal families of the bride and groom, plus the natal families of their parents, represented strongly by their parents' siblings and to a less extent by the children of these people.

Putting it in forcible if slightly exaggerated terms, weddings in their kin aspect, among the middle-class people we have studied, are parentally-oriented. It might be said with much truth that in such a wedding the parents of bride and groom invite their kin, whereas the bride and groom invite their friends.

Such a generalization is, of course, open to qualification. Some kin counted as friends, and would have been invited by the young couple accordingly. Again, they had many ties with their parents' siblings, who were their own uncles and aunts, and who were therefore often invited to attend on this basis. But there was often a process of assimilation, whereby they were closely integrated in idea with members of the natal family. The same might occur with their children as when a cousin was described as 'more like a sister' or brother.

The conversion of kin to friends is probably illustrated by the substantial number of affines who attended these weddings. These comprised not only siblings' spouses and the 'uncles' and 'aunts' married to parents' siblings, but also individuals from a surprising range of diverse categories. Apart from these and the spouses of first cousins, at least a dozen different kinds of affines were recorded, including such distant relatives as MBWZH and MZHZSW, as well as spouses of second cousins.

We have classified the kin among the wedding guests broadly in terms of their sex distribution and the closeness of their consanguinity or affinity to the marrying pair. But consider the distribution of these guests in terms of what is ordinarily called their generation, but what can be more properly called their kinship grade – without reference to relative age, whether in genealogical terms they are on the same level as the marrying pair, or above or below them. This may give some answer to the question as to whether a wedding is a celebration primarily in the interests of the marrying pair, and attended mainly by their age-mates, or whether, as sometimes alleged, it is a function for their elders, in the fulfilment of certain social dictates.

The result of this classification are given in Table 29. They show that while these weddings were attended by a considerable proportion of kin of the same kinship grade as the marrying pair, this amounted only to about 44 per cent of the total, and was exceeded significantly by members of the older generations, who contributed about 52 per cent of the total. Moreover, in the same generation as the marrying spouses, siblings and their spouses were responsible for more than half the total. Putting it in another less formal way, for every first cousin on the average who attended a wedding, there were two uncles or aunts. To kin of this senior generation attendance at a wedding probably not only renews kin contact and offers social support to bride and groom, but emphasizes a principle of social continuity. They commemorate a change of role by the young couple, and by their presence help to validate it. In the wedding they also see the promise of a new generation coming forward to follow in their footsteps – to assume the roles they themselves must soon lay down. They have the opportunity of keeping in touch with developments and not being overlooked. Moreover, attendance at a wedding often gives them the chance of introducing their own spouse or child to their wider kinship field.

The considerable number of spouses of siblings or parents' siblings who attended is interesting. It is by no means clear if the relationship involved was regarded as direct or indirect – if the affine concerned came to the wedding because of a tie with bride or groom or because of the tie with his or her own spouse – perhaps both. But the greater number of sister's husbands attending weddings as compared with brother's wives leads one to suspect that women are more successful than men in inducing their spouses to attend a function in which they are interested – such as a sister's or brother's wedding. (While brother's wives were more likely than sister's husbands to have young children to care for, the sisters presumably also had young children, yet were not inhibited from attending.) The excess of affinal aunts over that of affinal uncles would seem to contravert this proposition. But apart from attendance of some widows, what this probably meant was that the women were less able to induce elderly husbands to attend weddings with them than they were younger husbands, notwithstanding that the latter were at the most busy period of their lives.

TABLE 29

Wedding attendance by kinship grade (generation)

Kinship grade	*Category*	*Males*	*Females*		*Total*	*%*
Two grades above marrying pair	Grandparents	1	7	8		
	Gr's. siblings	0	2	2	10	2%
One grade above marrying pair	Parents	44	54	98		
	Parents' siblings	32	47	79		
	Their spouses	10	21	31		
	Other consanguines	3	9	12		
	Other affines	4	6	10	230	50%
Own grade	Siblings	36	51	87		
	Sib. spouses	25	16	41		
	1st cousins	14	27	41		
	2nd cousins	8	7	15		
	1st c. spouses	6	3	9		
	Other affines	3	4	7	200	44%
Grade below	Nephews/nieces	8	5	13		
	Other consanguines	2	1	3		
	Affines	4	0	4	20	4%
Total		200	260		460	100%

So far we have been considering the attendance of kin at these weddings primarily in individual terms, with reference to the relation of the particular kinsman or kinswoman to one or other of the marrying pair. But people often attend weddings not as separate individuals, but as members of small domestic units. It is clear that this was so in the cases under discussion, from the number of affines involved; the existing spouse link was obviously an important factor in their participation. If now we reorder the material given in several of the Tables above in terms of marital units we find that about 70 *married couples attended* these weddings on behalf of the bride and about 60 on behalf of the groom, the proportion of senior generation to that of the marrying pair being about 3 to 2. In addition about another 40 *domestic units* were *represented* by one or more people each on the bride's side, and another 25 units on the groom's side. In all, then, the 45 weddings for which we have most detail involved at least 200 families or domestic units in the kin field of bride and groom alone.

WEDDING PRESENTS

We have recorded few details about wedding presents. But the general significance of the present seems to be of multiple character. It expresses a relationship of amity with the young couple; it is an acknowledgement of their social recognition in sending the invitation; it is an economic contribution to their resources; it is a manifestation of the status of the donors. More specifically from the kinship point of view, some gradation of the value of the gift in accordance with relative nearness of kinship is regarded as permissible. Moreover, the wedding present can have a representative function – it is commonly a token of goodwill not simply from a single individual kinsman, but from a set or group of kin, such as a set of siblings or a family of parents and children.

In modern middle-class circles, however, the norms of present-giving do not seem too assured, and there is considerable variation in behaviour. It seems to be generally accepted that acceptance of a wedding invitation lays a strong obligation on the guest to furnish a present.[10] When a wedding invitation cannot be accepted, however, two schools of thought appear to exist. One is that a present should be sent all the same, since the invitation itself demands a concrete response, and the young people are getting married anyway. The other view holds that if one declines a wedding invitation this absolves one from the obligation of doing anything more concrete.

[10] Former standard middle-class custom was for the present to be sent before the wedding, and to be displayed ceremonially. Modern custom seems to dispense with the formal display. It still seems customary to send the present in advance, though in line with the general trend to greater informality in social matters the present is sometimes given to the married pair at the wedding reception, as would appear to be an American custom. The custom of a 'list' to help guests to choose an appropriate present now seems common in English middle-class circles.

These views epitomize two different attitudes towards kinship bonds in contemporary society. The first lays stress on the continuity in the relationship between the parties; the kinship tie endures, therefore the wedding should be recognized and celebrated by a present, irrespective of whether the kinsman can attend it or not. The other point emphasizes the essential reciprocity of social arrangements, even between kin; it is more literalist and narrow and, it may be argued, more in keeping with what are conceived to be the facts of modern urban life. Invitation letter has been answered by declining letter; non-attendance, therefore, needs no further action, certainly none which will involve the kinsman in expenditure of time and money.

We do not have the evidence which would enable us to answer the question as to which view prevailed quantitatively among all the cases under study. But it is clear that the more narrow economical position was not simply accepted by all our principals as justified. We had various references of an approving kind to kin who, invited and unable to attend the wedding, sent cheques or other presents; there were also references of a cooler kind to kin who though invited did not come and did not even send a present. To some degree, genealogical relationship was the determining factor. The obligation to send a wedding present in reply to an invitation, irrespective of attendance, was heavier on closer kin.

A more ambiguous situation occurs in a wedding to which a kinsman is not invited, but to one of whose principals he may feel bound by prior ties. Strict equity would seem to indicate that a present should not be sent; yet it was in some cases – possibly in reciprocity for earlier service. At a war-time wedding kin were not invited, but were notified. The husband told his two mother's sisters and his mother's brother, one sister and the brother being married. The married pair received only one present from that group, the mother's brother and his family. Later, when the mother's brother's son was studying in London and living in a bed-sitter, he visited the married couple three or four times, usually for supper, and wrote to them several times when he went abroad. When he married later the wedding was in the Midlands, and our couple were not invited; but they gave him a wedding present all the same.

In giving and receiving wedding presents there is a commingling of economic and social elements, of notions of economic reciprocity and of recognition of ties of kinship or friendship. But in whatever proportion these may be combined, it is evident that one of the important functions of a wedding present, for donors and recipients, is the symbolic representation of relationships which are felt to be significant and which are regarded as having continuity.

FUNERALS

A wedding is a time of merriment, a funeral a time of mourning; both are normally attended by kin. From the personal angle, the sentiments involved and the issues to be decided are very different. But viewing the situation analytically, we find some common patterns in the kinship alignment and kinship behaviour.

From the analytical point of view, one important feature which distinguishes a wedding from a funeral is the different source of initiative for attendance. For a wedding, it is from the central parties, the bride and groom, or their kin representatives, that the invitation to attend comes; it is for the other kin to wait to be asked, and their responsibility lies in acceptance or refusal. At a funeral, the situation is almost reversed, at least in appearance. The immediate kin of the dead person do not normally invite other kin to attend;[11] these kin are expected to take the initiative and by their presence at the funeral to demonstrate their sentiment for the dead and their support of the living. At a funeral, the presence of kin without a summons is regarded as a compliment; at a wedding it would be likely to be regarded as an affront. Not to invite to a wedding can offend; not to attend a funeral uninvited can also offend.

Yet even in this reversal of initiative in attendance there is a common feature – in both cases the presence of kin is a significant component. They help to establish the central party – bride or groom of the wedding; dead person of the funeral – in their proper social setting, to provide their social coordinates. They are part of the process of 'legitimization', to use the term in its broad Weberian sense, whereby those with responsibility for the proceedings – parents of the marrying pair, widow and children of the deceased, or other kin as may be – are confirmed in the actions they are sponsoring or carrying out.

Moreover, there is closer resemblance in some details of wedding and of funeral than might at first appear. Failure to send a wedding invitation can offend – but so also can failure to send a notification of time and place of a funeral. Failure to attend a funeral after such notification may be construed as neglect or insult just as may failure to reply to and act upon a wedding invitation. And even if it has been obvious that the kinsman concerned is in no position to attend either wedding or funeral, failure to send the appropriate communication

[11] A similar point is made by William E. Mitchell, in regard to Jewish kin gatherings in New York City (*American Anthropologist*, vol. 67, p. 981, 1965). But there are exceptions. One informant commented about family funerals, 'If we're asked, we go'.

to inform him of what is taking place may also be taken very much amiss. There are similarities also in the economic side. A wedding need not be very expensive, especially if the ceremony takes place in a Registry Office. But it is commonly celebrated by a 'reception', with food and drink. A funeral, though nowadays often conducted without much display, nevertheless requires substantial financial expenditure. Attendance at a wedding normally involves a present to the marrying pair. Though attendance at a funeral does not necessarily imply gifts, nearness of kinship to the deceased does tend by convention to suggest that flowers or a wreath would be proper, and this may mean a significant outlay. Again, though for a funeral no formal provision of food and drink equivalent to the 'wedding-breakfast' is customary, and certainly in middle-class London circles nothing of the Irish 'wake' celebration takes place, there seems often to be some meeting of relatives after the funeral and some refreshments, which it is the duty of close kin to provide. Moreover, in such a situation gloom may turn to jollity and a discreet party atmosphere develop, as at a wedding, as kin recall earlier days and renew acquaintance. (Case records of funerals as parties are mentioned later.) Finally, while there is no regular custom of inviting to a funeral, close kin of the deceased may exercise their discretion in admitting other kin and friends to the ceremony by declaring the funeral a 'private interment'. They can also limit the expression of grief and solicitude by making it known that they do not wish for flowers or for messages of condolence.

In all these ways, then, kin at a funeral can be controlled in their participation in parallel fashion to the control of kin at a wedding. In what might seem a free field for the expression of uninhibited sentiment at the loss of one of their number they tend to follow definitely patterned procedures, with sanctions of approval and disapproval to guide them.

We were interested in the patterning in the funerals described to us by our informants, especially in the assembly of kin. Altogether we accumulated data about some 80 funerals, but comparable kin details were collected for only 55 of these. (The reasons for the gap were: partly lack of sympathetic enquiry by our interviewers, mainly in the early phase of the study; partly the difficulty of pressing for details on a subject which might have had painful associations; and partly inability of our informants to remember what kin were present on occasions often quite a number of years past.) Of the 55 funerals, 29 were those of women and 26 of men. Since on the whole we gained much more of our data from women than from men it is not surprising that three-fifths of these funerals described were of kin of the wives in our sample. But the remaining score of instances, referring to funerals of kin of husbands and often described by them, provided evidence enough to indicate that our picture was not biased greatly, if at all, on the woman's side.

In considering these funerals as indices to kin relations and especially kin grouping, there are several questions to answer. Who are the kin whose funerals are attended? What is the size of kin assembly at a funeral, and what proportion do kin bear to the total participants? What are the types of kin whose funerals are attended and how wide is the range? How far do the kin in attendance represent the kin available? What was the nature of the relationship of these kin to the dead person and to one another before and after the funeral?

The range of kin seen as demanding formal recognition by funeral attendance was fairly narrow. Of the 55 funerals noted, slightly more than half were of parents of one or other of our informants. The remainder were distributed mainly among siblings, grandparents and parents' siblings. Very few other kin had funerals attended by our informants. These other kin comprised: of consanguines, a grandparent's sister, two first cousins and a father's first cousin; of affines, two sister's husbands, a father's sister's husband and a father's brother's wife. No funeral of even a second cousin was attended. Other funerals of kin attended by our principals but for which the record is less complete included a few kin of wider range, mostly affines of various types. In two of the few cases of remote affines the parties were Jewish: a woman with her husband attended the memorial service of her MBDHF; a man attended the funeral of his FFF2ndWDD. Here fairly strong family pressures seemed to account for participation. In the Christian field a man went to the funeral of his FZ1stHZH. The reason for this was not kinship sentiment, but because he was one of the executors of the will of the dead man, and wanted to meet the deceased's two sons, who were co-executors. The man's wife did not go to the funeral; she did not know the deceased, and as they were not Church believers there was no ceremony, just a small social gathering. She said it was 'difficult to go to this sort of thing if you are not close to the person who has died because you may be gay and the family may be offended'.

As regards kin attendance, the average size of the kin contingent at a funeral, from our data, was almost exactly 9 persons, or almost the same as the average kin attendance at weddings. In theory, such an average could have been produced by a few very large attendances and a great number of very small ones. Statements about the size of the funeral gathering did seem to indicate a bi-polar distribution. On the one hand, there was the suggestion of great gatherings to which 'everybody went' – 'every single adult relative in London would have been there' – 'dozens of old Auntie Hilda's and Uncle George's sort of thing!' On the other hand, there was mention of the very small private funeral – 'with only the immediate family'; 'a sad occasion and they didn't want a big crowd'; 'a fairly quiet funeral'. (For a wedding, the equation of a quiet occasion with few guests is easily seen; for a funeral, which one expects to be 'quiet' in any case, the equation does not seem so apt!) But this bi-polar distribution seemed to be something of a stereotype, as far as kin attendance was concerned. It is true that in a quarter of the cases attendance of kin members was below 5 in each case. But in nearly three-fifths of the cases kin attendance was between 5 and 15 persons; only half-a-dozen cases showed kin attendance of 20 and over, and the highest recorded figure of kin participation in a funeral was 32. Large funerals certainly occurred – one, the recent funeral of Mrs Herbert's father, a prominent man in public life in Eastern England, was described by her as the biggest gathering of its kind she had ever seen. 'Everybody came' including the Lord Lieutenant of the county, and she thought that her brother's wife catered for about 300 guests in the family home after the service. She wasn't sure of the proportion of relatives to friends at the service – 'it was fifty-fifty, perhaps... but that's just a guess, I don't really know'. In fact, from the account of the memorial service in *The Times* only about 30 kin could be identified by our analyst, i.e. about 10 per cent of the participants. It is probable, then, that with funerals as with weddings, the larger the gathering the smaller the proportionate kin component.

Out of a total of about 500 kin mourners of all kinds recorded as attending the 55 funerals taken for scrutiny, rather more than half were consanguine kin. Of these, about 100 comprised parents (a few) and sons and daughters of the dead person, with about another 100 siblings and nephews and nieces, and about a score of grandchildren. Other consanguines of more remote relationship were only about one-tenth of the total, the most remote were only second cousins or first cousins once removed. To the very large funeral already mentioned came a MBSD and a MZDD of the dead man (the latter being also by another line of kinship his FFBDD). Of the latter woman the daughter of the dead man said, 'She's a very distant cousin'. The daughter made an interesting remark in this connection – that a proof of her dead father's popularity was that not only people of his own generation came to his funeral, but also the children of people of his generation.

Remarkable in this series of figures of kinship attendance, and unexpected to our investigation, is the high proportion of affines of various kinds who were present. They totalled over 200 – 40 per cent of all kin attending funerals. Rather less than half of these were spouses of the siblings and sons and daughters of the dead person, with some spouses of the deceased. Over 100 were affines of a variety of other types – siblings of spouses, siblings of siblings' spouses, and spouses of cousins. What emerges here is the strength of the affinal tie, whereby a husband or wife takes on the responsibility of a spouse, with some spouses of the deceased. Over 100 were affines of a variety in conjunction with a consanguineal tie, whereby one sibling identifies with another and responds to an affinal tie as if it were his or her own.

Why do people go to funerals, including those of their kin? The reasons are multiple and complex. The possible inhibiting effect of the occasion must not be ignored. The idea of death and the associations of the ceremonial with death influence some people towards keeping away from funerals. A few of our informants found the whole subject distasteful. One described how she went to a Quaker funeral of her husband's father's sister: 'Everybody sits around doing nothing until they feel moved to get up and say something. A harrowing experience.' Another woman said she felt depressed at the thought of funerals – either by cremation or by interment; she 'couldn't bear the thought'. She had not been to any funerals yet, but would go to her mother's in due course. About her father's funeral she was uncertain – he would have his sister and his second wife to attend him. Yet the complex character of her emotional attitudes was illustrated when she mentioned the undertaker's premises at the bottom of Highgate Hill, and said she felt compelled to look in the faces of people in the cars following the hearses up the hill. Sometimes the death of someone very close is such a shock that attendance at the funeral cannot be borne. An elderly man whose wife died was too upset to go to the funeral – 'he couldn't face it' – so his son's wife stayed behind to look after him while his son and daughter went to what was a 'quiet' funeral.

But for the most part running counter to this aversion to funerals was the attitude of response to obligation, expressed by a considerable number of our informants. One of the most striking observations in this vein was that of Mrs Herbert. 'Near relatives come to a funeral because they must. The most remote ones come because they are friends.' What was particularly striking was the way in which a sense of obligation overcame distaste for such an occasion. Mrs Lark, who had had little experience of such matters, said of her attendance at her mother's funeral, 'I forced myself to go'. A man who went to his mother's half-sister's daughter's funeral said he did not go because he wanted to but out of a sense of duty: it was 'the last way of showing respect, I don't like it . . . but I go'. A woman went to her FBW funeral, because her father could not go. 'It's the only family funeral I've been to. I'm not a funeral-going person. She was the only relative in London. I didn't see how I could get out of it – I probably had pressure from my parents.'

But as the last quotation illustrates, this sense of obligation may have complex roots. It may involve respect for the dead, a last way of implementing kin ties and possibly of expressing gratitude for past favours. One man said, in explaining why he went to his mother's sister's funeral: 'I have a very strong sense of duty. I was fond of her. When my mother was alive I did not see her so much' – she was a kind of mother substitute. Other elements in the funeral procedures may be products of a sense of guilt. Informants have described expressions of exculpation in regard to a dead kinsman. 'When she was alive I would have done such and such, but – '. It has been suggested that over-compensation for guilt feelings may lead to very positive affirmations of duty and marked action in mourning the dead.

But the sense of duty may also be as much a recognition of obligation towards the living as towards the dead. Some of our informants, very clear and cool analysts of their own motives, had no difficulty in stating the issue quite cogently. One man, asked if he felt obliged to go to a family funeral, replied: 'Certainly! If my sister would die before me, I would have to go.' 'Why?' 'Because of the daughter . . . not because of the family reason; just to please the daughter.' (When his sister was ill, he had gone over to Switzerland every three months to see her.) Mr Waverley said he attended the weddings and funerals of his friends as a matter of course – his friends were the company he had chosen for himself. Family occasions were very different, but his FMZ (of whom he had been rather a favourite) would be deeply distressed if he did not go to them. This was a thing of duty; he went out of politeness; also parental pressure was very important. Another man, like the former, a non-practising Jew, said of his MBD that he had not seen her for several years – there was no reason to see her. But he attended her funeral. 'I don't believe in ceremonies. You go because you have a mother who insists, and because people feel a bit miserable at funerals and need cheering up. It would be better to burn the bodies and have done with it!' The other side of the picture was shown by Mrs Forsyth who told of the death of a father's brother. She and her father heard of this from another brother of her father. He later attended the funeral but they did not; the widow was disappointed that no other of the brothers had been present. Our informant commented in disapproval, 'Father should have gone; he gave the excuse that he had just come out of hospital!' But her attitude was based on no particular sentiment for the uncle in question; before his death he lived far away and was rarely seen. Recognition of obligation to attend a funeral may be thus spurred on by a double source of judgment – that of the close kin of the deceased and one's own close kin.

Sometimes attendance at a funeral may be an indirect response to a kin obligation. Mrs Pillerth explained that she disliked funerals intensely and didn't go if she could help it. When she did go it was as a 'mark of respect' and out of a desire not to hurt anyone's feelings. If anyone close to her died, she would try to keep the funeral as 'small' as possible. She attended her father's funeral from sentiment. But the reason she gave for attending her godmother's funeral was that she went to accompany her mother and an old cousin of her godmother's; she couldn't let them travel alone to the South coast town where the funeral took place.

People who acknowledged an obligation to attend a funeral were in a majority. But a few explicitly refused to accept it – at least in terms of a response to a social convention. One woman said that she didn't go to her mother's brother's funeral, adding rather apologetically, 'Well, mother went'. But then she continued to say that she would not have gone even if her mother had not attended; she had not seen him for an awfully long time. 'I wouldn't have gone out of a sense of duty . . . I wouldn't go to anyone's funeral for this reason.' If she had no liking for a person she certainly wouldn't go 'for appearances' sake'; she 'wouldn't be bothered'.

Attendance at a funeral was not, however, only a matter of paying respect to the dead or not wishing to incur the disapproval of the living. With a few of our informants a more positive, quasi-sociological explanation of attendance was given. Mr Gibbon said that he went to funerals because he believed that a large attendance 'makes the one that's left feel part of a group'. (He was not a sociologist by profession.) This interpretation of the situation, of funeral attendance giving support to the bereaved and maintenance of solidarity among the kin seemed to be of fairly general currency.

But certain factors were recognized as limiting the attendance of kin at funerals. Distance was one. To be far away from the scene of a funeral seems to have been regarded by all parties as a genuine excuse for not attending. But how distant is 'too far'? By several informants Scotland was held to be 'not close enough' to London to attend, e.g. a father's mother's funeral. As a general proposition, London and the Home Counties seemed about the limit for ordinary attendance at funerals of kin of second degree and beyond, but for kin of first degree – parents and siblings – people would travel considerable distances. Other physically limiting factors were illness and weather, while obligations of work were regarded as reasonable excuse. The wife of a busy professional man commented that he would go to the funeral of a close friend but 'I don't think just because an uncle died he'd go'. And a man who was a Trade Union Secretary did not attend his own brother's funeral allegedly because of his work – though he did go to the funerals of another brother, his mother and two of his sisters' husbands. Looking after children was put in much the same category as work. At the other extreme, holidays seemed to have priority over all funerals except those of very close kin – though they probably fell under the head of temporary distance. So a woman attended the wedding of one FBS who was married in the South because she thought not many kin would be there. She said she felt 'a kind of impersonal family feeling'. She did not attend the funeral of another FBS, who had been killed whilst trying to rescue two men from a well, as she was away on holiday at the time. Yet she continued to send the widow (whom she disliked) a Christmas card because 'I want her to feel that the family is behind her, and that in a disaster she should not feel forgotten'.

So tacit conventions exist about how physical factors should govern attendance of kin at funerals, and the size and composition of the kin gathering tend to be governed by such conventions.

But there are other funeral conventions of a more overt social kind. For the most part, it seemed to be agreed that children should not be expected to attend funerals. One woman said that her mother never made her go to funerals and even at the age of sixteen she didn't attend her own father's funeral. Yet there was an opinion that a child should learn about death and the way in which people leave the society of which they were members. This view was trenchantly put forward by one informant. She took her son to the funerals of her second husband's mother and mother's sister 'to see what a funeral's like'. She held that it was important that children should go to funerals. In the (Jewish) funeral of the Ghent family it was specifically noted that, though the children did not attend the actual burial of their grandfather, they came to the house for the prayers afterwards. This whole issue of children's participation in funerals is clearly a debatable one, and raises some interesting questions of social learning.[12]

We found also a conventional view among some people that women should not attend funerals. We met this opinion in three

[12] The issue was regarded as sufficiently interesting by the *New York Post* (14 May 1964) to merit an article in their Human Relations section 'Children and Funerals' by Dr Rose N. Frankblau. She made the pertinent point, ignored apparently by our North London informants, that children should be *asked* if they wish to attend the funeral service. The idea of adults 'taking' children illustrates the moral imperative which is commonly believed to attach to funeral participation by kin.

forms: personally idiosyncratic, rather vaguely held; local, that this used to be so especially in Scotland; and religious, that it is a Jewish practice. None of these views was widespread.

The idiosyncratic opinion was expressed by Mr Gibbon as 'funerals are more of a men's affair – women don't go to them much'. A variant of this was expressed by a woman who justified her non-attendance at the funeral of her MBW (who committed suicide) by saying, 'I think it's mainly because very few women go to funerals nowadays'. She also justified her attendance at her mother's brother's funeral by saying that she went because she knew of one other woman who was going – she didn't want to be the only woman there. As for local views, we were told by one woman that it used to be the custom in Scotland for women not to attend funerals – though our informant stated that a couple of years before this she herself had attended her brother's wife's funeral. Mrs Mitchie stated that she did not attend her first husband's funeral 'because in Scotland women do not attend funerals'. These views may well have a great deal of truth, but we were not able to pursue them.

With Jewish funerals, however, the evidence was much clearer. A general view was expressed by one of our informants that it is a tradition among Jewish families to go to funerals, but that tradition also restricts this role to the males of the family. A woman said flatly 'Women do not attend Jewish burials'. The conventional role of women kin in Jewry when a death occurs is to go to the house of close kin if it is thought that moral support is needed. Orthodox Jewry apparently thought it too upsetting for women to attend the actual burial. But there are usually prayers at the home after the funeral, and these the women attend; they also usually go to the grave afterwards. But as Jews know well, and as it was explained to us by informants, this funeral restriction is nowadays a custom only of orthodox Jews; it is not the case with Jews who belong to Reform or Liberal congregations

In the light of these opinions it is interesting to see just what was the distribution of men and women kin in the 55 funerals we took for examination in kin terms. So far from bearing out this view of masculine support, the average number of 9 kin present was divided in the proportion of five women to four men. In only one of the 55 funerals was no kinswoman present at all, whereas there were three funerals at which no kinsman was present. In two of these cases the dead person was a woman, but in the other it was the father of our informant, whose funeral was attended by his wife, two daughters and his niece. (This was a small affair, with no announcement, though close friends wrote to the daughter letters of sympathy, and after the formal ceremony the guests went to her sister's for tea.) It could be argued, of course, that the predominance of women in the overall figures is linked with the rather greater number of funerals of women. But do men tend to be in the majority at funerals of their own sex? This too is not borne out by the figures, at least as far as kin attendance goes. At approximately half the funerals of women, the majority of kin mourners were women; but there were twice as many funerals of men where female kin mourners were in the majority as there were funerals of men where male kin mourners were in the majority. So, in the general field of kin mourning, it is a myth that funerals are the affairs of men, and that women do not attend. Of course it is possible that among the friends, and especially the business associates, of the dead person, men may tend to predominate – though even here many wives apparently attend also.

It is interesting to note in particularly the actual practice of the Jewish families in our field of study.

Mrs Garson, a Jewish woman who had married out of her faith still adhered to the traditional custom; when her mother's brother's wife died she went to his house to keep him company, but when he himself died, she did not attend his funeral. (But she had attended, with her Anglican husband, memorial services of her MB, MZH, MBDHF and FMZH – a wide range of kin.) The Regan husband and wife regarded themselves as Liberal Jews but 'very unreligious'; but when Mrs Regan's father died about ten years ago neither she nor her mother attended the funeral. Only male relatives and friends went – 'I'm sure there must be a reason, religious I suppose', said she, with what an orthodox Jew would regard as infuriating vagueness. But when her husband's mother died a few years later she did attend, because lots of other women did too – the funeral service was conducted in a Liberal synagogue. In another case, where the husband's family was said to be orthodox, but the wife's family not so, the wife had attended the funerals of her mother's mother and father's brother; and mother's father's memorial service. Another husband and wife were both of Liberal views, and the wife had attended the funerals of her brother, her sister and her sister's husband in the last five years. Asked if she always went to funerals of relations she said 'It depends how closely connected we are'. For brother, sisters and first cousins, 'We should go to these, of course. It is not a thing you enjoy but with them it's a different matter'. She did say, however, that her husband attended more funerals than she did. In general, then, with the middle-class Jews in our field of study, for the most part having left the strict Orthodox tradition behind them, the notion that women did not attend funerals was a piece of traditional lore, by which they themselves did not necessarily abide.

What is of interest in this situation is the creation of a new custom, serving to test in some respects the strength of kin ties. If attendance at a funeral were simply an onerous obligation, with no compensating social satisfactions, then there is no reason why Liberal Jewish women should present themselves at such a potentially painful scene. But though forbidden by the stricter tenets of their religion, they clearly find some easement in attending personally to pay their last respects to their dead kin and to give some support to the living.

It may be thought that if it be a Jewish tradition for kin to attend funerals, and if the bar on the participation of women be removed, Jewish funerals of modern type are likely to have a larger kin participation than funerals of people of other religions. Our material is too sparse to allow of generalization. But it may be pointed out that of the four Jewish funerals for which we have kin details, three were attended by 15, 16 and 24 kin respectively, numbers which were well on the high side of the average. But the highest figure, 24 kin, was exceeded by the kin attendance figures for at least three other funerals, all Church of England.[13]

The Jewish funeral at which the largest kin attendance was recorded was interesting in several ways. It was the funeral of Mrs Ghent's father, a man who, like her mother, had been nominally orthodox but had discontinued the ritual practice. The Ghents, though regarding themselves as Jewish, did not belong to any synagogue and considered themselves to be 'non-practising'. The wife remarked 'I can't say I have any real religion. I don't go to a synagogue unless I'm invited for weddings or *barmitzvahs* – we're not anything, you can't even call us Liberals. We (she and her siblings) weren't really brought up like that. But although they (her parents) weren't religious, they liked to feel they belonged to the religion and the community and the synagogue; and tried to bring us up that way. We went to classes, Hebrew, but none of us seemed to take it seriously.' (Her siblings were later connected with a Liberal synagogue, primarily for the sake of their children, whose *barmitzvahs* took place there. Mr and Mrs Ghent had no children.) Yet to the funeral of the wife's father came a large number of people, and about 50 came to the house afterwards. Those at the funeral included three siblings of the wife, with two of their spouses and a son; three of her father's sisters, with two of their husbands; a FZS and FZD, each with spouse; three brother's sons of her father with two of their wives; and a father's half-brother's daughter with her husband. In addition, two nephews and a niece of the wife, a cousin (her MBS)

[13] But kin attendance figures for both the largest Jewish and largest Church of England funeral were for wife's kin only.

and two sons of another cousin (FBSS), who had not gone to the funeral, attended the prayers at the house. To the house also came a brother of the wife, who had been ill and so did not go to the funeral. 'He came on a quieter night, not on the biggest night. I thought it very sweet of him to come.' Now here was a case where religion provided forms of procedure for some people who in ordinary life had largely abandoned them, and in so doing the religion gave a rallying point for kin assembly. The wife remarked in this regard, 'More often you see relatives at funerals than at any other occasions'. Yet the composition of the kin assembly was significant. Although relatively large, it was still of fairly limited scope, being restricted almost entirely to siblings and children of the deceased, and the descendants of the siblings, all with spouses. It may be noted that its range was definitely less wide than that of the comparable non-Jewish funeral already mentioned.

Two related but somewhat contrasting principles have been indicated in this material on kin participation in funerals. One is that of conceptual solidarity marked by a personal symbol, or by representation. When actual presence at a funeral is not thought feasible or convenient, sending a wreath or a bunch of flowers is a kind of measure of second-grade participation. A woman who said she did feel an obligation to go to funerals and weddings had attended the funerals of her husband's mother and father, her own father and her husband's sister. But she and her husband did not go to the funerals of either her HMB or her HFFZ, though both of these were as close as Brighton; they 'sent flowers' instead.

But another method of indirect participation is by being 'represented' by another person. 'Representation' is a highly developed convention in official circles, as may be seen by funerals of people in public life. But this convention exists also at an unofficial level in our middle-class field. We have already given examples of this for weddings (p. 232) and the same principle operates for funerals. In a funeral described as a 'small family affair', a brother's son of the dead man 'represented the people from Northampton' who were recognized as not being able to travel to London for this occasion. In another case a woman specifically represented a man. A dead woman's brother was abroad, so his son's wife represented him at the funeral.

The other principle is that of personal support by physical attendance.

A common theoretical argument is that attendance of kin at a funeral gives support to the bereaved and makes them feel part of a group. This is probably true in a general sense. Yet the principle of representation, of symbolic attendance, is given validity; it is conceptual rather than physical solidarity which is emphasized. Moreover, the presence of specific kin may not add any particular weight if the bereaved person is not in a condition to perceive clearly who has attended. Sometimes he or she obviously does. But an elderly man who had lost his wife only six months before our enquiry had been in some distress and did not remember the details of who came beyond the fact that some of his wife's kin were there – some nieces and nephews he thought. One may infer from this, perhaps, that the *bereaved* are comforted by the presence of *close kin* at the time, and derive their sense of support from this and from the general gathering, whereas it is the *other kin* who obtain a sense of solidarity and a reinforcement of kin relations by noticing in detail whom of their number attend.

This point of view is strengthened by considering a further aspect of funeral attendance which was emphasized by a number of our informants – the opportunity it gave them for renewing kin contacts. Many of them said they 'saw' certain relatives only at funerals. Of a father's brother and family a woman said that there was no ordinary contact – 'they don't even congratulate us when we have a new baby'; but they were last 'seen' at her father's funeral. A man said of funerals 'the only time we have a get-together'.

With this renewal of kin contact was linked the custom of taking refreshment together after the funeral. Various accounts of funerals mention 'a little gathering after' in the form of 'tea', 'a meal at the house', a 'luncheon' at a hotel, a 'small meal' afterwards. This was thought by most informants to have traditional form.[14] But clearly for some of our informants, especially those with rural or North Country backgrounds, funerals were occasions of celebration and reinforcement of kin ties, once the formal rites of committal were ended. One statement pointed out explicitly how 'When you die up in Sheffield, everybody comes'. At a funeral of a father's sister many kin attended and, remarkably, everyone knew exactly in which order to go in. After the funeral all returned to the house of the dead woman for a meal. 'We enjoyed the party and meeting each other again.' Another opinion was, 'My husband has a theory that funerals always become cheerful and turn into real parties. I think he's right; certainly they are always a great time for getting together and meeting the family.'

[14] According to Mr. Woollcombe, the custom in farming families in East Anglia and Lincolnshire was to have a formal reading of the will of the deceased in the presence of relatives, farmhands and friends, and then to have a funeral dinner. In Yorkshire, according to the same informant, it was very different – the deceased was 'buried with ham' in a sumptuous meal with lots of alcohol. However idealized or dramatized be these pictures, they may well correspond to former local customs.

One is not entitled to conclude that such statements represent general patterns of behaviour: the contrast with the many 'small funerals' of a 'quiet' nature alone is proof of this. Nor can one conclude that some families of our sample were unfeeling about the death of their members. The relative age of the dead person is obviously one important factor, and his or her closeness of kinship. But manifest here are elements in the funeral situation – of catharsis, of reintegrative function of assembly – which, latent in many such situations, tend to come to the surface especially in large gatherings. Of particular interest is that these statements about funerals bringing relatives or 'the family' together refer only to the kin and not to friends. Friends, the implication is, need no such stimulus to come together – they seek their own occasions. But to bring kin together an *obligatory* social occasion is needed. Such an obligatory occasion is provided by a crisis of life, especially a wedding or a funeral. And though the one is a time of rejoicing and the other a time of sorrow, in social terms they have to some degree a common function. Both, by the contraints they are held to impose, recognize the uniqueness and value of the kin tie.

But this is only a general conclusion, the working of social process at a very broad level. At a more specifically operational level there is much variation in conduct, in the extent to which these kin constraints are held to be binding.

KIN GATHERINGS ON OTHER PERSONAL OCCASIONS

Personal occasions for kin gatherings so far discussed have involved some degree of ritualization, at least in their traditional form. Baptism, circumcision, marriage, funeral in our North London area are all still overwhelmingly religiously oriented – although in attenuated form they may be carried out in secular context. Ritual sanctions may therefore bring some kin to attend. But there are other personal occasions which are entirely social in character, completely devoid of any religious associations. These include the celebration of 'silver', 'golden' or 'diamond' weddings (25, 50 and 60 years married); a son's or daughter's 21st birthday, or a senior relative's three score and ten; engagement to marry; departure to or arrival from a foreign country. But no significant differences in kin participation appear between these kinds of occasions and the more ritualized crises already described. From consideration of about 25 such gatherings for which we have record, kin patterns similar to those we have already described emerge. For birthdays and 'silver' and 'golden' wedding celebrations the simpler gatherings comprised parents, siblings and their children, with possibly a cousin as well, and usually only kin present. At times the kin emphasis may take on an exclusive form. In one case four birthday parties were recorded as having taken place from 1959 to 1961: of our informant's mother and father (80th) and her sister's daughter and son (21st). In each case those participating were much the same: our informant's father and mother, her three sisters with husband or child each, and a MZD and her family. This was clearly a tightly knit family of parents and daughters. At one of the celebrations a family photograph was taken and at the back stood the husband of one of the sisters. 'We were annoyed' said our informant, – 'he is not the family, well not strictly, that is.'

Larger gatherings took in a wider kin range, and included guests who were not kin. One of the largest of which we have record was an engagement party for the daughter of the house, during the period of our study, when over 200 people attended. They included many kin, including the girl's mother's siblings from Vienna and Paris, and a MMFBSS – second cousin once removed – who happened to be in England.

Celebrations to mark arrival of kin from or departure to a foreign country seem to have attracted fairly extensive gatherings – up to about 15 kin in some cases, with friends in addition. But the range of kin involved was not great, rarely going beyond first cousins, and then nearly always limited to their spouses or children. Illustrative of these gatherings was a 'welcome home' party given by Mrs Offord for her mother and mother's sister when they returned from America. The kin comprised: mother, mother's sister and this woman's daughter, and her daughter's two sons (one with girlfriend); MB with his wife and son; and FZS and his wife. Also came a MBW, FZD and FZDD. Invited, but unable to come, were another mother's brother, and another FZD with her husband and son. A comparable party was given for our informant when she returned from America. (It is interesting to note that with this married couple, the husband being Anglican and the wife Jewish, there was no family gathering at Christmas, nor did the husband's family appear to have any other type of family gathering.)

SEASONAL GATHERINGS OF KIN

Conventional seasonal holidays, especially the 'holy days' of traditional Judaism or Christianity, tend to be associated particularly with kin gatherings. This is so partly because of the overt linkage between these religions and the cohesion and values of family life, and partly because the pause in ordinary work allows of the visiting of kin rather more easily than on other occasions. Even medical men with demanding hospital ward duties – of whom there were several in our sample – usually found time on Christmas Day, after they had carved the turkey for the patients' Christmas dinner, to attend a family party that evening or the following day.

On kin behaviour at religious seasons such as Easter or Passover, or the more secular festivals such as New Year, our collection of material was not very systematic. But our impression is that our subjects made little of these occasions for extra-familial kin gatherings, however much they may have focussed upon them as occasions for intra-familial celebrations. In one pattern Mrs Willmott gave the children in care of her father to take them off to spend Easter with their grandparents on a farm in Northumberland, while she stayed behind to look after her husband, who had to work. Another pattern was a kin gathering at our informant's own home. Mrs Savage and her conjugal family, her mother, her mother's sister and her brother and his family all assembled – giving 'the feeling of a large party'. With the Newells small informal family gatherings were held at the Easter weekend – Sunday lunch with a FBS and FBD of the wife's, with their spouses – 'switching around a bit' in a reciprocal arrangement. Passover seemed to have been celebrated correspondingly by the Jewish families. In a family of relatively orthodox Jews, the husband's father, a widower, usually came to stay for the festivals. In a mixed marriage, Mr and Mrs Waverley celebrated Passover at the house of his parents, having been 'bludgeoned' or 'blackmailed' into so doing by them. In the Arden family, where the wife was a convert to (Liberal) Judaism, though neither she nor her husband recognized Passover, she said that she knew that her husband's father and stepmother would have liked to invite them, but that she and Mr Arden couldn't stand the necessary abstention from smoking which acceptance would entail! (Tobacco can be a source of irritation socially as well as physically!)

The coming of the calendrical New Year was celebrated as a kin festival by few of our North London subjects. But unlike the official English New Year, the Jewish New Year is a rotating date, being fixed according to a lunar calendar. It also tends to have more ritual significance. In one orthodox household, 'the bits of the family that are in London do come together'. The husband, wife and two children went on Friday to the WMZ, and there met cousins of the husband. On Sunday the husband and wife took the children over to the WMZ in the day and invited the husband's cousins (his FFBD and her husband) for the evening. Even Mr Waverley and his wife, non-practising Jews, agnostic, with his brother and brother's wife, paid a visit to his parents at the Jewish New Year. 'It's the only occasion the six of us do meet.'

The most regular of all seasonal occasions for kin gatherings is undoubtedly Christmas. It is well recognized in England that Christmas is not just for Christians, and that for many middle-class people of various religious persuasions it is a prime occasion for social celebration. Where in these celebrations do kin ties enter?

Of the 90 households in our study 68, or rather more than two-thirds, regularly and purposely had kin relations outside the household over the Christmas season. Of the remainder, nine were Jewish or part-Jewish households in which the religious associations of Christmas were not taken to be relevant; some of these, as already described, celebrated religious festivals of their own at other times. Two other households were said specifically not to have had any extra-familial kin gatherings at this time, though they probably celebrated the season domestically; in one of these the husband, Mr Goodwin, gloomily remarked, 'We don't meet as a family except for funerals'. For the remainder no information is available.

Doubtless for a good proportion of those who keep Christmas as a form of family or kin gathering the religious significance of the festival is considerable; some signalize this by church-going. But it is generally accepted that Christmas is a social and not purely a religious occasion, and is associated with gifts to children and other recognition of family ties. Hence it is not altogether surprising to find among our cases a few in which Jews celebrate Christmas. We are not referring to simple instances of recognition of a public holiday, as where a Jewish husband and wife usually went away for a rest at that time; or where a Jewish doctor and his agnostic (Christian) wife did not keep a traditional Christmas but did drive over to his brother's house on Christmas Day to 'dump the presents'. Instances of real celebration were of the following calibre. A husband and wife, Liberal Jews both, went on Christmas Eve to his MMBD for a cocktail party, at which they saw her husband and son too, then had his parents to stay over the holidays. The wife's mother was not asked to come because she and the husband had quarrelled, and she resented this lack of invitation. 'Last Christmas I believe Mother went away; that was a bit of luck!' Still, she was to be invited the following year; the wife had hopes of an amiable party but was nervous. In a case where the wife was a convert to Judaism and the husband's family orthodox Jews, the husband's mother held a small family gathering before Christmas, attended by the husband and wife, and his brother and family. In still another instance Mr and Mrs Ghent, both Jewish though not practising, had a Christmas party of the wife's sister and her husband, wife's father's half-brother's daughter and her husband and son, wife's father's sister and two friends. The wife's aunt was invited specifically because 'she was always on her own' – an example of that integrative kin spirit common to Jews and Christians at such a time. (Note that this couple distinguished family gatherings from social gatherings of friends by saying that one could see relatives far more informally.)

The same acceptance of Christmas as a social occasion for recognition of kin ties was seen in some households of Christian background overtly professing themselves agnostic, atheist or non-religious. Various couples had the husband's parents; the husband's mother; the wife's parents; the wife's brother in to Christmas dinner or to spend the day or the period with them. The Maskells, atheists, were fully occupied on Christmas Day with the husband's professional work. But 'Boxing Day is our Christmas Day'. The husband's mother and sister came in, and the husband's father if he was in England; formerly the wife's mother and sister with husband and daughter also came. Other kin were also involved in a sharing arrangement, in reciprocal fashion. A mother's sister of Mrs Maskell gave a tea and then a theatre party, primarily for the children of the kin set, to include her husband, her two daughters with the two daughters of one and the husband and nine children of the other; her two step-sons with wives and three children of one of them; and our informants and their son. Another daughter of the mother's sister didn't come – she was not on speaking terms with her mother, and the daughter of our informant didn't attend for more personal reasons. But even then the party numbered 26 people (Fig. 9). A cocktail party given by one of the daughters of our informant's aunt was probably even larger since it included many of the same kin and other more distant relatives, such as some of his aunt's second husband's son's wife's kin.

The basic sociological function of Christmas gatherings, as of Christmas presents, is undoubtedly integrative. This is epitomized by a case in which when the wife's mother was alive Christmas was usually spent with her; all her children used to come, and it was one of the main occasions on which our informant's husband met members of his wife's family. (In those spacious times, before the War, 14 persons used to sit down to dinner. 'It was very nice. There were four maids and all six children.')

But much variety obviously exists in the amount and quality of Christmas performance as in the style of presents given or exchanged. The two main variations on which we wish to focus are the character of the contact between kin at this season and the range of kin involved.

Substantial differences of behaviour and subtle nuances of estimation lie in whether kin are invited to share Christmas Dinner, come to tea or supper, or stay the night. But ignoring this aspect of hospitality, a major difference of sociological interest is in whether people go to kin or have kin in to their homes for these events.

To a very considerable extent this is a function of family stage. Young people, when first married, tend to go to the parents of either – but oftener the wife's parents – to spend Christmas Day or some other part of the festive season. The decision as to which couple of parents (or surviving parent) to go to may sometimes pose an

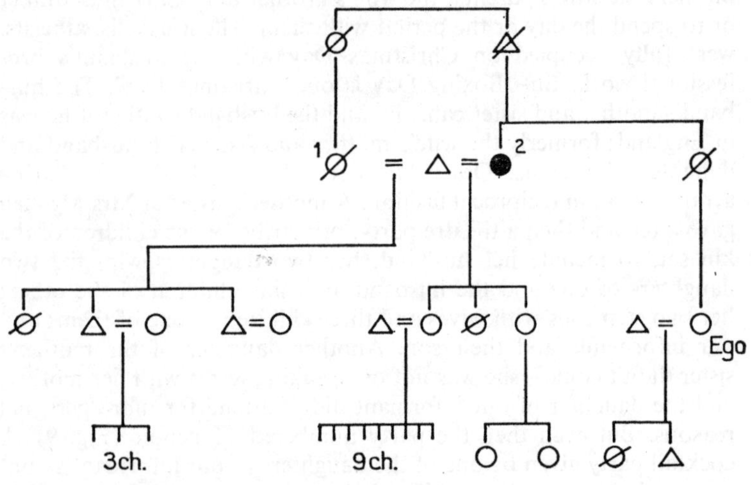

FIGURE 9. A Christmas Party

awkward problem. Mrs Gilroy said that formerly she and her husband went to her parents in Cornwall for Christmas; once they had small children they stayed at home. This solved a problem of choice between her own and her husband's parents; the arrival of children provided an excuse for not having to decide! Now, her mother invited her father's mother and sisters, who lived close, while the husband's parents had his brother for Christmas. This then is the second stage – when with young children the married couple either have a small family Christmas at home or as an alternative invite either one or both couple of their parents to come to them.

A third stage is reached when the parents of the married pair grow older and less able to provide entertainment or even less able to travel, and when the children of the married pair grow up, and become more mobile. Then a tendency is for the married pair with their children to visit one or both sets of their parents. Variants may occur at any stage with the death of one or other of the parents of the married couple. For this or reasons such as distance apart, an asymmetrical pattern of Christmas visiting tends to develop, as time goes on – at least as far as husband's and wife's parents are concerned. The situation is complicated by relations with siblings, by the growing independence of the children of the married pair, and by elements such as the need to care for aged aunts. But stage-patterns of this kind can be discerned in the Christmas arrangements of many of our subjects.

Overall, in our sample, of those who kept Christmas, households whose members stayed at home and had kin to visit them were about twice as many as those who went out to visit kin. This conforms to the situation of a good proportion of our subjects, who were in the family stage of having at least one dependent child. But there were a few cases in which reciprocal visiting took place.

In particular, the situation is changed by the death of a parent, especially if he or she has been widowed earlier. This often has a disintegrative effect on family assembly at Christmas, or makes for a re-orientation of relationships. It is part of the cycle of family development. Illustrative of this change in pattern were the Fortescue couple who used to spend part of Christmas in Norfolk when the wife's parents were alive, and who had the husband's father at their house when he was alive. For the last two years after their deaths, however, the Christmas guests had been the wife's FMZS and his wife, and the wife's mother's sister – the latter women being godmothers to the Fortescue children. This obviously involved a radical readjustment of domestic patterns in housekeeping, as well as a quite new human environment for the children at this time. In the Lark case 'Christmas would rotate' when the wife's mother was alive, between our informant's home and that of her brother; one year they would all spend Christmas with him and the mother would come to her daughter for New Year, while the next time the opposite would occur. 'Now all this is a bit in abeyance since she died.'

Widowhood presents special problems, but Christmas is a time above all when children try and secure that the solitary parent should not be left alone. When both husband and wife have a widowed parent some careful balance may be necessary. Both Mrs

March's mother and her husband's mother came for Christmas. The husband's mother went back to her own house in Highgate at the end of the day, while the wife's mother, who lived further away, stayed the night with her daughter. The decision often does not rest with the widowed person, but with kin. An elderly man, recently widowed, said to our interviewer a few days before Christmas 'I don't know what I'll do. No one's said anything about Christmas yet.' Would he go to his son's home? 'They generally have people over, or go over there' (to friends). But he thought he would probably hear from his son, and be invited over; he did not seem concerned about it and seemed to assume he would not be left alone. In fact, his confidence was fully justified; he did go over to his son's place on Christmas Day, to find his son, son's wife and child, two friends, a friend of his grandchild, and the brother of his son's wife, with wife and two children. The brother took the old man home by car since they lived near him. A great deal of forethought is apt to go into such arrangements made for elderly kin at Christmas.

The range of kin involved in Christmas hospitality shows considerable variation. We have not thought it necessary to list in total the actual numbers of kin concerned, but rather to consider the relative frequency of types of kin. The details are approximate, if only because people's memory of their Christmas entertaining was not always complete. But a rough index to kin participation can be constructed by listing the types of consanguine kin concerned in any one case (omitting their spouses and children) and counting the number of cases in which each type is found. This '*kin participation index*' gives the following results for the Christmas season, assuming some degree of continuity over the period of the few years before our enquiry was made.

TABLE 30

Types of kin involved at Chrismas Season (apart from spouses and children)

Wife's parents	23%	Wife's uncles and aunts	9%	
Wife's siblings	27%	Wife's other kin	11%	
		Total wife's kin		70%
Husband's parents	13%	Husband's uncles and aunts	1%	
Husband's siblings	12%			
		Husband's other kin	4%	
		Total husband's kin		30%
Total parents and Siblings	75%	Total uncles, etc.	25%	
		All		100%

Two facts are clear from this Table. In proportion of types of kin (not actual numbers) parents and siblings (with their spouses and children) form by far the greatest sector of Christmas guests among kin. Also, wife's kin rather than husband's kin have pride of place on this occasion. In addition, we have recorded a few cases where children (adult, mostly married) come to their parents' home for Christmas. This still further strengthens the conclusion that outside the conjugal families of parents and children in our sample, it is the members of the natal families of husband and wife, particularly of the wife, who constitute the major type of kin guest at the Christmas season. To put it crudely, Christmas in this respect can be looked at as a recapitulation of the childhood scene, especially of a woman's childhood scene.

But to regard it in this light is to overlook many of the nuances of the situation. Although the types of other kin involved are relatively few and the genealogical range is quite narrow, they are not insignificant, but form about a quarter of the total kin types involved. Moreover, they are not alternative to parents and siblings as guests, but additional. One implication here is that to some extent the members of the natal family are the 'obligatory' guests, and the other kin are the voluntary choice of the hosts. They represent the kinship spirit at large, so to speak, at the Christmas season, and operating freely and selectively they include uncles, aunts, first cousins and the spouses and children of all these, and a few more remote kin. (One of our households had a MBDD of the husband from New Zealand staying; this Christmas dinner had 17 or 18 people, about as much as the wife could manage!) Moreover, there is one important structural factor restricting kin participation at Christmas festivities which is lacking for participation in weddings and other such personal gatherings – Christmas is a general feast and so there may be immediate competition from the other kin ties of the people in question. Unless there is to be a continuous round of visits, people must select which visits they can conveniently make, and even so there may be some clash. For instance, to the house of one of our informants at Christmas there normally came her mother's brother, with his wife and son. But for one Christmas he did not come because of a competing claim – he had to go with his wife to her mother's place instead. Of necessity, then, Christmas tends to be a narrow-range kin gathering, and what is notable is the considerable body of extra-familial kin who do assemble for the occasion.

One final point must be made. Christmas tends to be a compulsive season in the sense that in general there is an obligation felt to celebrate it and to entertain in so doing. 'To have someone' for

Christmas is regarded as nearly essential by many families. To this may be added the appeal of 'being sorry' for people. It is a well-recognized principle that an acquaintance or friend should not be left solitary on Christmas Day, and a considerable amount of hospitality to 'lame ducks' is in fact given in response to this convention. Such a principle is applied even more strongly to kin. Aged aunts, distant cousins from the Commonwealth, affines who would not ordinarily be a matter of concern are likely to be incorporated into a Christmas gathering. This is one of the few occasions when the conventions of hospitality and the conventions of kin obligation coincide.

A brief review of the function of these various kinds of kin gatherings, and of the differences in the way they are treated, brings out the peculiar character of the kin tie, as understood by our informants. This is the quality of *obligation* which it carries: obligation to 'have to stay' at Christmas, to 'go' to a wedding or funeral, etc. It may be significant that the terms used in such contexts tend to be simple Anglo-Saxon words, suggesting a long ancestry in custom.

The obligation to attend such a gathering is sometimes linked with performance of a specific role for which a kinsman or kinswoman is regarded as peculiarly appropriate. At a wedding a bride's father is the 'correct' person to 'give her away', while her sister is a most suitable bridesmaid or matron of honour; similarly a groom's brother is a very proper 'best man' to him. It must be noted that these roles are all sex-specific: the bride must be given away by a man, not a woman, and can have a female but not a male attendant of her own generation. (Page boys are permitted to her, but they must be of a junior generation, equivalent to her 'flower-girls'; siblings' children often fill these roles.) Close kin are often invited to be 'witnesses' and to sign the marriage register, thus validating the union of the young couple. The bride's mother, usually without formal role except that of witness, has normally the very important role of organizing the wedding hospitality.

But for most kin the obligation to attend such a kin gathering is independent of the allocation of any special roles to be performed; much of their function is simply to *be there*. It is probably for this reason that in complex modern urban conditions the obligation is so unequally regarded, and that so much personal discretion is used in complying with it. The 'being there' means, on the part of a kinsman, that he identifies to some degree with the proceedings and the principal participants. Though he is not called on for special duties he is not simply a spectator; he is a participant. As such, his presence lends social weight to the proceedings, and may be thought therefore to contribute support to the principal participants, by paying in effect a tribute to their status. So much is regular sociological interpretation. It is on this kind of basis, presumably, that one would explain the behaviour of a man who attended a mother's sister's funeral, 'in spite of hating her guts', as it was reported. An explanation of the very frequent presence of affines at these gatherings is presumably also in analogous terms: by attendance at a wedding or funeral a husband or wife demonstrates solidarity with the spouse and the spouse's kin.

But the attendance may well be as much in the interest of the kinsman who attends as of him who is attended. We are not referring here to the claims of reciprocity, which may well mean that a defaulter in time pays for his failure to appear by lack of support for his own celebrations. There is another aspect of the matter which may be equally significant for the person concerned. His own status may be involved – failure to attend a kin gathering may be interpreted by others as an indication that he has been disregarded in the inviting or the dissemination of information about the forthcoming event. Moreover, in an allied sense, it affects his notions of incorporation into the social milieu. As one of our informants, a single woman, put it – going to family gatherings 'gives me a feeling of belonging'. The question as to why people should want to belong to some of the sets of kin of which they were apt to be very critical raises still deeper psychological issues.

9

Kin Sets and Kin Groups

The last Chapter dealt with *assemblies* of kin for specific social occasions; in this Chapter we are concerned primarily with kin *units* of more regular nature. So far in this study we have given plenty of evidence for social linkage between kin, both individually and in sets of varying size. But a question which remains is the significance of such linkage in collective and relatively persistent terms. In English middle-class life are there, outside the elementary family, kin groups or linked sets of kin of any continuity, with any enduring quality in common aims, interests and activities of their members? Do the individuals of our sample in their ordinary life base any of their acts and opinions on relations with such bodies of kin, whose movements and views represent a collective expression with intellectual weight and emotional loading?

The problem of identifying, defining and describing such kin groups or other associations of kin is not easy.

One reason is that, in this study, the greater part of our material is drawn from the conceptions of single informants. It is their view of their kin world which is presented to us, and their interpretation may overstress or understress the degree of unity in social relations among their kin. But from the mass of detail of each informant's relations with his or her kin regularities in pattern can be picked out and behaviour can be checked against opinion. Given also the considerable amount of indirect evidence we have as to kin relations, what seem reasonable inferences can be made about the existence and operation of kin groups as about other aspects of the kin situation.

But another source of some difficulty in handling this problem of kin groups and other forms of kin association is the confusion which still obtains about the terminology used, by both anthropologists and by others, in the description of such kin entities. Terms such as 'extended family', 'kindred', 'kin network' have been freely used in the literature; because they have not always been given the same meaning it is hard to compare the various studies closely and to align our work with that of others in this field.

A third difficulty is the obscurity surrounding the relevant processes of group formation, including the applicability of the notion of patrilineal descent.

PATRILINEAL TRANSMISSION OF RIGHTS

A formal principle of organization of kin in the English social system is given by the practice of every person having at least two names, a first name or personal name (possibly several of these) and a surname or family name. The surname, transmitted to children from their father, is a convenient built-in device for allowing recognition of continuity over generations (in contrast to, say, a Muslim system which uses patronymic for a single generation only). But while the surname is a useful means of identification of people patrilineally, the transmission of right to a father's name does not necessarily imply the transmission of any other kinds of rights, at least outside the elementary family. Nor does it imply a consistent principle of recruitment to operational kin groups. So while we may speak of a *patrinominal frame* for kin recognition, any patrilineal units which may be identified may be structural units only on paper, mere genealogical entities. They may have little relevance for social action, and may not correspond at all to the operational units of the kinship system.

The English kinship system has adopted a unilineal principle of transmission of rights in three main spheres: transmission of family name; inheritance of entailed landed property; and succession to hereditary high office. The first is general; both of the others are operative in only very restricted sectors of the society. In each sphere the principle, basically patrilineal, has been subject to considerable modification. A maternal kinsman's surname is usually assumed by children born out of wedlock, and occasionally by someone who accepts this as a condition of inheriting property or who wishes to emphasize some other link with his mother's family. Landed property has not always been transmitted in the male line; it has sometimes been handed on to a daughter who was an only child or to some other issue through a female. The patrilineal rule of succession to high office has been waived in specific instances, for Royalty as well as for peers of the realm, in favour of issue through females.

It is appropriate then only to a very limited degree to speak of the English system as being characterized by 'patrilineal descent'.[1]

For some sectors of British society separable named kin units

[1] W. H. R. Rivers (*Social Organization*, London, 1924, p. 86) did use this term; though he pointed out that such usage is hardly customary in such case.

extending beyond the elementary family have been historically significant in social reckoning and social action. Great aristocratic families such as the Cavendishes, the Howards, the Percys, have been recognized for generations as major bodies of kin, primarily of patrilineal connection, though their boundaries have not been precisely defined. At a village level also rural families bearing the same name and living in the same place often seem to have been recognizable over several generations as social units of collective force.[2]

In our London field of study the basic kin unit was indubitably the elementary conjugal or marital family. For many contexts this had a specific location, the household, with which for practical purposes it was usually identified. The common surname was symbolic of the social unity of the family, and served also as a mark of identification. Outside the domestic circle, what other kin units were in operation?

OLD HIGHGATE FAMILIES

We expected to encounter neither the land-holding political units of the 'great family' type, nor the highly localized face-to-face groups of the rural family. The Estate of Greenbanks was of recent social formation, so no enduring kin groups were expected there. But we did think it likely that we should find examples of 'old families' in Highgate, since we already knew of a few descendants from men who were living in Highgate in the early part of last century. As it happened, only a single representative of one of these turned up in our sample. Male members of this family had occupied important commercial and professional positions in Highgate for at least one hundred years, had married into other Highgate families and were very well known locally. The question of how far they and their families still constituted a coherent kin group, and how far they might

[2] But the concept of rural families of long antiquity in the same village may be to some extent an 'ideal pattern', since rural mobility has often been considerable. We have tested out the conventional village stereotype in a West Dorset parish. An analysis of the enumerators' schedules for the parish of Thorncombe in the Census of 1851 gave about sixty surnames. A review of these in 1962 revealed that only fifteen of these names were then directly represented in the parish by descendants in the male line, and only another five could be identified as having descendants through a female line. Thus, only about one-third of the families of 1851 were recognized as still surviving in the parish just over a century later.

Kin groups of a fairly strong corporate character have been described for some other sectors of Western industrial society, e.g. W. E. Mitchell, 'Descent Groups among New York City Jews', *Jewish Journal of Sociology*, vol. 3, 1961, pp. 121–8; E. Leyton, 'Composite Descent Groups in Canada', *Man*, 1965, No. 98.

differ in this respect from other people in our sample was therefore of considerable interest to us.

Our informant, Mrs Danby, said that when a child she used to play a lot with her cousins, about eight of them, children of her mother's sisters, mother's brother and father's brothers. She had been bridesmaid to another mother's sister's daughter. All lived in Highgate and 'we went around to all the relatives' houses fairly frequently'. One of her mother's sisters, a mother's brother and a mother's brother's son actually lived with her parents and her at various periods before the War. In more recent years she had lost close touch with her mother's relatives, with whom she had little common interest. Even with her mother's brother in Highgate she had not been on formal visiting terms for over ten years. Christmas cards, however, were exchanged with many of these relatives. On her father's side the ties were closer. 'All the family in Highgate meet at a gathering at least once a year.' But this was not a regular family gathering arranged solely to meet relatives; it just happened that there had been quite a number of wedding anniversaries, christenings, birthday parties and funerals attended by herself, her father, one of her father's three brothers, her father's sister, one of her father's brother's daughters and this woman's husband, and a father's brother's son.

'The family' or 'immediate family' in this sense meant primarily a set of consanguineal kin with a common ancestor two generations back. The significant point about them were:

1 They were kin of her father, a widower.
2 They all lived in Highgate, where members of this patrinominal family had lived for several generations – since 1820, it was said.
3 Our informant's tie with them was of different qualities:
   a She was very much attached to her father, whom she saw daily;
   b She was much attached to her father's brother's daughter, whom she also saw daily, and this woman's husband, whom she saw about twice a week.
   c She liked to see her father's brother and father's sister, but 'I wouldn't go out of my way to see them . . . I feel I ought to see them'. So she did occasionally.
   d She saw her father's brother's son only occasionally or on 'family occasions' such as weddings or funerals.

This set of people can plausibly be described as a kin *group*. It was a set of closely related consanguines, with an independent existence, not simply focussed on any single member, such as our informant. Residence in the same neighbourhood was an important link, but not a determining factor in their association. Historically, the elder members of the group had a property interest in common – their father's and grandfather's business – but this was not a tie among the younger members. What they did share and what primarily kept them in social relationship was a common interest in one another's doings, a common sense of obligation towards people of the same near patrilineal ancestry.

Several points of significance stand out here, and apply to other cases of consanguine kin groups in this Highgate situation.

1 It was the *idea* of 'family' that provided the basis of their continued social relationship.
2 This idea was reinforced by early association through residence in the same neighbourhood.
3 Ties between members of the 'family' were selective; because of either distance or lack of common interest some members were much 'closer', i.e. in more active and frequent social relationship than others, who were nevertheless still classed as members of the 'family'.

From this, an important feature of such kin groups emerges – that they are not units of clear-cut boundary but are rather configurations of people in varying intensity of relationship.

Moreover, as we have already pointed out in Chapter 6, a person's intimate kin, with whom most intense social relationships are shared, may not necessarily be consanguine kin. The notion of 'family' may be widened to include certain affinal kin, or if consanguines only are reckoned as 'family' then 'family' are not necessarily the closest kin. In the Danby case just described (see Figure 10), co-existent

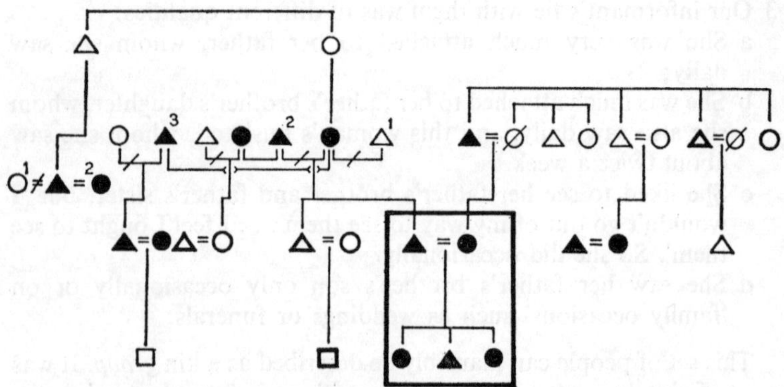

FIGURE 10. A Complex Collection of Intimate Kin
(Solid and heavy outline indicate degrees of intensity)

with strong ties with our informant's father and a FBD were very close relations with our informant's husband's father and this man's wife (stepmother of her husband) and also with her husband's mother; some more distant affines also were regarded as intimate.

All this bears on the concepts of 'extended family' and 'kin network' discussed later.

The only example in our sample of an 'old Highgate family' thus showed some solidary kin group characteristics, but not purely patrilineal and not of a very marked kind. What of other families without such local roots?

CONTRASTS IN KIN GROUPS

Here fairly highly integrated patterns of relationship among parents, siblings and their children sometimes occurred. In one outstanding example Mr Mitchie was an only child and he was described by his wife as not being a very family-minded person, knowing few of his relatives. In contrast, Mrs Mitchie had grown up surrounded by kin (see Figure 3). Her father, born in Scotland as one of a sibling group of four, was educated locally, worked on his father's farm after leaving school and was given his own farm by his father when he married. The wife's father's aim in turn was to give each of his children a farm of their own, and this he managed. The wife's mother was the daughter of a Scottish farmer also. The father was very anxious to see all his children well educated – even more his daughters than his sons because after all, he argued, the boys would farm whereas the girls would need a better education. (Two of the sons took university degrees in agriculture, however, while all three sisters went to university.) Farming and the professions, including schoolteaching, occupied many of the kin.

When Mrs Mitchie's two daughters were born the news was telephoned to her husband's parents, her parents, one of her sisters and five or six close friends. The general run of kin in Scotland were not notified separately because 'Father would put the news in his weekly letter' which circulated among all the siblings. Presents were received from Mrs Mitchie's two sisters, two brothers' wives, a FBW and FBD, while a brother and his wife sent a pram and a cot which had belonged to their last child. One daughter was given her mother's maiden name and the other her father's mother's maiden name.

Mrs Mitchie visited her parents twice a year (see p. 211); she usually wrote or telephoned to her father weekly. One of her brothers, a Member of Parliament, was seen eight or ten times a year, either visiting Highgate or when she, her husband and their children went and spent a weekend on his farm. Her eldest sister was a special favourite, and our informant, husband and children went to stay on her sister's farm three times a year at school half-term. The two sisters saw each other six or eight times a year and wrote or telephoned monthly. They formerly shared a house for some years. Mrs Mitchie said that there was no friend of hers of whom she was more fond than of her siblings. (But cf. Chapter 12, p. 426.)

She also had a special relation with certain other kin. Her father's brother's wife and daughter lived on a farm a few miles away from her parents. She was very fond of them and always saw them every time she went home, exchanged Christmas cards and received presents from them. Another FBD, again living a few miles away from her parents, was always seen when she went home and sent a Christmas card. Whereas she described her husband's kin as 'un-family' sort of people, viewing their relatives very objectively without warmth, hers were obviously seen with strong affective reaction and much contact was maintained with them.

Mrs Mitchie was very fond of her father and respected him greatly, feeling that she and all her siblings owed a great deal to him. Concerning her mother she was rather more critical. She thought her mother more stiff and rigid in her views, inclined to be a bit snobbish. She 'always got on with Father best – all girls do, I think.' The mother's father had been 'a big farmer', a great character, but the rest of her family weren't very successful, and as the mother was very keen on people getting on in the world this was perhaps the reason why her parents always had more contact with her father's than her mother's kin. Yet there was no rejection of the mother's kin. The mother's sister lived with Mrs Mitchie's parents until she died. Our informant felt responsible for her parents and thought all her siblings felt the same way.

This woman included her sisters and sisters' children also in her area of responsibility. When asked what arrangements would be made concerning her children if anything happened to her and her husband, she replied, 'I really don't know. We haven't made any legal arrangements. I would feel that my sisters would see that the right thing was done, but I haven't really thought about it.' She said she felt much less responsible towards her brothers and their children. Towards more distant kin she acknowledged no responsibility, feeling that if it were necessary it should be supplied by the State. Although seeming extremely fond of a number of her kin, she gave the impression that apart from her parents, whom she regretted not seeing more often, and possibly her sisters, she felt that twice a year was often enough for visiting and resented to some extent the claims made upon her. (Cf. Chapter 5, p. 142.) She said too that many of her relatives were very strict and censorious of kin who did not conform to their standards. Her father stood out in contrast to this. When she spoke of her 'family', she sometimes meant her conjugal family – just herself, husband and children – and sometimes her natal family – her parents and brothers and sisters – but she always talked about 'going home' to Scotland.

This is a case where the criteria of common activity and interests and multiple interaction clearly applied, and the group of parents, their children and grandchildren constituted a social unit which could be definitely regarded as a group. But there are two points to be noted. The situation was described from the point of view of our informant, and in our description, therefore, it is an ego-oriented group. Yet it seems fair to assume that a great deal of social interaction took place completely apart from Mrs Mitchie, as instanced by what we were told of the circulation of the father's weekly letter to all his children and his provision of farms for them. There were then nuclei of social activity in kin terms apart from the ideas and doings of our informant. Again, the level of social action among the members of the group was very uneven. Mrs Mitchie herself had been quite selective in her relationships. These had been particularly close with her two sisters, reasonably so with one brother and his wife and much less so with her other two brothers. Presumably her other siblings had roughly equivalent attitudes towards their parents and to one another. Structurally, this was a group of what may be called an extended family order (see Figure 3). Operationally, it was a kin unit with selective arrangements among the members, giving for each individual an inner and an outer circle of social relationships.

In the case just described the ties were clearly strong but selective and primarily between consanguineal kin. In a contrasting example (the March family, Figure 11) the ties were also strong but even more selective, and yet reached out to more distant kin, including affines. Mrs March's father had been a senior civil servant, Mr March's father a builder. Both wife and husband had a brother each. The wife's father was dead, her mother lived near the South Coast. The mother was seen once a month, letters were sent once or twice a week from both sides, and telephoning took place about once a fortnight. The mother came up to stay in London for a night or two quite often, and also spent Easter, Christmas and the basic summer holidays with the Marches. Mrs March sometimes went down to stay for a few days with her mother, and the three children also went in their holidays. The family very seldom went all together to stay with Mrs March's mother because there was not room enough to put them

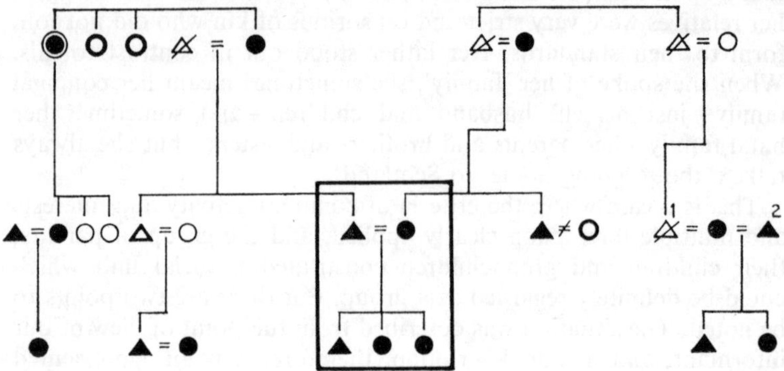

FIGURE 11. Ties with Distant Affines

all up, and it would have been tiring for her to have so many people descend on her at the same time. This was mainly why she came to spend so many of the holidays with the family, so that she would not have all the trouble of looking after and catering for so many people. Mrs March took especial care to see more of her mother because her father had died only recently and she didn't want her mother to feel too lonely. Christmas and birthday cards and presents were exchanged. Mr March's father was also dead, but his mother lived in Highgate and was seen by the family once or twice a week. The wife often dropped in to ask her mother-in-law if she wanted any shopping done or errands run, telephoned her about twice a week and took her to hospital for regular check-ups. Christmas and birthday cards and presents were exchanged. When children were born the elder daughter was given the wife's maiden name and the younger daughter the husband's mother's Christian name.

Mrs March had very close relations with her brother. This man had had a University education, including a period in Paris, began work as an antique dealer, then moved into insurance and banking, and finally became a teacher of languages in a Mediterranean country. Married, after a few years he separated from, then divorced, his wife. He had attended his sister's wedding and was godfather to one of her children. Letters were exchanged four or five times a year between him and his sister, and the family with Mrs March's mother all went out one Easter to spend the entire holiday with him. On his annual holiday he came to England. Christmas and birthday cards and presents were exchanged. Before he and his wife separated they had lived in Hampstead, and contact between them and the March family was much more frequent – once every two or three weeks.

The March family still maintained contact with the brother's divorced wife. This woman had visited her sister-in-law's family twice a year or so since the separation some years before, and always dropped in around Christmas time. If ever the Marches were in the West Country, where she worked, they called to see her, letters passed to and fro a couple of times a year and Christmas cards and presents were exchanged.

With Mr March's brother the affective relationship was rather different. He and his wife, living in the West Country, were seen about half-a-dozen times a year, usually in London. Mr March said rather curtly that these visits were more concerned with business matters than with wanting to meet each other. Letters and telephoning were purely on business and took place perhaps two or three times a year, depending on the situation. Christmas presents were exchanged, but it was recognized that there was no close emotional tie. Our informants were, however, quite fond of Mr March's brother's son and his wife, who also lived in the West Country. Christmas cards and presents were exchanged and they were seen about three times a year.

Other kin seemed to occupy a place in Mr March's field as much as did his brother. Three of his mother's sisters lived not very far away. They were seen perhaps rather formally about twice a year, and though no letters were exchanged Christmas cards were, and Mr March always gave his aunts quite large Christmas presents. One aunt (ringed in Fig. 11) had several daughters, but with only one and her husband and daughter was there a very close relationship. They were seen about eight times a year, telephoning took place every month or so, Christmas cards and presents were exchanged and the two families enjoyed meeting.

On Mrs March's side there was very uneven contact with her parents' siblings and their children – one father's brother with his wife and children had never been seen by our informants. He didn't get on well with Mrs March's father, and she didn't even know the names of his children, her own first cousins. Where a particularly close relationship did exist was with the former wife of one of the sons of another father's brother. This woman had married Mrs March's cousin, who died, and later she remarried. She and her second husband and their two children were seen at least once a year, and they came to stay for part of the summer holiday in a cottage owned by our informants. Letters were exchanged for Christmas and birthdays, and three or four times a year as well. They always exchanged postcards at holiday time and telephoning also occurred several times a year. Christmas and birthday presents passed to the children from both sides. This affinal tie rested in part on the recognition of early services. Said Mrs March about this woman, 'I am very friendly with her. When she was first married to my cousin, who was drowned young, I went up when I was twenty-one and I stayed there. I went once a year after that, and it was through a friend of theirs that I met my husband, and he is still a great friend of my husband's.' The tie between the two families seemed even closer because the former widow was godmother to Mrs March's youngest child, and Mrs March in turn was godmother to the woman's daughter. Mrs March felt that their regular and constant contact was helped by this fact.

The March case describes intimate relations with various kin outside the immediate family circle. But the configuration of relationships is very different from that described in the Mitchie case. From the structural point of view any extended family unit is here of a very incomplete kind. Husband and wife in this case had each only one parent and one sibling living, and only one of these siblings had children. Structurally, the kin in close relationship formed a very asymmetrical set – including the husband's first cousin and family, and the wife's first cousin's widow and second family, Unlike the situation in the Mitchie case, one cannot assume any particular social relationships between some of the components of the kin set concerned. As far as we know, Mr March's first cousin and Mrs March's first cousin's widow had no social contact whatsoever; they certainly did not form part of any unitary kin group. The close kin of our informants in operational terms were essentially ego-oriented. Selectivity occurred, not among a set of genealogically equivalent persons but among a set of genealogically assorted persons, some affines being preferred to most consanguines.

These cases have been cited extensively because, while not being precisely opposite poles in the kinship field, they do illustrate divergent ways of association with kin in group form.

TYPES OF KIN IN GROUP RELATIONS

We now enquire what is the position of our sample as a whole, what kinds of sets and groups of kin were to be found, and with what composition.

It must be emphasized again that at this point we are concerned with sets of kin in an operational sense. The groups we are looking for are not just structured arrangements of kin on a genealogical chart, but people related by kinship who meet, consult together, engage in common social activities, treat one another as part of the personal fabric of their lives. So from this point of view we have charted genealogically for each case in our sample the exact relationship to our informants – the members of the central elementary family – of all those persons who could be classed as intimate or 'close kin' in social terms. This definition was given primarily by the informants themselves in describing the activities they shared or were involved in, the services performed between them and the emotional attitudes they had towards these kin. It must be stressed that this intimacy or 'closeness', as our informants often described it, was not simply a matter of frequency of contact. There were kin – sometimes even a parent – with whom our informants were frequently in contact, but towards whom they had a somewhat 'distant' attitude – with reservations and lacking warmth.

We now summarize the results of this scrutiny of intimate kin from the point of view of what types of kin tended to form operational groups with the members of the elementary families of our sample.

Theoretically, one might expect to find that the wider operational kin group of the members of any conjugal family would be composed of all the members of the natal families of each member. So, for our informants and their children, this wider kin group would consist of the parents and siblings of the husband and the parents and siblings of the wife – the kind of group which might assemble at the christening of a new baby in the family, and which might continue to operate as a collective unit for many other social purposes. But against this in London society and generally in British society three factors militate. Demographic differences, in parents living or dead, siblings existent or not, make for differences in group structure; geographical dispersion for economic, educational and other reasons tends to prevent such regular functioning; and personal likes and dislikes tend to be sufficiently powerful to affect the way in which theoretical obligations are carried out.

In fact, theoretical structure and operational group just don't match. Out of the 30 Highgate cases *there was not one of the 'perfect' wider kin group*, with full complement of parents and siblings of both husband and wife, in intimate relationship with our elementary family.

In 2 Highgate cases only were all four parents – father and mother of husband and wife – reckoned as intimate kin of our informants. One of these, the Mitchie case already described, approximated on the wife's side fairly closely to the ideal pattern in that her siblings, aunt and cousins helped to compose the intimate kin group. On the husband's side, it is true, only his parents participated.

It might be put forward as an hypothesis that some degree of asymmetry in the formation of an intimate kin group is to be expected, that if the wife's relatives are strongly represented the husband's will be correspondingly lacking, and vice versa. There is some basis for this; individual cases show a kind of absorption of the elementary family in the kin of one side to the exclusion of the other. But as an overall pattern this is not borne out; in about half the cases the elementary family drew its intimate kin fairly equally from both husband's and wife's side. In the other case with all four parents as intimate kin no siblings were included. The husband insisted on an almost complete separation of his kin from his marital family; he had only formal relations with a half-sister and even with his own sister. The wife, who had no siblings, had her mother's sister and this woman's husband and daughter as part of her intimate kin group, and these people were also accepted by the husband.

Altogether there were 17 cases out of the 30 in Highgate in which at least one parent and at least one sibling of husband or wife figured in the set of intimate kin of the conjugal family; another 6 in which parents were prominent among the intimate kin, but no siblings were included; and another 5 cases in which siblings were prominent but no parents were included. To put this from another angle, in only 2 cases out of the 30 did the intimate kin of an elementary (conjugal) family of our informants contain neither a parent nor a sibling; in all the other 28 cases some member of the natal family of either the husband or the wife helped to form the set of intimate kin of the elementary family.

The material from Greenbanks gave a very similar picture.

Before proceeding, it is useful to outline the situation in these two exceptional Highgate cases. In one a primary reason for the sparse set of intimate kin was demographic circumstance. The husband had no traceable kin. Having been deserted by his parents in childhood he had been brought up by a friend of his mother's whom he had been taught to call his 'Aunt', to whom as to some of her relatives he was much attached; she was a quasi-kinswoman. He had a sister, but she had been lost to sight in childhood. Significant extra-familial relations were maintained for him by his wife. The wife's parents and only brother were dead; she had a very strong affective bond with her mother's sister, and with a cousin, the son of her mother's brother, She had never been very close to her own parents, even to her mother. She also had relations of some warmth with two other of her mother's sisters and with her dead brother's third wife and his child by his first wife. In these relations her husband shared, and kin ties were thus created for him. In the other case (Lander) the husband's mother was dead and he had been estranged from his father for over a decade, but his parents' sisters and the son of one of these were part of his intimate kin group. He had one brother, with whom he had quarrelled and whom he did not wish to see. The wife was out of sympathy with her parents, and also with her only brother, because she had become a convert to Catholicism. She still maintained relations of some strength with her father's sister, the widow of a father's brother, and her brother's wife, while she had a close and understanding relationship with one of her father's brothers. In both these cases, then, special circumstances were presumably responsible for the lack of members of the natal family in the intimate kin set.

But a very significant point has to be made as a corollary to this. Members of the natal family are a primary resource for building up an intimate group of kin, but they are not a resource used indiscriminately. A very high degree of selection goes on among them, presumably a kind of two-way process whereby each party exercises choice for a variety of reasons, including the attitudes of other kin. In the sample of 30 cases from Highgate there were only 5 cases in which every available parent or sibling had been included in the set of intimate kin of our informants. In 11 cases of the 30, one or other parent of husband or wife, though in theory available, was not included in the intimate kin category. In 7 of these cases one or more siblings had also not been included as well as in another 14 cases where no parents had been concerned. So, in two-thirds of the Highgate cases, one or more siblings had not been reckoned among a family's intimate kin.

It might be postulated that where parents were no longer alive to keep the children together, the body of siblings would tend to drift apart. The evidence does not seem to support this view. In the few cases where the parents of both husband and wife were either dead or divorced in our Highgate sample, the body of intimate kin seemed to utilize siblings neither more nor less than in those cases where parents were still alive and part of the intimate kin.

In this field the wives in our sample showed more disposition than did their husbands to create sets of intimates from their relatives. The 30 Highgate families showed a great range of intimate kin, from one person only reckoned in this category to 23 persons; the average was 7 per family. But whereas husbands had on the average just over 2 intimate kin, their wives had on the average 5 apiece. The mother–daughter relationship was clearly of considerable importance here; in over half the cases wives counted their mothers among their intimate kin. But to husbands their mothers were also very important, nearly half being among their intimate kin. But whereas more than half the wives included a sister or a brother among their intimate kin it was noticeable that the proportion of sibling intimacy was much less among the husbands of our sample. About a sixth of the wives in our sample, and about a third of the husbands had at least one brother or sister to whom they were indifferent, with whom social relations were minimal or lacking. This conclusion is reinforced by later data (Chapter 12).

When we turn to consideration of consanguine kin outside the natal families of husband and wife, it is noticeable how relatively little use was made of aunts and uncles, with the exception of mother's sisters, who were part of the intimate kin in about one-third of the 30 Highgate cases. Cousins did not appear a great deal among the intimate kin, but were not entirely lacking in the Highgate cases, even second cousins. Sometimes, as in the Arthur case, a cousin might be regarded as being as close as a brother or sister.

What was especially significant in this field was the important part played by relatives by marriage in helping to constitute some of the socially closest kin of a family. Husbands and wives of children, and of siblings, might be assumed to be drawn into the family's orbit by force of circumstances, though even here, as we have seen, selective arrangements were common, and by no means all such people were received with intimacy. But a whole range of people with whom there was much more discretion in the implementation of kin ties – spouses of aunts, cousins and even more distant kin, or siblings of step-parents – were included in the set of family intimates. (An example is given in Figure 11 and a more exotic one in Figure 10.) In total, in the 30 Highgate cases, more than half the total intimate kin of our informants were literally extra-familial – outside the natal families of husband and wife. They were either consanguines of a lateral order (cousins, parents' siblings) or affines of various degree (e.g. spouses of siblings of husband or wife or other kin of such spouses). Again, the Greenbanks material showed similar patterns.

Two points have emerged very clearly in this aspect of our study. One is the great degree of variation in extra-familial kin intimates, those people on whom a person is apt to depend a great deal for sociability, advice and personal services. The other point is the very considerable use made of kin outside the natal family of husband and wife. From the point of view of a theoretical understanding of English middle-class kinship, and also of those interested in the application of the results to problems of personal and social life, this would seem important. So much attention has been focussed upon the influence of the 'family' upon individuals that it is necessary to be more precise about the relationships of the persons so designated.

From this point of view we now want to consider how far these sets of people can be regarded as kin units and what terms are best used in describing them.

'THE EXTENDED FAMILY'

One term which formerly was fairly commonly used in describing sets of relatively close bilateral kin, especially consanguineal kin, was *kindred*; but partly because of obscurities in the definition of this term it has now tended to drop out of use except in a restricted sense.[3]

A term which has come to be fairly widely used, now that the importance of kin ties has come to be appreciated in British studies of domestic social relationships, is 'extended family'.

This term has had two main connotations, referring to different contexts of social relationships, or to different phases of a general process. One context or phase can be illustrated by views about the way in which large-scale kin units in Britain are thought to have disintegrated under the stress of modern economic and social pressures of industrialization, with the consequent trend to migration and premium upon individual freedom. It has been stated for instance by John Bowlby, whose views on family life command great respect, that social mobility, both economic and geographic, tends in modern conditions to break up the 'extended family'. Geoffrey Gorer, an acute observer of English family life, who has been quoted by Josephine Klein in support of her own opinion, has said that by practically every criterion the break-up of the extended family (i.e. the large kinship group which includes married brothers and sisters and cousins, etc.) has proceeded much further in the South of England than in the Midlands and the North.[4] The *process* to which these writers draw attention is doubtless a very real one. But the kin *units* to which they refer are not at all easy to identify. Structurally, it is not at all certain that it is *family* ties in any strict sense that have suffered. Sometimes it may have been large households containing an elementary family of parents and children with attached secondary kin all living under one roof that have been reduced in size over time. Sometimes the reference may have been to a greater individualization of property rights, the dissolution of *corporate ownership* of parcels of land or craft businesses by sets of siblings and their children. Sometimes, and we suspect most commonly, the idea may have been the

[3] See W. H. R. Rivers, 1924, p. 16; and for historical development and various uses of the term see J. D. Freeman, 'On the Concept of Kindred', *J.R.A.I.* 91, pp. 192–220, 1961; W. E. Mitchell, 'Theoretical Problems in the Concept of Kindred', *American Anthropologist* 65, pp. 343–54, 1963.

[4] John Bowlby, in a letter to *The Times*, 26 March 1965; Geoffrey Gorer, *Exploring English Character*, London 1955, pp. 45–6; Josephine Klein, *Samples from English Cultures*, vol. i, London 1965, pp. 131, 332.

weakening of general *ties of communication and other social relationships* between any consanguineal kin as they abandoned living in the same village or other common geographical area.

The other context often given to 'extended family' is almost the reverse. Kin strength, not weakness, is emphasized. What is regarded as so striking is not the break-up of the 'extended family' but its survival in industrial society and the functions it fulfils. Such treatment in effect gives an equation of the term with positive recognition of kin ties outside the elementary family. In one enquiry, for example, when subjects were asked to reveal their knowledge of and contact with members of their 'extended family', what was meant was 'their relatives', in practice, the set of people of three generations depth descended from the informant's grandparents.[5] In other enquiries conducted from the Institute of Community Studies, and making significant contributions to our understanding of kinship in London working-class and lower middle-class society, the notion of 'extended family' has been used in a much more restricted way, to mean those relatives who share the same dwelling as the members of an elementary family or who live near them and share much of their daily lives.[6] In still another investigation 'extended family' has been used to refer to any persistent grouping of persons related by descent, marriage or adoption, which is wider than the elementary family, in that it characteristically spans three generations from grandparents to grandchildren.[7]

The term 'extended family' is clearly a tempting one to those trying to describe kin relations outside the elementary family. But there are several important issues on which there is difference of usage. The extended family is understood to be composed of people who are kin, not the mere enlargement of an elementary family by the addition of a friend or dependent. But the elementary family of parents and children is a group; is the extended family to be considered as a group? And if so, in what sense?

In simple formal definition a human group is a number of persons standing near together or classed together or belonging together. In social usage the notion of 'togetherness' implies more than physical contiguity; it refers to a social contiguity, a nearness or touching of

[5] Margaret Stacey, *Tradition and Change: A Study of Banbury*, OUP, 1960, p. 117.

[6] Michael Young and Peter Willmott, *Family and Kinship in East London*, London, 1957, pp. 202–3 *et passim*; Peter Townsend, *The Family Life of Old People*, London, 1957, pp. 108–19; Peter Willmott and Michael Young, *Family and Class in a London Suburb*, London, 1960, pp. 48–9.

[7] Colin Rosser and Christopher Harris, *The Family and Social Change: A Study of Family and Kinship in a South Wales Town*, London, 1965, pp. 32, 199.

interests, with shared aims and common organized activities. Such common participation is particularly evident in what used to be called 'primary groups', where every member is able to interact with every other member.[8] In our contemporary Western society the family of parents and young children is clearly such a primary group. The basic role of this unit, which however embedded in other kin forms is practically universal, has been indicated by the range of terms applied to it. Reference to *simple, elementary, immediate* family indicates its basic structural character, while *primary, nuclear* and *focal* family indicate its basic function in the social process. The terms *conjugal* or *marital* family indicate that it is rooted in the procreative union of a married pair, while *natal* family or *family of origin* indicate that it is from this unit that the new generation springs. *Family of procreation* stresses its creative, forward-looking aspect; *family of orientation* its normative, backward-looking aspect. In this collection of terms national and other idiosyncratic preferences have been shown by anthropologists and sociologists. But whatever be the variation in the terms applied, there has been general agreement that in its structure of relationships this type of family operates in relatively solidary unitary fashion.

It does so through various mechanisms, which do not all apply in every case but most of which do. These include common residence, mutual co-operation in productive activities, sharing of a common income, acknowledgement of the authority of a common head, mutual socialization and response to moral norms. These mechanisms rest essentially on the linked concepts of a connubial relationship between the married pair, parental/filial relationship between them and their children, and a sibling relationship among these. (Such mechanisms may also have repressive effects, especially expressed through the authority of the parents, and hamper the development of individual initiative.)

Now 'extended family' literally should presumably mean a kin group in which these primary ties and mechanisms are replicated by a new generation of parents and children linked to the others in the same way, with similar roles and relationships. But two limiting criteria are introduced by this process of replication. To produce the second generation family one or more new spouses have had to be brought in; these people have parents and probably siblings too. So the children of each of these new spouses can belong to two extended families – one from the natal family of their mother, the other from the natal family of their father. But here a practical limitation comes in. Whereas the members of an elementary family usually live to-

[8] See e.g. George C. Homans, *The Human Group*, New York, 1950, pp. 85–7, etc.

gether – when the children are young anyway – and have intricate social communication, in Western industrial society this is not so feasible, and indeed is rare, when the family process extends. Two natal families linked together by the marriage of one of their sons and one of their daughters are very often settled at some distance from each other, and tend to lead very separate social careers. For any close unit of parents, children and grandchildren to work, there must be some selection of kin. An operational unit must crystallize out of the abstract theoretical set of kin available. In practice what usually happens in most societies is that by social convention either the mother's or the father's natal family is made more accessible to the children. So the extended family with which they have most to do is apt to be either of matrilateral or patrilateral kind. Sometimes, though probably less commonly, the children operate with both alternately.

Granted that the concept of 'extended family' should apply operationally to a set of kin in some type of close relationship analogous to that in the elementary family, what should be the criteria of such relationship?

The first criterion is the social effect of the group upon the behaviour of its members. Membership of a family means being influenced in a great variety of intimate social ways, both in opinion and in behaviour. Something of this quality should be identifiable in the relations between members of an extended family. Living in the same household with other kin may be presumed to imply such effect, but living near him or her, or seeing each other every day, does not of itself mean this. Indeed, as we know from ordinary family relations, siblings or parents and children may live apart and yet maintain this intimacy and powerful reciprocal influence upon behaviour, or live near and be at daggers drawn. In our view, to speak of a set of kin as an 'extended family' should imply something of this quality of relationship, and such a view is broadly in line with most anthropological opinion. Therefore, definitions which equate 'extended family' in our society with either the whole range of relatives in *both* mother's and father's natal families, or with the same set of them who live near to one another, irrespective of the degree of effect they have on one another's behaviour, seem inadequate. Definitions which see the critical element of 'extended family' membership in living near or in 'seeing' certain kinsmen very frequently are drawing attention to an important factor of communication. But they leave unstated the more important aspect of *quality* of communication, that is, degree of participation in social affairs, decision-making, opinion-forming.[9]

[9] A critical examination of this and other definitions has been made by Rosser and Harris, op. cit., pp. 30–1, 218–9.

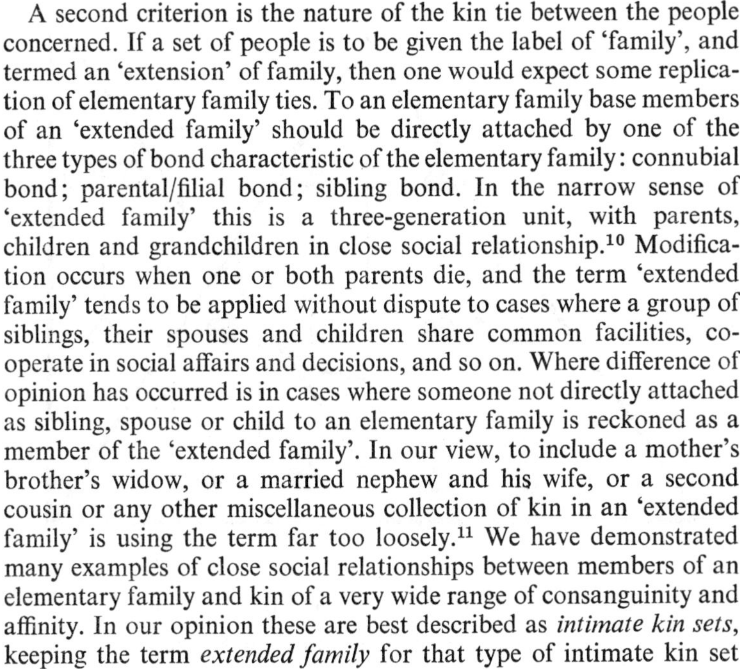

A second criterion is the nature of the kin tie between the people concerned. If a set of people is to be given the label of 'family', and termed an 'extension' of family, then one would expect some replication of elementary family ties. To an elementary family base members of an 'extended family' should be directly attached by one of the three types of bond characteristic of the elementary family: connubial bond; parental/filial bond; sibling bond. In the narrow sense of 'extended family' this is a three-generation unit, with parents, children and grandchildren in close social relationship.[10] Modification occurs when one or both parents die, and the term 'extended family' tends to be applied without dispute to cases where a group of siblings, their spouses and children share common facilities, co-operate in social affairs and decisions, and so on. Where difference of opinion has occurred is in cases where someone not directly attached as sibling, spouse or child to an elementary family is reckoned as a member of the 'extended family'. In our view, to include a mother's brother's widow, or a married nephew and his wife, or a second cousin or any other miscellaneous collection of kin in an 'extended family' is using the term far too loosely.[11] We have demonstrated many examples of close social relationships between members of an elementary family and kin of a very wide range of consanguinity and affinity. In our opinion these are best described as *intimate kin sets*, keeping the term *extended family* for that type of intimate kin set

[10] This unit has been called alternatively a *grandfamily* (Paul Bohannan, *Social Anthropology*, 1963, pp. 100–5). In English kinship studies the term was first used apparently by Raymond Firth in a note (unpublished) on kinship groups for a study in South London in 1947. The note read: '*Grand family*. This is an effective social unit, consisting of all the descendants of a married pair in the first and second generations. The Grand Family is the direct extension of the Simple Family by prolongation to a second generation. It normally maintains itself as a unit during the life of one or both grandparents. To the grand family are affiliated all spouses of children and grandchildren (with a special sub-affiliation for spouses who are separated or divorced). Intersection of grand families occurs since each of the spouses is a member of another such grand family.'

Note that this is a structural concept. What might be thought to be the corresponding term in French has been sometimes primarily a demographic concept. For example, *La Plus Grande Famille* was an association, formed in a period when the low birthrate in France was causing much concern, and composed of fathers and mothers of at least five children. The Association was recognized by law as being of public utility (by a decree of 21 August 1922) and issued publications advocating larger families.

[11] We thus find the definition offered by Rosser and Harris acceptable provided the element of direct descent is specified (op. cit., pp. 32, 199). Otherwise the definition pushes too many kinds of kin configurations into the same bag. (See also review of Rosser and Harris's book by T. H. Marshall, *Sociological Review*, vol. 14, 199, pp. 83–4.) Most of the material dealing with 'extended families' in their Swansea study does deal with the narrower range of parent-child-grandchild, and married sibling relationships.

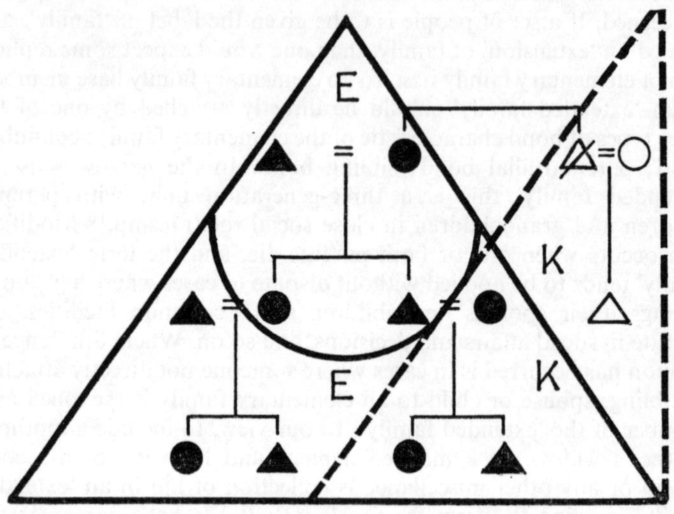

FIGURE 12. Extended Family and Intimate Kin Set
E=Extended Family, K=Intimate Kin Set

which is based on the direct family bonds as defined above (Figure 12).

Empirical recognition of the little sets of kin of varying composition who operate in close contact and influence one another's opinions and behaviour is of great importance in understanding the workings of English society. As we confirm here, it may be essential in understanding the social processes of the elementary family itself. But it blurs the situation unnecessarily to call all these sets of kin, irrespective of the ties which bind them together, 'extended families'.[12] By abandoning the distinction between 'family' and extra-familial kinship an important set of criteria for analysing types of social relationship is overlooked.

Moreover, some awkward problems are not faced. One such problem is that of estranged parents. Take the case of Mrs Lander,

[12] Townsend has seemed to press this point of view too far in his advocacy of the view that 'the extended family is indeed *the* primary group for a substantial proportion – we don't yet know exactly what proportion – of the populations of industrial societies'. 'Family and Kinship in Industrial Society: A Comment by Peter Townsend', *The Sociological Review Monograph* No. 8, pp. 89–96.

whose religious conversion had estranged her from her parents and her only brother. Intimate kin of her and her husband were father's brother, Mr Lander's father's sister and two mother's sisters, and one of his mother's sister's sons. To describe these as 'extended family' while ignoring the wife's parents and brother would be only a figurative usage which would seem to do violence to the concept of 'family' – yet it was these more distant relatives who filled the woman's need for social support and communication. It seems preferable to speak as we have done, of the 'intimate kin set' in this case, and point out that with the woman's estrangement from her natal family no extended family existed for her as an operational group.

Reviewing our Highgate material as a whole we have found three-generation extended family relations in three-quarters of the cases. But only 3 of these cases, one-tenth of the Highgate sample, showed a full pattern of intimate kin group of conjugal family with two parents and one or more siblings of either spouse. The common pattern was one parent of either spouse, with or without spouse's siblings. One-quarter of the cases showed no extended family structure, but had various other patterns of intimate kin sets. And most of the cases which had extended family structure showed other patterns of intimate kin relationships in addition.

Comparison of the simplified genealogies of two cases will illustrate the difference in typology. Figure 13 illustrates 'extended family'

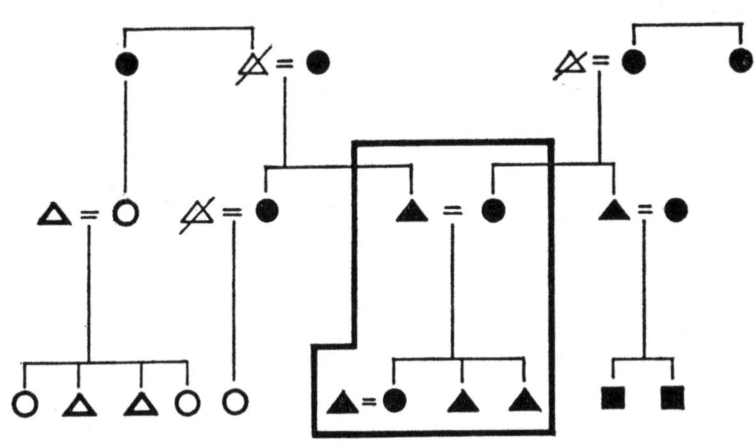

FIGURE 13. Symmetrical Spread of Intimate Kin
(Key to Figs. 13 and 14 as in Fig. 11)

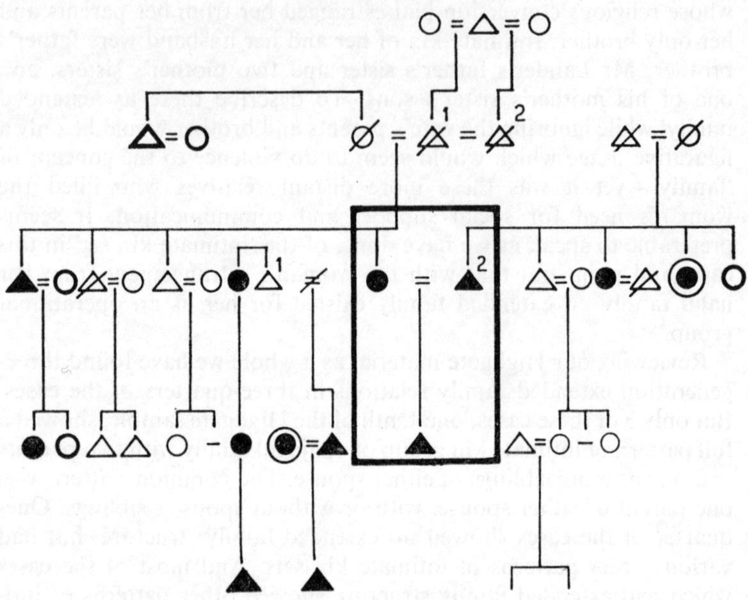

FIGURE 14. Ties with Kin of Divorced Spouse

relationships on both Mr Savage's and Mrs Savage's side, with a mother and a sibling on each side as family extensions. Additional kin support was given by husband's father's sister and wife's mother's sister, and the spouse and children of the wife's brother.

Contrast with this Mrs Lark's case (Figure 14). The close relatives outside the elementary family included Mrs Lark's son by a former marriage, and his wife and son; her brother and a daughter of his; and a sister of Mr Lark. But the person with whom Mrs Lark's relationship was most close was her first husband's sister's daughter; this woman's son was also very important to our informant. Not only is the genealogical pattern very different here from that of the extended family of parents and siblings; the social pattern is also very different. The intimacy of the kin relationship must be defined in different terms. The quality of relations with a divorced husband's sister may be no less strongly affective than with one's own sister, but since historically the relation has arisen only after maturity, and the initial link with the husband has since been severed, necessarily the relation has been differently structured. It must therefore of necessity have a different quality and possible also different function from a relation with a sister of one's own.

KIN NETWORK AND KIN SET

A further point of importance arises here. A family is a group, so an 'extended family' presumably has also some corporate character. But many of the sets of intimate kin described in this and in other British studies seem to have no particular group existence. They are what has been described as 'ego-oriented', that is, the various people concerned operate in this context primarily with reference to one central person. These may meet one another at his birthday party or in his house at Christmas, but otherwise they may have only a genealogical relation to one another. They may not operate in any truly corporate or collective sense at all. Most anthropologists would probably concur in the view that the merely temporary association of a number of kin at a birthday party, or a funeral, when perhaps many of them have met for the first time for years, and have no other corporate activities, can at most be described as occasional kin groups.[13] Kinship units defined primarily by some personal focus, and therefore relatively impermanent, are distinguished fairly clearly from those which operate as a totality in terms of some common rights and obligations of all their members, and are therefore relatively permanent.[14]

Another conceptualization of relations in an intimate kin set is also possible. Instead of forming a group for collective action with every member involved continually with aspects of group aims and group behaviour, or instead of coalescing only as a body on specific actions in a life crisis of one of their number, the members of a kin set may operate in a series of dyadic relationships, i.e. in two-person links. The relations of these people may then be conceptualized as a form of social network. The structure of their relationships may be such that A has relations with B, C and D, but not direct with E, F and G; B has relations with A, D and E, but not with C, F and G, and so on. The number and character of relationship which each person has with others of his kin set will vary according to the pattern of reticulation of the network, hexagonal, octagonal, irregular, etc.

[13] Raymond Firth, 'Bilateral Descent Groups: An Operational Viewpoint', 1963, p. 26; J. R. Fox, 'Prolegomena to the Study of British Kinship', *Penguin Survey of the Social Sciences*, 1965, p. 142. E. Goffman, *Encounters: Two Studies in the Sociology of Interaction*, 1961, p. 9, contrasts 'groups' with 'gatherings' or 'assemblages', a usage which H. W. Scheffler, *Choiseul Island Social Structure*, 1965, p. 43, has adopted. This is in line with general anthropological treatment.

[14] W. E. Armstrong, one of the first to make this point explicit, termed such units 'groupings' and 'groups' respectively (*Rossel Island*, 1928, p. 32). J. R. Fox, op. cit., pp. 129–31, seems to exaggerate the confusion in this field.

The idea of a kin network is a simple and appealing one, avoiding the assumption of group behaviour where in fact there is no collective action, yet maintaining the concept of social linkage between kin. It seems a useful concept if maintained as a general metaphor. But the various attempts made to give the concepts of social network greater precision as an instrument of analysis[15] have not been altogether satisfactory.

One advantage of the concept of network is that it need not imply the existence of a boundary, and this is helpful in considering kinship systems without clearly formulated and demarcated groups of lineage or analogous order. Network as a visual descriptive term has proved attractive, but as used in kinship analysis it tends to lay stress upon the form rather than upon the content of the relationships involved. Where the knots of the network are conceived as families this tends to assume that the family is an indivisible unit and to ignore the fact that every member of one family is not in identical relation to every member of another. Even where the knots are conceived as individuals, the analogy with a network breaks down in the sense that the ties of relationships between individuals linked by kinship may be of very different order, e.g. affinal as against consanguineal, or very different quality, e.g. aggressive and denigratory as against friendly and supportive. Moreover, the network concept tends to emphasize the formal static aspects of kin relationship and not bring out the continuing processes involved – the additions to a set of kin produced by marriage and procreation of children do not resemble in any apt way the modes of network growth.

So in this book we do not describe the extra-familial kin ties as a

[15] See J. A. Barnes, 'Class and Committees in a Norwegian Island Parish', *Human Relations*, vol. vii, pp. 39–58, 1954; Elizabeth Bott, 'Urban Families: Conjugal Roles and Social Networks', *Human Relations*, vol. viii, pp. 345–84, 1955; idem, *Family and Social Network*, London, 1957; E. J. Jay, 'The Concepts of "Field" and "Network" in Social Research', *Man*, 1964, no. 177. A. C. Mayer has distinguished between *network* as a field of social relations between people, and *set* or *quasi-group* as a collection of people in interaction. ('The Significance of Quasi-Groups in the Study of Complex Societies', *A.S.A. Monograph 4, The Social Anthropology of Complex Societies*, London, 1966, pp. 97–122.) An amusing semi-serious article by Nicholas Tomalin, 'Atticus discovers Networks' (*The Sunday Times*, 23 February 1963), discusses the social significance of networks (alliance by talent and self-interest) in contrast to clubs (alliance by status). Networks, by this account, are typically left-wing, middle-class intellectual formations of people whose early friendships have crystallized into maintenance of contact and mutual responsiveness and helpfulness. But one of our informants described merchant bankers as constituting a network!

The type of network analysis used as a management tool in research and development, with particular reference to timing of processes and cost, is of a different order. Although sociologically it looks rather pretentious and naïve, it has achieved a high degree of sophistication, especially in mathematical terms.

network, except in a very general loose sense. We have preferred to speak of the *effective kin set*, and *intimate kin set* to describe those kin in varying degree of relationship with our informants, leaving the *shape* or *pattern* of the relationship a matter of further specification. Between some sets of kin, relations are so structured in a series of dyadic ties that the term *kin network* is appropriate; between others more highly corporate activities and attitudes obtain so that the term *kin group* seems apt. Sometimes the kin group, or some sector of it, is such a direct projection of relationships from an elementary family that the term *extended family* seems to be that which is most fitting; sometimes no clear-cut group structure of kin seems to operate. Families and individuals differ very much in this respect. As Fox has pointed out (op. cit. p. 140), our society is not one composed of kin groups to which everyone must belong.

One point is very clear. In the recruitment of these sets of extra-familial kin, none followed a solely unilineal principle. It has been generally recognized by anthropologists that outside the transmission of surname, and a very limited range of property, titles and offices, the English kinship system is of a bilateral or cognatic order. What is also significant in the English field, and what seems to be characteristic of many other cognatic systems as well,[16] is the important operational role of kin related through a marriage tie. Formation of an effective kin set, including kin of an intimate relationship, may involve ties of an affinal kind. Hence we may speak in this context of an *affino-cognatic* system of kin set formation.

[16] Cf. Raymond Firth, 'Relations between Personal Kin (*Waris*) among Kelantan Malays' in *The Bonds of Kinship in East Asia and the Pacific: Homage to Lauristan Sharp*. Vol. I (ed. William G. Skinner & Robert J. Smith). In press.

10

Kin Terms and Status Relations

Study of the words by which people refer to or speak to their kin may seem to be about the dullest and least rewarding part of a kinship enquiry. But it is very revealing. When people use kin terms such as Father, Mummy, Aunt, they are in effect saying something about their conception of the relationship in which they stand to the person so designated. This is particularly so in a system such as the modern English one, which allows a considerable degree of flexibility in the use of (or abstention from) terms of kin relationship. When speaking *about* kin to others the ordinary terms of reference – father, brother, uncle, cousin, etc. – are available by custom and are convenient shorthand expressions to indicate relationships. But in speaking direct *to* such persons modern convention has dropped the use of quite a number of kin terms. As has been pointed out by Fowler,[1] the custom of using a kinship term by way of direct address is now common only with four words – father, mother, grandfather, grandmother. Not so long ago husband, wife, brother, sister[2] were also used as forms of address, but these fell into disuse during the nineteenth century, and the use of uncle, aunt and cousin as terms of address has survived mainly by prefixing them to the personal name of the individual spoken to.

Unlike the position in many primitive societies, though respect may inhibit the use of personal name alone as a mode of address to a senior kinsmen, there is in English usage no absolute taboo on this – even to a parent-in-law. If not always entirely polite, this does occur

[1] H. W. Fowler, *A Dictionary of Modern English Usage*, 2nd edn, revised by Sir Ernest Gowers, 1965, 'Names and Appellations', pp. 379–80; R. W. Chapman, 'Names, Designations and Appellations', *S.P.E. Tract* No. XLVII, 1936, pp. 233– 651.

[2] 'Brother' is still used by some siblings as a form of address, being what may be called an *accented term*. It is apt to be a self-conscious usage, semi-humorous, with a flavour of analogy with trade-union or other associational membership which lays stress on 'fraternal' unity. 'Sister' may be used similarly, perhaps less often, even in the abbreviated form 'Sis' which (used by a brother) was probably more common a generation or two ago. Sissy (Cissy), ultimately derived from sister, has now acquired the meaning of an effeminate boy.

to some extent with all types of kin relationship, concurrent with the spread of more general informality in most social relationships.

In this Chapter we concentrate primarily on kinship terms as modes of address, since this shows the different factors involved with greatest sensitivity. But before examining the material in this field empirically, we consider the structure of English kinship terminology in a general way. Brief analyses of the kinship system of the contemporary United States have been made. But as far as we know this is the first time that a systematic presentation of English usage has been published.[3] Here we emphasize that in this immediate context we are discussing the structure of terms generally available in the modern English language. Those used by our informants broadly conform to this, but we discuss our empirical evidence later.

TERMS OF REFERENCE

English terms of reference, i.e. used when speaking (or writing) of a kinsman to another person, are relatively standardized. Except in the speech of young children, and in the use of a few colloquial expressions such as 'my Dad', 'my Mum', 'your Grandma', which show some class differentials, the terms of reference to kin show few alternates and little variation.

The primary or basic terms of reference number thirteen (see Figure 15A). Eight of these can be applied within a nuclear family, either a natal family or a conjugal family, according to circumstances. Six of these are terms for consanguineal relationships and two for affinal relationships. In a natal family the available terms are: father, mother, brother, sister. In a conjugal family there are: husband, wife, son, daughter. For extra-familial kin, there are five primary terms: uncle, aunt, nephew, niece, cousin. (If cousin were differentiated by sex the system would be more symmetrical.)

With one exception, the term cousin, all these primary terms indicate differentiation according to three principles – generation, sex and lineation. As regards differentiation by generation, in the generation senior to Ego there are four terms: father, mother, uncle, aunt; in his/her own generation, also four terms: brother, sister, husband, wife; and in the generation junior to Ego, there are four

[3] Talcott Parsons, 'The Kinship System of the Contemporary United States', *Essays in Sociological Theory*, Glencoe, Ill., 1954, pp. 177–96; D. M. Schneider and G. C. Homans, 'Kinship Terminology and the American Kinship System', *American Anthropologist*, vol. 57, 1955, pp. 1194–208; D. M. Schneider *American Kinship*, 1968. An unpublished essay by Camilla H. Wedgwood, seems, alas, to have been lost during the War.

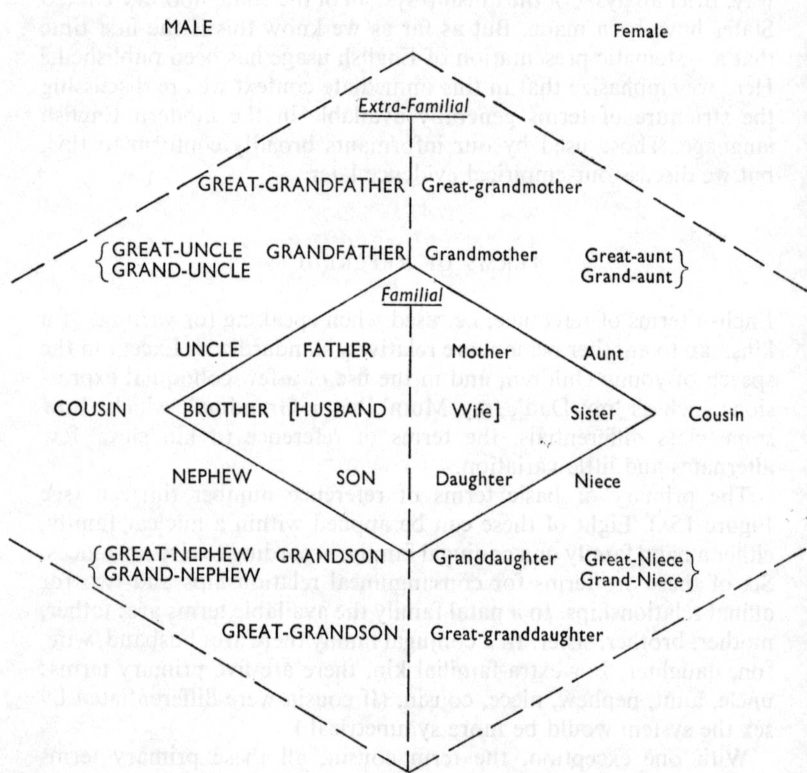

FIGURE 15A. Terms of Reference to Consanguine Kin

terms too: son, daughter, nephew, niece. (Note that the full range of terms of reference is available to any Ego, since he may refer to himself as a father, husband, etc. to some other kin person.) As regards differentiation according to sex, in some kinship systems the kin terms of reference between persons in the same generation indicate not the actual sex of the one referred to, but the nature of the relation between them – whether the person is of the same sex as, or opposite sex to, that of the speaker.[4] The English system follows another principle. It lines up kin terms for the most part with the actual sex of the person referred to – brother and uncle are male, daughter and niece are female, no matter who is speaking. (An exception is cousin which, unlike the corresponding French terms, does not specify by sex.) By implication the English are more interested in whether a relative is male or female than in the similarity or difference of sex quality in the relationship involved. As regards lineation, Ego's own ascendants and descendants – father, son (as with extensions of these primary terms – grandfather, grandson, etc.) – are distinguished from his collaterals – uncle, aunt, nephew, niece, cousin.[5]

Compared with many systems of kin terminology, the English system is rather sparse in basic categorization. There is no popular collective term for a set of brothers and sisters, similar to the German *Geschwister*, for example. The term sibling, meaning one who is kin to another, a relative, has a long history, together with various other developments from sib, but it is only from about the beginning of the twentieth century that it has come to be used with precision in the plural form to indicate individuals having a parent or parents in common.[6] (Anthropologists are probably the most frequent technical users of sibling in this sense.) There is a collective term parents, but strictly speaking this applies only to father and mother of a person; it is used only loosely to apply to both pairs of parents of a married couple. There is no term, as there is for example in Malay, to indicate the relationship between these two pairs of parents themselves. Again,

[4] In Tikopia, for instance, 'my *taina*' means a brother if a man is speaking or a sister if a woman is speaking; conversely, 'my *kave*' is a sister if a man is speaking or a brother if a woman is speaking.

[5] This was not always the case. Until about the end of the sixteenth century nephew and niece, in line with the Latin *nepos* and *neptis* from which they were ultimately derived, could refer to grandson or granddaughter or further descendants.

[6] The *Oxford English Dictionary* cites Karl Pearson (1897) and E. L. Thorndike (1905) as the earliest sources, and gives the primary meaning under this head as 'each of two or more individuals born to the same parents but not at the same birth'. This would exclude twins, but the broader meaning seems to have prevailed. Thorndike writes of 'ordinary siblings', in contrast to twins, who were presumably extraordinary siblings!

there are no terms to indicate seniority and juniority among brothers and sisters (as e.g. in Malay), still less to indicate seniority and juniority among kin in the father's generation (as e.g. among some New Guinea peoples). Further, no distinction is made in terminology between parents' siblings on the father's side and on the mother's side – both are uncle and aunt with only sex distinction noted. Finally, the term cousin is an all-purpose term. It does not assimilate parents' siblings' children, etc. to own siblings, as does the terminology of many kinship systems, but on the other hand it distinguishes neither sex – as the French term does – nor generation, as many kinship systems do. Moreover, it gives no indication of whether the person referred to is on the father's or mother's side of the kin universe.

The English system of kinship terms has often been characterized as a 'descriptive' system. But in fact there are only four terms – father, mother, husband, wife – which if used literally must refer to single individuals alone. It is in the set of secondary terms that the process of building-up characteristic of a descriptive nomenclature occurs. Here the system is very symmetrical. Three areas of terminology are involved: specification of ascendants and descendants outside the nuclear family; specification of collaterals; and specification of affinal relationship.

Specification of ascendants and descendants is done by an odd convention, the use of two prefixes etymologically suggesting size or status – *grand* and *great* – to indicate remoteness by generation from the term to which it is added. Common Indo-European usage involves one such prefix, and then other prefixes of a differentiating order for subsequent generations. But the English usage is to employ two prefixes with essentially the same original meaning: *grand* from the French, and *great* from Old English. These are sometimes used separately, sometimes together, but in an idiomatic way. *Grand* is applied mainly to terms of lineal relationship, of the parent and child order: grandfather, granddaughter, etc.[7] The dictionary gives also forms such as grand-aunt, grand-nephew, grand-niece, but in ordinary speech more commonly the prefix *great* seems to be used with such terms of collateral relationships, to indicate one degree of removal, as great-aunt, great-niece. But granted that great and grand can be equivalent with these collateral relationships, they are definitely not so for the lineal relationships. One can speak of grandfather and grandchild but nowadays not of greatfather or greatchild.[8]

[7] But the French use *grand* for ascending generations only and, more plausibly, *petit* for descending generations!

[8] But the *Oxford English Dictionary* gives greatfather, great-cousin, as obsolete forms.

(Nor can either prefix be applied to cousin, which is capable of enlargement only by descriptive phrases – see below.) Once past the second generation of remoteness, the indication of degree is given only by the prefix great, as great-grandfather, and the English mode of reference is to go on monotonously adding one more 'great' for every generational step. Moreover, there can be no inversion: one speaks of 'my great-grandson', not 'my grand-greatson', though the net significance should be the same.

Specification of cousinship uses a more logical numerical principle of order. The nearest cousin genealogically (cousin german) – father's (mother's) brother's (sister's) son (daughter) is a 'first' cousin; a father's father's brother's son's son (FFBSS) etc. is a 'second' cousin; and a FFFBSSS is a 'third' cousin. In each case the terminology 'first', 'second', etc. indicates the number of generations back from Ego which have to be traced to obtain the collateral relative, a sibling of Ego's forbear, from whom the cousin in turn traces his descent.[9] Differences of generation between cousins can be indicated by the additional descriptive phrase of 'once removed', 'twice removed', etc., though the exact character of the asymmetry cannot be so shown. For example, my first cousin once removed may be my FFBS – my father's first cousin, or my FBSS – my own first cousin's son.

Specification of affinal relationship involves the notion of a legal tie at the connecting point. In the English kinship system, unlike many other systems, there are no kin terms all components of which refer exclusively to persons related by marriage – except the two central words husband and wife. All the rest are borrowed or built up from consanguineal terms. Borrowed terms are uncle and aunt for spouses of parents' siblings – a kind of assimilation of affines.[10] Built-up terms are constructed simply from the corresponding consanguineal term with the suffix 'in-law' added. But the range of consanguineal terms so called upon is very limited, being ordinarily restricted to the six terms of nuclear family use: father, mother, brother, sister, son, daughter. Though aunts-in-law, cousins-in-law and grandmothers-in-law are created in effect by marriage quite often, their existence is not recognized by any regular kin terms – when a reference is so made it is in a joking way, with the presumption that this is stretching the conventional use of terms – though they have dictionary authority.

[9] The *Oxford English Dictionary* phrases it as 'descended the same number of steps in distinct lines from a common ancestor'.

[10] The *Oxford English Dictionary* defines aunt as sister of one's father or mother, also an uncle's wife, 'more strictly called an aunt-in-law'. In the *Shorter Oxford English Dictionary*, uncle-in-law as the husband of one's aunt is also given (from 1561, etc.)

The English use of nuclear family terms as the basis of affinal terminology of reference tends to stress two contradictory principles. On the one hand, the nearest affines are assimilated to members of the nuclear family – they are *like* fathers, mothers, brothers, sisters, sons, daughters. Yet, on the other hand, there is recognition overtly that they come into existence only by a legal act, that of marriage. It is not a coincidence then that this ambivalence can be found also in social relations between the parties, and finds reflection *inter alia* in the variability in terms of address (see Chapter 12).

A further aspect of kinship terms of reference is of tertiary rather than secondary order. This is where a breach has occurred in an original conjugal family by death or divorce, one parent has acquired another spouse, and further children are added to the family, either brought by the new spouse or born to the pair after the marriage. Here the prefix 'half-' indicates siblings who share one parent, while 'step-' indicates a person of sibling, parent or child status with whom there is no consanguineal relationship. The 'step-' relationship is analogous to an affinal one, in that it is created by the legal act of marriage (see later). But here the assimilation of the relationship to that within the conjugal family is terminologically more complete. Theoretically speaking, a step-brother is a brother 'in-law'. But the sociological fact that one of his *parents* and one of yours have formed a married couple implies a greater degree of unity than if one of his *siblings* and you have married. This is intelligible from a practical point of view since quite often the 'step-' siblings may be relatively young and occupy the same household with their respective parent and step-parent.

A good way of bringing out the significance of the English terms for affines and step-kin is to contrast them with the French terms. In both English and French a spouse's parents, brothers and sisters are referred to as if they are a kind of father, mother, etc. The husband or wife acquires as it were a new family through marriage, but since this is different from one's natal family the term is qualified. In English we refer to all these people as 'in-laws'. Historically the 'in-law' phrase seems to refer to the canon law of the Church. It indicates that while these people by origin are strangers there is now by religious rule an impediment to marriage with them (cf. p. 190). But the popular view seems to be not concerned with this. Rather the popular in-law notion is that of a relation with people who have been suddenly foisted on one by a legal act, who have family privileges without responsibility, contact with whom may involve difficulty and even dissension.

With the rather grim phrase 'in-law' contrast the French usage. A French husband or wife refers to his spouse's father and mother as *beau-père* and *belle-mère*. Now, in formal terms *beau* and *belle* mean that which pleases the eye or the spirit. So, literally, in France a wife's mother is a 'fine mother', a woman who is agreeable. Both English and French mothers-in-law are created by the legal act of marriage, but whereas the English ungallantly concentrate on stressing the fact that she is there by law (and presumably unavoidable), the French politely draw attention to her sterling qualities. But is there really a radical difference? According to the dictionaries,[11] *beau*, for example in the term for a son-in-law, *beau-fils*, is a term of affection which in the Middle Ages was used particularly for persons of whom one was fond. As the language developed it became attributed to terms of relationship by marriage. In the archaic language the ordinary kinship terms had been used with the suffix *astre* (as *marastre* for mother-in-law), but in time that suffix had acquired a decidedly pejorative sense. So a way out was found by using the *beau*, *belle* terms, which were those of affection. But now, did the French come to use these terms of agreeableness because of affection towards the mother-in-law or because they wished to placate someone who was recognized as a rather formidable person? It would seem the latter, because in the course of history the term *belle-mère*, despite its fair-seeming character, has apparently come to acquire in French a rather dubious sense, as mother-in-law has in English. What the French have done then is to have invented a respect term – analogous in some ways to usages found commonly elsewhere in the world.[12]

STEPMOTHER AND MOTHER-IN-LAW

The English and French systems of terms differ in one significant respect. The French include in a single category of *beau-père* and *belle-mère*, etc. those relatives whom we class separately as step-father, stepmother, etc. Logically, there is much to be said for this usage. A stepmother is a woman who has married a parent; a mother-in-law is a woman parent of someone one has married. It is also significant that in English the only terms which can consistently take the prefix *step-* (father, mother, son, daughter, brother, sister) are those to which exclusively the suffix '-in-law' can also be applied

[11] e.g. Littré, *Dictionnaire de la Langue Francaise*, ed. intégrale, Pauvert, 1956.

[12] But lest we think that only the French are polite about family relationships let us remember that where the French husband or wife speaks of a spouse as *ma moitié* – 'my (other) half', by tradition the English modestly call him (or usually her) 'my better half'. Note that sixteenth century Scots usage has *good-mother* for mother-in-law or step-mother, also *good-father*, *good-brother*, etc. for analogous affinal or step-kin.

regularly.[13] It is also interesting to note in view of the French analogy that in the English language until the fifteenth or sixteenth century father-in-law and mother-in-law were also used for what we now call stepfather and stepmother; indeed the usage continued occasionally right into the nineteenth century.

According to our dictionaries to call a stepmother mother-in-law is now incorrect. Yet structurally speaking, stepmother and mother-in-law do have something in common. In each case the existing parent/child relationship is complicated by the creation of a new marriage. But there are significant differences. With the mother-in-law it is the mother/son or mother/daughter tie which is cut across by a new marital tie in the *inferior* generation, that of the child. With the stepmother, it is the father/son or father/daughter tie which is cut across by a new marital tie in the *superior* generation, that of the parent. The responsibility for the situation is different. A mother-in-law is made by the act of her child. She herself has legally no say in the creation of the role (unless the child is a minor) – which is perhaps why she has such a lot to say afterwards! With the creation of a stepmother it is a child who has no say – and being in a junior position has less opportunity to protest. So, if there is any grievance to be felt it is likely to be primarily by the mother in the mother-in-law case and the child in that of the stepmother. From some points of view the child is more vulnerable, since when the father contracts the new marriage the child may be quite young and in real need of personal love, care and assistance. The classic stereotype of a stepmother is a woman who is lacking in this love and care required by children – in our fairy tales she is the cruel woman *par excellence*, especially if she has children of her own already on whom to lavish her attention.[14]

By contrast, a mother-in-law should be more independent, less susceptible to the shock of having to share her son or daughter with a newcomer. Yet she may be vulnerable in another way. Her son or daughter may be marrying at a time when she has hardly begun to appreciate her children's maturity and capacity to take their own decisions. Anxiety about their future may then be in the forefront of her mind. Alternatively, she may feel her own future threatened. She may have begun to recognize how important her children are as adult persons in her social life. Later, when perhaps her own powers are

[13] Ward Goodenough 'Componential Analysis', *Science*, 2 June 1967, pp. 1203–9, (p. 1205) speaks of these terms in this context as 'collectively a unit of reference' for deriving affinal terms.

[14] 'Stepmothers are famous – or infamous – throughout the world', Paul Bohannan, *Social Anthropology*, 1963, p. 81. As one of our informants more politely put it, 'You know stepmothers are not the same as a mother'!

beginning to wane, she may feel the need of economic contribution and, most of all, she may wish for their interest and affection as her own social life begins to narrow down. Here a mother has to rely more than before on son or daughter. Hence at any stage she may have what seems to her to be valid claims upon her child; of necessity she tends to interfere with the movements and decisions of her child's spouse. Hence, for a mother-in-law, the stereotype is not cruelty, as with the stepmother, but domination. Some mothers-in-law are so aware of this possibility, of acting out the stereotype, that they go to the other extreme and shut themselves away from their married children, or if they visit them creep about the house to give no trouble and are careful not to utter any controversial opinion.

But the structure is different in still another respect. A stepmother is a *substitute* for a mother, structurally speaking. A mother-in-law is an *addition* to a mother in structural terms. So while there may be more relief for a daughter-in-law who has her own mother to turn to, it may yet be more easy to adjust to a stepmother who may provide a real substitute. Putting it another way, in our English system of kinship, a person needs one mother, but not two. Where there are two there is often a tendency to polarize the relationships involved. Any relations with a parent may involve both affection and recognition of authority. With mother and mother-in-law, these two elements may be separated – the mother comes to represent the principle of affection, the mother-in-law the principle of authority.

For any particular case, as our material shows later, this may be an over-simplification. It may be that stepmothers were more frequent in England in Victorian times, when heavier mortality rates for young women in childbirth were likely. Nowadays they are more likely in countries where divorce is relatively common. When there is a stepmother, and the mother is not dead, but divorced, the issue is not easily predictable. Mother may be loved and father's new wife hated. But sometimes the advantages of having two parental households may be appreciated, and mother and stepmother be regarded as filling complementary but equally positive roles. (For further discussion of step-kin, especially in regard to mode of address, see later in this Chapter, pp. 328–30.)

From the empirical point of view, the material from our North London study is conformable with and bears out the generalizations on kin terms of reference given here. These generalizations themselves, though perhaps novel in some respects, have not raised any very contentious issues. The case is rather different with the material on terms of address.

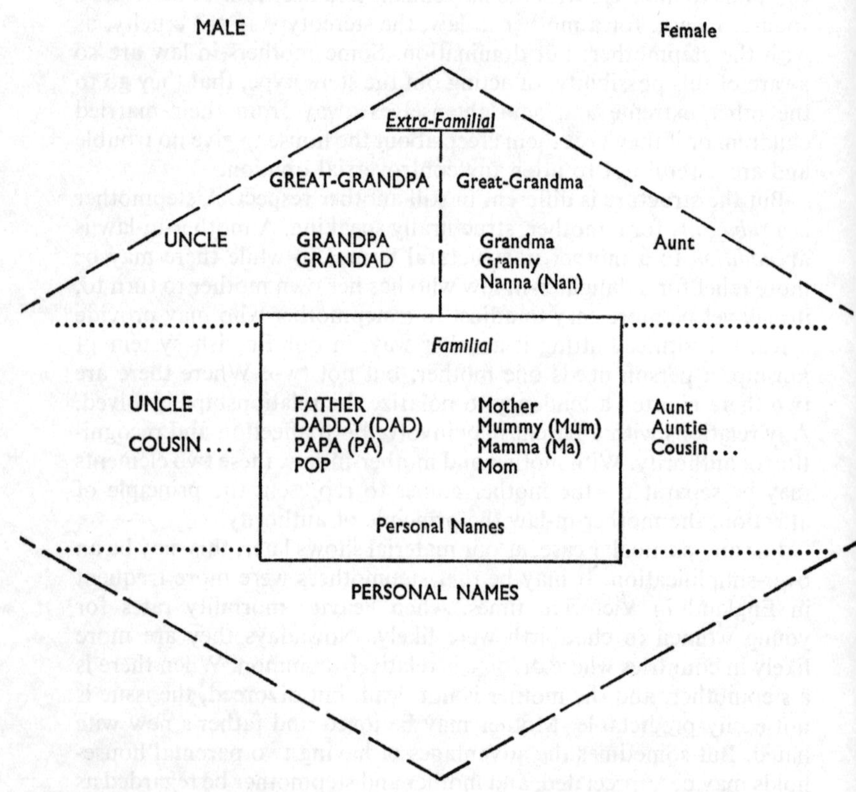

FIGURE 15B. Terms of Address to Consanguine Kin

Note. The figure is arranged in generation levels. For cousins and other kin of own generation and below personal names are used.

TERMS OF PERSONAL ADDRESS

In the English kinship system terms of personal reference are relatively specific and invariant, that is, a term ordinarily refers only to one category of relative, and there is only one term to refer to any category. 'My' husband, wife, father, mother, taken literally can mean only one individual in each case, and apart from colloquialisms such as 'my old man', 'my ma', etc. there are no other kin terms by which to indicate them. 'My' grandfather, grandmother, can refer to one of only two individuals in each case. Similarly, son, daughter, brother, sister, though possibly open to refer to more individuals, still each apply to only one category of very limited numbers of persons. Even uncle, aunt and cousin, though extended to include affines, still indicate persons whose relation can be fairly easily and unambiguously defined in genealogical terms. It is otherwise with the English kin terms of personal address. (Figure 15B.)

In the first place, there has been fairly wholesale borrowing of terms of address from the field of the natal family to use in extra-kin fields which seem to present some analogy with family relations and statuses. The use of 'Father', 'Mother', 'Brother', 'Sister' in addressing members of religious orders, either with or without the personal name in addition, or 'Sister' for a hospital nurse in charge of a ward, are common examples. The inverse pastoral form, 'my son', 'my daughter', from confessor to penitent is a specially interesting linguistic usage; what is ordinarily a term of reference is used as one of address, with the personal pronoun here indicating relative status in this context, not genealogical relationship. In all such cases where original kin terms have acquired special meanings, relative age and generation have become irrelevant to the terminology; it is role or status that are paramount.[15] Outside the natal family the terms uncle and aunt are often applied by children to friends of the parents, usually at their parents' instance (see later). Such pseudo-kin are assimilated thereby to the position of parents' siblings because of the apparent analogies in their role and status. A few terms of address derived from the natal family may be applied very widely indeed in

[15] Some of such re-applied kin terms may be used also as terms of reference, but then they tend to become category indicators, not indicators of personal relationship. One can speak of 'a sister' of a hospital or religious order, or 'a son' of the Church. To say 'my sister' of the hospital nurse could mean either that she was a sibling of yours or that she was in charge of a ward where one was a patient. But to say 'my son' if it be not a term of pastoral address would mean a child of one's own.

ordinary life. Here relative age is significant. The use of Dad to an elderly man and Mum or Ma to any elderly woman is common in working-class circles; this assimilates them to parental status, with its mixture of familiarity and respect. An inverse usage common in Australia and New Zealand, and apparently also in some sectors of England, is the use of Son as a generic form of address to a boy whose personal name is not known.[16] (Interestingly, daughter is not now used in corresponding way.)

A second point about English terms of personal address to kin is the extent to which they can be replaced or supplemented by personal (Christian) names. For all kin of a generation equal to or junior to Ego personal names are normally used in address. This applies to affinal as well as to consanguineal kin, in strong contrast to many other kinship systems, in which rules of avoidance require that an affine shall be addressed by a special kinship term and never by name. In the English system only to members of senior generations are kin terms of address used, and even here considerable intrusion of personal name and address has occurred during the past couple of generations. Broadly speaking, any term of reference to a relative of a senior generation can also be used as a term of address. But whereas for ascendants – parents, grandparents – the kin term alone is enough, for their collaterals the personal name of the relative addressed is commonly added – 'Aunt Emily', etc. Since a person can have only one father and one mother, biologically speaking, it seems obvious that no personal name is needed in addressing parents. The addition of personal name to uncle or aunt is wanted for identificatory or specificatory use. But this principle is not carried through rigorously, since while a person may have two grandfathers and two grandmothers it is not customary for him to specify each by personal name (but for use of surname see later). However, a practical consideration here may be that the likelihood of having four grandparents living is probably much less than that of having an equal or greater number of aunts and uncles.

The widespread use of forenames (personal names) as modes of address to kin is an important fact in the interpretation of the significance of kinship in English social relations. The orthodox view of kinship terms in social anthropology is that they provide a frame of classification for individuals in the society, indicating the appropriate types of behaviour in some reasonably consistent scheme. Making allowance for idiosyncratic relationships between individuals, kin term may be regarded as an index to more general patterns of social action. It is important then to note that to call a person by

[16] Colleagues in the linguistics field, Professor Eugénie Henderson and Dr George Milner, have supplied examples of this usage in England.

his name, as distinct from his kin relation, is to remove an indicator of appropriate social behaviour. This is particularly relevant in the English system, in which by convention juniors traditionally used kin terms in addressing their seniors, who for the most part used first names in return. Hence the modern extension of the 'first name' practice has meant that it is the verbal frame for the behaviour of junior to senior that gets dropped. This is in line with a more general tendency to re-definition of these relationships. The use of personal name, which has come to be a possible mode of address in all English kin relations, even if rare in some, is one facet of the phenomenon of variant alternatives in modes of address to kin which exist in some of our basic relationships.

But what do people actually call their kin? There is as yet in British anthropology no adequate description of what actual practice is in these matters, still less any proper analysis of the significance of the variations that we know to occur. Our aim in this Chapter is to provide at least an outline of the situation and a set of materials bearing on it. We begin with the parental terms.

MOTHER AND DADDY: A QUESTION OF AUTHORITY

An ordinary layman's view of the development of parental terms of address within a middle-class family might well be something of the following order. After some infant attempts, with more or less distortion, to reproduce what the parents offer as the terms by which to address them, most children settle down to Mummy and Daddy (Mum and Dad being the working-class equivalents); but a great proportion later change these youthful terms for Mother and Father. In a few cases, however, abbreviations, colloquialisms or nicknames for parents persist into adult life of the children, and in modern times a fashion for allowing children to use the first names of their parents has grown up.

The empirical picture presented by the data from our North London study is similar in outline to this, but is rather different in detail, especially when it comes to questions of variation and change. As part of our study we collected material wherever possible on the way in which kin, especially those of the immediately antecedent generation, were addressed by our informants and their children. This material is by no means a complete record, involving only about 160 individuals. But a total of over 800 'citations' was obtained, each mentioning how a specified type of relative was addressed, with many illustrations and much comment on the implications of the form of address used. In round figures, about 330 of these citations described how people addressed their parents, about 290 how they addressed their parents' siblings and about 200 their parents-in-law.[17]

The parental terms in particular showed a considerable range of variant forms of address: Mother, Mummy, Mum, Mamma, Ma, Momma, Mom, with corresponding forms for father – as well as first names and nicknames. But broadly they could be divided into formal terms, informal terms, personal names, and special forms of address, including nicknames. The relative distribution of the 330 instances is given in percentage figures in Table 31.

TABLE 31

Forms of address to parents

Mother	*Citations* %	*Father*	*Citations* %
Mother	32	Father	19
Mummy	32	Daddy	37
Mum	15	Dad	16
Mamma, Ma	9	Papa, etc.	9
Personal name	6	Personal name	6
Special term	6	Special term	13
	100		100

In general, the distribution between the categories is similar for both parents, as one might expect, save for one notable exception. Whereas Mother and Mummy share the field equally, Daddy stands out as a favoured appellation, with Father having only half this frequency. This discrepancy leads to the heart of a very interesting and important problem, that of the significance of kinship terms, particularly terms of address, as indices of concepts of relative status.

In discussing modern family relationships one is justified in assuming that questions of relative status, obligation and exercise of authority are apt to lie not far below the surface if they have indeed not erupted into active matters of dispute. They can co-exist with

[17] A 'citation' is in effect a single type description. In collating the results, for counting as a citation, each variant form of address used by a person was listed separately. But similar usage for more than one relative of the same type was aggregated, as was similar usage by children in the same family. These citations include terms used by informants for their ascendants and terms used by the children of informants. The age distribution is such that separation into two neat generation groups is not possible, though some broad differences are perceptible (see later).

strong emotional attachments between the members of the family; indeed, the very presence of such attachments may complicate the situation by giving a keener edge of conflict to the effort of any member of the family to meet what he or she regards as just claims. These problems may be symbolized by the kinship terms used in communication. In the face-to-face relations of family life people attach great importance to what they call one another. The linkage of personal name with sense of personal identity is obvious, and the various ritualizations which demonstrate this are well known to anthropologists. Much the same is true of kin terms of address, within the family most of all. People are apt to be very sensitive to the precise form of kin term used when they are spoken to, and conversely, the terms which they use to others of their family can also reveal sectors of their emotional life in which these others are concerned. The relationship is two-way: a person can choose what he would like to be called by members of his family, but he cannot impose his choice upon them; on the other hand, there is no point in using a particular form of address if the person spoken to will not respond. These issues often do not appear overtly, and convention, channelled through the guidance by parents at an early stage, often provides children with an equipment of kin terms which they do not themselves attempt to alter. Nevertheless, whether overt or not, social forces are at work.

Consider first the stereotype view, probably accurate a couple of generations or so ago, that Mummy and Daddy are the juvenile or nursery forms of address to parents,[18] and give place to Mother and Father as children grow up. As terms of reference this is clearly the case: few adult men or women of the English middle-class would care to speak to strangers about 'my Daddy' as a child would readily do, even though in the atmosphere of the home they might speak to other members of the family about 'Daddy'. In our case material children certainly had a predilection for Mummy and Daddy; the citations in which these terms were current among children were more than four times as frequent as those in which Mother and Father were used. Occasionally one can note a deliberate change from the more juvenile to the more adult usage. One middle-aged woman, Miss Lamb, described this. When she was young her parents were Mummy and Daddy. 'As we got older we spoke of our father as "the Pater" to each other. This was really just a growing-up stage. He was a Greek and Latin scholar and it probably came out this way to each other – "the Pater". Mother was "Mummy" then, and we consulted

[18] cf. *Oxford English Dictionary: Mummy*, a child's word for mother; formerly dialectal, in recent years fashionable in England. *Daddy*, a diminutive and endearing form of *Dad*, itself a childish or familiar word for father.

among each other and decided one day that we'd call her "Mother". We asked her what did she think, and she said it was all right, and was quite amused about it.' But in another context this woman said 'The modern thing today is no prefixes, isn't it? Children call their parents by their Christian name.'

But as terms of personal address Mummy and Daddy are not by any means just juvenilia. Of the persons recorded as using Daddy as a mode of personal address to a father, 35 were adult men and women, representing more than one-third of the adults from whom we got information in this section of our enquiry. Most but not all of these adults using Daddy were women. Those who used Mummy as a mode of address – again mostly women – were nearly as many. What is interesting is that while more preference was shown by the adults as a whole for Mother than for any other term of personal address to a parent, Daddy came next in order of usage, outstripping Father considerably.

What are likely to be the reasons for this? One plausible reason is the peculiar quality of the father–daughter relation, with its undertone of special intimacy and affection, for which Daddy seems to be regarded as an expression. But there is another plausible reason, which can help to account particularly for the retention of the form of address among men. The term Father as a mode of address apparently is thought by many people of the younger modern generation to be very stiff and formal; it is also held to suggest an authority pattern to which these young people are anxious not to concede too much weight. They tend then to use face-to-face terms which emphasize the informality and affective character of the father–child (especially father–son) relation. Daddy is one of these. Of the 40 citations of adult men's use of personal term of address for the male parent only 10 are for the use of Father; all the others are of Daddy and other informal terms. This interpretation is strengthened when one looks at the frequent use of Mother as a personal term of address. Here half the citations in which adult men address their female parent give this formal term, which can be reckoned as not to carry with it the same suggestion of authority. Women too are much more ready to use the basic maternal term; they use more formal address to the parent of their own sex than do men to theirs.

It is relevant also from this point of view to examine the question of consistency or parallelism in these parental terms of address. Ordinarily, one thinks of them going in pairs – mother, father; mummy, daddy; mum, dad; mom, pop. Rather more than half of the citations (including those of children's usage) did fall into such parallels. There is no doubt that as parallel pairs used by the same individuals, Mother and Father and Mummy and Daddy were by far the most favoured by our subjects. Of a total of 90 citations of such pairs, just half were of Mummy and Daddy – half of these again coming from children – and upwards of a third were of Mother and Father, while Mum and Dad accounted for only a sixth of the total. But a significant number showed some asymmetry – as a person who called his mother Mummy and his father Dad or Pop, or a family of children who called their mother Momma and their father by his Christian name. Prominent among these asymmetrical usages were those in which the mother was given the full status term Mother while the father was addressed by the more informal Daddy or Dad. Unconsciously, perhaps, for the most part, the father was stripped of his most formal attributes, but the mother was allowed to retain hers.

At the receiving end such informal terms, however, do raise questions of their propriety. To some people terms such as Mummy or Daddy, especially if used to them by adolescents or adults, savour of 'soppiness'; they are 'wishywashy'. Actually, few of our informants expressed themselves at all strongly on this point, and most seemed to have no objection to the continuation of such terms into adult life. One woman, however, did say that she disliked intensely 'the Mummy and Daddy business' and preferred that her children should call their parents by their Christian names. Against this view was the firm opinion of Mr Woollcombe, who regarded Daddy as a term which conserved his authority over his children, compared with their possible use of his Christian name. He said 'I don't like parents and children on Christian name terms. It's not right – suburbanites do it a lot – it's disrespectful . . . I want some authority in my home, so they (the children) call me "Daddy". I want some authority later.' This had point since informal as the term Daddy is, by convention it does convey a paternal status recognition, as against the use of forename, which conveys no idea of status at all. We shall return to the question of the use of forenames as terms of personal address later.

In the stereotype of parental terminology just mentioned husband and wife, each as adult member of a primary family, would address their own parents as Father and Mother, while their children address them as Daddy and Mummy. But lack of conformity to this pattern is most marked. We have material for 20 primary families which shows how husband, wife and child each addressed his or her parents. In only one case out of the score was the stereotype followed, though in one other case husband and wife combined Mother/Father terms with Mummy/Daddy terms. All the other cases of families show some variation. In a few, all members of the family use the same terms: in one, children as well as husband and wife use the Mother/Father terms of address; in a couple of others all use the Mummy/Daddy terminology. But all other cases show varying combination of terms. Three examples, taken haphazardly, illustrate this. Mrs Mitchie called her parents Mother and Father, her husband called his Ma and Pop and their small daughter called them Mummy and Daddy, occasionally also calling her father by his Christian name 'because she hears me saying it'. Mrs Lander called her parents Mother and Daddy, the children said Mummy and Daddy to the husband and wife, and the husband called his parents 'M' and 'D'. Mrs Lark called her parents Mamma and Daddy, the husband called his parents Mother and Father and their adolescent son addressed his parents as Mum and Pewter. (This last is one of the idiosyncratic forms which appear in some families as independent inventions. The etymology, according to his mother, was that the son when very small said once to his father 'You're pewterful' (? beautiful) and this, shortened to Pewter, remained as his description and pseudonym.)

It is impossible to elucidate determining factors in every variation. In half-a-dozen cases the terminology of parental address is the same for mother and child, but this pattern may be merely coincidental and is by no means a consistent one through the field. Regular progression neither by age nor by generation provides a sufficient explanation. What one is led to infer is that the raw materials for parent terminology supplied by general convention and by known example – Mummy, Daddy, Pop and the rest – are reworked in each family situation according to the interplay of status interests and other structural elements, and the climate of opinion which the members of the family have in matters of social relationships.

This is illustrated by two further features. One is the use of forename as a mode of address to parent by child. From a young child's point of view a kin term of address is a name, and it takes time to separate off category name = kin term, from personal name. There is no intrinsic reason why a child should not treat Daddy as a personal name for his father, like John or James. If it be objected that John and James are applied to single individuals, and Daddy to lots of individuals, the answer is that there are also lots of Johns and Jameses too. So conversely, John (or James) can appear to the child to be a suitable alternative to Daddy, if he hears other people around him using this name. But even in contemporary society few parents seem to have encouraged such a usage. Our records do contain cases of such use of forename by children for a parent, but relatively few. Among the 140 or so individuals for whom parental terms of address have been noted, only about 10 per cent used one or both forenames of their parents in speaking to them. This suggests what on other grounds one may imagine, that there has been a fairly strong built-in attitude of dissuasion of children from using their parents' forenames instead of kin terms. This attitude of disapproval sometimes finds specific expression in our records. Moreover, there is no marked evidence that this attitude has greatly altered in modern times; more than half of the few cases of forename use we have recorded were of people already adult, some even elderly; it is by no means only a recent phenomenon.

With parents, there is a sound sociological basis for this. Their disapproval does not take the form of an emotional outburst against lack of respect, as one might think, so much as a reasoned argument. For instance, Mrs Newfield in the course of discussion about use of names and kin terms said suddenly 'I'd have nothing against it if Ailsa (her small daughter) called me by my Christian name, but I don't think she would do it. She would not use it or pick it up. To her there is only one Mother, but there are two or three Mary's in our circle.' Miss Lamb explained the matter in much the same way from the other angle. 'This business of not calling people (by forename). . . . Mother, father or auntie is a nice relationship and why should it really go out? One would be losing something. I mean it keeps them on their relationship and gives them a bit more responsibility. Christian names – it immediately takes away the relationship basis because you can call any friends by Christian name. For example, if I think of a man as Walter (her father) he is a man, and I feel it is less close to call him that than "Daddy". I remember we tried this on as children.' One day her sister was heard calling 'Walter!' Their mother said 'Who are you calling?' Answer: 'Daddy'. Mother: 'But he's your father and you know him as Daddy and not as Walter.' Objection: 'But you call him that!' Mother: 'Yes, but I'm his wife.'

What the parent, and probably also the child, feels is that the uniqueness of the relationship is better preserved by a kinship term than by a forename, which gives no idea of status and role. It may be the child as well as the parent then who wants to keep to kin terms. But as will be shown again later when considering the treatment of parents' siblings, the issue of whether a senior shall be called by personal name by a junior is a broad one, with status notions deeply embedded, and with effects easily perceived.

A second feature illustrating the interplay of structural and conceptual elements in the determination of terminology of address to parents is the changes that occur according to the stage of the family cycle. As a child advances towards adult life the Mummy/Daddy terms may be replaced by Mother/Father in stereotyped fashion, or may be succeeded by the personal names of the parents. But a more striking change which involves a recognition of role substitution is the dropping of parental terms and use of grandparent terms instead; this can occur with the birth of children to the son or daughter.

Speaking in genealogical terms, it is nonsense for a daughter to call her own mother Grandma, but this is precisely what occurs in some cases. Sociologically, it makes good sense; what the woman is doing is to relate her mother to the new generation of children, to whom she is an important senior person, verbally as well as in other ways. Where this occurs, for the most part, it has appeared to take place without much conscious deliberation, but to have emerged as the family situation developed. But occasionally the change is conceptualized, as by Mrs Woollcombe, who had always called her parents Mummy and Daddy, but having produced several children in rapid succession was beginning to address them as Granny and Grandpa. 'We're beginning to call them (by) what they are to the children, otherwise it gets so confusing', she said. There is also another possible sociological reason for the adoption of the grandparental term; this is related to the difficulties of the affinal relationship (see pp. 418–22).

AUNTS AND UNCLES: A QUESTION OF RESPECT

The problems of kin terminology of address are less complicated with parents' siblings. In the terms themselves, there is little variation. However great the intimacy of relationship, the tie with uncle or aunt usually lacks that peculiar mixture of authority and affection which is apt to be a special quality of parenthood, and usually also that close daily contact characteristic of normal family life. So one may postulate that there is less incentive to find special terms to demonstrate this. Where, as in a large proportion of cases, kin terms of address are used to parents' siblings, Uncle has solid support; hardly any variation on this occurred in the 100 or so cases of our record. Perhaps primarily for linguistic reasons (its consonantal ending), however, Aunt is often given a diminutive suffix, and is converted to Auntie (or Aunty). The proportion of those who used Aunt as a term of address to those who used Auntie was about three to one, in a set of well over 100 users. (Otherwise, there was little variation on aunt, though a few people, usually from French or German background, used *Tante*.)

We discuss later the opinion of one of our informants that the use of the term Auntie is a breach of good manners, with a definite suggestion of class difference here. We found no other opinions to this effect. What we did find, on the other hand, was a sex bias in the use of the term. Of the users of Auntie, about 30 in all, four-fifths were female, suggesting that the use of the diminutive indicated not so much a class affiliation as a token of intimacy or familiarity, especially between women, or between women and girls, of different status. Some colour is given to this idea from various angles. Mrs Nudley, who called her parents' siblings Auntie, used to call her great-aunts Aunt . . ., presumably from greater respect. A young man who used to call his FBW Aunt . . . when he was a boy, now when he was grown up, she said, called her 'Auntie dear' – 'as a joke as I'm not much older than he is.' Another man and his siblings used to refer to their father's sisters as 'the Auntie Blokes', a jocular usage of familiarity which started when they were children and persisted – though presumably Aunt was used as a term of address.

The word Aunt or Uncle as a term of address is normally followed by the personal name of the relative spoken to. This has some identification value where more than one relative of the same category exists. But it would seem from our records that Uncle and Aunt are still in use occasionally as independent terms of address. Where this does occur, it would seem to be non-controversial, even if a little curt. While the omission of the personal name may be thought no more than odd, the omission of the category prefix – using personal name alone in speaking to aunt or uncle – is often looked upon with misgiving, even moral indignation. Opinions differ very much on the proprieties involved. But the views are apt to be quite forcefully expressed, showing a distinct interest in status questions.

A few of the many statements recorded will indicate the range and intensity of opinion on what might seem to be a rather superficial matter. A conventional position was that of Mr and Mrs Goodwin, who used Uncle and Aunt terms in addressing their kin, and also in speaking about each other's kin. Their children did the same. The husband said he kept up these terms of address as he felt 'odd' not using them. The Tomlinsons always used the terms as a mark of respect to parents' siblings; it 'avoids confusion where (personal) names are duplicated' – as they were in several instances in that family. 'We are very precise in these matters' Mrs Tomlinson said rather primly. Mrs Ghent said about her siblings' children: 'I think they should call me Aunt. The younger ones have to call me Aunt; I think it's respectful. But when they're in their late teens they can call me by my Christian name. They know I like this – my brother's children call their parents by Christian names – and I don't approve of it. They're different generations. To me the rudeness between generations today is appalling, and this is the public pressure of today; TV – appallingly rude manners. Unless they are shown respect at home, how can they expect to show it in the world later on?' Both she and her husband addressed their parents' siblings as Aunt . . . and Uncle . . ., and insisted that their first cousins' children as well as siblings' children should address them in the same way. Mrs

Regan said she disliked hearing small children address adults by their first names. She felt this was 'unthinkable', wrong and rather disrespectful. But when children reached their late teens she thought it all right if they dropped the Uncle/Aunt prefix. 'I think it's awful for little children to call grown-ups by Christian names. Awful! When small they (her brother's children) should call us Uncle and Aunt. But when older I'd not mind' – if they switched to calling her and her husband by their first names. (She and her siblings used to address their older relatives as Uncle and Aunt.) 'Respect' was also the keynote of usage in another case, though practice differed between parents and children here. The wife, of middle-age, always called her parents' siblings when she was young by their Christian names – 'that was the way it was in those days . . . parents were advanced and it was thought modern'. But now when she had adult children of her own she always talked of them as Uncle and Auntie So-and-so when she was discussing them with the children; she felt it was a sign of respect as they were so much older than these (adult) young people. But the son and daughter themselves called their own maternal uncle and his successive three wives all by Christian names.[19]

It is important to note sociologically that these ideas of respect, sometimes expressed with great fervour, attach on the whole in modern times at least to status by relative age rather than to status by genealogical position. In terms of the family cycle it is children primarily from whom the verbal tokens of respect are due. Typical of the behaviour of a number of aunts and uncles was the suggestion of one woman who, when her nephew reached the age of twenty or so and called her Aunt, said 'Let's drop it'. Similarly from the other side, as a child grows to maturity its view alters. 'You can't call them aunt and uncle when you are older.' The significance of childhood experience comes out in another way. Mrs Nebworth had always called a father's sister and father's brother by their forenames because she met them for the first time when she was no longer a child. 'You can't suddenly meet someone and start calling them Auntie', she commented – though she apparently felt she could use the Christian name quite happily on sudden meeting. Status of this uncle/aunt kind is then not automatic, but is a matter of growth, with a strong childhood referent. The ambivalence involved without the childhood context is illustrated by an experience of Mrs Regan. She said of her mother's sister that she always thought of this woman as Ethel, but always called her to her face Aunt Ethel, because she knew this woman expected her to and felt she should out of respect. She thought of this

[19] A very different point of view was expressed in another case, where a man's second wife was disliked by his junior relatives and called by her personal name, not Aunt, 'as a sign of *dis*respect'.

woman as Ethel because her mother always referred to her in this way, and our informant met her for the first time only ten years before when this aunt returned from South Africa on holiday. A more attenuated version of the 'respect' theme is given by cases where a parent has no strong views on children's conduct in this sphere, but persuades the child to adopt Uncle/Aunt terms less the feelings of the older person will be hurt.

In strong contrast to these views about courtesy and respect due to uncles and aunts being expressed by avoidance of their first names, at least when nephews and nieces are young, is the attitude that this is only a façade. One woman, mother of a whole brood of children, said that the Uncle/Aunt title prefixed to the first name showed a false sense of respect which didn't ring true, and she had preferred to dispense with it altogether. All her children had been encouraged to call their parents' siblings and friends by forenames, and the younger children went to a school where, with the approval of their mother, they addressed the staff also by first names. Mrs Maskell, who tended to call her own aunts and uncles by their first names, tried to prevent her own children from calling anyone aunt or uncle. She said of her own parental siblings 'We always called them by their Christian names . . . the only one not was Aunt Rachel and Uncle Oliver – we *did* call them auntie and uncle till we were about eleven . . . but that's not quite consistent; some were not. Emily (her mother's sister) was never auntie.' On her attitude towards her children's usage she said 'Aunt and uncle were severely quashed because I'm snobbish about it – I think it's awful. Mrs M (her mother-in-law) wanted Zoe (her daughter) at one time to call people aunt and uncle because she thought it was the conventional and right thing to do. Zoe did as she was told by Mrs M while I seethed in the background . . . and Zoe knew I was against it and wouldn't make her do it.' She then complained to her mother-in-law, made her objection clear 'and I squashed it'. So views *for* the use of first names by nephews and nieces in addressing their seniors can be just as strong as views *against* this. Opinions of a less analytical, perhaps more idiosyncratic kind are also expressed. An elderly single woman clearly had strong feelings on the subject. 'I won't be called Aunt, I loathe the term Aunt, I don't want to be an Aunt, it makes me feel grannified.' Mrs Vendor said that she called her parents' male siblings Uncle, except one father's brother, whom she called by his first name. 'He couldn't bear being called Uncle. Even his own children called him by his first name.'

Here then is a direct conflict of opinion, one side holding that the use of first names in addressing uncles and aunts is a modern usage, shows lack of respect and can only be condoned as nephews and nieces grow older; the other side arguing that the retention of these status titles shows only a false and superficial respect, and that significant social relationships are better achieved without them. Cutting across this opposition are various idiosyncratic views, but also the more reflective opinions of those who regard the usage as essentially tending to vary with difference in the social situation. An illustration of such a view is the statement by Mrs Willmott, mother of adolescent daughters, to the effect that she thought children went through a stage in their late teens when they did not care to use Aunt and Uncle terminology any more, even for parental siblings. She thought that children tended to become self-conscious about kin terminology at this stage, and to resent the acknowledgement of age and authority which these terms implied. But she added that she thought it was only a 'stage' and that most people grew out of it and were glad to use the kin terms again when they became adult. Perhaps this last sentiment involved a little wishful thinking, but it clearly embodies a very significant sociological reflection.

In the light of all this, what actual usage did we find in this field? The following table, though based on incomplete data, does represent a considerable body of evidence.

TABLE 32

Forms of address to parents' siblings

Used by	*Citation of* *Uncle-/ aunt-**	*First name alone*	*Mixed use*	*Total*
Adults:				
Women	38	3	14	55
Men	22	5	7	34
Young people	15	2	12	29
All	75	10	33	118

* Included in this are a couple of cases in which the French or German form of aunt (*Tante*) was used.

From this it is clear that as far as our data go, the notion that by modern custom young people use only first names to their uncles and aunts is just not correct. Young people who used only forenames to these relatives were, like the adults, only a handful, and those who used forenames even as alternates to the uncle/aunt terms, which they also used, were less than half. In all, those who used *only* some form of uncle/aunt terms of address comprised nearly two-thirds of the whole set recorded. So clearly 'modern' usage has not swept the board, even among the young; presumably the influence of general convention and of parents' guidance is still strong. Moreover, there are great variations in practice not simply in individual families, but even among individual people in regard to different aunts and uncles. Some are given the full formal treatment, others are called by their personal names, a few given nicknames. What we seem to be looking at in the field of kin term usage is a resultant of forces: status involvement; ideas of equality; age phasing as children grow to maturity; and perceptions of the impact of seniority and authority upon individuality. Expressive linguistic symbols, with the frame provided by convention and early upbringing, each tends to have assigned to it an idiosyncratic personal idiom.

Similar principles emerge in extensions of the Uncle/Aunt terminology to cover consanguineal kin wider than parents' siblings. Unlike cousin, aunt is a term of fairly precise connotation – it means basically mother's or father's sister, is expected to cover half- and step-kin of the same order, and by assimilation is applied also to the spouses of uncles – father's brothers' and mother's brothers' wives. But the term has conventional associations, including seniority by one generation. Hence a cousin who is very much older may be addressed as Aunt, even though other kin may disapprove. But the aunt role has much more to it than mere seniority. It connotes authority, but less than that of father or mother, and less responsibility, less intimacy, but still a friendly interest and the possibility of some flow of gifts and services. If nephews and nieces owe respect to their parents' siblings, the latter are typically regarded as a potential social asset. Hence there is a tendency for other senior female kin to be assigned to the aunt category if they tend to fill the stereotyped position, especially if parents' siblings are actually lacking.

We have several cases of this in our records. Mr Grant, whose father had no siblings and who met his mother's sister only once, when he was a child, referred to his FMBD as his second cousin (actually, father's first cousin) and called her Auntie Mary. This woman, two years older than our informant's father, had been brought up with the father in Highgate. 'They were more like brother and sister than cousins.' When she died she made her cousin the residual beneficiary of her will and left money to our informant and his two siblings. Mr and Mrs Grant also acquired her flat in Highgate, with much of her furniture and some of her oil paintings on the walls. More surprisingly, Mr Grant called his sister's husband's mother's sister Auntie Mabel; she was 'a marvellous old lady' of 89 years of age at the time of our study, living locally, and the ties with the sister's husband's kin were manifold and strong.

But for some of our informants the application of the aunt term had much more definite limitations. Mrs Offord had no siblings but a close relation with her father's sister's daughter, to whom she had been bridesmaid, and whom she saw at least twice a week. This woman's teenage daughter used to call our informant Aunt Joy, but as she grew mature this was rejected. Our informant told her not to, 'because it makes me feel old' and was firm that her first name alone should be used. The cousin, mother of the girl, agreed with this, saying that now the children were growing up there would be no need to use the aunt term. Here the rejection was based not on the genealogical inappropriateness of the term but on the changing age relation – just as with uncles and aunts of the ordinary category. But in an analogous case when Mrs Pillerth's FZDDs called her Auntie this infuriated our informant; she said, 'I can't stand this – as I'm not their aunt'. So the term 'aunt' does have for some people, probably for most, a fairly definite genealogical connotation, even if this does operate outside the immediate parents' sibling range.

Uncles and aunts of parents were very few. Some great-aunts had been assimilated to the aunt category, especially if they treated the children of their nephews and nieces with some of the same generous interest they bestowed on the nephews and nieces themselves. A man's mother's sister was 'very sweet' to his children. Unmarried, she lived with her brother in Scotland, and from time to time visited Edinburgh, where two of the children were at school, and took them out for an excursion. She also sent presents for the children, the second daughter being named after her. Whenever the family visited Scotland a visit to her was a 'must'. The children in return called her by a short form of her Christian name, like everyone else, and wrote to her as 'Dear Auntie . . .'.

Use of the terms uncle/aunt to the spouses of parents' siblings is a process of identification which is only part of a much more general tendency for spouses to merge their kin for many purposes. This process too can have its extensions, as when a spouse's sibling adopts the same terminology in turn for a husband's or wife's uncle or aunt.

PSEUDO-KIN AS UNCLES AND AUNTS

More than most words which are ordinarily kin terms, uncle and aunt tend to be used beyond the kin field, to apply especially to *friends* of one's parents. This is in line with a general connotation of these terms as implying seniority and respect yet some sort of familiarity, even service, as by gifts or advice. Metaphorically, the relation may often be described as 'avuncular'. We speak of such relationships as those of pseudo-kinship, because they counterfeit the forms of kinship, including the description – though this does not imply that there is necessarily anything false in the relationship. We distinguish pseudo-kin – friends who are given kin terms – from quasi-kin – people such as godparents – who are subsumed into the kin category. (Not only do godparents assume certain obligations approximating to those of the kin category; in some conditions marriage prohibitions apply to them and their children as if they were true kin.)

As with uncle and aunt in true consanguineal relationship, opinion varies as to what the pseudo-kin friends should be called by children. But in this instance there is not only the issue of respect versus familiarity; much of the argument turns on the propriety of using uncle/aunt terms at all for people who are not 'true' relatives.

The position of the purists on such a question was stated in one of its most extreme forms by Mrs Mitchie, mother of two young children. She herself didn't call anyone Aunt or Uncle who wasn't related; she thought that to do so was 'a dreadful practice'. She thought that people should be referred to by their Christian names or as Mrs So-and-so, etc. People who wanted unrelated children to call them Auntie were hypocrites, too full of their 'own sense of dignity'.

A more reflective approach to the problem was that of Mrs Danby, with three young children. She said that she and her husband got the children to refer to various relatives as Auntie . . . and Uncle . . . because the people concerned preferred it – 'one continues to do it because they like it'. But they wouldn't allow the children to refer to friends as uncle or aunt – such friends had to be called either Mr or Mrs – or addressed by Christian name. She and her husband didn't think it very logical for the children to refer to or address non-kin by kin terms. 'We decided this because we felt it was a little silly to call people who weren't your relatives Aunt and Uncle.' She added that such a practice served only to muddle a child because then eventually everyone in its environment was referred to by a kin term: ' "There's a new auntie over there . . ." ! It is confusing to the child, apart from anything else because it goes out and out in ever-widening circles' to include virtually anyone with whom the children come into contact. Another facet of this view was put by Mrs Newfield who, by origin, was a mid-European Calvinist. 'I hate this business of Aunt So-and-so, it does not mean anything. An aunt is somebody I could turn to. It means something. If you call everybody aunt, it is like Mr or Mrs, no special relationship.'

So the assimilation of friends to kin positions, even if only verbally, is disliked strongly by a number of people. But their reasons for disliking the custom are variously expressed – confusion of categories, hypocrisy of adults, confusing to the children, crossing the class barrier. Other people may discourage or would like to discourage their children from using the aunt/uncle terms for non-relatives, but find their children have created such pseudo-kin, either on their own initiative or because the friends have wanted to be so called. Mrs Nudley said that as a child she herself used to call 'everybody' aunt and uncle. When she grew older she dropped this usage entirely, and she began to call her parents' close friends by their first names, 'after an initial period of embarrassment when one didn't call them anything'. Her small daughter hadn't called her friends anything till recently, but was now beginning to say Auntie. The mother said she didn't really like making a little child call an unrelated adult Auntie – 'but they can't say Mr and Mrs and not all adults like children to call them by their first names'. She thought the outcome would depend on the adult's wishes. Again, there were others who disliked the custom though they themselves either called some of their parents' friends Aunt or Uncle or allowed themselves to be called such by children of friends. Another woman said, 'I don't like pseudo-titles – it is only forgivable if a person is a lot older than you are'. But she had one pseudo-aunt who was a friend of her parents, and whom both she and her small son called aunt. Mrs Outram felt quite strongly, she said, that her children should not use kinship terms for people who were not kin, yet her husband had a godfather of whom he was very fond, and whom he called Uncle. She herself was called Auntie by some of her own godchildren although she did not like it. Such instances of apparent discrepancy between opinion and action illustrate how complex this matter is; they also suggest how social strains can arise in seemingly trivial situations.

But in contrast to such disapproving views about the use of uncle/aunt terms towards non-relatives are other opinions of a much more positive kind. These maintain in effect that the use of uncle/aunt for non-kin is not really a confusion of categories, and does not assimilate friends to kin in anything more than name. It is a usage of courtesy and respect and, moreover, of convenience, providing an easy solution to the problem of how children shall address people who stand to them in a fairly close relationship without being actual kin.

Mrs Grant, with four children, said that she encouraged them to use the uncle/aunt terms towards all adults with whom their parents were on Christian name terms. This included those of the children's godparents who were non-kin. (One of the children told the interviewer how Uncle Ricky – a non-kin godfather – had taken him to the pantomime.) In this woman's view the practice was useful because she didn't think children should call adults by their first names. She didn't think that the use of a kin term for these people implied that they were particularly close, or that it put them in a 'kin' position. She herself still referred to a friend of her mother's as Auntie Mary. Some informants brought even the interviewer into the Auntie category – 'Show the auntie your photos'; 'Don't do that or the auntie will think you're a naughty boy', etc. But there was also discrimination. All the Woollcombe family friends were addressed by the two children as Aunt/Uncle, and it was made clear that this was purely a title of respect and didn't denote any kind of near-kin relationship; relatives and friends were thought of as separate. Moreover the children were not urged to call *anyone* Aunt/Uncle. Little Helen, laying the table for tea, asked her mother whether Auntie (the interviewer) would like a big or a small mug. The mother corrected her daughter, 'The lady, Helen dear, that's not Auntie'. The interviewer's comment was: 'The child (aged 3½) was still too young to distinguish who was and who was not an Auntie, and poor Helen didn't know how to address me after her mother's mild correction.'

Most commonly it is the parents of young children who take it upon themselves to begin the practice of using uncle/aunt terms for their friends. But occasionally the outsider willl take the initiative. In some cases the adult's presentation of himself or herself to the child might be bewildering. Mrs Fortescue said that she had been told to call all her parents' women friends Auntie; it was considered a term of respect in cases where her parents called their friends by their Christian names. 'There were hundreds of them. They referred to themselves as Auntie – for example, "I'm your Auntie Peg, dear, remember me?" – when one couldn't remember ever seeing her before.' But this custom, inhibiting as it might be, did have one advantage, she pointed out; it meant that one could be more familiar with their children – treat them like brothers.

On the whole, however, those people who approve of the uncle/aunt address to non-kin are fairly discriminating in the people they admit to this privilege, just as people who disapprove in general may allow certain exceptions to the rule.

In one type of context, rather neutral, the use of the Uncle/Aunt terms for non-kin is allowed to develop if there seems a place for it. Mrs Willmott said that her children did use these terms for some close family friends when they were young; she thought this might be partly explained by the fact that she herself had no brothers and sisters on whom they could use these terms.

In special cases in which services of an unusual kind had been rendered, the ties between pseudo-kin Uncle or Aunt and other party might be very close indeed. A man whose mother died when he was seven and whose father had deserted her earlier, was brought up by a close friend of his mother's, whom he called his aunt. 'I was very fond of her and called her Aunt and treated her as badly as any son treats his mother and with permanent extortions. . . . But she was unique in my life . . . the centre, the hub, the home, the hearth . . . she sent me to school and she was still the home . . . and I would feel that, as with my mother, I'd turn to her.' With all this, though he spoke of her later to his own children as his 'foster-mother' he did not, he said, think of her as a relative, nor of her relatives as kin to himself. 'It was always firmly put into me that I was not of the family, so I don't think of them as family . . . I kept my own name and that's a sufficient reminder in itself to a child . . . and it was done deliberately because my "aunt" was not married . . . though she was fifty when she took me on and there was little biological possibility of her being able to have a child; it was done therefore to save her reputation.' This case is interesting because it helps to show the great range which may be comprised under the aunt term. Here it was essentially the mother role which the woman assumed, yet she did not assume the term Mother, as presumably she might well have been able to do, by persuading the boy to call her this. Yet the boy had to call her something; if either Miss – or Christian name were inappropriate, as they might well seem from a boy of seven, then what? A kinship term was the obvious answer, yet one which maintained some nominal social distance between them, since she was a spinster who wished to preserve her good name.

In a few cases the opinion was expressed that while our informants themselves may have used the Uncle/Aunt terms in addressing non-kin, this custom is getting out of date now, and children call their parents' friends by Christian names. One woman put it in analogous fashion by saying that in her day parents' friends were referred to as Mr –, Mrs –, etc. whereas 'now of course there's been a complete change to Christian names'.

Our general figures do not bear out this suggested wholesale abandonment of parents' friends as pseudo-uncles and pseudo-aunts. Of our 90 cases we have information for about 70, and uncle/aunt terms for non-kin were used in just over 40 of them. In the remainder for the most part either formal titles or first names were used by children for parents' friends. It seems a fair inference that the advantages of the pseudo-kin usage still outweigh the objections seen to it. But the factor of relative age still persists nowadays as a very important determinant of the terminology. It was frequently reported that the children used to call some people Uncle and Aunt whom they now called by their Christian name, and that people who wished young children to call them Uncle and Aunt 'from respect' were willing to waive this as the children reached maturity. Even after maturity age may have its claims. One couple who had no children of their own used to tell their friends' children not to call them Aunt and Uncle – 'It's a bit silly when they get older – a left-over of when you were small. It's the sort of thing expected in the Victorian age.' Yet they themselves, in their fifties, always called Aunt an old lady who came to them for Christmas and Easter. She was an old friend of the woman's stepmother, and they said it sounded very formal to say Mrs. Yet they did not like to call her by her first name because of her age – an interesting instance of what may be called the 'respect imperative'.

To sum up, this issue of using kin terms for non-kin often poses a problem, if only a minor one, for the parents of young children. Many parents feel a reluctance to encourage the child to develop what they feel to be a false categorization. Yet they are faced by the dilemma of what to substitute for kin terms. Surnames are too formal, first names too familiar, and many of them are too hard for a small child to pronounce anyway. Moreover, many parents – and many children less consciously – wish to mark the special kind of relationship and services that may exist with family friends. For the child to use the senior kin terms of Aunt and Uncle is about the simplest solution,[20] and it is for their convenience as much as for any other reason that many parents seem to tolerate a usage that they dislike. But on one point they seem to be emphatic: while the anthropologist may think that use of the kin term implies that these people are thought of in some way as being kin, or like kin, the parents deny this vigorously. Relatives and friends are different, and use of the same words for each does not bring them together. What in effect they argue is that Uncle and Aunt have two separate meanings; the one is an extension of the other, but kin and friends as categories are not merged thereby.

This ability to use a common pair of terms for two separate categories of social relationship is a point of wider theoretical significance in the study of kinship, since too often anthropologists have tended to assume that same term implied not only shared role in some respects but also that the people concerned were thought of as being in some sense the same.

GRANDPARENTAL TERMS

There is less to be said about the use of most other consanguineal kinship terms. Siblings are called by first names, as for the most part

[20] In one case an adolescent boy called some of his parents' male friends 'Sir' – which his mother added with a smile 'is a very good sign of discipline in the young, I feel!' But then, the boy was going to Harrow!

are cousins of all kinds. The term cousin as a mode of address in combination with the first name has not, however, completely yet passed out of English usage, though it is rare. We have in our records about ten instances of this usage. A few informants described the custom as old-fashioned. One said that when she was younger she used the term Cousin in writing and sometimes in speech as a mode of address, but she thought that this usage had now died out. Another said that she was herself called Cousin Alice by the family of her MBS, and that she 'just thought it was funny'. Where the usage did occur it was primarily as a mark of respect to seniority, either to a cousin of a parent, or to a cousin of one's own who was so much older as to belong in effect to the uncle/aunt generation.[21] Sometimes the senior relative preferred this form of address. A schoolboy got from a couple of elderly female cousins of his father's letters signed 'from your cousin . . .', to which he replied sometimes 'Dear cousin . . .' and sometimes 'Dear . . .' His mother, Mrs Lark, commented: 'But I don't encourage all this cousin business . . . only if she was very old, as a sign of respect.' A FBD of the Tomlinson parents, an army officer, was called by her first name by all members of the family except the youngest son, a boy of nine, who called her Cousin Amy. The term cousin was introduced because the parents felt, they said, that it wasn't correct for him to call her by her first name alone and nothing else seemed appropriate. When a Canadian FBS of Mr Pillerth visited London with his wife and children, the two families had a discussion about what his children should call our informants; they decided on the Cousin terms. Our informants' children picked this up in turn and began to call the FBS and his wife Cousin . . . too. Their mother thought this 'rather nice', though she herself didn't call anyone cousin.[22]

Outside the parental field the greatest variation of kin terms of address lay in grandparental relations. At first glance developments in the two fields seem very similar. We can accept in principle the view put forward much earlier by Radcliffe-Brown and others that grandparents, while resembling parents in some characteristics, differ from them structurally in being much less concerned with authority over the child, hence the tendency is for the relationship between grandparents and grandchildren to be marked by especial familiarity, even if they are not equated. The basic grandfather and grandmother terms, therefore, tend to effloresce into a number of abbreviations and diminutives which reflect this familiar, informal

[21] See Chapman, op. cit., pp. 233–4.

[22] An idiosyncratic example of conscious decision about kinship terms was a man who called his FBD 'Sweet Cos' when he talked to her, and put 'Dear Cos' in his letters to her brother – 'but he was rather affected anyway'!

relationship. But there is a special problem here. A person has only one pair of parents, who are clearly distinguished as individuals in terminology as in role. But there are two pairs of grandparents, for whom in English one basic pair of terms must serve. Hence the proliferation of grandparent terms may have to serve an additional function than in the case of parents, by assisting in the differentiation of mother's parents from father's parents.

In many cases, of course, no problem of differentiation arises since not all the four grandparents are alive. Even where they are the problem is sometimes met by using surnames, or place-names, affixed to the grandfather terms. But commonly where the problem arises it is met by using different forms of the basic terms for mother's and father's parents.

About half a dozen variations on each of the two grandparents terms have been developed, but interest tends to be concentrated on only two or three of them. In a set of 100 citations for the term of address to grandmother, drawn haphazardly as the information was available, Grandma (Granma) and Granny (Grannie) made up about 70 per cent, each of about equal use. The next most popular form was Nanna (Nannie, Nan), with Grandmother, Grandmama, Grandmummy, Gran, Big and Little Gran, Grana, and special forms or nicknames all very low on the list. For about 70 citations of grandfather terms of address, the most popular was Grandpa (about 40 per cent) and then Grandad (Granddad, Granda) with about 20 per cent. Grandfather had considerably less popularity, while Grampie, Grandpop, Grandpapa and Granddaddy were used by only one or two people.

What is noteworthy is the number and range of special terms used for grandparents, especially grandfathers, by particular individuals. Grandfathers have been called variously, according to our records, Papa, Pops, Dandy, Buma, Pepe, Guido, Uncle Joe, Idle Jack (from a child's tale), as well as by a Chinese term for that relative, and by their initials. Grandmothers have had less variegated appellations, but they include Anoo, Oma, Giky, Gangan and Gala, as well as Aunt Queenie, and terms in Russian. A few of these terms, such as Oma (German *Omama*, Grannie) obviously derive from a different cultural usage; the child has picked up a foreign term which he has heard his mother use to his grandmother. Others are adult inventions. In one family the children called the mother's mother Granny, but the father's mother didn't want to be called this because it made her feel too old. So the children's mother thought up the name Giky for them to use when they were talking about the problem. Other terms were a child's own coinage. Gala illustrates how such a family term came into being. It originated with a woman's eldest child who when very young could not pronounce Grandmother in addressing her mother's mother; the nearest she could get was *Gamala.* The second child, a boy, took this up, but corrupted it still further to Gala, a word which came to be used in turn by all eight of the woman's children; moreover, it was adopted by the grandmother's whole group of descendants.

The asymmetry in the use of the terms for male and female grandparent should be remarked. In our material Grandma and Grandpa are a popular pair of terms, but equally so are Granny and Grandpa as a pair. Granny and Granddad are much less frequently paired, Grandma and Granddad hardly at all. Grandmother and Grandfather go together, but are rarely used. Granddaddy and Grandmummy were discovered in use once each – in separate families – but Grandmum not at all. The parallel with Granddad in frequency of use would seem to be Nanna[23] and its derivatives; but they are not linked necessarily; Nanna can be used with Grandpa, Grandad or Grandfather – it has no exact linguistic parallel of its own. Differentiation of grandparents by using separate terms for them therefore tends to follow no standard rule. What one might think to be an intelligible practice, that mother's mother should be assigned a less formal, more intimate term than father's mother is in fact followed in some cases: mother's mother is called Grannie[24] or Nannie; father's mother, Grandma. In the case just cited, it was the mother's mother who was called by the child's name Gala; the father's mother was called Grandmama.

The suggestion made by Goody, that Nanna (Nana, Nannie, Nan) is a term used for mother's mother, whereas Grandma or analogous term is used for father's mother, is borne out on the whole by our evidence. Of eleven cases of Nanna usage, nine were for the maternal and only two for the paternal grandmother; here a woman called her father's mother by this term and her children used the term for both grandmothers. (The class implications of this term are discussed later.) But it is probably significant that in our sample of a dozen Nanna usages, there were no men. Nanna was a term used by women and children only. Male children used it, but only when they were young. The association of the idea of Nanna (grandmother) with Nanny (nurse) put forward by Goody has some support from our material. Mrs Herbert indeed described her best nanny for the

[23] For an ingenious discussion of the etymology and use of Nanna see J. Goody, 'On Nannas and Nannies', *Man*, 1962, No. 288.

[24] *Grannie, grannie* – a familiar, endearing or contemptuous synonym of grandmother, probably formed on *grannam, grandam* (Oxford English Dictionary). In comment on this we should point out that we found no contemptuous use of this diminutive.

children as 'an auxiliary grandmother' – (but not a substitute grandmother)!

It would seem reasonable too that whereas grandmothers should be differentiated, there is less need to differentiate grandfathers, and they can be called by the same term. This too occurred in our material. But there were many variations. The nearest to a classic form of distribution of terms was the case where children called their father's father and (step)mother Grandfather and Grandmother and their mother's father and mother Granpa and Granma. Mrs Herbert called her mother's parents Granny and Granddad, and her father's parents Grandmaman and Grandpapa – the reason for the French terms being that she had a French nanny and spoke French before English. Her own children had called her parents Granny and Granddad, which is what she herself had called her mother's parents, and they called their father's parents Grandmummy and Grandpapa – just to make the difference from their mother's, she said. But the pattern through the generations was complicated by the fact that this woman's husband had a daughter by an earlier marriage. This daughter called her stepmother's parents Aunt Dora and Uncle Oram, thus dropping a generation for them, while the daughter's children called the stepmother – our informant and their step-grandmother – by her first name, while they called their grandfather Granddad. In the Danby kin group a special term was invented to cope with a step-grandfather. The Danby children called their mother's father Granpa, their father's father Granpa Danby (with his surname suffixed) and their father's mother Granma. But this woman had divorced her Danby husband and remarried. As the children already had two grandfathers, their father's mother thought up a term Gafa for her second husband, which was near enough to Grandpa for the children to use, but which would avoid confusion.

The need for differentiation of grandparents by their grandchildren is to some extent a function of the degree of contact between them. It is for this reason in some cases that terms for two grandmothers or grandfathers are allowed to be coincident. This may be quite a conscious process on the part of the parents. Mrs Vendor's children called her mother Grannie and their father's mother Grandma – 'to distinguish her from my mother'. They called their mother's father Grandpa and his second wife (he had been divorced) by her first name. But they called their father's stepfather Grandpa also, by the same term as that used for their mother's father. Their mother said that it wasn't necessary for the children to have a separate term for him because they saw so little of him.

The point of all this detail is to demonstrate how kinship terms such as those used for addressing grandparents can be used with flexibility and manipulated to meet varying social situations. This is particularly useful when dealing with children, for whom otherwise confusion might be caused.

A final point is that grandparental terms, like uncle and aunt, can be extended beyond the immediate frontier, even to affines. Mrs Neville, for instance, had very friendly relations with her FBSW, and called this woman's mother Grandma. Again, structurally, extension can be made to three or more generations by the addition of the prefix great-. We have two cases of living great-grandparents in our records. In one, a wife's mother's mother and father were called by her and her husband Granny and Granpa before the children were born; afterwards they addressed the old couple as Greatgranny and Greatgranpa, using the same terms as the children did. In the other case, however, the same process of telescoping a generation occurred as with great-aunt and aunt; the mother's mother's mother was called simply Gran (their mother's mother being called Grannie) or even apparently addressed by a short form of her first name. Occasionally, as happened to one of our interviewers, a grandparent term may be applied to a non-relative to create a convenient category for the child to classify a newcomer. But by far the most important use of grandparent terms is that made by affines, a point which will be discussed in another section of this Chapter.

TERMS FOR STEPKIN

A special problem of kinship terminology arises when a parent has contracted a second marriage. At one stroke, a person is confronted with a relationship with one or more strangers with whom possibly he has had no previous contact. The relationship so created is structurally ambiguous. These people are assimilated in position to close consanguineal kin, parents and siblings. Yet the assimilation has arisen simply by the acts of another person and by legal process. The individual affected has neither grown up with these new kin nor selected them for himself. How then shall he address them? Granted individual differences in the history of their relationships (a second marriage is sometimes contracted with a relative or a close friend, well-known to the family) and in personal temperament, in some cases there tends to be a stress on the assimilation aspect and in others on differentiation. (We leave out of account here relations with step-siblings who, on the whole, tend to be assimilated on a basis of equality by use of the first name in address.) The problem arises mainly with senior kin, stepmother or stepfather, or occasionally step-grandparent.

In ten cases clearly located in our records three methods of dealing with the situation appeared to be used. One was to call the step-parent by the parent term: in three of the ten cases a stepmother was called Mother or an equivalent. One of these was very striking. A man's son called his stepmother Mum, and called his own mother by her first name. He only knew his mother after he was practically grown up. When his father's first marriage split up (according to the stepmother, under the influence of the husband's mother) this grand-mother was determined that her son's wife should not get custody of the child. He therefore only came to know his mother much later on, and grew up hearing her referred to by her first name. We do not know whose idea it was that he should call his stepmother Mum, probably hers, in an attempt to get into personal contact with him. That his use of the term indicates an appreciation of her services to him is likely, since it was she who, thoughtful for the boy, traced his own mother and brought them together.

Another method of assimilation into the kin field, which does not, however, have the intimacy of the parental relationship, is the use of a term such as Auntie. This term had a meaning for one woman because her stepmother was, in fact, her mother's sister. But the retention of the aunt term indicated the step-daughter's attitude of preserving some social distance between them. The woman's father, left a widow, married his late wife's sister. When asked why she continued to call her new stepmother Aunt, the woman replied, 'I couldn't change it'. Her husband, who was present at the interview, commented, 'She would have loved you to have called her Mother'. The wife replied, 'It never entered my head to call her anything but aunt'. She said she had never considered the matter before, nor did her aunt expect to be called anything else. There had been little change when her father and aunt married, since they had been living in the same house for years before. 'Everybody thought it the right thing to do.' This was an obvious case of the acquisition of new status not being fully coincident with change of role, and consequently retention of the former terminology seemed appropriate. (Our informant had also another unorthodox 'aunt' relationship. Her mother's brother married one of her first cousins, a FBD, and she called this woman Aunt rather than by any other term, or by first name.) In another case the stepmother was addressed as god-mother by one of her stepdaughters, but this again reflected an already existing relationship; it gave a satisfactory solution to the naming problem.

In yet another case of extended aunt terminology a step-grand-mother was called Auntie. This telescoping of a generation was quite intelligible since the woman was the much younger second wife of a very old man, called Granddad by numerous grown-up grandchildren, and it would have seemed incongruous to have called her grandmother. The aunt term expressed relative age grading and the respect and familiarity due to their grandfather's wife.

The third method of dealing with the ambiguity in the step-parent relationship is the use of first names. In one of these cases a stepfather used to be called Daddy when his stepdaughter was young, but she called him by his first name as she grew up. Use of the first name in such cases, although superficially indicating some intimacy, may in fact be less an indication of familiarity than a method of dealing with a social problem. This is particularly likely to be so when all the parties concerned are adults in middle age or later. Here the use of first name for a father's second wife by his children who already have children of their own is one of the few simple methods of meeting the dilemma. Hence we find that while first names may be used for stepmothers, their stepchildren may really be very ignorant about them or even antagonistic towards them. The simplest demonstration of this is a statement by one of our informants that she called her father-in-law Dad and his second wife by her first name, and her husband also called his father Dad and stepmother by her first name – to her face; 'I won't say what he calls her in private.'

The same problem arises to a lesser degree with grandparents, and we have already given examples of the use of special terms to meet the situation (p. 325).

PARENT-IN-LAW TERMS: PROBLEM AND SOLUTION

With relatives by marriage the whole question of what to call them takes on a special significance. They are normally presented to a person in adult life, not as figures known since childhood. They come as the result of one's own choice of marriage partner, yet they themselves are not directly chosen. They come with the spouse – as one woman said rather acidly, 'When you marry you take over your husband's kin' – and there is a quality of inevitability about them. So tension is likely and the words in which the relationship is expressed often bear this out.

With affines of one's own generation the issue is not so acute – first names will serve and some show of familiarity is easy. But with affines of a senior generation, mother-in-law and father-in-law especially, constraint often appears.

A crucial fact and, when one thinks of it structurally, a surprising fact about people to whom one is related by marriage is that in the English kinship system there is no specific term by which to *address* them. They are spoken of as father-in-law, mother-in-law, etc., but are not ordinarily spoken to in such terms. This sets a problem, which for many people is serious and is often unsuspected by others: what to called these 'in-laws'? Affines must be addressed by terms borrowed from the consanguineal field, unless their names are to be used or some other device adopted. Use of first names presents no serious problem with people of the same generation or from senior to junior generation; but it can be a source of considerable embarrassment for sons-in-law or daughters-in-law who are addressing their spouses' parents. Yet surnames may sound stiff, and parental terms too intimate. The difficulty is the greater since this is a problem which strikes people in early adult life, without that childhood preparation which is usual with other kinship usages.

A few examples indicate some of the varieties of mode of address to 'in-laws'. Mr and Mrs Herbert each called the parents of the other by Christian names. The wife said it was particularly easy for her husband since he was not much younger than her mother, and it would have seemed strange had he used any other form. She said that the problem of what to call their parents-in-law was settled quickly, with the minimum of fuss. Mrs Mitchie called her husband's parents by their first names; she had known them before she met her husband and all his friends did so. But he called her parents Mr and Mrs with surname. She remarked that they were very much older than he was, and he didn't see them very often, and that anyway they were the sort of people who 'just wouldn't be called by their Christian names. They would think it very peculiar if anyone did'. In a further set of combinations Mrs Maskell, who had been widowed when young and later remarried, called her first husband's mother by her personal name, but wrote to her as Grandma – 'as a sort of joke' – adopting her child's term. When she herself was a child she called her parents Mummy and Daddy. She later began to call her mother Dally, which had been her small niece's adaptation of Dad-dad, which she had confused with Granny. This Dally term was then adopted by everyone in the family, including our informant's husband and the children. Her father was long dead. Her husband's father was addressed by his Christian name by everyone, the children included, but the husband's mother was called Doy (pronounced Doughy). According to her husband and his sister their grandmother was called Ho Mama and their mother Do Mama – 'because she was like dough!' This nickname of Doy was used by a lot of people, including her daughter and the children, though our informant called her by her first name to her face.

Lacking a specific kinship term for parental affines, there is a variety of patterns available in our society, any one of which may be adopted by junior affines in speaking to their fathers- and mothers-in law.

i Parent terms, formal or informal, adopting spouse's usage.
ii Surname, prefixed by Mr and Mrs, adopting stranger's usage.
iii First names, adopting familiar usage of equality.
iv Grandparent terms, adopting own children's terms, in familiar usage of junior to senior.
v Special terms of an invented or imitative kind, sometimes semi-humorous, in 'joking relationship'.
vi 'Nothing at all' – son- or daughter-in-law sedulously avoids using any term of address, practises a tacit avoidance, and uses personal pronouns only.

Some of these solutions[25] veer towards the side of respect and even social distance, others towards that of familiarity and even equality. In Chapter 12 we examine this problem of affinal terminology in detail.

KINSHIP TERMS AND CLASS CONSCIOUSNESS

In the course of our study we have come across a few indications that some kinship terms are regarded as having a class connotation. There is a popular view that Mum and Dad are *the* characteristic terms of reference as well as of address in working-class circles, and Goody (op. cit.) has suggested that Nanna is above all the term for a Mum's Mum – a kind of working-class counter to the upper-class Nanny, where role on a kinship basis has replaced role on an economic basis. Where do middle-class people stand in this respect?

Our analysis has been able to establish what are the patterns, empirically speaking, of a sample of North London middle-class people. But how far do their usages assume what may be regarded as a class form? This question is not easy to answer, if only because there has been very little specific investigation of kin term usage from such a point of view elsewhere in English society.

Without undertaking any elaborate historical enquiry one can see some evidence for past class differentiations in usage, as examplified by the Oxford English Dictionary's discussion of terms for mother and father. This authority is very cautious on the point for the most part, contenting itself with describing usage as 'fashionable' on the one side or 'unfashionable' or 'vulgar' on the other. Thus *Mam* is described as colloquial, a childish (formerly also a familiar or vulgar)

[25] R. W. Chapman (op. cit., p. 234) notes this problem but lists only four solutions.

word for mother; corresponding to *Dad* but now more strictly confined to infantine use or allusions to this. *Dad* is treated as a childish or familiar word for father, originally ranking with *Mam* for mother, but now less typically childish. It has occurred from the sixteenth or possibly the fifteenth century in representations of 'rustic, humble or childish speech' but may well have been in use much earlier. *Daddy* is given no class ranking. *Mummy*, a childish alteration of *Mammy*, formerly dialectal, has in recent years become fashionable, whereas *Mum* is listed as a vulgar variation of Ma'am, which itself is a colloquial shortening of Madam. (*Mum* is also allowed as a 'pet' name for mother.) *Mamma* (spelt Mama especially in the early nineteenth century) has attracted the most attention. An equivalent of mother, its status has always been the same as that of *Papa*. In the eighteenth century, though *Mamma* as used by young children was probably common, *Mamma*: seems to have been confined to the upper classes, and among them to have been freely used not only by children but also by adults of both sexes. In the nineteenth century its use was much extended and among the lower middle-class it was a mark of 'gentility' (the Dictionary's own inverted commas). Latterly in England it has become unfashionable, even as used by children. *Ma*, a childish and colloquial shortening of *Mamma* (used freely in the nineteenth century) is 'now often ridiculed as vulgar'. *Papa*, too, an equivalent of father, was in its first introduction from French, courtly and polite and used even by adults. It was long considered as 'genteel' but more and more left to children and in the second half of the nineteenth century was largely abandoned even by them.

So, officially speaking, there has been a downward class shift in *Papa* and *Mama*, then a tendency to leave them to the children who in the end have almost given them up. *Mummy* has become fashionable but *Mum* is vulgar, while *Dad*, apparently not so vulgar, has become more adult, and *Daddy* remains a classless term of childish endearment. Broadly, this could fit what we would guess to be regarded as the position in the U and non-U terms of Professor Alan Ross and Miss Nancy Mitford – that Mother and Father as formal terms of address, and Mummy and Daddy as informal terms tend to be middle-class and upper-class polite usage, while Mum and Dad epitomize the working-class terminology.

Now where do our informants stand in all this? It is clear from the earlier material, including the Table on p. 306, that they do not present a united front; they use among them a great range of terminology, fashion and unfashion, 'genteel' and 'vulgar'. Moreover, the same family and even the same person may use several forms. As far as parental terms of address are concerned, there is certainly a good sprinkling of Mums and Dads – about a seventh of the total citations by our subjects. But is this an indication of the working-class origin of a good proportion of our subjects, or of the spread of working-class terms up into the middle-class belt, or of developments in the direction of greater brevity and informality common to all classes in these modern times – or that the labelling of such kin terms as 'working-class' or 'upper-class' is perhaps itself too rigid? We are inclined to think that the latter suggestions are more likely correct.

In the first place, the more class-tinged terms in our samples were fairly evenly distributed among men, women and children, and between Greenbanks and Highgate. Moreover, for the most part the users of them were apparently without self-consciousness in this respect. In the only case in which we did get a spontaneous reaction in this field the implication turned out to be far from straightforward. Mrs Pillerth told us how when her children were small they called their parents Mummy and Daddy. Their father, a professional man whose own father had been in medicine, was at the time of our study still called Daddy or Pop or even 'You' – and the children wrote to their parents 'Dear Mummy and Daddy'.[26] But when the children were about thirteen they began to call their mother 'Mum'. A woman of good professional family, she was scandalized and at first refused to answer – she thought it so unpleasant. But they persisted and finally she did reply, in effect accepting the appellation though she hated it. She explained to our interviewer that she thought it was 'the influence of school' that made them use the term. In line with the hypothesis we are examining one might have expected they went to grammar schools – but one was a well-known boys' public school and the other a very select girls' private school! The daughter continued to use Mummy occasionally, the son not. Yet while their mother thought Mother a much pleasanter term than Mum she did say, 'I would feel very odd if they suddenly called us Mother and Father'.

So, if Mum and Dad be the hallmark of working-class kinship usage of personal address to parents, they are not exclusive indices. The use of them does not stamp a person as necessarily working-class, or even of working-class origins. What seems far more plausible is that the distribution of Mums and Dads – and analogous abbreviations – among the parental terms of address is a concomitant of a growing trend to informality in child – parent relations. Though there is retention of kinship terms by the child, for reasons already

[26] Our colleague Eugénie Henderson has suggested that while the term Daddy is classless, 'class' may come into the length of time that the use of it persists in a family.

discussed, informal terms are preferred; the terms selected therefore tend to include some representation of what has been formerly regarded as working-class usage, since relatively greater informality in parent or child relations would seem to have been characteristic of such families.

But the class issue arises also in other contexts. The most clear-cut pronouncement came from Mrs Herbert, a woman of county family, on the question of the use of Aunt terms. She was quite unequivocal that the diminutive Auntie (Aunty) had class connotations. When she herself was a child, she said, she called her parents' siblings Uncle and Aunt, and when she grew up she substituted first names for those of them whom she liked. When her own children were small they called their parents' siblings Uncle and Aunt also. 'They always say "Aunt" – *never* "Auntie"; "Auntie" makes us all shudder!' In her view it was 'definitely not done' to use this form. On the other hand, though she disliked the term Auntie intensely, she thought it was gaining ground, and that in the next generation it will have probably supplanted Aunt altogether. Equally vigorously, she expressed the view that neither she nor any of her children had ever called anyone Aunt or Uncle who was not 'a relation'. 'Never – it's definitely "non-U" to do this!' she remarked. Some of her friends had asked her children to call them Aunt – which made her wince – but although she had never said anything to her children about it, they never adopted this term for non-kin. However, she thought it might be a habit that is spreading gradually through all classes of society.

We were not able to follow up these ideas, and it is doubtful if they had any wide currency among our informants. Indeed, we had no other analogous expression of them, and it is clear from our last informant's own statements that some of her own friends did not share them. What they stand for is not then a representation of what class practice is, but rather what a sector of opinion in the class thinks it is or used to be or would like it to be.

What also seems fairly clear from such evidence as we have is that whatever may have been the position in the past, in modern times the trend of borrowing usage, if it does occur, is in the direction of movement upwards, from working-class to middle-class (and perhaps 'upper-class' also) in the matter of these kinship terms. This goes against the hypothesis of Goody (op. cit., note 23) that with class mobility and mass communications 'the usage of the upper classes inevitably tends to spread downwards. . . .' Moreover, the wide distribution of terms which we have found bears against any view that kin terms of address are particularly good class-indicators, at least as far as the middle class is concerned.

Three questions may be posed which bear on this class issue in kinship terminology:

i How far do the terms of working-class ascription, such as Mum, Dad, Nanna, Auntie tend to be coincident in usage in the same families?

ii How far do the families where they occur, either separately or in combination, appear to be of working-class origin?

iii How far do such families seem to have any particularly identifiable other characteristics – e.g. the warmth and solidarity sometimes attributed to working-class families?

The answer to the first question is relatively simple. In round figures out of 70 households for which we have reasonably full information about terms of address to the major kin, in 30 one or other of the Mum, Dad, Nanna, Auntie terms are used by some member. But what is very striking is the lack of any consistent pattern of combination of terms. About half the households are accounted for by the use of Mum and Dad only, or Auntie only, without each other or Nanna. In only two households are all four terms used, and even here not by all members: in one case the wife uses all terms, the husband none, and the children use Nanna and Auntie but not Mum and Dad; in the other case the wife uses three terms but not Nanna, the husband uses Mum and Dad but not the other two, and the child uses Nanna and Auntie only! So if these are working-class patterns, they are very fragmented in the area of our study, even in single families.

The answer to the question of whethe families with these linguistic usages for kin have been upwardly mobile or have working-class connections is less simple to give, but the evidence is fairly clear. We disregard those which use the term Auntie alone, and look at those which use Mum or Dad or Nanna or any combination of these terms. Of the 26 households in this category almost exactly half can be classed as having manual worker or small trader background in the husband's or wife's parentage or both. For instance, in a family where Mrs Neville calls her mother and father Mum and Dad and her children call her mother Nanna, her father was a cabinet-maker, her mother made shirts, and she made no bones about having been born into a working-class family in Bethnal Green. She listed among her kin a shop-assistant, a printer, an upholsterer and a garage hand. Though upwardly socially mobile – she had had a successful professional career herself – she gave no impression of being consciously concerned with improving her social position. Her husband, also in the public entertainment world, had a family background of non-classical musicians. A husband in another case of the Mum, Dad and

Nanna category, had a commercial traveller as his father's father, a railway worker as his father and a hansom-cab owner driver as a mother's father, while his wife's father was a warehouseman. But sometimes the background was very mixed. Where Mrs Grant used the terms Mum and Dad, and called her mother's mother Nanna, as did her children, her father had been the warden and her mother the matron of a hostel, her mother's father had been a teacher and her father's father had owned a box factory employing 40 men; her husband's mother's father had been a photographer in Turkey and his father's father a wheelwright.

But this working-class thesis of the genesis of these terms does not hold at all completely, in any direct sense. In the category of these Mum, Dad, Nanna users about half the households involved are indubitably of what may be called straightforward middle-class background. Take two cases where the wife called her mother's mother Nan or Nanna. The parents of Mrs Nudley when she was young owned an off-licence business, and her mother's parents kept a public house. But her father had turned to the off-licence when he was in poor health; previously he had helped his father, who owned a building business; her mother's brother, who had been very successful in the Port of London authority, had been knighted for his services. This might be categorized as a lower middle-class upbringing, since her mother's brother was described as 'having grown away from his family'. But in the other case Mrs Nebworth's father had been to Marlborough and belonged to a moneyed family in the West country, and her mother's father had been in the Army in India and afterwards worked in an insurance office. She said that her grandparents would have gone to private schools; even when she was young Council schools were for the really poor; if she and her brother had gone to a Council school they would have been ostracized! Her husband's father, a Cambridge man, had joined the HFF's legal business. In this case, as in others where the occupational and social background was that of the Army, Civil Service, rubber merchants, wine merchants, bank managers, offshoots of county families, the use of terms such as Mum, Dad, Nana cannot be put down to working-class origins. We are dealing with more subtle and more pervasive influences than those of crude class relations.

SUMMARY

The main theme of this chapter is an examination of the way in which in the English kinship system terms of address are not merely stereotyped linguistic labels, but are dynamic expressions of attitudes and relationships. They serve as indicators of relative status, and because they do so, and because relative status is not always agreed upon by the parties concerned, the use of kin terms is not automatic but can be a matter of adjustment and even of dispute. What is very striking about the terms of address used in the English kinship system when studied empirically is the range of variation which some of them display. We have emphasized that such variation is neither incidental nor trivial when viewed sociologically. The range of terms invoked serves a very useful social function, given a possibility of selection among them to match particular interests and social circumstances. Kin terms on the whole express either respect or familiarity, and some choice is usually open in the use of them. In figurative usage it is the stereotyped role which is ordinarily presented. 'To father a plan' means to initiate or to take responsibility for a scheme. 'To mother a person' means to take care of, give services to or cherish someone.[27] But while 'to mother' and 'to father' in figurative terms are well understood roles, the connotation of the kin terms covers a far wider range of ideas and functions. Even then, diminutives and colloquial expressions are felt to be necessary in order to express particular personal relationships. So also with other than the parental relationships. With aunts and uncles and grandparents various combinations of respect for age and authority, familiar and emotional ties, condition the use of kin terms. Even fear of ageing on the part of seniors may lead to the modification of a conventional kin term into one of a lower generation or to first names.

What emerges also from the study of kin terms is the tendencies to change which their use exemplifies. On the personal side there tends to be a transition from informal to formal within the family circle, and from formal to informal outside that circle as the children progress to maturity. The stage of any set of people in the whole family cycle is important here. There tends also to be a change from one generation to the next, with growth in recent times of relatively informal modes of address – though the recent nature of this change is sometimes over-estimated. The question has been sometimes posed as to how far kin terms reflect economic conditions, as illustrated by differences of class usage. Our general conclusions are that although 'class' elements can be perceived in some usages, they are not outstanding, and it is essentially differences in social rather than in

[27] It is pertinent to note that English does not provide for someone to 'sister' or to 'brother' another person. According to dictionaries to 'grandfather' does exist as a rare term and 'to grandmother' means to coddle. (But grandmotherly when used, especially of legislation, is said to mean excessively *paternal*, which is almost a contradiction in structural terms!)

economic situations which give rise to differences in kin modes of address. The social situations are of many kinds, but they refer basically either to relations between seniors and juniors with the respect/familiarity antinomy well marked or to situations of ambiguity – exemplified particularly by the mother-in-law dilemma, where elements of uncertainty and lack of conventional procedures complicate the issue. We have been able to demonstrate regularities in much use of kin terms, indicating that common problems are often solved by accepting the obvious, conventional solutions. But we have also been able to show a high degree of variation and to link this by means of our examples with the recognition of areas of distinct sensitivity. Not only relations between affines but also between parents' siblings and their nephews and nieces often have delicate implications – e.g. about the significance of relative ages or the significance of opinions on conduct, which to some extent may be reflected in the type of kinship terms used.

We do not argue that all these situations are self-consciously faced and the alternatives intellectually explored. But it is quite clear from our material that in some of these relationships there is awareness of the nature of the problem and of the stresses involved. There is also facility in expressing in words what the people concerned feel. It is clear from much of our material that in many situations these kin term usages are learned – children adopt either the practice or the instruction of their parents. But what also seems to be clear is that children themselves are not mere passive recipients of kinship terminology, but can be innovators and persistent users of terms even when their elders may not wish them to be. The very fact of their persistence and success in many of these cases is a further indication of how deeply linked is the use of kin terms, particularly terms of address, with the effort of the personality to express itself and maintain itself in separate individuality.

One final point. It is clear that to understand the use of English kin terms, particularly terms of address, it is necessary to study not simply such terms individually but to look at them in the form of systematic arrangements in which variations in usage by the different members of the kin set concerned can affect one another.

11

Kinship Situations and Concepts

This Chapter and the next are the heart of our study. We have already described people's general attitudes towards the subject of family and kinship, what people know about their kin and the amount of contact they have with kin. We have also examined the structure of terms by which people call their kin. Now we consider more specifically the meaning of kinship as it is expressed in action. First, we describe the major kinds of *situations* in which relations with kin are meaningful. Then we isolate and examine two basic themes which appear to underlie many relations with kin – support for oneself, responsibility to the other. Then in the next Chapter we examine the quality of kin relations as demonstrated in different kinds of *roles* in which individuals are involved, focussing particularly upon relations with members of the natal family compared with those with collateral kin, and upon relations with kin by blood compared with relations with kin by marriage. We also examine the variations in *family patterns* of kin relationship, including those associated with changes over time.

SITUATIONS WHERE KIN HAVE MOST MEANING

We have selected for special attention the following types of situations in which kin are involved: residential choice; career selection, with reference to education, occupation and marriage; property transactions; situations of crisis, with pregnancy and confinement as an example; and recreational situations, especially family gatherings and holidays.

LIVING WITH KIN

Residential kin links include living with kin, living near kin and living in continuity with kin by taking over a dwelling they have occupied. While living with kin is commonly regarded as a working-class pattern, our evidence reveals that it is by no means unknown in some forms in middle-class circles also.

Among our informants alone, in the 58 households with which we have been primarily concerned, 40 persons or almost exactly one-third of the total household members had lived with kin of some type after leaving the parental roof. The great majority of these were women. Throughout our whole sample we were specifically told of about 120 instances of kin who were living together or had shared a household at some stage. In all, about one quarter of these were young people staying with senior relatives away from home while they were in training or starting their working career. It seemed to be slightly more common for them to stay with a married sister, cousin or other kinsman of the same generation and rather less common to stay with an aunt or grandmother. About another quarter were siblings sharing a dwelling. In only a few cases did a brother share with a sister; in the great majority unmarried, widowed or divorced sisters lived together. Much of the emphasis was on shared services between persons of roughly the same capacity or on dependence of a young person upon an older one. In about 40 per cent of the instances, however, this situation tended to be reversed. A young person, man or woman, went to look after an older relative or such a relative came to live with someone much younger. In most cases this elderly relative was a parent, but in a few it was an uncle or aunt. In a further 10 per cent or so of cases a married son or daughter shared a dwelling with a parent or parents, or lived with parents-in-law.

Several general points can be made about this evidence. The first is that these situations reveal a pattern of change over time. The type of residence with kin tends to alter with the stage of the family cycle, though the pattern is by no means a rigid one.

In all circles in English society it is regarded as completely normal for a child to live in the same dwelling as the other members of its natal family. (This is not so in all societies; in some a boy or girl is expected to leave the natal home at an early age and go temporarily or permanently to live with relatives. Adoption, 'borrowing' of children, attachment to their mother's brother or similar practices may involve children as members of kin households other than those of their own family.) In our society what calls for attention is when a child of immature years is living away from the natal home.[1] When

[1] Our genealogies show for earlier generations a few children living with parents' siblings and being brought up by them in a kind of informal intrafamilial adoption. We came across no instances in the generation of our informants. Adoption, a nearly universal practice, involves in British conditions a permanent separation of child from original parents, whose identity and sometimes whose very existence may not even be known to the child – as distinct from the practice in some other societies where fairly free traffic obtains between original and adoptive parents. The British middle- and upper-class institution of 'boarding school', involving only periodic absence from the natal home, offers special problems with which we are not particularly concerned here.

children are placed in a situation of difficulty by the death or separation of their parents, or by their parents having to go abroad, kin, often grandmothers or aunts, are commonly sought as hosts for the child. This can have a marked, even traumatic, effect upon the child, who may feel that he or she has been rejected by the parents. It can also affect relations with the kin permanently. One woman told how she spent a few months with her mother's brother and his wife when she was a little girl, when her parents were moving round the country. According to her they were so strict that she was miserable and disliked them ever since, seeing them as little as possible.

When a son or daughter is adult the expectation that he or she will leave the natal home is strong, and the problem of where to live takes on a different form. The elements involved are the need of the young person for a home, the requirements of the chosen occupation, and the balance to be achieved between parental and filial sentiment and individual independence. There is much variation, but in the outcome kin often play an important role. A mother's or father's sister may provide lodging, but often it is someone of the same generation but socially more assured, that is, a married sister or married cousin. Such kin serve as an intermediate stage between the young person leaving the natal home and establishing himself completely independently. This pattern seems to be a very obvious one to follow when the job requirements of the young person lead him to the metropolis, but its very obviousness is a recognition of the significance of the kin bond as a useful social mechanism. Even in these days many middle-class families have a 'spare room' which could be available for a lodger and can be used by kinsmen who have come to London. But there is a distinction between 'staying with' kin for a time, and 'living with' kin indefinitely; on the whole, our middle-class instances are of the former practice.

There are many modifications of this pattern. For economic reasons a son or daughter may continue at home, obtaining lodging below the market rate and contributing to the family finances. Or the young person may prize independence more than kin sociability, and insist on a lodging free from all ties. But family sentiment may be strong, and the family itself may move residence in order to be with their son or daughter. The dynamic character of the situation is exemplified by Mrs Maskell's case in which her natal family moved house so that she, then aged fifteen, could be more accessible to her professional work; but two years later she asserted her independence by leaving home. This did not mean a final breach with her parents; when she had married and her husband died soon after, she and her newborn child went to live with her mother.

At a later stage in the family cycle siblings may share a dwelling, but more common is the pattern of junior and senior kin living together when the latter is aged.

The second point is the complexity of the social relationship and motivation underlying these residential patterns. In the only case in all of our sample in which a man, his wife and their two daughters were sharing the same house with his father and father's second wife – an example of an extended family in the fairly strict sense of the term – one might have expected this arrangement to have arisen from the affectionate interest of the parties in each other and in the children. So far from this being the case, the arrangement was disliked by both and existed from necessity, not from choice; if the young people could have afforded to have moved elsewhere they would have done so.

Each kind of relationship has its own advantages and difficulties, and an uneasy balance may obtain between sociability and independence. In many cases an option exists not only between living with kin or non-kin, but between living with different kinds of kin. A woman for preference lived with her dead husband's parents during the War, rather than with her own parents – the latter had been tried and 'did not work out very well'. The very closeness of the parent/child tie in itself can stimulate parent or child to reject an offer of a home. There are cases where quite definitely the sibling bond proves to be stronger than the parent/child bond, or the sibling relation has a more neutral character, and so living with a brother or sister proves easier. A woman went to live with her sister and husband after the death of her own husband, though she had a son with whom she could have lived. A man, after the death of his wife, went to stay with his daughter, but later preferred to be 'on his own' and decided to return to the family house which he shared with his sister. But joint sibling residence itself may have unexpected results – as when a brother, having gone to share a house with his sister, married her housekeeper, much to her surprise and indignation!

Some striking financial implications of kin relationship occurred when parental and affinal relationships were involved together. A son, earning and living at home, contributed to the family income, but the mother did not spend what he gave her and returned it to him in due course when he married. This is perhaps fairly common, though it depends upon the general financial situation of the parties. In a bizarre case a husband came to live in the same house as his wife's mother and wife's brother when he married, since he had no money to rent or buy a house and his wife did not want to leave her mother. The wife's brother, who had a half-share in the house with his sister, lived with them until he married, at which time the husband, who had accumulated some capital, was then able to buy him out.

But until this time the husband paid rent to his wife! This somewhat odd arrangement was, in fact, quite intelligible since the wife wished to make it perfectly clear to her mother that the house was hers and her brother's, and that the mother could feel that she rightfully belonged there.

Our evidence seems to indicate that a pattern which has been amply described for working-class families – members of the natal family when adults deliberately choose to live near one another – is by no means a common one among our middle-class subjects. Close residential contact between mother and daughter especially has seemed to be a critical feature. Of our 58 samples cases of families with dependent children, in 16 the wife's mother was dead. In only one of the remaining 42 cases did she live with the family, and in only 5 others did she live within a mile. In 9 other cases wife's mothers lived in North London and so were readily accessible; 3 others lived elsewhere in London and 10 others within fairly easy reach of London, mainly on the South Coast; 12 wife's mothers lived elsewhere in the United Kingdom and 2 abroad. In other words, a very small percentage of married women with children of their own lived near their mothers. About half of the rest had their mothers relatively accessible so that they could be visited if required at weekends. The middle-class pattern, then, is not for a woman to have intimate daily walking distance contact with her mother, but to be able to keep in touch with her at a moderate distance.

But people were not indifferent to where their close kin lived. We have about a dozen instances of a son or daughter moving or selecting a house in order to be near parents, and a few where propinquity to other kin, such as a father's sister, was a reason for choosing a residence. The existence of kin was also in some cases responsible for a decision to take over a house or flat, so providing a combination of economic and social services. In a few cases relatives lived near one another primarily because they were engaged in a family business, and this was a matter of convenience. The most marked of all our examples was a set of kin whose menfolk were all connected with the Army and who all lived in adjacent streets or even dwellings at Aldershot. Involved here were a MZ, MMZ, MMZD, MMMZD and two MMB, all with their families. As our informant described this, not inaptly, her childhood was 'a mass of seething relatives. We all lived on top of each other, practically in the same street, and the situation has not changed that much now.'

To sum up, living near kin was not a very common pattern among our middle-class families. But the residential claims of kinship were not denied. Depending on the stage in the family cycle, their households might give a home to a young relative at college or starting a job, or to an elderly relative deprived of companionship and services by death of a spouse. Intermediately, siblings might share a dwelling on a reciprocal basis, or a married son or daughter find temporary shelter. In general, it would seem that the command of independent income enjoyed by many middle-class people, including widows and old people, facilitated their choice of residence and lowered the incidence of living with kin.

CAREER SELECTION: CHOICE OF SCHOOL

Visitors from other countries where a State educational system is practically universal might be forgiven for thinking that the English middle classes have an obsessional interest in education. But it is a plausible generalization that a primary distinguishing characteristic of the English middle classes is their self-conscious attitude to education and to the career opportunities linked with it. In contemporary English society the class differentiation still to some extent built into the educational system can hardly be ignored. But apart from this, the different qualities of education provided by different schools (if not types of schools) is such as to focus the attention of parents who wish to give their children the best career opportunities. The financial situation of working-class parents makes them accept the State educational ladder as the normal means of progression for their children. With middle-class parents the problem is apt to be more acute. A good proportion have financial resources to give their children a private education (i.e. including in this term the 'public' schools). Since the private education system is linked to only a limited degree with local recruitment, the problem for these parents is where to send their children – factors of the child's aptitude and intelligence, the school's reputation and even ancillary matters such as religion can all enter in. But for many middle-class parents the financial problem complicates the situation. Giving a child an education outside the State scheme until he gets to University level may involve considerable financial sacrifice, so that comparison of this with alternative claims upon the parents' income becomes a very relevant factor.

First we discuss parental initiative and the extra-familial kin influence in this educational field. (Our material does not deal with the preparatory school situation.) In decision-making in an ordinary family the wishes of the parents are of very great importance. We have only one case in our records of husband and wife thinking public school education in one of the better and more expensive schools to be of such importance that they said that because of the cost they did not want to have any more children than their son and daughter. But other decisions of considerable significance did appear. A few cases of parents changing both job and residence to meet their children's needs were found. Refusal of jobs abroad while the children were young occurred, as did return from abroad when children were of school age in order that they should have 'the right kind' of education. A wife's brother and family came back from West Africa because they didn't want their children to go to boarding school and have to stay with relatives during the holidays. (The idea of their attending a local school obviously never arose.)

Normally parents chose what type of education the child should have and where. In the case of sons particularly the parents' choice appeared to have been affected by the experience of the father. Ties with the 'old school' accounted in many cases for the choice made on behalf of the son. A son was 'put down' for Rugby because of the family tradition – his father, his father's father and apparently also his great-grandfather all went there, as well as various of his uncles and cousins. Another man's grandfather had been Provost of Eton, and about twenty members of his family, including third cousins, could be traced to have gone there. Typical of the attitude in such a milieu was the statement of the wife of a man who went to Charterhouse: 'We were saying the other night we don't know why, because Rugby is the family school.' In a few cases, however, the school memories of the father were so unfavourable that he deliberately refused to send his son to a nearby public school, and preferred one at a distance.

But in most of our cases there was no 'family school'. Most of the people in our sample were educated at the lesser public schools or at grammar schools where the family tradition was less strong. Again, there was some scepticism about the value of a boarding school education in modern conditions. Then, too, the quality of education provided by a school seemed to be of more importance than the name of the school itself. One woman said that her boys' names were down for Eton though her husband had not been there. But she seemed to find it necessary to defend her attitude by saying, 'It *is* the best public school: Eton assimilates all types'. Most parents seemed to have fairly firm views about the kind of education their children should get, if possible. Ordinarily, the occupation that they followed did not seem to be relevant to the chances of acceptance of their child at any particular school; income was the main restricting factor.

Apart from income level, there is one aspect where the condition of the parents may have serious implications for the educational career of the middle-class child – in religion. In so far as middle-class parents may wish to utilize other than State education, the religious label that a child gets from his parents may affect his school entry. Catholics and Jews are mainly affected, but the effects are of opposite kinds. Catholics strive on the whole to send their children only to Catholic schools, and the choice open to them is therefore limited by their own exclusiveness. Jews, on the other hand, relying for their religious instruction primarily on the home and the synagogue, and with few schools of their own, tend to be victims of the limitations imposed by others. Some 'public' schools, e.g. Clifton, appear to have a Jewish 'house', some are indifferent to the religious and allied characteristics of the children they take. But others, especially if of long-established Church foundation, have a Jewish quota – or so it is alleged. Their argument seems to be that since they are ostensibly institutions with a specific Christian denominational charge, entry cannot be claimed irrespective of religion; their Jewish quota they regard as a concession to public policy, not an unwarranted restriction. The counter-argument is that whether they admit it or not they function as public rungs on the educational ladder. Hence their quota (if they have one) is discrimination against Jews, partly from general prejudice and partly because the Jewish zeal for education[2] pushes their children relatively in advance of the others. The argument of selection on religious ground would have more force if a distinction were drawn between practising Jews and those who are merely of Jewish background – but this does not seem to happen.

We are concerned here with the way in which this parental link, this unsought kinship handicap, for which the child has no responsibility, was related to the entry of children from our sample into the educational system. The matter may be viewed as presenting a set of alternative strategies for the child's kin.

The simplest way out of the dilemma would be to seek entry for a Jewish child into schools in the State-financed system, where no question of differentiation on religious grounds arises. Several Jewish families in our sample had in fact done this, but it would seem more because they disapproved of the private school system as such than because they despaired of their children's entry into it. Another way was to accept the quota restrictions and allow the child to compete under this handicap; a few parents with bright children did this. (To enter a child for a public school at birth was thought by some Jews to increase the chances of getting him on the quota.) Another strategy was to enter the child for a public school, but

[2] The point of view of a nominal Anglican defending the quota of one school was, 'It is a Church of England school, and the Jews are so clever that they would dominate the school if they were admitted on a merit system'. According to him, after a newspaper controversy in which the quota system was attacked a letter appeared from the Jewish head boy upholding the system.

register him or her as Christian of some denomination, as had been done by one non-practising Jewish family. When very young the children had been entered for both a day and a boarding school, and their mother, Mrs Waverley, said that she and her husband felt a bit hypocritical, because they had entered their children as C. of E. They had thought of putting down Protestant, without saying what they were protesting about, or Nonconformist, without going into what they did not conform to; but decided on C. of E. because they wanted to avoid any prejudice; they wanted their children to have a chance. The schools they chose were not ones which emphasized religious teaching. The wife said that her husband wanted the children to know he was Jewish, and did not want them to be ashamed of his Jewish background, but he intended telling them about it when they were older. Also, he did not want them to be taught Hebrew or the Jewish religion; he and his wife hoped it might be possible to teach the children a morality independent of religion if this were possible.

This type of solution had been rejected by another Jewish couple, the Regans. Talking about ways round the Jewish quota, about which she was outraged, the wife said, 'A number of Jews put down C. of E.' (on the child's entry form); and of another parent she said, 'They had the child baptized! It's awful! A Jew christened!' She and her husband wanted their son to go to Westminster, but said the school wouldn't put his name down because of the religious restrictions at present. She said she would pull all strings to get him in, but she hadn't any! Her brothers went to school at Clifton, which she disapproved of for Jews, because the tone of the Jewish house was naturally enough fairly orthodox, and more liberal-minded Jews were made to conform. Her brothers were fine sportsmen, but matches were always held on Saturday, and while the brothers weren't orthodox, the house officially was for Jews. So they could never play in matches held on Saturday! When asked whether she and her husband had considered sending their children to a Jewish school, she replied 'God, no! We'd not send them to a Jewish school. Never! Not for anything!' When asked why not, she answered, 'We live in a modern community – though I'd be unhappy if they married a non-Jew.' She and her husband were liberal Jews in diet and similar matters, so it would not be inconvenient to send their children to a non-Jewish school.

These two examples epitomize the difficulties faced by parents of Jewish, especially perhaps liberal Jewish, persuasion in trying to provide for their children an education which they consider to be desirable to place them on equal terms with the rest of society. The shifts to which some parents resort may seem bizarre, and may even arouse the wrath of some other Jews. But the problem is a complex one. In the case cited above, where the parents classified their children as C. of E. for school entry, neither husband nor wife had any religious affiliation at the time. The husband's parents and family were Jewish, and though his father was really agnostic, he had been brought up in orthodox style, but had not maintained this. The wife came from a Christian background: her father had been a Roman Catholic and her mother Church of England, and she herself had been brought up an Anglican. Since the religion of a child in England is not specifically determined by that of its male parent, there was no particular reason why the children should not have been classed by the religion of their mother, quite apart from a convention that for official religious entries C. of E. is an acknowledged description for many people of no particular faith. What of course is implied in this whole situation is that the label 'Jewish' refers not just to a religion but to membership of a particular kind of community and through kinship to only one parent. (Moreover, by Jewish rules, since the mother was non-Jewish, the children were non-Jews.)

So far we have been discussing instances of parental action in a child's educational field.

There are two spheres where the role of kin outside the immediate family circle appears most clearly in educational choice. One is in paying for a child's education. In about a score of cases – perhaps upwards of 20 per cent of the total – some financial help was given to parents by kin: e.g. a husband's mother paid for her grandson's education (at Harrow); a brother paid the fees for his younger brother and for his sister's children; a girl sent money to her father for her younger brother's schooling; parents or other relatives set up educational trusts or covenants for children; people borrowed from their parents to pay their children's school fees. That a general link between education and extra-familial kinship was seen by some of our informants is illustrated by a reflection of Mrs Underwood. 'I have a theory that families sending their children to boarding schools are those with grandparents financing them. Those who send their children to the minor public school near by have no help from grandparents.'

But a more widespread role of kin in the educational field was in providing consultation and opinion. The advice of kin on the education of children was often specifically not sought, or was rejected when offered unsolicited. But in many cases there was discussion with them about the whole educational problem, in particular the choice of schools and the choice of subjects. This was only to be expected since many of the kin had children of their own and, granted sociability between the parents, questions of comparative standards and achievements, both of schools and of scholars, were almost bound to be raised. This flow of information, comparison and advice, perhaps more freely given than asked, is one quite important function of relations between kin with young and adolescent sons and daughters. Moreover, kin expectations about the school to be attended and of performance, held by grandparents, aunts and uncles, whether these are explicit or implied, enter into the field of parents' judgment.

Among our records are these examples. A husband's father, who attached great value to education, would have paid for his grandson if necessary. His opinion was quoted with respect. 'He always said there is nothing more valuable than education because they can't take it from you.' A wife wished her son to go to the same school as her husband had attended, and she wanted all her children to have as good an education as possible. She said she had consulted none of her kin about this, but she also said that all the kin on her mother's side 'have a thing about education' and were anxious for their children to get a degree above all else; it seemed fairly clear that she had been influenced by their attitude. In another case a son was a scholar at Eton, and his mother said, 'Everyone in the family goes to Eton, and it makes it so difficult to send them anywhere else'. She added with justifiable pride, 'Never send a lazy boy to Eton'. The relationship of a child with its siblings and cousins may also affect the situation. An elder son was taken away from one school and sent to another, not because he was doing badly but because his younger brother was not suited to the former school; the parents didn't want the younger lad to think he was a failure, so 'We pushed them out together'. Another case illustrates several of these themes. The wife's father left money for the education of his grandchildren, the wife and her brother being joint trustees. (The existence of this trust was confirmed from external sources.) Educational advice was sought from the wife's brother. But in deciding about schools for the children the wife said, 'We steer off kin to avoid rivalry – we steer off sending them to the same school'.

These instances point to a further problem. Parental expectations may affect not only the choices parents make for their children at critical periods, but also may even react upon their day-to-day relations with their children. When parents point out to a son or daughter that a cousin is 'good at school', this may act as a spur – or it may merely exacerbate relations, not only with parents but perhaps with cousin and parent's sibling as well. The whole problem of educational achievement and the choices that are attached thereto bulk very large in English middle-class society, and it is here perhaps as much as anywhere that kin relations have their most subtle effect.

OCCUPATION

From the detailed occupational histories of the principals in our study and other material about many of their kin we have about 160 instances, in about 70 cases, where choice of occupation was related to kin attitudes or actions. It is not always easy to assess just what this relationship involved – it varied in different instances from a deliberate intention of kin not to interfere, or at most a mild approval of a job chosen, to a strong pressure towards a certain occupation, or an equally strong attempt at dissuasion. But the general outlines of the situation seem fairly clear. Broadly speaking, the kin factors of most positive effect may be grouped in four major sets: a general family tradition of occupation; the general influence of kin in a particular direction; the particular economic situation of a parent or other kinsman; the specific wishes of a parent or other kinsman.

Some indication has been given earlier (p. 132) of the types of family business into which a number of our subjects and their kin were able to fit. For brief illustration here, a cotton business in Liverpool passed down through four generations; a legal business passed down for three generations; a brewery was a family concern in which a man's FMB was chairman, to whom succeeded his brother's son, who was succeeded in turn by his son, other members of the family including our informant being directors. Even when a family firm did not provide occupational opportunities directly, the existence of a family tradition tended to steer people towards a particular kind of career – as when several siblings, following their father and father's father, entered Greenwich Naval Academy, or a set of brothers entered the Church one after the other (Figure 2).

Favourable conditions for occupational choice were supplied by a family business or a family tradition in about a quarter of the 160 instances of kin interest noted.

In the Regan case the wife's father's father and the wife's father's brother were tailors, one of her father's sisters married a tailor, another married a man who dealt in dress materials, and her father had gone into the underwear business with her mother. In another case, perhaps even more spectacular since it involved artistic talent as well as professional skill, the husband's father was a professor of music and the husband played the oboe; other professionals included the wife's father, a harpist, as were wife, her half-sister and half-brother; her sister's daughter, a pianist; her sister's daughter's husband and sister's daughter's two sons, violinists; while her father's brother, two father's brother's sons and sister's husband all played the double bass. Clearly in such cases the conditioning of a young person to follow the 'family line' must have been strong. But the conditioning may have been indirect. Acquaintance with the relevant experience rather than imitation of kin may have been the significant feature.

An important function was supplied by kin who by virtue of their own position were able to provide jobs for other kin or to make suggestions as to where suitable openings could be found. About half the instances of kin interest in occupations were of this type. Such actions may be partly a function of the non-local professional occupations sought by middle-class people. Local opportunities in the place of their birth or upbringing are often rare, and as an alternative to answering advertisements in an impersonal way the personal contact given by kin (and friends) is often very helpful. We have cases of a dentist inheriting his father's practice, of a doctor getting into a hospital partly on his uncle's name, of a man who interested his wife's brother in camera work and got him a job on a newspaper, of a woman's maternal uncle, an engineer, giving advice on the engineering training of her son, of a man who went to work in his FZH paper factory, and of a man who got a job for his wife's brother in a merchant bankers through his own connections in this business. Usually the kin connections involved were quite close – sibling or spouse's sibling or nephew. But occasionally the link was tenuous. One man, at a party given by his WMMZ, met for the first time her son, who put him in touch with a suitable post. Another man found a job in the city office of his WMBWD2ndHB. In such cases the job was not found primarily because the person seeking it was a kinsman. It was the fact that he was a kinsman and so in the appropriate social circle which placed him as a person to whom help should be given in getting a job.

A few occupational choices were determined by the economic situation of parent or other near kinsman. A daughter used to work as a telephonist, but after her father died came back to help her mother run the farm. A man was at University, but when he left his occupational choice was restricted because he had to provide for his mother who lived with him, and so he needed at once a steady job with prospects. A man wanted to be a quantity surveyor and go to Canada, but his wife objected so he did not, and became a bailiff for the owner of a stone quarry. Such early channelling of occupational choice does not seem in most cases to have militated against the rise of the person concerned in the economic and social scale. One instance of this was a man (the father of one of our informants) whose own father died and, as the eldest son, he decided to go out to work. He went first to an observatory and then later as an assistant to a firm of instrument makers; after a change to another instrument-making firm he became later managing director and then chairman of the board. This success story becomes more intelligible when one discovers that his father also had been a managing director of an instrument company, his uncle had been superintendent of the observatory concerned, as had also been his grandfather, and his great-grandfather had been a chief instrument mechanic who had invented important meteorological instruments bearing his name which are still in use in many observatories throughout the world. This man's rise to eminence in his profession was almost certainly not due to his kinship connections, but clearly they could indicate an obvious ladder up which he could climb, and they would not have hindered him!

The wishes of parents regarding their children's occupation took various forms. A man's father approved of his choice of the medical profession partly at least because the father's brother was a successful doctor; an ideal pattern had been set up on a kin basis and for the father this reinforced the son's choice, on partly irrational grounds. Another man was keen on the idea of his son's going into local government, and paid £350 for him to be articled to a town clerk. He said the fee was too high and it was a 'confidence trick', though the young man was paid a wage and so most of the money came back. But he also said he didn't object to paying this sum for his son's career because 'It feeds the ego to pay hard cash for everything'. In the event the son, a terrific worker with a very determined nature, took the opportunity to gain a law degree, then worked with various firms of solicitors and later set up successfully on his own. In this case the father could feel that while the son had not finally turned out exactly as he had planned, he had at least contributed materially to the son's advancement. Father and son could thus congratulate each other and themselves. In other cases men were anxious to give their sons a professional training so that these would not be unsuccessful business men like themselves, or modified their industrial plans to give their daughters a start in a career. In various cases children were encouraged by their fathers to follow their own career. Sometimes this was by reaction. One man's father had forced him to become a teacher against his wishes, which were to be an architect. So strongly did he feel this throughout his life that he was resolved that his daughter should choose her own way of life without interference.

Some sons and daughters persisted in having their own way against parental wishes. A father wanted his daughter to become a teacher as he was and as his father had been. But she said, 'I couldn't teach. I haven't got the patience', and she became a caterer and dietician. Another daughter was probably going to do medicine, as did her father, despite her mother's view, '– I told her one doctor in the family is enough'. Another woman's family had wanted her to be a doctor, but she didn't like the medical course so did psychology and education instead. The effects of such display of independence were sometimes to threaten the amity between parent and child. A man's father wanted him to go into accountancy because he didn't feel that advertising, which was the son's choice, was a good profession. The man was determined to take up advertising, did so and made a success of it, although the result was a lot of tension, not so much between him and his father as with his father's second wife. Another father tried to influence his son to enter the firm where he himself worked, but the son rejected this. Much later he was happy to have done so, because he said that he now got along with his father much better than when he was near and in close contact with him.

But contrarywise there were instances of a person who had succumbed to parental pressure succeeding in the career which he or she had entered against their own inclinations. One woman said that her father, knowing she wished to become a teacher, had insisted that she took Froebel training. 'I am very glad he did insist, though I loathed it.' The father of one of our subjects had wanted to be a doctor. But his father had thought it would be a good thing for him to enter law, and used his contact with a firm of solicitors to introduce him to it. In due course this man became a lawyer, rose to eminence and was knighted for his services.

Where parents did intervene, and they were the main kin who did so, it was primarily for one or more of four reasons. They wished the son or daughter to follow a family profession; they wished the younger generation to do better than they themselves had done; they liked the status or the money to be gained in the occupation of their choice; or they felt that there were certain disadvantages in the occupation chosen by their child.

Indication of changing family patterns was given by some informants. One elderly woman whose son was in the Civil Service said that her mother had wanted all the daughters to be teachers, and three out of four did so. 'My father had a business but my two brothers wouldn't touch it with a bargepole!' (One became a teacher, the other an engineer.) He was very disappointed, but, she said, 'in the old days they wouldn't have been asked'.

In these middle-class families the range of discussion about occupations centred primarily on business and the professions. Hardly a single case referred to a preference for a manual occupation – apart from the desire of small boys to be engine drivers. Parental and kin context obviously was relevant here. Another point is that in this middle-class milieu of the post-war period we were dealing with the choices of women as well as men. In a large proportion of our cases the women expected to have a career even after they married, and within their natal family were prepared to fight vigorously for the career of their choice – which again was usually a professional one. A further point is the evidence given of the fallibility of parental judgment at this critical stage. Many of our subjects seemed to lack a 'vocation' at the outset of their career. They seemed to have settled down quite comfortably into occupations which they had taken up either at the wish of their parents or through their parents' help. But a significant proportion of men and women were successful at and obviously enjoyed the careers which they themselves had chosen, either without reference to or in defiance of their parents' wishes.

The proportion of instances in our records in which kin ties definitely facilitated entry into a career was moderate. We take for clarity the position of the male principals in our study, 80 in all. Of these from our evidence almost exactly 25 per cent had been helped to their jobs by parents or other kin or (in a few cases) influenced in their choice of careers by family tradition. In about another 5 per cent of cases kin influence, primarily parental influence, had been brought especially and strongly to bear upon them but they had resisted and made their own choice against kin wishes. More generally, in about half the families of this middle-class sample, parents had fairly definite views as to the kind of occupation which it was desirable for their children to follow, though they expressed these views rather than insisted upon them. Many sons or daughters did choose the preferred line, either yielding to pressure or acting in accord with their own wishes. But the kinship influence was not always direct. It often tended to operate in subtle fashion, serving to crystallize rather than determine the actual choice of occupation; so that the resultant decision was the final move in a complicated intellectual and emotional game of family relationships and adjustments.

The upshot of our enquiry for this section of our study is that kinship reactions were a significant component of the social situation concerned with occupational choice. Though by no means a prime determining factor in the majority of decisions finally made, being apparently definite in not more than about 25 per cent of instances, these interests of kin in the choice were pervasive, with many side effects.

It is hard to evaluate the merits of this kin interest from even the very limited social point of view of success and job-satisfaction of the person immediately concerned. But such kinship influence as is exerted seems neither particularly useful nor particularly hampering. It often provides a channel for decision-making, but it is neither better nor worse than the other channels open. Sometimes parental interest in itself provokes a counter-reaction. But one should not argue from this that parents' interest, even anxiety, for the careers of their children is misplaced. It may not on the average be of any particular advantage to the children career-wise. But *as an index of the affective relation between them*, it may be of much greater importance. It is perhaps worse for a son or daughter to feel that their parents are uninterested in their choice of career than to feel pressure towards a particular choice, even against their own inclinations. Presumably the ideal for a parent would be to demonstrate interest without commitment, but it is clear from our material that this is characteristic of only a minor fraction of our cases.

MARRIAGE AND KINSHIP OPINION

In moving from education to occupation and then to marriage in this middle-class milieu we are moving along a diminishing scale of parental intervention and choice. (Parental emotional interest is often in inverse proportion.) Parents are largely responsible for the educational decisions made for their children; their views are of only very limited effect in the selection of their children's occupations; when it comes to marriage their views carry very little weight at all. Yet a marriage is a commitment which can affect parents deeply. It usually means a radical shift in family allegiance. As Mr Arthur said very pertinently, 'People don't like a marriage in the family because it alters the structure'. Moreover, unlike participation in a school or a job, that in a marriage can only be dissolved with great difficulty, usually with pain and disruption of a whole set of kin ties. Hence traditionally in many societies marriages have been arranged by parents. Ostensibly in the interest of son or daughter but often in their own interest as well, such marriages in modern Oriental conditions are often defended by the young people. But in modern Western conditions the personal commitment and responsibility of the individual in a marriage is conceived as paramount. So, though parents may feel more acutely and have stronger opinions about the marriage of their son or daughter than they have held about their education or their occupation, empirically their views may have relatively little effect in facilitating or blocking the marriage. What these views may do is to affect the general quality of relations between all the parties both before and after.

In earlier sections we have tried to assign some order of magnitude to our findings about the significance of kin relations in residence, education and occupational choice. In the field of marriage it is much less easy to find any quantitative measure of kin involvement, and we concentrate on a more qualitative type of analysis.

Very few of our informants seem to have met their future spouses through kin. One man met his future wife because she knew his parents politically; in a few other cases a wife met her future husband through her brother because the two men were colleagues. But in an overwhelming number of instances the future spouses met each other either through mutual friends or, for the most part, when thrown together by their occupation – including under this head a number who were University students together – or their interests, such as music. More generally from our material apart from the few people who married kin (see Chapter 6 and later p. 370), kinship played very little part in bringing future spouses together.

An interesting hypothesis in relating kinship to choice of spouse was put forward by one of our informants, without prompting from us, and clearly generalizing from her own experience. She said that from observing whom her friends at school had married she had reached the following conclusion. 'People who were happy at home married men who are in the same, or nearly the same, profession as their fathers. Those unhappy at home have married men with different occupations from their fathers. I've married a man very different from my father; I didn't really get on with him (her father).' She added emphatically about her husband – 'a man with a very different occupation to my father'. She continued that some people 'marry *against* their backgrounds – like me; people who find it difficult to get on with their families.' Then she added a rather startling suggestion, that similarity between husband and father led to growing more like mother, and conversely. 'People who've married men like their fathers are getting like their mothers. I'm certainly not getting like my mother. I hate playing bridge! I've married a man more like my grandfather!' She herself had had a rather unhappy childhood, having been brought up by a Nanny, and her grandparents having largely replaced her parents (partly owing to the War). She said she clashed with her parents socially, since they liked parties and card-playing and she did not, and she swore she would never marry a man with a bad temper, like her father. But after her marriage she had got on better with her parents, especially with her father. Her generalization can be taken then as largely a commentary on personality reactions to childhood unhappiness. (The hypothesis is worth further exploration, but requires more detailed data than we possess.)

What does appear quite markedly in our material is the extent to which kin judgment was expressed upon the suitability of particular marriages. Our records contain mostly opinions of disapproval –

which, however, had not inhibited people from marrying. On the average there was such an instance in nearly every case of our sample. They fell into four broad types.

In one type kin reaction followed a formal rule of the society, the most obvious application being where a proposed marriage might run counter to the legally prohibited degrees of kin. Marriage or attempted marriage within what was interpreted as a prohibited degree rarely occurs in our records. But in one such instance the husband of one of our informant's aunts (MZ) 'thought a great deal' of his wife's family, and when his wife died he wanted to marry the daughter of one of his wife's sisters. 'As this was not allowed by religious law, he couldn't.' (Actually such a union did not appear to be forbidden.) Our informant commented that she thought this was a pity as it would have been 'a good thing' for the niece materially; but then she added that she thought the niece didn't really want to marry him, so perhaps it didn't matter after all! In the end the man, of whom our informant was very fond, did marry again, a woman who was far from meeting with the approval of his first wife's family.

Another type of kin reaction was where the marriage was disapproved on personal grounds, of temperament, character or relative age. This type of kin attitude was often emotionally acute. A husband's mother tried to prevent a marriage and, to pacify her, since she was a very conventional woman, the marriage took place in church. The parents in another case each disapproved of the potential spouse. The girl had had a child by the man before marriage: her parents thought him irresponsible; his thought her not virtuous enough. A son wanted to marry a Welsh woman of whom his mother did not approve; he did not marry but when he later left this woman (for other reasons) and married elsewhere his mother said regretfully, 'She was better than the wife he has now'. But ordinarily there seems to have been some resolution of the situation involving rapprochement between the principals and their parents.

The reasons just given for kin disapproval of a marriage were the ostensible ones; it is usually not possible to judge how far any other elements underlie them. But the opinion of a third party may allow of a plausible interpretation in terms of self-interest of the objecting kin. Anxiety to see that a will is not disturbed may be one motive for kin to resist a marriage, though we have no direct instance of this in our records. Analogous to this, however, was an instance where the father's first cousin of our informant (FFBD) was said to have spent her life seeing that her father didn't marry again after his wife's death – because she wanted the home to herself. Strains of a less material kind were indicated occasionally. The mother of one of our informants had been very ambitious for her daughter, had idolized her, and had resented her marriage. The mother, who had emotional relationships with other – mostly unhappily-married – women, tried to get her daughter to postpone the marriage for a year or two to think about it, and then advised her daughter not to let her husband come near her and tried to impress upon her how unpleasant the physical side of marriage was. From this identification and attempt to restrain, the daughter escaped to her mother's sister's home, where with this substitute mother she found a 'normal happy atmosphere'.

A further type of marriage disapproved of by kin involved category factors, one of the most important being social class.

A few informants expressed themselves in general terms on this issue. One woman whose father had been a wine merchant and who was married to a chartered accountant, described herself as 'middle-class'. Her husband's family, she said, were 'not rich but not poor either'. She thought that people should keep to the same class when they married. 'If you're used to a nice home – not rich but comfortable – and then you marry into a poor family, it won't work.' She thought that most people did in fact keep to their own class. Sometimes 'you get boys marrying beneath them, but this isn't very often. You've got more in common with someone of your own class, haven't you? A boy or girl from a poor family might seem all right at first, but after a bit they might grate on your nerves.' Since she had a son in his late teens and a daughter just come of age she was possibly giving vent to her own fears here. The issue came up occasionally in specific terms. Mrs Danby said that her husband's father disapproved of his son's marriage because he didn't think she came from the same background as her husband, 'which is true'. She was not of working-class origin but was thought by her father-in-law to be not so well connected. Another woman said of her son's wife, 'She is an only child and from very bourgeois parents'. The traditional background of some families included stories such that a great-grandfather had been 'cut off' by the family for marrying a fireman's daughter. On the female side too women who contracted asymmetrical class marriages evoked disapproval. A female cousin married 'a Post Office clerk or something', and contact was lost; an aunt married the son of a local garage proprietor. A great-aunt 'let down the family tone' because she married a chemist: 'My grandmother was very upset and it was the scandal of the family – she married a mere chemist! Times have changed since then; chemists have become more respectable.' Another cousin – her father was Dean of Trinity and a bank director – ran away with a stoker from the Navy, and 'nobody heard from her for a long time'. Of a niece's husband it was said, 'It's a very declassé marriage, he is not upper-middle-class and has a Lancashire accent'. Another cousin disappointed her family by marrying a garage mechanic who did not eat with her and her cousins when they were guests, but separately in the kitchen – 'as though he resented eating any other way'.

But such instances of asymmetrical class marriage were relatively few throughout our range of cases – certainly less than 1 per cent of all marriages noted. Moreover, the reaction of the family concerned was not always unfavourable.

In general, such middle-class kin opinions on a choice of spouse from a 'lower' social class, though often strongly expressed, were of a relatively simple and conventional kind. Since so few of our principals were directly involved it is difficult to judge how far the kin most immediately concerned, the siblings and parents, made a rational adjustment when the marriage was concluded. But the emotions involved did not seem as a rule to be very deep.

KIN ATTITUDES TO MIXED MARRIAGES

Where the cultural background of spouses was very markedly different, in ethnic or religious background, the reactions of kin tended to be more manifest.

In a couple of cases ethnic factors gave dismay to kin. A sister of one of our informants, of mixed German–Jewish extraction, married a Malayan Chinese much older than she was. Although she had a daughter by him, and although he wished to have a family existence with her, his father in Malaya proved recalcitrant and refused to admit her as his son's wife. Though she and her husband continued to correspond there seemed no possibility of rapprochement, and she and her daughter took refuge in a kibbutz in Israel. One brother had tried to persuade her against the marriage. Another had disapproved of it – 'I didn't think it would turn out right', but as she was adult he thought she should make her own decision. He thought that one should not try and advise in such situation; 'it is their business'. In another case a distant relative (MBWZDS) married a Malay woman in Singapore. This was a matter of interest only to our informants, who had no direct contact. It was reported that the marriage distressed his mother, who had been most upset – not by the woman's ethnic origin but by the fact that in the home she had very different cooking and housekeeping habits. But it was said the mother felt much better after the birth of a child, who was 'very sweet'.

In a marriage where the parties were of different religions the reactions of kin were often complex, with great intensity of feeling. Some kin seemed to find it very difficult indeed to make a working adjustment to the marriage, and social relations tended to remain always a strain. On the whole, members of the natal families concerned seemed in the end to have adapted themselves to the union and to have maintained fairly frequent social contact with the married pair and their children. It seems to have been more distant kin who in some cases completely severed contact with the married couple. At first sight this seems a paradox since it may be assumed that emotionally they would be much less involved than the parents or siblings of the married pair. On the other hand, because of this very fact severance of relations could mean much less to them. In a modern metropolitan society there may not be any other links except those of kinship to bring them into contact, and so where the ideological framework of religion comes into conflict with this the religious element can be treated as paramount. Withdrawal of kin contact and interest may be painful, particularly if it means cutting away ties operating since childhood; but the range of alternative social relations can provide compensations. There is possibly an added factor. Kin who are not particularly close may feel that their relationship entitles them, even requires them, to mark their disapproval by concrete action. So they sever social relations.

In our study there were several marriages which had involved the conversion of one party to Roman Catholicism. Mr Gilroy's family had been Church of England but he became a Roman Catholic before he married, indeed before he even met his future wife, who was a Catholic. A friend who was a priest had been responsible for his conversion, and this friend later became a godfather to one of his children and influenced the married couple's selection of schools. No family friction appeared over religious differences and the Catholic wife's relations with her Anglican parents-in-law were very close and friendly. The religious situation in the two sets of kin concerned was interesting. The husband's brother too had married a Catholic. The wife's family two generations back had not been Catholic. Her father's father married a Catholic and brought his children up in his wife's faith, but their relations with other non-Catholic kin did not seem to have been affected – the wife's Anglican FFBD was her closest friend of all her kin. The only effect of difference in religious affiliation in this particular kin universe seemed to have been in the selection of godparents and in seeking advice on schools for the children.

Quite a thoughtful attitude was shown by Mrs Grant whose parents were Church of England but who, with her two sisters, had all become converts to Roman Catholicism, to which her husband also belonged. When the wife married she was still an Anglican, but she converted about two years after her marriage 'when I finally realized that "they" (the Catholics) were right after all'. She said that originally she had determined not to convert, but that she changed her mind after her son had been christened in a Roman Catholic Church. She began to realize how awful it would be to see her children growing up with a religion that she could not share. She didn't think that families should be divided over religion. After her conversion she found her Catholicism meant a great deal to her and was very happy about her decision. Her mother, it appears, had not objected when all of her three daughters converted. She was perhaps 'a bit hurt' that they all changed, but, it was alleged, thought that 'as long as you have a religion, it doesn't matter which'. The wife explained that her natal family situation had predisposed her in the direction she took, that her family had 'never been particularly against anyone and had no prejudices against Catholics or any other group. We knew all sorts of people, Jews and Mahomedans, through my father's social work.' Her mother had been brought up in a Liverpool district which had always been a Roman Catholic stronghold and knew many Catholics well. In this case, notions of conjugal family solidarity were clearly very important to the wife. The logical sequence to her was – make a personal choice of a partner for life, realize the religious implications of that choice for husband and children, and adjust her own religious convictions and practices accordingly.

The kinship situation was very different where a woman from a conservative family, many members of which had been in the textile business in the Midlands for several generations, married a man whose family was Catholic and strongly Irish. Mrs Lander's family, according to her, had not been at all religious; when she and her siblings were children they hardly ever went to church and her father never did. Notwithstanding this, there was trouble when she decided to become a Catholic and marry. Her parents' opposition, however, she felt was based as much upon their disapproval of the man she had chosen to marry as on religious grounds. There was a family quarrel – 'My mother and mother's side of the family virtually excommunicated me'. Her father's brothers' and sisters' attitude was less censorious, so her mother quarrelled with them too. Between Mrs Lander and her parents there was coldness for six years, during which time they didn't see one another, and exchanged letters very rarely. In Mrs Lander's view her mother's attitude was, 'We will forgive you if you apologize', and she commented that she had no intention of apologizing for something she had a perfect right to do; she felt that if anything the apology should be the other way round! Because of the quarrel her parents didn't go to her wedding. In the end a kind of rapprochement was made with them, and they offered to lend her and her husband a car when they were going on holiday to Scotland.

The young couple then spent a night with her parents, and Mrs Lander said it was 'awful, a terrible strain'. Kinship repercussions from this opposed marriage were considerable. On the financial side the wife said that though she and her husband had not asked for help her parents had been generous; she did not think her expectations of inheritance had been altered, although there might be in the will 'some funny clause' saying that the money was not to be used for Catholic education of her children. But the children were growing up with virtually no contact with their mother's parents except of a very formal kind. Mrs Lander's mother seemed worried by this, and wished she saw more of her grandchildren. The elder, about five years old, reciprocated this attitude and 'adored' her grandmother. But Mr Lander appeared to have strong views; he was very much against having more to do with her family, particularly her parents, and disliked his daughter's attachment to her grandmother. Outside the wife's natal family circle the quarrel also had effect (see Chapter 12, p. 439), especially with her mother's sisters. This breach meant that relations with her cousins on her mother's side had practically ceased. This instance brings out in strong relief how the structure of the kin universe may be altered by one critical act. The children of this couple were very unlikely to know anything of their mother's cousins on her mother's side, if indeed they succeeded in maintaining any affective relation with their mother's parents.

Although Catholicism has been treated as a unitary factor in the discussion of the kinship aspects of mixed marriages, selection among the various types of Catholic institution may take place and involve non-religious, perhaps aesthetic factors. In the case just discussed the parents said they would not think of having their children brought up in a non-Catholic school. But they did not attend the local Catholic Church. 'Good heavens, no! It's run by the very worst sort of Catholics – Irish Passionist types – awful!' They themselves attended Dominican services elsewhere which were much more austere.

Much of what has been said in general about mixed Roman Catholic and Anglican marriages and kin effects of conversion would seem to apply also to mixed Jewish and Christian marriages. But in the latter case the rigours of Jewish orthodoxy, where they are practised, seem to give an even stronger predisposition towards kin difficulties. In our sample there were few orthodox Jews: most were of Reform or Liberal background, and some might be regarded as completely agnostic in the religious field. Nevertheless, Jewish kinship factors were apt to affect social relations of the partners to a mixed marriage if only because even an agnostic often had some orthodox Jewish kin. Moreover, the existence of such Jewish kin gave opportunity for comment to any of the spouse's kin who might have anti-Jewish views. We obtained no material on cases where Jew and non-Jew had wished to marry but refrained because of the opposition of their relatives. But taking account of the fact that by definition we are dealing with cases where the parties concerned overcame or disregarded any such opposition, it still did seem that in modern conditions kin influence was usually not strong enough actually to prevent such a marriage from taking place. What happened was that relations between kin, even close kin, tended to become exacerbated and remain strained for a long period, with reactions upon the position of any children. But we also found such mixed-marriage situations viewed by some members of the kin group in relatively neutral, analytical terms. Many of our informants were interested in this problem and willing to generalize about it apart from their own cases.

As with Catholic/Anglican marriages, there was considerable variation in the kinship effects of Jewish/Christian marriages. In some cases there was very little reaction from kin. Mrs Neville and her natal family were Church of England, although not practising members. The husband was a non-practising member of the Jewish faith. There was mild kin objection but no real opposition to their marriage. The wife's parents said beforehand, in warning rather than protest. 'You are going to marry him, and he is a good bit older and a different religion!' They were uncertain whether the wife, only twenty, realized fully what she was doing, and apparently were reassured when they found she did. The person who did make rather tactless remarks was her sister, who said, 'You're mad! He's a good deal older than you.' But because of the sister's husband's lack of a settled job-interest the sister was reported to be now saying, 'I wish I had done the same.' The wife had decided when their son was born that the child would not be christened; he would be allowed in due course to choose his religious allegiance. But she then became very ill and while in hospital suddenly thought that the baby should be christened in case he or she died. The husband had not objected. When our interviewer asked the wife what her husband's religion was she said, in a startled voice, 'He's Jewish, does it matter?' But she had had a clash with her sister in which a slighting reference had been made to her Jewish connections (see Chapter 12, p. 433).

Another man, brought up in the Jewish faith, said he felt it had no relationship to this century or this part of the world so he broke away from it – the only member of his family to do this. His marriage to a non-Jewish girl caused a rift between his mother and himself which lasted for ten years. But in the end friendly relations were resumed and wife and mother got along together reasonably well. According to him, the relations with her Christian daughter-in-law were better than with her Jewish daughter-in-law.

In those circles where Jewish religious profession was taken relatively lightly family difficulties might still occur, though muted, without formal severance of social relations. One wife's parents, who were Christian, did not object in the least to her marrying a Jew. 'Father was a Catholic. There was some conflict here one generation back so he became irreligious. Mother was C. of E.' On the husband's side there was more objection. The husband described his father as 'peculiarly Jewish, but with a great deal of ambivalence. He is becoming more anglicized than his peers, though quite unashamedly Jewish.' But as regards religious practice he was 'really agnostic'. (Said the wife to the husband in a discussion on this whole matter, 'Your father *enjoys* ham!') According to the husband, for his mother the Jewish religion was Jewish family life. She used to go to synagogue; later she abandoned this and concentrated on burials, marriages and other formal events. The husband said of himself and his wife: 'We were both fairly anti-religious before we met; there has been no conflict with us. My mother was very much against it, but there were no rows.' To which his wife commented, 'I wouldn't say that.' The husband admitted, 'Well, there were tremendously long arguments', to which the wife added, 'She had one or two goes at me'. The husband said that whereas neither he nor his wife had altered their profession of faith, his brother had persuaded his fiancée to change her religion; she became Jewish though it didn't mean anything to her. His mother, not deeply religious, and with a great sense of family warmth, accepted this. It seemed obvious that our informant wished his wife had done likewise; he felt that it would not have mattered to his mother if the wife had just called herself Jewish – that would have been enough.

With the Newfields, where the wife had also not converted, both parties initially had faced great opposition to their marriage. They were of different nationalities, and this too was held up as a reason why the marriage was doomed. But, strongly attracted to each other, they went ahead despite violent disapproval from both sides. Once they were married and each spouse had been introduced to and stayed with the respective parents-in-law the disapproval tended to vanish, since when there had been a great deal of contact between both sets of parents and the married pair. It was with other more distant kin that embarrassment seemed to exist. The wife said rather ironically, 'No Jew wants a non-Jew in his circle, but with us the poor orthodox people feel they ought to do something about it. They objected to my husband's marriage and feel they ought to save us from our situation.' The orthodox kin of Mr Newfield tried applying a sanction by taking their business away from him, but some returned because of his high professional standing. They also tried taking him aside and suggesting a rabbi who could get his wife converted quickly! Mrs Newfield seemed to have rather ambivalent feelings towards her parents-in-law. She criticized her mother-in-law but was very fond of her father-in-law and felt much sympathy towards him for his sufferings during the War. She was of the opinion that it depended upon the status and education of Liberal Jews according to whether they objected or not to mixed marriages. She thought that those of better education and higher status were least likely to object.

Opposition on the part of relatives may be mitigated by conversion of the spouse to their religion, but not necessarily removed entirely. When first interviewed Mrs Arden said she was Jewish. Only when the non-Jewish range of names on her genealogy was questioned did she tell the story of her mixed marriage. She said that she was originally Church of England, as were her parents. 'My husband is Jewish by origin, but not by religion.' His family were orthodox, but he was not and therefore never discussed religion with them. Yet, she said, he would never stop being a Jew, and for that reason she decided to change her religion. She didn't like the idea of her sons being 'half and half'; she felt it was important that they took the religion of their father, and it was not good to have divided religion in the house. Also, she wanted them to have synagogue instruction, and this meant that according to the strict rules she would have to change and become Jewish. She said that it was a difficult decision to make. Her husband did not apply any pressure; it was entirely her own decision. She studied for nine months, and although she had not completed her studies she was pregnant at the time, so they hurried her acceptance ceremony. The rabbi made her promise that she would come back and continue, but she hadn't so far, mainly because of lack of time with three small children.

Mrs Arden's family showed no disturbance when she married a Jew, nor did they show any concern when she changed her religion; she didn't know if it meant anything to them. She thought it might have been hard for her father to take, but her mother helped him to digest the news before he saw his daughter. She suspected that her parents kept their feelings to themselves so as not to worry her too much. Her husband's family, she said, were quite pleasant to her, considering that they could have hated her on sight. Yet there was one member of the family who wouldn't acknowledge her – her husband's Aunt Miriam, a public figure who had been an intense and devoted worker for social causes. The wife said that she didn't run into the family much so it didn't affect her; she saw her husband's father and stepmother, but the other members only when she made an effort. But she and her husband were not asked to attend any orthodox gatherings.

The future of their children was a problem for this couple, who both sighed when the question was raised by our interviewer. It was a subject they thought a lot about, but had so far procrastinated upon. They both wanted the children to have a basic religious grounding, and in the circumstances wished it to be Jewish. They felt they 'had to' send the boys to religious classes, and they were under gentle pressure from Mr Arden's father to give them a proper religious education. They said they must really do something about it soon, because their eldest son, aged seven, who was going to a church school, was talking of being baptized! Mrs Arden said she wished the children to see both sides of the religious field, but that so far the boys had only been to church and not to synagogue. Mr Arden said he had been to a synagogue and was interviewed by the rabbis. He realized that the religious schools were not State-subsidized and had to get money where they could, but he objected to being asked by them how much he earned. According to his account, if they hadn't done this he would have been generous, but, he said, he felt they were interested only in his money and not in his children – so he walked out in a huff, and the situation had been shelved for the time being. (He was very sensitive about any questions concerning money.)

Here the mixed marriage was associated with a strong sense of parent–child relations, but little concern for wider kin ties. The wife had no siblings, the husband only one sister with whom his social contacts were few on account of bad relations with his brother-in-law. Aunts, uncles and cousins were of no great importance to the couple, whose society included several good old friends. Relations with their respective parents were adjusted to a workable level, and in fact the wife's relation with her mother seemed to have become closer after her acquisition of a husband had given her an alternative point of emotional attachment. In this case religion was respected, but made to serve an instrumental role, and the initial differences were composed in the interests of family unity.

In Jewish sentiment there is probably more feeling against the marriage of a Jewish woman to a non-Jewish man than where a Jewish man has married a non-Jewish woman. There were only two such cases of the former in our sample (as compared with six of the latter.) Neither involved much immediate family opposition. In one the wife, though not a practising Jew, was closely linked socially and emotionally with her mother and other kin, who were. There was some disagreement between the parents of husband and wife when her son was born, as to whether he should be christened or circumcised. The wife offered to have him christened 'to please my mother-in-law'; but her Christian husband objected, and in the end no action was taken. In the Garson case all the wife's kin were members of prominent Jewish families, but her upbringing had not been orthodox. Her parents were dead by the time of her marriage, but she continued to maintain close and affectionate relations with her siblings. With her more distant kin, especially on the father's mother's side, there was more constraint. Some of her father's mother's family were very orthodox, very strict, and these 'old family patriarchs' as the wife called them – a FMB, FMBS, FMBW and FMZ – strongly objected to her marriage. Relations with them were consequently infrequent and strained, though not completely severed. But there had been other marriages also outside the Jewish community to acclimatize them. Two sons of her FMB had married non-Jewish girls and had been completely cut off from the family by their father with a traditional announcement of death symbolizing the severance of all relationships. (This seems to have been a Jewish practice more characteristic of a generation or so ago than today.)

These examples of Jewish–Christian marriages make it clear that while anti-Jewish prejudice is responsible for some difficulties by kin, the exclusiveness of Jewish attitudes can be equally a serious cause of kin friction. In some cases religious differences may be used as a peg on which to hang differences of other, perhaps more personal, kinds. But that this does not arise simply as a retrospective attitude when a mixed marriage has occurred is attested by many general opinions.[3] These can be illustrated by some views of a Jewish young woman married to a Jewish husband. She said she didn't approve of mixed marriages, and she could not think of anyone in either her or her husband's family who had married 'out'. This view was not just an abstract one; she related it concretely to the situation of her daughter and son, about which she had very strong feelings. (They were still children.) She said, 'We all have our theories on prejudice. I would be far more unhappy if my daughter married a non-Jew than if my son did. I think the more common ground there is the better', adding rather pessimistically, 'marriage is difficult enough without different religions!' For her greater unhappiness should her daughter marry 'out' she gave the following reasons: 'I am of the opinion that a Jewish man makes a far better husband for a Jew than a non-Jewish

[3] For example, the rabbi of a London synagogue wrote in his quarterly magazine: 'Mixed marriage is the malady which more than any other affects the survival of Jewry . . . Not every intermarriage is doomed to breakdown or difficulty – but it is an inescapable conclusion, based on all the evidence, that as a general rule a mixed marriage creates serious difficulties' (quoted in *Hampstead and Highgate Express*, 18 February 1966.)

man; I think he provides more; what money he has, more of it goes to the home and the children – better food, the home more comfortable, more money on holidays than drinks at the pub. More like the life that our children are leading now. I won't say he would be more faithful. I suppose it's just the same with Protestant and Catholic mixed marriages – no! not the same as Catholics because then the children have to be brought up as Catholics. You can't work it out, as with a Jewish and non-Jewish marriage.'[4]

An additional kinship problem arises in regard to the religious future of the children of such a mixed marriage. In the Newfield family there were three daughters. The husband seemed to feel, in the traditional Jewish way, that women's place was in the home. He belonged to an orthodox synagogue where – though much less strict than in Poland, his homeland – his wife said incredulously, 'the women sit in the first floor of the house and peep down from a hole in the floor (actually from a gallery) at the men in the room below'. But he and his wife were bringing the children up as Liberal Jews. They had given them godparents, and intended to send them to non-Jewish schools and to bring them up in as English a way as possible in speech and behaviour. The idea was that later they would be so 'liberal in outlook' that they could choose for themselves whether or not to remain Jewish. But the wife felt that a very serious problem might arise when her daughters wished to marry if they wanted to marry in a synagogue. She gave a comparable example. The daughter of a Jewish man and non-Jewish woman had been brought up all her life as a Jew and attended synagogue every week, went to religious classes and observed religious restrictions. She was about to marry the son of a rabbi, who checked over her background and found that there was 'this business over the mother'. He had hired a hall and ordered kosher food, but the Kashrut Commission decided not to approve of the catering for the reception because the girl's mother was not Jewish. The rabbi apparently had a terrible row with the girl's parents, the girl, and his son, because he didn't want the latter to have such a bride. But eventually a compromise was reached. The rabbi said if the girl would again go through a course of training she would be acceptable. So, said our informant, for the 'sins' of the mother the young woman took this six months token course, at the end of which she was 'doubly' and 'safely' a Jew. She said, 'It was simply the fact he could not marry the girl because she was not quite the wife he should have had. It is so primitive, so ridiculous.' This

[4] With this may be contrasted the view of Mr Arden, a Jewish man married to a Gentile. He said that a Jewish woman controls the family and that is why he could never marry a Jewish girl. But in fact he treated his wife as if she still directed family policy!

was the opinion of someone who had been brought up as a Nonconformist and who could not be expected to see the matter from a Jewish angle. But from her own experience she thought that it was only in such a marriage with a 'key' Jewish figure where any serious objection to a synagogue ceremony was likely to arise.

The difficulty caused by having a mother who was not Jewish can be almost traumatic for a young person who has been brought up to consider himself or herself a Jew. The defect in one's kinship here is not easy to remedy because while Judaism allows for conversion, the stringency of its conditions is such that this is not easily obtained.

The reaction of kin to a mixed marriage has a certain analogy with their reaction to a union of two people who have not been married. In the stricter religious circles of say, Roman Catholicism or Judaism, a marriage to a person of another faith is imperfect and may be in their eyes no marriage at all.[5] (If celebrated in civil style only, for them any marriage is ecclesiastically invalid.) In such case part of the social strain may arise because the natal families of the two principals are in an ambiguous position – their affinal roles *vis-à-vis* one another are not clearly defined.

In our records we have a number of instances of kin of our principals living in an unmarried state with a domestic partner, and a few of our principals themselves occupied such a position at some period of their marital history. In no case does kin opinion seem to have functioned as an effective sanction. It seems to have been kin of the older generation for the most part who disapproved; members of the younger generation seem to have shown more tolerance. The attitude adopted by close kin of the same generation was realistic, matter-of-fact. The legal marriage tie was treated as of less importance than a satisfactory personal relationship. Kin were not looked on as guardians of morality but as supporters in social life.

KIN IMPLICATIONS OF A FIRST-COUSIN UNION

A marriage which is perfectly appropriate in modern English law but which sometimes attracts unfavourable popular attention is that of first cousins, the union of whom is thought (inaccurately) to react upon the offspring. As cited earlier (Chapter 6), there was only one case of such a marriage among the principals in our study, the

[5] Cf. the report of an even more stringent declaration by judges of the Jewish Orthodox ecclesiastical courts in London and Manchester that marriages solemnized by Liberal or Reform rabbis are not valid in Jewish law. (*Sunday Times*, 2 January 1966.)

Tomlinsons. The kinship implications of this were interesting. Since it was the marriage of patrilateral parallel cousins, children of two brothers, the husband and wife bore the same surname before marriage. The wife said this was sometimes a nuisance. When for official documents she had to give her maiden name, and it turned out to be her husband's surname too, an official would say, 'No, your maiden name . . .'; she got tired of explaining the circumstances. This made for some self-consciousness on Mrs Tomlinson's part. When asked what difference they thought the marriage had made to their kin relationships, both husband and wife said, 'None at all'. They argued, supporting each other, as follows. Family solidarity, they suggested, depended upon childhood background. In their case this had been intensified as they shared their childhood experiences in the same close-knit circle. When they married they had to form no new relationships, and this is why they said that being first cousins made no difference to kin relationships. (In marriages not between first cousins it was held possible to overcome the lack of shared experience in childhood by taking the spouse to visit the other's childhood scenes.) Our informants insisted that in the case of a first cousin marriage, when 'aunt' became 'mother-in-law', etc., it was only 'the legal relationship which is altered', not the personal one. Another effect of being first cousins as well as spouses which they considered important was that 'no strange close relation is likely to be flung at you unawares'. This problem is one which most people have to face early in a marriage, and which can create great difficulties; this they felt they had escaped – though they met it to a modified degree with distant relatives who had to introduce themselves. They felt that in their children's generation, however, their first cousin marriage did make a difference. 'The next generation as cousins are very used to each other. They literally share a large number of relatives, and have grandparents in common.' This close kinship was intensified, since the husband's sister was married to the wife's brother – creating a double first cousin union!

In this case husband and wife themselves had perceived much of the sociological implication of their conversion of consanguines into affines. But what was also interesting was that they reproduced this understanding very largely in terms of avoidance of disturbance by the outside world – thus denying in a way the value of more widespread external social contacts, and by implication one of the more general anthropological assumptions about marriage. This attitude was reinforced by the wife's view of her relations with her mother-in-law. The relationship did not appear to be an easy one. This woman, her 'aunt' before marriage, was her father's brother's wife, not her father's sister, i.e. not a member of the patrilineally recognized group. The husband explained his mother's position in somewhat denigrating terms: 'She was an only child brought up by maiden aunts and never really understood what belonging to a family like ours could mean.'

KINSHIP AND MONEY

It is tempting to adopt the epigram of one of our informants, 'Money always cleaves families', as the epitome of this section of our enquiry. But the quality of kin relations as expressed in monetary transactions and attitudes towards them is not so one-sided; it may be held indeed that money unites families as much as it divides them. This is borne out by our evidence concerning financial contributions made by sons and daughters to parents or occasionally sibling's support. Such assistance seems to have been given for the most part ungrudgingly, even cheerfully, and accepted by spouses as a necessary part of the obligations which they rightfully should incur.

It is sometimes assumed that one correlate of middle-class position, as contrasted with that of the working-class, is the possession of some inherited wealth by most families. It is interesting then to examine our material from this point of view. We have some data on inheritance by the principals in 66 households of our study; in just over half of these, 35 in all, there was some inheritance of money, or fairly definite expectations of inheritance from kin by one or more adult individuals in the households concerned. The average sums were not very large – about £1,500 inheritance per person in the dozen or so instances where precise financial details were obtainable. The range of inheritance was fairly considerable, however, varying from about £100 (or a 'forty-second share in three cottages' in one instance) to £15,000 in trust. In about 20 per cent of the cases where money or landed property was inherited it appeared to be of such amount as to yield a moderate private income, e.g. of the order of £400–£500 a year from houses and stock. Inheritance in Greenbanks seemed to definitely be on a smaller scale than in Highgate, where there were several cases of substantial capital of unspecified amount inherited.

Noteworthy in most of these cases was that only one partner in a marriage had inherited any money; in very few cases did both spouses come from families with property to pass on. From this point of view then these people may be regarded as lower and middle middle-class, rather than upper middle-class, where presumably it is more common for both spouses to bring inherited capital into the marriage or acquire it later. From this point of view too it is significant that in only one case, of the Herberts, did we receive any information about marriage settlements, though there were several other cases where trusts had been set up for children of a marriage by interested parties such as a husband's mother. In the Herbert case the wife said that all the women in her family had marriage settlements. 'Every family has them!' she commented, in glorious generalization. She added that they were very important, because the lawyers tie the capital so that it can't be 'blown' by either husband or wife, and constitutes a fund settled in trust on the children. Trustees, in her view, were usually relatives – a brother, an uncle, an aunt's husband. (In the appropriate circles, this is yet another important function of kin, including affines; the point was not stated, but it is customary for males only as a rule to serve as such trustees.)

In the 30 cases in which there was specifically no inheritance of money or landed property by our principals, there were still at least half a dozen in which personal belongings such as furniture, silver, jewellery, a grandfather clock or other property, sometimes of considerable value, had been handed down to them by kin (see Chapter 5). In sum then, for this range of middle-class London families, there was some inherited property in about two-thirds of the cases; only one-third had been without any such contribution.

The immediate point is that all this inherited wealth is a material token of kin interest (the cases of inheritance from a godparent or family friend were very few). Significant is the distribution of kin from whom the legacies came. With one exception, that of the brother of an elderly woman, all the kin from whom property had been inherited were of a senior generation. Taking all kinds of inheritance together – money, real property, heirlooms, etc. – parents were responsible for the legacies in three-fifths of the instances, parents' siblings in one-fifth, while in the remaining one-fifth the kin included mother's mother, great-aunt, and first cousin once removed (FMBD). It is noteworthy that no more distant kin were involved – the idea that most middle-class families have a remote kinswoman with money to leave to them seems to be a myth. We were told on several occasions of remote kinsfolk with money to leave to others – their own descendants or siblings – but our informants seemed pretty dispassionate about such occurrences, and obviously did not feel themselves to be concerned. A concrete indication that monetary transfer can imply kin interest is in those cases, of which several occur in our material, where a legacy is made conditional upon change of name, or the change is made in acknowledgement of a legacy.

Now as to the validity of the epigram that money always cleaves families. Reviewing all the material collected on wills, property relations, legacies and the like, including transactions or relations between any kin mentioned in our cases, we have found only about a score of instances of disputes. This means on the average one instance of quarrel or resentment displayed for every three of our cases. The instances that related directly to the principals of our study were very few; the proportion of conflicts due to their property transactions seemed less than 20 per cent, and no more significant than those due to religious difference.

The content and intensity of such disputes over property or monetary transactions as did occur varied a great deal. Some were private resentments which never came to open expression, let alone a quarrel between the parties. In a case of remarriage of a widower his son farmed the father's land. If the second marriage had not taken place he presumably would have occupied with his wife and children the big farmhouse; instead they had to live in a bungalow on the estate. When the second wife's married son and his wife (our informants, the Vendors) arrived to stay they were put up in the big house. The two step-brothers had been quite good friends from long before the marriage, but when they met in the big farmhouse the Vendors had 'a slight feeling' that they were intruding; they had never been invited to the bungalow.

Open bad feeling among kin over wills was recorded in about half-a-dozen instances. These seem to have occurred in two main kinds of situations – where one sibling was alleged to have obtained too great a share of a parent's property; or where a second marriage had complicated the inheritance. Such a dispute came to the surface particularly as an explanation of why certain kin were not in contact. One informant in the first interview said she thought one of her father's sisters was dead, but after discussing the matter with her parents found it was not so. She had not seen this aunt for about twenty years. The lack of contact was probably due to her father, she thought; he had quarrelled with all his sisters over his mother's will. When she died she did not leave a 'proper' will. Quite a big estate was involved, much of which went to her second husband and step-sons. According to our informant her father should have inherited the property, as the eldest son, but he did not. Moreover, the contents of the house were put up for auction, after his sisters had 'taken their pickings', as they lived near. The brother got practically nothing, hence the bitterness, even though one of the sisters later gave her brother some 'bits'. On our informant's mother's side there was also trouble over a will. Apparently, a sister of the mother went down to see their father during his last illness and, it was said, directed his hand as he signed the will. He did not leave much, but there was dissension in the family. 'My aunt got the cash, and we got a lot of old books.' After this, our informant's mother had little to do with her sister, and our informant did not go to her aunt's funeral. The feeling that may lie behind these disputes is sometimes vividly represented. Mr Forsyth had no contact with his father's sister; he didn't like her, though he had had a wedding present from her. More than twenty years before there had been a row over a family will, in which the aunt had 'done very well'. Mr Forsyth's father had looked after his parents for a long time, until they moved to the district where the daughter lived. 'This is where the dagger was put in the back!' – presumably the insinuations which deprived her brother of his rightful share of the inheritance.

Some of the most bitter disputes, however, appear to have occurred not over wills but over other property issues (see e.g. Regan, p. 410). One had a will as a background, but the issue was rather what was equitable outside the arrangements of the will. When Mrs Gamba's mother died, her share of her and her husband's property was divided between our informant and her two brothers. The father remained in the house and soon after remarried. The agreement between him and his children was that since they had received their mother's share of the joint property his share should in due course go to his second wife, much younger than himself. Our informant did not admit to any kind of resentment over this arrangement; she insisted that it was a fair agreement. The understanding, however, applied to the major property – money and land; all personal belongings such as books, silver, piano, photographs should be left to the children when their father died and not to the second wife. But with old age 'they get stingy and concerned with property and money', and the father omitted to state this provision in the will, which left everything to his second wife. So, after his death, his children could not collect any of their mother's personal belongings. The brothers, though resentful, decided to let things take their course. Not so our informant – she mobilized them, got a lawyer and sued her father's wife. The case was settled out of court, the stepmother keeping the silver, our informant receiving photographs, letters and some of the books, and the brothers the piano and other things. Our informant had never seen her stepmother again, and indeed our interviewer learned of the existence of this woman only when she asked about wills. 'I did not tell you my father had remarried because it is unimportant; she does not count!'

Most of these disputes over money and property seem to have cut fairly deep into kin relations. Some were not confined to the immediate parties to the issue but involved other kin as well, almost along factional lines. Mr Arthur's father died when he was very young and he was left as an only child, closely attached to his mother. It seemed that his father had left a will in which very little property was left to the mother, and the main beneficiaries were the father's two sisters. Mr Arthur thought that his mother hadn't minded too much, though it seemed that she had talked a great deal about the injustice of the situation. He said that his mother had brought him up to look upon these two aunts as black figures, and that he was rather prejudiced against them. The feud – so he described it – was sufficiently estranging for him not to have known a cousin, the son of one of these aunts, until this man walked into his office one day and identified himself. He had found this cousin a very able and upright man and they became quite friendly. Here, but for the initiative on the part of one member, the patrilateral cousin relations would have remained completely severed as a result of the thirty-years old dispute.

Complex alignments in connection with a set of property disputes arose from an inheritance whereby the three Potts brothers each received £15,000 and four sisters each £10,000 from an estate which originally had been much larger but had been denuded by poor management. It was administered by the children's mother, from whose family it had apparently come earlier. In addition to the inherited sums, which were held in trust, there had been some distribution of personal property, including family silver, paintings and other heirlooms, but the mother herself still controlled substantial resources. The children, long since grown up, had squabbled over the inheritance. One brother (not the eldest) was convinced he had been cheated and that he had received less than his rightful share; accordingly he continued to put pressure on his mother for additional benefits. As a result, he and another brother were not on speaking terms. One of the sisters apparently felt equally cheated. As daughter she had received less than a son, and she seemed to resent this more than did her sisters; she also put pressure on her mother. Because of her attitude she had cut herself off from all but one of her sisters, and even with this one her relations were not entirely smooth. A third brother, our informant, viewed all these manoeuvres with distaste. He said he strongly objected to these and other demands made by his brothers and sisters upon his mother, over and above the funds held in trust for them. Linked with this attitude was his view that only in very special circumstances would he turn to any of his siblings – and then only to one brother of whom he was very fond – for assistance in difficulty.

That monetary transactions and the distribution of property do not necessarily divide families is shown by the many instances in which such affairs were quite amicably arranged. Since amity is less spectacular than dispute, specific references to it are not so frequent in our records. But for about a quarter of the inheritance transactions recorded for our principals there is definite statement that they were effected without any trouble, and in at least half of the rest the context makes it fairly clear that amity obtained.

Most of these specific statements referred to relations between siblings, drawn forth as reflections on an apparently uneven distribution of property. The principle followed in the dispersal of the personal belongings in a large house of one fairly wealthy family, that of Mrs Garson, was that each of the five children should take what they wanted. This freedom caused no problems, partly because none of the siblings was in great need (e.g. Mrs Garson had received a house full of furniture from an old spinster childhood friend of her mother's), and partly because general relations between them seemed to be very good. Another instance concerned the privileged position of siblings. Money from a grandmother was to come to Mr Gamba and his brother through their mother. When the brother was considering divorce the mother, who disapproved strongly, threatened to cut him off from the inheritance. Mr Gamba talked her out of this, suggesting that if she left all the legacy to him alone it would cause resentment and spoil the friendship between the brothers. So the mother changed her mind, but instead of transferring the money to the brother directly set up a trust with Mr Gamba to administer it. As trustee he was left to decide whether the funds were to be handed over to his brother or reserved for the education of the brother's children. Here Mr Gamba's emphasis was on parity of treatment in the name of good kin relations.

In another situation the emphasis was on lack of parity, for similar reasons. When Mr Gibbon's mother died her house was sold for £500 (years ago). He took none of the money because he 'wasn't in need' and his sisters had looked after their mother. They had £250 each, and, he thought, appreciated their brother's generosity. But another reason why he acted in this way was that his parents had helped him financially to go to college, while his sisters had received only an elementary education. He felt that as he had had 'anything that was going' it was now their turn to benefit. Yet the principle of inequality in distribution related to difference of need was sometimes a matter of debate. Mrs Potts said that whatever property there was in her family should be divided among her two brothers,[6] because her husband should be responsible financially for her, whereas they had wives and children to support. This view was challenged by her

[6] Cf. another case in which it was reported that a wealthy father's sister left to a favourite niece, whom everyone thought would inherit from her, only heirlooms and no money. 'She had a very Victorian outlook – she believed that only men should inherit.'

husband, who thought that daughters should receive as much in inheritance as sons.

Several general inferences can be drawn from this material. In the first place, there was clearly a great deal of moral indignation displayed and presumably felt over the issues where property disputes occurred. In the second place, it is often very difficult for the external observer to see where a moral balance should be drawn, in terms of principle itself, let alone application of principle to a given case. Claims of wife presumably should have precedence over those of sisters in a property distribution, but what about those of second wife as against those of children of the first wife? How do long companionship and domestic care for a parent rate for recognition of the claims of one sibling to inherit favourably to the detriment of other siblings? These are questions where equity would seem to lie in a number of practical considerations balanced out. But what of the principle that sons should inherit 50 per cent more per share than daughters – is this to be justified on the basis that men have heavier financial responsibilities than women do, or rebutted on the ground that in our modern society men still have much greater opportunities of securing a substantial and stable income? And what is the validity in modern conditions of giving any weight to the traditional principle of primogeniture? These are questions to which no simple answer can be given from any neutral point of view, yet to which our informants and their kin did usually have relatively simple replies. These replies were often highly emotionally coloured. Moreover, they were often associated with long-term persisting attitudes of rejection of the other parties involved in the dispute. It seems likely then that these property disputes are often symptoms rather than causes of family or kin dissension – or that the property distributions do not actually generate disputes but rather spark off underlying tensions which then focus on the property issues. We examine later some of the conditions which seem to promote such tensions, especially between siblings, and between step-parents and step-children.

Yet to sum up in our sample of middle-class families, about two-thirds had some inherited property, for the most part of moderate value; and in a high proportion of the cases the inheritance was accomplished without dispute.

KINSHIP AND CONFINEMENT

A good test of the quality of kin relations is given by the reactions of kin to a crisis in the family. One type of crisis which offers the possibility of direct comparison among different cases is the birth of a child.[7] In our sample overall there were 58 families with at least one dependent child, and 130 children had been born to the mothers concerned. About two-thirds of the children were born in hospital or maternity home and the remainder at home. (According to standard National Health practice first babies only are expected to be delivered in hospitals.) Where the mother had a choice, reasons for hospital preference were need for special medical care, less trouble involved with no other children to worry about, and less expense. But preference seemed to be largely an individual matter. Those mothers who had their babies at home seemed to think that it was more comfortable in familiar surroundings; 'it was nice having friends and family around'. One argument was that home was preferable to hospital because it was better psychologically for the older children to have their mother with them at the time. But choice of home or hospital might also be determined by availability of kin. One woman said 'There is no point in having your babies at home unless you are rich or unless you have a mother in the family to look after you'.

It is at this time of a woman's life that a mother may play as important a role as at any other. There are two aspects of this situation. One might imagine that a mother would be particularly welcome for psychological support for the critical event of a woman's first baby. Again, it might be even more necessary for practical reasons at the birth of subsequent babies, to look after the earlier children. In fact, for first babies women's mothers gave some form of help in about 50 per cent, other kin helped in about 10 per cent, and in 40 per cent no kin help at all was received. For subsequent babies the picture was much the same. The role of wife's mother was partly a function of the stage she had reached in the family cycle; her assistance would have been increased by perhaps another 10 per cent if she had not been prevented from attendance by age or illness. Husband's mothers gave substantial help in a few cases only. Siblings gave little help in a confinement. Wife's sisters gave assistance in less than 10 per cent of the instances and husband's sisters helped hardly at all. There was a fairly obvious reason for this: the sisters were busy in employment or married with homes to look after and very often their own children as well.

In this situation of crisis husbands showed a fair amount of self-reliance. In a few instances they went to stay with their mothers, but in about a third of the 130 instances the husband managed in the house either alone or with the help of friends, neighbours or paid

[7] A more detailed study of kinship and other social factors in pregnancy and childbirth is being carried out by Jane Hubert (Mrs Jane Forge) with support from the Social Science Research Council. This prospect arose directly from the present study.

assistance. (In a couple of cases the husband helped to deliver the baby at home; in one he was not a doctor.) There was considerable variation in the form of paid assistance employed (in about one-third of the cases), varying from the technical aid of a nurse to the non-technical aid of an *au pair* girl, 'daily help' or 'cleaning woman'.

Several general descriptive points can be made here. First, if a woman has a baby in hospital, this involves a problem of provision for her dependants at home. Again, in all the arrangements concerned with pregnancy and confinement it is kinswomen and not kinsmen who are almost exclusively concerned. In a society which it is sometimes argued increasingly tends to equate the roles of men and women, the whole sequence of operations concerned with the birth of children – except the purely medical operations, with which either male or female doctors may be concerned – is still regarded as being primarily an affair of women. A further point is that the question of a kinswoman such as a wife's mother coming to stay and help in the house is to a considerable extent settled by whether or not there is a spare bedroom. This pattern may then be a function of space in middle-class dwellings, linked with middle-class geographical separation of mother and daughter. Where, as in a working-class milieu, a mother may live close to a daughter she does not need to move in, and in any case there may be no room for her in which to stay.

In some cases the woman having the baby felt the lack of kin assistance. Mrs Fortescue had her first child in hospital and then had a local nurse to help her when she returned home. Her mother would have come, but 'had a bad heart'; instead then the daughter went with her baby to stay with the mother for a month. The second child too she had in hospital and was helped for three or four weeks by the same nurse. She said that she felt the lack of relatives, especially young ones, who could have helped at a time like this – she had a brother but no sisters, and her husband had only one sister, who was not available. Services of kin on such an occasion were often expected, and failure to render them could be a matter of offence. One woman had her third child at home with no kin help at all. Her mother was a diabetic and could not come, nor could her sister. Her *au pair* girl had left and her husband and a neighbour did what was necessary when she was in labour. She had asked her husband's father's second wife, who was in the United States, to come over and help, but this woman said she could not leave her husband – which was judged to be only an excuse, and was resented.

Complexities of kin relations, however, are illustrated by instances where kin help was definitely not wanted at the time of confinement or was regarded as of dubious value. Mr Vendor looked after himself during the first confinement, and before the second confinement his mother, a doctor, gave some help but had to return home before the actual birth. The wife's mother then arrived, bringing with her two dachsunds, which involved the household in 'a chaotic situation'. Rather despairingly the wife said of her approaching third confinement, 'It's no use depending on relatives. You can't depend on your family, they just don't come.' So she engaged a nanny and an *au pair* girl. The complex implications of kin presence on such an occasion are illustrated by the history of Mrs Waverley's confimenents. Her first daughter was born in hospital and she wanted to have her mother around for sentimental reasons. But it was disastrous: the mother was a helpless person and needed much attention. The wife's sister could not help since she was just married. For the second confinement the sister came to look after the elder daughter and stayed three weeks and the mother stayed later when the baby was some months old. But this really meant looking after the mother rather than having her to look after the child. At the time of our study the wife was pregnant again, but definitely didn't want her mother to come to her aid. Her husband's mother would have come but had a coronary attack. Her husband's father's sister would have come with avidity, but she felt that at the slightest opportunity her husband's other kin would 'move in'! Another more cynical observation was by a woman who got a girl friend of hers to come and look after her husband and son while she was having her baby. The friend fitted into the household very well and stayed two years. 'You can always choose a friend but you can't choose a relative' the wife said.

One further element in kin relations at such a time is the notion of reciprocity which lies behind some services, particularly between sisters. When Mrs Mitchie came out of hospital with her baby her sister stayed for a week. The wife said that when she was younger she used to slave over her two sisters' children and used to tell her sisters that she was going to have triplets to get her own back! So when her baby daughter was born her sister 'could hardly not have come'. The notion of reciprocity is closely linked with that of equality. With Mrs Outram it took a bizarre form. She learnt that her father had paid for her brother's wife to have her baby in a nursing home. She therefore demanded equality of treatment, but had the baby at home without any female kin to help and only paid assistance; she bought a washing machine with the money instead!

Various other patterns are perceptible in kin relations concerned with birth. When his first child was born, Mr Gibbon telephoned his wife's mother and then went out with the wife's brother for a drink 'to wet the baby's head'. This was the only instance we found of such an expression. But celebration of some kind was common; in particular news of the birth was telephoned to close kin. Acknowledgment of the birth was normally followed by presents given for the baby, in particular by kin. Except for babies born in wartime, there was hardly any instance in which no presents at all were given by kin. Two points about this were clear: that a very wide range of kin was often involved – e.g. clothes were given by WFFBD, WBW, WFFZ and D, WMMBS; on the other hand, present-giving was highly selective and by no means even all the closest kin always made gifts. It was recognized too that female rather than male kin were involved. Two comments illustrate this. For one birth a brother sent nothing, 'as his wife was dead and it is usually women who send presents'. Another brother wrote a note of congratulation 'but as a bachelor he didn't send anything'. Relative poverty was regarded as a reason for lack of a gift and a letter was accepted as a substitute. Frequently, too, knitting clothes for the baby was a recognized and acceptable, less expensive method of celebrating the birth than any other present. The whole process of acquisition of clothes for the new child clearly had a sentimental aura in addition to ordinary material significance. 'Passing on' of clothes and baby furniture was widespread, and though it involved a measure of economy it also combined kinship sentiment. This was exemplified in another way by a mother keeping her own childhood dresses for her daughters to wear and hoping that they too in turn would pass them on to their own children. The only discordant though still sentimental note on this point came from a woman who mildly complained at the amount of baby clothing she was given, with the comment, 'A pity, because it's so nice buying baby clothes'. It was common for kin to give equipment in addition to clothing and consultation frequently took place to avoid duplication of gifts. So, a wife's mother bought a bed, the wife's mother's sister a pram, the husband's mother a big cot, the husband's sister a high chair and the husband's half-sister a play pen. In a significant number of cases – about one-third in the Highgate sector – money was also given to be put into a post office or other bank account on behalf of the child.

Patterns of differentiation, however, were also perceptible. The view of one woman that 'Mothers are always more interested in their daughter's children than in their son's', was not confirmed by our cases. It did not seem that a daughter always got priority over a daughter-in-law in this field of kin interest in pregnancy and confinement. But it did seem clear that the interest of kin tended to diminish as the number of births in a family increased. A concept of the marginal utility of babies did seem to operate. One woman noted that whereas for her first and second child 'more or less everyone' sent gifts; for the third and fourth, presents were few and far between. 'I think people were getting a bit bored at my producing babies by the time Viola was born.' The Roman Catholic prohibition on birth control seemed to awake gloomy expectations in the minds of some kin. One woman, a Catholic, had both her wife's mother and her husband's mother to help her with the first confinement. They were in poor health when she had her second baby, which was born at home, and no kin at all came to help. 'They decided there were going to be lots of children and lost interest.' (The kin judgment in this case was prophetic because for her third confinement she had twins!) Some mothers also held that the first child was more advertised among kin than the later ones. 'I think people tend to give more for the first child than for the later ones.' The general situation among the set of kin may also be relevant here, as where it was held there was no great interest in a baby because its parents were not young and there had been many babies in the whole family previously. The birth of this particular child, however notable to its parents, was not considered as a major event by their families.

For a woman pregnancy and confinement is the period when she feels perhaps most of all the need for mobilization of her resources. Utilization of kin services is part of her strategy. Failure to utilize such service may indicate the lack of close kin or a calculation that on balance the strains are likely to be more severe than the benefits received. Here the personal relation between the woman and her mother, sister or other kinswoman is of prime importance. But other elements may also enter into the calculation, as when she may be anxious about how her husband will get on with her kinswoman in her own absence. In nearly two-thirds of the cases in our sample, positive considerations outweighed the negative ones and a kinswoman outside the marital family was called upon to give assistance. Such assistance was commonly one element in a long-term series of relations between the parties.

There is a point here of general relevance, even to the whole national accounting system. To a considerable degree the services of a kinswoman represent a substitute for paid services. It is impossible to assign any precise figures here, if only because of the lack of the cost of any alternative services which such kinswomen might perform elsewhere. But it is reasonable to think that since kin spend on an average at least a fortnight helping in the home at confinements for even half the approximately three-quarters of a million births per annum, on a national basis these maternity services performed by kinswomen are worth several millions of pounds a year.

KINSHIP AND HOLIDAYS

The last type of situation to be analysed in this context is recreation.

Our extensive material on family gatherings is discussed in Chapter 8. Some of these were distinctly recreational, but here we deal only with behaviour in non-ceremonial holidays. Such recreational situations serve as a foil to the birth situation, since in the latter help is necessary and therefore to some extent not a matter of choice, whereas on holidays choice is expected to be free. So it is of interest to see how far people tend to be associated with their kin at such times.

About a quarter to a third of the subjects of our study tended to avoid their kin when they went on holiday, or to choose their place of holiday irrespective of kin considerations. A man said he did not like to have to use his holidays to visit relatives, even to see his parents; he wanted to rest and to go away with his wife and child alone. A woman said, 'My idea of a holiday is to be on our own – to relax'; as one reason for avoiding holidays with her kin she said, 'You live in dread of the children quarrelling with each other'.

Yet remarkable in this situation is the high proportion of people who, at some time or another, did take holidays with kin outside their marital family. Most of these kin were members of the adult's natal family. Though the patterns were very diverse, they often preserved a rough balance between husband's and wife's kin. In one case at Easter the wife took the children to stay with her mother for ten days, leaving the husband to fend for himself; in alternate summers the wife's sister usually stayed with the family for a time and the husband's sister came to stay for several weekends in the year. In another case a man went weekly to a cottage in the Midlands to be with his sister and friends; his wife did not often go but their son used to spend his holidays with his father's sister and his mother's sister. There was a distinct tendency for patterns to be repeated periodically. In a family with 'county' connections there were shooting parties on the wife's brothers' and sister's husband's estates and the wife's parents usually spent their summer holidays at a shooting lodge which the husband and wife rented in Scotland. 'It was a definite pattern for my parents', and her siblings also used to go there in turn.

Among the roles that kin can play in the holiday field are the provisions of holiday company, holiday quarters, and services while parents go away alone. Some children were looked after by incoming kin (in one instance a MFBD) when their parents were on holiday, so that they should not have to be transferred to a strange house as well as have their parents absent.

The degree to which holidays were spent with kin varied according to family stage. When children were very young it was often more convenient for them to stay with relatives than among strangers. So a husband, wife and child would sometimes spend their holidays with his sister, but as the children grew older and the family had more money they preferred to stay in hotels. When the children of another family were small the husband and wife had holidays by themselves and the wife's parents took charge of the children, a nanny and the animals. When the children were older they began to go on holidays with their parents; 'they needed us more'. Then at a still later stage they began to go on holidays without their parents. Significant here is the role of extra-familial kin as social intermediaries, introducing the child to coping with the outside world apart from its parents.

For the most part relations with kin on holiday appeared to arise from mutual pleasure in one another's company. Sometimes, however, economy was an object as when a family went to the husband's mother's house in the country, 'especially if there was no money to pay for the holiday'. But there was often a deliberate view that it was a good thing to maintain kin relations – as with one couple who annually spent a week's holiday at the seaside with the wife's sister, feeling that they ought to do this otherwise relations would 'grow strange'.

BASIC IMPLICATIONS OF KINSHIP: SUPPORT AND SOCIABILITY

Two of the main implications of behaviour towards kin, as revealed by our material, are the notions of support and of responsibility. They may be antithetical or complementary according to circumstances. Personal support is expected to be derived from kin, personal responsibility to be assumed for kin, and they can be regarded as opposed or positively linked.

An important component of support by kin is the sociability they provide. Sociability is a quality attaching especially to friends, with whom by definition there is expected to be a positive affective relationship of social contact. But considering that kin are a given factor in one's scheme of things, and as such may be resented, it is interesting to see how much they are relied upon for relations of sociability. Occasions vary greatly, from casual exchange of news by telephone or by 'dropping-in', to regular outings together and fairly formal kin gatherings. The affective quality of these contacts and occasions may be quite complex. Whereas with friends attitudes are definitely positive (superficially, at least, on the conscious level), with kin some degree of ambivalence is much more frequently and overtly indicated. News may be communicated between sisters with undertones of triumph or resentment at the relative achievements of each other's children. Calling on one another at fairly regular intervals may occur partly in order to avoid giving the impression of neglect and so providing a basis for accusation. When kin go out together in a group it may be a pleasure for some but an ordeal for others. Questions of choice – where to go and who shall pay – may provide subject for recrimination or later domestic discussion and reproach. But there still is often an almost compulsive need to remain on sociable terms with kin and to regard frequent contact with them as a necessary, if somewhat onerous, part of social life. Going outwards from a conjugal family, this sociability aspect is apt to display itself commonly in regard to the kin of either husband or wife, but more rarely of both.

It is difficult to separate relations of sociability from those of support. It may be argued that quite apart from the maintenance of any direct physical relationship with kin, the very knowledge of their existence in one's social universe can be a factor of reassurance, an element in the definition of the self as an entity not completely isolated in a potentially hostile world. This may seem an exaggeration, and doubtless many people prefer to think of themselves as completely independent, and regard the ties of kinship as fettering their freedom of social action. But it does seem clear from the way in which many people talk of their kin, without necessarily being in close relation with them, that they regard these relatives as a kind of extension or support of themselves in the outer world. Kin represent persons on whom theoretically they may call in need, whether or not in practice they use their kin in this role. As our material demonstrates, however, it is quite usual for kin to be in more active relationship – to be a kind of sounding-board to listen to one's troubles, give approval to one's actions, give opinions which will enable one either directly or by reaction to come to decisions, furnish information in strange situations or environments.[8]

It is significant that kin are regarded as especially appropriate for these functions. Friends are often used in this way, but the tie of friendship seems to be conceived as definitely positive, affective. Some of the kin roles may well involve receiving unpalatable views; and tension may be generated between the parties. The friendship bond is looked upon frequently as too frail to bear much weight of tension and negative affect. With kin, however, a certain imperative appears. They 'ought' to be available to supply this separate role; even if a certain amount of tension, criticism and unpopularity is risked in this exchange of views, this tends to be regarded as a proper risk. This attitude, which forms an important part of the quality of

[8] Cf. P. Willmott: 'The kindred may be an important source of companionship and support in the heart of the modern city.' (p. 126), 'Kinship and Social Legislation', *British Journal of Sociology*, vol. IX, 1958, pp. 126–42.

kin relations, would seem to be associated with the recognition of the kinship bond as one marked by continuity. Pragmatically, it can be broken at the social level, as by blunt refusal to have any more social relationship with the kin concerned. But at whatever level the relationship be denied, the genealogical tie is usually given some social weight. A very refusal to discuss with an outside observer a brother or sister with whom one has severed relationship implies the recognition of an ultimate tie – one which only death can dissolve.

An important point about this aspect of support is that it is often conceived as one-way. If the ideal of friendship is equality, the ideal of a kinship relation allows of asymmetry. Differences in age, capacity and economic position may be all regarded as valid reasons why one party should give and the other receive, without necessary reciprocation.

This point of view was expressed in an interesting way by Mrs Pillerth. She had an elder sister with whom relations had grown closer as they grew up and the relative age gap decreased. Both sisters had married, divorced and later re-married, each facing much parental opposition at the divorce, and turning to each other for comfort and support. After her divorce our informant lived for a time with her sister and was re-married from her sister's house. Molly was really very good to me – she's always been very kind.' When Molly's marriage broke up in turn she came to stay with her sister, who also looked after the children during their school holidays. The sisters continued to see or telephone each other every day. Although our informant was the younger she seemed to regard her sister as the more dependent of the two. She said she wouldn't ask her sister for moral support 'because she needs it more and it's not fair to extract it back again'. She believed, she said, that moral support cannot be reciprocated – either one is the type of person who gives it (and she saw herself as that type) or one is the type of person who receives it. Seeing herself as a dispenser of help rather than a receiver of it, she was therefore rather disconcerted at our interviewer's question as to whom she would turn in a serious crisis – she replied 'To prayer!' But she then said she would first turn to her sister and then to some very close friends.

It is in this light that social situations involving kin have to be regarded. The quality of these relations is complex, composed of elements of friendship, companionship, recognition of services, feelings of obligation and responsibility, as well as of criticism and hostility. Often with much asymmetry, the tie of kinship is yet recognized as a valid link, operating almost as a kind of magnet, attracting people towards a renewal of their social contacts despite frequent friction and disappointment.

We now attempt to isolate further and assess the significance of some of the more important of these elements in kin relations.

LOVE OR DUTY – SENTIMENT OR STRUCTURE?

Conventionally, the overt concept which most characterizes the relations of extra-familial kin is perhaps thought to be that of some form of fondness or affection. This point of view is exemplified by Margaret Stacey, 'Such ties as exist within the extended family derive less from customary obligation than from affection born in the immediate family. But this need not be maintained after the immediate family has broken up. If they are maintained it is because the affection is maintained.'[9]

Two important features of extra-familial kinship are embodied in this statement. One is the lack of any clearly defined customary rules specifying the behaviour appropriate to kin of a certain category – unlike the position in most primitive societies. The other feature is the tendency for kin ties outside the family to be a reflection of the quality of relationships at an earlier stage, primarily in childhood, inside the family. Our records contain many instances of relations with parents, siblings and some other kin described as 'close', or 'fond', and based as the person concerned saw it, upon recognition of childhood service, companionship and affection. Such affection may extend beyond the natal family. A woman said of her FBDs, 'We are more like sisters than cousins'. They saw one another very frequently, with much reciprocal visiting, their children were very friendly and at an earlier stage the father's brother had been like a father to the woman. There was thus a strong positive affective bond, of multiple character.

Yet the statement quoted from Mrs Stacey's interesting study expresses only a part of the truth. Where a tie between adult members of a natal family and even more between extra-familial kin is maintained it is apt to be characterized not just by affection, but by a much more complex set of attitudes. 'Affection' may well be a component; but so also may be respect, and a sense of obligation and responsibility. There may be also a sense of being bound by the very fact of lifelong continuity of shared experiences and interests.

Mrs Nudley was a woman who was 'in constant touch' with her mother. She obviously relied on her mother a great deal for services such as care of her child, helping with the washing, shopping, and loans of cash, and her mother called round regularly four days a

[9] Margaret Stacey, *Tradition and Change: A Study of Banbury*, OUP, 1960, p. 132.

week. Yet although she saw so much of her mother and relied on her so much, she didn't feel so very close to her. 'She's not all that much of a friend.' Personal matters were not discussed with her mother – 'there's not that bond of confidence'. When she was with her mother she often gave the impression of being slightly irritated, and during the time that our interviewer saw them together there were several minor disagreements, chiefly over the child. Here maintenance of kin ties clearly had an affective component but this was not simply 'affection' in the conventional sense. There was rather an exchange of two different kinds of services yielding satisfactions of different order – with emotional satisfactions for the mother and economic satisfactions for the daughter being prominent. Yet both involve kin support for the individual.

From this point of view it is useful to adopt a phrase suggested by one of our interviewers and to speak of a '*link of convenience*' as opposed to a '*link of affection*'. This is illustrated by the behaviour of Mrs Dingle (Figure 1, p. 107–9) who visited her FZH in hospital because she was asked to do so by the man's daughter, her own cousin, of whom she was very fond. If her relation with her cousin was a link of affection, her relation with her father's cousin's wife (FFBSW) was a link of convenience. She used at first to go and see this woman, who was old and in a nursing home, mainly because she wanted to keep in touch with that side of the family, and from the old woman she got news. Later, annual letters and Christmas cards were exchanged. But this became a one-sided arrangement. So 'I don't think I'll bother this year', she said 'because she hasn't answered the last two.' Now that the channel for news of other relatives was no longer operative her notion of keeping in touch died away. Once the 'link' had ceased to be one of convenience, the kin tie was no longer maintained.

FULFILMENT OF RESPONSIBILITY

As indicated in Chapter 4 on kinship ideology, responsibility was a concept very much to the fore in the discussions of our informants, who used the term, or spoke of 'duty', 'obligation', 'conscience' or, more generally, of 'family feeling'. Some of them specifically separated the concept of obligation or duty from that of affection or 'closeness', using the former terms to apply to help given to relatives with whom they felt they had little in common.

The expression of a sense of responsibility or obligation may be direct or indirect. In the direct form, the kin tie is maintained and implemented in some concrete way because the kinsman is thought to be in some need, or because the social pattern itself dictates appropriate action. A frequent instance is the conscientious way in which some aunts send presents to their nephews and nieces. The converse situation is when a person maintains relations with an elderly aunt who would otherwise be left without help or comfort. Indirect responsibility rests upon the conception of obligation to a third party, for whose sake a specific kin relation is maintained. Mrs Nudley, who was very close to her brother, when asked how she got on with the brother's wife, replied: 'I don't think about it, on principle. I *have* to get on with her – she's my brother's wife.'

Responsibility may be felt towards a specific relative or it may be more diffuse. Mrs Underwood said she felt some responsibility towards her mother's sister. She went to see her about three times a year (making a visit during the period our interviews took place), exchanged Christmas and birthday presents with her and wrote to her about every six weeks. She was also an executor for her aunt's will, though her brother administered the aunt's finances. According to our informant, 'the family' always took responsibility for this old aunt and she used to stay a lot at our informant's parents' house. When they were alive the aunt was their responsibility; now that they were dead she felt that she herself had inherited that responsibility. She added, 'I don't think that duty makes up for affection. All the same, when it comes in practice you do feel an obligation to your family. Your family must not be allowed to sink – not just the immediate family, but the whole family. You probably feel it the older you get. We are looking for an alternative place for Aunt Tabitha. I was up there last week, and we are going to a great amount of trouble over her.' Saying that she felt that she must attend her aunt's funeral when she died, Mrs Underwood added, 'There is no one left of that generation.'

But the fulfilment of responsibility had fairly definite limitations in the kin field. One limitation was genealogical distance from the person concerned. Another was personal like or dislike founded on early experiences. Mrs Danby differentiated very firmly between her responsibilities to her father's and her mother's kin. She was very close to her father, who had been left a widower, and he was very aware of his relatives and very interested in them. She was never very close to her mother, who had been an invalid until her death; and she had little interest in her mother's kin, with whom she had had little contact for many years. So 'to a much lesser degree would I help my mother's relatives, if necessary, but I wouldn't feel such a tremendous responsibility; it's not the same sense of responsibility as I have towards my father's family.'

Another limitation on the acknowledgement of responsibility was shortage of time and energy. A simple instance was that of Mrs Mitchie, who said that she had seventeen nephews and nieces, and that if she tried to send Christmas and birthday cards to all it would be too much work. But this limitation appears in a much more complex way in its connection with the restrictions placed on the development and freedom of the individual assuming the responsibility.

This raises some of the most difficult problems in the whole kinship field. Granted that there is recognition of a sense of duty to elderly kin a dilemma is often created by the practical question – where does duty lie? Miss Lamb, a senior social worker with a great deal of experience, gave a very telling instance. A friend of hers in her middle-age had elderly parents in the country. The father wanted this daughter to give up her job and look after them. This woman had given the suggestion considerable thought and finally decided not to. This was partly for the sake of her mother, who was arthritic and who would give up household chores if the daughter took over the housekeeping; this might tend to immobilize her. Moreover, if the daughter gave up her job now and had only her pension, should anything happen to her parents she would find it extremely difficult to get another good job. She visited her parents every weekend and helped them, and she had two sisters who were able to help the parents during the week. So for the time being she left arrangements as they were. Our informant, who thoroughly approved of this decision, concluded, 'It is a question of balance between emotions, affections and so on, as to whether it is best for a person to give up a career. And what will happen to the person if they say, "My *duty* lies in giving up my job"? I don't relish it. That person won't be much good to the older person after a bit, because they will feel so frustrated and restricted that they're not much good to the older person either. So every situation must be balanced.' The problem of where duty lies is not simply one-way. Kin, especially elderly kin, may have before them the question of what is reasonable or fair to ask of their younger relatives who, in the conventional expression, have their own lives to lead.

One further aspect of the concept of responsibility for kin is its possible ambivalence. As pointed out in Chapter 4, admission of obligation to a kinsman, despite the lack of affection – or even when affection is present – is not at all incompatible with a sense of grievance and resentment at having to shoulder the burden. This condition tends to be exacerbated by two factors. One is the feeling of giving support to a kinsman when others, equally closely related, are not contributing their share. The other factor is when the responsibility is indirect, particularly when an affinal tie is involved. When a widowed mother or father is brought to stay with son or daughter who has been newly married the strains thrown upon the spouse may be very great. The legitimate feeling of responsibility which son or daughter feels towards parent almost inevitably comes into conflict with the interests of the spouse, and the latter may be torn between loyalty to husband or wife and a feeling of being exploited in favour of someone for whom they feel little sympathy (see Chapter 12).

But it is possible for responsibility to a third party to have an integrative and not a divisive effect, especially when a group of siblings or other close kin are involved. Here it is the notion of being responsible *to* rather than responsible *for* one's kin which acts as a sanction for behaviour – what may be termed a *principle of accountability* is at work. This in part explains the situation of a family in which individual personal relations are not particularly good but which presents a common front against the external world. One woman whose father, divorced from her mother, she had not seen for many years, characterized her siblings as a 'united family against anyone outside, but inside everybody hates everybody's guts. Nobody likes or approves of anybody else, but they all stick together.'

An analysis of two extended illustrations will show the complexities involved in the fulfilment of obligation to kin. The Newell couple disclaimed any strong kin feelings or sense of kin unity and regarded their obligations as definite only towards parents. Said the husband, 'I think other people are much more family-minded than we are'. He said that his siblings felt the same way as he did. 'We all grew up fairly independently.' In a dire emergency, of course, he would help his siblings, and he and his wife had in fact given his sister a home for a time when she was in trouble. 'We were more or less called upon to help Hester and we did.' But otherwise 'I would not offer my brothers and sisters a home'. The wife had no siblings, so the problem did not arise in such form. But she had her father living with them, and when her mother's brother lost his wife by suicide she and her husband invited him to stay. 'He was left high and dry, and he was always a great friend of my father's.' They had a spare room and they just did not feel they could let him go back to his flat after his wife's tragic death. In discussing this matter with our interviewer the husband said to his wife, 'It was really out of consideration to your father'. The wife agreed, but said that even so, they could not have let her uncle go back on his own. When asked if they would have done the same for a friend in that situation the wife replied, 'Well, I don't know about offering them a home'. Her husband reminded her that they had done just this for a friend, for three years. This couple, who had no children, were obviously acting from a diverse set of considerations. They cherished their independence, and thought of themselves as not strongly bound emotionally or in terms of social and economic responsibility to any kin except their parents. Yet at the same time their joint sense of responsibility to others in a socially weak position was evidently well-defined. Moreover, the relations they maintained with one person in their kin sphere were partly determined by other kin, in an interlocking system. So the wife said that since her uncle came to live with them he brought them more into contact with other kin because they used to take him out in the car to see them.

Here is responsibility exercised for a kinsman outside the natal family, and indeed outside the group of what could be termed extended family on a strict definition. In principle, obligations to kin were reckoned to be restricted to members of the natal family, but in practice were extended further. Moreover, the reasoning involved a mixture of attitudes of consideration for a third party, the wife's father, in having the wife's mother's brother to stay, mingled with sympathy for his sudden widowed state and recognition of a moral claim upon husband and wife's aid. But within the assertion of the general principle of non-involvement, husband and wife left themselves free to respond as they thought fit in a positive way.

A telling instance of the significance of third party considerations is given in the account given by Mrs Neville of her quarrel with her sister (see p. 433). They did not see each other for over three months, and this was a strain for their mother, who had to see her daughters separately. Mrs Neville herself had missed seeing and talking to her sister. But she said she also felt relieved because when she drove over her young son used to fret if, as often happened, he had not been allowed to play with his cousins. She said, 'If there wasn't any family, that's it!', meaning that this would have been the end of any ordinary non-kin relationship. The sisters had stopped telephoning each other and any news had to filter through their mother. She said she made up the quarrel mostly for her mother's sake. Her mother was ill and the row was upsetting her. Also 'because our family had never argued; we're a very close family and my mother was worried that her sister and all that family would know we weren't together'. Her mother had said that although the sister was the elder, and though she had been in the wrong, why did not Mrs Neville make the first move towards a reconciliation. So she did; one day she went round to see her sister and they both acted as if the whole business had been forgotten; neither ever referred to it again.

These are examples of different types of sanctions. In the first, kinship had its effect in reinforcing the moral claims of a wife's mother's brother on the sympathy and practical help of a married couple. But the pressure exercised by the wife's father seems to have been slight and indirect, if at all; the moral sanctions were largely 'internalized', and expressed by the married couple as their own reactions to a situation of stress in which the kinsman had been placed by his wife's suicide. In the second case the sanction appeared to be largely external – the overt, direct pressure exercised by the mother, reflecting in part the influence of wider kin opinion, without which the daughter would not have attempted a reconciliation with her sister. Or so it seems. Yet the mother's arguments were felt by the daughter to have moral force – no economic or social pressures were used – and 'internalized' in the sense of being re-interpreted as a just concession in view of her concern for the mother's health. Moreover, the operation of the sanction of the mother's interests and welfare may have been more subtle than just this. As noted by our interviewer at the time, our informant may have felt that her mother's ill health was a good excuse for mending the separation – a kind of face-saving device. So part of the set of sanctions involved may well have been her own wish not to be deprived for too long of the sociability and support which she had been used to expect from her sister. This interpretation is strengthened by a remark of our informant that she wouldn't like to be without her family. On the other hand, it seems very probable that she felt so wounded by her sister's insulting gibe that without their mother as intermediary and mediator she would not have taken the initiative in approaching her sister and tacitly agreeing to overlook the episode.

It is important to be clear at this point what is involved in our interpretation of the operation of sanctions in these cases. It is not argued that such sanctions and such subtle face-saving devices occur only with kin relations. But it is argued that the continuity and moral value of the kin relationship – especially among members of a natal family – combined with the interest of a third party also a kinsman, provides a special kind of channel which promotes the flow of actions of responsibility. This can be so even where 'affection' or some similar description of the quality of the relationship may seem inadequate. There is one further aspect of the analysis – that while we infer certain intellectual and emotional conditions from the statements and actions of our informants, what we are primarily concerned with are the sequences of speech and action themselves as indicators of the quality of the kin relations.

A special context of the kin tie is demonstrated by the behaviour of professional men in our sample. A solicitor did legal work for about a score of his relatives including his mother, sister, father's sister and her sons, a mother's brother's son, as well as his wife's mother, brother and mother's sister. While the other kin were ordinary paying clients, those mentioned had their legal work done free or at a reduced rate. One medical man looked after his mother's health for ten years or so as her registered doctor, and gave medical advice to several of the wife's kin without charge, as a private matter. Another helped his father's brother, his mother's sister's son and daughter and some of his wife's kin with advice about various ailments, especially with suggestions as to whom they might consult. None of these kin paid for the services they received. Professional etiquette was maintained, but a special concession was given to kin which would not so easily have been granted to others. But entering into professional relations with kin did offer special problems. An architect said that he would be a bit careful about giving professional help to kin; it could be embarrassing. They think they will get a house for very little and ask something almost impossible for the money they want to pay. To make the job economical the architect has to charge a substantial fee, and this makes him feel embarrassed. On the medical side one doctor said that most doctors try not to have kin as patients; another, that he made a point of not offering medical advice to any members of his family – 'poking around and trying to offer advice in family medical matters was a sure way to make trouble'. He did not treat his own children, though he specialized in pediatrics. Apparent contradiction in this is easily understood. Some people are willing to tackle the problems involved in professional relations with kin and give special concessions on the basis of kin relations; others are unwilling to be involved in the problems created by the privileged position of kin. Clearly there is a special character in the kin tie which means that professional relations with kin are not expected to be simply of the impersonal, economic kind normal in relations with other clients.[10]

The precise form which acceptance of responsibility or carrying out of service should take may be pertinent to an interpretation of kin relations. This is a matter of context. When a very junior relative visits a senior one, some material provisions such as a bed for the night, a meal or even a gift of money may be appropriate. But conversely in order to render a gift acceptable it may be necessary to clothe it in the language of commerce, and give the transaction the appearance of direct reciprocity. A striking illustration of this was when Mrs Neville's mother acted as baby-sitter for her child. She

[10] It is understood that a man in the medical profession will have his wife and children treated by a colleague; the possibility of professional judgment being clouded by emotional considerations is thus avoided. Such treatment is without fee. (But a substantial Christmas present, e.g. of wine, may give an acknowledgement of the service.)

always paid her mother for this service because she knew that this was the only way in which she could give her mother money. 'My mother's very proud; she won't accept money for nothing, so I pay her when she looks after Peter.' This transaction had its undertones. For some years Mrs Neville's sister had been giving their mother all the groceries she needed from a shop the sister's husband owned, on the pretext that the mother did so much baby-sitting for them too. Now the husband had begun saying that his mother-in-law should pay for her groceries. 'My mother doesn't mean anything to him, and *she's* ill; she looks after his children on Friday and *she's* not paid.' So our informant suggested to her mother that she should charge the son-in-law baby-sitting rates and earn a little money. Here, as the angle of view altered, the transfers of money to the mother were treated either as gifts or as payments for service rendered.

In other circumstances it may be time and personal attention, not money, that are required. Mr Regan had been very generous in sending money to his MZD and her husband in the United States, doing this through his mother as a more tactful method than direct gift to these people, who were much less well-off than he was. He also used to give his mother money. But his wife felt keenly about this, contrasting his attitude with her own. 'My husband would have given his mother anything but time – money. But it appals me. He treated his mother in a way without respect. He'd send her home in a taxi, but wouldn't drive her home' (because it took up too much time). For the wife, time spent on and with one's parents was of far greater value than any amount of money. (See also Chapter 12, p. 409.)

The response to a call for the expenditure of personal time is one of the best tests of attitudes towards kin. Some people give their time ungrudgingly, acknowledging a personal commitment of their energies and capacity to the service of the kinsman. Others give their time, but reluctantly, regarding themselves as responding to demands of doubtful legitimacy and really committed intellectually and emotionally elsewhere. Others still, as in the instance just mentioned, evade the call upon their time by substituting some other form of response. One result of this evasion may be that another kinsman, perhaps a spouse, feels compelled to assume the responsibility instead, but this enforced giving of time and energy may be a source of resentment against the person regarded as a defaulter.

Among the variables involved in the quality of a kin relationship, reciprocity is important (see Chapter 4, p. 110). In kin as in non-kin relations it is seen commonly in the exchange of Christmas cards and birthday presents, and in reciprocal visiting and dining. Responsibility assumed for kin, especially elderly kin, is often looked at as delayed, diffused reciprocity for services performed by the elder kinsman at a much earlier stage. The rationale of services performed for parents is primarily derived from the recognition of their devotion in bringing up their children.

Relations with extra-familial kin often consist very largely of chains of reciprocal services, each party adding further links in response to a complex set of pressures. In the Regan family again the husband had relatives in the United States who suddenly wrote saying they were going to be in London for the holidays and would like to call. 'In principle although I think a family should be close, I don't in practice; I'm too lazy', commented Mrs Regan. 'If someone wanted to turn up I'd feel like postponing it. The people at Whitsun – we felt "Oh, no! How awful!" So naturally we cursed like mad when they said they were coming on Whit Saturday. But you can't curse if they come from America.' Though she and her husband rather dreaded having these kin, they felt they should have them over for a meal and drive them round London in their car. This they did and in fact liked the relatives when they met; the 'chore' turned into a very pleasant occasion which both parties seemed to have enjoyed. Mrs Regan also said she knew that when the growing children of these American kin wanted to come to England she would be expected to allow them to stay in her house. 'I'd probably wriggle a bit if asked to have a boy for three months. We're going to get a little stream of this from America – the relatives. I'm not too keen on having people staying, but I like the privacy.' But she and her husband were expecting to give this hospitality.

Now there were at least three elements involved in their decision to take these actions. There was a general feeling that everyone should take some responsibility for relatives. 'Everyone should help a bit. Some should do a little and some should do more. Money is the easiest thing. But one must be prepared to put people (relatives) up, and for more than a weekend. It will arise with the youngsters from America.' The second element was that of direct reciprocation – husband and wife had themselves visited the young people's parents in America and been given hospitality. The third reason was for the sake of their own children. 'It's essential for our children to get to know the family. Everyone *needs* a family – it's practically like religion. You run there when you're in trouble – at least some of us do.' So, present service performed and future demand expected to be fulfilled are offset against past service received and future benefit hoped for. The chain of reciprocities carries its own sanction, as Malinowski has pointed out long ago, and also serves to give expression to the quality of kin relations.

12

The Quality of Kin Relations

We have already given much incidental material on the roles played by individual kin. But we need to look more closely at the problem of the particular quality of these individual relationships. What is a mother, a mother-in-law, an uncle, an aunt, a cousin – as an ideal type, and as a concrete relationship? There are some conventional notions in literature and in popular talk – stereotypes one might call them – associated with the concept of each of these types of relationship. What we want to do here is to see how far such stereotypes exist in our North London field, and the degree to which our empirical material corresponds to them. We want also to sort out the kinds of ways in which one category of kin differs from another category. The best procedure for tackling these questions is to combine presentation of selected case materials with general summaries of the overall position.

One important point must be emphasized from the start. Consideration of any individual kin role means considering personal relations in the context of family interaction. This means also considering relations not simply at any particular period, but over the passage of time. To understand the meaning of a mother's role for one of our woman informants we have to consider not only her relations to her own children and to her own mother; we have also to bear in mind that her mother is her husband's mother-in-law and one of her children's grandmothers. It is the configuration of this total set of ideas, attitudes and actions that helps to determine how the mother's role can operate. Moreover, one of the features of our study is consideration of kin relations between adults. There is a vast difference between the scope and intensity of a mother's activities in regard to a daughter still under the maternal roof and to one that is married with a separate home of her own. Whatever be the emotional involvement of the mother and the daughter, their implementation of it must be radically affected by time and changing circumstances. In the last Chapter we have described analytically the major types of situation in which people are concerned with their kin and the ideas of responsibility and obligation which lie behind this. In this Chapter we consider how far particular kin are selected from the range available and fitted into the situations or themselves initiate, conform to or contribute to the order of events.

In indicating these patterns of kin orientation we give detailed illustrations from our case data to show how families cope with their problems and work out their adjustments in reference to their kin. But these illustrations must not be taken as 'typical'. Families with one or more living parents of husband and wife, some siblings of the parents and children of these, constituting uncles, aunts and other kin with whom significant relationships were maintained were plentiful among our cases. But as exemplars they were nearly all idiosyncratic. Husband or wife had a foreign parent, or had married a Jew, or had turned Roman Catholic. One was an orphan, another had no brothers or sisters, another had been involved in a succession of divorces. Nearly every family had some circumstances which made it unique and introduced some complication into the pattern of kin relationships. What we have done then is to take a set of examples to illustrate a *range of variation* in kin patterns, not a typicality.

We focus first of all upon parental roles, in particular that of the mother in relation to a married daughter.

GENERAL QUALITY OF RELATIONS WITH PARENTS

Many examples have demonstrated already that the relationships between members of a conjugal family and their kin outside the family cannot be regarded as based upon any simple set of factors. They are the resultant of a number of forces, including the pressures exerted by other members of the elementary family. But at an objective level relations between any pair of kin can be isolated to some extent and summed up in a crude but meaningful way as being 'good' or 'bad', or in some qualified form of these. As we show later, any such crude moral expression has to be broken down empirically into a number of behaviour components, verbal and non-verbal. But on the negative side when a person says that he 'does not get on with' a relative this has certain concrete referents such as not visiting, tendency to quarrel when they meet, or in extreme cases not even speaking to the relative in question.

In our society one of the basic kin relationships outside the immediate family and household is that of a married person with his or her parents – who in middle-class sectors normally live separately. The stereotype of such relationships is that of friendly contact, affection and mutual support. Variants of the stereotype point to financial help from the parent to the married son or daughter or, alternatively, from the child to the parent where necessary. A particular situation in which son or daughter is expected to support a parent is when the latter is widowed. As one woman said, the only relatives she felt she ought to see were 'the two mothers. I can't say I ought to see the others'. She felt she should see her own mother and her husband's mother because both were elderly people and had 'lost' their husbands. This made them rather lonely. They were no longer surrounded by family, and it was in this sort of situation she felt children should make the effort to 'see something' of their parents and let these see the grandchildren.[1]

In actual fact, what are the relationships which do exist between parents and children when the latter are adult? In order to ascertain this we charted from our material the quality of the relationship with parents as specified by our informants. We restricted the examination to the 30 cases from Highgate and the corresponding 28 cases of families with dependent children in the Greenbanks sample. In some of these cases parents had been long dead and the material in regard to them was too indeterminate to allow of useful classification. From the 58 cases, however, we obtained data on 168 parents. These comprised 42 wife's fathers, 52 wife's mothers, 33 husband's fathers, 41 husband's mothers. Relations between these parents and their sons or daughters were good or reasonably equable in a high proportion (85 per cent) of cases. (We consider later the more precise significance of this.) But in at least 26 cases, 15 per cent of the whole, relations were described as bad, or non-existent; or there was dislike by the married son or daughter for the parent without this necessarily being reciprocated or even understood.

This negative affect is worth a special note. It might be argued by conventional moralists that once the period of adolescent rebellion was over, natural affection between parent and child would be such that only in very rare cases, primarily with delinquent behaviour on the part of the child, would the tie of affection be denied. Yet our material shows that relations between parent and adult son or daughter, like relations between other kin, can be subject to extreme

[1] One of our informants, whose background was Continental and who did not fall in the sub-sample which we had examined for quantitative purposes, expressed the conventional view of relations to parents clearly and forcefully. She said she felt the most important thing parents should do was to provide a child with all that made it possible to lead a happy life. They should make every effort to make a child secure in the world and in a place fit for it. This could not be done by money or education alone. The relationship between children and parents was reciprocal. 'You always get back what you put in.' Parents received from their children the treatment corresponding to the effort they themselves had made earlier.

difficulty leading in some cases to near or complete breach; and that this can occur with people who in other respects would be regarded as of normal social behaviour. In other words, in adult life the parent/child tie is subject to similar strains as occur in the general kin field. One difference, however, is that the strains are apt to be endured at a much greater intensity or for a much longer time than in the case of other kin before a breach occurs.

In detailed categories, the 26 'negative' cases comprised: bad relations between husband and his father, 3; between wife and her father, 8; between husband and his mother, 6; between wife and her mother, 9. In view of stereotypes of mother–child relationship, especially mother – daughter tie, it is important to note that bad relations or a breach between mother and child made up more than half the cases, one-third of them being between mother and daughter.

An important reason given for lack of effective relationship of married son or daughter to father or mother was lack of support in early years. The most specific index to this was divorce or desertion by the parent. of the 58 cases of immediate concern here, parents of husband or wife had been divorced or separated in 8 instances. Relations with one parent had completely broken down in 3 instances (in each case with wife's father) and were strained in 2 more, though they were definitely good in the other 3 instances. Where relations with one parent were bad or very distant, some degree of identification with the other parent was usual.

It was desertion of child rather than divorce from mother or father which seemed to produce most social distance in the married son or daughter in later years. In the Grant family we have one marked instance of a deserter father whose tentative efforts at reconciliation were rejected by his daughter. In a complex case where Mrs Nebworth had broken with her father, her parents had quarrelled constantly when the children were young, but they didn't finally break up and get divorced until after the children had left home. Mrs Nebworth said that family life had been a misery when she was young. The children hated to hear their parents quarrelling and family meals were an ordeal, often ending in quarrelling, with the children leaving the table one by one crying, to go upstairs. While this resulted in great solidarity within the sibling group, they all left home as soon as possible. As a result of this experience she had strong views on family amity. She felt it wrong to say that a couple should stick together and not get divorced, because children suffer far more when the parents hang together disliking each other and quarrelling all the time. From this early experience too she said her own dislike of quarrelling in the family circle of her husband and children arose. But it was not her father's divorce as such which separated her from him; it was one of his later marriages. With his second wife Mrs Nebworth was in friendly relations, but this marriage too broke up. Our informant really disliked the third wife, whom she accused of spiteful gossiping about the family. Their relations seemed to be those of mutual mistrust, each putting the worst construction on what the other said or did. Because of this Mrs Nebworth no longer saw her father, whom she identified with his wife in this.

Re-marriage of a parent after divorce or death of spouse was sometimes heartily approved of by son or daughter. Mr Danby's mother had married young, then divorced and married the man who became his father. This marriage later broke up, and each spouse re-married, the mother's third husband having also been married and divorced before. Mr Danby was much attached to his mother, and to his stepfather, and also to the stepfather's son by his former marriage. At one time he had been in bad relations with his own father and the father's second wife, not because of the father's marital affairs but because his father tried hard to push him into entering a profession he disliked, and also disapproved of his fiancée. When in the course of time the son made a success both of his career and of his marriage the father's opposition disappeared, and relations between all the parties was very friendly.[2]

In the Vendor case there was a double second marriage. The husband's mother married again after the death of her first husband; the son was very pleased about his mother's second marriage and Mrs Vendor found her stepfather-in-law 'an absolute darling'. Mrs Vendor's own parents had been divorced and her father re-married. She was not pleased when she heard about this, not because she disapproved of the marriage itself but because she was annoyed at her father getting married secretly and not telling her about it until a year later. Apart from this annoyance she thought that for him to marry again was one of the most sensible things he ever did. He had been much happier, the second wife, a very sweet, unselfish working-class girl, was devoted to him and looked after him very well.

But in such a re-marriage several parties may be involved, and

[2] In a few cases it was not the parents' but the child's divorce which disturbed relations. In one case a mother, described by her daughter as a very rigid woman, was thoroughly upset about the daughter's divorce – she thought divorce was absolutely wrong whatever the circumstances. But in this case she grew more tolerant with age, and in fact approved very strongly of her daughter's choice of a second husband. 'They felt that if I *had* to marry again then David was the nicest person I could choose.' Note that the structural breach made by divorce here in separating daughter from husband could have thrown daughter back to mother. Yet the attitude was complicated by the positive value attached by the mother to the daughter's marriage.

profit to one may mean loss to another. Her mother was very bitter about this re-marriage, and never stopped saying unpleasant things about her ex-husband and his new wife. The daughter sympathized with the way that her mother must feel. 'After all, she had nothing.' But she had been critical of both her parents, especially her mother, since when their marriage was breaking up originally neither of them had bothered to write to their children more than about once a year, and she and her sister used to feel very unwanted. So whereas in later life her mother became very dependent upon her, she herself found it very difficult to respond. 'She's been very vicious and selfish towards me.' Accordingly, though desperately sorry for her, she did not love her mother except in a 'filial' sort of way. '*She is* my mother, but I cannot love her as a person.' She said she felt people had a duty to look after their parents, however unsatisfactorily the latter may have treated them. Though critical also of her father she was much fonder of him and more indulgent. Concrete events such as divorce and re-marriage are just surface indications of underlying tensions of quite complex character, but whether, how and when the tensions involve the children may depend upon a range of other circumstances.[3]

Temperamental factors responsible for breach between mother or father and adult son or daughter might be one or other of polar opposites. Interference with the personal life of the growing child – including obsessive preoccupation with domestic detail – or aloofness and distance from the child's development might be equally deleterious. Mothers who were sweet and sympathetic to children while handing them over to be brought up by nurses or relatives, or who read detective novels all day and said the sooner they were off her hands the better, seemed still to be remembered with resentment by children. In a case which showed definite neurotic elements a man was very bitter about how he was treated by his parents as a child, and heaped the blame for all his troubles on to his mother. He said she was a very dogmatic, cramping sort of person who could not bear untidyness or dirt in the house, kept her children much too warmly dressed even in summer and showed a lack of cultural interest which he resented very much as he grew up. From other evidence his mother appeared to be a rather insensitive woman with no knack of gauging subtleties in family relationships and with an almost pathological phobia about cleanliness, a possessive hoarder who never invited her son's wife or children to her house. His wife's parents were in contrast to this. The wife's mother was a very countrified person who loved gardening, jam-making, bottling, baking and making clothes. She was very sympathetic and

[3] We have no case in our records of physical assault between parent and child.

her children felt quite happy and secure with her. The wife's father, however, a schoolteacher of musical tastes, tended to leave his children alone to be dealt with by his wife. 'He never took a personal interest in us, he always criticized rather than praised, he could be very damping indeed.' Once when his daughter took home some paintings which had been praised by her teachers, she found her father looking through them; he turned to her with the sole comment, 'Remember a straight line is always a straight line'. Loved by his pupils – other people's children – he remained almost distant and rather impersonal to his own. Inclined to be irritable, he was an uncommunicative man and his daughter was never close to him.

The Gilroy case demonstrated parent–child role clash in a severe form. The daughter had been brought up in a boarding school while her parents were abroad, and had learned to be independent. Later, even after she had married, she wanted support and affection from her mother, but found her mother willing to give this only at the price of wanting to make decisions for her. Conscious of her independence, the daughter resisted such interference as she saw it; the result was tension sometimes so extreme that mother and daughter did not speak to each other. Of her parents the daughter said, 'It is not that I do not like them', and her husband added, 'It is not that she is not close to them'. But in making personal decisions she tended to turn to her mother-in-law instead. The husband in turn had had difficulties with his father, who wanted his sons to work with him and conform in other ways to his ideas. After a struggle with his father the son was free to pursue his own career, but he still tended to regard his father with circumspection and preferred not to have to rely on him too much lest he jeopardize the independence he had gained.

The passage of time and the coming of grandchildren had ameliorated some situations of friction, and relatively harmonious relations had been restored after a period of non-contact between parent and child. Though our instances are few, reconciliation between mother and son or daughter seems to have been more common than between father and son or daughter. To this degree the conventional image of relative closeness of mother to children may be supported. 'Children lean more to the mother anyway, don't you think'? is a comment that, while not borne out completely, does seem to have some relevance.

But what is particularly significant in the social relations of parents to married children is the way in which superficial harmony covers a range of disparate attitudes. Common in our material was the expression on the part of married son or daughter that relations with a parent were friendly but superficial; that he or she liked the parent but did not feel they could discuss intimate matters with him or her. As one woman put it, despite her affection and admiration for her mother she could never go to her with her troubles – 'we are on a different wave-length'. In such situations elements of affection and of obligation tend to be closely linked. Many of our informants expressed this feeling of duty to parents: e.g. the husband who sees his mother every week though he finds her dull, because he knows how much it means to her; the wife who visits her mother out of a sense of duty although the older woman refuses to enter her daughter's house.

A number of informants also seemed to have feelings of guilt in regard to their parents – that they did not do more for them, or that they did not feel more emotional warmth towards them. Mrs Fortescue's father became ill after her mother died and needed constant attention. His daughter decided it would be the best thing to have him live with her, but he refused to leave his country cottage. At last he was induced to spend Christmas with them, and tricked into staying on. He developed loss of memory, continually tried to escape and had to be brought back, and did not recognize his daughter. She said this 'broke her heart' and she would go upstairs and weep at night. She asked her brother if he would share the burden of keeping their father, but he refused. The strain then became too much for her and she had her father put in a nursing home. All the time he was there, until his death, she bore the full cost of the nursing. But she said she had terrible guilt feelings because she put him there, although she felt she had no other course.

A further element in the complex set of factors relating to attitude to a parent was the feeling by some sons and daughters – especially the latter – that the parent was making claims which were in one sense inequitable but in another were difficult if not impossible to resist. This is what more than one of our informants described as 'emotional blackmail'. Mrs Waverley spoke of the happy memories of her childhood and the close family relationships then, and the way in which her parents exploited these memories of hers later in order to get her to do things, such as maintain contact with kin in whom she now had no special interest. Another woman spoke of the way she worked in her parents' shop, how she wished to leave and felt she could not do so because of her realization of how much her parents depended on her. Any mention of her wish for a freer occupation upset her parents. 'I just dropped the subject. It's rather awful really, such a position for a daughter. Much as one's fond of one's parents it's a bit thick to work for them if you don't like it. They have an emotional claim on you.' This was a case where an external stimulus provided the solution. 'The war was a release for me. Without upsetting my father I could leave. It would have been unkind just to walk out on him.'

The complex pattern of relationships, personal evaluations and interpretations in which one type of conduct is regarded as subtly transformed into or representing another is illustrated by cases such as the following. When talking about her relationship with her mother Mrs Savage said her mother was a very strong personality with a tendency to 'run' everyone. She doesn't 'run' people in the sense of commanding them, but is very enthusiastic about ideas she has and goes on at people until they have either agreed or disagreed with her. Our informant said that as a child she developed a passive resistance against this habit of her mother's – in contrast to her brother, who was both more under his mother's influence and more violent in rebellion against her if he disagreed. The daughter didn't argue against her mother but just didn't comply with her wishes. Another facet of a mother's activities was presented by Mr Lark who felt very close to his mother, much more so than to his father. 'A strong feature of my family history is the preponderance of the place taken in it by my mother.' She lived deliberately in and for her children, at immense cost, and for her death her son was completely unprepared. Yet as time went on he came to see how much his mother by her devotion helped to isolate him and his siblings from their father; consequently, close as he was to his mother, he began to feel much more sympathetic towards his father. (This man's wife had different views: she said her mother-in-law, however admirable, made her feel like 'an illiterate Hottentot', and treated her like that too!) A theme of maternal fission of the sibling group emerged in another case when a woman commented that her mother had behaved in a highly secretive way, keeping each child in ignorance of the actions of the others. She had encouraged each of her children, even when grown up and married, to tell her all their grievances about the others, and listened and agreed to their complaints instead of trying to correct mistaken impressions. In this way she managed to keep her children apart from one another, yet each tied to her, even at the adult stage. Our informant said that she had only recently 'tumbled' to this procedure, when her mother came to stay, and she discovered how each was played off against the others. Since then she had become very friendly with her sister, with whom formerly she had not been on good terms.

A central point in all this is that instead of dealing with conventional stereotypes of 'mother-love', 'Mum', 'father-figures' or whatever, our evidence shows a set of highly complex patterns of relationship between married adults and their parents. Fathers and mothers are people formerly in the domestic circle for whom on the whole there is a very great deal of affection, admiration and respect, and willingness to commit much time and energy in gratifying their wishes. At the same time, while it is recognized that they have a prior right to make demands, such demands may be resented, even while being fulfilled. Again, the foibles of fathers and mothers may be overlooked or shrugged off, but they may cause plenty of irritation and lead to some rejection of claims. Moreover, some demands may be regarded as excessive, as blackmail, employing as instruments those emotional ties which are felt to be properly a free, not enforced, tribute to affection and gratitude. Yet very rarely is there sufficient explosion of resentment to lead to complete breakdown of social relationship between married son or daughter and parent. The upshot is often a kind of elaborate strategy of relations, in which there is much manipulation of personal wants and resources against the background of admitted social obligation.

AFFINES: A SURFEIT OF MOTHERS-IN-LAW

We now turn to consideration of the position of affines – relatives by marriage. By the act of marital union, the immediate consanguineal kin of the spouse are brought into a special position which simulates to some extent the position of a person's own close kin. In particular, English law and the law of the Church forbids subsequent marriage with certain of these people (cf. Chapter 6, p. 191). But while assimilated in some ways, affinal kin are sharply distinguished in others, and complex forces of social and psychological order operate, often making it hard to maintain equable relationships.

A detailed example from the Regan family illustrates the complex pattern of attractions and pressures. Mr Regan was a manufacturer, born in Germany, then apprenticed to a trade in England; his father was a tradesman in Germany, then the United States, then England; his mother was dead. His wife, first at a private school, later did secretarial work; her father (dead) had been in the clothing trade; her mother was a business woman. They had two children, and the family was Jewish.

Here the kin pattern was affected by two major circumstances. Mrs Regan belonged to a well-to-do Jewish family the father of whom was proud of being English. His parents had emigrated here from Holland, not as refugees – and so he differentiated himself from his daughter's husband, a refugee and a foreigner. He was opposed to the marriage. He had indulged his daughter's every whim and sent her to private schools, but saw to it that she was brought up in a disciplined way. He died soon after his daughter's wedding. Her mother, who had inherited from her parents a clothing shop and with her husband developed the business, was extremely capable; she had preferred to work with her husband rather than stay at home and bring up the children, so she employed a maid and a nanny, to attend to the family. Mr Regan was sent over as a refugee from Germany in 1933, and his parents joined him some years later. But his father, a shoemaker, could get no employment in Britain, so emigrated to the United States; while the son built up a business here, his mother stayed to look after him. She had died only recently. So, crudely, the existing parental pattern of our informants was: resident wife's mother; immigrant husband's father – in a Jewish setting.

But the actual lines of kin relationships were very different in some respects from a conventional stereotype of Jewish kinship as a closely-knit group of relatives.

To begin with, the major affinal relationships revealed basic personal incompatibility. Mr Regan had been very attached to his mother when she was alive, and telephoned her every day. She used to be seen every Saturday afternoon for tea, and sometimes during the week too. Their visiting was one-sided: for six months Mrs Regan would visit her mother-in-law, and then for the next six months the elder woman would visit her. 'It depended on the age of the children. At one time we were in daily telephoning. It was hell! An awful grind. She could tell by my tone of voice if the children were ill' – and this used to upset the mother-in-law. Telephoning 'was a duty call; she wanted it, and my husband wanted it.' Mrs Regan said that although she admired her mother-in-law, 'I never liked her. My husband and his mother were very close, and his upbringing was very different. It seemed to me fantastic that she'd devoted her life to her son, not to her husband. The old people were fond of each other but fought like cat and dog. She was a strong personality and domineering. I'm stubborn and secretive. We thought differently, and I didn't like her. I was as dutiful a daughter as he was a son. I was conscience-ridden – terrible – but I never liked her.'

The reason given for this complex emotional attitude was briefly the discrepancy which the wife felt between her husband's great affection for his mother and the manner in which he treated her. He was an only child and she adored him – 'her life was to serve her son – to do what he wanted. She served him like a wonderful wife in a way, and it was her absolute life and pleasure to do what she could. He thought nothing of it. It wasn't strange; he was devoted;

there was never a cross word. She is fantastic and has to be admired; to be feared, but a wonderful woman.' She felt that her husband's response was to take this service for granted, and to put business before his mother's comfort (cf. also Chapter 11, p. 396). Yet it was clear that his mother wished it this way. But what disturbed the wife, it seemed, was the thought that her husband could act so. When the mother-in-law was ill and near her end Mrs Regan said, 'My husband wouldn't see that she was ill. It worried me. She's someone I don't like, she's only my mother-in-law. I'd take her to the hospital and visit her frequently.' Her husband gave her money but didn't take her to the hospital because he was busy at work. Even the night she was operated on the husband and wife went out on business entertaining. The mother-in-law didn't want her son to see her so ill, nor did she want the comforts of a nursing home. But the wife felt guilty on her husband's behalf for the time he didn't spend with his mother, so put herself out to do things she would probably not have done if her husband had been there to do them. Because he and his mother were so close, this disturbed the wife all the more.

There way well have been elements of hypersensitivity here, due to a projection from the wife's feelings for her own mother, and perhaps from some criticism of her husband in other directions. But what this illustrates is the manifold elements in an affinal relationship in which there is a strong component of obligation.

With her father-in-law Mrs Regan had little in common. She had no real affection for him, and put up with him from a sense of duty. 'He's really like a piece of furniture. He's got a good appetite and likes a cigar. And he's deaf. He's no trouble and he always hears what he shouldn't! It's difficult to communicate with him. He doesn't have any friends.' (Stimulated by our interviewer, who talked with him, he seemed very lively, to the obvious surprise of husband and wife.)

The flamboyant element in the family relationships was supplied by wife's mother and the husband. The wife appeared to feel great affection for her mother and admired her business ability. She saw her mother every week and telephoned her more often. But she felt torn between her mother and her husband. 'My mother and Francis – do not see eye to eye; they have certain similarities and they clash. To my mother he says "You don't do enough for your daughter financially" and she says "You don't do enough for my daughter. She slaves for you." ' The mother argued that Mr Regan ought to give his wife a dress allowance, instead of paying for her clothes individually as she got them. Mrs Regan had a small personal income from capital given to her by her parents, and used this on occasion, leaving her husband to contribute or not as he thought fit. She said she preferred this to a dress allowance, thinking she got more from him that way. But this seemed very unsatisfactory to her mother, who continually raised the matter. There was quite a fuss after one of our informant's birthdays, because her husband gave her a cheque for £20 to spend as she wished. The wife's mother became angry again, saying 'Twenty pounds! You ought to give her £100. Look at her. What she is doing for you. Entertaining your acquaintances, bringing up your children.' Our informant added rather wryly, 'Money really is the root of all evil!'

The mother-in-law's criticism of the husband to his face and the general disagreements about money seem to have stemmed from the time soon after the marriage when Mr Regan asked his parents-in-law for a gift of £4,500 to help him buy a house. They offered him a loan. But he pointed out with some brusqueness that they had given their daughter no dowry, though they could well have afforded one, and that it would be bad policy to withdraw money from his business to repay such a loan. He was under-capitalized and what he wanted was an outright gift. He applied such pressure that in the end he got what he wanted. But the parents were not used to such conceptions or methods. They preferred to make gifts to their children as occasion arose, at their own discretion, and disliked having their hand forced in this way. The husband, on the other hand, resented what he regarded as their meanness; with his German background he had expected a dowry.

Since then relations had been strained. The wife said emphatically of her husband, 'He doesn't like my mother. I definitely try to put it out of my mind. They antagonize each other. It's hell.' One difficulty was that the husband and the mother used to take out their dislike of each other on the wife, who tried to act as intermediary. The result was that she tried as far as possible to avoid having them meet. This meant that she gave up having her mother round at weekends or for Christmas when her husband was home, because each was rude to the other and the wife couldn't stand the constant bickering. She preferred to see her mother alone while her husband was at work, so that their meeting would be fairly peaceful and harmonious. If her husband was at home and she said she was going to see her mother he would declare he was not going; on the other hand, he disliked being left alone. When her mother seemed likely to come over for the day on Sunday he declared he would spend the day in bed. But her efforts at keeping the disputants apart reacted upon the wife – her mother resented not being asked over for Christmas, thinking that she ought to be invited.

The broad picture then was one of very limited kin relationships. The wife felt she should try and get on with her parents-in-law, but her husband apparently felt no such obligation towards his wife's parents and siblings. The wife had certain standards of conduct towards kin, but allowed these to be overborne by the more forceful attitudes of her husband. 'In principle although I think a family should be close, looking back since you (the interviewer) started this, although I thought it should be close-knit, I don't in practice; I'm too lazy.' This is clearly not what is often regarded as a typical Jewish attitude towards family and kin ties. But the evidence for what is typical has not yet been clearly presented. It might be argued that this is a case of a Liberal Jewish household, reflecting the spirit of freedom from traditional behaviour. This particular couple were Liberal Jews and 'very unreligious', going rarely to synagogue. (Said our informant, 'Let's face it, Liberal Jews are Jews only in name'.) Whether the disinterest in their kin was a consequence or only a concomitant of their Liberal spirit is impossible to determine. But what is evident is that for both husband and wife kin ties apart from parental ties were of relatively small social significance. They saw far more of their friends than they did of their relatives. The husband epitomized the situation rather caustically by saying that he had a hard enough time getting his wife to keep up with their friends whom they wanted to see, let alone relatives in whom they were not interested. Yet the parent/parent-in-law ties bulked very largely in their life.

MOTHER-IN-LAW STEREOTYPE

The quality of kin relations is well illustrated further by examining the contrast between consanguineal and affinal kin – particularly between parents and parents-in-law.

In this examination we include attention to some of the linguistic aspects. Patterns of language are not complete guides to patterns of thought or behaviour, but the social categories they indicate reveal elements which may be critical in our thinking. Some of these elements have already been exposed in Chapter 10, and others will appear later in this Chapter.

In the field of kinship generally, looked at on the comparative plane, many societies use labels for categories of kin in what anthropologists have called a 'classificatory' manner. A word which in European language would ordinarily be translated as 'mother' is applied to a whole set of women of the equivalent senior generation, including not only the person's own mother but also his mother's sisters and some or all of her female cousins. (Such systems often also separate relatives whom we class together; many societies, e.g., classify mother's brother differently from father's brother, whereas we lump them both together under the common term 'uncle'.) There is a difference of opinion as to how far such linguistic usage permits or inhibits the highly individualized personal affection between mother and child which is the stereotype in European society. But it is clear that overtly such usage of a set of 'mothers' tends to distract attention at the linguistic level from the unique bond between natural mother and her child. In like measure the relationships created by marriage fall into similar classificatory categories. A man in our society has only one mother-in-law – he would look with horror at, say, the Tikopia custom of having a whole group of them. Yet when the same 'mother-in-law' term is applied to a number of women, and the same name-avoidance and respect-behaviour adopted toward them all, this does tend to mean rather less of a focus of one woman, the wife's mother, on the unique relation with her daughter's husband. (There are also more clear-cut rules for treating all one's in-laws.)

The mother-in-law is often regarded as the key figure in affinal relationships, the stereotype of difficulty in the marital situation. Does the sex alignment in the affinal relation make a significant difference? For a mother about to become a mother-in-law, the loss of her married daughter may seem less severe than that of her married son. The old saying, 'A son's a son till he takes a wife, a daughter's a daughter all of her life', has much point. Yet if it were completely true then relations between mother-in-law and daughter-in-law might be expected to be worse than those between mother-in-law and son-in-law. More grounds for conflict should occur where an alien woman has come in and married the son than where an alien man has married the daughter. And yet we have the impression that most of the popular jokes refer to the bad relations between a *man* and his mother-in-law. Is this because wives suffer their mothers-in-law more patiently than do their husbands? Is it because the very closeness of the mother/daughter tie puts the husband at a disadvantage? Or is it because of the husband's masculine pride? Does he think he becomes rather easily the helpless outsider in his own home, finding the vital decisions taken in the light of his wife's mother's opinions and advice rather than of his own? One may think that the focus of the mother-in-law stereotype upon relations with son-in-law rather than with daughter-in-law is due to ideas of opposition between sex roles and of masculine superiority being built into the popular idea of the relationship.

Let us recall the stereotype with a few examples. Last century the English mother-in-law was the well-known butt of jokes in the music-halls of the day. The Oxford English Dictionary quotes a slang definition from a newspaper gag, which those who have drunk

English beer will understand. 'Mother-in-law – the drink of this name is composed of equal proportions of old and bitter.'[4] This general popular idea of spouse's mother as acid, a termagant, goes back a long way in England – a citation of 1688 refers to 'The ever-lasting Din of Mothers-in-Law', and a sixteenth century author remarks, 'It is said that mothers in lawes beare a stepmother's hate unto their daughters in lawes'.

But why the mother-in-law rather than the father-in-law? This seems to be a reflex of the special role of the mother in a family. It is she who is generally credited with the more intense interest in the children and with watching over their development more closely than does the father. This proposition can certainly be challenged in modern times, when many fathers can give the bottle and change the nappies as skilfully as can the mother. But historically in Western society it certainly had much truth. So, the intense interest of the mother is carried through into the dominating role of the mother-in-law.

We all know that what looks on the surface to be a very simple kind of family situation has, in fact, quite complex principles of social relationships. But what we have tried to show consistently in this book is that what to many people may seem purely personal matters of individual temperament have in fact some very general underlying social patterns. In many societies studied by anthropologists these patterns are much more strongly marked than in our own: the structural stress between mother-in-law and son-in-law for instance is often marked by behaviour of respect which goes so far as actual avoidance of personal contact. The rule that no son-in-law should go anywhere near his mother-in-law, behave or speak rudely to her, renders a 'mother-in-law row' almost unthinkable. We consider from our empirical material how far the English mother-in-law stereotype, especially contrasted with that of the mother, is borne out in middle-class life. First we describe some of the general attitudes towards mother and mother-in-law, and then focus particularly on some linguistic aspects of the situation.

Some of the opinions given about relatives in our study express the stereotype very well. Our record of one woman is that: 'She speaks of her mother with admiration when she speaks of her at all, and she speaks of her mother-in-law with bitterness.' Another woman said she got on very badly with her husband's mother and heartily disliked her, 'but now I have learnt to stand up to her'. Another described her mother-in-law as a vindictive woman and, generalizing from her own experience, said, 'I keep away from mothers-in-law, if you know what I mean – like all in-laws, I suppose'. Still another

[4] *Daily Telegraph*, 3 July 1886.

view was expressed by a woman who said, 'We have been very lucky really with our in-laws', the kind of remark which many people use about the lack of stormy weather on a holiday, a fatalistic attitude that mothers-in-law are an act of God or a matter of chance rather than choice and free will.

These are representative views, backed up by a lot of evidence from concrete behaviour. They show two kinds of attitude. There is a view that affinal relationships are, so to speak, occupational risks. They are something given by an act of marriage. One takes over the social debts as well as the social assets of the marriage partner – and his or her parents may represent a pretty solid social liability. What is interesting is that the situation is seen, if only vaguely, by some people in structural terms. They recognize it is not just particular mothers-in-law who are difficult, but that the affinal role in itself has certain in-built sources of tension. Others, on the other hand, lay the weight of responsibility for the relationship on personality difficulties or temperamental incompatibility.

But what is also interesting from our material is that the attitudes associated with the affinal role may be reversed. There are cases where husband or wife admire and respect a mother-in-law and may be very fond of her. This may occur in contrast to the attitude to the person's own mother. We found people often surprisingly objective about their parents. Mrs Maskell, who left home at seventeen because she clashed with her mother, did not get on well with her mother later and said so. She described her mother as a very jealous and slightly stupid woman, and visited her only out of a sense of duty. The mother complained that her daughter's house was not kept clean and tidy, and would enter it only to help when her daughter was ill. By contrast, our informant got on well with her mother-in-law, whom she regarded as not possessive, not jealous and with a wealth of similar interests of an artistic and cultured kind. Husband and wife were united in their affection for his mother and in their toleration of the wife's mother for whom they felt, at best, a rather pitying sympathy. Mrs Danby, whose own mother had been an invalid and very trying for a long while before she died, got on excellently with her husband's mother. 'Mother-in-law relations', she said, 'usually have a slight touch of jealousy, but not in this case. I should like her as a friend whether or not she was my mother-in-law.'

Parallel instances could be given of the relations of men to their mothers-in-law. To revert to a point raised earlier, despite the stereotype, we found no evidence to suggest that relations betwen a husband and his mother-in-law were significantly better or worse than those which a wife had with her mother-in-law. A similar varied range of attitudes occurred: the man who said he saw his mother-in-law all too often; the man who found his wife's mother very trying, tolerated her because he knew she was empty with no resources, and saw her only for his wife's sake; and the man who liked his wife's mother very much. One husband used to have a great deal of difficulty in getting along with his wife's mother because she wanted to organize their house. Relations improved when children were born, and 'she is now more interested in the grand-children than in the staircarpet'. Wives' views on their husbands' relations with their mothers showed similar distinction. Of one husband and her mother his wife said, 'I would not leave them alone together for long'. But of another, the wife's mother thought there was no one in the world like him; he was the favourite 'blue-eyed boy'; 'he is the only one who can break a plate in my mother's house without being made a misery.'

It is evident then that what we could call the *mother-in-law syndrome* is a complex condition with strong possibilities of positive as well as negative symptoms. How were these distributed over the whole series of cases?

FACTORS IN BEHAVIOUR TO PARENTS-IN-LAW

In the Greenbanks and Highgate material we got a lot of evidence of people's attitudes towards their parents-in-law, and how they saw the relations with them. Take the relations with the mother-in-law alone. Of 70 odd cases, with husbands and wives represented fairly equally, less than one quarter could be described as primarily negative, that is, bad relations existing between the parties. In the other three-quarters of the cases, the husband or wife got along tolerably well with the mother-in-law; in nearly half of all the cases, relations could be described as definitely good. The popular stereotype existed, but it was in a very definite minority.

Some people referred to the stereotype in the abstract, though they denied it in their own case. One woman, who admired her husband's parents very much, said that there was nothing 'in-law-ish' about her relations with them. She thought the classical picture of the disagreeable mother-in-law was nonsense. 'A mother-in-law can be a very good friend. It depends on both sides.'

But relations were often not clearcut. One woman tolerated her mother-in-law, indeed quite liked her in some ways, but thought she had a phobia about cleanliness, found her interminable chatter boring, and had a sense of relief when she departed after staying with them. Another woman admired her mother-in-law for strength of character and independence, but was a bit frightened of her, did not feel comfortable with her, would not visit her alone and wrote to her only to thank her for presents.

The time factor could play a very important part in the development of mother-in-law relations. In the case just mentioned, the husband's mother had tried hard to prevent her son's marriage. She ignored her daughter-in-law completely for a long while, but then, especially after a child was born, her attitude changed and the woman became her favourite daughter-in-law. In another case a man said he used not to get on well with his wife's mother who was a rather dominating woman, but in time he became fond of her 'because of the great help she has been with the children'.

But the time factor could operate also in a negative way. In many human relations, of friendship as well as of kinship, great importance attaches to the *duration* of social contact as well as its quality. There seems to be a notion varying with different types of relationships of what is a *tolerable period* of intimate social contact. In the elementary family of parents and young children it is assumed that continuity of intimate relationship should endure – though as the children grow up this assumption may be looked at differently by them and their parents. With affinal kin the notion of a tolerable period takes on great importance. People can stand their mothers-in-law in the house for a limited period, but after a time feel they have had enough. How long is enough? is the critical question to which there is no formula answer. But in many cases relations with the mother-in-law seemed to be equable enough so long as they remained fairly formal, fairly brief and well spaced out.

Time and social distance have been singled out as significant factors in the characterization of relations between in-laws. Other factors of a relatively objective kind can also be identified – whether the parties live close together or far away, whether the mother-in-law is in good health or not, whether she has resources to maintain herself or needs economic support. Demographic factors also can be significant, such as relative age. If the mother-in-law has other children to absorb her interest this may relieve pressure; if there are grandchildren these can be a very powerful mollifying factor. More subjective elements – common interests of a cultural kind; equable character and temperament which play down aggression, dominance or jealousy; a sense of responsibility and obligation – may all lead to the maintenance of relations which otherwise would be severed.

So far we have spoken of relations of husband or wife with their parents-in-law alone. But it has been stressed that such relations operate in the context of other relations in the family circle, parents in particular. Popular formulations are not much guide here, since they may turn out to be diametrically opposed. 'Daughters are always closer to their mothers' is one such formula. But another is 'girls always get on better with their fathers', and the woman who gave us this aphorism added for good measure, 'It's all Freudian, I'm sure'. Equally disparate hypotheses can apply to the mother and mother-in-law situation. Relations of a woman with her mother-in-law can be modelled on those with her mother. Where she finds the temperament, experience and authority of an older woman incompatible with the development of her own mature life, she reacts against the mother-in-law much as she reacts against her own mother. Alternatively, if she finds relations with her mother compatible and supporting, she may duplicate this by the creation of new ties with a woman in parallel standing. In the couple of dozen cases we have where relations with mother and mother-in-law can be directly compared, half show parallel attitudes to the mother and the mother-in-law – nearly all favourable. In the other half, the attitudes to the senior women are contrasted. Either the wife has affectionate relations with her mother and is at odds with her mother-in-law, or, almost equally, is at odds with her mother and relies affectionately on her mother-in-law. There were quite definite indications in some cases that a wife found in her husband's mother a refuge from her own mother. Such a distribution suggests two points. The first is a very strong feeling that in such family relations between women of different generations there ought to be an equable adjustment made by the younger, the daughter or daughter-in-law. This is the ideal; the reality is different. The second point of implication then is that many people find it difficult to maintain such a balance and find a solution in a kind of compensatory mechanism. Either woman of the senior generation is taken as a point of attachment; the other by contrast is used as a foil. One senior woman must be selected for positive relations, especially as a confidant, for support; so, almost of necessity, negative aspects of relations with the other tend to be stressed. Such contrast of relationships seems less marked between men, possibly because they are less preoccupied with the domestic universe than are women.

But in the relations between husband or wife and the mother-in-law, the position of the other spouse may be very relevant. Possessiveness of the spouse's mother towards her son or daughter, leading to jealousy of her daughter- or son-in-law, are often components. A complicating factor may be the emotional involvement of the spouse with his or her own mother, using her as a defence against or a retreat from the spouse or as an external standard of judgment in domestic affairs. Relations with the mother-in-law may be maintained simply out of loyalty to the spouse, who may recognize the sacrifice. But mild friction between husband and wife, as when one wishes the other would visit the mother-in-law more often, is probably common. Differences of view between husband and wife about the character and behaviour of the mother-in-law may lead to more serious strains between the spouses. A wife resents the mother-in-law's hold over her husband, feeling he has not yet thrown off the ties of his natal family; a husband feels that his mother-in-law comes between his wife and himself on decisions which the pair of them could make alone. In such conditions the third party is an irritant, not a co-operating or mediating factor.

NAMES: WHAT DO YOU CALL YOUR MOTHER-IN-LAW

The interplay of forces in this whole set of relationships is illustrated by ways in which the different parties address one another. Much of the argument of this section could be epitomized by the answers to the question, 'What do you call your mother-in-law?' This is in fact a question which we asked the subjects of our kinship study. The replies were revealing, and from them we can now predict a probable range of answers in any English middle-class situation.

First let us repeat (cf. p. 331) that one of the odd things about the in-law relationship in the English kinship system is that there is no particular rule about what one should call such people. We speak *of* them as father-in-law, mother-in-law, etc., but no one would think of speaking *to* them in such terms unless in a joking way. This sets a problem which in England anyway is often quite serious for young people when they get married. In itself the absence of such a rule, by not giving a clear guide, poses a problem for each newly married pair afresh. They must work out for themselves what they must do. The so-called primitive societies manage things much better; as anthropologists know, most of them lay down quite definite ways of addressing mothers-in-law and fathers-in-law. These ways usually avoid all forms of personal name, employ parental terms and incorporate special expressions of respect as a polite dual or plural.

In Chapter 10 we have isolated six different ways in which one may address one's parents-in-law. One can call them Mother or Father, or informal equivalents, following one's spouse; one can use the surname with Mr or Mrs, as strangers do; one can use first names (forenames) or other personal names (including what are rather oddly called Christian names), adopting the familiar terms of equality; one can use grandparent terms (after children are born), adopting the children's own terms and emphasizing the junior/senior relationship; one can use nicknames or other special names; or one can avoid using names at all. So, one can be informal or formal, egalitarian or status conscious.

The six styles of addressing parents-in-law can be arranged in a variety of ways. But essentially they represent three main types of classification of these new people brought into relationship with oneself. A mother-in-law may be assimilated with one's own kin by using the term Mother or Grandmother or variants of these forms. She may be classed in effect as a friend by calling her by her first name or by a nickname. She may be classed as a stranger by calling her by her surname with Mrs prefixed – or even by refraining from calling her by any term at all. We have arranged our material to bring out these contrasts.

In our study we collected in all 214 instances of how people addressed their parents-in-law. These people (just over 100)[5] included about equal numbers of husbands and wives, and a few widows. The original figures are given in Table 33, with general percentages for mother-in-law and father-in-law distribution separately.

TABLE 33

Forms of address to parents-in-law

Used by	*Mother-in-law*							*Father-in-law*							*Total instances*
	M	*G*	*P*	*N*	*S*	*O*		*F*	*G*	*P*	*N*	*S*	*O*		
Wife	26	8	11	6	4	4	59	21	4	9	6	4	1	45	
Husband	14	7	15	9	12	7	64	7	2	15	6	13	3	46	214
Totals %	33	12	21	12	13	9	100	31	6	27	13	19	4	100	

M/*F* = mother/father terms *G* = grandparent terms *P* = first/personal name
N = nickname *S* = surname with prefix *O* = 'nothing at all'

What stands out from this material is that in our field of study no single solution, nor indeed any dominant solution, had been adopted to the problem of what to call parents-in-law. Broadly, over the whole range, mothers-in-law were treated verbally as kin in rather more than 40 per cent of the cases, as friends in rather less than 40 per cent and as strangers in about 20 per cent. Fathers-in-law were assimilated as kin in rather less than 40 per cent, were treated with familiarity in rather more than 40 per cent, and were treated as strangers in over 20 per cent of the cases. But what is really marked is the difference between what husbands called their parents-in-law and

[5] Representing rather fewer than the 70 cases mentioned on p. 336, since our information about naming was not complete.

what wives called them. Wives were strong on the use of parental terms for both mothers-in-law and fathers-in-law, only medianly so on the use of familiar names, and used surnames for address hardly at all. Husbands showed only limited use of parental terms for mothers-in-law, even less so for fathers-in-law, but were quite strong on personal names and nicknames, and on surnames. In other words, towards parents-in-law wives showed an inclination to treat them as kin of family type, whereas husbands divided their behaviour largely between familiarity and stand-offishness. Such a range of behaviour in terms of address conforms to what one might expect in the affinal situation of authority between junior and senior in the absence of any firm rules.

On the other hand, in so far as social distance is expressed by use of surname by junior to senior, and even more by avoidance of any term of address at all, it is notable that all such instances still made up less than a quarter of the total. So, though the relation of 'in-laws' at the parent-son/daughter level might be fraught with difficulty and strain (as much evidence showed) only relatively few people refused to make a terminological adjustment, and kept their parents-in-law at a distance. By far the great majority, something like three-quarters, made some concession, whether in the name of general good relations or in order to placate the spouse. They gave the new connections a kin status or a special personal name or nickname, or got on a footing of equality with them on first-name terms. If wives were more ready than their husbands to admit their spouse's parents to kin status, husbands were more ready to admit theirs on a friendly basis.

In our material the avoidance of any term of address at all was in some ways the most interesting – and unexpected – point. In about 7 per cent of the instances the son-in-law or daughter-in-law used what they described as 'nothing at all' to the father- or mother-in-law. They spoke to these people as 'you' if they had to, but it was quite clear that they avoided even this wherever they could. A woman who had been married for about 15 years with three children called her father-in-law by his Christian name, and her husband did the same with her father and mother. But about her mother-in-law she said, 'It's rather an awkward question because I really don't know what to call her: "Nan" or "Mother Brown". I think it is because they are much more relative conscious. She is of a different generation.' Another wife said her husband called her mother 'Mother' if he had to call her anything – 'but he manages without calling her anything at all', and he tried not to call her father anything. Another husband called his wife's parents 'nothing unless driven to it'. When the wife wrote to her parents he added a postcript to avoid the embarrassment of addressing them as anything. If he had to, he called his wife's mother Mrs Brown, while his wife called his parents M and D, using initials for Mum and Dad as he did. Another wife called her parents Mam and Tad and her parents-in-law Mr and Mrs Smith, while her husband called his parents Mother and Father and hers 'nothing unless he has to', though he used Mam and Tad when writing to them. In fact, said our informant, neither of them used a name for each other's parents in speaking to them unless they had to face the problem. Quite often they got round the difficulty when writing by addressing them as 'Dear Both'! This didn't imply any intention of being distant, she said, relationships were good all round. And she added the significant sociological point that she thought there would be less of a problem when there were children as the grandparental terms could then be adopted. (Cf. Schneider, 1968, p.84–5.)

The impression given by these examples of stumbling ineptitude in handling social relationships throws up on strong light the basic dilemma of many people in regard to their parents-in-law. It is not so much that they dislike their parents-in-law or have ambivalent attitudes towards them; it is rather they just wish they weren't there. One way of dealing with this source of social embarrassment is to refuse to face their social existence by not giving them any names.

But this negative attitude is often overcome as the family cycle develops. With the birth of a child a way of compromise, of re-identification, opens up. With many people it is clear that grand-parent terms are grasped at as a way of avoiding an embarrassing choice. Some of our informants were themselves quite sophisticated about this. Mrs Pillerth told us that her husband, a medical man of middle years, called his mother-in-law Grannie. She said this was the 'perfect solution' to the problem of what to call in-laws. She didn't know what her husband called her mother before the children were born (about 15 years before) – 'I don't think he called her anything!' Her father he always addressed as Sir. Yet the mother-in-law was no gorgon – another daughter's husband called her by her Christian name and she didn't seem to mind. Mr Woollcombe was quite assertive on the point. When he married, his parents-in-law wished him to call them by their Christian names. He refused. 'I told them there would be children, so I would not call them by their Christian names. I tried to avoid calling them anything. Now I call them Grandma and Grandpa – the same as the children.' Yet factors of personal prejudice and choice tend to operate also in affecting the use of such terms. Mrs Nebworth used to call her mother Mummy and now, following her children's habit, calls her Granny. This woman wants her son-in-law to call her Granny too, but he has refused; he doesn't like the practice and calls her Mrs Jones, using her surname. His wife commented tolerantly 'Well, you can't unless you are used to it'.

We cannot explain precisely in every case why people chose one mode of address to parents-in-law rather than another. But in general terms the Mother and Father forms or their variants were often found where son-in-law's or daughter-in-law's own parents were dead. The grandparent terms seemed to be associated solely with situations where children had been born to the young couple, and first name terms seemed to be facilitated by a relatively small age gap between senior and junior in-laws. But factors of personal temperament, and particular elements in the son- or daughter-in-law's own natal family situation seem to have also been of importance. We now examine this last point a little further.

CONTRAST WITH PARENTS

This spread of terms of address for parents-in-law indicates the ambiguity which exists when people have to take on a new social relationship with others of a senior generation – people bound by intimate ties to the person they have married. One difficulty here is that the entry of these new senior people on the social scene inevitably raises comparison with one's own parents. This is illustrated by embarrassment which often arises in the use of parent terms for in-laws. It's due not so much to an inability to find a title which one thinks suitable for them, as to a desire to avoid having to apply to them the one title which some of them seem to want – that of Mother or Father. People often baulk at this. Mrs Gamba, when adult, used Mother and Father to her own parents but said she had never been able to call her in-laws by the same terms; she preferred to use their Christian names. Another woman always called her own mother Mother and she used the same term for her mother-in-law. because she knew this woman wanted to be called that. The mother-in-law was a Victorian type and if she had been called anything else but Mother would have 'fainted in a heap'. 'Yet' said our informant, 'there should be some other word for it because after all you can only have one mother.' Another woman, when we asked her what she called her mother-in-law, said, 'I call her Mother, though it nearly chokes me'. She said she used this word 'because she is my husband's mother', and since she was very fond of her husband she did what she knew he wished. Mrs Gibbon never had a term for her mother-in-law when they talked together. She wrote to her as Mother, but she could never bring herself to use this term in conversation. She found it very difficult, she said, and used to wish there were a special term one could use. She felt that 'If you have got a mother of your own it doesn't seem right to call someone else Mother', so sometimes she used the children's term Grannie. She said her son's wife was in the same position with her – of not having any name for her. 'I know how she feels because I felt the same about my mother-in-law'. But in strong contrast to the views of many people was that of Mrs Gilroy who addressed her parents-in-law as Mother and Father. Her relationship to these people was very close and comfortable. She was one of the few informants who seemed to respond to this question without hesitation or indication that there had been difficulty in the selection of terms of address. Her relation with her own mother was distant and impersonal, so it is a fair inference that the term Mother was not charged for her with much emotional familiarity. In support of this it can be mentioned that when asked to whom she would turn in an emotional crisis this woman replied at once 'my husband's mother', and she did in fact rely on her a great deal.

What is interesting here is not only the spread of terms but also the kind of balance they often showed and the range of variation. There was no case in our series in which both pairs of parents-in-law were simply called Mother and Father by both sides. Reciprocal pairing was also rare. Only a couple of really straightforward cases occurred where husband and wife each used for their in-laws the terms which the other used for parents, e.g. wife's mother and father were called Mama and Papa by both husband and wife, while husband's parents were called Mum and Dad by both.

What seems to be involved in many of these cases is a rather ill-formulated reluctance to confuse categories – an inability to share what is felt to be a very special, unique expression for parents with those who are parents only by law. So when a person does adopt 'parent' terms for spouse's parents these terms may emerge as different from the terms for his own parents.[6] A mother-in-law was called Mom by her own children and the daughter-in-law used the same term. She said this made things easier, as it wasn't mother, which she really would not have wanted to use; her own mother was called Mother or Mummy. People got up to some odd dodges in this naming of in-laws. This woman called her father Jim from a name in a story which they used to read together as a child. So her husband

[6] A neat if somewhat dry mode of expression was reported by one of our nformants. She recollected that her son-in-law ordinarily didn't call her anything at all. But when he wrote to her a few weeks before, he had headed the letter 'Dear Mother (in-law)'! Another method of differentiation – of which, however, we have only very few examples – is to call the mother-in-law Mother Jones, following the kin term by the surname. We have an impression that this is a mode of address adopted by men rather than by women.

too called his father-in-law Jim and, by logical extension, called his mother-in-law Mrs Jim. Another husband called his mother Mother, and his wife too called her Mother. But the wife differentiated her own parents; she called her mother Mimp, a pet name; her father she called Dad. But as for her husband: 'I don't know what he calls my father'. After some thought she said she had never heard him call her father anything. 'I think he compromises and calls him Sir.'

But we think it is no accident that as another method of meeting this problem of differentiation, in about half the married pairs we studied, the terms used by the two spouses for their respective parents-in-law fell into completely different categories. If surnames were used by the husband then Christian names or grandparental terms were used by the wife; if Christian names by the husband, then parental names by the wife, etc.

The point in all this is that such variation of names is not just casual or random. The lack of formal naming rules as exist in some societies may give flexibility, allow adaptation to personal circumstances and temperament. But while there are no precise rules there are expectations and there are patterns of behaviour. As part of the pattern, each different set of persons has an internal consistency in modes of naming. What we have here is an ingenious process of filling an institutional gap. In the absence of a standard kinship term or other conventional expression for parental affines, each married couple has faced the problem and found some individual solution. They have not created new terms (though some nicknames might almost rank as such); they have drawn on the existing material, recognizing the overriding kinship quality of these important social relationships, but in such a way as to maintain the differentiation between them. Whether or not such a solution is consciously introduced and understood by the parties concerned it has distinct social functions. It helps to provide a means of identification or specification of different kinds of relatives within the wider family field. It helps to bridge over some awkward category gaps which our conventions do not properly fill. And while serving as an aid to communication it helps to preserve an individual personal form of relationship in circumstances of some delicacy.[7]

[7] A couple of incidental comments may be made here on possible generation differences:

There was probably more formality in the mother-in-law/son-/daughter-in-law relation in Victorian times in England than today, and the problem of what to call mother-in-law would then have been less acute – the Mr and Mrs terms were probably the common solution (cf. R. W. Chapman, op. cit., p. 234). Young people of today may find the general relation with parent-in-law easier to handle, especially if they have known their prospective in-laws in advance. But even so, a few spontaneous comments from young people, in New Zealand and the United

This brief comparison of relationships with mother and mother-in-law throws light on the truth and falsity of family stereotypes. Relations between husband or wife and a parent or parent-in-law vary greatly. But they are neither random nor a question of simple personal compatibilities. There are significant structural factors which lay down the framework within which relationships are generated and worked out. But the structure itself is not a simple one. Many elements are involved and the actual relations worked out in any case are the resultant configuration of these elements. Any single relation is apt to be a kind of compromise between convention and personal feeling, and it is interesting how firm the convention still is.

EQUALITY AND CLOSENESS IN SIBLING RELATIONSHIP

Relations between siblings are regarded as having a special quality of their own, very different from that thought to exist between parents and children, but also meriting particular social respect. In some circumstances this quality may assume a quasi-mystical value. If a man says of another 'he was like a brother to me', this implies a peculiar intimacy, understanding and support, a simulacrum of the ideal type of behaviour regarded as appropriate from a sibling.

The sibling bond differs from that with a parent in several structural respects. It lacks the built-in status asymmetry characteristic of the tie between parent and child, which assumes an initial dependency of the child and a later compensatory obligation towards the parent. The relation between siblings is essentially, in ideal terms, one of equality. Again, the effects of time are different. Between parent and child, time makes for a revolution in powers. As the child grows to adult life the parent ages; as the child advances to maturity the parent declines beyond it; as the child grasps authority the parent loses it. With siblings the initial age disparity tends to be corrected by time, and they advance together, with no such reversal of their roles. A further difference is the degree of variation possible in sibling numbers – one cannot really have multiple parents, but

States as well as in England, have made us aware that the problem is not unfamiliar to them. Some societies which encourage the marriage of cousins, such as sectors in Islam, mitigate the severity of the mother-in-law problem thereby; she may be already an aunt, and as such has been familiar from childhood. But what is interesting sociologically is that, from some evidence we have, in such cases the nomenclature and formality of the mother-in-law relation are apt to take precedence. (In the case of the first-cousin marriage in our sample the wife, who called her mother-in-law 'Aunt Gertie' before marriage, called her 'Mother' or 'Little Gran' (because of the children) afterwards.)

multiple siblings are common and offer a range of variation for behaviour.

Between siblings, as between parent and child, there is expected to be affection, but according to convention there should be no element of erotic interest in this. Modern psychologists and social workers know better. But erotic components in either relationship are of different order between parent and child than between siblings. Moreover, the affective aspects of the relations offer different possibilities. A structural factor which may be sometimes overlooked is the reverse parallelism in the situation. Rivalry between father and son for the mother's affection, between mother and daughter for the father's affection, is well understood; sibling rivalry for the affection of either parent, especially that of the mother, is also commonplace. But in a family with say, two sons and two daughters there are ten structural possibilities of dyadic competition[8] using different combinations of symmetry or asymmetry of sex, and of authority. These include, for example, a symmetry of sex and asymmetry of authority in the father–son rivalry for affection of the mother; and an asymmetry of sex and symmetry of authority in brother–sister rivalry for her affection.

In this complex field, what the anthropologist looks for, *inter alia*, is evidence which will indicate whether in the adult world the forces of competition between siblings – perhaps originating in competition for parental affection, but not necessarily so – or the forces of alliance – against the parents or against the world in general – appear to be the stronger. He also wishes to see how far sex difference among siblings appears to be relevant to this issue.

We now illustrate some of the views expressed by our North London informants on these relationships, showing the value they attach to the sibling relationship and the weight they give to various factors in the situation, both personal and general.

We begin with the statement of Mrs Mitchie, who said there was no friend of whom she was more fond than of her siblings. She was the youngest of a sibling group of six. 'It was nice being the youngest – I was spoilt by everyone.' At first she said she got on with all her siblings equally well; as she later admitted, she felt much closer to her sisters than to her brothers – 'I don't know why; it just happened' Her eldest sister was a 'special favourite'; 'in a way she was like a mother to me when I was a little girl'. Later: 'I don't know how far she influenced the others in their views, but she certainly influenced me.' In this sibling group there appeared to be some division between

[8] I.e. brother/brother, brother/sister, sister/sister in regard to father or mother; father/son, father/daughter, mother/son, mother/daughter in regard to other parent.

the more conservative and more radical sections, the latter having a similar outlook on life and seeming more alike in character. Two of the brothers in particular had a more conventional attitude. With the brother nearest in age to our informant, 'We didn't get on; he was a boy and four years older than me, so we fought all the time'. General relations among all the siblings appeared equable, but not without mild criticism: the radicals 'often have a bit of quiet gossip against them' – the conservatives.

The Garson case illustrated the difference in the sibling situations of husband and wife, though both had close relations with these kin. The husband had only one sister, who was according to himself and his wife, the most important person in his life outside of his wife. Two years older than he, she had been his closest companion during most of his adult life. When they were young, especially in their teens, the relationship was not so smooth, but there was always an alliance against parental wishes and parental decisions. As a child he spent most of his time at his mother's mother's house, because his father was away at the War and his mother was working full time. As he grew up there was tension in his relations with his mother, who was very set in her ways; although he liked her he had a struggle to assert his independence. The sister married quite some years before her brother, and her house became his real home. Whenever possible he went there for his vacations and weekends, unless he felt he ought to visit his mother. Not long after his marriage his sister was widowed, and he assumed responsibility for her, helped her financially and her children.

Mrs Garson had two sisters and a brother, and though they were all close to one another she remarked that the quality of the relation was very different from that between her husband and his sister. The members of this sibling group were not so dependent on one another. (Both informants agreed with our interviewer that the greater unity of parents and children in this case might have tended to give the different tone to the sibling relationship.) The closeness of the wife to her siblings was based in her view on similarity of character and sharing of experiences, but with different elements in each case. To her younger sister she felt extremely close. She wanted her own children to like her sister's children, and to share the common family background. While she felt this to be a terribly demanding type of interpersonal relation, very intangible, she obviously felt it to be very important. From her elder sister she stood more apart. Though she would help her sister if need arose, there would always be a certain amount of rivalry in the relationship, going back to problems of seniority and authority as children. Our informant as a child did not want to 'be bossed around', and perhaps wanted to be the one to boss. In the upshot the sister found support from their brother, who was very outgoing and close to all the sisters. Our informant's relation with her brother was one of mutual help and advice; before his marriage he had been dependent on her for companionship and support.

But there were complexities even in a situation of harmonious sibling relationships. Mrs Gibbon was the fourth in a sibling group of five, her husband the youngest of four. She said that both she and her husband were 'ones for families', and characterized both sibling groups as 'close'. Before her marriage she, her elder sister and her two brothers used to go round together; they formed a 'little gang' in a rather unconventional society to which they belonged because it organized rambles, 'socials', theatre-parties and dances. 'People wouldn't think we were all one family – they were always surprised when they found we were related.' Both she and her sister met the men they later married at these dances. Her elder sister and a brother married and moved away from London, and our informant blamed the spouse in each case for this separation. This brother was always her favourite, but her dislike of his wife practically cut her off from him, and from his children. By contrast she was in closer touch with the other brother, never a great favourite of hers, whom she described as selfish and greedy, but who lived very near and was seen fairly often. Relations with her sisters were similarly multi-stranded. She always got on better with her younger sister, who was 'very understanding', much less 'bossy' and 'managerial' than her elder sister, who used to have to run the home when their mother was often ill. But her younger sister suffered from ill-health and was often trying. Having stayed for a time with the eldest sister, the youngest wished to return to London and seek a job, and to stay with our informant meanwhile. But this had its difficulties. 'I don't *want* her to live with me, though I wouldn't want her to be alone.' Yet neither of the brothers was thought to be suitable, so it seemed as if there was no good alternative. Mrs Gibbon thought that it was always sisters who stick together anyway; she felt much closer to her sisters than to her brothers. Despite this, it was not her own sisters but her husband's sisters with whom she got on better. With her own sisters there was 'a strong bond', but with her husband's sisters there was a placid stable relationship. Her husband was very fond of his sisters, and she and her sisters-in-law were very close friends.

Three themes emerge in this case. One is the view that sisters are always closer to one another than are brothers, no matter what the precise quality of the relationship at any one time. Another theme is the ambivalence perceptible in many sibling relationships – the feeling of obligation, even of attachment, implemented in the performance of services; and yet the feeling of criticism, possibly resentment, expressed in a range of opinions. The result is a kind of unstable equilibrium, in which a single even small occurrence can have marked effect in altering the relationship definitely in one way or another. The third theme is the relative weight of husband's and wife's sibling relationship with her husband's sisters as a kind of victory for the husband's side. She thought that spouses always tended to have more contact with one side than the other, depending on who was the more forceful character. In her case her husband 'always got his own way' and that was why she spent so much time with his sisters who had been unfailingly kind and helpful.

We can now examine these themes and other possibilities in the light of the general empirical evidence from our North London study. We first look briefly at the amount of sibling contact in our Greenbanks and Highgate samples overall, differentiating by sex, though not by age. Taking contact simply as any form of communication (as already discussed in Chapter 7), adult sibling relations were at a very high level. Contact between sisters indeed was almost complete for the entire sample. In other words, complete lapse or severance of social ties with grown-up siblings was very rare; the bond of membership in the same natal family implied the maintenance of *some* form of social relationship.

TABLE 34

Contact of siblings

Siblings	*Total*	*In contact*	%
Brother – brother	78	68	87
Brother – sister	143	136	95
Sister – sister	91	90	99
	312	294	94%

But the *quality* of this relationship might vary a great deal.

For more specific data on these aspects of sibling relationships we rely primarily on the 58 random sample cases from Greenbanks and Highgate in which elementary families with dependent children were involved. This eliminates a number of variables in the cases of single women, widows, etc. which we studied at an early stage (though scrutiny of these has not shown any marked differences in the quality of sibling relations). Our procedure has been as follows.

From the lengthy accounts of relations between our informants and their individual siblings we have classified the relations with each sibling under three heads: positive; indifferent; negative. *Positive* includes a range of interaction from warmly affectionate and very close to relatively cool and reserved but good-humoured acceptance of the kin bond. Quarrelling may occur, but good relations are soon restored; no great enthusiasm may be expressed but the maintenance of contact is regarded as normal and obligation to render some services is acknowledged. *Negative* refers to relationships which are explicitly stated to be hostile. The parties may maintain some contact, but this is minimal, perhaps conceded because of some other relative; or no contact has occurred for a long time, and no particular effort is made to initiate it. *Indifferent* applies to intermediate conditions. No active dislike is expressed, some contact is maintained, but on a neutral level of affectivity. It may be explicitly stated by the informant that he has no particular interest in whether the social tie is kept up or not.

The measures are rough, but do seem to correspond fairly closely to distinctions made by our subjects themselves.

The total number of our informants in these 58 North London cases was 116. Of these 7 husbands and 10 wives, making 17 in all, were each the only child in their natal family. The 99 other informants had a total of 224 siblings; 16 of these died long ago, and no adequate information could be obtained about them. In quality of relations with the 208 siblings about whom data were obtained the distribution was as follows:

TABLE 35

Quality of sibling relations

Relation	*Numbers*			*Total*	*% by each category*			%
	Positive	*In-different*	*Negative*		*Pos.*	*Ind.*	*Neg.*	
H – B	30	14	6	50	60	28	12	
H – Z	37	12	4	53	70	22	8	
Hus/Sib.	67	26	10	103	65	25	10	
W – B	40	12	4	56	71	21	8	
W – Z	41	7	1	49	83	15	2	
Wife/Sib.	81	19	5	105	77	18	5	
[Bro/Sis.	77	24	8	109	70	22	8]	
Totals	148	45	15	208	71	22	7	100

From this set of more than 200 instances of sibling relationships it is clear that the ideals of closeness, support and mutual obligation between brothers and sisters are borne out in practice, in a majority of cases. The forces of alliance seem to be very definitely stronger than the forces of competition and rivalry, at least in so far as these may come to expression in overt conflict. But in a substantial minority, nearly one third, any very positive relationship is lacking, and is replaced by indifference or, in a small number of instances, by actual hostility. What is noteworthy is that men tend on the whole to have rather poorer relations with their siblings than women do, and that women's relations with their sisters seem to have the best record of all. Quite apart from any far-fetched notions about a greater degree of male aggression and male sibling rivalry, there would seem to be serious economic reasons why relations between brothers, and to a less extent between brothers and their sisters, could often be more strained than those between sisters. Men are all engaged in some form of business or professional activity; less occupied with domestic affairs and children in the working day than are their wives, they need less support in this field, and have therefore less incentive to maintain contact with their siblings. On the other hand, there is perhaps more likelihood of conflict arising in their greater involvement in the handling of common property.

Empirically, in general terms, the reasons for maintenance of positive relations between siblings included general sociability, support in crises and even in the minutiae of family decisions, and services for the children. In a few cases there was a strong emotional identification, as by an elder sister for a younger brother, or by a younger sister for an elder sister. Relations between a pair of identical twins in our sample, Mrs Waverley and her sister, were very close; they had an agreement that if anything happened to either the other would look after the children, and they expected to rely on each other in a crisis. But our informant thought her mother had been wrong to dress them identically and in other ways to emphasize their likeness; since they were not treated as separate individuals there was quite a wrench when they had to separate.[9]

Reasons for indifference between siblings were not easy to find, given the convention of maintenance of relations on an affective basis. Temperamental factors of general lack of expressive behaviour seemed to be involved in some cases, and predisposing conditions seemed to be in particular those of distance, both geographical and social. Siblings living in different continents for years tended to lose

[9] We have a record of adolescent twins, boy and girl, who disliked each other and fought; they had had an unsettled early childhood, culminating in their parents' divorce.

contact or at least to reduce it to the minimum of the Christmas card and occasional message. Siblings separated by a great age gap tended to regard each other with much less social interest than those close together in age. A special form of social distance had occurred in a few cases where a sister had joined a closed religious order, in which her loyalties were engaged explicitly to the detriment of her family ties. What did not seem responsible to any significant extent for coolness between siblings was social mobility – though it would seem to have been a factor in reduction of social ties with more distant kin. What did emerge in a few cases, however, was evidence of some embarrassment, or at least some caution, in relationships of a financial order if the siblings were in markedly different income levels. With the twins just mentioned, our informant had lent her twin sister a cot, pram, bath, maternity jacket and other materials for confinement, but she expressed reluctance to help her sister financially. On the whole, however, even with a considerable age differential, or social distance of other kinds, at least minimal social relations were maintained between siblings.

The two most important factors which seemed to be involved in the more severe breaches of sibling relationship were jealousy and rivalry from an early age; and the third-party element of spouses. Illustrations of this will indicate the kind of complexities encountered. The two Offord brothers, in business together, did not get on very well; they could not agree on how affairs should be run. When things financially came to a head there was 'a flaming row', and one brother walked out and set up another business. But he had difficulty in getting his money out of the original firm, and at the same time was pressed by his brother in regard to the finance of his house; this was bought originally by a loan from the family business and was now claimed as the firm's property. Relations between the brothers were very hostile.

In general, the sibling-versus-spouse situation seems to have been resolved along relatively viable lines. But there were instances where relations with the sibling were definitely worsened or severed because of difficulties with the sibling's husband or wife. Mr Grant had one brother, many years older, with whom relations were very cool. Christmas cards were exchanged but, 'I could see my brother on a bus and not say hello to him'. But an intensifying element to the social distance was the sister-in-law, who was thought to be very dominating. 'I would see more of my brother if it were not for his wife.' Mr Arden had had a close relation with his sister and a business connection with her husband. But there was some difference of views, and the sister's husband refused to settle an account. In the end Mr Arden sent a solicitor's letter, 'and that is unforgivable'. The brother-in-law then forbade his wife to see her brother. Matters were patched up for a time and a dinner party was held at Mr Arden's flat. But before the end of the evening the brother-in-law had created a scene (probably through jealousy of Mr Arden's success in business) and the feud was on again. The sister was forbidden by her husband to come to Mr Arden's wedding, and was very upset. Later they ran across each other occasionally in the City, where both worked, but the sister did not tell her husband she had seen her brother. Mr Arden, though regretful, said he felt his sister had made her bed and must lie on it.

In a number of cases no single factor or event in disturbance of amicable relations was discernible. An illustration occurs in relations between Mrs Neville and her sister. As a child Mrs Neville was ordered around by her elder sister. 'She was the bigger sister and acted the bigger sister.' She issued ultimatums. 'If we went shopping with my mother and I'd be playing in the street all covered in dirt, she'd say "If she's going like that, I'm not!" ' This usually resulted in the younger sister being left behind. On the other hand, our informant seems to have been more the centre of her mother's attention, was given training for a profession and launched on a career. Her mother always talked about how marvellous the younger sister was, and her elder sister's husband, when he first met her, said how he'd loathed her from all he'd heard about her from her mother's adulation. When some years afterwards the two sisters fell out, friction over their children, culminating in a sneer at the younger sister's Jewish connections, had been ostensible reasons for the breach (cf. p. 364). But the relationship had been complicated by the sister's husband. He hoped to get into television through the help of his sister-in-law and her husband, but their reluctance to promote him (they felt he hadn't the talent) exacerbated family relationships. Owning a shop with a prosperous business, he was tending to neglect it in favour of his ambitions, which for a man with a wife and small children to educate seemed to his sister-in-law and her husband to be ridiculous. The elder sister's growing perception of her husband's situation made her unhappy; though Mrs Neville did not mention it directly to our interviewer, this seemed to have brought the sisters closer together again.

The complexities in this case have been only cursorily sketched, but they illustrate one important feature of many sibling relationships – the way in which they change over time. Mr Woollcombe illustrated how the early disagreements of childhood tended to fall into the background when siblings reached maturity. 'I resented my brother as a child. I had been an only child for six years. There was much trouble when we were young ,between nine and three.' Later they were at different schools, and then the elder was away at work. But once they were adult, had been through similar experiences in the War, and their parents were dead, they found they were closer than before. Their tastes were different, and the elder brother seemed rather to despise those of the younger, but he was tolerant of the general situation. 'We have not got common interests. He likes flowers very much; I don't like flowers at all. Our reactions to everyday problems are the same, but he's more artistic and interested in the arts than I am. He's not interested in doing things with his hands as I am. He isn't really practical. His reaction to the family and children and family affairs is the same as mine, but our interests are rather different. We are brothers; our emotional reaction is very similar.' The younger brother had been looked after by the elder and his wife when he fell ill at an early period when he returned from a job abroad. He got on well with his sister-in-law who remarked: 'But he says I'm a very expensive sister-in-law because of all the children whom he has to get presents for.' In this case the conversion of early sibling rivalry into a relationship of affection was aided by the fact that the younger brother, as a bachelor, had remained free from other possibly complicating ties and had found in the patterns of kin relationship a periodic source of support.

This case illustrates also the ambivalence which enters into very many sibling relationships – the compound of criticism, affection and sense of obligation which characterize a social situation which is seen to be more or less viable in different phases. That the balance may tip in the direction of less rather than more contact in such circumstances is shown by a further instance. It concerned two brothers who saw very little of each other partly because each was extremely busy but partly also because of the elder's view of the younger's irresponsibility. The latter, according to his brother, was 'a nice chap, kind, perhaps too kind', who was always doing things for other people which involved him in great expenditure of time and sometimes extravagance in money. That the people concerned did not always merit the effort added to the elder brother's disquiet, which he had expressed on occasion. While their mother was alive they used to see much more of each other, but her death removed one tie. Yet despite the serious differences of opinion between them as to the way in which the younger brother led his life, the latter sent Christmas presents to his nephew and niece, and birthday presents too when he remembered, and was expected to turn to his elder brother if he ever wanted help.

How far is plurality of siblings likely to affect the quality of the relationship? Do people with only one brother or sister tend to keep up good relations with this one sibling, whereas do people with more than one show less interest, be more selective or discriminating? The question is of some theoretical interest because if a person kept up good relations with all siblings irrespective of their number, this would imply that there was something in the sibling relation itself which commanded respect and acknowledgement sufficient to overcome any forces of conflict and dispersion. The data from our study do give some answer on this point. In our 58 cases there were 45 people with only one sibling apiece, and 54 people with more than one sibling, with almost equal distribution among husbands and wives. Of those with only one sibling, two-thirds were in good relation, and only one-third in indifferent or bad relationship. But of those with more than one sibling, half were in indifferent or bad relationship with one or more. There was some tendency then, albeit only a slight one, for people to be rather more careful not to be alienated from their only brother or sister than to be in good relations with all their brothers and sisters if they had more than one. Moreover, wives maintained a distinctly better record of relationships with their siblings, whether multiple or single, than did husbands with theirs. Yet it is to be noted that husbands were in relatively better relationships with single siblings than with all their multiple siblings. There were no patterns of complementarity in sibling relations as between husband and wife; there was no evidence that if relations with wife's siblings were maintained and good those with husband's siblings were not maintained or bad. Selectivity seemed to proceed primarily on a personal, not a structural, basis.

What is noteworthy is that though relations of indifference or bad feeling seemed to prevail fairly frequently among siblings, in hardly any groups of multiple siblings (only 3 out of 50) were relations of our informants negative with all their siblings. In general, it appeared as if individuals tended to pick out one at least of their siblings for some positive social relations – and sometimes pick out another as a focus for their frustrations and aggressions.

A final example of multiple sibling relations illustrates this, and indicates once again how the patterns of early childhood are carried through into adult life.

Mrs Ghent said, 'I never really liked my brother John. I liked listening to good music. *He* liked listening to jazz or some very bad music. If I had a station on (the radio) he'd change it. We just weren't very good at living together.' John and her brother James 'didn't have a lot in common. They had completely different outlooks and interests. They used to blow up when they didn't see eye to eye over something. And they shared a room too, which was bad for their relationship.' She 'got on well with my brother James. I used to compare my boy friends with him, and they were never as nice as him. He was the nicest of them all. That's why I didn't marry for so long. He also helped me form my tastes. Perhaps that's why we're friends – but not my other brother, John.' She had a younger sister, June. 'I used to quarrel madly with her the whole time. We must have hated each other – and now we're so fond of each other.' The reason she gave for their mutual dislike as children was 'because we shared the same bedroom. I was always tidy and cherished my possessions. Her nature was the opposite – untidy and she never treasured any possessions. And she'd do things with my things too, and that was our bone of contention. My mother should have given us separate rooms (if she'd been able to). If we had to live with each other now it'd probably happen all over again.' Her sister had been the youngest child of the family, and our informant may have been jealous of her absorbing the family attention. 'In my ignorance as a child, when she wanted to be friends with my friends I was annoyed. But I was very childish. We must have been very cruel. My sister used to make eyes at my friends. She was so pretty – and I used to say "I don't want to go out with my nasty sister; I want to go out with my friends." '

With her sister the relationship improved markedly as they got older, especially when the elder sister started working and had other distractions. In time a close relationship developed between the spouses and families of Mrs Ghent and of June and James. Even though they did not see eye-to-eye on political matters, they enjoyed one another's company. With the other brother John it was different. In the early years of his marriage relations were friendly, but later a coolness developed, ostensibly over money. He let it be known that he thought his relatives only got in touch with him when they wanted money, and this rankled. On the other hand, his sister thought he should have assumed more financial and social responsibility for their aged father when he became ill, and wrote to him in these terms. So brother John ceased to visit his siblings. He did not come when they invited him for meals or family gatherings. Nor did he 'do anything' for his nephews. 'He should send presents to his nephews when it's their birthdays, but he didn't. I think it's awful.' The brother's reaction may have been exacerbated by his divorce, from a wife with whom his siblings got on well. But Mrs Ghent's attitude may have been coloured by the fact that from the other side pressure was being put upon her and her husband to take care of Mr Ghent's father. She and her husband got on well with her husband's sister but difficulty had arisen with the sister's husband, who had been suggesting that he might be relieved of the burden of his father-in-law who had been living with them for the last five years. Mrs Ghent was rather unsympathetic to this view, forgetful of the predicament she and her husband had been in over her own father. 'He suddenly feels it's enough. But of course it's his *duty*. And there's no way out. And the daughter very much likes having her father there, and this has set up stress (between husband and wife).'

This epitomizes one important aspect of the 'sibling syndrome' in many cases – that friction is focussed, if indeed it does not arise, over the question of maintenance of parents. It is not simply a matter of possible rift between spouses over the care of the parent of either; where there are siblings it is the problem of *apportionment* of responsibility between different households which may provide the bone of contention. And since looking after the home is ordinarily part of the primary role of a wife, it is the daughter rather than the son – and consequently the son-in-law rather than the daughter-in-law – who tends to be the bearer of the initial burden.

What does seem to stand out from our material is that with parents, the obligation of peculiar quality of kinship is recognized and implemented to some degree even though son or daughter may be highly critical of the parent. Only in most exceptional circumstances is it ignored. But with siblings the *critical threshold* is considerably lower. If relations with a brother or sister become strained, if neither party takes the initiative for a time, then social contact may be severely reduced or dropped altogether and no effort made to revive it. But where the relation is maintained with some degree of regularity it tends to take on the character of some intimacy. Experiences are shared, there is consultation in decision-making, and services are performed reciprocally. All this affects the patterns of social relationships within the ordinary conjugal family.

UNCLES AND AUNTS, NIECES AND NEPHEWS

So far we have been concerned in this Chapter with kin who, while outside the conjugal family circle of our adult informants, were formerly part of their natal family – their parents and their siblings. Now we examine the quality of relationship with people who at no time formed part of our informants' natal families, people of secondary relationship – the siblings of their parents and the children of their siblings.

The categorization of these kin by terms of address has been considered in Chapter 10 (pp. 312–18). It has already been indicated there that the terms 'Uncle' and 'Aunt',[10] basically applying to siblings

[10] Dictionaries confirm this usage, but also give *aunt-in-law/uncle-in-law* as sixteenth century alternatives for uncle's wife and aunt's husband. The position of honorary 'aunts' and 'uncles', not kin but friends of the family, has been discussed in Chapter 10.

of the parents, are also freely used to the spouses of these siblings, so giving four consanguines and four affines under this head. This usage is a correlate of the fact that in British custom the concept of aunt or uncle has no very specific role attached to it. In particular, no distinction of status or service is drawn between aunts and uncles on the mother's side and on the father's side. This is contrary to usage in very many non-European societies, where mother's brother and father's sister are each especially distinguished by title and role from father's brother and mother's sister, in accordance with well-defined structural principles and functions. The indefinite role character of the uncle–aunt concept in the British field is shown by the lack of special position for spouses of parent's siblings. These are either assimilated to the people to whom they are married (if an aunt gives a present, it is probably her husband who has paid for it and shared in the sentiment) or, if given a personal position, their behaviour is seen to be consonant with that of 'true' uncles and aunts. It is a question how far an 'aunt', say, is regarded as standing in a direct relation to her nephew or niece or as related to them only by her position as mother's or father's sister. Operationally, the distinction may be of some significance in lending a quality of personal 'belonging' to the aunt relation in the former case. To answer this question adequately is beyond our ability here. It would need a kind of componential analysis of non-verbal as well as verbal behaviour in material which was beyond our powers of field observation to collect. But in so far as we can give an answer from the data available it would seem that both aspects are involved – the category of 'aunt' has an autonomy beyond that of parent's sister, though this is a basic component.

But what is the appropriate behaviour of uncles and aunts in British kinship? Structurally, they are of senior generation; not members of the natal family but closely associated with parents, they imply respect without authority. Functionally, they have no clearly defined roles, but broadly imply support and friendly social contacts. A common pattern among our informants was that when they were children their uncles and aunts – or some of them – gave birthday and Christmas presents, and provided a home to stay during holidays. Such early contacts also often established a basis for subsequent relations with cousins – though sometimes too much propinquity when young led to later aversion.

Aunts and uncles may act as quasi-parents, or parent substitutes, especially on the death of parents. Mrs Garson used to see her mother's brother and his wife several times a year and send them Christmas and birthday cards and presents. When she was small she was often sent to spend weekends in their country home. As she grew older she lost interest, but with the death of her parents contact was re-established. 'I suppose because then one can do it on one's own and they do not invite you because of your mother or father.' This mother's brother and his wife (he was one of three brothers) made a special effort to keep in touch with her and her siblings after their parents died, even though their nephews and nieces were now grown up. They offered to marry off our informant from their house but she decided to have a small wedding instead. Later, she did not assume responsibility for them since they were in a good economic position and were in any case looked after by the wife's nephew. But she visited them a great deal and was quite fond of them. Mrs Maskell kept in close touch with her father's sister, telephoning her weekly or corresponding with her. 'I do write to her if I'm away – the only one except my mother.' She sent her aunt Christmas presents and very much enjoyed visiting her, saying, 'I have to look after her because she's very old. I feel rather bad when I don't see her because she lives alone.' She said that the aunt was 'a very important Mummy-figure to a vast quantity of people'.

Part of the attraction which some aunts and uncles seem to have had seems to be due to their relative neutralism. They are close enough to parents to be interested in the family affairs, yet detached enough to be a useful resort for complaint or advice. The rather vague 'avuncular' role of convention (there is no corresponding *amital* role) probably owes much to this structural position.

But a marked feature of the relation with parents' siblings is the range of variation that occurs. The role of aunt or uncle is not only relatively undefined; it is also an optional, not an obligatory, one. It is left very much to the discretion of the relative concerned as to how it shall be played. There is a stereotype of 'aunt' or 'uncle' but by no means every aunt or uncle conforms to it.

So, of Mr Mitchie's two mother's sisters one, living in New York, had always been a very conscientious aunt, sending presents to her nephew until he grew up, and then to his daughters until she retired and could no longer afford it. Christmas cards and occasional visits continued to be exchanged. But with the other mother's sister there was no contact at all. She lived in Canada, but didn't get on with her sister, so there was no correspondence between them or between her and her nephew. Mrs Lander had a mother's brother and a mother's sister, with neither of whom was there any contact, and three father's brothers and two father's sisters, with only two of whom was there any regular contact. Distance had grown between uncles and aunts, and niece, ever since our informant had changed her religion on her marriage (see Chapter 11, p. 362). One father's sister was visited whenever our informant went north and was written to on holidays, but there was an element of 'should' in these visits. The other had not been seen for some time, after she sent an indiscreet letter which made her niece very angry. With two of the father's brothers relations had not been close for some years. The other father's brother was visited whenever the niece went up north to see her parents. A bachelor, he lived in a guesthouse, and his niece looked on him with great affection. He was the only person of whom she said without qualification that she went to see him because she liked him. He had been the only member of her family to come to her wedding 'at great cost', in the face of much family opposition, because he wished to show his support for her. He thought that the family quarrel was silly, and that some member of the bride's family should be present. In this case, a personal decision on the part of the junior relative had been the precipitating element in tending to crystallize social relations into patterns of a tenuous or a relatively strong kind.

Analogous decisions had been taken by some of our informants who had obtained divorces, and shocked their uncles and aunts thereby. Mrs Pillerth saw her mother's brother and his wife 'as little as possible', even though they lived near her mother south of London. When she was a little girl she had spent some months with them while her parents were moving around the country, and had been very miserable, because her uncle and aunt were so strict. She had disliked them ever since, and they were appalled when our informant divorced her first husband – 'they never really got over it' and regarded her as a black sheep. Yet here the norms of politeness were observed whenever they met, and Christmas cards were exchanged as if relations were quite amiable. Personal temperaments were clearly responsible for much of the social distance, since relations with a father's sister continued to be very close and our informant regarded this aunt's house as her 'second home'.

Sanctions involved in the maintenance of such social relations seem to be relatively weak, depending partly upon the relations between the siblings of the upper generation and partly upon the development of the interests of the younger generation. Mr Forsyth explained that he saw one of his mother's sisters about once a year; his mother tended to ask him round when she knew her sister was coming to see her. This man sometimes telephoned his aunt if he had heard from his mother that she had been ill. He remarked 'we have nothing in common. Their interests are narrow and few. They are not the type to smoke or drink gin and tonic – they would be embarrassed at parties. They never go out in the evening.' With his mother's other sister there was no contact, probably owing to his laziness. 'I have no interest in keeping contact. We have our own circle of friends, and they don't fit into it. I have not much respect for them. They make no attempt to contact me.'

The direction of development of personal interests is evidently a very important element in the quality of relationship between uncle/aunt and nephew/niece. A section of dialogue between Mr and Mrs Waverley illustrates this. The wife commented on the fact that her husband's brother, while having little time for his cousins, did allow the occasional aunt into his house.

Husband: Oh! How awful! You can have them in when I'm not here.

Wife: They're your aunts. Mine in fact come uninvited. Zoe (her father's sister) just arrives on the damn doorstep.

H: You're more soft-hearted than I am; not that we dislike them. But in principle they have to prove themselves to have a special claim, before we are friendly. . . . The aunts resent it very much, that we don't invite them over.

W: There's rivalry, because there are so many of them. Only one of them comes, the others want to come, and then you spend your whole time seeing them.

H: It's ludicrous to spend time this way. Every time we see them, there's more sorrow than reproach. Harriet is very fond of me.

W: Mary likes me. But we've outgrown them. We've changed and some of them haven't.

H: The thing is, that they'd make demands, and because of their different concept of the family, seeing them would involve demands that we're not prepared to meet.

W: I've got five aunts that I'd quite like to see.

H: I've got four. It would take most of our time, just to see them. It's a quantitative problem.

This last point is quite a serious one, of more general structural importance. Most people seem to have a personal concept of a limited time and energy supply, with only a fraction of it available for 'seeing' relatives. With parents it is relatively simple; there can only be four at the most for both spouses. But the multiple character of parents' siblings – nine aunts alone in the case just cited – can be a real deterrent to the maintenance of kin relations of any great intimacy with all. Hence there is a noticeable tendency to selectivity, on the basis of geographical nearness, early experiences, temperamental compatibility or lack of distractions (as when uncle or aunt is unmarried). As with other types of kin, relations with an aunt or an uncle might depend upon attitudes towards this person's spouse.

Noticeable also is that despite the negative factors operating against the recognition of aunts and uncles as part of the social universe, there are many instances of social relations maintained out of loyalty to parents, sense of obligation for past services, sympathy for the growing helplessness of the ageing, as qualifying elements to the recognition of kinship as such. We have various instances of care for aged aunts in return for their earlier care of a household when a mother had died or was away. In several of these there was no particular affection for the aunt. Said Mrs Danby, 'she was a difficult person to know, which made it not very easy to be affectionate towards her – but she looked after me very well and I kept up with her, visiting her and writing to her, till there was no point' (when the aunt, in a mental home, had got beyond the stage of recognition of her niece). Services of considerable variety may be performed in this field. One woman saw her mother's sister, a cripple, twice a year, with occasional telephone calls in between. Among the services done our informant tended the grave of her aunt's husband, keeping it free from weeds.

In the sphere of parents' siblings, are aunts more important than uncles? Some of our informants thought so. Mr Waverley commented that he and his wife were agreed on this: 'It's all the women who count; the men are dim figures.' This was partly a reflection of the fact that those women belonged to a generation who did not go out to work, and so had more time for relatives. In general: 'I suppose aunts do tend to take more of a role; the men wouldn't try and force the issue.' With a dozen aunts and uncles of various types between him and his wife, he had plenty of basis for judgment. Broadly speaking, our own material on contact between all our informants and their parents' siblings tends to bear out this view (see Chapter 7, pp. 201–2). Contributory to this situation was probably the greater preoccupation of the aunts with domestic affairs than the uncles, involving greater contact of nephew or niece with aunt than with uncle in early years. Linked with this is the more marked role of aunts than of uncles in initiating and managing ceremonial occasions demanding preparation of food, such as birthday parties, Christmas and New Year parties or family gatherings in general. The acknowledged leadership of wife and mother as prime controller of the commissariat tends to give her the foremost place in the arrangements of children who attend such parties as nephews and nieces, and such early attitudes often persist. Linked further with the more domestic role of women is the tendency for an aunt to act as source of knowledge about kin and mobilizer of kin on periodic occasions. Both of these are functions performed more by women than by men in general, hence more by aunts than by uncles.

We have been concerned primarily in this section with the relations between our informants and their parents' siblings, i.e. with kinship relations between adults. But much the same range of variation seems to have occurred in the relations with our informants as aunts and uncles towards their own nephews and nieces. In many cases the informant declared a fondness for a brother's or sister's child, sent presents for Christmas and birthday, provided hospitality for holidays and sent invitations to social gatherings. When nephew or niece was adolescent or young and unmarried, as a student or starting a job away from home, the aunt in particular performed various helping services and assumed some responsibility. Mrs Nedd, for instance, had a brother's daughter from Scotland staying with her for a week, showed her round London and took her to a theatre one evening. She complained that relatives were always coming and that she had so much to do, but seemed nevertheless to enjoy her niece's company. She also had a sister's daughter working in London, on whom she kept an eye, as the girl was young and unprotected. She telephoned her niece every few days and had her over to a meal about once a week.

Yet such initiative on the part of our informants seemed to be regarded as voluntary, with no very strong sense of obligation. To a considerable extent relations with nephews and nieces were an extension of those with brothers and sisters. Many of our informant's siblings, like themselves, had growing children who tended to be seen when, and only when, visits took place between the parents. At this stage, relations tended often to become generalized, that is, the children were treated as a set, without very much individual differentiation. Various of our informants confessed that they 'had rather given up birthdays' of their nephews and nieces – ceased to send cards and presents, and ceased also often to remember the dates, thus removing one of the major identifying symbols for children. Such dissolution of personal contact, often owing to sheer numbers of kin at the particular grade (see Chapter 11, p. 391), is clearly an important factor in the general process of loosening of kin ties in the extra-familial sphere.

But selectivity could be seen to operate here as in other kinship fields. Illustrative of this is Mr Potts's case. He had four married sisters and two married brothers. The sisters were very much older than he, and relations between them were fairly distant (cf. Chapter 11, p. 376); their children, married in their turn, were nearer the age of our informant, and contact with them was therefore more informal. But it was still mostly sparse. Several were seen only on family occasions, and no Christmas cards were sent to them. One niece, however, who used to visit her uncle and his wife before her marriage, was much liked and was sent a Christmas card; she was one of the few relatives they wished to see more often. One brother had married twice. His first wife had asked for a divorce in order to be free to marry someone else; the family disapproved of this and all contact with her was cut off. Since the children of the first marriage remained with her, our informant had lost all touch with these nephews and nieces, though he had been godfather to one who still remained in London. With the children of the second marriage contact was maintained. In effect then a process of filtration had taken place which eliminated from the effective kin field the larger number of nephews and nieces.

RELATIONS WITH COUSINS

Structurally considered, relations with cousins are of a different order from those with siblings because they are of tertiary, not primary, connection. Cousins may be regarded as close kin, but their closeness is not regarded as a legal impediment to marriage. (Note the case in our sample in which our informants, husband and wife, were first cousins; with their respective sister and brother also married to each other, p. 371). Relations with cousins of the same generation may obviously have something of the quality of those with siblings; a number of our informants specifically said that they regarded a particular cousin 'as close as a sister to me', 'as close or closer than brother or sister'. It might even be postulated that the attraction of a cousin as a marriage partner owes something to the notion of being able lawfully to convert a sibling into a spouse. The well-known prejudice against the marriage of first cousins would seem to be based sociologically upon an unformulated objection to such confusion of roles – with the idea of harm to the children of such a marriage as a rationalization.

Social relations with cousins in our North London sample operated over a wide spectrum. Some of our informants professed themselves to be very fond of their cousins and bore this out by constant visiting and many services. Others said they felt they ought to see their cousins, but in fact managed to pass the greater part of their lives under this moral burden without much apparent strain. Others still never met their cousins 'unless they could not avoid it', and others simply had no contact at all nor any wish for it. To some extent a differentiation could be made between families which took an interest in relatives outside the household circle, and those which did not – kin-loving and anti-kin families. Such a differentiation could be related in particular to the character of early experiences in childhood.

But in fact very few families displayed such a wholesale acceptance or rejection of their cousins. Most showed discrimination between individual cousins on the basis of propinquity, compatibility of temperament and interests, response to the wishes of parents, aunts or uncles. Mrs Outram had a mother's sister to whom she sent a regular Christmas card and whom she telephoned occasionally. She said she was just too lazy to do more. 'I am always meaning to write to her but I never really get around to it.' This aunt had three daughters and a son. The Outrams went to the son's wedding some years before, but had almost no contact with him afterwards. One daughter was divorced and lived in East Africa. Our informant did not like her cousin and had no contact with her. To another daughter she sent a regular Christmas card and said she would see more of her cousin if she lived closer to London; but they had no other contact. The third daughter was our informant's favourite cousin and they corresponded frequently. She too had been divorced, but this had not affected the relationship. Our informant would have liked to see much more of this cousin. 'She is an interesting person – most of my relatives are such dull middle-class people.'

Analogous situations occurred among quite a number of our informants. One had close friendship with a MBS, whereas a FBS and FBD were 'an awful lot'. They had a small business in South London, and tastes and interests very far apart from those of their cousins. A MBS was distinguished as 'nasty Arthur' from 'nice Arthur', a MBDS. Whereas a MBD was met only when it was unavoidable but was sent a 'civil' Christmas card, with a FZD relations were strong and friendly; they exchanged Christmas cards but not presents, having a 'non-aggression pact' in that respect. But when another MBD was reported to our interviewer, the husband said, 'I've never heard of her', to which the wife replied, 'Why should you?'.

Cousinship is often important to children and adolescents. It provides playmates if they live near and built-in occasions for sociability. Older cousins may act as godmothers for younger cousins, responsibility may be assumed when they are away from home. Another use of cousinship is to provide a channel for communication and for entry into another society. We have in our records a number of cases of kinship ties re-activated on the basis of cousinship when people came to London from overseas. Cousins again are commonly regarded as appropriate for invitation to large family gatherings such as weddings, and their presence at family funerals is also treated as normal. Here too there is much variation in behaviour. But the tie of cousinship, while not regarded as being significant enough to demand regular contact, is held to have some weight when it comes to family celebrations or crises of life.

We have mentioned already that some cousins of one's own generation may serve as quasi-siblings, especially if a person has no brothers or sisters, or these show very great disparity in age. The significance of this generation factor was illustrated by an informant who had no siblings nor first cousins on her father's side. She said, 'I didn't know any young relatives, only old ones. This worried me as a child. I thought they'd all die and I'd be left alone.' An illustration of the way in which a cousin might be equivalent to a sibling was given by a woman who described her family as being reasonably close, saying that her sister could be called on in an emergency and that in time of trouble there would always be someone there. 'If the house burned down any one of my cousins would take the children', and she would do the same for them. There was nothing tangible in this arrangement, but it gave a sense of security which she felt was important and should be communicated to children.

In many cases persistence of social relations with cousins in adult life seems to have been dependent primarily on kin contacts in childhood, and some of our informants specifically stated this as their view. One, for instance, said that she used to see a great deal of her mother's sisters, especially during holidays, and thought this was one reason why she kept in close contact with their daughters in recent years. Contrarywise, another informant said her parents' lack of contact with their relatives in turn affected her contact with them. As a consequence, she had not met her maternal second cousins.

People who do not maintain any relationship with a close cousin may feel it incumbent upon them to defend or explain away their behaviour. One of our informants, saying there was no contact with the daughter of her mother's brother, added 'even though she is a first cousin'. Another said of her husband's FBS and his wife, 'We don't see them in years', adding that this was because when her husband and his cousin were young they were trained in the same business. Then her husband started a business of his own and this created jealousy and 'quite a lot of feeling' in the cousin. Hence, they were now seen only if somebody dies.

As with all other relationships, the attitude of the spouse tends to affect relationships with cousins. In practically all cases spouses pool their cousins in the sense that social contact with them is regarded as a joint affair. Rarely does one spouse maintain regular contact with a cousin whom the other spouse never sees. This can have its repercussions within the domestic field. Even where relations are most amiable, one spouse may jokingly express a mild critical attitude, as illustrated by Mr Herbert, who remarked good-humouredly, when his wife was describing how one of her own cousins of a junior generation had spent the winter with them: 'I am just a hotel keeper to my wife's cousins.'

The general patterns of relationships with cousins can be best illustrated by considering attitudes of our informants to their living first cousins. Social relations with them can be differentiated in terms of: *intensive*, close, with regular contact; *moderate*, with occasional visiting; *rare*, with casual occasional visits; no ordinary contact, meeting only on *family occasions*; no ordinary contact, relations maintained by Christmas cards or New Year cards, infrequent *correspondence* and news through other kin; *no contact* whatsoever. If the total living first cousins of the 58 sample households referred to earlier be arranged by reference to spouse, sex and mother's or father's side, the following Table results.

TABLE 36

Attitudes to first cousins

	Intensive	*Moderate*	*Rare*	*Family occ. only*	*Corresp. etc. only*	*No contact*	*Total*
Wife's	19	34	54	52	39	134	332
Husband's	3	38	75	43	14	102	275
Female 1st C	16	42	70	52	29	102	311
Male 1st C	6	30	59	43	24	134	296
Mother's side	11	44	74	52	36	116	333
Father's side	11	28	55	43	17	120	274
Totals	22	72	129	95	53	236	607
	15%			45%		40%	

Out of approximately 600 living first cousins of all kinds of both spouses then, there was rather more intensity of contact on the wife's side than on the husband's, with female rather than with male, and on the mother's rather than on the father's side. But the differences were not to any very marked extent since all the cousins in regular or moderate contact only amounted to about 15 per cent of the whole. In the English system there is no discrimination in term between cousins of different sex (compare the French *cousin*, *cousine*), nor between cousins on the mother's and on the father's side. We did not find in our sample any significant difference in behaviour towards cousins on mother's or father's side as such. If, however, separation is made throughout in terms of male/female, then out of 80 wife's female first cousins on the mother's side 17 were in regular or moderate social relations as compared with only 7 husband's male first cousins out of 53 on the father's side – i.e. 21 per cent as compared with 13 per cent.

GENERAL OBSERVATIONS

The quality of kin relations can be characterized in affective terms as being relatively close or distant. But in more empirically observable terms a distinction can be drawn between various types of social contact. There may be purely geographical contact, 'seeing' kin literally, or as the vivid colloquial expression has it, 'running across them'. There may be contact through the requirements of economic organization, as when relatives meet over the business concerns of, say, a family firm. Formal family gatherings of christenings, birthday parties and weddings provide occasions for many contacts which otherwise might not occur. Here the occasion is set by external circumstances, but with a strong element of voluntary kind in the gathering. Of different type are the crisis gatherings where the occasion is set involuntarily by the illness or death of a relative. Here the emphasis is not upon the obligation to invite so much as upon the obligation to appear or at least to communicate with the kin concerned. 'Seeing' in the social sense of visiting is apt to be an index of some affective relationship, or at least of the acknowledgement of social obligation towards the relative concerned, since the occasion is voluntary by one or both parties. Correspondence ranging from the Christmas or other greeting card to the letter may have a dual function. It may be regarded as the only means of maintaining social contact with people who are geographically too separated to be personally seen. On the other hand, it is often treated as a substitute for social contact of a more intimate kind. The interpretation of kinship obligation requires the maintenance of some contact, but the norms of the society provide contact by letter or still more by greetings card as an acceptable substitute for more personal approaches.

In drawing out the quality of kin relationships from the material given here, a number of points seem clear.

1 *Conventional stereotypes* of kin relationship are *inadequate* to characterize what actually happens. Affection for the mother, respect for the father, intimacy with brother or sister certainly occur. But lack of these qualities in relations with such kin is also observable, and freely discussed.

2 Many of the relationships with kin indicate an *ambivalence* of quite an overt kind. People can be fond of their kin, yet feel they are a drag upon freedom of action. People may not particularly like their kin, yet feel a strong sense of obligation towards them. One of our informants said: 'Relatives are the only people you can dislike but

still be on good terms with' – a symptomatic if not wholly accurate statement.

3 Attitudes and behaviour towards kin show a high degree of *selectivity*. There is very little category behaviour, that is, treating all members of the same category alike. Relations with one cousin may be very close, with another very distant; even one brother or sister may be ignored, never visited or written to, while with another communication may be warm and frequent.

4 This selectivity is often associated with a notion that there is a kind of *finite reservoir of time and energy* available for social relations, and therefore some selection is necessary on personal grounds between kin for maintenance of contact.

5 In all these relations with kin a great deal of importance is attached to what may be called *petty services*. Massive services such as gifts or loans of money, or major contributions of time and labour involved in looking after houses and children for long periods do occur. But on the whole it is the visiting, the running out in the car, the shopping, the Christmas card and the letter which bulk very large in the mental ledger of services which nearly every person seems to keep as a measure of specific kin relations.

6 Behind a great deal of the quality of kin interaction lie concepts of *relative status* – a judgment of the self as being up-graded or down-graded by what is said and done by others. A feature of kin relations is that they seem to show very great sensitivity in this sphere – as if we can take from the strangers opinions and acts which those already connected to us by a permanent tie cannot be allowed to demonstrate unchallenged.

13

General Aspects

In this Chapter we summarize our main findings from this enquiry into the kinship of middle-class families in North London, and offer some additional comments on general questions.

STRUCTURAL FEATURES

From the data we have assembled and analysed the main structural features of one sector of English middle-class kinship are clear.

To begin with, it is evident that we can properly speak of the kinship of such people as a *system*. Behaviour towards people recognized as 'relatives' is not random; it tends to follow prescribed conventions, to be repetitive and to form part of articulated series of relationships in which ties with any one kinsman are affected by those with other kin.

To anthropologists, this English kinship system is structurally of a relatively simple character. It is of shallow genealogical depth and relatively close lateral boundaries. Few people trace back further than their grandparents or further out than their second cousins. The system is one in which consanguines are fairly well individualized. In formal terms, parents are uniquely separated, sibling terms are confined to members of the natal family, and grandparental terms apply only to the two pairs of parents of a person's mother and father. Category terms exist, e.g. 'uncle', 'aunt', 'cousin', but here too there is a distinct tendency to individualize them in application by combining them with the personal name for superior generations. (For kin of the same or inferior generation, such as most cousins, nephews or nieces, personal names are always used in address.) Since preferential mating is lacking, and marriage is very rarely with someone already a kinsman, affinal and consanguineal conceptions are fairly sharply differentiated. Yet partly because their origin is so different, affines can be assimilated in basic terminology to the existing set of consanguines. Instead of a fresh set of terms to designate or differentiate them (as in many other societies) they are semi-identified as 'father', 'mother', 'brother', 'sister', 'son', 'daughter', with the suffixed 'in-law' to indicate their special status. The custom of use of personal name for addressing people of equivalent or inferior kinship grade avoids difficulty with affines of sibling or child grade. But the ambiguity in the position of parental affines is seen in the range of variation of terms for addressing them, and the uneasy situation in which many people find themselves when confronted with the possibility of calling them by parental names. What stands out in this English system is the tendency all the way through to specify persons individually, not give them a category term. Many societies seem to categorize kin and even to assimilate non-kin as quickly as possible into the kin-category scheme. They rarely use personal names even to children. All old men are 'grandfather'; all middle-aged men are 'father' or 'uncle' or 'father-in-law' . . . and so on. The middle-class English system can only do this in an informal context. In any formal context relatives must be properly pinpointed as individuals, with category label carefully qualified to bring out the personal aspect. In this sense the English kinship system can be called a *specifying system* as against the *categorizing systems* of many other, especially non-industrial, societies. But its specification is of individual persons, not statuses and roles. There is not, for example, the distinction as occurs in many systems between siblings on the ground of their relative seniority and relative authority; all are brothers or sisters with no overt indication of birth order.

STANDARDS OF CONDUCT BUT LACK OF RULES

The structural simplicity of this kinship system allows for a great deal of variation in content. Genealogical knowledge and the counting of kin differ greatly among different people, not only due to demographic and generational factors (e.g. single child in a family, bachelorhood or spinsterhood, old age) but also to factors of social discrimination on family and personal grounds.

On the ideological plane, there is in general a decided sentiment about the basic significance of consanguineal kinship bonds, and some generalized, fairly standardized canons of responsibility towards kin. But there is no very precise set of rules for social behaviour in putting these notions of responsibility into effect, and the application of them in practice tends to be very restricted, often to members of a person's natal family. For parents, certain legal prescriptions exist about the feeding and care, discipline and education of their children. For children, when adult, there are certain normal social expectations which for the most part do not exist in legal form, about what they will do for their parents if the latter are in want or ill. The pressures of society also tend to be felt by siblings if a brother or sister is in similar distressed circumstances. But apart from certain legal specifications regarding 'next of kin', the great body of extra-familial kin are free from any general social formulations about expected behaviour to relatives. There are norms of respect or familiarity for kin who are of senior, of equivalent or of junior grade, but these are not formalized to any high degree; nor are they associated with any firm code of privilege and obligation. The statuses and roles associated with different kinship positions are of a rather indefinite order.[1] Neither the type of kin who should or need not be helped, nor the nature of the things to be done for those kin who are recognized to require services are laid down. Again, there is no general agreement even as to how far the rules that exist in minimal form shall be carried out – the degree of sacrifice that ought to be made in order to do what is right and proper. Moreover, where social expectations exist, they are backed by no particular sanctions. In modern urban conditions of an industrialized society, especially in a metropolis, ignorance of the social milieu of one's friends and neighbours is such that it is practically impossible to check whether or not they are carrying out even such minimal rules of behaviour towards the kin they recognize.

Now the lack of clear-cut rules of obligation and behaviour towards kin, and particularly of any specification of when and where the somewhat vague series of social expectations do not apply, is liable to create difficulties of choice and decision. There are choices of a direct kind – whether or not to assume responsibility for a relative in poverty or other distress, having regard to one's own resources of time, finance, house-room, etc. There are also choices of a more indirect, perhaps more subtle, kind – how far an offer to lend a helping hand may offend or injure the individuality of the relative concerned, and allow him or her to lapse from an invigorating struggle and personal focus of energies; how far help to one relative may offend another and disturb a delicate balance of social forces. These are not merely choices in the field of expediency – they may have a moral connotation as well, and the attempt to arrive at a decision on grounds of what it is right to do may present a very difficult problem. As McGregor and others have pointed out, kinship is not a structural feature of modern British society. But in the very fact that it is not lies precisely a considerable difficulty. Obligations and responsibilities have to be assessed in the light of personal judgment, not formal

[1] This was pointed out by W. H. R. Rivers, *Kinship and Social Organization*, 1914, London, p. 13 (reprinted London School of Economics Monographs on Social Anthropology, No. 34, 1968, p. 46).

rule. Claims are made, expectations are presented, duties conceived, with no clear guide for their resolution in action. Much of the peculiar quality of kinship lies in this.

The middle-class English kinship system is then a *permissive*, not an *authoritarian* system. The relative lack of role categorization and formal obligation also means that the system is on the whole a selective one. People have a range of kin available to them, but the decision to implement these relationships is primarily a matter of mutual adjustment on the basis of personal selection. Taken into consideration are such factors as temperamental compatibility, feeling of moral obligation, deference to the views of other kin, geographical accessibility.

KIN CONTACTS AND FLOW OF SERVICES

Yet it is important to note that although no firm ideology exists in regard to obligations to different categories of kin, and there is no consistent attempt to instruct children about their kinship relations in any systematic way, there is on the part of most people considerable knowledge of the existence of distant relatives and a desire to maintain connection with at least some of them. Information gained about kin in early life does not seem to be lost even if the informant is not consciously interested in 'his family'. Childhood playmates may be forgotten, but kin whom one has known in childhood are usually remembered. Moreover, not only is there memory of kin, there is contact with kin. Not one of the people in our study was without some social relations with kin. This is facilitated by the fact that relations with kin tend to be multi-stranded. Although kin may be lost to sight for years, a family crisis such as the death of an elderly member may reactivate the acquaintance. The kinsman is not just part of the world of one's childhood; he belongs to the world in which one has grown up. So, contact with many kinsmen is retained because of its multiple associations, not because of any conscious attempt to maintain it. Our informants often expressed surprise when confronted with their genealogies, drawn up after repeated interviews; they did not imagine they could have remembered so much.

Such knowledge may be utilized in many ways. We have shown the variety of ways in which people implemented their knowledge of their kin. Most people assumed some responsibilities for members of their natal families, and many did this also for extra-familial kin. Much material has already been given to show the range, quality and frequency of services involved, and considerable expenditure of time, energy and resources upon the affairs of kin. The planning of relations with kin occupies a considerable sector of people's activity. In a high proportion of the households we studied, influences on behaviour and roles in decision-making were not restricted in the kin field to the elementary family.

In a relatively abstract sense kinship is a structure. But it is also a flow. It is not simply a flow of women in marriage, as Lévi-Strauss seems sometimes to imply in his more concentrated phases of analysis. It is not even a flow of exchange of goods and services in any strict accounting 'transactional' fashion. The notion of generalized or diffuse reciprocity does apply to a considerable amount of kin relations. But it fails to take account of the fact that some kin services rest primarily upon the basis of response to obligation without anything comparable being involved in return then or later. A flow of not very well defined social actions – interest, support, participation, advice – characterizes relations between kin in our field of study. Just being there at a wedding or a funeral is a form of social service to the major participants – the wedding breakfast or the funeral luncheon are not conceived of as any direct return for this. Even less positive action may be significant – just listening to complaints about husband or child or sibling may be a very important form of personal support. (The same is true of non-kin, but with relatives such service is apt to be treated more as a right.)

In this field marriage is very important, not especially because it involves a transfer of women – one might regard the transfer of men as equally significant in some cases – but because it attracts kin. The affines that a person acquires through marriage may have a very distinct influence upon his social behaviour whether he wishes this or not. Even the consanguines of affines (or the affines of consanguines), who form a kind of outer circle and for the most part are ignored, can be mobilized or can erupt on to the family scene of action. In some cases a block of these affines may form the person's most intimate kin.

Looked at from the point of view of social development of an individual, kinship can be seen from our material to vary in significance at different periods of life. When very young a child seems to regard all adults as kin – or rather to form part of an undifferentiated category of persons related to the parents; in later childhood separation occurs and some are specifically identified as grandparents, uncles and aunts. As a young person gets to maturity he or she may often use kin for more definite services, such as giving a lodging away from home, or help in finding a job. Kin may also help in introducing the young person into a wider social universe – though from our evidence they take little or no part in opening up a marriage market. At this period, although physical contact may be maintained and some services provided by kin, intellectually and emotionally kin may count for little in the lives of young people. When they marry, the situation often changes fairly radically. Wedding itself may bring around them more closely many kin with whom their contacts have so far been fairly remote. And in particular they are brought into inescapable relationship with an entirely new set of people – the kin of the spouse. If the impact of affines is unsought at the outset of marriage, when children are born their parents often are led to implement and even revive kin ties. Interest of kin in the children, and desire to provide a known social milieu for the children may lead to a re-shaping of domestic and extra-familial patterns of behaviour. Some people indeed, either on behalf of their children or in pursuit of their own power interests, may seek to exploit the potentialities of extra-familial kin ties to such a degree that they become in effect 'kin imperialists'.

With advancing age, parents see a tendency to recapitulation of their own experience in the social relations of their children, and endeavour to fortify this, or alternatively to modify kin relations in reaction from what they recollect or imagine themselves to have suffered. As old age advances interest in kin often tends to increase, but also often tends to become more selective. In particular, as a person reaches old age there is often a shrinking of genealogical knowledge. Grasp of the details of kin of lower generation tends to be lost and kin information and contact often become progressively imperfect, save for children or a few other close kin. In our middle-class field of study this cycle of kin relations has been very perceptible, and it is clear that it is one of the more significant cycles in the social life of the people concerned.

CONCEPTUAL FRAMEWORK

In the course of our analysis we have shown the need for a more adequate conceptual framework for the study of kinship in urban Western society, and have put forward some suggestions for this. Here is a further comment.

Studies of kinship in urban industrial society normally start from consideration of the family. Different views have been strongly asserted here. It has been stated, as by Parsons, Nimkoff or Goode that modern industrial structure favours the development of nuclear or independent families and bears against the continued existence of extended families. Industrialization and urbanization are believed to result in loss of functions of the family, and atrophy of extra-familial kin links.[2] Strong reaction has been expressed against such propositions, as by Townsend,[3] who has found it hard to accept any idea of the extended family 'giving way' to some variety of the nuclear family. But as Barić has pointed out,[4] there is no necessary contradiction between these views. If by extended family is meant a group of kin of three generations or more with a fairly well-defined corporate linear character involving co-operation in productive activities, common ownership of assets and recognized common responsibilities, such units are almost entirely absent from the modern urban industrial scene. But if, as Townsend would seem to mean, extended family in a very loose sense means those extra-familial kin who maintain a relationship of some intimacy with members of a nuclear family, then such entities do persist even in fully developed urban conditions. Yet whether or not urban kin ties may be thought to have been maintained or have weakened or declined, they certainly have changed form with greater dispersion and greater economic independence of kin.[5]

But an issue in kinship theory has tended to arise because of confusion at times between these two social forms, an extended family group and a set of extra-familial kin. If one applies the test of where authority is exercised, the difference becomes plain. In an extended family, as observed comparatively in many societies, authority is normally exercised by the head of the family who is the senior male, commonly the father or grandfather of the consanguine family members. In the set of extra-familial kin authority is dispersed, the kin in each independent nuclear family having their own responsibility for productive activities and control of assets. In this sense Parsons and those who have thought along the same lines have been correct. Except for family firms and some control of joint property, decisions in the set of extra-familial kin in a modern Western urban society are made in nuclear family units, however influenced they may be by kin ties outside. Parsons's view has sometimes been interpreted to mean that once the children in an elementary family have grown up, married and moved away a process of fragmentation sets in and ties between them and their consanguine kin soon tend to disappear. It

[2] Talcott Parsons (on the American family) in Talcott Parsons and Robert F. Bales, *Family, Socialization and Interaction Process*, Glencoe, 1955, p. 9; M. F. Nimkoff, *Comparative Family Systems*, Boston, 1965, pp. 343 et seq.; William J. Goode, *The Family*, Englewood Cliffs, N.J., 1964, p. 108.

[3] Family and Kinship in Industrial Society: A Comment by Peter Townsend. *Sociological Review Monograph*, No. 8, Keele, 1964, pp. 89 et seq.

[4] Lorraine Barić, in M. Freedman, (Ed) *Social Organization: Essays Presented to Raymond Firth*. London, 1967, pp. 2–4.

[5] Raymond Firth, Family and Kinship in Industrial Society, *Sociological Review Monograph*, No. 8, 1964, p. 87.

is true that he has emphasized the strength of the independent family of procreation at the expense of other kin ties. But that Parsons did not ignore the significance of these is indicated by the fact that he himself was one of the first to draw attention to the significance in American society of kinship outside the elementary family. He also indicated how on the sociological side family studies at that date (1943) were overwhelmingly oriented to problems of individual adjustment rather than to comparative structural perspective.[6] This said, we re-emphasize the importance for sociological thinking of attention to the set of extra-familial kin. Since work in this field began some twenty years ago sociologists and anthropologists in many countries have demonstrated the importance of such kin.[7]

Various ways can be imagined of characterizing the set of extra-familial kin of a family in English middle-class society. We have shown the inadequacy of the cliché 'extended family' as a blanket term for all kinds of kin attached to or linked with a conjugal family. They can hardly be regarded as a series of formal corporate groups – as in many societies – and the concepts of quasi-group or kin network, though useful in some respects, are not completely satisfactory. In different contexts the set of extra-familial kin can be classed with reference to size, integration, level of services among members, etc. But such classification does not easily yield any simple set of types. Only at a superficial level can one speak in this middle-class universe of such polar types as large or small families, open or closed kin groups, integrated or dispersed sets of kin. From the point of view of residence, jobs, reciprocal services, influence in decision-making, the circumstances and personality of the various members of the elementary family and their associated kin are such that a great variety of combinations of factors is possible.

There has been much debate in recent years on the issue of descent theory versus alliance theory in the interpretation of kinship.[8] Argument has been complex, often very abstract, and most of it has been concerned with segmentary kin groups and positive marriage rules –

[6] 'The Kinship System of the Contemporary United States', *Essays in Sociological Theory*, rev. edn 1954, Glencoe, Ill., pp. 177–96.

[7] One of the latest studies in Belgium, for instance, confirms their significance. Jean Rémy, 'Persistance de la famille étendue dans un milieu industriel et urbain', *Revue française de sociologie*, vol. 8, 1967, pp. 493–505.

[8] The major protagonists include Dumont, Fortes, Goody, Leach, Lévi-Strauss, Needham, Schneider. For references see e.g. David M. Schneider, 'Some Muddles in the Models', *The Relevance of Models for Social Anthropology*, A.S.A. Monographs, 1, London 1965, pp. 25–85; Robin Fox, *Kinship and Marriage*, Pelican Books, 1967, *passim*. A recent statement by Maybury-Lewis, 'The Murngin Moral', *Trans. New York Academy of Sciences*, ser. II, vol. 29, pp. 482–94, comments further on this issue.

conditions which are not applicable to the English kinship system. But a fundamental question has been involved – the extent to which any kinship system is concerned with the ordering of kin along genealogical lines, with serial procreation and internal group structure as the foci, or with the ordering of relationships between groups, with marriage as the prime mechanism of linkage.[9]

Our analysis has some relevance to this issue. From perspective of kinship in this sector of an urban industrial society it would seem that both aspects are important. Analysis of our English kinship material primarily in terms of descent group theory does not carry us very far. Consanguineal group solidarity is weak. The groups are small and shallow and on the ground do not conform to any strict unilineal principles. On the other hand, to regard the kinship system as primarily one which exists as a symbolic expression of group relations – exemplified by transactions in which *inter alia* women are moved around in marriage – would involve serious distortion. In our field there is no form of prescriptive marriage – women are not pushed around as pawns, and there are relatively few group transactions. There is ample empirical evidence of the pervasiveness of individual choice in marriage and in other situations. (The single instance in our material of quarrel over the giving of a dowry (not offered) illustrated not so much relations between two different kin groups as the exasperation of a man from a different cultural background at meeting the English lack of appreciation of the significance of dowry for marriage relations.)

In general terms, what we have found is that parent–child ties are very strong, but surprisingly without illusion. Notions of filial sentiment do operate, but not at the level of the popular emotionally sticky, undifferentiated attachment. Particularly with son or daughter, at the overt level there is apt to be a very cool rationalistic appreciation of the parent's virtues and faults and an almost clinically analytic attitude at times towards responsibility for parents. As far as sibling ties are concerned, those between sisters are markedly close, but those between brothers, or between brothers and sisters, are highly selective. In all cases there is an expectation in our middle-class circles that parental and sibling ties, while not denied, shall be subordinated to the marriage bond. When a London middle-class girl marries she expects to live in her own house or flat, and even in these days of professional women's independence, to accompany her

[9] The basic position was stated in essence many years ago by C. N. Starcke, *The Primitive Family*, London, 1889, p. 274. 'The development of the family was not merely advanced by the relations which existed between its members; it was rather the different family relations of the two parents which paved the way for this development.'

husband to his occupational area, not to remain closely associated with her parents and siblings. The 'Mum-complex' described by various writers on aspects of London society has little meaning in residential terms for our North London people.

The significance of consanguineal bonds is seen from another angle, in the great importance attached to affinal ties. There is hardly anyone in the area of our study who has not fairly regular contact with some of his or her spouse's kin – which is a demonstration of the persistence of the spouse's consanguineal ties. But the affinal relations tend to be strong and intimate with only one spouse's consanguines. There is some balancing in the household, but the kin field often is furnished predominantly by either husband or wife, and still further from the relatives of one parent of these only.

So the notion of unilineal descent as an integrative principle is replaced by that of consanguinity, and the significance of the affinal principle rests ultimately not on the idea of transactional alliance between groups but of marital alliance between individuals.

CORRELATES OF MIDDLE-CLASS KINSHIP

The question of what is specifically middle-class about the kinship patterns we have demonstrated is not easy to answer. But we can indicate some possible correlates.

The wide range of variation we have found, and the very considerable flexibility in interpretation of kinship norms is clearly to some degree a reflex of the cultural, religious and even in part ethnic difference of background over our field. Our middle-class subjects were definitely a composite set of people. But they were primarily professional in occupation, and so tended to share a common set of values about work and its standards, about training and education generally, and about the importance of individual skill, initiative and judgment. To a considerable degree their selective interest in kin tended to follow along similar lines.

Their occupational level and specialization tended to be associated with an income level which allowed them a fair degree of choice in social affairs. In their own education and that of their children especially, their command of moderate wealth, largely from earned income, allowed them a good range of choice irrespective of local residence. Geographical mobility indeed has been often part of the ethic of the professional middle-classes and even more the aristocracy, exemplified in the early sending away of boys to school. In many cases educational mobility was assisted by kin, who provided the necessary finance. Wealth counted in another way, by allowing some freedom of choice in accommodation. The size of a middle-class house commonly allowed of a 'spare room' or other accommodation for a dependent kinsman; but many of these middle-class people could afford to pay for accommodation for a widowed mother or other relative elsewhere. So kin responsibility did not need to be demonstrated in residential proximity.

But the inherited wealth of our subjects was for the most part very moderate. Where they had links with land-owning families or families rich in financial or commercial resources these links tended to be of junior membership, as children of younger sons or on the distaff side. So while they lacked the intricate network of marriages and job influence which seems to be characteristic of the more traditional upper-class circles, they also tended not to display either the kin contests for wealth and power or the sharp differentiations of primogeniture which also seem to be manifest in such circles.

Another characteristic of our middle-class families affecting their patterns of kinship behaviour was the literate intellectual quality of their culture. There was considerable variation here. But many of them had been brought up in an atmosphere of books and general discussion about social issues, and were accustomed to a somewhat self-conscious analytical attitude towards their social relationships with their kin. With the husbands for the most part in professional occupations, many of their womenfolk came also from similar families and themselves had often work of a professional nature which gave them intellectual interest outside the home. The family ethos then tended to be one of individualism and concern for personal freedom.

Their kinship system was affected by these characteristics. Their ideology of personal fulfilment meant that they tended to be highly selective in their implementation of kin ties, according to compatibilities of interest and temperament. But their articulate conceptions of morality led them to be very conscious of kin responsibility. The result was a flexible system of kin relationships, in which the habit of letter-writing served to keep them in touch with those kin, even at a far distance, with whom they wished to maintain contact. The notion of kinship was considered as elastic, not needing nearby residence nor continual operational expression to maintain it. What may be termed this middle-class kinship mode would seem to have drawn some of its character from the mode of friendship. Kin and friends were sharply differentiated in some contexts. But the structure of friendship in the middle-classes operates over time and distance – people can remain friends despite long severance in distant countries, and a local focus in friendship though often thought desirable is not deemed essential. Attitudes to kin have something of this same quality, of a bond with selected people thought to persist irrespective of geography, and maintained by periodic activity, perhaps mainly by correspondence. But while friends are an alternate resource to kin in the field of selected personal relationships, to the tie with kin is attributed a durability of a peculiar kind.

SOME OBSERVATIONS FOR APPLICATION

This study was not undertaken from any particular 'problem-oriented' point of view. We set out to chart and analyse what seemed to us to be an important and often ignored aspect of middle-class social life, not to draw any practical conclusions as to how this life can be lived better. But in so far as our account of kinship has indicated a significant dimension of much decision-taking in domestic and personal life, it is pertinent to draw attention to some of the practical implications.

A conception of kinship as a flow of social behaviour rather than a structural set of positions is of particular relevance to our understanding of social processes. It has long been clear in discussions of social issues that any consideration of the problems of individuals has to be made in the context of family circumstances. But 'family' has been generally understood to be the elementary nuclear family of parent and resident children. What has not been so clear is that in many social circumstances 'family' is understood by the people concerned to include some kin outside the domestic circle. We have demonstrated in previous Chapters how significant for individual and family contact are such extra-familial kin ties. They may be very important for the transmission of social values. They can play an important part in the developmental history of individuals. They can provide a very important recreational field, especially for holidays, where small children are involved. They can be of prime importance in periods of transition or life crises – as at the birth of a baby or in sickness. They can influence critical decisions – about migration to a new job or choice of schools for children. They can afford support or they can depress by criticism when highly personal emotional issues arise, such as choice of a marriage partner or change of religion. They can provide regular material for sociable activity and help thereby to maintain individuals in viable social relationships. Conversely, by too active interference with members of the family – or too marked withdrawal from interest – such kin may help to stimulate tension and conflict, and contribute to the social deterioration of the individuals to whom they are related.

Our material has gone to show that in the middle-class society we have been examining the significance of extra-familial kinship is expressive rather than instrumental. Although concrete assistance is of considerable importance – in helping towards choice of school or job, giving financial aid or performing small services, as for aged parents – it is primarily as a means towards fuller expression of a personality that such kinship ties are maintained. Moral obligations are recognized in this wider kin field, but they are relatively unformalized and so allow a great deal of selectivity in their fulfilment. This in turn involves some degree of uncertainty not only as to what may be legitimately claimed from kin, but also as to the extent to which such claims will be acknowledged and acted upon. This means that there is very little to put forward in the way of clearcut principles in this field which will apply to particular cases. Statistical regularities can be indicated but to understand the operation of family and kinship in any one case specific enquiry must be made.

All this is relevant to problems of social administration. It is often stressed that all social workers are increasingly aware of the significance of the family as 'an important dynamic organism' and as 'a unit of concern' in the field of social work. It is also recognized that the increasingly protective role of the State in the provision of educational, health and welfare services has tended to reduce the area in which family and kinship provision is required.[10] Studies of English working-class society have indicated that, despite this, kin outside the family have important roles to play. It might be argued that in middle-class circles greater family prosperity would make it less necessary for extra-familial kin to supplement the functions of the State. But as our study has demonstrated, middle-class families too have their areas of social relationships in which neither their own financial prosperity nor the protective intervention of the State can adequately replace the contribution given by kin. There are the problems of the aged and the sick. Now that de-hospitalization has become a recognized aim in the Health Services, the problems of home care, always considerable, are increased. No matter how efficient and widespread be the provisions of the State and of voluntary agencies in the convalescent and geriatric field,[11] there is still much room for a whole series of amorphous, miniscule services which count for so

[10] Olive Stevenson in *The Family in Modern Society* (New Barnett Paper No. 1 n.d.) (1964) pp. 57, 62; O. R. McGregor and Griselda Rowntree, 'The Family' in *Society: Problems and Methods of Study*, ed. A. T. Welford et al., London, 1962, pp. 397–428; Raymond Firth, op. cit., 1964.

[11] The significance of extra-familial kinship for an understanding of the social and economic position of the elderly has been appreciated by the organizers of the Social Survey Cross-National Survey of Older People in Great Britain a few years ago. The interview schedule included questions about 'family and relatives' both in and outside the household, and the services they performed. Reference was made *inter alia* to siblings, nieces, cousins, sisters-in-law, grandchildren.

much in the evaluation of personal comfort. Such services can be and are provided to a very considerable extent by kin. Again, much especially mental illness, is associated with adverse social factors. Miller and his colleagues wrote of the problem families they studied in Newcastle-upon-Tyne that disturbed behaviour in childhood was considerable in various forms. They found that 'Its origins were deeply rooted in the personalities of children and parents and in their ideals of family life and standards of behaviour. Only in a few cases are they seen and treated by the family doctor, many pass unrecognized.' Most families care for their children faithfully and well, but 'a considerable proportion of parents are beset with illness or instability in their personal relationships'.[12]

This was in a working-class environment and a very special case. But to a lesser degree similar observations would appear to apply to any set of families randomly chosen in this country. Even in areas quite outside the clinical range some degree of relative instability or stress in parents in a family seems to have been related in many cases to their own relationship with parent or sibling or other kin. Hence, in order to understand any social problems arising from a family situation it is advisable to study the complete kinship pattern and not simply relationships within the elementary family itself.

The relevance of such a viewpoint for work in the social services should not need to be underlined. But it is symptomatic of initiative as well as enlightened interest in such questions that, while the pioneering studies in the significance of extra-familial kinship in Western societies were made for the most part in Britain, it has been in the United States that the first full-scale enquiry into its directly practical implications has been made.[13] The results of this study showed very clearly that research on the kinship relations of clients outside the nuclear family could broaden the conceptual framework and perception of social process held by social workers, and thereby increase their capacity for diagnosis and thereaputic action. Only slowly is the perception of this growing in the British social services field.[14]

To conclude: the results of this enquiry may not seem spectacular; but they reveal aspects of our society which have not so far been

[12] F. W. Miller, S. D. M. Court, W. S. Wallen, E. G. Knox, *Growing Up in Newcastle-upon-Tyne*, O.U.P., 1960, p. 255.

[13] Hope Johnson Leichter and William E. Mitchell, op. cit. Their project was sponsored jointly by the Russell Sage Foundation and the Jewish Family Service, New York, at the request of the latter.

[14] It is expected that the enquiry on kinship and personal support in pregnancy and confinement being carried out by Jane Hubert (Mrs Jane Forge) will furnish substantial evidence to this effect.

adequately studied and which are highly significant for an understanding of much social behaviour. This book is large, but we have thought it essential to document as full as possible the range and variation in the kinship patterns we have uncovered. In the course of the study we have suggested a framework for the collection and analysis of relevant social data in this field, and have put forward a set of basic interpretations of kinship in a metropolitan middle-class context. The results apply in the first instance to British society, but they suggest a wealth of comparable situations and problems in other Western countries especially the United States, which with all its diverse cultural background, shares a common basic language. Many of the problems raised here still demand much further investigation, but we believe that this book offers a basic approach to such research.

Appendix

References to cases cited most frequently

Index

The International Library of

Sociology

and Social Reconstruction

Edited by W. J. H. SPROTT
Founded by KARL MANNHEIM

ROUTLEDGE & KEGAN PAUL
BROADWAY HOUSE, CARTER LANE, LONDON, E.C.4

CONTENTS

PRINTED IN GREAT BRITAIN BY HEADLEY BROTHERS LTD
109 KINGSWAY LONDON WC2 AND ASHFORD KENT

GENERAL SOCIOLOGY

Brown, Robert. Explanation in Social Science. *208 pp. 1963.* (*2nd Impression 1964.*) *25s.*

Gibson, Quentin. The Logic of Social Enquiry. *240 pp. 1960.* (*3rd Impression 1968.*) *24s.*

Homans, George C. Sentiments and Activities: Essays in Social Science. *336 pp. 1962. 32s.*

Isajiw, Wsevelod W. Causation and Functionalism in Sociology. *165 pp. 1968. 25s.*

Johnson, Harry M. Sociology: a Systematic Introduction. *Foreword by Robert K. Merton. 710 pp. 1961.* (*5th Impression 1968.*) *42s.*

Mannheim, Karl. Essays on Sociology and Social Psychology. *Edited by Paul Keckskemeti. With Editorial Note by Adolph Lowe. 344 pp. 1953.* (*2nd Impression 1966.*) *32s.*

Systematic Sociology: An Introduction to the Study of Society. *Edited by J. S. Erös and Professor W. A. C. Stewart. 220 pp. 1957.* (*3rd Impression 1967.*) *24s.*

Martindale, Don. The Nature and Types of Sociological Theory. *292 pp. 1961.* (*3rd Impression 1967.*) *35s.*

Maus, Heinz. A Short History of Sociology. *234 pp. 1962.* (*2nd Impression 1965.*) *28s.*

Myrdal, Gunnar. Value in Social Theory: A Collection of Essays on Methodology. *Edited by Paul Streeten. 332 pp. 1958.* (*3rd Impression 1968.*) *35s.*

Ogburn, William F., and **Nimkoff, Meyer F.** A Handbook of Sociology. *Preface by Karl Mannheim. 656 pp. 46 figures. 35 tables. 5th edition* (*revised*) *1964. 45s.*

Parsons, Talcott, and **Smelser, Neil J.** Economy and Society: A Study in the Integration of Economic and Social Theory. *362 pp. 1956.* (*4th Impression 1967.*) *35s.*

Rex, John. Key Problems of Sociological Theory. *220 pp. 1961.* (*4th Impression 1968.*) *25s.*

Stark, Werner. The Fundamental Forms of Social Thought. *280 pp. 1962. 32s.*

FOREIGN CLASSICS OF SOCIOLOGY

Durkheim, Emile. Suicide. A Study in Sociology. *Edited and with an Introduction by George Simpson. 404 pp. 1952.* (*4th Impression 1968.*) *35s.*

Professional Ethics and Civic Morals. *Translated by Cornelia Brookfield. 288 pp. 1957. 30s.*

Gerth, H. H., and **Mills, C. Wright.** From Max Weber: Essays in Sociology. *502 pp. 1948.* (*6th Impression 1967.*) *35s.*

Tönnies, Ferdinand. Community and Association. (*Gemeinschaft und Gesellschaft.*) *Translated and Supplemented by Charles P. Loomis. Foreword by Pitirim A. Sorokin. 334 pp. 1955. 28s.*

SOCIAL STRUCTURE

Andreski, Stanislav. Military Organization and Society. *Foreword by Professor A. R. Radcliffe-Brown. 226 pp. 1 folder. 1954. Revised Edition 1968. 35s.*

Cole, G. D. H. Studies in Class Structure. *220 pp. 1955. (3rd Impression 1964.) 21s. Paper 10s. 6d.*

Coontz, Sydney H. Population Theories and the Economic Interpretation. *202 pp. 1957. (3rd Impression 1968.) 28s.*

Coser, Lewis. The Functions of Social Conflict. *204 pp. 1956. (3rd Impression 1968.) 25s.*

Dickie-Clark, H. F. Marginal Situation: A Sociological Study of a Coloured Group. *240 pp. 11 tables. 1966. 40s.*

Glass, D. V. (Ed.). Social Mobility in Britain. *Contributions by J. Berent, T. Bottomore, R. C. Chambers, J. Floud, D. V. Glass, J. R. Hall, H. T. Himmelweit, R. K. Kelsall, F. M. Martin, C. A. Moser, R. Mukherjee, and W. Ziegel. 420 pp. 1954. (4th Impression 1967.) 45s.*

Jones, Garth N. Planned Organizational Change: An Exploratory Study Using an Empirical Approach. *About 268 pp. 1969. 40s.*

Kelsall, R. K. Higher Civil Servants in Britain: From 1870 to the Present Day. *268 pp. 31 tables. 1955. (2nd Impression 1966.) 25s.*

König, René. The Community. *232 pp. Illustrated. 1968. 35s.*

Lawton, Denis. Social Class, Language and Education. *192 pp. 1968. (2nd Impression 1968.) 25s.*

McLeish, John. The Theory of Social Change: Four Views Considered. *About 128 pp. 1969. 21s.*

Marsh, David C. The Changing Social Structure in England and Wales, 1871-1961. *1958. 272 pp. 2nd edition (revised) 1966. (2nd Impression 1967.) 35s.*

Mouzelis, Nicos. Organization and Bureaucracy. An Analysis of Modern Theories. *240 pp. 1967. (2nd Impression 1968.) 28s.*

Ossowski, Stanislaw. Class Structure in the Social Consciousness. *210 pp. 1963. (2nd Impression 1967.) 25s.*

SOCIOLOGY AND POLITICS

Barbu, Zevedei. Democracy and Dictatorship: Their Psychology and Patterns of Life. *300 pp. 1956. 28s.*

Crick, Bernard. The American Science of Politics: Its Origins and Conditions. *284 pp. 1959. 32s.*

Hertz, Frederick. Nationality in History and Politics: A Psychology and Sociology of National Sentiment and Nationalism. *432 pp. 1944. (5th Impression 1966.) 42s.*

Kornhauser, William. The Politics of Mass Society. *272 pp. 20 tables. 1960. (3rd Impression 1968.) 28s.*

Laidler, Harry W. History of Socialism. Social-Economic Movements: An Historical and Comparative Survey of Socialism, Communism, Co-operation, Utopianism; and other Systems of Reform and Reconstruction. *New edition. 992 pp. 1968. 90s.*

Lasswell, Harold D. Analysis of Political Behaviour. An Empirical Approach. *324 pp. 1947. (4th Impression 1966.) 35s.*

Mannheim, Karl. Freedom, Power and Democratic Planning. *Edited by Hans Gerth and Ernest K. Bramstedt. 424 pp. 1951. (3rd Impression 1968.) 42s.*

Mansur, Fatma. Process of Independence. *Foreword by A. H. Hanson. 208 pp. 1962. 25s.*

Martin, David A. Pacificism: an Historical and Sociological Study. *262 pp. 1965. 30s.*

Myrdal, Gunnar. The Political Element in the Development of Economic Theory. *Translated from the German by Paul Streeten. 282 pp. 1953. (4th Impression 1965.) 25s.*

Polanyi, Michael. F.R.S. The Logic of Liberty: Reflections and Rejoinders. *228 pp. 1951. 18s.*

Verney, Douglas V. The Analysis of Political Systems. *264 pp. 1959. (3rd Impression 1966.) 28s.*

Wootton, Graham. The Politics of Influence: British Ex-Servicemen, Cabinet Decisions and Cultural Changes, 1917 to 1957. *316 pp. 1963. 30s.*

Workers, Unions and the State. *188 pp. 1966. (2nd Impression 1967.) 25s.*

FOREIGN AFFAIRS: THEIR SOCIAL, POLITICAL AND ECONOMIC FOUNDATIONS

Baer, Gabriel. Population and Society in the Arab East. *Translated by Hanna Szöke. 288 pp. 10 maps. 1964. 40s.*

Bonné, Alfred. State and Economics in the Middle East: A Society in Transition. *482 pp. 2nd (revised) edition 1955. (2nd Impression 1960.) 40s.*

Studies in Economic Development: with special reference to Conditions in the Under-developed Areas of Western Asia and India. *322 pp. 84 tables. 2nd edition 1960. 32s.*

Mayer, J. P. Political Thought in France from the Revolution to the Fifth Republic. *164 pp. 3rd edition (revised) 1961. 16s.*

CRIMINOLOGY

Ancel, Marc. Social Defence: A Modern Approach to Criminal Problems. *Foreword by Leon Radzinowicz. 240 pp. 1965. 32s.*

Cloward, Richard A., and **Ohlin, Lloyd E.** Delinquency and Opportunity: A Theory of Delinquent Gangs. *248 pp. 1961. 25s.*

Downes, David M. The Delinquent Solution. A Study in Subcultural Theory. *296 pp. 1966. 42s.*

Dunlop, A. B., and **McCabe, S.** Young Men in Detention Centres. *192 pp. 1965. 28s.*

Friedländer, Kate. The Psycho-Analytical Approach to Juvenile Delinquency: Theory, Case Studies, Treatment. *320 pp. 1947. (6th Impression 1967). 40s.*

Glueck, Sheldon and **Eleanor.** Family Environment and Delinquency. *With the statistical assistance of Rose W. Kneznek. 340 pp. 1962. (2nd Impression 1966.) 40s.*

Mannheim, Hermann. Comparative Criminology: a Text Book. *Two volumes. 442 pp. and 380 pp. 1965. (2nd Impression with corrections 1966.) 42s. a volume.*

Morris, Terence. The Criminal Area: A Study in Social Ecology. *Foreword by Hermann Mannheim. 232 pp. 25 tables. 4 maps. 1957. (2nd Impression 1966.) 28s.*

Morris, Terence and **Pauline,** assisted by **Barbara Barer.** Pentonville: A Sociological Study of an English Prison. *416 pp. 16 plates. 1963. 50s.*

Spencer, John C. Crime and the Services. *Foreword by Hermann Mannheim. 336 pp. 1954. 28s.*

Trasler, Gordon. The Explanation of Criminality. *144 pp. 1962. (2nd Impression 1967.) 20s.*

SOCIAL PSYCHOLOGY

Barbu, Zevedei. Problems of Historical Psychology. *248 pp. 1960. 25s.*

Blackburn, Julian. Psychology and the Social Pattern. *184 pp. 1945. (7th Impression 1964.) 16s.*

Fleming, C. M. Adolescence: Its Social Psychology: With an Introduction to recent findings from the fields of Anthropology, Physiology, Medicine, Psychometrics and Sociometry. *288 pp. 2nd edition (revised) 1963. (3rd Impression 1967.) 25s. Paper 12s. 6d.*

The Social Psychology of Education: An Introduction and Guide to Its Study. *136 pp. 2nd edition (revised) 1959. (4th Impression 1967.) 14s. Paper 7s. 6d.*

Homans, George C. The Human Group. *Foreword by Bernard DeVoto. Introduction by Robert K. Merton. 526 pp. 1951. (7th Impression 1968.) 35s.*

Social Behaviour: its Elementary Forms. *416 pp. 1961. (3rd Impression 1968.) 35s.*

Klein, Josephine. The Study of Groups. *226 pp. 31 figures. 5 tables. 1956. (5th Impression 1967.) 21s. Paper 9s. 6d.*

Linton, Ralph. The Cultural Background of Personality. *132 pp. 1947. (7th Impression 1968.) 18s.*

Mayo, Elton. The Social Problems of an Industrial Civilization. With an appendix on the Political Problem. *180 pp. 1949. (5th Impression 1966.) 25s.*

Ottaway, A. K. C. Learning Through Group Experience. *176 pp. 1966. (2nd Impression 1968.) 25s.*

Ridder, J. C. de. The Personality of the Urban African in South Africa. A Thematic Apperception Test Study. *196 pp. 12 plates. 1961. 25s.*

Rose, Arnold M. (Ed.). Human Behaviour and Social Processes: an Interactionist Approach. *Contributions by Arnold M. Rose, Ralph H. Turner, Anselm Strauss, Everett C. Hughes, E. Franklin Frazier, Howard S. Becker, et al. 696 pp. 1962. (2nd Impression 1968.) 70s.*

Smelser, Neil J. Theory of Collective Behaviour. *448 pp. 1962. (2nd Impression 1967.) 45s.*

Stephenson, Geoffrey M. The Development of Conscience. *128 pp. 1966. 25s.*

Young, Kimball. Handbook of Social Psychology. *658 pp. 16 figures. 10 tables. 2nd edition (revised) 1957. (3rd Impression 1963.) 40s.*

SOCIOLOGY OF THE FAMILY

Banks, J. A. Prosperity and Parenthood: A study of Family Planning among The Victorian Middle Classes. *262 pp. 1954. (3rd Impression 1968.) 28s.*

Bell, Colin R. Middle Class Families: Social and Geographical Mobility. *224 pp. 1969. 35s.*

Burton, Lindy. Vulnerable Children. *272 pp. 1968. 35s.*

Gavron, Hannah. The Captive Wife: Conflicts of Housebound Mothers. *190 pp. 1966. (2nd Impression 1966.) 25s.*

Klein, Josephine. Samples from English Cultures. *1965. (2nd Impression 1967.)*

1. Three Preliminary Studies and Aspects of Adult Life in England. *447 pp. 50s.*
2. Child-Rearing Practices and Index. *247 pp. 35s.*

Klein, Viola. Britain's Married Women Workers. *180 pp. 1965. (2nd Impression 1968.) 28s.*

McWhinnie, Alexina M. Adopted Children. How They Grow Up. *304 pp. 1967. (2nd Impression 1968.) 42s.*

Myrdal, Alva and **Klein, Viola.** Women's Two Roles: Home and Work. *238 pp. 27 tables. 1956. Revised Edition 1967. 30s. Paper 15s.*

Parsons, Talcott and **Bales, Robert F.** Family: Socialization and Interaction Process. *In collaboration with James Olds, Morris Zelditch and Philip E. Slater. 456 pp. 50 figures and tables. 1956. (3rd Impression 1968.) 45s.*

Schücking, L. L. The Puritan Family. *Translated from the German by Brian Battershaw. 212 pp. 1969. About 42s.*

THE SOCIAL SERVICES

Forder, R. A. (Ed.). Penelope Hall's Social Services of Modern England. *288 pp. 1969. 35s.*

George, Victor. Social Security: Beveridge and After. *258 pp. 1968. 35s.*

Goetschius, George W. Working with Community Groups. *256 pp. 1969. 35s.*

Goetschius, George W. and **Tash, Joan.** Working with Unattached Youth. *416 pp. 1967. (2nd Impression 1968.) 40s.*

Hall, M. P., and **Howes, I. V.** The Church in Social Work. A Study of Moral Welfare Work undertaken by the Church of England. *320 pp. 1965. 35s.*

Heywood, Jean S. Children in Care: the Development of the Service for the Deprived Child. *264 pp. 2nd edition (revised) 1965. (2nd Impression 1966.) 32s.*

An Introduction to Teaching Casework Skills. *190 pp. 1964. 28s.*

Jones, Kathleen. Lunacy, Law and Conscience, 1744-1845: the Social History of the Care of the Insane. *268 pp. 1955. 25s.*

Mental Health and Social Policy, 1845-1959. *264 pp. 1960. (2nd Impression 1967.) 32s.*

Jones, Kathleen and **Sidebotham, Roy.** Mental Hospitals at Work. *220 pp. 1962. 30s.*

Kastell, Jean. Casework in Child Care. *Foreword by M. Brooke Willis. 320 pp. 1962. 35s.*

Morris, Pauline. Put Away: A Sociological Study of Institutions for the Mentally Retarded. *Approx. 288 pp. 1969. About 50s.*

Nokes, P. L. The Professional Task in Welfare Practice. *152 pp. 1967. 28s.*

Rooff, Madeline. Voluntary Societies and Social Policy. *350 pp. 15 tables. 1957. 35s.*

Timms, Noel. Psychiatric Social Work in Great Britain (1939-1962). *280 pp. 1964. 32s.*

Social Casework: Principles and Practice. *256 pp. 1964. (2nd Impression 1966.) 25s. Paper 15s.*

Trasler, Gordon. In Place of Parents: A Study in Foster Care. *272 pp. 1960. (2nd Impression 1966.) 30s.*

Young, A. F., and **Ashton, E. T.** British Social Work in the Nineteenth Century. *288 pp. 1956. (2nd Impression 1963.) 28s.*

Young, A. F. Social Services in British Industry. *272 pp. 1968. 40s.*

SOCIOLOGY OF EDUCATION

Banks, Olive. Parity and Prestige in English Secondary Education: a Study in Educational Sociology. *272 pp. 1955. (2nd Impression 1963.) 32s.*

Bentwich, Joseph. Education in Israel. *224 pp. 8 pp. plates. 1965. 24s.*

Blyth, W. A. L. English Primary Education. A Sociological Description. *1965. Revised edition 1967.*

1. Schools. *232 pp. 30s. Paper 12s. 6d.*
2. Background. *168 pp. 25s. Paper 10s. 6d.*

Collier, K. G. The Social Purposes of Education: Personal and Social Values in Education. *268 pp. 1959. (3rd Impression 1965.) 21s.*

Dale, R. R., and **Griffith, S.** Down Stream: Failure in the Grammar School. *108 pp. 1965. 20s.*

Dore, R. P. Education in Tokugawa Japan. *356 pp. 9 pp. plates. 1965. 35s.*

Edmonds, E. L. The School Inspector. *Foreword by Sir William Alexander. 214 pp. 1962. 28s.*

Evans, K. M. Sociometry and Education. *158 pp. 1962. (2nd Impression 1966.) 18s.*

Foster, P. J. Education and Social Change in Ghana. *336 pp. 3 maps. 1965. (2nd Impression 1967.) 36s.*

Fraser, W. R. Education and Society in Modern France. *150 pp. 1963. (2nd Impression 1968.) 25s.*

Hans, Nicholas. New Trends in Education in the Eighteenth Century. *278 pp. 19 tables. 1951. (2nd Impression 1966.) 30s.*

Comparative Education: A Study of Educational Factors and Traditions. *360 pp. 3rd (revised) edition 1958. (4th Impression 1967.) 25s. Paper 12s. 6d.*

Hargreaves, David. Social Relations in a Secondary School. *240 pp. 1967. (2nd Impression 1968.) 32s.*

Holmes, Brian. Problems in Education. A Comparative Approach. *336 pp. 1965. (2nd Impression 1967.) 32s.*

Mannheim, Karl and **Stewart, W. A. C.** An Introduction to the Sociology of Education. *206 pp. 1962. (2nd Impression 1965.) 21s.*

Morris, Raymond N. The Sixth Form and College Entrance. *231 pp. 1969. 40s.*

Musgrove, F. Youth and the Social Order. *176 pp. 1964. (2nd Impression 1968.) 25s. Paper 12s.*

Ortega y Gasset, José. Mission of the University. *Translated with an Introduction by Howard Lee Nostrand. 86 pp. 1946. (3rd Impression 1963.) 15s.*

Ottaway, A. K. C. Education and Society: An Introduction to the Sociology of Education. *With an Introduction by W. O. Lester Smith. 212 pp. Second edition (revised). 1962. (5th Impression 1968.) 18s. Paper 10s. 6d.*

Peers, Robert. Adult Education: A Comparative Study. *398 pp. 2nd edition 1959. (2nd Impression 1966.) 42s.*

Pritchard, D. G. Education and the Handicapped: 1760 to 1960. *258 pp. 1963. (2nd Impression 1966.) 35s.*

Richardson, Helen. Adolescent Girls in Approved Schools. *Approx. 360 pp. 1969. About 42s.*

Simon, Brian and **Joan** (Eds.). Educational Psychology in the U.S.S.R. *Introduction by Brian and Joan Simon. Translation by Joan Simon. Papers by D. N. Bogoiavlenski and N. A. Menchinskaia, D. B. Elkonin, E. A. Fleshner, Z. I. Kalmykova, G. S. Kostiuk, V. A. Krutetski, A. N. Leontiev, A. R. Luria, E. A. Milerian, R. G. Natadze, B. M. Teplov, L. S. Vygotski, L. V. Zankov. 296 pp. 1963. 40s.*

SOCIOLOGY OF CULTURE

Eppel, E. M., and M. Adolescents and Morality: A Study of some Moral Values and Dilemmas of Working Adolescents in the Context of a changing Climate of Opinion. *Foreword by W. J. H. Sprott. 268 pp. 39 tables. 1966. 30s.*

Fromm, Erich. The Fear of Freedom. *286 pp. 1942. (8th Impression 1960.) 25s. Paper 10s.*

The Sane Society. *400 pp. 1956. (4th Impression 1968.) 28s. Paper 14s.*

Mannheim, Karl. Diagnosis of Our Time: Wartime Essays of a Sociologist. *208 pp. 1943. (8th Impression 1966.) 21s.*

Essays on the Sociology of Culture. *Edited by Ernst Mannheim in co-operation with Paul Kecskemeti. Editorial Note by Adolph Lowe. 280 pp. 1956. (3rd Impression 1967.) 28s.*

Weber, Alfred. Farewell to European History: or The Conquest of Nihilism. *Translated from the German by R. F. C. Hull. 224 pp. 1947. 18s.*

SOCIOLOGY OF RELIGION

Argyle, Michael. Religious Behaviour. *224 pp. 8 figures. 41 tables. 1958. (4th Impression 1968.) 25s.*

Nelson, G. K. Spiritualism and Society. *313 pp. 1969. 42s.*

Stark, Werner. The Sociology of Religion. A Study of Christendom.
Volume I. Established Religion. *248 pp. 1966. 35s.*
Volume II. Sectarian Religion. *368 pp. 1967. 40s.*
Volume III. The Universal Church. *464 pp. 1967. 45s.*

Watt, W. Montgomery. Islam and the Integration of Society. *320 pp. 1961. (3rd Impression 1966.) 35s.*

SOCIOLOGY OF ART AND LITERATURE

Beljame, Alexandre. Men of Letters and the English Public in the Eighteenth Century: 1660-1744, Dryden, Addison, Pope. *Edited with an Introduction and Notes by Bonamy Dobrée. Translated by E. O. Lorimer. 532 pp. 1948. 32s.*

Misch, Georg. A History of Autobiography in Antiquity. *Translated by E. W. Dickes. 2 Volumes. Vol. 1, 364 pp., Vol. 2, 372 pp. 1950. 45s. the set.*

Schücking, L. L. The Sociology of Literary Taste. *112 pp. 2nd (revised) edition 1966. 18s.*

Silbermann, Alphons. The Sociology of Music. *Translated from the German by Corbet Stewart. 222 pp. 1963. 32s.*

SOCIOLOGY OF KNOWLEDGE

Mannheim, Karl. Essays on the Sociology of Knowledge. *Edited by Paul Kecskemeti. Editorial note by Adolph Lowe. 352 pp. 1952. (4th Impression 1967.) 35s.*

Stark, W. America: Ideal and Reality. The United States of 1776 in Contemporary Philosophy. *136 pp. 1947. 12s.*

The Sociology of Knowledge: An Essay in Aid of a Deeper Understanding of the History of Ideas. *384 pp. 1958. (3rd Impression 1967.) 36s.*

Montesquieu: Pioneer of the Sociology of Knowledge. *244 pp. 1960. 25s.*

URBAN SOCIOLOGY

Anderson, Nels. The Urban Community: A World Perspective. *532 pp. 1960. 35s.*

Ashworth, William. The Genesis of Modern British Town Planning: A Study in Economic and Social History of the Nineteenth and Twentieth Centuries. *288 pp. 1954. (3rd Impression 1968.) 32s.*

Bracey, Howard. Neighbours: On New Estates and Subdivisions in England and U.S.A. *220 pp. 1964. 28s.*

Cullingworth, J. B. Housing Needs and Planning Policy: A Restatement of the Problems of Housing Need and "Overspill" in England and Wales. *232 pp. 44 tables. 8 maps. 1960. (2nd Impression 1966.) 28s.*

Dickinson, Robert E. City and Region: A Geographical Interpretation. *608 pp. 125 figures. 1964. (5th Impression 1967.) 60s.*

The West European City: A Geographical Interpretation. *600 pp. 129 maps. 29 plates. 2nd edition 1962. (3rd Impression 1968.) 55s.*

The City Region in Western Europe. *320 pp. Maps. 1967. 30s. Paper 14s.*

Jackson, Brian. Working Class Community: Some General Notions raised by a Series of Studies in Northern England. *192 pp. 1968. (2nd Impression 1968.) 25s.*

Jennings, Hilda. Societies in the Making: a Study of Development and Redevelopment within a County Borough. *Foreword by D. A. Clark. 286 pp. 1962. (2nd Impression 1967.) 32s.*

Kerr, Madeline. The People of Ship Street. *240 pp. 1958. 28s.*

Mann, P. H. An Approach to Urban Sociology. *240 pp. 1965. (2nd Impression 1968.) 30s.*

Morris, R. N., and **Mogey, J.** The Sociology of Housing. Studies at Berinsfield. *232 pp. 4 pp. plates. 1965. 42s.*

Rosser, C., and **Harris, C.** The Family and Social Change. A Study of Family and Kinship in a South Wales Town. *352 pp. 8 maps. 1965. (2nd Impression 1968.) 45s.*

RURAL SOCIOLOGY

Chambers, R. J. H. Settlement Schemes in Africa: A Selective Study. *Approx. 268 pp. 1969. About 50s.*

Haswell, M. R. The Economics of Development in Village India. *120 pp. 1967. 21s.*

Littlejohn, James. Westrigg: the Sociology of a Cheviot Parish. *172 pp. 5 figures. 1963. 25s.*

Williams, W. M. The Country Craftsman: A Study of Some Rural Crafts and the Rural Industries Organization in England. *248 pp. 9 figures. 1958. 25s.* (*Dartington Hall Studies in Rural Sociology.*)

The Sociology of an English Village: Gosforth. *272 pp. 12 figures. 13 tables. 1956.* (*3rd Impression 1964.*) *25s.*

SOCIOLOGY OF MIGRATION

Humphreys, Alexander J. New Dubliners: Urbanization and the Irish Family. *Foreword by George C. Homans. 304 pp. 1966. 40s.*

SOCIOLOGY OF INDUSTRY AND DISTRIBUTION

Anderson, Nels. Work and Leisure. *280 pp. 1961. 28s.*

Blau, Peter M., and **Scott, W. Richard.** Formal Organizations: a Comparative approach. *Introduction and Additional Bibliography by J. H. Smith. 326 pp. 1963.* (*4th Impression 1969.*) *35s. Paper 15s.*

Eldridge, J. E. T. Industrial Disputes. Essays in the Sociology of Industrial Relations. *288 pp. 1968. 40s.*

Hollowell, Peter G. The Lorry Driver. *272 pp. 1968. 42s.*

Jefferys, Margot, with the assistance of Winifred Moss. Mobility in the Labour Market: Employment Changes in Battersea and Dagenham. *Preface by Barbara Wootton. 186 pp. 51 tables. 1954. 15s.*

Levy, A. B. Private Corporations and Their Control. *Two Volumes. Vol. 1, 464 pp., Vol. 2, 432 pp. 1950. 80s. the set.*

Liepmann, Kate. Apprenticeship: An Enquiry into its Adequacy under Modern Conditions. *Foreword by H. D. Dickinson. 232 pp. 6 tables. 1960.* (*2nd Impression 1960.*) *23s.*

Millerson, Geoffrey. The Qualifying Associations: a Study in Professionalization. *320 pp. 1964. 42s.*

Smelser, Neil J. Social Change in the Industrial Revolution: An Application of Theory to the Lancashire Cotton Industry, 1770-1840. *468 pp. 12 figures. 14 tables. 1959.* (*2nd Impression 1960.*) *50s.*

Williams, Gertrude. Recruitment to Skilled Trades. *240 pp. 1957. 23s.*

Young, A. F. Industrial Injuries Insurance: an Examination of British Policy. *192 pp. 1964. 30s.*

ANTHROPOLOGY

Ammar, Hamed. Growing up in an Egyptian Village: Silwa, Province of Aswan. *336 pp. 1954.* (*2nd Impression 1966.*) *35s.*

Crook, David and **Isabel.** Revolution in a Chinese Village: Ten Mile Inn. *230 pp. 8 plates. 1 map. 1959.* (*2nd Impression 1968.*) *21s.*

The First Years of Yangyi Commune. *302 pp. 12 plates. 1966. 42s.*

Dickie-Clark, H. F. The Marginal Situation. A Sociological Study of a Coloured Group. *236 pp. 1966. 40s.*

Dube, S. C. Indian Village. *Foreword by Morris Edward Opler. 276 pp. 4 plates. 1955. (5th Impression 1965.) 25s.*

India's Changing Villages: Human Factors in Community Development. *260 pp. 8 plates. 1 map. 1958. (3rd Impression 1963.) 25s.*

Firth, Raymond. Malay Fishermen. Their Peasant Economy. *420 pp. 17 pp. plates. 2nd edition revised and enlarged 1966. (2nd Impression 1968.) 55s.*

Gulliver, P. H. The Family Herds. A Study of two Pastoral Tribes in East Africa, The Jie and Turkana. *304 pp. 4 plates. 19 figures. 1955. (2nd Impression with new preface and bibliography 1966.) 35s.*

Social Control in an African Society: a Study of the Arusha, Agricultural Masai of Northern Tanganyika. *320 pp. 8 plates. 10 figures. 1963. (2nd Impression 1968.) 42s.*

Ishwaran, K. Shivapur. A South Indian Village. *216 pp. 1968. 35s.*

Tradition and Economy in Village India: An Interactionist Approach. *Foreword by Conrad Arensburg. 176 pp. 1966. (2nd Impression 1968.) 25s.*

Jarvie, Ian C. The Revolution in Anthropology. *268 pp. 1964. (2nd Impression 1967.) 40s.*

Jarvie, Ian C. and **Agassi, Joseph.** Hong Kong. A Society in Transition. *396 pp. Illustrated with plates and maps. 1968. 56s.*

Little, Kenneth L. Mende of Sierra Leone. *308 pp. and folder. 1951. Revised edition 1967. 63s.*

Lowie, Professor Robert H. Social Organization. *494 pp. 1950. (4th Impression 1966.) 50s.*

Mayer, Adrian C. Caste and Kinship in Central India: A Village and its Region. *328 pp. 16 plates. 15 figures. 16 tables. 1960. (2nd Impression 1965.) 35s.*

Peasants in the Pacific: A Study of Fiji Indian Rural Society. *232 pp. 16 plates. 10 figures. 14 tables. 1961. 35s.*

Smith, Raymond T. The Negro Family in British Guiana: Family Structure and Social Status in the Villages. *With a Foreword by Meyer Fortes. 314 pp. 8 plates. 1 figure. 4 maps. 1956. (2nd Impression 1965.) 35s.*

DOCUMENTARY

Meek, Dorothea L. (Ed.). Soviet Youth: Some Achievements and Problems. *Excerpts from the Soviet Press, translated by the editor. 280 pp. 1957. 28s.*

Schlesinger, Rudolf (Ed.). Changing Attitudes in Soviet Russia.

2. The Nationalities Problem and Soviet Administration. Selected Readings on the Development of Soviet Nationalities Policies. *Introduced by the editor. Translated by W. W. Gottlieb. 324 pp. 1956. 30s.*

Reports of the Institute of Community Studies

(*Demy 8vo.*)

Cartwright, Ann. Human Relations and Hospital Care. *272 pp. 1964. 30s.*

Patients and their Doctors. A Study of General Practice. *304 pp. 1967. 40s.*

Jackson, Brian. Streaming: an Education System in Miniature. *168 pp. 1964.* (*2nd Impression 1966.*) *21s. Paper 10s.*

Jackson, Brian and **Marsden, Dennis.** Education and the Working Class: Some General Themes raised by a Study of 88 Working-class Children in a Northern Industrial City. *268 pp. 2 folders. 1962.* (*4th Impression 1968.*) *32s.*

Marris, Peter. Widows and their Families. *Foreword by Dr. John Bowlby. 184 pp. 18 tables. Statistical Summary. 1958. 18s.*

Family and Social Change in an African City. A Study of Rehousing in Lagos. *196 pp. 1 map. 4 plates. 53 tables. 1961.* (*2nd Impression 1966.*) *30s.*

The Experience of Higher Education. *232 pp. 27 tables. 1964. 25s.*

Marris, Peter and **Rein, Martin.** Dilemmas of Social Reform. Poverty and Community Action in the United States. *256 pp. 1967. 35s.*

Mills, Enid. Living with Mental Illness: a Study in East London. *Foreword by Morris Carstairs. 196 pp. 1962. 28s.*

Runciman, W. G. Relative Deprivation and Social Justice. A Study of Attitudes to Social Inequality in Twentieth Century England. *352 pp. 1966.* (*2nd Impression 1967.*) *40s.*

Townsend, Peter. The Family Life of Old People: An Inquiry in East London. *Foreword by J. H. Sheldon. 300 pp. 3 figures. 63 tables. 1957.* (*3rd Impression 1967.*) *30s.*

Willmott, Peter. Adolescent Boys in East London. *230 pp. 1966. 30s.*

The Evolution of a Community: a study of Dagenham after forty years. *168 pp. 2 maps. 1963. 21s.*

Willmott, Peter and **Young, Michael.** Family and Class in a London Suburb. *202 pp. 47 tables. 1960.* (*4th Impression 1968.*) *25s.*

Young, Michael. Innovation and Research in Education. *192 pp. 1965. 25s. Paper 12s. 6d.*

Young, Michael and **McGeeney, Patrick.** Learning Begins at Home. A Study of a Junior School and its Parents. *About 128 pp. 1968. 21s. Paper 14s.*

Young, Michael and **Willmott, Peter.** Family and Kinship in East London. *Foreword by Richard M. Titmuss. 252 pp. 39 tables. 1957.* (*3rd Impression 1965.*) *28s.*

The British Journal of Sociology. *Edited by Terence P. Morris. Vol. 1, No. 1, March 1950 and Quarterly. Roy. 8vo., £3 annually, 15s. a number, post free.* (*Vols. 1-18, £8 each. Individual parts £2 10s.*

All prices are net and subject to alteration without notice

1268 H.B.